LATIN AMERICAN PEASANTS

THE LIBRARY OF PEASANT STUDIES

EVERYDAY FORMS OF PEASANT RESISTANCE IN SOUTH-EAST ASIA
edited by James C. Scott and Benedict J. Tria Kerkvliet
(No.9 in the series)

NEW APPROACHES TO STATE AND PEASANT IN OTTOMAN HISTORY
edited by Halil Berktay and Suraiya Faroqhi
(No.10 in the series)

PLANTATIONS, PEASANTS AND PROLETARIANS IN COLONIAL ASIA
edited by E. Valentine Daniel, Henry Bernstein and Tom Brass
(No.11 in the series)

NEW FARMERS' MOVEMENTS IN INDIA
edited by Tom Brass
(No.12 in the series)

CLASS, STATE AND AGRICULTURAL PRODUCTIVITY IN EGYPT
Study of the Inverse Relationship between Farm Size and Land Productivity
by Graham Dyer
(No.15 in the series)

TOWARDS A COMPARATIVE POLITICAL ECONOMY OF UNFREE LABOUR
Case Studies and Debates
by Tom Brass
(No.16 in the series)

PEASANTS, POPULISM AND POSTMODERNISM
The Return of the Agrarian Myth
by Tom Brass
(No.17 in the series)

AN APARTHEID OASIS?
Agricultural and Rural Livelihoods in Venda
by Edward Lahiff
(No.20 in the series)

LATIN AMERICAN PEASANTS

Edited by

TOM BRASS

FRANK CASS
LONDON • PORTLAND, OR

First published in 2003 in Great Britain by
FRANK CASS PUBLISHERS
Crown House, 47 Chase Side, Southgate, London N14 5BP, England

and in the United States of America by
FRANK CASS PUBLISHERS
c/o ISBS, 5824 N.E. Hassalo Street
Portland, Oregon 97213-3644

Website http://www.frankcass.com

British Library Cataloguing in Publication Data

Latin American peasants. – (The library of peasant studies; no. 21)
1. Peasantry – Latin America 2. Peasantry – Latin America – History.
I. Brass, Tom
305.5′633′098

ISBN 0 7146 5384 5 (cloth)
ISBN 0 7146 8319 1 (paper)
ISSN 1462-219X

Library of Congress Cataloging-in-Publication Data:

Latin American peasants / editor, Tom Brass.
p. cm. — (Library of peasant studies ISSN 0306-6150 ; no. 21)
Includes bibliographical references and index.
ISBN 0-7146-5384-5 (hardback) — ISBN 0-7146-8319-1 (pbk.)
1. Peasantry—Latin America. 2. Agricultural laborers—Latin America. 3. Latin America—Rural conditions. 4. Land reform—Latin America. 5. Peasantry—Latin America—Political activity. 6. Agricultural laborers—Latin America—Political activity. I. Brass, Tom, 1946- II. Series.
HD1531.L3 L37 2002
305.5′633′098—dc21

2002015545

This group of studies first appeared in a Special Issue on 'Latin American Peasants' of *The Journal of Peasant Studies* (ISSN 0306 6150), Vol.29/3&4 (April/July 2002) published by Frank Cass and Co. Ltd.

Printed in Great Britain by MPG Books Ltd., Bodmin, Cornwall.

For Amanda,
and for
Anna, Ned and Miles.

Contents

Acknowledgements

In the 29 years since its foundation, *The Journal of Peasant Studies* has published special issues and books based on them on an increasingly regular basis: two in the 1970s, five in the 1980s, and seven in the 1990s. With the exception of two (Ottoman History, South Africa), all the special issues that appeared over the last decade of the twentieth century were edited by me, either alone or in conjunction with others, on the basis of which experience it is possible to observe incontrovertibly that the task of editing themed volumes is both rewarding and onerous. The total of fourteen special issues of the *JPS* that have been published thus far – together with the book versions – are wide-ranging in their thematic and geographical coverage, devoted as they are to a variety of agrarian issues (feudalism, plantations, sharecropping, everyday forms of peasant resistance, the state and the peasantry, new farmers' movements, the agrarian question, rural labour relations) in all the major areas of the globe, except two: Latin America and China. Accordingly, this first special issue of the journal to be published in the new millennium is also the first devoted specifically to peasants in Latin America; the contributors represent a mixture of established and younger scholars, some of whom have published in this journal before, and all of whom have conducted fieldwork in rural Latin America.

Thanks are due to a number of people who in different ways have helped see this volume to its conclusion. To Graham Hart of Frank Cass Publishers, who steered it through the production process; to two members of the editorial advisory board of the journal – Professor Olivia Harris of the Department of Anthropology at Goldsmiths College, London University, and Professor Alan Knight of the Latin American Centre at Oxford University – for small but important acts of assistance in organizing this special issue; and, for reasons which they know all too well, to Amanda, Anna, Ned and Miles.

Tom Brass
Richmond, Surrey

Introduction

Latin American Peasants – New Paradigms for Old?

TOM BRASS

'We were exhausted from a long, painful trek; more painful than long, to tell the truth … We had lost all our equipment, and had trudged for endless hours through marshlands and swamps. We were all wearing new boots and by now everyone was suffering from blisters and footsores, but new footwear and fungus were by no means our only enemies. We had reached Cuba following a seven-day voyage across the Gulf of Mexico and the Caribbean Sea, without food, plagued by seasickness and aboard a far-from-seaworthy vessel.' – Ernesto Che Guevara [1967: 9] on the privations experienced by the guerrilla forces prior to the 1959 Cuban revolution.

'I get up, I give interviews and then it's time to go to bed.' – Subcomandante Marcos [2001: 74], leader of the 1990s Zapatista Movement in Chiapas, Mexico, in reply to a question about his average day.

Over the past decade, those with a passing intellectual acquaintance with peasants and peasant movements in Latin America might be forgiven for making two assumptions: that the only rural agency south of the Rio Grande was confined to the state of Chiapas in Mexico, and that the only analyses of agrarian mobilization were being written by postmodern theorists.[1] As the contributions to this volume attest, neither of these assumptions is correct. What is undeniable, however, is the extent to which the study of peasants, peasant movements and agrarian transformation in Latin America during the latter part of the twentieth century has undergone a profound change. Like their counterparts in Asia, peasants and rural workers in Latin America are, we are constantly informed, not what they were once thought to be, nor is their agency designed to attain the objectives previously attributed to them. In rural Latin America, therefore, just as everywhere else nowadays, new movements are said to be emerging, composed of new rural

---

Tom Brass formerly lectured in the Social and Political Sciences Faculty at the University of Cambridge, UK. E-mail address: tom@tombrass.freeserve.co.uk.

subjects exercising new forms of agency in keeping with apolitical 'new' postmodern populist objectives.

The latter designation, which signals a conceptual (and political) abandonment not only of mass mobilization (= revolution) aimed at the capture/control of state power, but also of the possibility/desirability of systemic transcendence (a transition from capitalism to socialism), stems from an equally marked process of epistemological confluence. This extends from an academically resurgent neoliberalism and neoclassical economic theory to a variety of currently still fashionable social frameworks informed or influenced by postmodernism (subaltern studies, everyday forms of resistance, post-development, post-structuralism, post-colonialism).[2] What all these paradigms have in common is not only their unabashed celebration of a rural 'voice-from-below' engaged in quotidian/local/(mostly individual) resistance based on ethnic/gender/ecological/peasant essentialisms, therefore, but also its characterization as a new and empowering form of identity/agency that occurs within capitalism.[3]

Because of the academic influence currently exercised by these 'new' paradigms, this introduction will attempt to situate the argument made by each contributor to this volume in relation to each of the two main analytical frameworks that have dominated the study of Latin American peasants. The first of these are the 'new' theories themselves, and their claims about peasant identity/agency/empowerment, while the second concerns the older debate over the agrarian question involving rival *campesinista* (= peasant persistence) and *descampesinista* (= peasant disappearance) interpretations.[4] To some degree, the eclipse of the latter approach, and the corresponding rise of the former, have coincided with a decline in land reform undertaken by the state, as Keynesian demand management gave way to neoliberal economic policies. It was this shift that contributed in part to the replacement of peasant-as-economic-subject by earlier concepts of peasant-as-cultural-subject. Finally, the political nature and economic role of the peasant/state relationship is considered briefly, not least because it is a complex history and one that much 'new' theory about Latin American peasants tends either to simplify or to ignore.

I

It is now clear that the post-war decline in peasant economy has been accompanied in the academic discipline of development studies by a conceptual re-essentialization of the peasantry: first by neoclassical theory as an economic subject, and then as a cultural subject by postmodernism. The latter in particular has shifted the analytical focus of the study of peasants away from political economy and history and towards literature and culture, an approach which entailed both the conceptual deprivileging of economic development ('post-development'), and the political rejection of Marxism, meta-narratives, and European Enlightenment discourse ('post-Marxism'). The profound implications of this change were evident from the emergence and consolidation in the 1990s of the 'new' populist postmodernism, a form of analysis-lite that has led to the dumbing down of the development debate, or the substitution of celebration for investigation.[5] Such views, it could be argued, have led to the uncritical espousal of what are unambiguously populist theories about the attainment of from-below empowerment, and have consequently not only reified false consciousness, but – in discarding concepts such as rural class formation/struggle/consciousness – have also eroded the emancipatory objectives associated historically with development discourse.[6]

Prior to the 'development decade' of the 1960s, the study of peasants was confined largely to anthropologists and historians. The theoretical construction of 'peasant society' was strongly influenced by anthropologists conducting fieldwork in Latin America, for whom the peasantry constituted a cultural system. For example, Foster's concept of 'limited good', Redfield's 'folk culture', and the 'culture of poverty' thesis advanced by Lewis, were all applied to rural communities in Mexico in the 40-year period from the 1920s onwards.[7] The same kind of epistemology informed Murra's theory of Andean 'verticality', applied by him and others subsequently to the study of Peruvian rural communities.[8] In these kinds of framework, peasants were depicted as being economically backward because they chose to be so, and for non-economic reasons to do with the culture and nature of peasant society itself. Rural social systems also occupied the attention of historians during the 1950s, albeit in a different way. Here the point of interest was the role of peasants in economic development, but with reference to case studies of agrarian transition long past. Examining how and why in particular contexts (Europe, Japan) feudalism had been replaced by capitalism, historians such as Dobb and Hilton focused on issues such as the relative importance to these transitions of endogenous versus exogenous variables such as trade and class.[9]

The post-war rise to academic prominence of development studies, and the central role in economic transformation allocated to the peasantry in what were still mainly rural Third World nations, was due to a renewed emphasis on the desirability of capitalist development in the Third World generally and its agriculture in particular. Because of the fear among policy-makers in industrial nations caught up in the Cold War that economic stagnation leading to peasant uprisings in underdeveloped countries would facilitate the spread of communism throughout the Third World, mainstream development strategy from the 1960s onwards required the implementation of agrarian reform programmes in many Latin America countries.[10] Economic growth linked to domestic accumulation depended in turn on the extension of the internal market, which required increasing the purchasing power of peasants. For this reason, agrarian reform in the post-war era became a political issue, and it was from this background that economic analyses of peasants emerged.

Accordingly, the debate about the peasantry, agrarian change and economic development (and thus transition) underwent a multiple shift. Instead of being concerned with peasant society and culture, or with specifically historical instances of transition from feudalism to capitalism, therefore, it was conducted now largely within the domain of the social sciences, where the focus was both on peasant-as-economic-subject and on obstacles to contemporary capitalism in underdeveloped countries.[11] The rise of neoliberalism in the 1980s, however, signalled a shift to export-led economic growth and a corresponding decline in the economic role of the state, consequences of which were the increased economic importance of national/international agribusiness enterprises and a decreased economic role for agrarian reform generally and smallholding agriculture in particular.[12] In Latin America as elsewhere, opposition to this process – both political and intellectual – took a populist form, and was accompanied by a return to earlier concepts of peasant-as-cultural-subject.

NEW PARADIGMS, OR THE BLINDING DARKNESS OF LITE

Until recently, most analyses of Latin American populism acknowledged the importance of peasant identity in this discourse, not least because of a recognition of the importance of this rural dimension in Europe, North America and especially Russia.[13] In the last context, Chayanov long ago argued that an homogeneous peasantry composed of self-sufficient petty commodity producers constituted a pan-historical socio-economic category which, in theoretical and political terms, was the mirror image of the classical Marxist view.[14] Unlike Chayanov, contemporary variants of peasant essentialism incorporate both semi-proletarianized and economically efficient family farms, arguing that the former should be helped to resist capitalism while the latter constitute a commercially viable alternative to capitalist production.[15] Perhaps because the peasantry in general is no longer thought of as politically important, however, more recent analyses of populism in Latin America have tended to overlook the historical significance and implications of this rural category in such mobilizations, and thus also of the powerful way in which this kind of discourse addresses both the identity and the socio-economic position of small and medium family farmers.[16]

Rather than a rural discourse that is backwards-looking, antagonistic to economic development and politically reactionary, therefore, the more usual interpretation of Latin American populism has been of it as an urban and forward-looking ideology compatible with anti-imperialism and national economic development. A variation of this theoretical approach has been applied to Latin America by, among others, Octavio Ianni and Otilio Borón, both of whom argue that following the 1929 capitalist crisis populism was a form of Bonapartism that was a pro-development and thus a politically progressive discourse.[17] Historically, however, Bonapartism shares many of the same characteristics not just with populism but also with fascism, and indeed, is in many instances synonymous with them: thus, for example, it is unashamedly nationalist, it rules in the name of 'order' (imposed on a mobilizing or mobilized urban industrial working class), it receives its main support from an actual/erstwhile rural petty bourgeoisie (peasants, lumpenproletarians) threatened by economic crisis, and it is a form of strong government which designates itself ideologically in the classic populist manner as 'above parties' and 'above classes'.[18] It is precisely all the latter aspects that have been appropriated by the 'new' postmodern populism, and not only applied to rural agency in Latin America but also recast in a progressive mould, either as 'new social movements' or as 'everyday forms of resistance'.

Unconnected with class, systemic transformation, and the eradication of rural poverty, the target of 1990s populist discourse (and in particular its postmodern 'post-colonial' variant) seems to be economic development itself.[19] In a postmodern framework, therefore, an imposed and disempowering economic backwardness which its rural subjects attempt to transcend is reconfigured as a chosen and empowering form of cultural 'otherness', to be retained/reproduced at all costs. Instead of attempting to realize the economic fruits and benefits of development (as Marxists argue), peasants are depicted by postmodernism as engaged in a twofold struggle: to remain subsistence producers, and against economic development.[20] Peasants and workers throughout the so-called Third World, and especially those in Latin America, are now being invited by exponents of the 'new' postmodern populist framework to forgo economic development, and to accept as a substitute for this a celebration of their existing cultural identity. It is towards the attainment of the latter, the 'new' postmodern populism asserts, that all 'from below' grassroots agency in Latin America (and elsewhere) – whether it takes the form of micro-level resistance or macro-level new social movements – is now geared.

In much current postmodern/populist analysis of agrarian mobilization, therefore, the prevailing view is that rural grassroots empowerment always and everywhere constitutes an unproblematically desirable end, a position arrived at without asking by whom and for what such a process is conducted. Thus the 1994 Chiapas uprising led by Subcomandante Marcos has been hailed as an exemplar of the 'new' agrarian mobilization, on the grounds that it represents a novel oppositional form (= the internationalization/electronification of opposition to capitalism), based not on class but on indigenous 'self-activity'/'self-valorization', is anti-development (= 'the refusal of development') and pro-ecology.[21] Peasant movements, exponents of the 'new' postmodern populism claim, have involved struggles by petty commodity producers against capitalism simply to defend the existing pre-capitalist relationships and institutions which protect them against economic hardship and starvation (the 'moral economy' argument). More recently, this position has been extended to include the view that the most effective peasant agency is not about revolutionary systemic overthrow but rather a continuous and clandestine kind of struggle ('everyday forms of resistance') to survive under feudalism, capitalism and socialism.[22]

In an attempt to disguise the conservative implications of this paradigmatic shift, postmodernism has pointed to the radical nature of its methodological approach: deconstruction, presented by exponents as an act of subversion that involves questioning everything. Accordingly, the recasting of peasant agency as 'everyday forms of resistance' has been accompanied by an ubiquitous tendency on the part of postmodern theory to label any identity/agency as 'subversive', an overworked and now largely meaningless concept which fails to ask the second and third of three important questions: not that something is being challenged, with a view to overturning it (the first and easiest one), therefore, but *why* this challenge is being mounted, and *what politics* inform this action and prefigure its outcome (the second and third, more difficult questions). Those who ask only the first question, and let the issue rest there, generally slot both agency and agent into a progressive framework, and consequently leave the politics of what is invariably categorized as 'resistance' unasked. Only by raising and then interrogating the politics of this latter process, however, is it possible to understand that 'resistance' is not necessarily progressive, and can be a form of struggle conducted as much by reactionaries on the political right as by progressives on the left.

Empowering Peasant Agency?

Perhaps the most influential contemporary approach to the peasant agency in the so-called Third World is the subaltern studies series.[23] Questioning the relevance of universals and the emancipatory object of the historical process, it supports the postmodern/post-colonial view of a culturally empowered peasantry as a 'natural' category outside and against history, and thus confers epistemological acceptability on the struggle ('resistance') of its constituent subjects to retain their traditions.[24] The same is true of the new social movements framework, which claims that contemporary rural activism is also mainly about cultural empowerment, and thus constitutes a break with the politics and practice of the past.[25] Farmers' movements which emerged in a variety of different national contexts (India, Mexico) during the 1980s and the 1990s are regarded by postmodern theorists as examples of an authentically new and classless form of agrarian radicalism that is both apolitical and anti-state, part of the new social movements composed of tribals, peasants, environmentalists and women.[26] In Latin America, it is claimed, such movements are authentic 'from below' phenomena, rural grassroots struggles the aim of which is to reproduce peasant economy, to celebrate ethnic identity, and to protect traditional culture.[27] However, as some of the contributions to this volume suggest, this claim is both open to question and – where true – politically problematic.[28]

McNeish, de Souza Martins, and Nugent all highlight the role of NGOs and other external forces in the ideological foregrounding of ethnic identity, thereby confirming that – *pace* postmodernism and subalternism – this particular form of 'otherness' is not simply a 'from below' phenomenon. Thus McNeish argues that it was the neoliberal structural adjustment programme, imposed on Bolivia during the mid-1980s, which undermined rural trade union organizations and left-wing politics, creating a space for traditional indigenous authorities and discourses to reassert their political power. He shows not only how the reassertion of ethnic identity in the municipality of Santuario de Quillacas in the Bolivian Highlands during the 1990s enabled better-off peasants to avoid having to share their economic resources with the inhabitants of poorer rural communities in the vicinity, but also – and more importantly – that it was outsiders (NGOs, anthropologists) who reintroduced Quillacans to their history, thereby providing the better-off elements with the very weapons necessary for this politically conservative process of 'reinventing Andean tradition'. Much the same point is made by de Souza Martins, who attributes to external 'mediating groups' (the church, political parties) an important role in the ideological formulation and emergence in Brazil of a conceptually homogeneous 'new' rural subject, notwithstanding the historical and regional diversity of the agrarian structure and workforce. Like de Souza Martins, Nugent also maintains that the essentialist notion of an homogeneous Amazonian peasantry is a concept reproduced in the main externally – by, for example, the MST (the Sem Terra Movement) as a result of the agrarian struggles taking place in the south of Brazil.

This view is complemented by Brass who, in his critique of the historiographical transfer from South Asia to Latin America of the subaltern framework, indicates how a search for an 'authentic' grassroots identity has led to the (re-)discovery by Latin American exponents of subalternism of a traditional form of rural cultural 'otherness' associated with the reactionary politics of the 1930s. In addition to the familiar economic objections made by Marxists to the theory of peasant economy, therefore, Brass insists there is also a basic *political* difficulty – that historically an essentialist concept of a 'classless' peasant has been (and is still) a central ideological emplacement of the political right – which most contemporary Marxists either ignore or of which they remain unaware.[29] It is this, as much as anything, which led to a recuperation by some variants of Marxist theory of peasant economy during the 1960s and 1970s, and a consequent epistemological inability in the 1980s and 1990s to combat the appropriation by the emerging 'new' postmodern populism of a discourse proclaiming the culturally empowering role of peasant economy.[30] Not the least of the many ironies is the fact that, historically and contemporaneously, the political right – its opposition to the 'foundational' universal categories associated with a socialist politics (class formation/struggle/consciousness that transcend national boundaries) notwithstanding – subscribes to what amounts to its own form of conservative internationalism: the agrarian myth, at the centre of which is an essentialist concept of peasant economy and culture.[31]

Just how conservative are claims made by this 'new' postmodern populism about the empowering nature of 'from below' forms of cultural resistance conducted by an essentialist notion of Latin American peasants emerges from the critical analysis by Jansen and Roquas of the ideological and political role of devil pact narratives in Central America. Taking issue with the work of Taussig and Edelman, both of whom conceptualize the devil pact narrative as a discourse connected not with class but with gender or as evidence for an empowering resistance by peasant smallholders to capitalism, Jansen and Roquas argue that this discourse is much rather a politically conservative way of expressing grassroots antagonism about rural class inequality and wealth.[32] Rather than being a straightforward exchange between the devil and a particular individual who swaps his soul for wealth, therefore, it is clear that in Central America the pact with the devil entails not one but three very different kinds of symbolic exchange, each with its own class relation.[33] By attributing wealth to supernatural origins, however, the devil pact avoids confronting head-on the material basis of rapid capital accumulation within a particular rural community, and thus epistemologically locates this process in a (non-temporal) domain where – peasants can maintain plausibly – nothing can be done to alter surplus generating social relationships. Against the claim that devil pact narratives in Central America are empowering 'from below' forms of resistance to capitalism, Jansen and Roquas argue that such a discourse is much rather a politically *dis*empowering form of false consciousness.[34]

What the contributions to this volume in their different ways suggest is that all attempts by neoliberalism, populism and postmodernism to locate empowerment within capitalism are based on a misplaced view of the latter as a static, harmonious, crisis-free and thus essentially benign system. In pleading for a return to a 'kinder'/'caring' form of capitalism, therefore, exponents of these 'new' theories forget that, because the contradictions inherent in the accumulation process generate both economic crisis and its attendant class struggle, there is not (and cannot be) a 'steady state' tension-free capitalism suspended in a permanent equilibrium. The political difficulty now faced by born-again liberals (many of whom either used to be – or indeed continue wrongly to regard themselves as – Marxists) is as a consequence simply stated. No longer socialists, but still wedded to the idea of progress, they find themselves caught between having to support either the continued onward march of capitalism (= economic development) or reactionary anti-capitalist discourses/regimes currently opposed to further 'globalization' and 'Westernization'. For those who remain Marxists, however, no such dilemma exists: dismissing these two positions as a false dichotomy, Marxists – now as in the past – insist socialism constitutes the only form of systemic transcendence that goes beyond both capitalism and its reactionary anti-capitalist opponents. The dynamic of this systemic transcendence is itself located in the agrarian question, a debate that many exponents of 'new' postmodern populism dismiss as an 'old' (= irrelevant) paradigm.

II

The agrarian question is a longstanding debate between neopopulism and Marxism about the role of peasants in two kinds of systemic transition: from feudalism to capitalism, and from the latter to socialism. In the classical texts of Marxism – the main Marxist contributions to the debate were made in 1899 by Lenin and Kautsky – the process of accumulation that constitutes capitalist development is itself premised on an agrarian transition, which releases a marketed agricultural surplus that is transferred to industry.[35] Differentiating the peasantry into its rich, middle and poor components, Lenin argued that capitalist development in agriculture converted the former into a rural bourgeoisie and the latter into a proletariat, while middle peasants (or petty commodity producers) were 'depeasantized', and over time also became landless labourers. He also argued that, historically, capitalist penetration of a latifundist agriculture followed two distinct paths. The first was the Prussian model, in which the development of landlord capitalism on the estate system led to the impoverishment or eviction of its tenants. Labour-service relations between landlord and tenant continued, no new techniques were adopted, and agricultural production remained low. In the American model, by contrast, it was the better-off estate tenants who became capitalist producers and expropriated their landlords. The abolition of rent enabled these rich peasants to invest surpluses in new technology and thus to increase output.[36]

The significance of Lenin's two-path model of agrarian transformation for debates about rural development in Latin America lies in the historical importance there of the large landed estate (*hacienda*, *fundo*).[37] Although elaborated with reference to agrarian transitions in nineteenth-century European countries, the Prussian/American model is relevant to an understanding of landlord/tenant struggles leading to a transformation of large landed estates in the Andean regions of Latin America, notably the *hacienda* system in Peru and Chile during the twentieth century. Latifundia and plantations were the target of the three main agrarian reforms in Latin America, carried out in Cuba (1959–63) by the revolutionary government of Fidel Castro, in Chile (1964–73) by the civilian Presidents Frei and Allende, and in Peru (1969–75) by the military regime of President Velasco, all of whom redistributed land and converted tenants with usufruct rights into peasant proprietors, a pattern which lends credence to the American path.[38] Nugent, Assies and de Souza Martins, however, argue that – in contrast to the Leninist model – peasant economy in Bolivia and Brazil did not precede capitalism but much rather was introduced and reproduced by it.

OLD PARADIGMS – PARADIGMS LOST?

Assies outlines how, in the case of Bolivia, the economic decline of rubber tapping during the 1930s was accompanied by the emergence of peasant economy linked to Brazil nut gathering on small plots of land leased by estate-owners to their rubber tappers. The inexorable decline in rubber prices, a trend reversed briefly only during the Second World War and the 1970s, made Brazil nut gathering by Bolivian rubber tappers and their families an increasingly important alternative source of income. Much the same was true of Brazil where, as de Souza Martins shows, it was a commercial export-oriented agriculture which introduced specific forms of petty commodity production: the *colonato* system in the case of the São Paulo coffee plantations, the *seringuero* system in the case of rubber extraction in Amazonia, and the *cambão* relation on sugar plantations. In all these contexts, therefore, petty commodity production was implanted as a result of capitalist penetration, and is accordingly not pre-capitalist in origin. Where rubber estates and sugar or coffee plantations were concerned, the object of ceding usufruct rights to members of the workforce on the part of landlords and/or planters was to obtain additional workers for capitalist agriculture, in the shape of labour-power belonging to family members, usually women and children. The historical roots of the present agrarian crisis in Brazil, as represented by movements for the repossession of and/or the right to work on the land, are to be found – de Souza Martins maintains – in the earlier process of agrarian restructuring, whereby capitalist producers dispossessed/expelled members of the existing permanent workforce who had usufruct rights to land, and replaced them with temporary/casual/seasonal labour that was landless.[39] Rather than reasserting ancient property rights, therefore, struggles for land in Brazil are of a more recent provenance.

Accounting for the historical invisibility of a specifically Amazonian peasantry where ethnographic analysis is concerned, Nugent argues that this absence is due to a number of interrelated causes: the fact that cultivation is and has been combined with other forms of economic activity (hunting/gathering, goldmining, fishing), that the indigenous population of tribals is not a peasantry while Amazonian peasants are themselves composed of non-indigenous immigrants, and the predominance of an environmental deterministic discourse (smallholders are perceived in terms of ecological 'carrying capacity'). Like de Souza Martins, Nugent emphasizes that peasants in Amazonia have their origin in migrants escaping from the declining plantation economy of the northeast who became rubber tappers and, following the decline of the rubber extractive economy, reconstituted themselves as petty commodity producers combining multiple occupational roles with providing food for workers employed on development schemes in the region.[40] For this reason, the peasantry in Amazonia has not been depeasantized so much as transformed, along the lines suggested by Mintz for Jamaica – a 'reconstituted peasantry', but one that is reconstituted from a distance (migration). Like Murray (see below), however, Nugent expresses doubts about the long-term viability of peasant economy, as largescale/mechanized agribusiness enterprises shift to pasture, and thus increasingly monopolize large tracts of land as unproductive reserves, as a consequence of which the latter cease to be available for smallholding cultivation.

A related matter concerns the role of peasant producers in the world economy, and the implications of this for the *campesinista/descampesinista* debate and the agrarian question. The combined impact on rural Latin America of, on the one hand, a decline in land reform and, on the other, the implementation of neoliberal economic policies is evident from the contributions by Crabtree on Peru and Murray on Chile. Crabtree outlines how, in the case of Peruvian agriculture during the 1980s and 1990s, it was peasant smallholders who were economically most dependent on the existence of a buoyant and stable demand in domestic urban areas for the commodities they produced. When this domestic demand for the output of peasant agriculture contracted, either as a result of wage-cutting neoliberal industrial policies, or was met by cheap imports from abroad (again the result of market liberalization by the Fujimori government), the consequence was an inevitable economic decline on the part of petty commodity production and a corresponding increase in the incidence of rural poverty.[41] A twofold process thus characterizes the Peruvian countryside: impoverishment means that *minifundización* is combined with working for others and/or migration to the towns/cities, while other rural producers have been and are doing quite well. Into the latter category come large-scale export-oriented agribusiness enterprises (agro-industry producing for 'niche' foreign markets), those cultivating coca for the international drug trade, and rich coffee-growing peasants who have benefited from exporting into world markets, all of which have consolidated and even expanded the amount of land they operate.

That not even relatively better-positioned peasants are now able to survive in the world market as independent smallholders is a point made by Murray with regard to Chile, where the neoliberal counter-reform imposed by the military dictatorship after 1973 created a sector of small-to-medium-sized commercial proprietors (*parceleros*) from agricultural land that had been collectivized/cooperativized. Cultivating cash-crops (apples, grapes) for export, these peasant farmers were contractually tied to and (increasingly tightly) controlled by the national/international agribusiness enterprises which not only provided growers with capital investment but also marketed their output. Over the 1980s and 1990s, however, as capitalist competition and overproduction increased globally, many of these Chilean peasant farmers were engulfed by crisis, which resulted in the economic differentiation of the peasantry. The latter process took the form of disguised proletarianization and/or full proletarianization: increasingly, therefore, indebted *parceleros* were required to sell their land to agribusiness enterprises to which they owed money, and either continued working on land they no longer owned or sold their own labour-power (and that of their kinsfolk) off-farm in order to generate additional income.

The case made by Murray in this connection – that in economic terms the peasant survival threshold is probably much lower than thought – in effect precludes the reproduction of what many observers (especially postmodernists) and development theorists (especially neopopulists and neoclassical economists) have regarded as viable peasant agriculture. It is clear from this Chilean case-study, therefore, that in a *laissez faire* global market peasant producers throughout Latin America have to compete both in international markets and in their own domestic ones with agricultural exports from advanced capitalist countries, a situation which casts doubt on the long-term capacity of the peasant family farm to reproduce itself economically. This problem also underlines the central difficulty faced by those Marxists who continue to theorize the agrarian question at the level of the nation state: while peasant cultivators in Latin America (and elsewhere in the so-called Third World) may indeed be economically efficient when compared to unproductive landlords in their own countries, this is not the case when they have to compete with efficient high-tech international agribusiness enterprises in world markets.[42] In other words, a consequence of limiting the agrarian question to national social formations is that crucial processes – of class formation, surplus generation and transfer – occurring within agriculture that license the continued reproduction of international as distinct from national capital (that is, the *systemic* logic of capitalism) can mistakenly be declared to be at an end.

(Dis-)Empowering Labour Regimes

Linked to this is the debate about transformations occurring in the labour regime, an issue that also touches not just on the agrarian question itself but also on the debate about the connection between capitalist development and the employment of unfree labour. Evidence from many Latin American contexts suggests that an important effect of the neoliberal economic policies applied during the last three decades of the twentieth century has been a strong trend toward part-time work and a pronounced gendering of the workforce, a pattern confirmed here by Assies, de Souza Martins, Crabtree and Murray with regard to Bolivia, Brazil, Peru and Chile. Where current employment patterns involving poor peasants are concerned, therefore, peasant smallholders and/or members of their families offer their labour-power for sale to larger agrarian units and/or off-farm employers on a temporary/casual basis, because employers themselves now only want a casualized/feminized workforce.[43] That the latter is not necessarily, always and everywhere a proletariat, however, is point made by Assies, de Souza Martins, and Jansen and Roquas. Assies demonstrates how in the Northern Bolivian Amazon region the *habilito* system of labour contracting has been – and continues to be – utilized by agribusiness enterprises to obtain workers. This form of recruitment is based on a system of cash advances made by a merchant or producer to a worker, whose resulting indebtedness prevents him either – when he is a peasant smallholder – from selling commodities he produces on the free market in order to realize the highest price, or – when he is mainly an agricultural labourer – from selling his labour-power (his only commodity) in the free market in order to obtain the highest wage.

Part of the problem is that the 'transition' paradigm – the assumption that unfree labour is everywhere and always a pre-capitalist relation – is one to which both neoclassical economic historiography and certain kinds of Marxist theory adhere.[44] The result is that, for exponents of both, where debt bondage exists, capitalism cannot be present, and where capitalism is present what exists can only be free labour.[45] Thus, for example, Assies notes that in certain important respects the epistemological distinctions between apparently dissimilar analyses (by Barham and Coome, Weinstein, and Stoian) of production relations structuring rubber extraction in Bolivian Amazonia are not that great. All of them reject the interpretation of debt bondage as a coercive relation, and subscribe instead to what might be termed the combined 'risk-avoidance'/'subsistence guarantee' view, whereby both parties to the relation (merchant and/or employer, rubber tapper) benefit economically from the arrangement. The dynamic of the latter is consequently reinterpreted: the debt relation ceases to be a forcible method of extracting surplus labour (= a form of unfree labour), and thus a source of acute and continuing struggle between tapper and merchant or employer, and becomes instead a non-coercive, tension-free – and thus benign – form of patron/clientage, a mutually-beneficial arrangement freely entered into by all concerned.[46]

In a similar vein, Jansen and Roquas show not just how capitalist accumulation by a wealthy landowner in Honduras is centrally dependent on debt relations with his workers, but also how this relationship prevents them from linking their poverty to his riches, attributing the latter instead to supernatural causation in the form of a pact with the devil. Rather than promoting class consciousness, therefore, the existence of debt relations contributes to a situation of false consciousness, whereby rural workers reify their relationships with capital. Much the same point is made by de Souza Martins with regard to the Amazon region in Brazil, where the workforce employed by advanced multinational agribusiness enterprises is recruited and retained by means of debt peonage, a pattern that suggests a process of restructuring whereby dispossession (= depeasantization) accompanied by casualization generates not free but rather unfree relations of production.

Relevant to the way in which such labour regimes in the Amazon region have been and are reproduced is the teleological link between peonage and what might be termed the 'tropical nastiness' doctrine, or arguments to the effect that in Amazonia tropical disease/climate hinder/preclude the existence of 'normal' agricultural production and social relations, an issue considered here by Nugent. Just as for employers a discourse about the innate climactic 'otherness' of Amazonia licensed slavery and peonage, therefore, so nowadays abolitionist NGOs and postmodernists (such as

Taussig) deploy the same epistemology but for different ends. The latter infer that only its own form of 'other' – an indigenous subject that is conceptualized these days as the ubiquitous 'subaltern' – is truly able to survive economically in Amazonia. Both positions – the first political economy and the postmodern version of the 'green hell' discourse – in effect exclude the economic activity and/or relational forms encountered in the wider (non-Amazonian) society, and (unlike the second political economy version adhered to by opponents of coerced labour) each adheres epistemologically to the same discourse of Amazonia-as-untameable-Nature.[47]

(Dis-)Empowering Rural Agency

The politics of the agrarian question concern the revolutionary agency by the three components of the peasantry (rich, middle and poor) – distinct in terms of class, and thus in opposite political camps – in two systemic transitions (from feudalism to capitalism, and from the latter to socialism). In general terms, classical Marxism has always questioned the revolutionary potential of an undifferentiated peasantry, allocating to it a subordinate political role in a worker/peasant alliance. Some, such as Lenin and Kautsky, advocated merely the political neutralization of the peasantry, while others – such as Trotsky and Luxemburg – regarded it as actively counter-revolutionary, maintaining that once they became proprietors, peasants would oppose further attempts to socialize the means of production.[48] In contrast to 'new' postmodern populists, therefore, Marxism has always regarded identity/agency connected with peasant smallholding as neither progressive politically nor viable systemically. What Marxists do accept, however, is the ideological potency of peasant identity, particularly when deployed in the course of agrarian struggles as a populist mobilizing discourse to disguise the different (and potentially antagonistic) class positions and interests of the participants.

Thus a central role was played in Latin America by better-off peasants in mobilizations with socialist objectives (the 1959 Cuban Revolution, and the 1979 Sandinista Revolution in Nicaragua) as well as non-socialist ones (the 1952 Bolivian Revolution), all of which resulted in extensive agrarian reforms. With the demise of the landlord class as a result of post-war land reform programmes, agrarian populism shifted to reflecting the political and economic interests of capitalist farmers and rich peasants who – like landlords during the pre-war era – were similarly faced with potential or actual challenges from poor peasants and landless agricultural labourers. Populism was the mobilizing ideology deployed by Latin American rich peasants engaged in cash-crop cultivation. In Peru, it was used by tenants growing coffee for the world market in the 1960s and by better-off peasants growing coca for the international drug trade in the 1980s, and also in Colombia, by coffee-growing small agrarian capitalists during the 1970s.[49] All these peasant movements not only possessed as their main objective a redistribution of land but also continued to exhibit a powerful combination of nationalist and agrarian populist ideology.

During the 1990s rural grassroots movements have changed their emphasis, away from land redistribution (although this objective remains on the political agenda of poor peasants and agricultural labourers) and towards a combination of opposition to neoliberal policies, declining crop prices, the power of the state and higher taxation, and a concern with environmental and identity politics (sustainable economic development, biodiversity, ecofeminist and gender issues, ethnicity). This is true not just of peasants in Latin American countries (the Zapatista Army of National Liberation in the Mexican state of Chiapas, the Landless Rural Workers Movement in Brazil), but also of rural producers and inhabitants plus urban consumers in industrialized Europe and North America (the Countryside Alliance in the UK, farmers' movements in France, the anti-capitalist mobilizations against the World Trade Organization). Against postmodern/populist interpretations of these movements as 'new', however, exponents of 'old' paradigms would make the following two points: first, some of these rural mobilizations still represent the class interests of rich peasants and commercial farmers, and where this is not the case, mobilize on the basis of a non-progressive ideology; and second, all these 'new' movements raise the question of the class instrumentality of the state.[50]

III

That the institution of the state, and the instrumentality of its class politics, remains a central issue in any history of the Latin American peasantry is clear from the contribution to this volume by Petras and Veltmeyer.[51] Rejecting currently fashionable analysis, much of which is interested only in empowerment achieved within the existing bourgeois polity (= 'redemocratization'), and consequently either ignores the role of the state altogether (as in the case of postmodern approaches to the peasantry), or else downplays the significance of class in its instrumentality (preferring instead to focus on the state as a 'strong'/'weak' institution, and whether or not it practices 'good governance'), they contend that the major function of the state in Latin America throughout history has been and remains to shape the agrarian economy in the interests of the ruling class.[52]

At times, Petras and Veltmeyer argue, this has required a pro-peasant stance, such as promulgating agrarian reform legislation and the provision of credit and other inputs, while at others it has entailed an equally powerful anti-peasant intervention. The latter has taken either a direct form, such as the exercise in periods of acute class conflict of violence and/or military repression against guerrilla movements and rural-based armed struggle, or an indirect (but more insidious) form based on the political strategy of co-opting peasant movements and/or leaders. The main strength of the neoliberal state in Latin America, Petras and Veltmeyer suggest, derives paradoxically from the weakness of its rural opponents: the incapacity of contemporary anti-systemic movements in Brazil and Mexico, which contain a sizeable and socio-economically heterogeneous rural following, to build significant political support/alliances in the cities, coupled with the mass exodus of peasants from Ecuador, Colombia, Central America and the Caribbean.

THE STATE OF THE PEASANTRY?

Broadly speaking, there currently exist at least four different theories about the political nature and economic role of the peasant/state relationship: Marxist, Keynesian, neoliberal and what might be termed a culturalist version. Although there are obvious differences of emphasis, these four models all circulate within the domain of political economy, and either currently attract or have attracted in the recent past the attention of those with an interest in Third World and/or Latin American economic development. Their politics notwithstanding, these four concepts generate two distinct – and actually opposing – views about the peasant/state relation: whereas in Marxist theory the state is ranged against the peasant smallholder, in their different ways Keynesianism, neoliberalism and culturalism all correspond to frameworks in which the state intervenes on behalf of the peasantry.

Because for Marxism the peasantry is internally differentiated in terms of class, the first model of peasant/state relations does not allocate smallholders as such either a progressive role or an independent voice where the instrumentality of the state is concerned. Both the latter characteristics are extended by Marxism not to peasants but rather to agricultural workers and rich peasants in their respective roles as representatives of labour and capital engaged in class struggle, initially for the control of the state apparatus and subsequently through the state apparatus itself. Thus the revolutionary seizure of the state is historically the political objective of two different classes. As an ascendant bourgeoisie composed of small capitalist producers, rich peasants are in the course of a capitalist transition engaged in conflict against the state which represents the political interests of the landlord class, only to be dislodged in turn from state power by the proletariat and poor peasantry in the course of a transition to socialism. Since in the course of this class formation/struggle a peasantry is subject to a continuous process of 'depeasantization', it cannot discharge a similarly autonomous historical role; for this reason, an homogeneous/undifferentiated peasantry is not considered by Marxism to constitute an independent revolutionary force capable of realizing its own specific interests/programme as a result of seizure/exercise of state power.[53]

In the second model of peasant/state relations – the ECLA (United Nations Economic Commission for Latin America) or Keynesian – by contrast, smallholders are the economic beneficiaries of state intervention, but only incidentally so. Whereas many still adhere to the view that, in the debate about state planning versus the free market, ECLA was firmly in the camp of the former, its position was rather more complex. Arguing that the existing monopoly of agricultural land by unproductive landlords prevented this resource from becoming available to the economically more efficient smallholders who would cultivate it and sell the crops they grew, some of those connected with ECLA advocated political intervention by the state: the latter, it was argued, would expropriate landlords, thereby enabling land to be converted into a commodity available to the most efficient producer.[54] The dual assumption was, first, that an efficient agricultural market would involve only domestic producers, and second, that commercially-minded peasant smallholders would as a consequence be the main beneficiaries of this politically interventionist policy undertaken by the state. In short, ECLA was not opposed to the market as such but favoured state intervention in order to make the market work. The primary objectives of this Keynesian policy were economic: land reform would not only break the monopoly over land exercised by inefficient landlords but also turn land into a commodity. Only insofar as they were economically the most efficient producers, however, would Latin American peasants gain advantage from this process.

Much the same is true of the third approach to peasant/state relations in Latin America: the neoliberal model, widely applied throughout Latin America during the 1970s and 1980s. As with the Keynesian policy of ECLA, it is also necessary to question a widely held view about neoliberal economic theory. Although it is commonly assumed that the market was the institution around which neoliberal theory circulated, the focus of its discourse was – like that of ECLA – on the role of the state.[55] Where agriculture is concerned, monetarists perceive the state as discharging a dual but limited role: on the one hand a positive one, to guarantee the reproduction of private property relations and the free market; and on the other a negative one – the simultaneous prevention of monopolies, precisely since the formation/operation of the latter precludes the freedoms embodied in each of the former (individual property, the market).[56] If it is the case that agricultural commodities are being produced efficiently for the market by medium- or small-scale peasant farming, then the latter is an economic category that is as acceptable to neoliberalism as any other kinds of rural enterprise. In terms of political objective, therefore, the monetarist policies applied to the Latin American peasantry during the 1970s and 1980s represent to some degree a continuity of and not a break with earlier ECLA development strategy: namely, using the state to ensure the functioning of the market.

The fourth approach to the state is one which, despite (or, indeed, perhaps because of) its nineteenth-century origins, has until recently attracted little interest. It involves what might be termed the culturally specific state, in which this institution coincides with and therefore represents the political and economic interests of a particular ethnic group.[57] According to this conceptualization, the nation composed of a culturally homogeneous 'people' united by common language, customs and ethnicity, both precedes and need not necessarily ever result in the formation of the state.[58] Whereas the existence of the state is itself dependent on a pre-existing 'people' who themselves form a nation, the presence of a linguistically/culturally homogeneous 'people' does not of itself lead to or require state formation/reproduction. Nationhood, or the active realization of a nation within the boundaries of the state, happens when a 'people' formally asserts its 'national spirit' and 'national will', as a result of which the state henceforth embodies 'a collective personality, legal and political', and can thus be said, first, to have come about as a consequence of a 'people' exercising agency as such, and second, to constitute the political expression of this particular unity.[59]

States of Uncertainty?

The implications for the peasantry in contemporary Latin America of these different theories about the role of the state are not difficult to discern. If there is a space for peasants *qua* peasants in Marxist theory about the state, then it is a politically reactionary one: namely, their role in Bonapartism, a situation usually (but not necessarily only) of economic crisis in which independent peasant proprietors are to be found in the vanguard of the counter-revolution.[60] This pessimistic interpretation is borne out by the role of Latin American peasants in a number of different contexts over the latter half of the twentieth century. Once they had become proprietors as a result of agrarian reform, therefore, the unionized rich tenants who led the peasant movement against the landlord class in the eastern lowlands of Peru during the early 1960s not only ceased to be union members but also turned on poor peasants and agricultural labourers (their erstwhile allies in the anti-landlord struggle), and in the post-reform era deployed many of the same kinds of exploitative/oppressive practices/mechanisms as had landlords (low agricultural wages, land evictions, bonded labour relations).[61]

In a similar vein, attempts by the three most significant left-wing regimes in Latin America – Castro's Cuba from 1959 onwards, the Chilean Popular Unity government of Allende of the early 1970s, and the Nicaraguan Sandinista government during the 1980s – to plan/regulate agricultural production/distribution on behalf the urban and rural working class by, for example, extending the existing agrarian reform programme to include poor peasants and agricultural labourers, improving wage levels received by urban/rural labour, and controlling basic commodity prices, was in each case either opposed, blocked or undermined by better-off peasants.[62] This was possible because, in the case of Cuba, the sector of privately owned farms was not only considerable but composed of average sized units far in excess of those elsewhere in Latin America, a situation which in turn contributed to the rapid expansion of the black market, and – from the late 1980s onwards – decollectivization and land privatization.[63]

It could be argued that a main shortcoming in the Keynesian approach of ECLA to peasant/state relations in Latin America was the assumption that a global division of labour would separate countries in the Third World, where the focus would be on agricultural production, from those in metropolitan capitalist contexts, where nations would concentrate on industrial production. What Keynesian theory failed to understand was that an effect of the spread of capitalism would be that Latin American peasants had to compete with commodities produced by the advanced agriculture in metropolitan contexts, and it was into this theoretical gap, about the boundaries of the market in which Latin American peasants would compete economically, that neoliberalism inserted itself. Only peasant proprietors who were better-off managed to do this, while those who did not featured increasingly in the fourth model of peasant/state relations: the culturally-specific state.

The reasons for re-emergence towards the end of the twentieth century of a nineteenth-century view about the realization of both nationhood and statehood in the form of a culturally-specific state, are too obvious to require much elaboration. From the Balkans to the erstwhile Soviet Union, the break-up of the existing state has resulted in a process of political decentralization not of the state itself but much rather of national identity, which has in turn given rise to claims to nationhood/statehood on the basis of ever-smaller and much older territorial units. In short, a process which involves the reassertion by those claiming to form a 'people' possessing ancient territorial rights, on which the realization of a nation within the boundaries of the state are now increasingly based.[64] In the case of Latin America, this kind of state (re-)formation has been advocated historically both by socialists (José Carlos Maríategui, Hildebrando Castro Pozo) and by populists (Victor Raúl Haya de la Torre), all of whom insisted on building independent nations on the basis of what they perceived as an 'authentic' indigenous form of 'Inca communism'.[65] More recently, the idea of a culturally-specific state has been advanced by *indigenista* theorists now associated with the application of a postmodern subaltern studies project to the study of Latin American peasants.[66] This view has been supported by, among others, Albó with regard to the Bolivian Aymara, on the grounds that smallholding peasants belonging to that indigenous group had a culture and viable economic organizational forms that were specific to it, and as such constituted a nation that preceded Spanish colonialism.[67]

NOTES

1. Symptomatic postmodern theoretical approaches to the study of peasants and/or the subject of economic development in the so-called Third World would include not only those by Clark [1991], Friedmann [1992], Foweraker [1995], Escobar [1995], Brohman [1996], and Williams [2001], but also many of the contributions to the collections edited by Eckstein [1989], Foweraker and Craig [1990], Escobar and Alvarez [1992], Galli [1992], Pieterse [1992], Schuurman [1993], Booth [1994], Sinclair [1995], and Fox and Starn [1997]. The literature about the 1994 Zapatista uprising in Chiapas and its background is vast, and includes Clarke and Ross [1994], Reygadas *et al.* [1994], Cleaver [1994], Tello Díaz [1995], Gilly [1998], Díaz Polanco [1998], Harvey [1990; 1998], Otero [1999], Burgete Cal y Mayor [2000], Weinberg [2000], Nash [2001], and Hodges [2002].
2. Rather touchingly, some neoclassical economic interpretations of the peasantry continue to puzzle over whether or not peasants act as 'rational economic agents'. This, as every serious scholar of the peasantry knows, is a deeply patronizing and now wholly discredited argument about whether or not peasants are stupid; that peasants are not stupid, and do the best they can with the economic resources at their disposal (i.e., those which they can afford to purchase) is an uncontroversial proposition which nowadays occupies no-one apart from a few out-of-date neoclassical economic historians. It is, to put it bluntly, of the same epistemological order as the medieval theological debate about how many angels can fit on the head of a pin, and about as relevant to contemporary concerns. Because neoclassical economic historians focus on 'choice-making' individuals exercising 'subjective preferences', they fail to ask what is nowadays the more interesting question: why do peasants generally have only these and not other economic resources? The latter is a question that, historically, has always been asked by Marxists.
3. Even neoclassical economic historians [*Fogel*, 2000; *Sivakumar*, 2001: 57, note 32] acknowledge the existence of an epistemological overlap between their own views and those advanced by the 'new' populist postmodernism. Thus, for example, Fogel – whose marginalist economic framework informed the conservative and highly influential revisionist account [*Fogel and Engerman*, 1974] of *antebellum* plantation slavery as non-coercive/'benign'/'mild' – deploys the familiar anti-foundational argument of postmodernism in support of his present and equally conservative claim that poverty is no longer about material but spiritual deprivation [*Fogel*, 2000]. In his view, therefore, grassroots agency (= assertiveness/resistance) should henceforth be aimed at the realization of cultural empowerment (= postmodern agenda), which according to him has now replaced economic empowerment (= modern agenda) within the context of capitalism. The reactionary role of postmodernism in this discourse is evident from the following [*Fogel*, 2000: 2]: 'The agenda for egalitarian policies that has dominated reform movements for most of the past century – what I call the *modernist* egalitarian agenda – was based on material redistribution. The critical aspect of a *postmodern* egalitarian agenda is not the distribution of money income, or food, or shelter, or consumer durables. Although there are

still glaring inadequacies in the distribution of material commodities that must be addressed, the most intractable maldistributions in rich countries such as the United States are in the realm of spiritual or immaterial assets. These are the critical assets in the struggle for self-realization' (original emphasis).

4. The periodic attempt by some commentators [*Friedland*, 1991; *Buttel*, 2001] to move beyond the rival populist/Marxist interpretations of agrarian political economy by declaring them intellectually redundant, have failed precisely because of the inescapable epistemological and political importance of this dichotomy. Although Buttel [2001] wants to replace populist and Marxist paradigms, what he ends up with amounts to a perception of capitalism-without-class, an eclectic epistemological mishmash ('cultural-turn rural studies', 'actor-network studies', 'agri-food regulationism', postmodernism, post-developmentalism, etc.) that, on closer inspection, turns out to divide into the rival paradigms he so desperately wishes to transcend.
5. As has been pointed out elsewhere [*Brass*, 2000], in contexts where even a half-hearted socialist politics has been defeated, it is all too easy for the existing and/or continuing antagonism/opposition to capital to be channelled in a reactionary populist direction. Thus, for example, a better illustration of just such a populist mobilization than that undertaken by Osama bin Laden is difficult to imagine. To begin with, he himself is a rich and powerful capitalist who nevertheless espouses a backwards-looking ideological worldview, projecting a combination of anti-modern discourse/agency on behalf of the rural poor in an underdeveloped country on the one hand and an endorsement of traditionalist belief plus religious purity on the other. More importantly, both he and his anti-materialistic/anti-socialist/anti-Western views were first privileged and then reproduced from above, by the USA in furtherance of its struggle against a secular and materialistic communism in Afghanistan.
6. Marxists have long warned against this kind of nonsense, but to little avail. Those who were excluded from the academy during the 1990s for criticizing postmodernism as a form of neoliberalism, and pointing out its unambiguously conservative (not to say reactionary) political antecedents and effects, are currently witnessing an entirely predictable form of academic venality. Now that these Marxist criticisms have been vindicated, therefore, and the postmodern/neoliberal bandwagon has as a consequence begun to slow down, some anti-Marxist neoliberal postmodernists have surreptitiously watered down or shed their neoliberalism/postmodernism, and not only joined the ranks of its critics but also claimed that they were there all along! This kind of opportunism suggests that erstwhile postmodernists/neoliberals have little to learn from their fabled precursor, the Vicar of Bray.
7. For examples of the peasant-as-cultural-'other' approach of anthropology, see among many others the classic texts by Redfield [1930; 1941; 1956; 1958], Foster [1962; 1965] and Wolf [1966; 1971]. Historically, such culturalist images of peasant society have been particularly dominant in the case of Puerto Rico and Mexico, where the peasantry were depicted by anthropologists as belonging to (and constitutive of) a self-contained and hermetically sealed socio-economic system [*de Alcántara*, 1984]. Such 'folk peoples', according to Redfield [1930: 2], 'enjoy a common stock of tradition; they are the carriers of a culture [which] preserves its continuity from generation to generation … such a culture is local'. Similarly, the concept 'culture of poverty' – associated with the work of Oscar Lewis [1962; 1966; 1967a] – attributed rural poverty to psychologically innate negative cultural traits, while for Malinowski the participation in or withdrawal from market activity by Mexican peasants was governed by cultural factors, and not competition or declining prices/profits [*Malinowski and de la Fuentes* 1982: 177–9]. In responding to Stavenhagen [1967: 490], who accused him of saying 'being poor is terrible, but having a culture of poverty is not so bad', Lewis [1967b: 499] not only seems almost to agree but also to anticipate the postmodern celebration of culture-as-empowerment when he states: 'I am also suggesting that the poor in a pre-capitalistic caste-ridden society like India had some advantages over modern slum-dwellers because the people were organized in castes and *panchayats* … [p]erhaps Ghandi [*sic*] had the urban slums in mind when he wrote that the caste system was one of the greatest inventions of mankind.'
8. Applied by Murra [1972] to the organizational modalities of smallholders in the Peruvian

highlands, the concept 'verticality' refers to exchanges between peasants, rural communities, or land-based kin groups (*ayllus*) occupying different Andean ecosystems, where survival not surplus is the object of agricultural production. It is argued – again, largely by anthropologists [e.g., *Fioravanti-Molinie*, 1973] – that culturally determined reciprocity embodied in traditional community institutions (*mink'a*, *ayni*, *compadrazgo*) constitute an indigenous levelling mechanism which guarantees the subsistence of the rural population. It also prevents capital accumulation and peasant differentiation, and thus accounts for the continued existence of the Andean peasantry. For more on Andean 'verticality' and more generally the role of traditional institutional forms in rural communities, see Crabtree, Assies, Jansen and Roquas, and McNeish (this volume).

9. See Hilton [1976].
10. Both the 1949 Chinese Revolution and the Cuban Revolution a decade later contributed to this anxiety.
11. The prevailing orthodoxy in the 1960s/1970s debate about the mode of production in Latin American agriculture – a debate which in theoretical and political terms closely mirrored that taking place with regard to India [*Rudra* et al., 1978; *Thorner*, 1982] – was that economic stagnation, low growth rates, and inflation were all due to the continued existence of an economically backward feudal/semi-feudal agrarian sector (for similar claims by Stalinist historiography, see Afanasyev *et al.* [1974], Ulyanovsky [1974: 328, 329, 334, 350, 354], and Rutenberg [1988: ch.VII]). Consequently, exponents of this view argued, an as-yet absent process of capital accumulation could begin only when the expropriation of unproductive *latifundia* permitted the redistribution of under- or unused land to economically productive (but pauperized) smallholders throughout rural Latin America. The political subtext of this dualistic framework – itself a variation on other similarly dichotomous economic models ('market'/'subsistence', 'modern'/'traditional', etc.) – is, argues Borón [1981: 57–8], that 'a landowning fraction of the bourgeoisie would appear or outwardly perform as a decadent landed gentry. Indeed, the whole social structure of each formation, its culture, State and ideology, reflected the overdetermination of the nascent capitalist order by archaic social relations. So powerful were these feudal aristocratic elements that, for a whole epoch, there was an unfortunate and widespread belief among popular forces that the socio-economic system in Latin America was not capitalism but feudalism.' Among those who challenged this orthodoxy at that conjuncture were Frank [1967: 221–42; 1969: 350–61; 1979], Stavenhagen [1968], Vitale [1968], and Petras [1970: 381–2].
12. For the details of this process in Latin America, see Burbach and Flynn [1980] and Teubal [1987].
13. Whereas the text by di Tella [1965] on populism and Peronism makes no mention of a rural dimension to this discourse, the accounts by Hennessy [1969: 36ff.], about Latin American populism generally, and by Cotler [1971], about populism and the military in late 1960s Peru, do.
14. The most influential neo-populist theoretician has been and remains A.V. Chayanov (1888–1937), who at the beginning of the twentieth century denied that capitalist penetration of agriculture in Russia entailed 'depeasantization'. Instead he argued, first, that peasant economy remained the same despite exogenous systemic transformations (feudalism, capitalism, socialism) to which it was impervious, and second, that the economic reproduction of each individual peasant family farm was determined endogenously, by its demographic cycle. According to Chayanov [1966; 1991], the basic aspects of rural economic organization such as landholding size, food output, and work motivation ('self-exploitation') by sociologically undifferentiated petty commodity producers were governed by a specific combination of factors. These were the size of the peasant family itself, the ratio of working to non-working household members (or the labour/consumer balance), and the necessity of having to provide all the latter with their subsistence requirements (the drudgery of labour).
15. For examples of the argument attributing 'peasant persistence' to economic efficiency in the case of Colombia, Guatemala, Mexico, Ecuador, and Peru, see Reinhardt [1988], Gordillo [1988], Glover and Kusterer [1990], and Korovkin [1997]. Over the last two decades the

most influential exponents of Chayanovian views [*Lipton*, 1977; *Bates*, 1981, 1983, 2001: 30ff.; *Shanin*, 1990] have argued with particular reference to India and Africa that rural development and food production should be based on efficient peasant smallholding cultivation. Any economic failure on the part of the latter is attributed by Lipton and Bates to 'urban bias', or the conceptualization of appropriation and conflict not as intra-sectoral but rather as inter-sectoral (the countryside, agriculture and peasants all ranged against the state, the city, industry, urban workers, bureaucrats and industrialists). In order to off-set urban bias, they advocate the adoption in Third World countries of pro-peasant policies such as higher crop prices, lower taxation and larger agricultural price supports and subsidies.

16. See, for example, Cardoso and Faletto [1979: 127ff.], Collier [1979], Stein [1980], Coniff [1982], Loaeza [1995], Mayorga [1995], Perruci [1995], Cammack [2000], Philip [2000], and Demmers, Fernández Jilberto and Hogenboom [2001]. The analyses of agrarian populism in Mexico by Sanderson [1981] and Knight [1998] are exceptions in this regard, and more typical is the assessment by Coniff [1982: 13, 20] who, despite noting the populist antecedents of *indigenismo*, nevertheless maintains that '[p]opulism was urban in Latin America … populist movements and programs nearly always appeared in major cities'. Most recent analyses of Latin American populism remain mired in the epistemology structuring the earlier text on the subject by Laclau [1977: 143ff.], beyond which none have managed to move theoretically. The political significance of this is not difficult to discern: in his analysis of populism, therefore, lie the roots of the subsequent rightwards trajectory followed by Laclau [1985; 1989; 1990; 1992], for whom socialism, class and class struggle have now been abandoned, and replaced by (bourgeois) 'redemocratization' as the desirable end of grassroots action. The latter is for Laclau now the only possible form of agency: that is, a populist/postmodern form of mobilization based on 'new social movements', a plural-identity/non-class form of empowerment within (and thus compatible with) capitalism.
17. See Ianni [1975] and Borón [1981].
18. That Bonapartism is virtually indistinguishable from populism is clear from the observation by Marx [1979: 194] about the role of the former in the 1848 French revolution: 'Bonaparte looks on himself … as the representative of the peasants … [and he] wants to make the lower classes of the people happy within the framework of bourgeois society'. The political role of Bonapartism during the early stages of the Russian revolution was outlined by Trotsky [1934: 663] in the following manner, which suggests that he, too, regarded it as populist: 'The design had been by common consent to establish above the democracy and the bourgeoisie, who were paralysing each other, a "real" sovereign power. This idea of a master of destiny rising above all classes, is nothing but Bonapartism. If you stick two forks into a cork symmetrically, it will, under very great oscillations from side to side, keep its balance even on a pin point: that is the mechanical model of the Bonapartist superarbiter.' The link between Bonapartism on the one hand, and populism and fascism on the other, emerges from the case of 1930s Germany, where the same concept was applied by Trotsky [1975: 454] to the intermediary political regime that replaced bourgeois democracy and pre-figured fascism: 'a government of the sabre as the judge-arbiter of the nation – that's just what Bonapartism is. The sabre by itself has no independent programme. It is the instrument of "order". It is summoned to safeguard what exists. Raising itself *politically* above the classes, Bonapartism … represents *in the social sense*, always and at all epochs, the government of the strongest and firmest part of the exploiters' (original emphasis).
19. Unsurprisingly, academic assessments of the positive/negative impact of populism on the direction of grassroots mobilization in Latin America have been influenced strongly by the prevailing intellectual climate within the academy itself, a point that can be illustrated with reference to the case of Brazil. Hence the marked contrast between the pessimistic view of de Kadt [1970], who regarded the populism of Catholic radicals as contributing to the political weakness of rural agency in Brazil at the end of the 'development decade', and the over-optimistic/endorsing approach to this same mobilization subsequently on the part of Lehmann [1990], who also saw Catholic *basismo* as populist but – at the height of the postmodern reaction against development – celebrated this as a positive feature, characterizing *basismo* as an 'authentic' process of 'from below' empowerment. The more recent reassessments by Burdick [1993] and Hewitt [1998], however, have restored an

element of intellectual seriousness to this debate: not only do they show how conservative base Christian communities are, and how these kind of organizations have in effect depoliticized grassroots agency in Brazil, but their negative and critical interpretations vindicate the earlier less positive prognosis. (One can only smile at the bafflement now expressed by adherents of the overoptimistic view [*Lehmann and Bebbington*, 1998]: 'In an unexpected convergence, the anti-statism of neo-liberalism has found partners in the *basista* hostility to bureaucracy cultivated by the NGO movement'.) The correctness of the pessimistic interpretation – much 'new' grassroots discourse is neither grassroots, new, nor empowering – is borne out by many of the contributions to this volume.

20. The result has been to reinstate a view of rural life in Latin America not so dissimilar from an earlier and long-outdated perception of this as a tension-free rural arcadia, epitomized in the following idealized description of the Chilean *hacienda* system at the beginning of the twentieth century [*Mills*, 1914: 98, 132]: 'The [rural] working classes, apart from sudden ebulitions of temper, are a docile, easily-led people, without much social or political ambition … there is no tyranny, for the *inquilino* [= labour-service tenant] is in no way tied to the land, and can move off whenever he likes … The same leisurely and wasteful ways persist in every direction. But it must be confessed that life on the *hacienda* is often very pleasant. Many of them are large, well built, delightfully equipped, and money is plentiful.'
21. For these views about the Zapatista National Liberation Army in the Mexican State of Chiapas, see Cleaver [1994]. This kind of uncritical approach to Zapatista ideology leads Cleaver [1994: 147] to a positive assessment of 'from below' identity politics: 'Among the Indian nations and peoples of the Americas … the affirmation of national identity, of cultural uniqueness, and of linguistic and political autonomy is rooted not only in an extensive critique of the various forms of Western Culture and capitalist organization which were imposed on them through conquest, colonialism and genocide, but also in the affirmation of a wide variety of renewed and reinvented practices that include both social relations and the relationship between human communities and the rest of nature.' Unsurprisingly, this results not only in a corresponding idealization by Cleaver [1994: 153, 154] of the golden age myth ('In traditional Indian society life was not so hard') but also to abandon the notion of class differentiation ('What is unusual and exciting about these developments is how … struggles are not being … subordinated to "class interests" … [and represent instead] a workable solution to the post-socialist problem of revolutionary organization and struggle'), a view which ignores the fact that coffee production – albeit by peasant cultivators – has in many Latin America contexts licensed the emergence of small agrarian capitalists.
22. Each of these two approaches, which attribute an efficacy to 'moral economy' and to 'everyday forms of resistance', is associated with the work of Scott [1976; 1985]. Both are about the agency – consisting of smallscale, quotidian and individual acts of resistance – undertaken by peasant family farmers to reproduce themselves as an ubiquitous middle peasantry, and also the ideology – 'moral economy' – deployed by them in defence of such acts. The difficulties arising from any attempt to classify all acts/forms of 'from below' cultural resistance as inherently progressive politically, however, are evident from a collection [*Duncombe*, 2002] which attempts to do just this. For examples of 'resistance' theory as applied to rural Latin America, see Rasnake [1988], G. Smith [1989], Gould [1990], C. Smith [1992], Urban and Sherzer [1992], Mallon [1994], Wade [1999], and Korovkin [2000].
23. Associated with the series edited by Guha [1982–89], this framework has had a profound impact on the historiography of South Asia. As a number of commentators [*Lemelle and Kelley*, 1994; *Howe*, 1998] have pointed out, a not dissimilar process has also taken place with regard to Africa, where an innate African cultural identity is now constructed/celebrated by exponents of an essentialist 'from below' Afrocentric cultural nationalism.
24. Unsurprisingly, therefore, the neo-populist/neo-classical economic project of A.V. Chayanov [1966], which essentializes peasant family farming as a pan-historical category, also finds its realization in the postmodern theory dealing with rural agency in Latin America and India.

25. Although 'from below' agency as new social movement was a framework initially applied by Castells [1977; 1983] to urban contexts, the categorization of peasant mobilizations in Latin America as new social movements can be traced to the collection edited by Slater [1985].
26. Any lingering doubts about the spurious nature of the left-wing credentials attributed to Subcomandante Marcos [2001] are dispelled by what he himself has said in a recent interview with the Colombian novelist Gabriel García Márquez. Not only does Subcomandante Marcos espouse what are unabashed populist beliefs, therefore, but he also condemns the political left, and maintains an eloquent silence about socialism as a desirable objective of mobilization. That the agrarian mobilization in Chiapas raises difficult questions (the idealization/essentialization of ethnic/peasant identity, the predominance of religious ideology) about the political direction of the Zapatistas and Subcomandante Marcos is clear from Berger [2001] and the exchange between Hellman [1999; 2000] and Paulson [2000]. Most worryingly, in India an analogous discourse about rural cultural empowerment deployed by the new farmers' movements is one that has much in common with that of the Hindu nationalist BJP (the Bharatiya Janata Party) and the RSS (the National Volunteer Corps).
27. See, for example, Lehmann [1996].
28. It must be emphasized that not all the contributions to this volume agree as to how current agrarian mobilizations in Latin America should be interpreted: thus, for example, Petras and Veltmeyer regard the movements in Brazil and Mexico as possessing shared aims and characteristics, whereas de Souza Martins denies this.
29. Arguments made in defence of an undifferentiated peasantry and/or peasant economy by those on the left have frequently proved vulnerable to the positive characterization by conservatives and landowners – those opposed to socialism, in other words – of peasant culture as an empowering identity, a claim that not only takes many socialists by surprise, but has also led the latter to the erroneous conclusion that those who advanced such claims were becoming more progressive politically. The effectiveness of this line of argument in terms of class struggle waged from above derives from the fact that the ideological defence by conservatives and/or the political right of plebeian cultural 'otherness' enabled them similarly to defend their own (aristocratic or bourgeois) forms of tradition/privilege/hierarchy, also in the name of cultural 'otherness'.
30. Even now it is not clear that this lesson has been fully learned by those who continue to regard themselves as politically on the left. Thus, for example, in their introduction to a recent collection the avowed object of which is to reassert the value of Marxist political economy, Lem and Leach [2002: 1–2] glibly brush aside the debates of the last decade, observing that the '[t]urn of the twentieth century populist and liberal critiques, as well as more recent poststructuralist, feminist, and Foucauldian assaults on Marxist analysis (and also responses to them) have come to be so familiar, and to some extent mantric, that to review them here would be an exercise in redundancy.' One might justifiably enquire of Lem and Leach, first, where exactly were they when that particular conflict between Marxism and postmodernism was being waged, and what heroic deeds did they perform on the field of battle. In a similar vein, one might also ask why, if their purpose is to restore a specifically Marxist approach to economic development, Lem and Leach have included in their collection a chapter by Roseberry, who – having endorsed the theoretical approach to the study of rural Latin America of postmodernists such as J.C. Scott and Taussig [*Roseberry*, 1993] – was earlier aligned precisely with those very same 'assaults on Marxist analysis'.
31. Not only does this essentialist concept of an ahistorical peasant economy/culture replace the concept of depeasantization that is historically central to any Marxist theory about the dynamic processes of class formation/struggle and systemic development/transformation, therefore, but – as argued by Brass in his contribution to this volume – it is a category that has been deployed throughout the twentieth century by the political right in Europe (Germany, Spain, the UK) and the United States as well as Latin America (Peru, Bolivia, Argentina). A major obstacle to understanding this fact has been the tendency to depict as absolute the landlord/peasant divide, an approach which fails to appreciate that ideology

corresponding to the agrarian myth possesses both an aristocratic and a plebeian variant. Each variant of the agrarian myth – the landlord/aristocratic no less than the peasant/plebeian – valorizes and recognizes the hierarchical immanence of the other. Indeed, it could be argued that landlords object to peasants only when they cease to be peasants, and become either agrarian capitalists or landless rural workers: it is in the latter capacity, as *class*-specific rural subjects, that erstwhile peasants mount a challenge to the landlord class.

32. Jansen and Roquas also point out that, by maintaining that devil pact narratives in Central America correspond to peasant resistance against capitalism, Taussig is in fact defending an essentialist concept of peasant economy, whether or not he realizes that this is the case. For his part, Edelman attempts to explain the contradiction – between a rich landowner who is said by the rural poor to have a pact with the devil (= negative), and the fact that these same rural poor nevertheless identify with him, and thus perceive him in a positive light – by arguing that the pact is not about wealth but about sexual predation. For instances of devil pact narratives in rural Peru and Bolivia, see Lara [1973].

33. The three kinds of exchange are as follows. The first type involves a situation where the subject concerned himself enters into a Faustian pact, exchanging his own soul for riches and power. The second is structurally the same, except that in this case the object is to enrich or empower not oneself but rather someone else. Both exchanges involve no one other than the person entering the pact and the devil. These two variants have to be distinguished from another and structurally very different kind of pact, in which the same subject also enters into a pact with the devil, but instead of exchanging his *own* soul for wealth and power, he exchanges that of *others* – his own workers, who die suddenly and for no apparent reason, or that of his kinsfolk. In terms of class, these three exchanges give rise to equally different kinds of discourse. Accordingly, the first two types, where the subject involved exchanges directly with the devil, can be acceptable ideologically to peasants and workers, since in these cases the subject concerned bargains with his *own* property (his soul). Someone who becomes rich but forfeits eternal salvation may redistribute some of the riches gained thereby to poor peasants and agricultural labourers, in the process giving rise to the discourse about patronage which circulates about those who become rich as a result of being in a pact with the devil. Similarly, the person who enters into the Faustian pact can be said to have sold his soul for the benefit of others. Such transactions generate or reproduce the notion of ‘self-sacrifice’, ‘generosity’ and ‘selflessness’, all of which lend credibility to the concept of an exchange between a landowner on the one hand and a poor peasant or worker as an equal one, involving reciprocity. In short, they can be – and are – perceived by the poor at the rural grassroots as *virtuous* exchanges, from which others (and themselves) benefit materially. For this reason, these two narratives generate a discourse which both recognizes yet simultaneously legitimizes (and thus accepts) material inequality and wealth, a fact which gives rise in turn to the apparently contradictory element of patronage. In terms of class, therefore, the first two kinds of exchange are also very different from third, since what is bargained in the latter case is not the property of the exchanger – his own soul – but rather that of others: *other* souls, the property of *others*. It is this exchange that comes within the ambit of capitalism, where surplus-value (= soul) is extracted from the worker and appropriated by the capitalist (= rich peasant/landowner = the devil). In structural terms, it is the same as the European vampire legend, where Count Dracula, also a landowner, sucks the blood of peasants in order to benefit himself. In both cases (Faust, Dracula), therefore, it is the property (souls, blood) of others (peasants, the poor) which is appropriated for private (= capitalist) gain. This kind of transaction involves its subject exchanging indirectly that which is not his to exchange, and generates what is the most negative (and, from the point of view of the village poor, threatening) variant of the Faustian legend: someone is said to be not so much in a pact with the devil (= from which he suffers and others might benefit) as in league with the latter (= from which others suffer and only he benefits), i.e. an agent of darkness/evil/(capitalism).

34. The element of false consciousness is linked directly to the discourse about free choice in the Christian narrative: humanity can choose to be bad if it wants to be (= enter a pact with the devil), and reject ‘good’ (= God), but in doing so it forgoes salvation and eternal life. In

other words, those who are – or become – rich/'different' are permitted to be so by Christianity, since the latter extends them the right of choosing to be so. This is the way in which consciousness becomes false: disagreement and condemnation is permitted, but outright opposition – in the form of agency to rectify the situation – is not. Much rather, rectification or the pursuit of justice is something which is the preserve of God in heaven (not humanity on earth). It is indeed conservative, being also passive and fatalistic, and in this way it generates false consciousness among the rural poor. In other words, opposition to the landowner is symbolic only: the Faustian pact narrative recognizes the injustice of – but does not challenge – the basis of economic inequality (along the lines of 'we know it is unfair, but it is something about which we can do nothing').

35. The relevant texts are by Lenin [1964] and Kautsky [1988].
36. Other Marxists took a slightly different view. Kritsman [1984] focused on exploitative relationships within peasant households, and Kautsky [1988] maintained that although large farms were economically more efficient than smallholdings, they did not necessarily displace them. The reason for this was that a large agribusiness enterprise drew its (mainly seasonal) workforce from the surrounding peasant family farms. In some important respects, the American road in Lenin's two-path model of agrarian transformation is similar to the ECLA model. Whereas ECLA saw land reform as a means of avoiding revolution, by giving land to all the peasantry (and thus buying them off), Lenin by contrast saw it as a means of hastening revolution, since it would lead to open and increasingly acute struggle between capitalist peasant farmers and landless agricultural labourers.
37. For debates about the agrarian question in Latin America, see among others de Janvry [1981], Harris [1978; 1992], Winson [1978; 1982], and Reynolds [1997]. Although by no means all Marxists, most of the contributors to this volume both refer to and accept the importance of the agrarian question as having something to say about the way in which peasants in Latin America are transformed. By contrast, most 'new' postmodern populists either ignore the agrarian question altogether, or else deny that it is any longer relevant to an understanding of the peasantry in contemporary Latin America.
38. The subsequent fate of most land reforms in Latin America and elsewhere during the second half of the twentieth century, however, challenges the optimism of those who advocate the long-term economic viability of peasant family farming. None have survived, not even in China or Cuba, and all have been swept away by market forces. This suggests not that the reforms were wrong, but that *any* reform which fails to pose questions about systemic change – that is, the capitalist system itself – cannot hope to survive.
39. This dynamic is not dissimilar to the one outlined by Baraona [1965] with regard to Ecuador, where an historical process of internal/external encroachment (*asedio interno, asedio externo*) onto rural estates occurred, involving erstwhile labour-service tenants deprived of their usufruct rights to *hacienda* land, who were re-employed as landless casual workers, and then began to occupy estate land.
40. Given the widespread conflict over Amazonian land rights (on which see the contributions by Nugent, Assies and de Souza Martins), and the resulting insecurity of tenure faced by smallholding cultivators in the region, it would perhaps be inappropriate for this reason alone to characterize such petty commodity producers as independent proprietors. Against this image of an innately ephemeral form of agrarian existence, however, Nugent argues that – like those who work in the urban informal sector throughout Latin America, about which there is a large literature – peasants in Amazonia are not economically marginal, but engage in similar kinds of informal economic activity (harvesting Brazil nuts, mining gold) beyond the gaze/regulation/control of the Brazilian state.
41. As Crabtree points out, an important factor in this process was a decrease in state intervention in the agrarian sector, and a concomitant reduction in credit provision to smallholders. Murray makes much the same point with regard to Chile.
42. This problem, of defining the agrarian question at the level of national economies, has been noted by Watts and Goodman [1997: 6], who rightly criticize Byres and Bernstein for their narrow focus 'on the internal dynamics of [agrarian] change at the expense of what we now refer to as globalisation … the agrarian question for Byres is something that can be "resolved" (see also Bernstein …) [which] seems to imply that once capitalism in

agriculture has "matured", or if capitalist industrialization can proceed without agrarian capitalism ... then the agrarian question is somehow dead'.

43. This view is in keeping with those who attribute the continued resilience of the peasant family farm to an exogenous cause; its role as a source of an agricultural or industrial reserve army of labour, which provides agribusiness enterprises or rich peasants with a supply of seasonal and/or casual workers.
44. That neoclassical economic historiography should deny the existence/efficacy of bonded labour is in a sense unsurprising, since it is a theoretical framework the epistemology of which posits the existence of an individual choice-making subject always engaged in the exercise of subjective preferences in the context of what neoclassical economic historiography regards as unproblematically free exchanges between capital and labour in the market place (see, for example, the neo-classical economic analysis by Ortiz [1999] of rural labour markets in Colombia). More surprising, however, is the adherence of a particular variant of Marxism, the semi-feudal thesis, to this same epistemology, a difficulty attributable in part to low standards of scholarship (on which subject see Brass [2002]).
45. There is a way out of this dilemma: as has been argued elsewhere [*Brass*, 1999], the production relations capital strives to reproduce are in certain circumstances not free but unfree ones.
46. As Assies points out, this is why neoclassical economists, such as Barham and Coome, object to Weinstein's claim that the relations of production during the Bolivian rubber boom were pre-capitalist and resembled a feudal mode of production. Barham and Coome can then argue that, because these relations are 'chosen' by 'those below' and not enforced 'from above', they are in essence free, and thus what exists systemically is not an economically inefficient pre-capitalism but much rather an economically efficient form of capitalism – based on a free labour relation 'chosen' by and to the benefit of all.
47. Although these 'tropical nastiness'/'green hell' claims have been refuted empirically, as Nugent points out, it is important to distinguish between three distinct versions of this argument. The first two circulate within the domain of political economy, but each is politically distinct, while the third – which is postmodern – shares an epistemology with the first. The first political economy variant claims that Amazonia is a place the 'otherness' of which precludes the kind of economic activity and relational forms encountered in the wider society. Agricultural production in such contexts by non-indigenous subjects is impossible, it is argued, and for this reason work in such contexts must be undertaken by Indians. Not only is the indigenous subject constituted as the only suitable source of labour, therefore, but a result of the workforce being composed of what in the same discourse is 'Indian-as-untameable-Nature', work itself requires 'exceptional' measures (= coercion, brutality). This familiar discourse, in which Indian-as-untameable-Nature merges with and becomes part of the Amazon-as-untameable-Nature, is a variation on the 'green hell' argument, and one that has been used by employers everywhere – for example, cotton planters in the *antebellum* American south – to justify coercive relations the necessity of which derive from other causes (capitalist competition leading to overproduction and declining profitability). It is a variant of the labour shortage argument, the focus of which is on the supply (and not the demand) for workers. Whereas the first political economy variant has been deployed historically by conservatives (rubber planters/employers) who – as defenders of slavery and peonage – argue that since no one in their right minds would work in these tough conditions, economic activity required 'abnormal'/'exceptional' relations of production, the second version of the same discourse recognizes the environmental constraints, but denies that the environment precludes 'normal' economic activity and – particularly – relational forms. The second of the two political economy variants, therefore, has been and is deployed by radical opponents of unfree labour, both within and outside Brazil. They agree about the toughness of the conditions, but disagree about the necessity of relations such as slavery, debt bondage and peonage, arguing that if conditions do indeed amount to a form of 'tropical nastiness', then labourers must be paid more to do this kind of work. Here it is not so much the shortage as the cost of labour that is at issue.
48. Trotsky [1962] argued that since peasants did not constitute a class, they should be seen as a revolutionary force only insofar as they ceased to be peasants, and – like Preobrazhensky

[1980] – he warned that because one of the first acts of a revolutionary government headed by workers would be to expropriate all private property, the peasant proprietor should be regarded not as passively conservative but rather as actively counter-revolutionary. Much the same point was made by Rosa Luxemburg [1961], who opposed land seizures by peasants, since this created a new and powerful strata of proprietors in the countryside who would – with greater success than a small group of landlords – block further attempts to socialize the ownership of agricultural land.

49. For these peasant movements in Peru and Colombia, see Fioravanti [1974], Palmer [1992], and Zamosc [1986]. The same was true of India, where agrarian populist ideology was invoked by rich peasant tribals in West Bengal during the late 1960s and early 1970s, and also by the new farmers' movements which emerged in the Green Revolution areas during the early 1980s [*Brass*, 1995].

50. Thus, for example, the Landless Rural Workers movement in Brazil not only eschews party affiliation, and targets only unused land for occupation, but also includes among its ranks small farmers who, it transpires, may in some cases own/operate holdings of up to 100 hectares in size [*Stedile*, 2002]. In his contribution to this volume, Assies indicates that some peasants in the rural communities of the Northern Bolivian Amazon region also possess holdings of a similarly large size.

51. Elsewhere Petras [2002] reminds us of the important role discharged by the State in the reproduction of imperialism. For the role of the Latin American State in restructuring the domestic working class on behalf of national/international capital, see Vilas [1995].

52. For the concept 'redemocratization', and the attempt to recuperate a notion of a viable 'steady-state' capitalism (= 'a citizen-based alternative'), see Biekart [1999] and Dierckxsens [2000]; just how acceptable Latin American 'redemocratization' is to conservatives is evident from the defence of this process by one such [*Hawthorn*, 2002]. From the 1970s onwards an empowering 'redemocratization' by means of resistance was the avowed objective of anti-communist movements in eastern Europe (see, for example, Havel *et al.* [1985]), many of which turned rightwards once they gained power, and embraced not just capitalism but also neo-liberal economic policies and reactionary nationalist politics/ideology. It is perhaps significant that the postmodern/populist call for 'redemocratization', or the realization of all political empowerment within the confines of the existing capitalist state, has been taken up enthusiastically by Lipset [2001], who commends those whom he terms wrongly 'socialists' for their ideological pluralism and their acceptance of the market as a non-transcendental 'fact'. Like postmodern/populist theorists, he too celebrates 'new social movements' as a vindication of a 'post-Marxist' agency, claiming that henceforth this is the only viable form of grassroots action, noting that 'issues revolving around gender equality, multiculturalism ... and supranational communities push individuals and groups in directions that are independent of their socio-economic position' [*Lipset*, 2001: 84]. In other words, capitalism and its state can accept (and survive) every form of opposition except one: that based on class. His first conclusion [*Lipset*, 2001: 84-5], that '[a]ll this should make for more conservative and smug societies', is accurate in a way that his second ('These post-Cold War conditions bode well for democratic stability and for international peace') is not.

53. With one notable exception, these views were advanced by all those in the classical Marxist tradition. Marx [1979] himself placed the peasantry in the camp of reaction when writing about the 1848 revolution in France, while Engels regarded farm labourers, rather than tenants or peasant proprietors, as the most natural political ally of the urban industrial proletariat. For the process of 'depeasantization', and its connection with class formation and the struggle for the state, see Lenin [1964]. A constant theme in Kautsky's writings on the agrarian question from the 1880s onwards was that, as the smallholder was doomed economically, under no circumstances should an agrarian programme implemented by a socialist government seek to revitalize peasant farming [*Salvadori*, 1979; *Hussain and Tribe*, 1984]. Given the current enthusiasm on the part of 'new' postmodern populists for 'redemocratization', the words written by Kautsky [1902: 50–51] one century ago are prescient indeed: '[Small property owners] have despaired of ever rising by their own exertions, they expect everything from above, and look only to the upper classes for

assistance. And as all progress threatens them they place themselves in opposition to all advance. Servility and dependence upon reaction make them not simply the willing supporters, but the fanatical defenders of the monarchy, the church and the nobility. With all this they remain democratic, since it is only through democracy that they can exercise any political influence, and obtain the assistance of the public powers. ... This reactionary democracy has taken many of its ideas from the socialist thought, and many have therefore come to consider these as but beginnings which indicate an especial transition from liberalism to socialism. The untenableness of this position is clear today [= 1902]. Socialism has no bitterer enemy than the reactionary democracy.' During the 1920s Preobrazhensky [1980] warned the Soviet government against raising producer prices for foodstuffs, on the grounds that such a policy would benefit better-off peasants (*kulaks*), or precisely those elements opposed to socialism. The sole exception in this regard is Eduard Bernstein [1961], the founder of 'revisionist Marxism', who in a debate with Kautsky during the 1890s rejected Marxist argument about class differentiation (= the vanishing 'middle strata' composed of small traders, shopkeepers, artisans and peasants) on the grounds that the small farmer had not only not disappeared but continued to be economically viable. 'There can be no doubt', Bernstein said, 'that in all of Western Europe and, by the way, in the eastern section of the United States, the small and medium-sized agricultural enterprises are growing in numbers, while larger or giant enterprises are declining' [*Gay*, 1952: 193–4]. Others who adhered to this view (Eduard David, Friedrich Otto Hertz) argued that as socialism amounted to no more than 'general well-being and spiritual culture (*geisteskultur*)', such an objective could be realized by productivity-enhancing aid/support provided by the state to small and medium farmers [*Gay*, 1952: 195].

54. This, for example, was the view of Kaldor [1964: 233ff.], as outlined in a report submitted to ECLA about the economic difficulties facing Chile in the mid-1950s. See the contribution by Murray to this volume for additional information on this point.
55. Since for neoliberalism, the twin evils of planning and inflation that undermine the market derive from the inability of the state to control the money supply. Because for monetarist theory the very fact of market supply creates its own demand, economic growth requires that the market be permitted to operate freely, without state 'interference' (regulation, taxation, etc.). The role of the state in liberal economic theory is summed up thus by Robbins [1952: 193]: 'For the Classical liberal the characteristic function of the state ... is the establishment and the enforcement of law ... so far as the general organization of production is concerned, his essential conception of the role of the state is the conception of law-giver.' Long before its claimed 'discovery' by Isaiah Berlin, this element of positive/negative freedoms embodied in the State was outlined by Hobhouse [1911: 190]: 'Excess of liberty contradicts itself. In short, there is no such thing; there is only liberty for one and restraint for another. If liberty then be regarded as a social ideal, the problem of establishing liberty must be a problem of organizing restraints; and thus the conception of a liberty which is to set an entire people free from its government appears to be a self-contradictory ideal.'
56. On the subject of agricultural economic growth and the state, the following is a symptomatic neoliberal statement [*Friedman and Friedman*, 1979: 3]: 'The fecundity of freedom is demonstrated most dramatically and clearly in agriculture ... During most of the period of rapid agricultural expansion in the United States the government played a negligible role. Land was made available – but it was land that had been unproductive before ... the main source of the agricultural revolution was private initiative operating in a free market open to all.' Ironically, a similarly negative view of the state is held by many of those who subscribe to Latin American subalternism, to an 'everyday forms of resistance theory', and/or to a new social movements framework.
57. Perhaps the most influential exponent of this view is Bluntschli [1885: ch.II], Professor of Political Sciences at Heidelburg in the late nineteenth century, whose ideas about the genesis and nature of the state, and the process leading to its formation/reproduction, developed at the same time as Germany became unified.
58. Hence the view [*Bluntschli*, 1885: 86] that: '[A people] is a union of masses of men of different occupations and social strata in a hereditary society of common spirit, feeling and

race, bound together, especially by language and customs, in a common civilization which gives them a sense of unity and distinction from all foreigners, quite apart from the bond of the State.'

59. According to Bluntschli [1885: 87], '[w]e are justified, then, in speaking of a national spirit (*Volksgeist*) and a national will (*Volkswille*), which is something more than the mere sum of the spirit and will of the individuals composing a Nation.' In many ways, his concept of transition, from nation-in-itself (= people) to nation-for-itself (= State), mimics that of classical Marxism, from class-in-itself to class-for-itself.
60. This much is evident from Marx's critique of Bonapartism during the 1848 revolution in France. He regarded the Bonapartist state as backward-looking and reactionary, or the rule by 'the sabre and the cowl' on behalf of a peasantry and lumpenproletariat (= depeasantized peasants) menaced by economic crisis (taxes, debt, landlessness, alienation), a situation in which existing and erstwhile smallholders struggle to restore their earlier position and/or old property relations [*Marx*, 1979: 106, 149, 189]. The current idealization by postmodernism and subalternists of grassroots agency (= 'resistance') undertaken by peasants in defence of their status as traditional smallholders confirms the prescience of this critique [*Marx*, 1979: 188]: 'The Bonaparte dynasty represents not the revolutionary, but the conservative peasant; not the peasant that strikes out beyond the condition of his social existence, the smallholding, but rather the peasant who wants to consolidate this holding; not the country folk who, linked up with the towns, want to overthrow the old order through their own energies, but on the contrary those who, in stupefied seclusion within this old order, want to see themselves and their smallholdings saved and favoured by the ghost of the empire. It represents not the enlightenment, but the superstition of the peasant; not his judgement but his prejudice; not his future, but his past; not his modern Cévennes, but his modern Vendée.'
61. The details of this 1960s Peruvian peasant movement, plus the post-reform continuation and/or reintroduction by capitalist peasants of practices/mechanisms used by the landlord in the pre-reform era, are outlined in Brass [1999: 47ff.; 2000: 65ff.]. It should be emphasized that the latter case-study is not a unique occurrence, since this pattern of post-reform fragmentation of a peasant movement united solely in its opposition to a landlord class happened in many other contexts at that conjuncture. Much the same occurred in the case of the peasant movement which took place in Colombia during the 1970s [*Zamosc*, 1986], and also in the Indian state of Kerala, where a new class of rural capitalist emerged from among the ranks of tenants who had themselves been active in anti-landlord struggles, and were the beneficiaries of the land reform carried out during the 1960s [*Krishnaji*, 1986]. Conflict arose subsequently within this anti-landlord front when, on the wages question, agricultural labourers encountered fierce opposition from their rich and middle peasant employers, activists who had been in the vanguard of the earlier struggles.
62. For the radical nature of the agrarian reform programmes carried out in Cuba, Chile and Nicaragua over the latter half of the twentieth century, see among others de Vylder [1976], Peek [1983], Kaimowitz [1986], Kay [1988], Ghai, Kay and Peek [1988], Habel [1991], Mesa-Lago [1994], and Enriquez [1997]. For the imposition of an economic blockade by the United States against these three Latin American countries, see Morley [1987]. Contrary to the claims made by opponents of Latin American socialism – see, for example, the exchange between Colburn [1986], and Harris [1987] – the shortages (of labour and goods) that arose in Chile during the time of Allende, Nicaragua during the Sandinista era, and Cuba under Castro, were due not to the economic inefficiencies of planning but rather to external blockade coupled with the internal expansion of employment and the increased wage levels. In the case of Chile, for example, the availability of foodstuffs in 1972 was some 27 per cent higher than in 1970, while in Cuba over the 1958–62 period real disposable income of the working class rose by a quarter, and that of the poorest social groups doubled.
63. In the mid-1970s one-third of cultivated land in Cuba was in the non-state sector, where some 125,000 peasant proprietors owned an average of 12 hectares each, while as late as 1989 some 26 per cent of all land was in the private sector [*MacEwan*, 1982; *Deere, Pérez and Gonzales*, 1994]. This facilitated the emergence and expansion of the black market in Cuba, both in the 1980s and during 'the Special Period in Peacetime'. When in 1980 the

Cuban government permitted a free peasant market to operate alongside the existing system of state planning/procurement, peasant farmers started to decollectivize agriculture, proprietors leasing out land on a sharecropping basis rather than undertaking direct cultivation themselves. When state-provided inputs were diverted into private production, the free peasant market was closed down during the mid-1980s, because it threatened to undermine the egalitarian objectives of the Cuban revolution.

64. As Bluntschli [1885: 82] himself makes clear, nationhood and statehood to which it gives rise involves nothing more than the re-assertion of a more 'authentic' historical identity underlying existing nations/states. Hence the view that 'the Germans in the middle ages were at once a people (*nation*) and a nation (*Volk*), while in the last few centuries [= the eighteenth and nineteenth] they ceased to be a nation, and were rather a people divided into a number of different states, countries, and one may almost say nations. Today [c.1870] the German nation (*Volk*) has come to life again, although individual parts of the German people form parts of non-German nations and states.' He concludes, somewhat ominously given the events of the 1930s, by stating that '[a]lthough in our time the sense of nationality is stronger than ever before, yet even now the ideas of "people" and "nation" nowhere fully coincide.'
65. For a critique of the concept 'Inca communism', see Espinoza and Malpica [1970: 155–8], who blame Mariátegui for its idealization ('*Mariátegui ha contribuido en mucho a la idealización del Imperio del Tahuantinsuyo. Fue uno de los primeros en calificar su sistema de tenencia agraria como "comunismo inkaico" y considerar al Imperio como el antecedente más remoto de los gobiernos socialistas*').
66. This issue is discussed further in the contribution by Brass.
67. The views of Albó are examined by McNeish and Brass in their contributions to this volume. The political significance of this theory about peasant/state relations should not be underestimated, as is clear from the case of India, where the same kinds of argument are currently being deployed by the right-wing BJP and RSS in support of a specifically Hindu nation. It is clear that, in the case of India, two important exponents of reactionary Hindu chauvinism, Vinayak Damodar Savarkar and Mahadav Sadashiv Golwalkar, were both strongly influenced by Bluntschli's concept of a culturally-specific State [*Jaffrelot*, 1996: 32, 53–4]. A recent defence of the BJP by Elst [2001: 306–9] attempts, wholly implausibly, to argue that the influence of Bluntschli on Golwalkar was both minimal and 'innocent', and thus possessed no political implications.

REFERENCES

Afanasyev, L., *et al.*, 1974, *The Political Economy of Capitalism*, Moscow: Progress Publishers.

Baraona, Rafael, 1965, 'Una tipología de haciendas en la sierra Ecuatoriana', in O. Delgado (ed.), *Reformas Agararias en America Latina*, México, DF: Fondo de Cultura Económica.

Bates, Robert H., 1981, *Markets and States in Tropical Africa: The Political Basis of Agricultural Policies*, Berkeley, CA: University of California Press.

Bates, Robert H., 1983, *Essays on the Political Economy of Rural Africa*, Cambridge: Cambridge University Press.

Bates, Robert H., 2001, *Prosperity and Violence: The Political Economy of Development*, New York: W.W. Norton & Co.

Berger, Mark T., 2001, 'Romancing the Zapatistas: International Intellectuals and the Chiapas Rebellion', *Latin American Perspectives*, Issue 117.

Bernstein, Eduard, 1961, *Evolutionary Socialism: A Criticism and Affirmation*, New York: Schocken.

Biekart, Kees, 1999, *The Politics of Civil Society Building: European Private Aid Agencies and Democratic Transitions in Central America*, Amsterdam: Transnational Institute.

Bluntschli, J.K., 1885, *The Theory of the State*, Oxford: Clarendon Press.

Booth, David (ed.), 1994, *Rethinking Social Development*, Harlow: Longman Scientific & Technical.

Borón, Otilio, 1981, 'State Forms in Latin America: Between Hobbes and Friedman', *New Left*

Review, No.130.
Brass, Tom (ed.), 1995, *New Farmers' Movements in India*, London and Portland, OR: Frank Cass Publishers.
Brass, Tom, 1999, *Towards a Comparative Political Economy of Unfree Labour: Case Studies and Debates*, London and Portland, OR: Frank Cass Publishers.
Brass, Tom, 2000, *Peasants, Populism and Postmodernism: The Return of the Agrarian Myth*, London and Portland, OR: Frank Cass Publishers.
Brass, Tom, 2002, 'Rural Labour in Agrarian Transitions: The Semi-Feudal Thesis Revisited', *Journal of Contemporary Asia*, Vol.32, No.4.
Brohman, John, 1996, *Popular Development: Rethinking the Theory and Practice of Development*, Oxford: Blackwell Publishers.
Burbach, Roger, and Patricia Flynn, 1980, *Agribusiness in the Americas*, New York: Monthly Review Press.
Burdick, J., 1993, *Looking for God in Brazil*, Berkeley, CA: University of California Press.
Burgete Cal y Mayor, Aracely (ed.), 2000, *Indigenous Autonomy in Mexico*, Copenhagen: IWIGIA.
Buttel, Frederick H., 2001, 'Some Reflections on Late Twentieth Century Agrarian Political Economy', *Sociologia Ruralis*, Vol.41, No.2.
Cammack, Paul, 2000, 'The Resurgence of Populism in Latin America', *Bulletin of Latin American Research*, Vol.19, No.2.
Cardoso, Fernando Enrique, and Enzo Faletto, 1979, *Dependency and Development in Latin America*, Berkeley, CA: The University of California Press.
Castells, Manuel, 1977, *The Urban Question*, London: Edward Arnold.
Castells, Manuel, 1983, *The City and the Grassroots: A Cross-Cultural Theory of Urban Social Movements*, London: Edward Arnold.
Chayanov, A.V., 1966, *The Theory of Peasant Economy* (edited by Daniel Thorner, Basile Kerblay and R.E.F. Smith), Homewood, IL: The American Economic Association.
Chayanov, A.V., 1991, *The Theory of Peasant Cooperatives*, London: I.B. Tauris.
Cheater, Angela (ed.), 1999, *The Anthropology of Power: Empowerment and Disempowerment in Changing Structures*, London: Routledge.
Clark, John, 1991, *Democratizing Development: The Role of Voluntary Organizations*, London: Earthscan Publications.
Clarke, Ben, and Clifton Ross (eds.), 1994, *The Voice of Fire: Communiqués and Interviews from the Zapatista National Liberation Army*, Berkeley, CA: New Earth Publications.
Cleaver, Harry, 1994, 'The Chiapas Uprising', *Studies in Political Economy*, No.44.
Colburn, F.D., 1986, *Post-Revolutionary Nicaragua: State, Class, and the Dilemmas of Agrarian Policy*, Berkeley, CA: University of California Press.
Collier, David (ed.), 1979, *The New Authoritarianism in Latin America*, Princeton, NJ: Princeton University Press.
Coniff, Michael L. (ed.), 1982, *Latin American Populism in Comparative Perspective*, Albuquerque, NM: University of New Mexico Press.
Coniff, Michael L., 1982, 'Toward a Comparative Definition of Populism', in Michael L. Coniff (ed.) [1982].
Cooper, Frederick, Florencia Mallon, Steve Stern, Allen Isaacman and William Roseberry (eds.), 1993, *Confronting Historical Paradigms: Peasants, Labor, and the Capitalist World System in Africa and Latin America*, Madison, WI: University of Wisconsin Press.
Cotler, Julio, 1971, 'Crisis política y populismo militar', in Fernando Fuenzalida Vollmar *et al.* [1971].
Cox, Terry, and Gary Littlejohn, 1984, *Kritsman and the Agrarian Marxists*, London: Frank Cass Publishers.
de Alcántara, Cynthia Hewitt, 1984, *Anthropological Perspectives on Rural Mexico*, London: Routledge & Kegan Paul.
de Janvry, Alain, 1981, *The Agrarian Question and Reformism in Latin America*, Baltimore, MD: Johns Hopkins University Press.
de Kadt, Emanuel, 1970, *Catholic Radicals in Brazil*, London and New York: Oxford University Press.

de Vylder, Stefan, 1976, *Allende's Chile: The Political Economy of the Rise and Fall of the Unidad Popular*, Cambridge: Cambridge University Press.

Deere, Carmen Diana, Niurka Pérez, and Ernel Gonzales, 1994, 'The View from Below: The Cuban Agricultural Sector in the "Special Period in Peacetime"', *The Journal of Peasant Studies*, Vol.21, No.2.

Demmers, Jolle, Alex E. Fernández Jilberto and Barbara Hogenboom (eds.), 2001, *Miraculous Metamorphoses: The Neoliberalization of Latin American Populism*, London: Zed Books.

Desai, A.R. (ed.), 1986, *Agrarian Struggles in India after Independence*, Delhi: Oxford University Press.

Di Tella, Torcuato, 1965, 'Populism and Reform in Latin America', in C. Veliz (ed.) [1965].

Díaz Polanco, Héctor, 1998, *La rebelión zapatista y la autonomia*, México, DF: Siglo Veintiuno Editores.

Dierckxsens, Wim, 2000, *The Limits of Capitalism: An Approach to Globalization without Neoliberalism*, New York: Zed Press.

Duncombe, Stephen (ed.), 2002, *Cultural Resistance*, London: Verso.

Eckstein, Susan (ed.), 1989, *Power and Popular Protest: Latin American Social Movements*, Berkeley, CA: University of California Press.

Elst, Koenraad, 2001, *The Saffron Swastika: The Notion of 'Hindu Fascism'*, 2 Vols., New Delhi: The Voice of India.

Enriquez, Laura J., 1997, *Agrarian Reform and Class Consciousness in Nicaragua*, Gainsville, FL: University Press of Florida.

Escobar, Arturo, 1995, *Encountering Development: The Making and Unmaking of the Third World*, Princeton, NJ: Princeton University Press.

Escobar, Arturo, and Sonia E. Alvarez (eds.), 1992, *The Making of Social Movements in Latin America: Identity, Strategy, and Democracy*, Boulder, CO: Westview Press.

Espinosa, Gustavo, and Carlos Malpica, 1970, *El problema de la tierra*, Lima: Biblioteca Amauta.

Fioravanti, Eduardo, 1974, *Latifundio y Sindicalismo Agrario en el Perú*, Lima: Instituto de Estudios Peruanos.

Fioravanti-Molinie, Antoinette, 1973, 'Reciprocidad y economía de mercado', *Allpanchis*, Vol.5.

Fogel, Robert William, 2000, *The Fourth Great Awakening and the Future of Egalitarianism*, Chicago, IL: University of Chicago Press.

Fogel, Robert William, and Stanley L. Engerman, 1974, *Time on the Cross: Volume I – The Economics of American Negro Slavery*, London: Wildwood House.

Foster, George M., 1962, *Traditional Cultures*, New York: Harper & Brothers.

Foster, George M., 1965, 'Peasant Society and the Image of Limited Good', *American Anthropologist*, Vol.67, No.2.

Foweraker, Joe, 1995, *Theorizing Social Movements*, London: Pluto Press.

Foweraker, Joe, and Ann L. Craig (eds.), 1990, *Popular Movements and Political Change in Mexico*, Boulder, CO: Lynne Rienner Publishers.

Fowler-Salamini, Heather, and Mary Kay Vaughan (eds.), 1994, *Women of the Mexican Countryside, 1850–1990*, Tucson, AR: The University of Arizona Press.

Fox, Richard G., and Orin Starn (eds.), 1997, *Between Resistance and Revolution: Cultural Politics and Social Protest*, New Brunswick, NJ: Rutgers University Press.

Frank, Andre Gunder, 1967, *Capitalism and Underdevelopment in Latin America: Historical Studies of Chile and Brazil*, New York: Monthly Review Press.

Frank, Andre Gunder, 1969, *Latin America: Underdevelopment or Revolution?*, New York: Monthly Review Press.

Frank, Andre Gunder, 1979, *Mexican Agriculture 1521–1630: Transformation of the Mode of Production*, Cambridge: Cambridge University Press.

Friedland, William H., 1991, 'Shaping the New Political Economy of Advanced Capitalist Agriculture', in William H. Friedland *et al.* (eds.) [1991].

Friedland, William H., Lawrence Busch, Frederick H. Buttel and Alan P. Rudy (eds.), 1991, *Towards a New Political Economy of Agriculture*, Boulder, CO: Westview Press.

Friedman, Milton, and Rose Friedman, 1979, *Free to Choose: A Personal Statement*, New York: Harcourt Brace Jovanovich.

Friedmann, John, 1992, *Empowerment: The Politics of Alternative Development*, Cambridge, MA: Blackwell.
Fuenzalida Vollmar, Fernando, Julio Cotler, Jorge Bravo Bresani, Alberto Escobar, Augusto Salazar Bondy and José Matos Mar, 1971, *Perú, Hoy*, México, DF: Siglo XXI Editores.
Galli, Rosemary E. (ed.), 1992, *Rethinking the Third World: Contributions to a New Conceptualization*, New York: Crane Russak.
Gay, Peter, 1952, *The Dilemma of Democratic Socialism: Eduard Bernstein's Challenge to Marx*, New York: Columbia University Press.
Ghai, Dharam, Cristóbal Kay and Peter Peek, 1988, *Labour and Development in Rural Cuba*, London: Macmillan.
Ghose, A.K. (ed.), 1983, *Agrarian Reform in Contemporary Developing Countries*, London: Croom Helm.
Gilly, Adolfo, 1998, *Chiapas – la razón ardiente: ensayo sobre la rebelión del mundo encantado*, México, DF: Ediciones Era.
Glover, David, and Ken Kusterer, 1990, *Small Farmers, Big Business: Contract Farming and Rural Development*, London: Macmillan.
Goodman, David, and Michael Watts (eds.), 1997, *Globalizing Food: Agrarian Questions and Global Restructuring*, London: Routledge.
Gordillo, Gustavo, 1988, *Campesinos al asalto del cielo: de la expropriación estatal a la apropriación campesina*, Mexico, D.F.: Siglo Veintino Editores.
Gould, Jeffrey L., 1990, *To Lead as Equals: Rural Protest and Political Consciousness in Chinandega, Nicaragua, 1912–1979*, Chapel Hill, NC: The University of North Carolina Press.
Guevara, Ernesto Che, 1967, *Episodes of the [Cuban] Revolutionary War*, Havana: Book Institute.
Guha, Ranajit (ed.), 1982–89, *Subaltern Studies I–VI*, New Delhi: Oxford University Press.
Habel, Janette, 1991, *Cuba: The Revolution in Peril*, London: Verso.
Harris, Richard L., 1978, 'Marxism and the Agrarian Question in Latin America', *Latin American Perspectives*, Issue 19.
Harris, Richard L., 1987, 'Evaluating Nicaragua's Agrarian Reform', *Latin American Perspectives*, Issue 52.
Harris, Richard L., 1992, *Marxism, Socialism and Democracy in Latin America*, Boulder, CO: Westview Press.
Harvey, Neil, 1990, *The New Agrarian Movement in Mexico, 1979–1990*, London: Institute of Latin American Studies.
Harvey, Neil, 1998, *The Chiapas Rebellion: The Struggle for Land and Democracy*, Durham, NC: Duke University Press.
Havel, Vaclav, *et al.*, 1985, *The Power of the Powerless: Citizens Against the State in Central-Eastern Europe*, London: Hutchinson.
Hawthorn, Geoffrey, 2002, 'Liberalisation and Democracy in Latin America', *Estudios Interdisciplina de America Latina y el Caribe*, Vol.13, No.1.
Hellman, Judith Adler, 1999, 'Real and Virtual Chiapas: Magic Realism and the Left', *Socialist Register 2000*, Rendlesham: The Merlin Press.
Hellman, Judith Adler, 2000, 'Virtual Chiapas: A Reply to Paulson', *Socialist Register 2001*, London: The Merlin Press.
Henessy, Alistair, 1969, 'Latin America', in Ghita Ionescu and Ernest Gellner (eds.) [1969].
Hewitt, W.E., 1998, 'From Defenders of the People to Defenders of the Faith: A 1984–1993 Retrospective of CEB Activity in São Paulo', *Latin American Perspectives*, Vol.25, No.1.
Hilton, Rodney (ed.), 1976, *The Transition from Feudalism to Capitalism*, London: NLB.
Hobhouse, L.T., 1911, *Social Evolution and Political Theory*, New York: Columbia University Press.
Hodges, Donald, 2002, *Mexico Under Siege: Popular Resistance to Presidential Despotism*, London: Zed Press.
Howe, Stephen, 1998, *Afrocentrism: Mythical Pasts and Imagined Homes*, London: Verso.
Hussain, Athar, and Keith Tribe (eds.), 1984, *Paths of Development in Capitalist Agriculture: Readings from German Social Democracy, 1891–99*, London: Macmillan.

Ianni, Octávio, 1975, A *formação do estado populista na América Latina*, Rio: Civilização Brasileira.

Ionescu, Ghita, and Ernest Gellner (eds.), 1969, *Populism: Its Meanings and National Characteristics*, London: Weidenfeld and Nicolson.

Jaffrelot, Christophe, 1996, *The Hindu Nationalist Movement and Indian Politics, 1925 to the 1990s*, London: Hurst & Company.

Jones, Steve, P.C. Joshi and Miguel Murmis (eds.), 1982, *Rural Poverty and Agrarian Reform*, New Delhi: Allied Publishers Private Limited.

Kaimowitz, David, 1986, 'Nicaraguan Debates on Agrarian Structure and their Implications for Agricultural Policy and the Rural Poor', *The Journal of Peasant Studies*, Vol.14, No.1.

Kaldor, Nicholas, 1964, *Essays on Economic Policy – Volume Two (IV. Policies for International Stability, V. Country Studies)*, London: Gerald Duckworth & Co. Ltd.

Kautsky, Karl, 1902/[1916], *The Social Revolution*, Chicago, IL: Charles H. Kerr & Company.

Kautsky, Karl, 1988, *The Agrarian Question*, 2 vols, London: Zwan Publications.

Kay, Cristóbal, 1988, 'Economic Reforms and Collectivization in Cuban Agriculture', *Third World Quarterly*, Vol.10, No.3.

Knight, Alan, 1998, 'Populism and Neo-populism in Latin America, especially Mexico', *Journal of Latin American Studies*, Vol.30, Part 2.

Korovkin, Tanya, 1997, 'Taming Capitalism: The Evolution of the Indigenous Peasant Economy in Northern Ecuador', *Latin American Research Review*, Vol.32, No.3.

Korovkin, Tanya, 2000, 'Weak Weapons, Strong Weapons? Hidden Resistance and Political Protest in Rural Ecuador', *The Journal of Peasant Studies*, Vol.27, No. 3.

Krishnaji, N., 1986, 'Agrarian Relations and the Left Movement in Kerala', in A.R. Desai (ed.) [1986].

Kritsman, L.N., 1984, 'Class Stratification of the Soviet Countryside', in Terry Cox and Gary Littlejohn (eds.) [1984].

Laclau, Ernesto, 1977, *Politics and Ideology in Marxist Theory: Capitalism, Fascism, Populism*, London: NLB.

Laclau, Ernesto, 1985, 'New Social Movements and the Plurality of the Social', in David Slater (ed.) [1985].

Laclau, Ernesto, 1989, 'Politics and the Limits of Modernity', in Andrew Ross (ed.) [1989].

Laclau, Ernesto, 1990, *New Reflections on the Revolution of Our Time*, London: Verso.

Laclau, Ernesto, 1992, 'Beyond Emancipation', *Development and Change*, Vol.23, No.3.

Lara, Jesús, 1973, *Mitos, leyendas y cuentos de los Quechuas*, Cochabamba: Los Amigos del Libro.

Lehmann, David A., 1990, *Democracy and Development in Latin America*, Cambridge: Polity Press.

Lehmann, David A., 1996, *Struggle for the Spirit: Religious Transformation and Popular Culture in Brazil and Latin America*, Oxford: Polity Press.

Lehmann, David A., and Anthony Bebbington, 1998, 'NGOs, the State and the Development Process: The Dilemmas of Institutionalization', in Menno Vellinga (ed.) [1998].

Lem, Winnie, and Belinda Leach (eds.), 2002, *Culture, Economy, Power: Anthropology as Critique, Anthropology as Praxis*, New York: State University of New York Press.

Lemelle, Sidney, and Robin D.G. Kelley (eds.), 1994, *Imagining Home: Class, Culture and Nationalism in the African Diaspora*, London: Verso.

Lenin, V.I., 1964, 'The Development of Capitalism in Russia', *Collected Works*, Vol.3, Moscow: Foreign Languages Publishing House.

Lewis, Oscar, 1962, *The Children of Sánchez*, London: Martin Secker & Warburg.

Lewis, Oscar, 1966, *La Vida: A Puerto Rican Family in the Culture of Poverty*, New York: Random House.

Lewis, Oscar, 1967a, 'The Children of Sánchez, Pedro Martínez and La Vida', *Current Anthropology*, Vol.8, No.5.

Lewis, Oscar, 1967b, 'Reply', *Current Anthropology*, Vol.8, No.5.

Lipset, Seymour Martin, 2001, 'The Americanization of the European Left', *Journal of Democracy*, Vol.12, No.2.

Lipton, Michael, 1977, *Why Poor People Stay Poor: A Study of Urban Bias in World*

Development, London: Temple Smith.

Loaeza, Soledad, 1995, 'Mexico's Populist Heritage', *Journal für Entwicklungspolitik*, Vol.XI, No.1.

Luxemburg, Rosa, 1961, *The Russian Revolution and Leninism or Marxism?*, Ann Arbor, MI: University of Michigan Press.

MacEwan, Arthur, 1982, 'Revolution, Agrarian Reform and Economic Transformation in Cuba', in Steve Jones, P.C. Joshi and Miguel Murmis (eds.) [1982].

Magnus, Bernd, and Stephen Cullenberg (eds.), 1995, *Whither Marxism? Global Crises in International Perspective*, London: Routledge.

Malinowski, Bronislaw, and Julio de la Fuentes, 1982, *Malinowski in Mexico: The Economics of a Mexican Market System*, London: Routledge Kegan & Paul.

Mallon, Florencia, 1994, 'Exploring the Origins of Democratic Patriarchy in Mexico: Gender and Popular Resistance in the Puebla Highlands, 1850–1876', in Heather Fowler-Salamini and Mary Kay Vaughan (eds.) [1994].

Marx, Karl, 1979/1852, 'The Eighteenth Brumaire of Louis Bonaparte', in Marx and Engels [1979].

Marx, Karl, and Frederick Engels, 1979, *Collected Works*, Vol.11, London: Lawrence and Wishart.

Mayorga, René Antonio, 1995, 'Neopopulist Actors and Democracy in Latin America', *Journal für Entwicklungspolitik*, Vol.XI, No.1.

Mesa-Lago, Carmelo, 1994, *Breve Historia Económica de la Cuba Socialista: Políticas, Resultados y Perspectivas*, Madrid: Alianza Editorial.

Mills, George J., 1914, *Chile*, London: Sir Isaac Pitman & Sons, Ltd.

Morley, Morris H., 1987, *Imperial State and Revolution: The United States and Cuba, 1952–1986*, Cambridge: Cambridge University Press.

Murra, John V., 1972, *El 'Control vertical' de un Máximo de Pisos Ecológicos en la Economía de las Sociedades Andinas*, Huanuco: Universidad Hermilio Valdizan.

Nash, June C., 2001, *Mayan Visions: The Quest for Autonomy in an Age of Globalization*, London: Routledge.

Ortiz, Sutti, 1999, *Harvesting Coffee, Bargaining Wages: Rural Labor Markets in Colombia, 1975–1990*, Ann Arbor, MI: The University of Michigan Press.

Otero, Gerardo, 1999, *Farewell to the Peasantry? Political Class Formation in Rural Mexico*, Boulder, CO: Westview Press.

Palmer, David Scott (ed.), 1992, *The Shining Path of Peru*, London: Hurst & Co.

Paulson, Justin, 2000, 'Peasant Struggles and International Solidarity: The Case of Chiapas', *Socialist Register 2001*, London: Merlin Press.

Peek, Peter, 1983, 'Agrarian Reform and Rural Development in Nicaragua, 1979–81', in A.K. Ghose (ed.) [1983].

Perruci, Gamaliel, 1995, 'Neopopulism in Brazil's Democratic Consolidation: A Comparative Analysis', *Journal für Entwicklungspolitik*, Vol.XI, No.1.

Petras, James, 1970, *Politics and Social Structure in Latin America*, New York: Monthly Review Press.

Petras, James, 2002, 'A Rose by Any Other Name? The Fragrance of Imperialism', *The Journal of Peasant Studies*, Vol.29, No.2.

Petras, James, and Maurice Zeitlin (eds.), 1968, *Latin America: Reform or Revolution?*, Greenwich, CT: Fawcett Publications.

Philip, George, 2000, 'Populist Possibilities and Political Constraints in Mexico', *Bulletin of Latin American Research*, Vol.19, No.2.

Pieterse, Jan Nederveen (ed.), 1992, 'Emancipations, Modern and Postmodern', a special issue of *Development and Change*, Vol.23, No.3.

Preobrazhensky, Evgeny A., 1980, *The Crisis of Soviet Industrialization: Selected Essays*, London: Macmillan.

Rasnake, Roger N., 1988, *Domination and Cultural Resistance: Authority and Power among an Andean People*, Durham, NC: Duke University Press.

Redfield, Robert, 1930, *Tepoztlan, a Mexican Village: A Study of Folk Life*, Chicago, IL: University of Chicago Press.

Redfield, Robert, 1941, *The Folk Culture of Yucatan*, Chicago, IL: University of Chicago Press.

Redfield, Robert, 1956, *Peasant Society and Culture*, Chicago, IL: University of Chicago Press.

Redfield, Robert, 1958, *The Little Community: Viewpoints for the Study of a Human Whole*, Chicago, IL: The University of Chicago Press.

Reinhardt, Nola, 1988, *The Peasant Question and Family Farming in the Colombian Andes*, Berkeley, CA: University of California Press.

Reygadas, Pedro *et al.* (eds.), 1994, *La Guerra de Año Nuevo: crónicas de Chiapas y México 1994*, México, DF: Editorial Praxis.

Reynolds, Laura, 1997, 'Restructuring National Agriculture, Agro-food Trade, and Agrarian Livelihoods in the Caribbean', in David Goodman and Michael Watts (eds.) [1997].

Robbins, Lionel, 1952, *The Theory of Economic Policy in English Classical Political Economy*, London: Macmillan.

Roseberry, William, 1993, 'Beyond the Agrarian Question in Latin America', in Frederick Cooper, Florencia Mallon, Steve Stern, Allen Isaacman and William Roseberry (eds.) [1993].

Ross, Andrew (ed.), 1989, *Universal Abandon? The Politics of Postmodernism*, Edinburgh: Edinburgh University Press.

Rudra, A., *et al.*, 1978, *Studies in the Development of Capitalism in India*, Lahore: Vanguard Press.

Rutenberg, Victor (ed.), 1988, *Feudal Society and Its Culture*, Moscow: Progress Publishers.

Salvadori, Massimo, 1979, *Karl Kautsky and the Socialist Revolution 1880–1938*, London: New Left Books.

Sanderson, Steven, 1981, *Agrarian Populism and the Mexican State*, Berkeley, CA: University of California Press.

Schuurman, Frans J. (ed.), 1993, *Beyond the Impasse: New Directions in Development Theory*, London: Zed Books.

Scott, J.C., 1976, *The Moral Economy of the Peasant*, New Haven, CT: Yale University Press.

Scott, J.C., 1985, *Weapons of the Weak: Everyday Forms of Peasant Resistance*, New Haven, CT: Yale University Press.

Shanin, Teodor, 1990, *Defining Peasants*, Oxford: Basil Blackwell.

Sinclair, Minor (ed.), 1995, *New Politics of Survival: Grassroots Movements in Central America*, New York: Monthly Review Press.

Sivakumar, S.S., 2001, 'The Unfinished Narodnik Agenda: Chayanov, Marxism, and Marginalism Revisited', *The Journal of Peasant Studies*, Vol.29, No.l.

Slater, David (ed.), 1985, *New Social Movements and the State in Latin America*, Amsterdam: CEDLA.

Smith, Carol A. (ed.), 1992, *Guatemalan Indians and the State: 1540 to 1988*, Austin, TX: University of Texas Press.

Smith, Gavin, 1989, *Livelihood and Resistance: Peasants and the Politics of Land in Peru*, Berkeley, CA: University of California Press.

Stavenhagen, Roberto, 1967, 'Review', *Current Anthropology*, Vol.8, No.5.

Stavenhagen, Rodolfo, 1968, 'Seven Fallacies about Latin America', in James Petras and Maurice Zeitlin (eds.) [1968].

Stedile, Jão Pedro, 2002, 'Landless Battalions: The Sem Terra Movement of Brazil', *New Left Review*, (Second Series) No.15.

Stein, Steve, 1980, *Populism in Peru*, Madison, WI: University of Wisconsin Press.

Subcomandante Marcos, 2001, 'The Punch Card and the Hourglass', *New Left Review (Second Series)*, No.9.

Tello Díaz, Carlos, 1995, *La rebelión de las Cañadas*, México, DF: Aguilar.

Teubal, M., 1987, 'Internationalization of Capital and Agroindustrial Complexes: Their Impact on Latin American Agriculture', *Latin American Perspectives*, Issue 54.

Thorner, Alice, 1982, 'Semi-feudalism or Capitalism? Contemporary Debate on Classes and Modes of Production in India', *Economic and Political Weekly*, Vol.17, Nos.49–51.

Trotsky, L.D., 1934, *The History of the Russian Revolution*, London: Victor Gollancz.

Trotsky, L.D., 1962, *The Permanent Revolution and Results and Prospects*, London: New Park Publications.

Trotsky, L.D., 1975, *The Struggle Against Fascism in Germany*, London: Penguin Books.

Ulyanovsky, R., 1974, *Socialism and the Newly Independent Nations*, Moscow: Progress Publishers.

Urban, Greg, and Joel Sherzer (eds.), 1992, *Nation-States and Indians in Latin America*, Austin, TX: University of Texas Press.

Veliz, Claudio (ed.), 1965, *Obstacles to Change in Latin America*, London: Oxford University Press.

Vellinga, Menno (ed.), 1998, *The Changing Role of the State in Latin America*, Boulder, CO: Westview Press.

Vilas, Carlos, 1995, 'Forward Back: Capitalist Restructuring, the State and the Working Class in Latin America', in Bernd Magnus and Stephen Cullenberg (eds.) [1995].

Vitale, Luis, 1968, 'Latin America: Feudal or Capitalist?', in James Petras and Maurice Zeitlin (eds.) [1968].

Wade, Peter, 1999, 'The Guardians of Power: Biodiversity and Multiculturality in Colombia', in Angela Cheater (ed.) [1999].

Watts, Michael, and David Goodman, 1997, 'Global appetite, local metabolism: nature, culture, and industry in fin-de-siècle agro-food systems', in David Goodman and Michael Watts (eds.) [1997].

Weinberg, Bill, 2000, *Homage to Chiapas: The New Indigenous Struggles in Mexico*, London: Verso.

Williams, Heather L., 2001, *Social Movements and Economic Transition: Markets and Distributive Conflict in Mexico*, Cambridge: Cambridge University Press.

Winson, Anthony, 1978, 'Class Structure and Agrarian Transition in Central America', *Latin American Perspectives*, Issue 19.

Winson, Anthony, 1982, 'The "Prussian Road" of Agrarian Development: A Reconsideration', *Economy & Society*, Vol.11, No.4.

Wolf, Eric J., 1966, *Peasants*, Engelwood Cliffs, NJ: Prentice-Hall.

Wolf, Eric J., 1971, *Peasant Wars of the Twentieth Century*, London: Faber and Faber.

Zamosc, Leon, 1986, *The Agrarian Question and the Peasant Movement in Colombia*, Cambridge: Cambridge University Press.

The Peasantry and the State in Latin America: A Troubled Past, an Uncertain Future

JAMES PETRAS and HENRY VELTMEYER

INTRODUCTION

One of the ironies informing the study of peasants over the past three decades is that, while there exist a plethora of analyses of both *the* peasantry and *the* state, there is still no adequate theory of the relationship between them as formed and changed over time. Numerous monographs chronicle the history of the state in terms of its formation/support/reproduction as a macro-level political institution, or of the peasantry as a socio-economic category with (or without) a history in specific micro-level situations/contexts, but – except when peasant and state are engaged in violent conflict (with one another or against a third party) – neither feature in each other's history except peripherally as a fleeting appearance in someone else's 'grand' narrative.[1] This is why the first part of this article briefly examines the debate on the state, evaluating diverse views and arguments in terms of their adequacy in explaining peasant–state relations in Latin America.

In the second section we discuss the practice of the state, specifically the dialectic between the state and the peasantry in Latin American history as seen 'from above', a relationship that has been complex and changing. It is a truism, albeit an important one, that the role of the state with regard to the peasantry is deeply influenced by the type of production unit that is dominant and its relation to the market. The role of the state *vis-à-vis* the *latifundio* with its smallholders, tenant farmers, sharecroppers and migratory forms of landless or near-landless workers is significantly

James Petras is Professor Emeritus in Sociology, Binghamton University, New York, USA, and Henry Veltmeyer is Professor of Sociology and International Development, St. Mary's University, Halifax, Nova Scotia, Canada. The authors extend their thanks to Tom Brass for his helpful suggestions and comments on an earlier draft of this article.

different from that involving the plantation system with its seasonal but 'stationary' wage labour force. In the latter half of the twentieth century, the rise of a quasi-industrial bourgeoisie sharing power uneasily with labour and sectors of the agricultural elite, redirected the role of the state towards the promotion of import substitution industrialization financed by the export earnings of the agro-export sector. The role of the Latin American peasantry within this scheme – the 'subordination of agriculture to industrialization' – was designed to supply cheap labour to the cities and low cost food for the urban labour force. The state in this context was compelled to introduce a series of social and political reforms that would at once not only accommodate the interests of the agrarian and industrial bourgeoisie and, concomitantly, incorporate the urban middle and working classes into the economic and political system, but stave off pressures for more radical change.

With the advent of neo-liberalism in the 1980s, the relationship between the state and the peasantry in Latin America took another turn. Under the neo-liberal doctrine of free markets, structural adjustment and globalization [see, *inter alia*, *Veltmeyer and Petras*, 1997; 2000], the reversal of previously instituted reforms is accompanied by a massive displacement of small and medium rural producers and rural workers at a time of declining urban-industrial employment, engendering a new set of conflicts and confrontations between the peasantry and the state.

The third part of the presentation explores the relationship between the state and the peasantry in terms of a 'from below' response by the latter against the 'from above' imperatives of the former. Considered are three specific forms of agency involving peasants: repression, displacement and revolution. The generally repressive role of the state *vis-à-vis* the peasantry is contextualized, so as to identify its particular and changing forms. In this connection, the displacement of the peasantry from the land, from the agricultural sector entirely, and increasingly decanting them across national boundaries, is not simply a matter of 'individual choice' but of a systemic imperative driven by state policy defined by its dominant classes. The long-term, large-scale direct and indirect involvement of the state in the exploitation, repression and displacement of the peasantry has engendered rebellions, reforms and revolutions in which peasants have been the major protagonists. In colonial Peru, Haiti and Mexico the enslaved, indentured and enserfed rural labour force challenged colonial state power throughout the eighteenth and early nineteenth century. In the late colonial or post-colonial liberal reform period of history in Central America (El Salvador, Honduras, Nicaragua, Guatemala), the state instituted legislative, policy and repressive measures to bring into line (squash labour disorders) – and keep under control on the rural estate system – rebellious peasants, indigenous peoples and landless rural workers protesting against state actions in favour of the landed oligarchy [*Wheelock Román*, 1985; *Gould*, 1983; *Amador*, 1990: *Mahoney*, 2001]. And in the twentieth century, social revolutions in Mexico (1910), Bolivia (1952), Cuba (1959) and Nicaragua (1979), had peasants playing a major role in overthrowing the existing state.[2] In other contexts, peasants and landless workers were major actors in stimulating the development of a comprehensive – albeit limited – agrarian reform programme. This was the case, for example, in Chile (1965–73), Peru (1958–74), El Salvador (1980–85), Ecuador (the late 1960s into the 1970s) and Brazil (1962–64).[3]

The fourth section of the article examines both the power and also the limitations of peasant movements in their struggle with the state. The key issues raised in the discussion will be how the state has affected the peasantry, and the degree to which the state has been a friend or enemy at different times and in different countries over the last half century. From the mid-1980s onwards, peasant and rural landless workers' movements as well as rural guerrilla movements, have moved on to the centre stage of a protracted struggle throughout Latin America against neo-liberalism and its imperial backers.[4] In this struggle, the reforms and revolutionary changes wrought by the peasantry have been vulnerable to reversals, and peasants have suffered harsh repression, being forced to migrate in large numbers from their communities as the result of changes in the configuration of state power. The unfolding of this process is particularly clear with regard to developments in Brazil: as a consequence of neo-liberal structural adjustments to the economy, it is estimated [*INCRA*, 1999] that in the next five years over a million landless or near-landless peasants or workers will join the five million or so that migrated to the cities from 1986 to 1996, a year into Fernando Cardoso's presidency [*FAO*, 1998: 23; *Petras and Veltmeyer*, 2001b: 97].

THE STATE IN/OF THEORY

It is a commonplace that in Latin America, as elsewhere, the state has been and is essential to the operation of markets and the defence or transformation of the dominant social relations of production. In each specific form of agricultural production, the state has been instrumental in the foundation, extension, reproduction and transformation of the system involved, benefiting some classes – most often the large landowners – and disadvantaging others (mainly workers and peasants).[5] The essential theoretical point here is that the market is inexorably linked to an 'activist state', whether the principal agricultural unit be the large landed estate (the *hacienda* or *latifundio*), the plantation, the family farm, the peasant economy, or a combination of these production systems.[6] Before examining the latter, however, it is necessary to consider the state in (or, perhaps, of) theory, and particularly how and why there is still no adequate framework for understanding peasant/state relations.

Much recent theory about the peasantry has tended to oscillate between two competing and politically very different perceptions. On the one hand, there is the view that regards the peasantry as an entirely passive entity: it is either the disempowered object of various kinds of state agency (legislation, taxation, agricultural production regimes, systems of regulation, macro-economic planning, etc.) emanating from above and elsewhere, or the equally disempowered recipient of state patronage and inputs. On the other hand, a rival perception of the peasantry views it as an active and empowered entity, the grassroots agency of which contests both the effects of state action (revolutionary mobilization, rebellion, everyday forms of resistance, etc.) and what is received or on offer from the state (economic resources, infrastructural developments, etc.). This distinction is perhaps accurately reflected in the current epistemological gulf between varieties of on the one hand Marxism, and on the other postmodernism. For Marxism, therefore, the peasantry is mainly an economic category that corresponds to a transitional or archaic organizational form, destined always to be on the point of vanishing into the dustbin of history, and whose presence on the world stage is effected now in other disguises (as a rural proletariat, as an urban lumpenproletariat trapped in the proliferating informal sector, or as 'wage-labour equivalents' everywhere).

In much postmodern theory about the so-called Third World, by contrast, the peasant is recuperated mainly as a cultural category, whose identity as the disguised 'other' of Eurocentric metanarratives has been rescued – by, among others, exponents of post-colonial, post-development frameworks and the Subaltern Studies project – and given new life as the emblem of an irreducible alterity that is erased by misguided or inappropriate economic development.[7] Not the least problematic aspects of this approach are the following. First, postmodern analyses of acts of resistance privilege the element of identity-based particularities, which – when ethnicity replaces class – brings them into the orbit of conservatism and even the political right.[8] Second, the acts deemed by postmodernism to be empowering are invariably localized and/or small-scale, an approach which avoids posing questions about the role/function/reproduction of the state apparatus. And third, by refusing to address both the issue of class, and therefore the instrumentality of the state through which a class exercises power, postmodernism leaves the state intact, for either a landlord class or a bourgeoisie to use against peasants as and when it so wishes.

For its part, theory about the state has generally avoided issues to do with the peasantry. In the case of non-Marxist theory, where peasant/state relations are considered, they have invariably been viewed through the prism of establishing or re-establishing nothing more than bourgeois democracy. Thus the focus of an early and important analysis was on the way in which the process of agrarian transition led either (in the case of Asia) to communism or fascism, or (in the case of France, England and North America) to capitalist democracy.[9] More recent analyses that plough the same political furrow have as their objective not the establishment but rather the *re*-establishment of bourgeois democracy and its capitalist state. Here the focus is on 'resistance' by new social movements, leading to the re-democratization of the existing state apparatus [*Fox*, 1990; *Hartlyn*, 1998; *Lievesley*, 1999; *Grindle*, 2000; *Haagh*, 2002], in the process forming a 'civil society' that enables 'good governance' or 'hegemonic' rule to occur.[10] Linked to this are two other approaches, with similar objectives. The first is the Gramscian notion of 'hegemony', whereby control of the state is achieved by constitutional (= parliamentary) means, a method that was tried and found wanting in Chile during the early 1970s.[11] The second is the currently fashionable concept of the 'weak' or 'failed' state (particularly in Africa), where the object is similarly to constitute or reconstitute the formal apparatus of the bourgeois state.[12] Insofar as peasants and agricultural labourers are included within the ranks of these new social movements, and participate in the resistance mounted by such mobilization against the 'weak' or 'failed' state, the inference is that the rural poor necessarily benefit from such agency.

The absence of peasant/state relations from much Marxist theory about the state has been due in part to the fact that the focus of the latter over the past three decades has been on the formation/reproduction/role of the state either in advanced capitalist societies or in areas of the so-called Third World where capitalism is well established.[13] In neither of these kinds of context has a consideration of peasant/state relations been paramount, not least because epistemologically the presence of capitalism has tended to exclude the existence of peasants, and vice versa. For those Marxists with an interest in underdevelopment, therefore, the theoretical decoupling of Third World capitalism from the peasantry meant that the political object of agrarian struggles was to unite peasants in what was deemed to be a pre-capitalist countryside with elements of the 'progressive' national bourgeoisie in the towns against a 'feudal' (or 'semi-feudal') landlord class and its colonial state.[14] The aim, in short, was for the peasantry to help the urban bourgeoisie to achieve power, so that capitalism could then be established or 'deepened' in rural areas. Just as the focus of non-Marxist theory about the role of the state is on the 'weak' or 'failed' state – the object being to attain or re-attain bourgeois democracy and capitalism – so for Marxist and Marxisant theory the focus has been on the 'strong' (or in the case of Latin America, the 'bureaucratic authoritarian') state, seen as an impediment to the realization of bourgeois democracy, and thus to a socialist transition.[15] The 1970s saw a gradual change of emphasis, the idea of a 'strong' and class-specific state giving way to the concept of an 'autonomous' state; the rule by class of class associated with the 'strong' state was accordingly replaced with the notion of a 'plural' state, through which no particular class was powerful enough to be able to rule.[16] During the 1980s and 1990s this trend saw its apogee in postmodern theory, which denied both the efficacy of class and – consequently – state instrumentality.

Ironically, therefore, the development in Marxist theory of notions such as an 'autonomous'/'plural' state resulted in a de facto merger with non-Marxist theory: both now subscribed to a non-instrumental view of the state, against which were arraigned not specific classes but rather multi-class new social movements, henceforth pursuing not revolutionary aims (the overthrow of the existing social order) but engaged rather in everyday struggle in and against the state. It is time, therefore, to remind ourselves of two things: not just that the role of the capitalist state is essentially a coercive one (= the enforcement of *class* rule), but also that in Latin America – historically and currently – the target of this particular kind of non-hegemonic instrumentality has been and remains peasants and workers. The threefold object of the presentation which follows is accordingly to reinstate the agency of the state, to link this to the enforcement of class rule over peasants and workers, and to connect the latter in turn with challenges by peasants and workers to class rule and state power. From the state in theory, therefore, we turn to the state in practice.

AGRICULTURAL SYSTEMS AND THE STATE

The origins in Latin America of the earliest form of large-scale agricultural production, on the landed estate, were based on three combined processes: the forcible seizure of the land by the colonial state, the coerced conscription – again by the colonial state – of labour belonging to indigenous populations, small producers or imported slaves, and the development – yet again by the state – of a marketing and transportation infrastructure so as to facilitate exports [*Bauer*, 1975; *Pearse*, 1975]. A patrimonial state, a mercantilist economy and the *latifundio/hacienda* land tenure system served to fuel the European, and later US, accumulation process, which in turn generated nineteenth-century forms of industrial capitalist development and its adjunct – the 'old imperialism' of an exchange of raw materials and cheap labour for manufactured goods.

Rural Labour Regimes and the State

The key to the whole system was the availability and exploitation of labour-power, achieved *via* state coercion of workers, primarily native peoples and African slaves.[17] Exploitation was generally based on the expropriation of surplus in the form of rent rather than profit, and was more 'extensive' than 'intensive' – that is, an extended workday predominated over technological change.[18] Given the abundance of land *vis-à-vis* people and the labour conditions of super-exploitation, the only means by which the *latifundio* could operate and expand (and with it the whole export–mercantilist system) was through a system of overwhelming force and total state control.

The internal structure of the *latifundio* was based on a closed social system in which all of the rural labour force interactions took place within the *latifundio* and with the 'patron' – the boss (the landowner, his overseer or manager) – thus isolating the dominant class from the multiplicity of commercial, financial and manufacturing activities which might foster discontent, flight or rebellion. To retain rural labour involuntarily within this allegedly 'paternalistic' and closed social system, violent coercion was routinized, indiscipline was arbitrarily punished, and protest was savagely repressed with exemplary violence. The impressionistic view, held by some scholars, of 'reciprocal relations' and 'mutual obligations' based on an apparently harmonious 'moral economy', derived from the tightness of this control and its 'normalization' inside a closed social system where obedience was enforced under the threat (rather than the actualization) of violence. The appearance of everyday normality was maintained by the ever-present threat, and only the occasional reality, of a machete beheading.[19]

Two theoretical points need to be understood here. First, the existence of coerced labour was not, as is sometimes supposed, part of the organic evolution typical of 'feudal' or 'semi-feudal' systems.[20] Rather, local and world market opportunities, and the diverse and growing economic activities, encouraged large landowners to resort to coercion and total control as a means of maximizing exports and trade, securing thereby a supply of labour under conditions of an unfavourable land/people ratio. The object was to pre-empt/prevent competition for workers, which – if permitted – would raise the cost of labour. This is not to say a market in labour-power was non-existent, only to say that where it did exist it was controlled by landowners, who frequently exchanged between themselves the labour-power of their own workers (tenants, poor peasants and their kinfolk), an arrangement that operated independently of worker consent. Secondly, and for this very reason, the system of 'feudal', 'paternal' or 'reciprocal relations' on large estates was little more than a facade for forced labour, a form of control made necessary by the desire of most labourers to secure their independence and own plot of land, as evidenced by the history of escaped slaves in Brazil, Guyana and elsewhere in the Caribbean, and the search for refuge by Indians in the Andes and Central America [*Rodney*, 1981, Ch. 2].[21]

The plantation system, in fact, was a 'rationalization' and 'transformation' of the *latifundio*-based agricultural system.[22] In no case were these two systems ever in 'contradiction', either in violent civil wars or in bitter and prolonged political conflicts. The plantation system functioned adequately with different kinds of worker: slave, indentured and wage labour (see Best and Levitt [1975] and Thomas [1984] on the plantation economy). In all these labour regimes, the state's virtual monopoly over the means of violence in securing the prevailing social relations of property in land and other means of production severely limited either the formation or the reproduction of an independent peasant economy. The peasantry, in effect, served as a huge reserve army of labour, subsisting on tiny plots of land adjoining the larger productive units, thereby enabling what neo-liberal ideologues call 'flexible production'. Employed only during planting and harvesting, they subsisted on their own plots in the 'dead season', saving their landlords the cost of their social reproduction.[23] Nevertheless, the smallholdings served as a meeting ground for organization, and occasional large-scale land seizures and protests; the economic advantages to the landowners of this arrangement had a political price.

Theoretically, the transition away from coerced labour led not to a wage labour system, or to a peasant economy, but rather to a system of wage labourers who were also peasants.[24] When they rebelled against their landlords, therefore, it was as workers, but their demands on such occasions were those of peasants – for land. The role of the state in such circumstances was to facilitate land use for specialized production of exported commodities and, given the precariousness of the commodities produced (their harvest time was short), to apply the maximum force needed to ensure that labour produced 'just in time'. Given the fact that the plantations were largely foreign owned – particularly by investors from the imperial country (the United States, Britain) – the state operated as a 'comprador' institution: its economic activities were geared toward facilitating the movement of capital and commodities as well as policing the workforce composed of peasants.[25]

Policing certainly involved repression, but in an important sense that has been a constant in the history of state/peasant/landlord relations, notwithstanding occasional shifts in state power to pro-peasant regimes. But the level, intensity, content and purpose of state policing have all metamorphosed with changes in the dominant form of agricultural production. Policing under the *latifundio* system was essentially local, supplemented by state power in cases of 'emergency' involving widespread rural rebellion. The purpose was to maintain the 'closed social system' of the *latifundio* in which tenants and labourers only interacted with the patron, minimizing external (and 'politically contaminating') linkages. The only exception here would have been the military conscription of peasants who, because of their contacts with the urban centres, frequently became the bearers of dissident views.[26] In effect, policing under the *latifundio* system was directed towards immobilizing the peasantry and confining them to a closed social system.

In the plantation system, however, the role of the state was twofold: on the one hand to provide a certain flexibility of movement while at the same time trying to limit contact between rural and urban labour, and on the other to ensure a docile stable peasantry by providing it with subsistence farming during the 'dead season'. While 'local policing' continued, therefore, the great concentration of landless labourers, their greater accessibility to 'outside' ideas and organization, and the capacity for concerted large-scale action, all led to greater degree of 'national state military intervention'. Local military officials, judges and prosecutors, all of whom were politically and socially intertwined with plantation owners, were in the course of employer–worker disputes frequently called upon both to set in motion and to legitimize the use of state violence and, subsequently, punishment (detention without trial, imprisonment). The crucial strategic weakness of the plantation owners was the vulnerability of their crops during harvest season: a strike of only a few days' duration could lead to the decline or destruction of the harvest. This fact was well understood by rural organizers of the plantation workforce. Given this strategic asset favouring the workers, plantation owners turned to the state for help, and solicited its repressive intervention – 'exemplary' and 'preventative' violence – so as to pre-empt/prevent any action at harvest time.

Plantation markets were largely international, US or European, and as tropical production sites multiplied and competition intensified, working conditions deteriorated and new lands were expropriated from untitled local producers. In this political situation, market dynamics led to intensified conflict between the owners of expanding plantations and peasants, as well as between the former and plantation workers. And once again, the state played a crucial role. First, evicting de facto peasant squatters, using the judicial device of 'untitled land'; and second, pushing displaced peasants on to reserves set aside for indigenous peoples, thus opening up additional land for extensive agriculture in the future. The state also promulgated labour legislation outlawing the right to strike during the harvest season, and subsequently institutionalized (= 'normalized') collective bargaining between plantation owners and 'domesticated' leaders of the plantation workforce.

Agriculture and the 1930s Capitalist Crisis

The plantation model of agrarian development was so successful that it spread from one section of the Latin American imperial domain to another; because it was an advanced system of agricultural production, however, it was ironically prone to economic crisis. Events in the 1930s had an enormous impact on agro-export production systems, leading to a virtual disintegration of export markets and the emergence of popular rebellions in the context of widespread hunger. In a manner that is reminiscent of what happens today (not just in the Third World but also in metropolitan capitalism), the 1930s capitalist crisis was – as Marxists argued then and since – the effect of over-accumulation, overproduction, and the consequent devalorization of existing means of production, a combination which in turn precipitated a financial crisis in the banking sector.[27] With the collapse of export markets, and commodity prices hitting rock bottom, the crisis of the 1930s dealt a powerful blow to plantation agriculture. Some foreign owners sold their large rural properties to the local elite, while others retained their holdings but sub-contracted them to local farmers; yet others abandoned their lands in part to peasant squatters. All plantation owners faced varying degrees and forms of rural insurgency and peasant uprisings, and many of them diversified their portfolios, diverting investment into urban real estate, finance and (in a few cases) newly protected 'import substitution' industries. Although the state played a crucial role in the suppression of rural uprisings (see below), it also – and equally importantly – facilitated the transition to new forms of agricultural production and urban sites. Unsurprisingly, therefore, the 1930s crisis and the consequent economic decline of the liberal agro-export sector had a major impact on peasants and rural workers in Latin America.

The 1930s crisis of the liberal agro-export system led to the emergence of a new 'import-substitution' model, which harnessed agro-exports to local industrial production without changing the domination of the agricultural elite over the peasantry and the rural labour force. In effect, the ascendancy of the urban bourgeoisie and petty bourgeoisie involved a trade-off in which the agrarian oligarchy accepted its political subordination in exchange for continued control in the rural sector. Agrarian reform – supposedly a 'democratic demand' of the 'progressive bourgeoisie' – had no part in the social pact between the urban bourgeoisie and the agrarian oligarchy. In any case, politically, the period from 1930 to 1964 in the case of Chile, and within more or less the same timeframe in other countries, saw the gradual decline of the agrarian oligarchy as industrialization advanced and capitalism more fully penetrated the countryside, converting important elements of the landed oligarchy into an agricultural bourgeoisie committed to a more complete capitalist transformation of agriculture.[28] In this kind of situation, the role of the state was twofold: first, it was committed to industrialization based on a process of import substitution, transferring resources and investment capital from mining and agriculture into urban-centred industry; and second, to ensure the availability of cheap foodstuffs and other wage goods.

The import substitution model without agrarian reform led to the first wave of rural to urban migration, beginning in the late 1930s and 1940s and accelerating from the 1950s onwards.[29] In this new situation, the federal state channelled resources into industry, allocating foreign exchange earned by the primary sector to the importation of capital and intermediary goods for the burgeoning consumer goods industries. At the regional or local level, the big landlords retained control over state power and so managed to pass the 'costs' of their political subordination on to the peasantry. In the same context, while Marxist or Communist parties endorsed the notion of a worker–peasant alliance, in fact they were generally seeking alliances with the so-called 'national' bourgeoisie in pursuit of a productionist strategy, or were engaged in strictly 'workerist' struggles and organization.[30] The emergence of peasant-based movements in this context owed little to the urban-based left or populist parties – at least to their mainstream leaders and organizations (some local organizations and individuals excepted).[31]

The State, Capitalist Modernization and Agrarian Reform

In a very real sense the economic crisis of the 1930s as this affected the agrarian sector in Latin America was not itself 'resolved' until the 1960s, when a programme of land reform was initiated by the state: this was done as a defensive response to the lessons of the 1959 Cuban revolution, and thus designed to prevent the emergence of more radical demands for change among the peasantry. In this political climate, the state in almost every country initiated a broad programme of agrarian reform, an additional political objective being to incorporate the peasantry within a dual agenda: not just to divert existing and future dissent into constitutional channels, where it might more easily be co-opted by the state, but also to bring smallholders into the orbit of a specifically capitalist development project, thereby offering them a rival to the socialist alternative. Generally speaking, under the rubric of agrarian reform legislation designed to modernize agriculture, the ownership of productive tracts of land has been further concentrated, redistribution occurring only within the peasant sector itself, leading to a process of internal differentiation.[32] The latter has involved the emergence of a small stratum of rich peasants, some of which are converted into rural capitalists, a somewhat larger middle stratum of self-sufficient 'peasant farmers' with productive capacity *vis-à-vis* the domestic market, and a rural proletariat, composed in most instances of a huge mass of semi-proletarianized – that is, landless or near landless – migrant workers. In most contexts, however, these attempts at accommodation and co-optation, including unionization from above and the setting up of parallel or government-controlled peasant organizations, either failed or were only partially successful: usually, they tended to unleash class conflicts that continued into another and more radical phase of land reform.[33] For this and other reasons, Latin American governments at first instituted a land reform programme, but then devoted their energies to preventing its radicalization, using a combination of strategies ranging from corporativism (unionization from above), attempts at controlling peasant organizations, co-opting their leadership, to outright repression.[34]

In each phase of capitalist modernization – that is, in the transition from haciendas to plantations, and from export-oriented to import-substituting industrialization – the state played a crucial role in promoting, financing and protecting the dominant 'modernizing' classes from the threat of peasant and rural worker movements, forcing the rural proletariat and peasantry to bear the costs of 'transition'. These dynamics reappeared in the 1980s, in the context of a transition towards a neo-liberal New World Order facilitated by the so-called 'globalization process'. Among the categories disadvantaged by the application of neo-liberal measures in Latin America, the peasantry and rural workers have been the most adversely affected [*Veltmeyer and Petras*, 2000].

From Neo-liberalism to Neo-mercantilism

With the advent of neo-liberal reforms in the 1980s and 1990s, governments in the region acquired a new set of weapons in their confrontations with peasant-based and/or peasant-led organizations and movements, and in short order, according to some observers, the era of radical – even liberal – land reform was over.[35] This, at least, is how it has appeared to those in control of the state apparatus, or to the economists who serve the state in the capacity of policy advisers. In short, the issue was no longer one of a redistributive land reform, let alone one which entailed new non-individualistic or non-private property relations, but rather the modernization and capitalist development (= productive transformation) of agriculture, a process to take place without a change in property relations or non-market redistribution of agrarian resources/assets.[36] To this end, governments in the region enlisted the support of non-governmental organizations (NGOs) to encourage peasant organizations and communities to make greater use of the 'market mechanism' (land titles, land banks, etc.)

and, in their politics, to eschew direct action and utilize instead 'the electoral mechanism' – in other words, to adopt peaceful/legalistic forms of struggle in pursuit of their interests (sustainable livelihoods) [*Veltmeyer and Petras*, 1997; 2000].[37]

The reality of today's world economy has little to do with 'free markets' and even less with a 'globalization' in any of its permutations [*Petras and Veltmeyer*, 2001a].[38] The world is now divided into three competing and cooperating imperialisms, headed by the US and including the European Union (EU) and Japan. The nature of these imperialisms is essentially neo-mercantilist, although their interests are cloaked in rhetoric of a 'marriage [between] the free market and liberal democracy' [*Domínguez and Lowenthal*, 1996]. Neo-mercantilism puts the imperial state at the centre of economic activity – much to the disadvantage of rural producers in Latin America, particularly smallholders and rural workers. The essence of neo-mercantilism is a two-pronged strategy: at home, imperial state protection of domestic capitalists who are not competitive, and abroad the forced opening of markets in the Third World under conditions that are prejudicial to other imperial competitors. Among the most protected and state subsidized sectors is agriculture. Imperial policy-makers spend tens of billions of dollars, Euros and yen directly and indirectly subsidizing producers and exporters, while establishing a variety of protective measures, from explicit quotas on agro-imports to so-called 'health concerns', so as to curtail or exclude imports from competitors and Third World countries.[39]

Latin American peasants and rural labourers have been undermined by this neo-mercantilist system in a number of fundamental ways. First of all, the subsidies allow agro-exporters to sell cheaper, *via* subsidized electricity, water, extension programmes, etc., than peasant and farm producers in the Third World, thus driving millions of peasants into bankruptcy. Cheap food imports supposedly produced by more 'efficient' (= subsidized) US farmers have driven over two million Mexican and Brazilian peasants off their farms in the 1990s [*Petras and Veltmeyer*, 2001b]. While the USA and the EU heavily subsidize their food and grain exporters, the IMF and World Bank demand budget cuts and free trade from Latin American countries, leading to precipitous declines in budget funding for agriculture and the flooding of domestic markets with cheap subsidized imports.

State-imposed overt and covert quotas on farm imports into the EU and the USA undermine potential agro-exporters in Latin America who, in turn, cut back on the work conditions, payment, and even the employment of rural workers, in effect increasing the number of rural destitute. The non-reciprocal nature of the trading rules that are 'agreed to' by Latin America regimes reveals their 'colonized' nature. These colonized states play a crucial role in raising the gate for foreign imports, cutting credit and investment funding in the rural sector (except for a few specialized sectors that complement EU and US agriculture). In addition to 'draining resources from the countryside' to meet foreign debt obligations to EU and US bankers, the colonized state in Latin America is also assigned several other crucial roles: to police the displaced peasants and destitute rural workers, denationalize landownership, and privatize economic enterprises in key economic sectors.[40]

Having examined the way in which the state in Latin America has ordered and re-ordered agriculture 'from above' – first in the interests of a landed rural oligarchy, then on behalf of an agrarian bourgeoisie, and latterly so as to favour foreign and domestic agribusiness enterprises – it is necessary to consider the 'from below' response on the part of peasants and rural workers to all these developments: that is, the resort by the latter at different conjunctures to rebellion, revolt, and revolution.

REBELLION, REVOLT AND REVOLUTION

From the very beginning of colonialism and throughout its history – the Spanish and Portuguese conquest, and the subsequent military incursions by British, French and US forces – the peasantry has been the mainspring of popular rebellion, revolts and revolutions in Latin America.[41] While the forms of popular rebellions varied, and on the surface took on the appearance of 'archaic' or 'millenarian' movements by 'primitive rebels', the reality was much more complex, both in substance and motivation.[42]

The Modernity of Peasant Agency

The early rebellions, symbolized by the uprisings led by Túpac Amaru, were unquestionably attempts to oust the Spanish colonial rulers and restore elements of pre-Columbian society. The key issue here was not the non-viability of the latter, but rather the thrust of a popular rural uprising aimed against imperial power. One cannot simply impose on this rebellion an archaic restorationist symbolism, since peasants rebelling to free themselves either from labour-service obligations (*mita* or *repartimiento*) and other extra-economic coercive mechanisms of the *encomienda* system, or from the burdens of tenurial labour-rent (*inquilinaje*, *ponguaje*, *huasipunguero*), created the possibility of constructing a peasant-based subsistence agricultural system [*Pearse*, 1975]. But, as Bauer [1975] points out with regard to Chile, the constraints and oppressive conditions of a pre-capitalist (and pre-modern) agrarian structure informing the *latifundio/minifundio* complex, and consequently the prevalence of tenurial relations binding a smallholding peasantry with only usufruct rights to a landlord class (the *hacendados*), for the most part prevented the evolution of an independent – and modernizing – peasantry.[43]

The clearest and most advanced example of the inherently modernist tendencies of an enslaved rural labour force is found in the Haitian revolution which occurred at the end of the eighteenth century.[44] The anti-slavery revolution was also anti-colonial and, at least among the masses, strongly influenced by egalitarian sentiments favouring land redistribution. The subsequent wars of Independence in Latin America operated on two levels: struggles by merchants and landlords to secure state power (= political independence), to liberalize the economy, expand trade and appropriate native lands, and – on a different plane – struggles by slaves, peons and smallholders both to secure access to land and also to free themselves from coercive and exploitative social relations of production binding them to landlords (= socio-economic emancipation).

The post-Independence era during the nineteenth and early twentieth century is a period of repression coupled with modern rebellion. By that we mean the following dialectical process. On the one hand the dominant rural oligarchies engaged in a process of 'primitive accumulation' involving the seizure of native communal land and the abolition of any legislative protection against and thus constraints on the exploitation of rural labour, particularly that of indigenous peoples. On the other hand, the popular rebellions were 'modern' not in an ideological or programmatic sense but with reference to their collective attacks on the oligarchy's monopoly of landownership, state power, trade, and credit. The reclaiming of territory and defence of pre-existing native property rights (usually community or cooperative in origin and function) prefigured and were, in effect, dress rehearsals for the modernist claims being made, not just today but over the past decade, by indigenous peasants in Bolivia, Ecuador, Mexico and elsewhere in Latin America for self-determination, autonomy, and social justice. 'Local' or decentralized forms of rebellion were characteristic of all 'early modern' urban and rural revolts in the nineteenth century. The key point here is that, in substance, peasant–peon revolts were blows against a liberal export model of agricultural development linked to world markets, as opposed to production and trade of foodstuffs for local markets.

The savage repression that accompanied the seizure of land and control of post-slavery labour was met by mass resistance in Mexico and elsewhere.[45] The successful repression by the state of these mass collective mobilizations had as its aftermath the fragmentation and dispersal of the dispossessed peasantry and the formation of bands who were later dubbed 'primitive rebels', a label – as Wolf [1969] points out – which obscures much more than it reveals about the sequencing of collective action.[46]

There is no question that the armies of the oligarchic government were formed by peasant and peon conscripts, and that there were varying lapses of time between revolts and rebellions; nevertheless, there were oral traditions that transmitted tales and legends of earlier periods of emancipatory struggle, between generations and throughout the region.[47]

The modernist nature of rural revolts is confirmed by the Mexican peasant revolution of 1910.[48] By the end of the eighteenth century, Mexico had gone furthest in terms of integration into world markets, penetration by foreign capital, and in the formation and dissemination of liberal ideology – *los cientificos* – cultivated by the Porfiriato.[49] The brutal and savage forms of torture and labour control – graphically portrayed in the novels of B. Traven and the popular prints of Posada – were not part of an archaic (or 'feudal') dynastic order exercising a benign form of authority over the Mexican countryside and its denizens, but the means of maximizing profits for modern capitalists in Europe, North America and Mexico City.[50] At least with regard to its popular sectors, then, the Mexican revolution was not merely a land reform movement but had an anti-imperial character – the first major revolution against a burgeoning US imperialism. Ironically, the trajectory of the Mexican revolution highlights both the tremendous revolutionary potentialities of the peasantry, and also the strategic weakness of the latter, particularly with regard to the question of state power.[51]

Even though the peasantry has formed the backbone of virtually all revolutionary armies, its basic economic interests have found expression in only a few regional armies, namely the Zapatistas. While the peasant armies were successful in overthrowing established power, they constantly resorted to 'pressuring' the urban-based political regime to implement political pacts. The state thus became a point of 'mediation' between conflicting bourgeois and peasant demands, not a strategic resource to be reconfigured and transformed in the service of a political economy, so reflecting a new peasant-based economy. At the peak of each peasant revolutionary mobilization, the bourgeois state responded with concessions and promises, even radical legislation. But when the bourgeoisie and military regrouped, and peasant mobilization weakened, the state reverted to type: that is, it either reversed the reforms, or failed to implement them.

The phenomenon of mass collective action – mobilizing against the state, displacing incumbent office holders and securing concessions, via pressure on the state without changing the class configuration of the state – was a characteristic feature of peasant movements throughout the twentieth century. Nevertheless, the nature, the leadership, and the demands of rural-based movements have changed over time.

Peasant Revolt, the State and Revolution

In the 1930s, significant peasant-based mass movements emerged in Mexico, El Salvador, Nicaragua, Colombia, Brazil and Peru.[52] Rural workers, particularly sugar workers in modern plantations in Cuba, the Dominican Republic and Puerto Rico, as well as Guyana and elsewhere in the Caribbean engaged in class warfare [*Post*, 1978; *Canterbury*, 2000]. In each instance, extremely violent and repressive measures were taken by the state, either to suppress or to destroy these rural rebellions, or – as in the exceptional case of Mexico under Cardenas – agrarian reform was extended to include hundreds of thousands of poor rural families. In El Salvador the peasant uprising was crushed and some 30,000 were killed, with a similar 'development' in Ecuador under almost identical circumstances and with the same devastating effects on an incipient class struggle.[53] In Nicaragua, the Dominican Republic and Cuba, the US occupation army and its newly anointed tyrant-presidents – Somoza, Trujillo and Batista – slaughtered thousands, decimating the burgeoning peasant and rural workers' movements. In Brazil, the Vargas regime defeated Prestes' rural-based guerrilla army while pursuing a strategy of national industrialization; in Chile, the Popular Front of radicals, socialists and communists aroused – and then abandoned – the peasant struggle, together with demands for agrarian reform in an implicit gentlemen's pact with the traditional landed oligarchy.[54]

In the best of cases, peasant-based revolutions have been able to secure extensive institutional reforms in the agrarian sector – namely, land redistribution. In the case of Mexico, agrarian reform was a sporadic and prolonged process that began in the early 1900s and reached its high point in the 1930s.[55] In Bolivia, the 1952 revolution of miners and peasants led to a sweeping agrarian reform that resulted in the expropriation of most large estates.[56] In Cuba at the end of the 1950s, the victory of the 26th of July movement led by Fidel Castro ended with the confiscation of most of the US- and Cuban-owned plantations, the land either collectivized or distributed to smallholders.[57] In Peru during the 1960s, Chile over the 1966–73 period, and Nicaragua from 1979 to 1986, substantive land distribution took place, largely as a result of mass peasant mobilizations and direct action [*Cotler*, 1978; *Kay*, 1981; 1982; *Midlarsky and Roberts*, 1995; *Vilas*, 1995].

However, with the exception of the 1959 Cuban revolution, these advances by peasants and landless workers suffered severe setbacks over the medium and long term. The key problem, as always, was the relation of the peasant movements to the state. In practically all the revolutions, the agrarian reforms listed above were reversed. In Mexico, Bolivia and Peru a prolonged process of state disinvestment in the reform sector culminated in legislation that provided incentives to agro-export monopolies, alienating community lands (the *ejido* in Mexico) and stimulating cheap (= subsidized) imported foodstuffs. The politics of alliances, in which the peasantry was generally subordinated to the urban petit bourgeoisie and bourgeoisie, would often secure an initial round of redistributive reforms and state assistance. Subsequently, however, peasant movements tended to fragment and divide along an 'official' and 'oppositional' line in which the former became a transmission belt for state policy. The state, in this context, either played upon or actively created these divisions. The inability of a peasant movement to transcend its sectoral and/or 'economistic' consciousness confined it to militant 'pressure group politics' in which other urban classes took hold of the reins of power, using the peasant movement as a battering ram to clear the way for a kind of capitalist 'modernization'. Only in the case of Cuba was the peasantry able to consolidate its position and prosper, largely due to the socialist nature of the urban leadership and its efforts to invest and develop the countryside as the 'motor of development'.

The second factor leading to the decline of the agrarian reform movements is intimately related to the first: the lack of state investment in the infrastructure, credit, marketing and extension of services which are essential for the development of cooperatives or individual land reform beneficiaries. The 'maximum act' of the state was the awarding of land titles in ostentatious ceremonies. The promise of future investments never materialized or, as in the case of Mexico and Chile, was selectively distributed as part of an electoral-patronage system. In the case of Nicaragua during the 1980s, the US–Contra war destroyed many of the state-sponsored agrarian reform support services, while forcing the Sandinista regime to reallocate budgetary funds from agricultural development to military defence [*Walker*, 1997].[58] Lacking credit, the beneficiaries were hard pressed to finance capital investments; lacking roads and transport, they could not market at a profit. The high costs of private credit and transport ruined many rural households that had benefited from earlier land redistribution, and the lack of state investment in irrigation facilities plus the (state sanctioned) usurpation of water rights by better-off members of the new agrarian classes, undermined growth. With the advent of neo-liberalism, the elimination of price supports and subsidies, together with the importation of cheap foodstuffs, delivered the coup de grace to the descendants of the initial land reform beneficiaries [*Vilas*, 1995].

Counter-revolution and the State

Over time, the state turned increasingly to stimulating the reconsolidation of landownership and the promotion of agro-export sectors. For example, in northern Mexico, the Santa Cruz region of Bolivia, in Peru, and Nicaragua and especially in Chile, land reforms were reversed, and old owners recovered their land while new ones purchased their holdings, all with the support of counter-revolutionary or counter-reform regimes.[59] This process of land reconcentration and reform reversal was itself facilitated by the co-optation of peasant leaders and the incorporation of bureaucratized peasant organizations as a subordinate component of the party-state. This, for example, was the case in Mexico with the PRI (*Partido Revolucionario Institucional*, or the Institutionalized Revolutionary Party) and Bolivia with the MNR (*Movimiento Nacionalista Revolucionaria*, or the Revolutionary Nationalist Movement).

The key theoretical point here is that revolutionary peasant movements (with the exception of Cuba) have been unable to seize state power and recreate the society and economy in their own image – at least in a manner that consolidates and expands both their kind of social forces and political interests. Armed peasant revolts with revolutionary programmes have seen their leaders accept the blandishments of the urban elite, concern themselves with modernizing reforms ('land titles,' etc.) or succumb to the temptations of capital and patronage.[60] In the case of Nicaragua during the 1980s, Chile in 1973, and the Dominican Republic in 1965 armed US intervention – not so covert and via Marines or mercenaries – was an important factor in the destruction of pro-land reform regimes and the institution of corporate agribusiness [*Kay*, 1977, 1981; *Vilas*, 1995; *Walker*, 1997].

The crux of the problem can be summed up thus: *the principal vehicle for any and all agrarian reform programmes in Latin America has been peasant influence over the state; the principal weakness, by contrast, has been the failure to consolidate state power so as to sustain the reform and make it irreversible*. In both its positive and negative outcomes, therefore, the fate of Latin American peasant movements is inextricably and unavoidably bound up with the state. The point is that a revolutionary vision that takes account of the links between agriculture and the commercial, financial and monetary system is essential. The only successful case of revolution in consolidating the position of land reform beneficiaries has been Cuba, which managed to transform the urban economy in the context of a far-reaching radical agrarian reform program.[61] The question is whether the new and dynamic agrarian movements that now dominate the political landscape in the Latin American countryside have learned the lessons of the past.

CONTEMPORARY RURAL MOBILIZATION AND THE STATE

By the end of the twentieth century, a new configuration of dynamic rural movements took centre stage in Latin America [*Petras*, 1997; *Petras and Veltmeyer*, 2001c]. Such movements are found throughout Latin America, including Ecuador, Bolivia, Paraguay, Brazil, Colombia, Mexico, Guatemala, the Dominican Republic, Haiti and, to a lesser degree, Peru, Chile and North Argentina. Most significantly, it is these peasant movements – frequently with a significant indigenous component – that have led the opposition to neo-liberalism.

As in the past, the growth and radicalization of the major peasant and indigenous movements is intimately related to state policies. In the case of Mexico, for example, the inauguration of NAFTA (North Atlantic Free Trade Area) was the detonator for the launching of the uprising by the EZLN (the Zapatista Army of National Liberation) in 1994.[62] Similarly, the major Indian-peasant uprising and takeover of Quito, the capital of Ecuador, in January 2000 and a year later was in large part a response to the neo-liberal policies implemented by the national government [*Ceriza*, 2000; *Lluco Tixe*, 2000; *Lucas*, 2000; *Macas*, 1999, 2000; *Hernandez*, 2001]. In Brazil, the Landless Workers Movement (*Movimiento dos Trabalhadores Rurais Sem Terra*, or MST) has combined land occupations and mass demonstrations in order to put pressure on the government to legalize and finance the redistribution of land [*Petras and Veltmeyer*, 2001b; *Robles*, 2001]. Movements employing similar tactics such as *Federación Nacional Campesina* have formed in Paraguay, where direct action land redistribution tactics are combined with confrontations with the state to legalize and finance agricultural credits and inputs [*Informativo Campesino*, No. 91, April 1996; *Fogel*, 1986]. In Bolivia, Colombia and Peru peasant movements have been in the forefront of the struggle to develop or maintain alternative crops (for example, coca) as a source of livelihood in the face of the neo-liberal free market policies that have inundated local markets with cheap imports. The military and their paramilitary auxiliaries, with the active support and approval of Washington's client regimes, have spearheaded the US-directed offensive against coca farmers. The irony is that every client regime and its generals have been the major drug traffickers in the region, while leading US and EU banks are the major launderers of drug money.[63]

However, most important is the fact that the contemporary peasant movements mentioned above differ substantially from those in the past. First, they are all independent of electoral parties and urban politicians. Second, their leaders are not part of and subordinated to a bureaucratic apparatus, but are the product of grassroots debates and accountable to popular assemblies. Third, they link sectoral struggles with national political issues. For example, the MST in Brazil calls for agrarian reform, nationalization of the banking system and an end to free market policies. The same is true for CONAIE (National Confederation of Indigenous Nationalities) in Ecuador and other movements. Fourth, most of the movements have developed regional linkages (via CLOC, or *Coordinadora Latinoamericana de Organizaciones del Campo*) and international ties (the *Via Campesina*) and frequently participate in anti-globalization forums and demonstrations [*Edelman*, 1998; *Desmarais*, 2002]. Fifth, the new peasant movements have been assiduous in their search for urban allies and building electoral strength in national parliaments. Finally, these movements have learned much from each other, particularly in terms of tactics – for example, the widely practised action of setting up and maintaining roadblocks (*cortas de ruta*) – that are now used even by recently formed movements of the unemployed urban workers in Argentina.

Because the neo-liberal economies depend on mining, forestry, agro-export enclaves, assembly plants and external markets and finance, they have weakened the economic position not only of the peasantry as a vital part of the economy but also (and thereby) of urban workers: food imports lead to de-peasantization, which in turn ensures that peasant dispossession unloads more surplus labour onto an already flooded urban labour market. In response, peasants have resorted to massive and direct forms of action, involving among other things the cutting of major highways, blocking the circulation of commodities essential for the neo-liberal economies, reducing foreign currency earnings available for debt payments, and putting pressure on overseas lenders. Roadblocks by peasants and rural workers are the functional equivalent of strikes by workers in strategic industries: they paralyze the flows inward and outward of commodities destined for production and trade.[64]

The deepening of the economic crisis, particularly severe in rural Latin America, has had two major consequences, both of them particularly evident in Colombia. First, there is the radicalization and expansion of the struggle in rural areas – particularly the growth of guerrilla armies now totalling over 20,000, mostly peasant fighters. Second, there is an increase in the number of agrarian producers involved in the struggle. At the end of July 2001 in Colombia, farmers, peasants and rural workers joined together in a national strike, blocking major highways in protest over debts, cheap imports, and lack of credit. Similarly, in Bolivia and Paraguay, alliances involving peasants, coca growers (*cocaleros*), Indian communities, farmers and urban sectors (trade unions, civic groups) have cut highways and marched on the capital to confront the state.

The response of the state to these rural mobilizations has been substantially the same in each case: the militarization of the countryside, the extension and deepening of the presence of US military personnel and other federal policing agencies, and negotiations designed to defuse but not resolve basic demands. In Mexico, for example, massive urban support for the Zapatistas led to a process of 'negotiations', and an agreement on which the government reneged immediately after the pressure lessened. Similarly, in Ecuador the government negotiated an agreement with CONAIE during the occupation of Quito and then, with the Indian withdrawal to the highlands, failed to comply with those parts of the agreement that came into conflict with earlier undertakings made by the government with the IMF and World Bank.

Given the growth of international human rights concerns, US military missions have increasingly encouraged Latin American armies to work with 'paramilitary' forces in order to carry out acts like village massacres and assassinations of dissident trade unionists or human rights workers.[65] In this context, the case of Colombia is a classical replay of Vietnam. In 2000, Washington provided US$1.3 billion in aid to the Colombian government, and followed this with over US$600 million the following year; further, Plan Colombia makes provision for the deployment in Colombia of over 1,000 US military advisers and subcontracted 'private' mercenaries. Although presented as fighting the war against narcotics, the Plan is actually directed against suspected peasant sympathizers of the political left, and peasant guerrillas linked to the latter. The use of paramilitary forces to repress civilians allows Washington and its military clients 'plausible denial' (in fact Washington even criticizes the 'paras') while channelling arms, funds and protection via the Colombia military command.

In the last two decades, particularly with the introduction of neo-liberal and neo-mercantilist policies, Latin American regimes have rejected land reform as a policy solution to rural poverty. Unlike the 1960s, when agrarian reform was perceived by some regimes as a method of pre-empting revolution, in recent decades the state has sought to reverse what reforms had taken place over the past 50 years. Growing international linkages and markets, the re-colonization of the state, and a new Latin American 'transnational capitalist' class are responsible for the roll-back of these agrarian reforms as well as the growing impoverishment and militarization of the countryside in the interest of containing the growing rural insurgency. The rollback in the countryside is itself part of a more general process of denationalization of industry and the privatization of public services and enterprises. Nonetheless, the development of opposition has been uneven, with the urban working class lagging behind the advanced detachments of the peasantry and rural workers. Urban mass movements do exist, such as the COB (*Central Obrera Boliviana*) in Bolivia, the CTA (*Confederación de Trabajadores Agricolas*) and the unemployed workers' movements engaged in mass roadblocks in Argentina (*Movimiento de Trabajadores Desocupados*), the PIT-CNT in Uruguay and the *Frente Patriotico* in Ecuador and Paraguay. However, in some cases, like Argentina, Chile and Brazil (not to speak of the corrupt corporate unions of Mexico), the official trade union confederations are controlled by corrupt right-wing bureaucrats associated with neo-liberal regimes (the *Confederación General de Trabajo* or CGT in Argentina, *Forza Sindical* in Brazil) or politically moderate officials (the CUT in Brazil, Colombia and Chile) who, while criticizing 'neoliberalism', live off state stipends and have neither the incentive nor the will to mobilize their followers. Given these adverse circumstances (state repression and laggard support), the demands and achievements of the rural movements are extraordinary. In Colombia, for example, the FARC-EP (the Revolutionary Armed Forces of Colombia-People's Army), a movement of peasant-based guerrillas, have secured a demilitarized zone the size of Switzerland where social forums are held and noted scholars, government officials and others debate vital issues such as land reform and alternative cropping patterns. In addition, the guerrillas have major influence in over one-third of the municipalities of the Colombian countryside [*FARC-EP*, 2000].

The notion of territoriality is central to all of the indigenous peasant movements. For example, a key Zapatista demand has been and remains legal recognition of Indian autonomy, and the control by the indigenous populations over the natural resources in their regions. Similarly, CONAIE in Ecuador, the Ayamara and Quechua nations in Bolivia, and the Maya nation in Guatemala, have all pressed their demands for national cultural autonomy and economic control – demands resisted both by the rulers of the client states and by US and EU extractive agribusiness enterprises. This issue of national autonomy grows out of the increasing frustration with the neo-liberal state, the constant military incursions and massacres, as well as a growing reaffirmation of a national cultural identity.

The second major advance made by contemporary peasant movements in Latin America is the anti-imperialist content of their struggles. The massive and continuing US penetration of the Latin American state, and a desire to reassert control over important natural/national resources is the mainspring of this resurgent anti-imperialism in rural areas. For example, the aggressive US anti-drug campaign involving the direct role of the Drug Enforcement Agency, the CIA and the Pentagon in destroying the livelihood of 40,000 coca farmers in Bolivia and over 100,000 in Colombia has certainly fuelled anti-imperialist sentiment. The US promotion and financing of sweeping fumigation programmes that have adversely affected the health of the rural population in Colombia, and destroyed traditional crops throughout the southern part of that nation, has further heightened anti-imperialist consciousness. Similarly, former US President Bill Clinton's admission of 'guilt' for complicity in the genocidal war on Guatemala, where over 250,000 – mostly Mayan Indian peasants – were slaughtered, has certainly not endeared US imperialism to the *campesinos*.

This combination of self-determination, anti-imperialism and opposition to neo-liberalism, is present in the advanced detachments of all the Latin American peasant movements. Among the rank and file activist peasants, however, the focus is on immediate local demands, particularly land reform, credits and prices and – in some regions – the right to cultivate coca. Leaders of the movements are only able to retain support on the basis of their militancy and honesty in sustaining the struggle for immediate demands. Not surprisingly, the Latin American state has not remained indifferent to this dual process of 'from below' policy formulation and grassroots mobilization. Thus the government of Mexico under President Salinas Gortieri attempted to drive a wedge between the popular movement and its peasant constituency via a programme (Pronasol) of 'poverty' subsidies. In Brazil the Cardoso regime has launched an Agrarian Bank to finance a commercial land-purchasing scheme in a failed attempt to draw peasant support away from the MST. Hitherto, these and other such moves on the part of the state against peasant movements of today have failed, unlike similar attempts made in the past against peasant organizations and movements, which, more often than not, succeeded in weakening or dividing them.

CONCLUDING COMMENT

Both the history of and present forms taken by peasant/state relations in Latin America underline the folly of ignoring or underestimating the instrumentality of the state and also the class-based nature of its institutional agency. Claims about the 'plurality' or 'autonomy' of the state notwithstanding, it is clear that it has in the past acted on behalf of the capitalist class, one that is either indigenous or external to Latin America, and continues to do so in the present. Arguments about whether the state is 'strong' or 'weak' miss the point, since it is the *politics* of the state – as embodied in its project and support – which is central. Insofar as the state is not merely the object but also the product (and, indeed, the producer) of conflict, therefore, it is both a participant in and a cause of struggle. Much current non-Marxist – and especially postmodern – analysis of the peasantry, however, either ignores the state altogether, or recognizes its presence and impact but denies that such agency is based on class. The latter position gives rise to two equally problematic interpretations. One reproduces an epistemologically simplistic state/self dichotomy that, because it fails to differentiate the act of resistance to the state in terms of class, wrongly privileges all forms of grassroots resistance as necessarily progressive. The other focuses on the desirability of formal re-democratization, an outcome which similarly dissolves the contradiction between capital and labour that is present so long as accumulation and surplus extraction continue to be systemic imperatives: whether the state discharges 'good governance' in the context of a liberal democracy or exercises 'strong' government on behalf of neo-liberal economic objectives is in the end irrelevant, since capitalism decrees that both these forms are merely two points on the same systemic continuum. Sooner or later, therefore, the liberal democratic state in which peasants and workers attempt to realize their political interests electorally (that is, 'choose' to be something 'other' than that desired by national/international capital) *becomes of necessity under capitalism* the 'strong' state administering the neo-liberal economy.

Historically and contemporaneously, the state in Latin America has played, and continues to play, a major role in shaping the agricultural economy, either following or setting an agenda that is for the most part directed against the peasantry. In a few specific contexts, the state has – for tactical reasons – supported an agrarian reform programme, but such ostensibly pro-peasant interventions have been both time-bound and spatially limited, with little actual redistribution involved. For its part, the peasantry has alternated between local struggles and confrontations with the state, at times playing a major role in confronting the incumbent governing class. In this kind of situation, any positive achievements – such as securing land redistribution – tend to be counter-balanced by incapacity of the peasant movement to shape the permanent institutions of the state, and consequently the medium and long-term reversal of reforms secured in periods of intense mobilization. This is not merely a debilitating factor where past agrarian mobilizations are concerned, but also a problem that persists to this day. For example, the Brazilian MST which, in the course of a protracted class struggle, managed to secure the expropriation of thousands of landed estates, has recently encountered a major setback, in the form of a sharp reduction of credits, which has in turn bankrupted – or threatens to bankrupt – otherwise viable agrarian cooperatives.

The problem of breaking out of the constraints imposed by sectoral class struggles is not an easy one for contemporary peasant-based movements in Latin America. Today, unlike in the past, many of the peasant leaders recognize that the financial system, the export regime, and macro-economic policy directed by the state, are all major obstacles to any peasant-based development. Yet the construction of durable and consequential political alliances remains elusive. It is important, however, to understand that this particular weakness is not due to what happens in the agrarian sector alone. In most Latin American countries, therefore, the growth of precarious and informal forms of labour has led to the decline of urban-based industrial unions and the weakening of their capacity for collective action on anything but wage demands. Even where the potential for mass urban organization is present, however, there is the constant reality of state repression, hindering the deepening of any revolutionary urban–rural alliance. In Colombia during the peace agreement of 1984–90 between the FARC and President Betancourt, for example, the Left attempted to organize a mass electoral party. Some 4,000–5,000 activists and two presidential candidates were killed, and scores of municipal officeholders were murdered by the military-backed death squads, forcing the surviving militants to rejoin the guerrilla movement and to resume the rural-based armed struggle. In Central America (Guatemala, El Salvador), the former guerrilla commanders were effectively incorporated into the electoral process, but only at the cost of abandoning the peasant struggle and remaining a marginal force in the Congress.[66]

Faced with this dilemma of co-optation or repression, Latin American peasant movements have responded in several ways. First, they have radicalized the struggle by engaging in sustained and extensive roadblocks, affecting the shipment of foodstuffs to the city and primary materials for export. Second, they have brought the struggle to the city: the MST, for example, has organized national marches into Brasilia of over 100,000 people, recruiting urban supporters as they march. In Mexico, the Zapatistas marched to the national capital, mobilizing over 300,000 in Mexico City itself. In Ecuador the CONAIE has occupied Quito and even 'taken the Congress', establishing a short-lived 'popular junta' with progressive junior military officials. Similar demonstrations and peasant marches have taken place in the Bolivian and Paraguayan national capitals, La Paz and Asunción. These demonstrations of force usually result in securing a negotiating session with the government, and not only generate a set of agreements that are honoured in the breach but also lead inevitably – for the time being, anyway – to demobilization. What all these examples underline is the centrality of both the urban sector and its state to the success or failure of agrarian movements.

However, the mass show of force does serve peasant organizations as a negotiating tool, to exert pressure on the existing regime in order to modify its neo-liberal agenda. Its revolutionary appearance notwithstanding, therefore, because of the subjective or objective realities it is in fact a reformist strategy. Many of the leaders of contemporary peasant movements, like Vargas of CONAIE, have for almost a decade engaged in the cyclical ritual of mass-protest/negotiation/agreements/broken-promises/mass-protest. It is clear that the pursuit of mass pressure politics instead of revolutionary struggles for state power is a sign of ineffectualness rather than strength: in short, these tactics are dictated by the weakness in the cities, and/or the limitations in the strategic thinking of the leaders concerning the nature of the state.

Compounding the complexity of the peasant struggles are divisions within peasant movements and weak coordination among peasant organizations, factors that play into the hands of a divide-and-conquer strategy pursued by the state. In Bolivia the personal rivalry between Evo Morales of the *cocaleros* and Quispe of the peasant movements is a case in point. Similar divisions exist in Paraguay, and to a lesser degree in Brazil. The most striking case of fragmentation, however, is Mexico, where each state has its own independent militant organization, and sometimes as many as two or three, according to region. In this kind of situation, the state frequently offers agreements or concessions to one organization at the expense of others, thus driving a wedge between them all in terms of future unity of action.

Nonetheless, there have been a number of successes: some efforts at forging tactical alliances between different rural organizations have paid off. In Colombia, for example, in August 2001 there was a successful agrarian strike (*paro agropecuario*) that included everyone from coffee growers to day labourers, and managed to paralyze major highways throughout the Colombian countryside. Similarly, a number of Indian organizations in Mexico have formed a national federation that articulates their collective interests and expresses their solidarity with the EZLN. Together with the growth of regional solidarity among peasant movements, these alliances and unified actions are a major step forward. However, the problem of confronting US-backed client states and their military forces remains a formidable challenge. The current efforts of the Zapatistas in Mexico and the MST in Brazil to build counterpart organizations in the cities have yet to be successful. While urban-based religious and human rights groups, leftist parliamentary deputies, academics and trade unionists do provide valuable support, they do not constitute an anti-systemic force that could aid revolutionary peasant movements in transforming the state.[67] For one thing, unlike the peasant movements, these organizations do not have an anti-systemic agenda. The most promising development in this regard is the *barrio*-based urban movement of the un- and under-employed in Argentina, and the community-based Coordinator of Popular Organizations (COPS) in the Dominican Republic. Both have demonstrated an ability to undertake national coordinated mass action that effectively paralyzes the urban economy, and this despite savage repression.

One current alternative to rural insurgency and the savage state repression it provokes has been what might be termed passive grassroots agency, which takes the familiar form of rural displacement and mass overseas migration. Over two million Colombians have been displaced by the US-backed paramilitary/military scorched earth policy, and today there are more El Salvadorians in the US and Mexico than in their home country.

A massive exodus of peasants from Ecuador, Colombia, Central America and the Caribbean is the 'passive/negative' response to the failed neo-liberal experiment coupled with state repression. Except for President Chávez in Venezuela, who speaks of a massive agrarian resettlement of rural migrants – a back to the countryside movement – no state in Latin America has either the resources or the political will to reverse the current decline in and crisis of agriculture as a whole, and of peasant economy in particular. Integrated into world markets, subordinated to Washington, the Latin American state has continued to pursue policies designed to 'empty the countryside', confiscating fertile peasant lands and transferring them to big landowners and/or agribusiness enterprises, and then repressing those who dare to object to this process by taking part in the burgeoning mass movements. The dislike is mutual, and the element of stand-off palpable: no mass peasant movement is currently aligned with any state in Latin America, and no state formation 'speaks for' the peasantry. If nothing else, this situation underlines the importance of developing an adequate understanding of peasant/state relations.

NOTES

1. A partial exception to this is the late Eric Wolf [1969; 1982; 1999], whose scholarly and insightful work on the peasantry in general and that in Latin America in particular transcended the stereotypically ahistorical and micro-/macro-level polarity that so often inform rural ethnography written by anthropologists. However, even this relatively sophisticated approach to the study of rural society was unable to develop a theory of peasant–state relations.
2. The leading role in the 1959 Cuban revolution, arguably, was undertaken by a rural proletariat composed of sugar workers (on which see Zeitlin [1967]), but even in this situation the peasantry was a critical factor in the rural social base of the revolution. With regard to Nicaragua see Ortega [1990].
3. The literature on the dynamics of these agrarian reforms is voluminous but see, *inter alia*, Gutelman [1974] and – more broadly – De Janvry [1981] and Stavenhagen [1970]. A number of commentators have identified up to three different agrarian reform programmes in Chile: the first (from 1982 to 1967) pre-capitalist in form; the second, under Frei and Allende (1967 to 1973), involving a transition towards a capitalist agriculture; and a third (from 1973 onwards) based largely on a return of landed properties to their former owners, many of whom were converted into capitalists of the Junker variety [*Castillo*, 1982].
4. We have noted and argued this point elsewhere (see, in particular, Petras [1997]), challenging the position taken by many Marxists like Munck [1984: 198], who draws the conclusion from developments in Chile and elsewhere that 'the centre of gravity of the class struggle in Latin America has shifted decisively from the countryside to the city.'
5. On this rather obvious point see, *inter alia*, Feder [1971] and Huizer [1973]. However, many scholars of peasant rebellion, like Huizer [1973], make broad reference to the prevailing 'culture' of repression in the Latin American countryside rather than document the specifics of state repression.

6. This point is made in more general terms by Karl Polanyi [1944] in his pathbreaking research into the social and political institutionality of market systems.
7. There is now a large and expanding literature that applies a postmodern framework to the analysis of Latin American peasants. For critiques of this approach, see Veltmeyer [1997] and also the contributions to this volume by Nugent and Brass.
8. See Brass, this volume. This danger is also clear from what Saul [1976: 98] observed, presciently as it turns out, about Africa a quarter of a century ago: 'For "tribalism" (the politicisation of ethnicity which is all too characteristic a pathology of dependent Africa) does not spring primarily from the bare fact of the existence of cultural differences between people. Rather, it has been teased into life, first by the divide-and-rule tactics of colonialism and by uneven development in the economic sphere that colonialism also facilitates and, second, by the ruling petty-bourgeoisie of the post-colonial period. The latter, too, seek to divide and rule – better from their point of view that peasants should conceive the national pie as being divided, comparatively between regions and tribes, rather than (as is in fact much more clearly the case) between classes.'
9. The text in question is Moore [1966].
10. The main exponent of this kind of anti-state 'resistance' theory is James Scott [1976; 1985; 1990; 1998]. Although Scott himself writes mainly about Asia, others who have adopted his analytical approach have applied this same 'resistance' framework to Latin America [*Nugent*, 1998; *Joseph and Nugent*, 1994]. Scott's concern with 'from below' agency notwithstanding, currently fashionable postmodern theory refuses to address the question of peasant/state relations, preferring instead to focus on the minutiae of quotidian grassroots resistance, which is invariably depicted as empowering. In our view, an approach that does not address the interrelated processes of imperialism, the agency of the state, and class rule, cannot understand the extent to which the exercise of 'from above' power necessarily poses limits to any and every kind of 'from below' empowerment. For typically conservative approaches to the issue of redemocratization, both at a theoretical level and in relation to the Third World, see respectively Cohen and Arato [1992] and Held [1993]. The latter text is in many ways a return to the earlier approach associated with Bendix [1964], for whom the object of Third World development was nothing more than the realization of (bourgeois) citizenship within the context of the (capitalist) nation-building process.
11. Under this rubric comes 'Eurocommunism', or the view that in western European nations such as Spain and Italy socialist objectives could be achieved with the support of the bourgeoisie, a political consensus amounting to the exercise by the working class (and peasant) of 'hegemony' in a capitalist democracy. Just how fragile a concept 'hegemony' proved to be was all too evident from the attempt by the Chilean bourgeoisie to undermine the constitutional rule by the Unidad Popular government in the period 1970–73, and from the military coup that ousted President Allende. What happened in Chile had a profound impact on leftists worldwide, and gave a renewed impetus to a longstanding debate: that is, whether the parliamentary or revolutionary path was the most appropriate to achieve socialism. In Europe, many of those who opted for the parliamentary road later abandoned the objective of socialism altogether. However, the debate about the feasibility of two distinct attempts to capture state power – a parliamentary road as distinct from extra-parliamentary agency – is one which still has currency in much of Latin America.
12. The sub-text to the concept of a 'weak'/'failed' state (see, e.g., Sandbrook [2000] and de Rivero [2001]) is that underdeveloped nations – especially those in Africa – are not yet capable of running a bourgeois state apparatus, and therefore in some sense not yet ready for the benefits of capitalist democracy. At an abstract level, not only is this kind of argument potentially (and always inadvertently) racist, but it also overlooks the active role of western imperialist nations in destabilizing and/or undermining for their own specific ends what used formally to be bourgeois democratic states in the Third World.
13. Much of the debate that took place in the 1970s was restricted to a consideration of the

state as it existed in western capitalist countries (see, for example, Holloway and Picciotto [1978], Wright [1978; 1989], Jessop [1990], Clarke [1991], and Barrow [1993]).

14. Perhaps the best-known debate in Western academic circles is that about the mode of production in Indian agriculture [*Thorner*, 1982]. Much of the debate about the role of the state, however, concerned Africa; see, for example, Beckman [1982] and Saul [1974] for a discussion of some of these issues with regard, respectively, to Nigeria and Tanzania, and the reply to Saul by Ziemann and Lanzendörfer [1977].
15. The concept of a 'bureaucratic authoritarian' state, which was academically in vogue during the 1980s, is associated with the influential work of O'Donnell [1979; 1988; 1992] on the development of a 'strong' state in the southern cone countries of Latin America – especially Argentina – in the period from the mid-1960s onwards. His argument is that in Latin America the 'bureaucratic authoritarian' state was the result of a combination of processes: on the one hand the emergence of what he terms the 'popular sector' on to the political stage as an electoral force, and on the other the simultaneous transnationalization of the capitalist economy. Caught in a pincer movement between these two antinomic forces – the 'popular sector' wants citizenship and democracy, and is able to realize this desire electorally, whereas the bourgeoisie does not, because citizenship and democracy interfere with or hinder accumulation – a 'strong state' is established (by the military, but with a technocratic civilian component) and claims to rule in the 'general interest'. In the words of O'Donnell [1988: 31], '[t]he specificity of [bureaucratic authoritarianism] in relation to other, past and present, authoritarian states in Latin America lies in this defensive action by the dominant classes and their allies to crises involving the popular sector that has been politically activated and is increasingly autonomous with respect to the dominant classes and the state apparatus.' The theoretical usefulness of this concept for the understanding of peasant/state relations, however, is limited. Of the many difficulties with this theory, three can be mentioned here. First, the concept 'popular sector' – or 'the people' (*pueblo*) – has been criticized as too all-embracing and amorphous, composed as it is of 'the disadvantaged sectors' (a designation which includes the peasantry), the 'urban middle sectors' and the urban bourgeoisie, all of which are arraigned against a 'foreign oligarchy'. Second, as O'Donnell [1988: 36, note 2] himself admits, the concept *pueblo* is based on the extremely problematic formulation by Laclau of the analogous concept 'the people'. And third, the analytical objective of this framework is the realization not of socialism but of that political chimera – an elusive yet much sought after 'steady state' capitalist liberal democracy, in which liberal state policy is equally acceptable to labour and to capital and the liberal state consequently governs with the amicable consent of both.
16. This distinction is reflected in the debate between Miliband and Poulantzas, which took place in the *New Left Review* during the decade following 1973; Miliband [1969] upheld the class-specific institutional role and instrumentalist view of the state, whereas Poulantzas [1975], by contrast, maintained that the state was autonomous, and independent of rule by a particular class. That Poulantzas should take this view is in a sense unsurprising, since he came from the same theoretical stable as Althusser, whose attempt to redefine Marxism as a non-determinate form of structuralism anticipated the aporetic theory propounded in the subsequent decade by the strongly anti-Marxist postmodernists.
17. The dynamics of this process in both the early colonial and the postcolonial period of national independence has been fairly well documented (see, for example, Reyeros [1949], Chevalier [1963], Bowser [1974], Florescano [1975], Rout [1976], Góngora [1975], Duncan, Rutledge and Harding [1977], Cole [1985], and Klein [1986]). As for the more recent capitalist penetration of Amazonia in the Brazilian context see, *inter alia*, Davis [1977], and Hall [1989]. See also the contributions to this volume by Assies, Nugent and de Souza Martins.
18. On some of the theoretical – and political – issues involved here in determining the form and conditions of exploitation see, *inter alia*, Laclau [1971].
19. For examples from different Latin American contexts of the use of violence to control rural

workers during the nineteenth and twentieth centuries, see Stein [1985], Taussig [1986], Mallon [1983], and Mendes [1992]. Despite its frequent romanticization, the phenomenon of rural banditry was another instance of violence and coerciveness underwriting the *hacienda* regime [*Sánchez and Meertens*, 2001; *Tocancipá-Falla*, 2001].

20. On this point, see the seminal and still important exchange between Frank [1969] and Laclau [1971] over when and whether capitalism was present in Latin America. The degree to which rural labour in Latin America has been coerced, and thus unfree, is also a subject of debate. Thus, for example, Bauer [1979a; 1979b] considers that, historically, agrarian relations of production have wrongly been classified as coerced or unfree, and are more accurately interpreted as free, the result of choice exercised by the workers or peasants concerned. This interpretation has been challenged by, among others, Loveman [1979] and Brass [1999], who maintain that such production relations were indeed unfree.
21. This is the case made by Nieboer [1910], who pointed out that where land remained an open resource, available to all, agricultural production necessarily entailed coercive relations, since this was the only way in which existing producers held on to their workers.
22. On the economic and social structures of diverse systems of agrarian production see, *inter alia*, Barraclough [1973].
23. On this theoretical point in regard to Latin America see Veltmeyer [1983] and – more generally – Meillassoux [1981].
24. Hence the frequent resort to the word 'semi-proletarianization,' a term which recognizes the difficulty of categorizing members of a rural workforce either as 'pure' peasants or as 'pure' workers.
25. Not the least important role of the state during the early part of the twentieth century was the purchase and stockpiling of agricultural commodities in order to maintain prices at their existing level. For an account of this process – known as the 'defence' of a particular crop – in the case of Brazilian coffee, see Rowe [1932: 22ff., 28ff.].
26. As happened in the 1917 Russian revolution.
27. Not just Marxists but Keynesians, it might be added. A case in point was coffee cultivation in Brazil, as is clear from a report by Rowe [1932] who, together with John Maynard Keynes, co-wrote a number of influential analyses of the way in which economic conditions in the late 1920s generated crisis, and in particular how more effective state intervention in agricultural commodity markets (stockpiling surpluses in order to maintain high prices) might avoid this outcome. Following the bumper coffee crop of 1927, 'the vast majority of the planters had more money in their pockets by the end of 1927 than they had ever had before in all their lives...[t]his superfluity of cash led to...new planting [and] the operation of a general trade boom, with the inevitable accompaniment of an expansion in bank credit to a most dangerous extent' [*Rowe*, 1932: 12]. This led to extensive planting, which in turn generated another bumper crop in 1928, resulting in falling commodity prices. The degree to which this was so is evident from the decline in the price of Brazilian coffee on the New York market: it went from over 20 cents per lb. in the period 1924–9 to only 13 cents in 1930 [*Rowe*, 1932: 86, Table IV].
28. On this point, see Orlove and Custred [1980].
29. This rural-to-urban movement was the effect of a proletarianization process that proceeded apace with the advance of capitalism into the countryside [*Bartra*, 1976; *Cancian*, 1987; *Sullivan*, 1995; *Veltmeyer*, 1983]. The transition towards full proletarianization went ahead slowly and unevenly, with extra-economic coercion persisting well into (and in some cases beyond) the 1960s in most Latin American nations. By 1970, a large part of the rural population in many countries was partially or wholly proletarianized, a situation which generated a new wave of political protest and peasant insurgency. As pointed out by Paige [1975] and discussed below, different categories of peasants (tenants, sharecroppers, rich/middle/poor cultivators) responded differently to this process; thus the key issue in rural struggles might be land, land reform, access to credit or technology, higher wages and better working conditions, or indeed any combination thereof.

30. In this context the position of the Communist Party in Chile is symptomatic of a widely held view on the Marxist Left that the first order of the day in the rural sector is to secure 'the end of the latifundios' and support the bourgeoisie in attacking the serious low-productivity problem – 'to organise the new agriculture with the central objective of increasing agrarian production' (cited in Castells [1976: 358]). For a critique of this strategy as applied in Chile under Allende, see Palacios [1979]. It was this politically reformist view – that Latin American agriculture was still in a pre-capitalist (= 'feudal' or 'semi-feudal') stage – against which Frank [1969] aimed his celebrated critique at the end of the development decade.
31. The question of the relative spontaneity of peasant rebellions and social movements has been heavily debated over the years and remains unsettled. For example, it is clear that the Zapatista uprising in Chiapas in 1994 was the product of a major – albeit hidden – decade-long organizational and political effort, but the upsurge of anti-systemic activity, both by Mexican peasants in the early 1970s and by peasants elsewhere subsequently, are generally regarded as owing little to the organizing efforts of Leftist or populist parties.
32. To take the not atypical and well-studied case of Chile, in the mid-1960s the Inter-American Committee of Agrarian Development published a survey [*CIDA*, 1966] that showed the inequality both of the land tenure system and of income derived from rural property ownership. In this survey the *latifundistas*, or landowning oligarchy, represented barely two per cent of the rural population but received a third of all income; rich peasants, or the rural bourgeoisie, represented seven per cent of the population and received 15 per cent of total income. Middle peasants, however, constituted 21 per cent of the population but received only 12 per cent of total income, while various forms of smallholder made up the remaining three-quarters of the rural workforce but accounted for less than a third of total income. The question is what impact the land reform programme has had on this social structure and pattern of income distribution. Indications are, and several partial studies suggest [*Barraclough*, 1973; *De Janvry*, 1981; *Ghimire*, 2001], that the overall impact of the land reform programmes of the 1960s and 1970s on this structure has been negligible.
33. The dynamics of this process were well analysed in Kay [1977].
34. On this tactic of 'from above' unionization, see Thorpe *et al.* [1995: 131–43].
35. Exponents of this view – the 'end of land reform' – include Lehmann [1978] and Kay [1999].
36. CEPAL's model of 'Productive Transformation with Equity' [*CEPAL*, 1990] applies principally to industry, but policy-makers in the region have extended it to agriculture as the basis for a more socially inclusive and participatory form of development that, unlike the neo-liberal model, interprets the role of the peasantry in the production process in terms of social as well as economic criteria.
37. On the dynamics of this kind of rural development process, at the level of theory and practice, see, *inter alia*, Amalric [1998], Chambers and Conway [1998], Ghimire [2001], Liamzon *et al.* [1996], and UNRISD [2000]. For the impact of neo-liberal economic policies on Peruvian and Chilean peasants, see Crabtree and Murray (this volume).
38. On this point, see the critique by Petras [2002] of the 'globalization' thesis advanced by Hardt and Negri [2000] under the spuriously radical label of 'empire'.
39. For more details on these points, see Petras [2002].
40. The dynamics of this process are evident across the region, but are particularly clear in Brazil under the presidency of Ferdinand Cardoso [*Petras and Veltmeyer*, 2001b].
41. In fact the term 'peasant' – then as now – encompasses diverse forms, both of social relations and of rural production and labour, most often in Latin America working the land under the constraint of debt-peonage that structured the *encomienda* system. Under these conditions, the concept 'peasant' generally referred both to those smallholders settled *within* large estates, where they were leased plots on a sharecropping arrangement or as labour-service tenants, and those independent cultivators settled *outside* the estates, but

periodically drawn upon by the latter units as a source of seasonal or part-time labour. The peasantry so understood constitutes a broad social grouping characterized, most often, by a combination of subsistence and simple commodity production, but also including among its ranks a huge rural proletariat and semi-proletariat composed of landless or near landless workers. The theoretical issues involved in categorizing peasants in terms of class are outlined by, among others, Duggett [1975], Foweraker [1978], de Janvry [1981], Brass [1991; 2000], Berger [1992], and Kearney [1996]. In the Latin American context, that of a politically weak and subjugated peasantry and the predominance of the *latifundio*, a rural petit bourgeoisie composed of independent farmers did not develop to the same extent as it did, under very different conditions, in North America. On this issue of the alternative paths of agrarian development in Latin America see, *inter alia*, de Janvry [1981], Kay [1981] and Mead [1991].

42. Both the nature of and limits to rural millenarian movements undertaken by 'primitive rebels' are examined in the important text by Hobsbawm [1959].
43. This touches on an issue that should be central to any discussion about rural transformation in Latin America: the agrarian question, or whether the *junker* or farmer path of transition prevails in particular countries, and why. Raised over a century ago – in 1899 – by Lenin [1964] and Kautsky [1988], the agrarian question addressed the way in which European agriculture at that conjuncture was being transformed, and in particular what kind of relational changes this process involved, and how this in turn permitted a surplus to be generated and transferred out of agriculture for the purpose of industrialisation. According to Lenin, the *junker* path was the less conducive to capitalist development, because its oppressive relations of production prevented smallholder accumulation, which in turn blocked market expansion. By contrast, the farmer (or peasant) path allowed this to happen, with the result that smallholding became differentiated in class terms, and the better-off cultivators that emerged under this system purchased labour-power and generated surpluses for reinvestment in productive capacity. One hundred year on, these remain important issues for those with an interest in Latin American development, and the past two decades have seen the publication of some important texts analysing the agrarian question in relation to specific countries in the region (see, for example, Harris [1992], Harris *et al.* [1978], and de Janvry [1981]). For a useful analysis of current theoretical problems raised by the agrarian question, see the collection edited by Goodman and Watts [1997].
44. For this event, see the classic account – initially published in 1938 – by C.L.R. James [1980], who noted that 'working and living together in gangs of hundreds on the huge sugar-factories…[slaves] were closer to a modern proletariat than any group of workers in existence at the time' [*James*, 1980: 85–6].
45. Many historians in their reconstruction of events have tended to ignore or downplay the significance of these and other such struggles and, in the case of Mexico, of a virtually 'unbroken tradition of revolutionary protest' [*Knight*, 1985: 2]. Unless they could be tied to some decisive revolutionary change in, for example, the state, the class struggles, acts of mass resistance and peasant rebellions that accompanied the process of 'primitive accumulation' (forcible seizure of land, etc.), and that characterized the 'popular movement'in post-colonial times, in the *ex post facto* accounts of these 'events' given by historians like Ruiz [1980] the dynamics of mass struggle tend to disappear, outweighed by institutional changes. Again, in the case of developments leading up to and following the 'Mexican revolution,' the more nuanced 'class struggle' approach of the 'new Marxists' (Cockcroft, Gilly, Semo), with all their conceptual stretchings and over-generalizations, did at least restore to the historical record the centrality of class struggle and mass revolutionary action in the process of change, particularly as relates to the state [*Cockcroft*, 2001]. On the vicissitudes of this notion of 'revolutionary action' and the surrounding debates see Knight [1985].
46. It is important to remember that a similarly stigmatizing label – that of 'vagabond' (=

'masterless man') – was attached historically to dispossessed peasants in England, a designation which was used by the state to justify legal controls on their freedom to sell their labour-power, their only commodity.

47. A good example of the historical dynamics and legacy of an oral tradition of emancipatory struggle is provided in the popular movements inspired by Emilio Zapata and Zapatismo which, notwithstanding the localized and limited nature of the 'peasant rebellion' involved (reluctance to seize state power, perhaps a 'fatal weakness'), did, as Knight [1985: 9] points out, constitute a 'mobilisation of the rural masses behind a genuinely popular programme' and a serious confrontation with the state that 'significantly helped in ...[its] dissolution'. Zapatismo, in this context, inspired generations of later mobilizations including those of Lucio Cabañas and the Ejército Zapatista de Liberación Nacional.
48. Important contributions to the historiography of the Mexican revolution include Knight [1986a; 1986b], Hart [1987], and Katz [1988].
49. For the prefiguring ideological influences on the revolution, see Cockcroft [1968].
50. The justly celebrated 'jungle' novels written during the 1920s by Traven [1974; 1981; 1982; 1994] are about slave labour in the mahogany camps (*monterias*) in tropical Mexico at the time of the Mexican revolution. For the popular prints of Posada, see Rothenstein [1989].
51. That this has continued to be a problem, particularly where the question of new social movements in Mexico is concerned, is clear from Davis [1994].
52. On this point, see the relevant sections in the important collections edited by Stavenhagen [1970], Landsberger [1969; 1974], the Commission Internationale d'Histoire des Movements Sociaux et des Structures Sociales [1976], and Roseberry, Gudmundson and Samper [1995].
53. For El Salvador, see Dunkerley [1992: 49ff.].
54. For a critical analysis and overview of the dynamics of these struggles, see Castells [1976], Kay [1981], and Loveman [1976].
55. Early and still useful accounts that chronicle this process include Simpson [1937], Whetten [1948], Silva Herzog [1959] and Tannenbaum [1968].
56. For the antecedents and effects of the 1952 Bolivian revolution, see the important political analyses by Lora [1963; 1970; 1967–70], the contributions to the collection edited by Malloy and Thorn [1971], and the more recent monograph by Dunkerley [1984]. Texts that deal specifically with the Bolivian agrarian reform include Beltrán and Fernandez [1960] and Dandler [1969].
57. For the details of this process, see, *inter alia*, McEwan [1981].
58. This was also true of the Cuba revolution during the 1960s, when resources had to be allocated to defend the island from US invasion.
59. For this process, see among others Teichman [1995] and Crabtree and Murray (this volume).
60. This is what happened in the case of the better-off peasantry in eastern Peru after the agrarian reform there in the early 1960s [*Brass*, 2000: Ch. 2].
61. It is easy to overlook the longevity of Cuban socialism. The Soviet Union lasted 72 years, and the Chinese revolution some 27 until the death of Mao: the Cuban revolutionary regime – which has so far lasted 43 years – comes between these two.
62. On this, see Harvey [1994; 1995].
63. Colombia is an obvious case in point, but there are others. For example, Bolivia, where the Banzer dictatorship, which ruled the country for most of the 1970s, had strong links with the drug trade based in the coca-growing semi-tropical region of Yungas and Chapare. The military uprising which took place in 1980 was known as the 'cocaine coup' because all the senior officers who took part were involved in the illicit trafficking of cocaine [*Latin American Bureau*, 1980].
64. Similar kinds of direct action have been undertaken by new farmers' movements in India.
65. This is now stated US policy in many other parts of the world. Whenever the USA is

engaged in foreign conflict, therefore, as in the case of Afghanistan, its preferred strategy is to arm and support a suitably pliant internal opposition to the existing government, against which hostilities are targeted. It is important to remember, however, that – from Guatemala in the mid-1950s to Chile in the early 1970s – this has to some degree always been true of US involvement in Latin America.

66. In the case of El Salvador this is the view, and political position, of the leaders of the ADC (*Alianza de Campesinos Democráticos*), a highly representative national amalgam of 24 peasant organizations that is informally aligned with the FLMN, who the authors interviewed in a series of research visits to El Salvador in 1996.
67. Not least because so many of those who adhere to NGO activity or parliamentary methods now eschew the possibility and the desirability of a revolutionary overthrow of capitalism and its state.

REFERENCES

Amador, 1990, *Un siglo de lucha de los trabajadores en Nicaragua*, Managua: Centro de la Investigación de la Realidad d América latina.

Amalric, Frank, 1998, 'Sustainable Livelihoods, Entrepreneurship, Political Strategies and Governance', *Development*, Vol.41, No.3.

Barraclough, S., 1973, *Agrarian Structure in Latin America, A Resumé of the CIDA Land Tenure Studies*, Lexington, MA: Lexington Books.

Barrow, Clyde W., 1993, *Critical Theories of the State*, Madison, WI: The University of Wisconsin Press.

Bartra, Roger, 1976, '¡Si los campesinos se extinguen!' *Historia y Sociedad*, No.8, Winter.

Bauer, Arnold J., 1975, *Chilean Rural Society from the Spanish Conquest to 1930*, Cambridge: Cambridge University Press.

Bauer, Arnold J., 1979a, 'Rural Workers in Spanish America: Problems of Peonage and Oppression', *Hispanic American Historical Review*, Vol.59, No.1.

Bauer, Arnold J., 1979b, 'Reply', *Hispanic American Historical Review*, Vol.59, No.3.

Beckman, Björn, 1982, 'Whose State? State and Capitalist Development in Nigeria', *Review of African Political Economy*, No.23.

Beltran, Fausto, and José Fernández, 1960, *¿Donde Va la reforma Agraria Boliviana?*, La Paz: Talleres Gráficos Bolivianos.

Bendix, Reinhard, 1964, *Nation-Building and Citizenship: Studies of Our Changing Social Order*, New York: John Wiley & Sons.

Berger, Guy, 1992, *Social Structure and Rural Development in the Third World*, Cambridge: Cambridge University Press.

Best, Lloyd and Kari Levitt, 1975, *Pure Plantation Economy*, St Augustine, Trinidad: Institute of International Relations (mimeo).

Bowser, Frederick P., 1974, *The African Slave in Colonial Peru, 1524–1650*, Stanford, CA: Stanford University Press.

Brass, Tom, 1991, 'Moral Economists, Subalterns, New Social Movements and the (Re) Emergence of a (Post) Modernised (Middle) Peasant', *The Journal of Peasant Studies*, Vol.18, No.2.

Brass, Tom, 1999, *Towards a Comparative Political Economy of Unfree Labour: Case Studies and Debates*, London and Portland, OH: Frank Cass Publishers.

Brass, Tom, 2000, *Peasants, Populism and Postmodernism: The Return of the Agrarian Myth*, London and Portland, OH: Frank Cass Publishers.

Cancian, Frank, 1987, 'Proletarianization in Zinacantan 1960–83', in Morgan Maclachan (ed.), *Household Economies and Their Transformation*, Lanham, MD: University Press of America.

Canterbury, Dennis, 2000, 'Political and Social Forces in Guyanese Working Class Development', unpublished PhD thesis, Department of Sociology, Binghamton University, Binghamton NY.

Castells, Manuel, 1976, *Movimientos sociales urbanos en América Latina: tendencias históricas y problemas teóricos*, Lima: Pontífica Universidad Católica.

Castillo, Leonardo, 1982, 'Chile's Three Agrarian Reforms: The Inheritors', *Bulletin of Latin American Research*, Vol.1, No.2.

CEPAL (UN Economic Comission for Latin America), 1990, *Productive Transformation with Equity*, Santiago de Chile: CEPAL.

Ceriza, Alejandra, *et al.*, 2000, 'Análisis de casos: la revuelta indígena en Ecuador,' *OSAL-Observatorio Social de América Latina* (Junio), Buenos Aires: CLACSO.

Chambers, Robert and Gordon Conway, 1998, 'Sustainable Rural Livelihoods: Some Working Definitions', *Development*, Vol.41, No.3.

Chevalier, François, 1963, *Land and Society in Colonial Mexico: The Great Hacienda*, Berkeley, CA: The University of California Press.

Chilcote, Ron and Dale Johnston (eds.), 1983, *Theories of Development*, Beverley Hills, CA: Sage Publications.

CIDA, 1966, *Chile: Tenencia de la tierra y desarrollo socio-económico del sector agrícola*, Santiago de Chile: Talleres Gráficos Hispano Suiza Ltda.

Clarke, Simon (ed.), 1991, *The State Debate*, London: Macmillan.

Cockcroft, James D., 1968, *Intellectual Precursors of the Mexican Revolution, 1900–1913*, Austin, TX: University of Texas Press.

Cockcroft, James D., 2001, *América latina y Estados Unidos: historia y política país por país*, México DF: Siglo Veintiuno Editores.

Cohen, Jean L., and Andrew Arato, 1992, *Civil Society and Political Theory*, Cambridge, MA: The MIT Press.

Cole, Jeffrey A., 1985, *The Potosí Mita, 1573–1700: Compulsory Indian Labor in the Andes*, Stanford, CA: Stanford University Press.

Collier, David (ed.), 1979, *The New Authoritarianism in Latin America*, Princeton, NJ: Princeton University Press.

Commission Internationale d'Histoire des Mouvements Sociaux et des Structures Sociales, 1976, *Les Mouvements Paysans dans le Monde Contemporaine*, (Vol.3) Naples: ISMOS.

Cotler, Julio, 1978, *Clases, estado y nación en el Perú*, Lima: Instituto de Estudios Peruanos.

Dandler, Jorge, 1969, *El Sindicalismo Campesino en Bolivia*, México: Instituto Indigenista Interamericano.

Davis, Shelton H., 1977, *Victims of the Miracle: Development and the Indians of Brazil*, New York: Cambridge University Press.

Davis, Diane E., 1994, 'Failed Democratic Reform in Contemporary Mexico: From Social Movements to the State and Back Again', *Journal of Latin American Studies*, Vol.26, Part 2.

De Janvry, Alain, 1981, *The Agrarian Question and Reformism in Latin America*, Baltimore, MD: Johns Hopkins University Press.

De Rivero, Oswaldo, 2001, *The Myth of Development: The Non-Viable Economies of the 21st Century*, London and New York: Zed Press.

De Walt, Billie and Martha Ress with Arthur Murphy, 1994, *The End of Agrarian Reform in Mexico: Past Lessons and Future Prospects*, San Diego: Center for US–Mexican Studies.

Desmarais, Annette-Aurélie, 2002, 'The Via Campesina: Consolidating an International Peasant and Farm Movement', *The Journal of Peasant Studies*, Vol.29, No.2.

Dominguez, Jorge I., and Abraham F. Lowenthal (eds.), 1996, *Constructing Democratic Governance: Latin America and the Caribbean in the 1990s*, Baltimore, MD: The Johns Hopkins University Press.

Duggett, Michael, 1975, 'Marx on Peasants', *The Journal of Peasant Studies*, Vol.2, No.2.

Duncan, Kenneth, Ian Rutledge, and Colin Harding (eds.), 1977, *Land and Labour in Latin*

America: Essays on the Development of Agrarian Capitalism in the Nineteenth and Twentieth Centuries, New York: Cambridge University Press.

Dunkerley, James, 1984, *Rebellion in the Veins: Political Struggle in Bolivia 1952–82*, London: New Left Books.

Dunkerley, James, 1992, *Political Suicide in Latin America*, New York: Verso.

Edelman, Marc, 1998, 'Transnational Peasant Politics in Central America', *Latin American Research Review*, Vol. 33, No.3.

FAO, 1998, *Yearbook*, Vol.51, Rome: FAO.

FARC-EP, 2000, *Historical Outline – International Commission Revolutionary Armed Forces of Colombia Peoples Army*, Toronto: Fuerzas Armadas Revolucionarias de Colombia-Ejército del Pueblo, International Commission.

Feder, Ernest, 1971, *The Rape of the Peasantry: Latin America's Landholding System*, New York: Doubleday & Co.

Florescano, Enrique (ed.), 1975, *Haciendas, Latifundios y Plantaciones en América Latina*, México, DF: Siglo XXI.

Fogel, Ramon Bruno, 1986, *Movimientos Campesinos en el Paraguay*, Asunción: Centro Paraguayo de Estudios Sociologicos (CPES).

Foweraker, Joseph W., 1978, 'The Contemporary Peasantry: Class and Class Practice', in Howard Newby (ed.) *International Perspectives in Rural Sociology*, New York: John Wiley and Sons.

Fox, J. (ed.), 1990, *The Challenge of Rural Democratization*, London: Frank Cass.

Frank, André Gunder, 1969, *Capitalism and Underdevelopment in Latin America*, New York: Monthly Review Press.

Ghimire, Krishna B. (ed.), 2001, *Land Reform and Peasant livelihoods: The Social Dynamics of Rural Poverty and Agrarian Reform in Developing Countries*, London: ITDG.

Gilly, Adolfo, 1971, *La revolución interrumpida. México 1910–1920: una Guerra campesina por la tierra y el poder*, México: El Caballito.

Góngora, Mario, 1975, *Studies in the Colonial History of Spanish America*, Cambridge: Cambridge University Press.

Goodman, David, and Michael Watts (eds.), 1997, *Globalising Food: Agrarian Questions and Global Restructuring*, London: Routledge.

Gould, Jeffrey, 1983, 'El trabajo forzoso y las comunidades indígenas nicaragüenses', in *El café en la historia de Centroamérica*, Hector Pérez Brignoli and Mario Samper (eds.), San José: FLACSO.

Grindle, Merilee S., 2000, *Audacious Reforms: Institutional Invention and Democracy in Latin America*, Baltimore, MD: Johns Hopkins University Press.

Gutelman, Michel, 1971, *Réforme et mystification agraires en Amérique latine: Le cas du Mexique*, Paris: François Maspero.

Gwynne, Robert and Cristóbal Kay (eds.), 1999, *Latin America Transformed*, New York: Oxford University Press.

Haagh, Louise, 2002, *Citizenship, Labour Markets and Democratization: Chile and the Modern Sequence*, Oxford: Palgrave.

Hall, Anthony L., 1989, *Developing Amazonia*, Manchester and New York: Manchester University Press.

Hardt, Michael, and Antonio Negri, 2000, *Empire*, Cambridge, MA: Harvard University Press.

Harris, Richard L., Anthony Winson, Florencia Mallon, Rosemary Galli, Alain de Janvry and Lynn Ground, and Roderigo Montoya, 1978, 'Peasants, Capitalism, and the Class Struggle in Rural Latin America (Part II)', *Latin American Perspectives*, Vol.5, No.4.

Harris, Richard L., 1992, *Marxism, Socialism, and Democracy in Latin America*, Boulder, CO: Westview Press.

Hart, John Mason, 1987, *Revolutionary Mexico: The Coming and Process of the Mexican Revolution*, Berkeley, CA: University of California Press.

Hartlyn, Jonathan, 1998, *The Struggle for Democratic Politics in the Dominican Republic*,

Chapel Hill, NC: University of North Carolina Press.

Harvey, Neil, 1994, *Rebellion in Chiapas: Rural Reforms, Campesino Radicalism and the Limits to Salinismo*, San Diego: Centre for US–Mexican Studies.

Harvey, Neil, 1995, 'Rebellion in Chiapas: Rural Reforms and Popular Struggles', *Third World Quarterly*, Vol.16, No.1.

Held, David (ed.), 1993, *Prospects for Democracy: North, South, East, West*, Cambridge: Polity Press.

Hernandez, Virgilio, 2001, 'Reflexiones preliminares sobre el levantamiento de los bases indigenas y campesinas', *Boletin ICCI 'RIMAY'*, No.3 (February).

Hobsbawm, Eric J., 1959, *Primitive Rebels*, Manchester: Manchester University Press.

Holloway, John, and Sol Picciotto (eds), 1978, *State and Capital: A Marxist Debate*, London: Edward Arnold.

Huizer, Gerrit, 1973, *Peasant Rebellion in Latin America*, London: Penguin Books.

INCRA [Instituto Nacional de Colonização e Reforma Agrária], 1999, *Balanço da Reforma Agraria e da Agricultura Familiar 1995–99*, Brasilia: Ministério do Desenvolvimiento Agrário.

James, C.L.R., 1980, *The Black Jacobins: Toussaint L'Overture and the San Domingo Revolution*, London: Allison & Busby.

Jessop, Bob, 1990, *State Theory: Putting Capitalist States in their Place*, Cambridge: Polity Press.

Joseph, Gilbert M., and Daniel Nugent (eds.), 1994, *Everyday Forms of State Formation: Revolution and Negotiation of Rule in Modern Mexico*, London and Durham, NC: Duke University Press.

Katz, Friedrich (ed.), 1988, *Riot, Rebellion, and Revolution: Rural Social Conflict in Mexico*, Princeton, NJ: Princeton University Press.

Kautsky, Karl, 1988, *The Agrarian Question*, 2 Vols., London: Zwan Publications.

Kay, Cristóbal, 1977, 'The Development of the Chilean Hacienda System, 1850–1973', in Kenneth Duncan, Ian Rutledge, and Colin Harding (eds.) *Land and Labour in Latin America: Essays on the Development of Agrarian Capitalism in the Nineteenth and Twentieth Centuries*, New York: Cambridge University Press.

Kay, Cristóbal, 1981, 'Political Economy, Class Alliances and Agrarian Change in Chile', *The Journal of Peasant Studies*, Vol.8, No.4.

Kay, Cristóbal, 1982, 'Achievements and Contradictions of the Peruvian Agrarian Reform', *Journal of Development Studies*, Vol.18, No.2.

Kay, Cristóbal, 1999, 'Rural Development: From Agrarian Reform to Neoliberalism and Beyond', in Robert Gwynne and Cristóbal Kay (eds.) *Latin America Transformed*, New York: Oxford University Press.

Kearney, Michael, 1996, *Reconceptualizing the Peasantry*, Boulder, CO: Westview Press.

Klein, Herbert S., 1986, *African Slavery in Latin America and the Caribbean*, New York: Oxford University Press.

Knight, Alan, 1985, 'The Mexican Revolution: Bourgeois? Nationalist? Or Just a "Great rebellion" ', *Bulletin of Latin American Research*, Vol.4, No.2.

Knight, Alan, 1986a, *The Mexican Revolution: Volume 1 – Porfirians, Liberals and Peasants*, Cambridge: Cambridge University Press.

Knight, Alan, 1986b, *The Mexican Revolution: Volume 2 – Counter-revolution and Reconstruction*, Cambridge: Cambridge University Press.

Laclau, Ernesto, 1971, 'Feudalism and Capitalism in Latin America', *New Left Review*, No.67.

Landsberger, Henry A. (ed.), 1969, *Latin American Peasant Movements*, London and Ithaca, NY: Cornell University Press.

Landsberger, Henry A. (ed.), 1974, *Rural Protest: Peasant Movements and Social Change*, London: Macmillan.

Latin American Bureau, 1980, *Bolivia: Coup d'Etat*, London: LAB.

Lehmann, David, 1978, 'The Death of Land Reform: A Polemic', *World Development*, Vol.6,

No.3.

Lenin, V.I., 1964, 'The Development of Capitalism in Russia', *Collected Works*, Vol.3, Moscow: Foreign Languages Publishing House.

Liamzon, Tina (ed.), 1996, *Towards Sustainable Livelihoods*, Rome: Society for International Development (SID).

Lichbach, Mark, 1994, 'What makes Rational Peasants Revolutionary? Dilemma, Paradox and Irony in Peasant Collective Action', *World Politics*, Vol.46, No.3.

Lievesley, Geraldine, 1999, *Democracy in Latin America: Mobilization, Power and the Search for a New Politics*, Manchester: Manchester University Press.

Lluco Tixe, Miguel, 2000, 'La aplicación tortuosa del modelo neoliberal en el Ecuador', *Boletin ICCI 'RIMAY'*, No.2 (January).

Lora, Guillermo, 1964, *La Revolución Boliviana*, La Paz: Difusión SRL.

Lora, Guillermo, 1967–70, *Historia del Movimiento Obrero Boliviano* (3 vols. 1848–1900, 1900–23, 1923–33) La Paz: Editorial Los Amigos del Libro.

Lora, Guillermo, 1970, *Documentos Políticos de Bolivia*, La Paz: Editorial Los Amigos del Libro.

Loveman, Brian, 1976, *Struggle in the Countryside: Politics and Rural Labor in Chile, 1919–1973*, Bloomington, IN: Indiana University Press.

Loveman, Brian, 1979, 'Critique of Arnold J. Bauer's "Rural Workers in Spanish America: Problems of Peonage and Oppression"', *Hispanic American Historical Review*, Vol.59, No.3.

Lucas, Kintto, 2000, *La rebelión de los indios*, Quito: Abya Yala.

Macas, Luis, 1999, 'Los desafíos del movimiento indígena,' *Boletin ICCI 'RIMAY'*, No.1 (April).

Macas, Luis, 2000, 'Movimiento indígena Ecuatoriano: una evaluación necesaria,' *Boletin ICCI 'RIMAY'*, No.3 (December).

Mahoney, James, 2001, *The Legacies of Liberalism: Path Dependence and Political Regimes in Central America*, Baltimore, MD: Johns Hopkins University Press.

Mainwaring, Scott, Guillermo O'Donnell, and J. Samuel Valenzuela (eds.), 1992, *Issues in Democratic Consolidation:The New South American Democracies in Comparative Perspective*, Notre Dame, IN: University of Notre Dame Press.

Mallon, Florencia, 1983, 'Murder in the Andes: Patrons, Clients, and the Impact of Foreign Capital, 1860–1922', *Radical History Review*, No.27.

Malloy, James M., and Richard S. Thorn (eds.), 1971, *Beyond the Revolution: Bolivia Since 1952*, Pittsburgh, PA: Pittsburgh University Press.

McEwan, Arthur, 1981, *Revolution and Economic Development in Cuba: Moving Towards Socialism*, New York: St Martin's Press.

Mead, Walter, 1991, *The Low Wage Challenge to Economic Growth*, Washington, DC: Economic Policy Institute.

Meillassoux, Claude, 1981, *Maidens, Meal and Money*, Cambridge: Cambridge University Press.

Mendes, Chico, 1992, 'Chico Mendes – The Defence of Life', *The Journal of Peasant Studies*, Vol.20, No.1.

Midlarsky, Manus and Kenneth Roberts, 1995, 'Class, State and Revolution in Central America: Nicaragua and El Salvador Compared', *Journal of Conflict Resolution*, No.29, June.

Miliband, Ralph, 1969, *The State in Capitalist Society*, London: Weidenfeld and Nicolson.

Miliband, Ralph, and John Saville (eds.), 1974, *The Socialist Register 1974*, London: The Merlin Press.

Miliband, Ralph, and John Saville (eds.), 1977, *The Socialist Register 1977*, London: The Merlin Press.

Moore, Barrington, Jr., 1966, *Social Origins of Dictatorship and Democracy: Lord and Peasant in the Making of the Modern World*, New York: Beacon Press.

Munck, Ronaldo, 1984, *Revolutionary Trends in Latin America*, Montreal: Centre for

Developing Areas.

Newby, Howard (ed.), 1978, *International Perspectives in Rural Sociology*, New York: John Wiley and Sons.

Nieboer, H.J., 1910, *Slavery as an Industrial System*, The Hague: Martinus Nijhoff.

Nugent, Daniel (ed.), 1998, *Rural Revolt in Mexico: US Intervention and the Domain of Subaltern Politics*, London and Durham, NC: Duke University Press.

O'Donnell, Guillermo, 1979, 'Tensions in the Bureaucratic-Authoritarian State and the Question of Democracy', in David Collier (ed.) *The New Authoritarianism in Latin America*, Princeton, NJ: Princeton University Press.

O'Donnell, Guillermo, 1988, *Bureaucratic Authoritarianism: Argentina, 1966–1973, in Comparative Perspective*, Berkeley, CA: University of California Press.

O'Donnell, Guillermo, 1992, 'Transitions, Continuities, and Paradoxes', in Scott Mainwaring, Guillermo O'Donnell, and J. Samuel Valenzuela (eds) *Issues in Democratic Consolidation:The New South American Democracies in Comparative Perspective*, Notre Dame, IN: University of Notre Dame Press.

Orlove, Benjamin S., and Glynn Custred (eds.), 1980, *Land and Power in Latin America: Agrarian Economies and Social Processes in the Andes*, New York: Holmes and Meier Publishers.

Ortega, M., 1990, 'The State, the Peasantry and the Sandinista Revolution', *Journal of Development Studies*, Vol.26, No.4.

Paige, Jeffery M., 1975, *Agrarian Revolution: Social Movements and Export Agriculture in the Underdeveloped World*, New York: The Free Press.

Palacios, Jorge, 1979, *Chile: An Attempt at 'Historic Compromise'*, Chicago: Banner Press.

Pearse, Andrew, 1975, *The Latin American Peasant*, London: Frank Cass.

Petras, James, 1997, 'The Resurgence of the Left', *New Left Review*, No.223.

Petras, James, 2002, 'A Rose by Any Other Name? The Fragrance of Imperialism', *The Journal of Peasant Studies*, Vol.29, No.2.

Petras, James, and Henry Veltmeyer, 2001a, *Globalisation Unmasked: Imperialism in the 21st Century*, London: Zed Press / Halifax: Fernwood Books.

Petras, James, and Henry Veltmeyer, 2001b, *Brasil de Cardoso: expropriação de un pais*, Petrópolis: Editorial Vozes.

Petras, James, and Henry Veltmeyer, 2001c, 'Are Latin American Peasant Movements Still a Force for Change? Some New Paradigms Revisited', *The Journal of Peasant Studies*, Vol.28, No.2.

Polanyi, Karl, 1944, *The Great Transformation*, New York: Reinhart.

Post, Ken, 1978, *Arise Ye Starvelings: The Jamaican Labour Rebellion of 1938 and Its Aftermath*, The Hague: Nijhoff.

Poulantzas, Nicos, 1975, *Classes in Contemporary Capitalism*, London: New Left Books.

Revista Koeyu Latinoamericano, koeyu@cantv.net

Reyeros, Rafael, 1949, *El Pongueaje: La Servidumbre personal de los Indios Bolivianos*, La Paz: Empresa editora 'Universo'.

Robles, Wilder, 2001, 'The Landless Workers Movement (MST) in Brazil', *The Journal of Peasant Studies*, Vol.28, No.2.

Rodney, Walter, 1981, *History of the Guayanese Working People, 1881–1905*, Baltimore, MD: Johns Hopkins University Press.

Roseberry, William, Lowell Gudmundson, and Mario Samper Kutschbach (eds.), 1995, *Coffee, Society, and Power in Latin America*, Baltimore, MD: Johns Hopkins University Press.

Rothenstein, Julian (ed.), 1989, *Posada – Messenger of Mortality*, London: Redstone Press.

Rout, Jr., Leslie B., 1976, *The African Experience in Spanish America: 1502 to the Present Day*, Cambridge: Cambridge University Press.

Rowe, J.W.F., 1932, *Studies in the Artificial Control of Raw Material Supplies: No. 3 – Brazilian Coffee*, London: The Royal Economic Society.

Ruiz, Ramón Eduardo, 1980, *The Great Rebellion: Mexico, 1905–1924*, New York: Norton.

Sánchez, Gonzalo, and Donny Meertens, 2001, *Bandits, Peasants and Politics*, Austin, TX: University of Texas Press.

Sandbrook, Richard, 2000, *Closing the Circle: Democratization and Development in Africa*, London and New York: Zed Press.

Saul, John S., 1974, 'The State in Post-Colonial Societies: Tanzania', in Ralph Miliband and John Saville (eds.) *The Socialist Register 1974*, London: The Merlin Press.

Saul, John S., 1976, 'African Peasantries and Revolutionary Change', in Joseph Spielberg and Scott Whiteford (eds.) *Forging Nations: A Comparative View of Rural Ferment and Revolt*, Michigan: Michigan State University Press.

Scott, J.C., 1976, *The Moral Economy of the Peasant: Rebellion and Subsistence in Southeast Asia*, London and New Haven, CT: Yale University Press.

Scott, J.C., 1985, *Weapons of the Weak: Everyday Forms of Peasant Resistance*, London and New Haven, CT: Yale University Press.

Scott, J.C., 1990, *Domination and the Arts of Resistance*, London and New Haven, CT: Yale University Press.

Scott, J.C., 1998, *Seeing Like a State: How Certain Schemes to Improve the Human Condition Have Failed*, London and New Haven, CT: Yale University Press.

Semo, Enrique, 1978, *Historia Mexicana: economía y lucha de clases*, México.

Silva Herzog, Jesús, 1959, *El agrarismo mexicano y la reforma agraria: Exposición y crítica*, México, DF: Fondo de Cultura Económica.

Simpson, Eyler N., 1937, *The Ejido: Mexico's Way Out*, Chapel Hill, NC: University of North Carolina Press.

Spielberg, Joseph, and Scott Whiteford (eds.), 1976, *Forging Nations: A Comparative View of Rural Ferment and Revolt*, Michigan: Michigan State University Press.

Stavenhagen, Rodolfo, 1970, *Agrarian Problems and Peasant Movements in Latin America*, New York: Anchor Books.

Stedile, Joao Pedro, 2000, Interview with James Petras, May 14.

Stein, Stanley J., 1985, *Vassouras: A Brazilian Coffee County, 1850–1900*, Princeton, NJ: Princeton University Press.

Sullivan, Kathleen, 1995, 'Rural–Urban Restructuring Among the Chamula People in the Highlands of Chiapas', in June Nash *et al.* (eds.), *The Explosion of Communities in Chiapas*, Copenhagen: International Working Group for Indigenous Affairs (IWGIA).

Tannenbaum, Frank, 1968, *The Mexican Agrarian Revolution*, New York: Archon Books (first published in 1929).

Taussig, Michael, 1986, *Shamanism, Colonialism, and the Wild Man*, Chicago: University of Chicago Press.

Teichman, Judith A., 1995, *Privatization and Political Change in Mexico*, Pittsburgh, PA: University of Pittsburgh Press.

Thomas, C.Y., 1984, *Plantations, Peasants and the State*, Los Angeles: Centre for Afro-American Studies, University of California / Kingston: ISER, University of West Indies.

Thorner, Alice, 1982, 'Semi-Feudalism or Capitalism? Contemporary Debate on Classes and Modes of Production in India', *Economic and Political Weekly*, Vol.XVII, Nos.49–51.

Thorpe, Andy *et al.*, 1995, *Impacto del ajuste en el agro Hondureño*, Tegucigalpa: Posgrado Centroamericano en Economia de la Universidad Nacional Autónoma de Honduras.

Tocancipá-Falla, Jairo, 2001, 'Women, Social Memory and Violence in Rural Colombia', *The Journal of Peasant Studies*, Vol.28, No.3.

Traven, B., 1974, *The Rebellion of the Hanged*, New York: Hill and Wang.

Traven, B., 1981, *The Carreta*, London: Allison & Busby.

Traven, B., 1982, *March to the Monteria*, London: Allison & Busby.

Traven, B., 1994, *Trozas*, London: Allison & Busby.

UNRISD [United Nations Research Institute for Social Development], 2000, 'Civil Society Strategies and Movements for Rural Asset Redistribution and Improved Livelihoods', (UNRISD – Civil Society and Social Movements Programme) Geneva: UNRISD.

Veltmeyer, Henry, 1983, 'Surplus Labour and Class Formation on the Latin American Periphery', in Ron Chilcote and Dale Johnston (eds.), *Theories of Development*, Beverley Hills, CA: Sage Publications.

Veltmeyer, Henry, 1997, 'New Social Movements in Latin America: The Dynamics of Class and Indentity', *The Journal of Peasant Studies*, Vol.25, No.1.

Veltmeyer, Henry and James Petras, 1997, *Economic Liberalism and Class Conflict in Latin America*, London/New York: Macmillan/St Martin's Press.

Veltmeyer, Henry and James Petras, 2000, *The Dynamics of Social Change in Latin America*, London: Macmillan Press.

Via Campesina, 1996, 'Managua Declaration, 1992', *The Proceedings of the II International Conference of Via Campesina*, Brussels: NCOS Publications.

Vilas, Carlos, 1995, *Between Earthquakes and Volcanoes; Market, State and Revolutions in Central America*, New York: Monthly Review Press.

Walker, Thomas (ed.), 1997, *Nicaragua Without Illusions: Regime Transition and Structural Adjustment in the 1990s*, Wilmington, DE: Scholarly Resources Press.

Wheelock Román, Jaime, 1975, *Imperialismo y dictadura: crisis de una formación social*, Mexico City: Siglo Veintiuno Editores.

Whetten, Nathan, 1948, *Rural Mexico*, Chicago, IL: University of Chicago Press.

Wolf, Eric R., 1969, *Peasant Wars of the Twentieth Century*, London: Faber & Faber.

Wolf, Eric R., 1982, *Europe and the People Without a History*, Berkeley, CA: University of California Press.

Wolf, Eric R., 1999, *Envisioning Power: Ideologies of Dominance and Crisis*, Berkeley, CA: University of California Press.

Wright, Erik Olin, 1978, *Class, Crisis and the State*, London: Verso.

Wright, Erik Olin (ed.), 1989, *The Debate on Classes*, London: Verso.

Zeitlin, Maurice, 1967, *Revolutionary Politics and the Cuban Working Class*, Princeton, NJ: Princeton University Press.

Ziemann, W., and M. Lanzendörfer, 1977, 'The State in Peripheral Societies', in Ralph Miliband and John Saville (eds.) *The Socialist Register 1977*, London: The Merlin Press.

From Rubber Estate to Simple Commodity Production: Agrarian Struggles in the Northern Bolivian Amazon

WILLEM ASSIES

Facts are simple and facts are straight
Facts are lazy and facts are late
Facts all come with points of view
Facts don't do what I want them to
Facts just twist the truth around
Facts are living turned inside out
[Talking Heads, *Crosseyed and Painless*, 1980]

INTRODUCTION

In October 2001 the Bolivian government convoked an 'Earth Summit' (*Cumbre de la Tierra*), to be held a month later. The previous years had seen an escalation of peasant unrest. In the Andean highlands the peasantry had turned increasingly to militant action with strong ethnic overtones. In the eastern tropical lowlands a colonists' movement had gathered strength, and in the year 2000 a movement of landless peasants had erupted, eliciting a violent response from large landowners who, in turn, pressured the government with their own claims. By the end of June that same year indigenous people of the tropical lowlands had initiated their 'Third March' under the banner of 'Land, Territories and Natural Resources' and were joined by peasants from the region.[1] The 'Earth Summit' ended in failure. Conditions were hardly propitious as in early November a clash between landless peasants and alleged paramilitaries had claimed seven lives, and peasant organizations were suspicious about the intentions of a government

---

Willem Assies, El Colegio de Michoacán, Centro de Estudios Rurales, Martínez de Navarrete 505, 59699 Zamora, Michoacán, México. Email: assies@colmich.edu.mx. The author thanks Javier Aramayo, Ana Cecilia Betancur, René Boot, Roxana Cuevas, Armelinda Zonta and many others for their aid in locating sources for this article and for their stimulating discussions. I would like to thank Tom Brass for his inspiring comments on an earlier draft of this essay. Final responsibility is of course all mine.

that had recently signed an agreement with the *Camara Agropecuaria del Oriente* (CAO), representing the large landowners and cattle-raisers of the Santa Cruz region, which ran quite counter to peasant interests. In the course of November the 'Summit' was renamed 'Encounter', reflecting reduced expectations, and when it took place by the end of the month some of the principal peasant organizations made a show of absence and announced that they would organize a summit of their own.

What the surge of peasant and indigenous people's movements made clear was that the agrarian and forestry legislation introduced in 1996 had failed to resolve the problems it was meant to address. The extremely slow, patchy, and often landlord-biased implementation of the 1996 *Ley del Servicio Nacional de Reforma Agraria*, also known as *Ley INRA*, generated frustration. Moreover, this law failed to address the problems that had accumulated in the Andean highlands since the 1953 Revolutionary land reform, and it is hard to apply in other specific regional contexts. The *Ley Forestal* generated its own set of conflicts. Forestry concessions that had been granted overlapped with territorial claims by indigenous peoples, and in 1999 the Banzer government had issued a decree allowing the conversion of rubber estates in the northern Amazon region into concessions under the 1996 Forestry Law, opening the way to a consolidation of a neo-latifundist tenure structure to the detriment of the local peasantry. This was one of the direct motives for the indigenous-peasant 'March for Land Territories and Natural Resources' which successfully pressured the government to repeal the decree and to modify the regulations for the implementation of the *Ley INRA*.

In this article I will focus on the specific constellation in the northern Bolivian Amazon region that provided a major incentive for the 'Third March', and I will seek to relate the issues at stake in the region to the broader debate on agrarian and forestry legislation. The history of the region has been marked by the rubber economy that arose in the final quarter of the nineteenth century. By 1985, however, rubber extraction entered into a final crisis. This heralded the beginning of a process of economic reconversion marked by changes in labour relations and forms of resource use. In the first section of this article I will outline the rise and demise of the rubber economy and show how, with the decline of the rubber estate system independent peasant-extractivist communities emerged, while at the same time control over and access to resources, rather than control over people on which the estate system was based, became increasingly important. In the next section I will sketch the rise of a new regional economic constellation after 1985, when the production of Brazil nuts became a major economic activity in the region. The third section of the article offers a further analysis and discussion of the regional transformations in the labour regime, in patterns of landholding, and access to resources. This analysis delineates the latent tension between 'owners' of *barracas* (former rubber estates) and the emerging *comunidades libres* (free communities). This conflict of interests became manifest when the 1996 land and forestry legislation started to be implemented in the region. Section four discusses this new legislation, shows how it triggered the 'Third March', and examines the outcomes of this peasant-indigenous mobilization. The concluding section sums up the argument and looks at the future prospects for the region.

THE RISE AND DECLINE OF THE RUBBER TRADE

This section provides a brief introduction to the region and describes how, alongside the rubber estates, a sector of free communities has come into existence and competes for resources with the established local agrarian elite. For convenience the century in which rubber production dominated – from around 1880 until 1985 – is divided into three periods. The first covers the rise of the rubber economy and the consolidation of the 'Suárez Empire', which came to dominate the region until it disintegrated after 1940. The period from 1940 to 1985 is characterized by the emergence of a much more fragmented system of *patron*-run estates, while in the interstices of this system the first free communities emerged. This constellation changed drastically as a result of the final collapse of the rubber trade after 1985. The new Brazil nut-centred economy would be built from the rubble left after the collapse of the rubber economy.[2]

The Rise of the Rubber Trade and the Consolidation of the Casa Suárez (1880–1940)

Until well into the nineteenth century what nowadays is the northern Bolivian Amazon region was still designated as 'land to be discovered'. The national border with Brazil was ill defined. The 1867 Ayacucho Treaty mentioned a line running from the confluence of the Beni River and the Mamoré, which then forms the River Madeira, to the unknown headwaters of the Javari River. This rainforest region was inhabited by various indigenous peoples – such as the Araona, Cavineño, Tacana, Ese Ejja, Chácobo Pacahuara and Yaminahua – descendants of whom can still be found in the region. Other groups have been decimated or displaced [*Lema*, 1998; *Stoian*, 2000a: 82, 123; *Weber*, 1994]. To the south the rainforest gives way to the Moxos plains, a swampy savannah region interspersed with patches of forest. This had been a region of Jesuit missionary effort that resulted in the establishment of some 25 mission-towns. After the expulsion of the Jesuits in 1767, *mestizo* cattle ranchers became the dominant class in the region. Only a few missionaries and some explorers in search of El Dorado ventured into the rainforest to the north, and often lost their lives there.

In the course of the nineteenth century, however, the rainforest region was incorporated into the world economy. The extraction of forest products, particularly cinchona bark (for quinine), brought new incursions, but all this paled beside the rubber boom. The perfection, in 1839, of the vulcanization process opened the way for new applications, resulting in growing demand for this commodity from the industrializing countries. In 1888 Dunlop invented the pneumatic tyre, first used for bicycles. It was the emergence of the automobile industry at the end of the century, however, that triggered the rubber boom between 1900 and 1913. Rubber extraction swept through the Amazon region following the river systems. From the north, Brazilians made their way upstream along the Juruá, Purus and Madeira rivers, and from the south Bolivians went downstream along the Beni River.[3] When Brazilian and Bolivian rubber exploiters met, boundary conflict ensued and resulted in war. In 1903 Bolivia saw itself forced to sign the Treaty of Petrópolis, by which it ceded the territory of Acre to Brazil. A new national border was thus established, which delimited the northern Bolivian Amazon. The town of Riberalta, founded in the late nineteenth century, became the most important regional centre. The present-day province of Vaca Díez in the Department of Beni, and the five provinces in the Department of Pando, constitute the bulk of the Bolivian Amazon region, and it is on this area that this article will focus.

By the late nineteenth century Bolivian explorers entered the northern rainforest region to engage in the rubber trade. One of them was Antonio Vaca Díez, the 'Bolivian Cecil Rhodes', who in 1897 would drown together with the notorious Peruvian rubber baron Fitzcarraldo, whom he visited on returning from a business trip to Europe. In 1880 Vaca Díez had sponsored an expedition by Edwin Heath who found that the Beni River effectively flowed into the Madeira, a discovery that greatly increased the feasibility of rubber production in the region since it provided a route toward the Amazon and thereby to the Atlantic trade. These pioneers explored the rivers and staked out the areas they took possession of by marking some trees on the riverside and claiming all that was behind as part of their estates or *barracas*. Then workers would be recruited and shipped to the rubber region. They were the last link in a chain of *habilitos* in which goods were advanced in return for the future delivery of rubber. This system, which will be discussed in more detail below, reached down from the large trade-houses in Belém and Manaus, through the patrons of the rubber estates, to the rubber tappers.[4]

The *barracas* consisted basically of a main-house on the riverside, where administration, storage facilities and the *pulpería* (company store) were concentrated, and a number of *centros*, settlements of a few huts in the forest from which the rubber trails would start. Each worker would be assigned a number of trails to work: in the morning he made incisions in the trees on which were affixed small pots to collect the rubber; in the afternoon he returned to collect the produce, and then coagulate it above the smoke of wood chips to form balls of wild rubber. These would then be delivered to the main-house every fortnight or so in exchange for a new supply of basic necessities such as rice, sugar, manioc and other essentials.

Rubber production in northern Bolivia eventually came to be dominated by the Casa Suárez (the House of Suárez). In 1882 the Suárez brothers, who were engaged in river trade, established their headquarters in Cachuela Esperanza, a strategic location on the Beni River, as it was the only place where navigation was completely interrupted by rapids that had to be bypassed by a short detour along the river bank. Until the late nineteenth century the Casa Suárez was hardly involved in rubber production. It advanced goods against future delivery of rubber and many a *barraquero* (estate owner) became indebted to the Casa Suárez. From 1895 onward, however, the Casa Suárez started taking over *barracas* from their indebted owners, and by 1916 the Suárez empire was consolidated. The Casa Suárez became a highly integrated enterprise, which at the height of its power laid claim to about 75 per cent of the Bolivian Amazon region and handled some 60 per cent of Bolivian rubber production. The company had offices in London and a number of other cities. Its headquarters in Cachuela Esperanza came to include a radio-telegraph station, residential blocks, a hotel, a restaurant, a cinema, a hospital under Swiss direction, and a number of large machine shops. Including its holdings in Beni, dedicated to cattle-raising to supply the rubber estates to the north, the enterprise extended for about 180,000 square kilometres. Patriarch Don Nicolas Suárez became known as the 'Rockefeller of the rubber trade' [*Fifer*, 1970; *Pacheco*, 1992; *Roca*, 2001: 241–255 *Sanabria*, 1988].

As we shall see in more detail below, the 1913 crash in rubber prices, due to competition from plantation-produced rubber from the British and Dutch colonies, triggered important changes in the organization of production. In the first place, as imports became more difficult, local agriculture became more important. In the second place, Brazil nut production emerged as a complementary activity. Brazil nuts are harvested between December and March, the rainy season when rubber tapping is not possible. However, in contrast to the tendency toward fragmentation into smaller estates that could be observed in other rubber producing regions [*Costa*, 1992: 59; *Martinello*, 1988: 47–61], the Suárez empire remained largely intact during the interwar period.

The Fragmentation of an 'Empire' and the Rise of the First Free Communities (1940–85)

Rubber production in the Amazon region saw a brief upsurge during the Second World War, but then resumed its secular decline in the face of competition from plantation produce and synthetic rubber. Brazilian exports dropped by about 40 per cent from 1945 to 1946 [*Martinello*, 1988: 293]. Production of native rubber in the region was saved from total collapse by price support policies implemented by the Brazilian government, both in response to pressures by estate owners and rubber traders and also for strategic reasons. Domestic consumer prices in Brazil might be up to three times the world market rate [*Pinto*, 1984]. Bolivian producers also benefited from these schemes, and this was formalized in the 1958 Roboré Treaty [*Pacheco*, 1992: 255–6]. The 1970s saw another brief upsurge in rubber prices in the context of the oil crisis, but thereafter the Brazilian price support scheme again became its main prop until the system was abandoned in the mid-1980s.

Meanwhile, however, Nicolas Suárez, the patriarch of the Casa Suárez had died in 1940, and this set the stage for the disintegration and fragmentation of the Suárez empire [*Roca*, 2001: 255–64]. Its estates were sold off or simply taken over by the administrators. The entrepreneurial organization of Casa Suárez gave way to what Pacheco [1992] calls *barracas patronales*, of various sizes. Where before Nicolás Suárez had been 'the patron' whose *barracas* were managed by 'administrators', the number of smaller *patrons* now proliferated. The emergence of the *barraca patronal* basically meant a simplification and, according to Pacheco, often a harshening of labour relations. Borrowing the imagery evoked by Aramburu [1994: 85], we might say that the 'golden age' of the 'big patrons' was over. At the time of the Casa Suárez the labour force had been relatively diversified. Some sectors received cash salaries and there was even something resembling a social policy. With the decline of the rubber trade, and the demise of this entrepreneurial mode of organization, relations were simplified to those between the *patrones* and *trabajadores empatronados* [*Pacheco*, 1992]. The infrastructure of earlier times fell into disuse and gradually decayed. Abandoned and overgrown machinery and dilapidated barracks can still be seen in Cachuela Esperanza. The Riberalta-based Seiler Company, earlier the Braillard Company and by the late 1960s taken over by the Hecker family, remained as a more or less 'entrepreneur-type' venture.

Alongside the *barracas patronales* a sector of *comunidades libres* started to expand, either as a result of the abandonment of *barracas* by their patrons or through the settlement by rubber tappers in areas not controlled by patrons.[5] The households in these communities relied on rubber tapping, small-scale agriculture and Brazil nut gathering; the complementary set of activities of a year-round agro-extractive cycle [*Assies*, 1997a: 8–10]. At the same time the disintegration of the Suárez empire opened the way for the emergence of a system of independent river-traders who came to play an important role in a complex web of *habilitos*, centred in the town of Riberalta and linked to Brazilian trade circuits. This trade web tied together the various components of a much more fragmented system.

Using data from the 1984 Agrarian Census, held just before the final collapse of the rubber trade, Ormachea and Fernández [1989: 30] calculate that there were 5,523 agricultural establishments in the region, covering 3,120,833 hectares out of a total of 8,626,100 hectares for the whole region. The average size of the holdings was 565 hectares, but distribution was rather skewed, with 88 per cent of the holdings smaller than 500 hectares and occupying 9 per cent of the land, and 4 per cent of the holdings larger than 2,500 hectares occupying 79 per cent.[6] Of the 5,523 establishments, about 3,200 were dedicated mainly to rubber and Brazil nut extraction. Data from a smaller sample suggest that about half of them were smallholdings, possessing up to 499 rubber trees and relying on family labour. The other half were *barracas*, relying on 'outside', but mainly resident, labour and accounting for 78 per cent of the rubber trails. Among the *barracas*, 95 per cent were classified as small, possessing between 500 and 4,999 rubber trees [*Pacheco*, 1990; 1992: 177].

The Collapse of the Rubber Trade after 1985

After 1985, the Sarney government in Brazil started dismantling the state agency regulating the rubber trade, and some years later the Collor government virtually abandoned all price support schemes. Rubber prices dropped to a historical low, and the rubber trade came to a virtual standstill. This had a dramatic impact on the emerging constellation described in the foregoing section.

The collapse of the rubber trade was accompanied by an accelerated spatial relocation of the population. Since rubber production disappeared as the mainstay of year-round economic activity, the *barraca* system ceased to be the main mode of socio-spatial organization. The *barraca* 'was doomed as an institution; it only remained as a geographic space', as one *barraca* owner put it. The more remote *barracas* in particular saw a decline in their population, which tended to move to or establish *comunidades libres*, or to migrate to the urban areas. The collapse of the rubber trade also implied a contraction of the itinerant trader networks, since there was little to trade any more for most of the year. This further contributed to a modification of rural settlement patterns, since the *comunidades libres* tended to establish themselves at strategic and more accessible sites alongside the rivers, and at a later stage along the roads that began to be improved by the late 1980s.[7] While rubber production had sustained a dispersed settlement pattern, its decline prompted a clustering of the population and, whereas rubber extraction had been the cornerstone of the agro-extractive cycle, agriculture now became the central element with Brazil nut gathering as an important source of cash income. Agriculture would be primarily subsistence-oriented, although depending on the location and the distance from markets, it might be articulated in a complex fashion with market exchanges [*Assies*, 1997a: 59–64].[8] Alongside the peasantry, particularly in the vicinity of the urban centres, one finds medium-sized farms (*granjas*), often dedicated to fattening of cattle or the production of some commercial crop. It is estimated that the cultivated area in the region expanded from 21,000 hectares in the early 1980s to around 48,000 hectares in the early 1990s [*Henkemans*, 2001: 52].

Another, no less important, consequence was massive rural–urban migration. Census data from 1976 and 1992 indicate a decline of the rural population in all the provinces of the Department of Pando, while the urban population in the Province of Nicolas Suárez, that is the town of Cobija, grew at a rate of 5.8 per cent annually. The urban population of the Province of Vaca Díez in the Beni Department, that is the towns of Riberalta and Guayramerín, also increased at a rate of 5.1 per cent per year. The Vaca Díez province was the only province where the rural population increased, at a rate of 0.5 per cent per year. This reflects a clustering of the *comunidades libres* around the towns [*Assies*, 1997a: 45–6]. While these national-level census data indicate the transformations in the region, some authors [*Henkemans*, 2001: 65; *Pacheco and Ávila*, 2001: 60; *Stoian*, 2000a: 193] include local data referring to 1985. Such data suggest that the latter year was a turning point, after which migration greatly accelerated. The collapse of the rubber trade thus may be assumed to have been a major push factor in the migration process. The main point is that the urban population in the region grew from 33,508 in 1976 to 81,161 in 1992 and, according to preliminary census data, to 117,559 in 2001, respectively making up 44, 66 and 71 per cent of the total regional population.[9]

THE RISE OF THE BRAZIL NUT TRADE

It was from the debris of the rubber economy that a new regional economy arose, this time centred largely on Brazil nut production. As we have seen, Brazil nut production started from the 1920s onwards, and by the 1950s it had become an important economic activity in northern Bolivia, with a total value often equalling and sometimes surpassing that of rubber exports

[*Stoian*, 2000b: 281]. Some *beneficiadoras* (processing-plants where nuts are shelled) had been established from the 1930s onward, by the Casa Suárez among others. Processing capacity went through some ups and downs during the following decades, but around the mid-1980s all *beneficiadoras* had closed due to the difficult economic and political situation in the country and the decline of the regional economy [*Assies*, 1997a: 46; *Bojanic*, 2001: 60–63; *Coesmans and Medina*, 1997: 149–50; *Stoian*, 2000b: 280–85].

The panorama changed radically during the second half of the 1980s. Various factors contributed to this development. By the mid-1980s some US importers had 'discovered' northern Bolivia as a source of Brazil nuts that could be purchased at a price between 30 per cent and 40 per cent below Brazilian export prices. In 1987 a British firm began importing Bolivian nuts on a massive scale [*Holt*, 1992].[10] The expansion of the new trade was also facilitated by the structural adjustment policies implemented by the Paz Estensorro government in 1985. Improvement of road connections to the Pacific also contributed to Bolivian exports, as did the reputation of Brazil nuts as a forest friendly product [*Assies*, 1997a, 1997b]. By the end of the 1990s some 20 *beneficiadoras* were operating in northern Bolivia, the great majority in Riberalta, and about five more outside the region.[11] Total export volumes soared from 10,000 metric tons in 1986 to over 30,000 metric tons by the late 1990s. More importantly, whereas in 1986, when all *beneficiadoras* were closed, the nuts were exported in-shell, by the late 1990s virtually the total volume of exports consisted of shelled nuts. The total value of exports had risen from about US$ 9 million in the late 1980s to about US$ 30 million ten years later. Bolivia had overtaken Brazil as the world market supplier of Brazil nuts, which should arguably have been renamed 'Amazon nuts' [*Assies*, 1997a: 1]. Brazil nut production became the driving economic activity in northern Bolivia.

Two other economic activities also became important in the region. One is palm heart production, which surged from 1992 onward. By the late 1990s it contributed some US$ 7 million to the regional income but then disappeared, even before depletion of the stock, due to international competition and the drying up of the Brazilian market after some Brazilians allegedly died after consuming the Bolivian product. The other activity is timber production. The value of timber exports from the region increased from about US$ 1 million in the mid-1980s to about US$ 20 million by 1997 [*Stoian*, 2000b: 291].[12]

A small group of *beneficiadora* owners have become the key players in the new regional economy, displacing the *barraquero* sector. *Beneficiadora* owners largely finance the Brazil nut harvest through a revamped *habilito* system, and some of them are also involved in the timber or palm heart industry. Some *beneficiadoras* have been set up with local capital, others are owned by large Bolivian corporations, which may also be involved in other ventures such as soya production. By the early 1990s the *beneficiadora* owners set up an organization of their own, the *Asociación de Beneficiadoras del Nordeste* (ABAN) which later fused with the *Camara de Exportadores del Norte* (CADEXNOR). These organizations partly replaced the *Asociación de Productores de Goma y Almendra* (ASPROGOAL), which had been founded in 1973 to represent the then locally dominant *barraqueros*. ASPROGOAL membership declined from some 160 members to about 40 around 1995. Occasionally, however, ASPROGOAL rises from the ashes, as we will see in the following section.

The *beneficiadoras* process the Brazil nuts and finance a good part of the harvest. Processing is done with the help of small manually operated cracking devices.[13] Initially the units of production often were no more than sheds, but quality concerns have brought improvements, also to some labour conditions. For processing the Riberalta *beneficiadoras* employ some 4,000 to 6,000 individuals, mainly women, for about seven to eight months of the year [*Coesmans and Medina*, 1997]. Shelling nuts has become the main source of urban employment in Riberalta. By the time of the harvest season the *beneficiadoras* have often processed and marketed their stock of nuts, and lay off their workforce, many of whom join their husbands during the nut harvest.

Raw material for the *beneficiadoras* basically comes from two sources. *Barracas* contribute an estimated 60 to 65 per cent and *comunidades libres* the remainder. An outstanding feature that should be borne in mind in discussing the configuration that emerged after 1985 is the change in urban–rural relations. As noted, the collapse of the rubber trade brought the demise of the *barraca* as the dominant mode of socio-spatial organization and triggered an unprecedented process of demographic relocation. The rapid shift of population to the urban centres meant that an urban labour pool, or reserve army of workers, became available, and has come to play a significant role in the emerging Brazil nut economy. The permanent population of the *barracas* has declined dramatically, and sometimes only a caretaker is left. Urban-based labour gangs have come to play a key role in the Brazil nut harvest in the *barracas*, as well as in the exploitation of other forest products. Each year, in December, between 5,000 and 6,000 people leave Riberalta's peripheral neighbourhoods for the Brazil nut harvest.

The section below outlines the changes in labour relations in the course of the process of economic transformation outlined above, and at the competition over access to land and resources between *barraca* owners and the *comunidades libres*.

LAND, LABOUR AND THE AGRARIAN STRUCTURE

Labour Relations during the Rubber Era

The workforce during the early rubber era was mainly recruited outside the region. The local indigenous population was hostile and mostly unwilling to work on the *barracas* carved out on their territories. In a recent letter the heir to one of the enterprises that arose alongside the Casa Suárez affirms:

> For in case you do not know, Monsignor, nearly all the people that worked for the Braillard Enterprise, later Seiler and then Hecker, were people that we brought from Apolo, Ixiamas, Tumupasa, Reyes, Rurrenabaque and from various communities along the Beni river up to Puerto Linares. You can recognize them by their way of dressing and because it was they who introduced the custom of the 'tipoy' and they were organized under the command of a Captain, who they elected from among themselves, and every fortnight in their traditional ceremonies on Thursday thcy would use the drug 'hallahuasca,' a custom that still survives in some places. All the men that we brought from Caupilan had the right to a paid return once they had paid off their advances. Very few returned. I am talking in the plural because I do not conceal what my father and grandfather did; I acknowledge and accept it. [...] With the exception of the indigenous peoples that the priests managed to evangelize, among them those of Puerto Cavinas on the Beni river, all other 'savages' that lived on the navigable rivers were exterminated once the repetition rifle became available, because thanks to this tremendous weapon the 'white man' gained supremacy and thanks to it he could practically exterminate all tribes. Before this invention the savage had the advantage. [...] A hundred years ago genocide was committed in our region, a killing without mercy in the search for rubber lands where the only obstacle to their exploitation was the savage man, who had to be killed by all possible means.[14]

Once the first *barracas* had been staked out workers would be recruited, mainly in the Santa Cruz region and among the indigenous population of the Beni plains, often by deceit if not by force [*Sanabria*, 1988: 95–6]. After being transported to the *barraca*, the worker would be supplied with the basic tools for work and survival, and an account was opened to keep track of the debt thus incurred, as well as for the future purchases at the *pulpería* in exchange for the 'black gold'.

At the height of the rubber boom a large part of the goods sold to the rubber tapper was imported. Thus Sanabria [1988: 131] asserts that Bolivians imported Chinese rice, Cuban sugar and Brazilian coffee and *cachaça* (cane alcohol), which totally displaced similar products earlier imported from Santa Cruz. In order not to divert the workforce from the main activity, and to enforce relations of dependency, subsistence farming by rubber tappers was, often effectively, discouraged on the estates though patrons might supervise the centralized production of some staples on a *chaco patronal* (plot cultivated under patron supervision) during the off-season. On the other hand, in times of high rubber prices the tappers may have preferred to buy imported luxury food [*Romanoff*, 1992: 131; *Stoian*, 2000a: 77].

An issue that requires attention here is the controversial question of the relations of production and the role of the *habilito* system. A question that often emerges in the literature on the Amazonian rubber economy is why it was not 'rationalized', and why it did not give rise to fully capitalist relations of production and a plantation system. Labour relations in the context of rubber production have often been described as a coercive and harsh system of debt peonage. Weinstein [1993], however, reconsidered this view and attributed the persistence of 'pre-capitalist' relations and the system of debt peonage to an alliance between rubber tappers and traders based on mutual self-interest. Due to various circumstances such as the dispersion of material resources, the mentality of the rural population, the initial scarcity of capital, and the enormous distances to be overcome, she argues, an economic system emerged in which production largely remained under control of the direct producer and surplus extraction occurred at the level of exchange. Patrons and traders were unable to establish direct control over the labour force, and for its part the labour force resisted such direct control. Weinstein's view, in turn, has been challenged by Barham and Coomes [1994a; 1996], who adopt a neo-institutional economic perspective, and argue that the debt system, or debt-merchandise contract as they call it, was relatively efficient in terms of transaction costs and risk reduction. Wage labour, they argue, would be inefficient in the context of the rubber boom since it would involve high transaction costs in monitoring the efforts of a highly scattered workforce to ensure the full delivery of the produce, because rubber tappers might be tempted to sell it to itinerant traders. On the other hand, the mark-up on supplies and the discounts on rubber were justified by risks such as product loss in transport or the loss of labour time of the tappers due to illness, desertion and tapper mortality rates of 25–30 per cent (and occasionally as high as 50 per cent). The clients, in return, would be assured of the delivery of needed goods and insurance (or leniency, I would say) in times of illness or other mishaps.[15]

Recently, Bojanic [2001] and Stoian [2000a], in their studies of the northern Bolivian region, have taken up this lead in order to challenge the usual view of the *habilito* system as 'brutal, unfair, exploitative and thus as an undesirable bondage system' [*Bojanic*, 2001: 93]. Their work invites further scrutiny of the forms of labour recruitment, labour relations, and their transformation in the region. I will first focus on the early rubber era and then on the transformation and current forms of the *habilito* system.

One of the most surprising features of Stoian's [2000a] argument is his assertion that Bolivian rubber tappers chiefly received fixed monthly wages in the early rubber era, and that therefore they should be considered proletarians in a context of 'primitive capitalism'. Only at a later stage were these fixed wages replaced by piecework rates. According to Stoian, the payment of fixed wages in northern Bolivia deserves special attention, since it suggests that labour relations in this region were less exploitative than is 'often assumed in a general way' about conditions during the rubber boom. This view, he argues, is rooted in the idea that rubber tappers received piece-rates, an arrangement that transfers 'the risks of illness and adverse weather to tappers, who reputedly received only nominal prices for the rubber delivered'. The payment of fixed wages, moreover, would be remarkable in view of Barham and Coomes' argument about transactions costs, and it refutes Weinstein's view that relations of production during the rubber boom were pre-capitalist and resembled a feudal mode of production. Conditions in northern Bolivia during the early rubber era were less exploitative than might have been the case elsewhere and fully, though 'primitive', capitalist labour relations predominated [*Stoian*, 2000a: 62–3, 123–6].

Stoian, however, overstates his case, both for 'primitive capitalism' and the extent of 'proletarianization' of the labour force. On the basis of a contract reproduced in Pacheco [1992: 237–8], for example, he argues that eight indigenous labourers hired from their apparent owner, a Mr C.M. Barbery, by the Casa Suárez, 'were granted sick leave of up to one month without losing their wage', but fails to note that it was Mr Barbery himself who received these wages [*Stoian*, 2000a: 63n].[16] In fact, the contract suggests conditions of indigenous slavery. Most of the contracts cited by Stoian refer to activities other than rubber tapping, for example a muleteer's contract; and the one that *does* refer to rubber tapping stipulates a piece rate for rubber production and a fixed wage for off-season activities. On the other hand, he is right in pointing to stipulations regarding medical assistance, though here one may raise the question as to whether this was anything more than legal formality (see below). And, despite often citing Sanabria, he fails to note that this author precisely sets apart the rubber tappers when stating that among the overall workforce these 'were not salaried in the strict sense of the term' [*Sanabria*, 1988: 129].[17]

Stoian's [2000a: 77] objection to the 'prevailing image' of rigid forms labour control as a 'subtle form of slavery' is not that convincing. Let us look at some of the features of the early rubber era. As noted, the local indigenous population was mostly antagonistic to recruitment into rubber tapping, and in a report on his expedition to the region in the late 1890s General Pando recommended their extermination, though finally some uneasy balance of mutual tolerance was achieved [*Fifer*, 1970; *Roca*, 2001: 229; *Stoian*, 2000a: 80–83]. The labour force came from elsewhere, and was recruited in various ways. During the early rubber era, when the pioneers established their estates, there was something like a 'rubber rush'. People, including shop-owners, professionals, public servants and craftsmen, left the impoverished Santa Cruz region for the 'rubber fields' on their own account, and often found work there in the administrative sector of the *barracas*, or as overseers or subcontractors, etc.; and they were salaried [*Sanabria*, 1988: 93–4, 99]. Recruiting rubber tappers and boatmen required for transport, however, was another matter. A number of them were recruited, often forcibly, from among the indigenous population of the Moxos plains that had been subject to missionary efforts. Others were recruited in and around the urban area of Santa Cruz under the *enganche* regime: that is, literally, by being 'hooked up'. Let us look at those two groups, which came to constitute the bulk of the workforce, and who were not 'salaried in the strict sense of the term'.

The indigenous peoples of the Moxos plains had been converted to Christianity by the Jesuits from the end of the seventeenth century. After the expulsion of the Order in 1767, *mestizo* farmers and ranchers took control and set the population to work, as cattle ranching expanded in these savannah-lands. Some had become involved in the cinchona trade but the situation changed dramatically after 1860, when the rubber trade took off and boatmen and rubber-tappers were needed. When forcible recruitment became widespread, many fled southeastward to the Securé forests. By 1887, Andrés Guayocho, a local shaman, started to call on the indigenous population to leave the town of Trinidad, and establish itself in the nearby townships of San Lorenzo and San Francisco. A messianic movement emerged which took off on a search for the *Loma Santa* ('the sacred hill'), a place without evil where they could re-establish contact with their saints, and would be free from suffering and exploitation. In the view of the dominant class the following gradual but uninterrupted exodus from Trinidad was nothing less than the beginning of an insurrection. They formed a 'War Committee', led by, among others, Nicolás Suárez, usually depicted as the empire builder and benevolent patron who brought progress to these remote lands. An armed column marched on San Francisco in order to force the Indians to mend their ways. They met with resistance, however, and 21 were killed, after which a punitive expedition of 150 men was sent out from Trinidad. This time, the indigenous population chose to flee into nearby forest areas where they were cruelly persecuted. Andrés Guayocho was captured and brutally whipped to death. Meanwhile, in the Securé region rumour had it that the Indians were preparing a rebellion. They were surprised while attending mass and the men received between 500 and 600 lashes apiece, while the women received between 200 and 300. Nine men and one woman died as a consequence. Many of those who could escape capture, or worse, fled towards the Chimane forest in search for the *Loma Santa*. Forced recruitment soon resumed [*Jones*, 1995: *Lema*, 1998: 11; *Roca*, 2001: 119–33].

In Santa Cruz labour recruitment took place through the *casas de enganche*. By various means people were lured into signing a contract, after which they would receive an advance payment, but would also be locked up until they could be shipped to the rubber fields. Once sufficient recruits had been contracted for a shipment, they would be walked out of town under armed surveillance through Beni Street 'from where people go, never to return'. Outside the town they were chained together and then marched for five or six days to the harbour of Cuatro Ojos from where they were shipped up north [*Sanabria*, 1988: 96]. While General Pando, after his expeditions to the North, recommended the extermination of local indigenous peoples, he was moved by the conditions of those who had been 'hooked' in this manner, and initiated legislation to protect those recruited on *enganches*, which was adopted in 1896. The *Ley de Enganches* stipulated that rubber tappers should receive a monthly or annual salary, their trip to the rubber fields should be paid for by the employer, they should receive free medical assistance, be provided with a register of their current account, receive a return ticket, could not be transferred to another employer without their consent, and a limit put on the payment advanced. A register of 'hooked' recruits was to be established by the Security Police, preference was to be given to contracts extending to workers conditions such as the freedom of labour, and 'hooking' indigenous people was prohibited.[18] The law pinpointed many of the abuses in contracting rubber tappers [*Roca*, 2001: 117], and it was to be honoured in the breach [*Sanabria*, 1988: 97]. Roca [2001: 110] reports that, according to the norms of the contemporary Civil Code on the freedom of contract, a clause could be inserted by which the contracted party explicitly foregoes 'any benefit' in his favour, and quotes several contracts in which the benefits of the 1896 law are annulled. Furthermore, the rubber barons filed recourse with the Supreme Court, which declared the law anti-constitutional since it applied only 'north of the fourteenth parallel' and not nationwide.

Forced labour recruitment continued. During one of his visits to Riberalta in the early twentieth century, P.H. Fawcett, a British colonel and member of the Royal Geographical Society who worked on the Peru–Bolivian boundary survey, witnessed the arrival of one such 'cattle' transport, and learned that the workers concerned were not sold through public auction, like Indians, but by way of private transactions for the value of their debt [*Paz*, 1999: 156–8].[19] The Prefect of the Beni Department was involved in the trade, and connived at the forcible recruitment of workers, peasants and Indians, who were dressed like soldiers to be illegally shipped to the 'rubber fields'. In response to such abuses an organization, the 'Social Defence', was created in 1906 in Santa Cruz. It denounced these forms of recruitment and sometimes prevented shipments of workers. By presidential order the organization was denied legal status and declared 'seditious'. Forced recruitment declined only after the rubber price crash in 1913, and the completion of the Beni–Mamoré railway, which reduced the need for boatmen [*Roca*, 2001: 118–19; *Sanabria*, 1988: 137–43; *Souza*, 1980].

When, after 1909, the British government started to investigate the denunciations against the Peruvian Amazon Company for atrocities committed in the Peruvian Putumayo region, a delegate was also sent to the Bolivian rubber region. Although in London representatives of the Casa Suárez had declared that their *barracas* would be open to inspection by anyone, the delegate – a Mr Gosling – was received in Cachuela Esperanza and Riberalta for some days but was not allowed to travel to the rubber fields. He denounced the debt-peonage in the northern Beni region as a form of undisguised slavery and noted that debts were heritable. The reports on the Bolivian rubber region noted widespread abuse, but surmised that things were not as bad as in the Putumayo, since the high market value and the relative scarcity of labour in Bolivia made it 'uneconomical to treat human life lightly' [*Fifer*, 1970: 137–40; *Roca*, 2001: 179].

The picture that emerges shows, in the first place, that some sectors of the workforce, particularly those not engaged in rubber tapping, received fixed wages while at the same time being engaged in debt relations, but contracts do not say how accounts were settled, or if – and when – cash appeared in the process. However, there is no indication that, in contrast to other rubber regions, Bolivian rubber tappers 'chiefly received fixed wages in the early rubber era' [*Stoian*, 2000a: 63]. In the second place, the account thus far calls into question the rejection of the interpretation of debt bondage as a coercive relation in favour of a view according to which both parties to the relation benefit from the arrangement, as implied by Weinstein [1993], Barham and Coomes [1996] and also by Stoian. The latter asserts that 'only if we acknowledge the varied and often contradictory factors that have led to the emergence of such systems – entailing advantages and disadvantages for all parties involved – we can do justice to the people who, after all, keep these systems alive', and affirms that the survival of such systems, albeit modified, is due to their 'functional significance' [*Stoian*, 2000a: 119].

One issue is that the neo-institutional/neo-classical economists argument hinges on the assertion that the rubber trade was competitive rather than monopolistic [*Barham and Coomes*, 1996: 33; *Stoian*, 2000a: 110]. In northern Bolivia, by contrast, it was much rather monopolistic.[20] Given the belief in competition for clients, these authors re-interpret the debt bondage relation. Downplaying the indebtness and bondage aspects, therefore, they view the *habilito* as credit that 'enables' the rubber tapper to do his job and thus gain an income. It ceases to be a coercive method of extracting surplus labour, and thus a source of acute and continuing struggle between rubber tapper and employer, and becomes instead a non-coercive, tension-free – and thus benign – form of patron-clientage, a mutually beneficial arrangement freely entered into by all concerned. Occasionally one even finds hints about debt bondage as a source of difficulty – distress, even – for the benign employer. The *habilito* system is viewed by such authors as a rational economic response to imperfections in the markets for credit, insurance, information, and factors of production since it reduces transaction costs [*Barham and Coomes*, 1996: 68; *Stoian*, 2000a: 111]. It is precisely from such a perspective that Barham and Coomes [1996: 65–8, 109] object to Weinstein's claim that the relations of production were pre-capitalist and resembled a feudal mode of production. They argue that these relations are *chosen* by 'those below', rather than enforced 'from above', and are therefore in essence 'free'. What exists systemically is not an economically inefficient pre-capitalism but rather an economically efficient form of capitalism, based on free labour relations chosen by and to the benefit of all.

Stoian [2000a: 122, 125], on the other hand, criticizes the feudalism thesis, arguing that labour was separated from the land and from the means of production and that it received a fixed wage or a piece rate. I do not think, however, that it is very useful to frame the issue in terms of a feudalism/capitalism debate, or to assume that unfree labour is everywhere and always a pre-capitalist relation. It is not the place here to rehearse the debate over capitalism and labour regimes or forms of labour control. I will limit myself to quoting Marx who, in his essay on pre-capitalist economic formations, affirmed that 'If we now not only call the plantation-owners in America capitalists, but [affirm] that they *are* [capitalists], this is because they exist as anomalies within a world market based upon free labour' [*Marx*, 1974: 358].[21] To understand the relations between rubber tappers and their patrons/employers, and the role of the *habilito* system, I think it is more helpful to turn to the concept of simple commodity production, and in particular Chevalier's [1983] argument that specific forms of simple commodity production can be treated as variations of capitalism, and therefore as subjected to a flexibly defined process of labour's subordination (formal and real) to capital. This view of simple commodity production may be combined with the notion of 'captivity', which suggests that patrons created a 'virtual' or 'captive' market where the exchanges in fact are a barter, but are symbolized in monetary value through the 'book of accounts' [*Geffray*, 1995; *Lescure, Pinton and Emperaire*, 1994]. To be sure, patrons claimed ownership of the object of production – the forest – although the legal status of such claims was somewhat obscure, and in fact their claims were rooted in 'custom'. Rubber tappers, on the other hand, 'owned' some means of production with which they were provided on arrival, and the cost of which they had to pay off subsequently with their produce rather than their labour-power.[22] They maintained a degree of control over the production process in the absence of mechanisms of real subsumption due to the dispersed nature of wild rubber collection. The debt peonage system thus can be viewed as a variety of simple commodity production, formally subsumed under capital, and characterized by the extraction of absolute surplus value through monopolized exchanges. Viewing rubber tappers as a specific 'captive' category of 'self-employed' labourers also sheds light on their struggle for more autonomy. The *habilito* system was accompanied by a 'moral economy' of its own, and was wrapped up in a discourse about paternalist ties of patronage and *compadrazgo*. But paternalism and its doctrine of reciprocal obligations, as Genovese [1976] has shown, develop as a way of mediating irreconcilable class and racial conflicts.[23]

Until now the focus has been on production relations as they emerged during the early rubber era and the boom period and, in passing, it has been noted that at the height of the rubber boom many consumer goods that were previously imported from Santa Cruz were displaced by foreign imports after the 1913 crash. As imports became more difficult, local agriculture tended to expand and the rubber estates sought to diversify their trade by engaging in the production of Brazil nuts, which became significant in northern Bolivia around 1930. Woortman [1996] describes this process as one of 'internalization of the conditions of reproduction', and suggests that agriculture and Brazil nut gathering at this conjuncture may have constituted 'functional equivalents'. While in some cases subsistence agriculture among rubber tappers might be tolerated, in other cases agricultural production would be centralized under the control of the patron/employer while rubber tapper households would be set to gather Brazil nuts and then exchange the latter produce for subsistence goods in much the same way as rubber [*Lescure*, 1993: 15; *Lescure, Pinton and Emperaire*, 1994; *Woortman*, 1996].[24]

Although economically speaking both the patron and the *barraca* organization mostly held their own, the main elements of a year-round agro-extractive cycle of complementary activities that could potentially sustain a rubber tapper's household were now in place.[25] In northern Bolivia rubber tapping was confined to two phases in the dry season (April to December). The first lasted from April to June. During the latter phase, when economic activity in the region was affected by the cold winds from the south, rubber extraction was suspended, only to be taken up once again in October, until the rainy season which starts in December made further extraction impossible. From mid-December until March was the season for Brazil nut gathering. The period when rubber tapping was suspended, from July to September, could be dedicated to related agricultural labouring tasks, mainly the preparation of fields by clearing and burning the forest. The onset of the rainy season from the end of November marks the sowing season for dry rice and corn that can be harvested from February to April. Other important staple products would be manioc and bananas [*Assies*, 1997a: 8–10]. Hunting and fishing provided proteins.

The mention of households in this context is not fortuitous. A further 'sign of the crisis' as Woortman [1996: 14] calls it, was the increasing presence of women on the rubber estates and the emergence of family life among rubber tappers. If during the first period a predominantly male workforce had been recruited, now family life would be encouraged in order to tie the rubber tappers to the estates.[26] While rubber tapping remained a mainly male economic activity, therefore, women and children came to play an important economic role in the emerging subsistence agriculture and/or in complementary activities such as Brazil nut gathering.

By making it necessary for rubber tappers to expand their agricultural operations – sometimes controlled by the patron and sometimes under control of the rubber tapper household – in order to enable the unit of production (= the rubber tapping household) to reproduce itself economically, the decline of the rubber trade brought about what one may call a 'peasantization' of the rubber tapper. This tendency gathered momentum with the disintegration of the Suárez empire, and the emergence of a new organizational constellation made up of on the one hand patron-run estates, and on the other emerging free communities. The collapse of the rubber trade after 1985 brought a further decline of the estates as a form of social organization, and led to the consolidation of the free communities and a rapid increase in urbanization. It was from this situation that the Brazil nut economy emerged.

The Transformation of Labour Relations after 1985

In considering the way in which the production relations in the northern Bolivian Amazon were transformed, it is necessary first to consider changes to the labour regime in the *barracas*. Whereas formerly the latter were populated all year round, now many *barracas* have been virtually abandoned. *Barracas patronales* continue to exist, but with an often strongly reduced number of inhabitants. In her recent study Henkemans [2001] describes one such *barraca* and the way the *habilito* system still works there. Many of its inhabitants have left, and those remaining have ambiguous feelings about the patron who, in their opinion, has evolved into a mere merchant who no longer takes care of his labourers, which forces them to develop new ties of mutual support and social security. The patron, in turn, depends heavily on the presence of cheap labourers:

> He needs to give the labourers incentives to stay on the barraca or to prevent them from leaving in another way, for example by causing them to be indebted to him. The habilito system still works well for that purpose, because the remote barraca remains almost completely isolated from urban centers, and the patron can largely control the transportation of outgoing extractive products and incoming food products. The whole system is based on making the labourers indebted to him, or making them think they are. As long as this is the case, many workers do not dare to leave. The veterans in the barraca have ambiguous feelings about their position. On the one hand, they are proud of the fact that they have become confidants of the patron due to their long service. On the other hand, they regret that they never had the courage or the ability to leave and become independent. [*Henkemans*, 2001: 92]

While in this case a group of permanent inhabitants has remained, in other *barracas* only a caretaker is present most of the time. By the time of the Brazil nut harvest, the *zafreros* (Brazil nut harvesters) arrive. Nowadays they are largely contracted in the urban areas, mainly Riberalta, and in this context the *habilito* system has taken new forms.

If the *beneficiadoras* own their *barracas*, they may provide a *habilito* to labour contractors who, in turn, recruit gang labour. Otherwise, the *habilito* may go to a *barraquero*, who may either contract workers himself or do this through a labour contractor. They provide the workers with an advance, the new *habilito*, which is often used for large expenses, such as the purchase of new clothes, new shoes, and school utensils for the children. By mid-December the harvesters, often accompanied by various family members, are shipped to the distant *barracas*, to return two or three months later. Riberalta harbour is bustling with small boats loaded with rice, noodles, cooking oil, toothpaste, soap and other essentials, the workers themselves sitting on top. Others may travel in trucks. During their stay in the *barracas*, where living conditions generally are dismal [*Henkemans*, 2001: 90–91], harvest labourers will collect nuts and deliver them to the central storehouse or to the *payoles*, storage facilities located deeper in the forest, where an account will be kept of their deliveries and expenses. These accounts will be settled in the city at the end of the harvest. By the mid-1990s about two-thirds of the Brazil nut harvesters, or some 5,000 to 6,000 persons, were recruited in urban areas, mainly Riberalta. Employment opportunities are scarce in these towns, especially for male workers, and casual labour is rampant [*Verheule*, 1998].

Thus, in urban contexts the *habilito* still plays a role in the recruitment of labour, and until recently debt obligations continued to be an important aspect of this process, as revealed in surveys carried out in 1994 and 1996, which show that harvesters ran up debts and felt obliged to work them off, either by remaining in the forest longer than planned or by promising to work for the same contractor the next harvest [*Assies*, 1997a: 54; *Verheule*, 1998: 87]. However, while the latter sources already point out that the *habilito* system was running into difficulties in urban contexts, Stoian [2000a: 118] and Bojanic [2001: 87–106] describe how the rupture of the close patron ties that prevailed in the *barracas* has resulted in an outright crisis of the *habilito* system. Workers may take the advance payment without fulfilling their obligations, contractors may cheat in the post-harvest settling of accounts or not settle them at all. During the harvest, contractors attempt to mislead workers, and vice-versa, over the volume and weight of nuts collected; food consumed may also be overpriced. The climate is one of widespread distrust in which all parties seek ways to deceive the other, setting off a spiral of fraudulent transactions. Nonetheless, Bojanic argues, hardly any unskilled jobs will be done if no advance payment is made, which leads him to the conclusion that the *habilito* system will persist in the near future but that it needs to be modernized, along with a formalization of labour relations. Whether that can be done remains problematic. Employers may be interested in disciplining the workforce involved in the Brazil nut harvest, but at the same time informal labour relations in the context of extensive underemployment [*Verheule*, 1998] contribute to the profitability of the Brazil nut industry [*Assies*, 1997a: 56–9].[27]

Communities and Estates: The Latent Conflict

The other source of raw nuts in the northern Bolivian Amazon are the *comunidades libres*, which account for 35 to 40 per cent of the harvest. As has been noted, these communities came into being in the context of the disarticulation of the *barraca* system, and they rely on a combination of peasant agriculture and extractivism. The relative economic importance of agriculture in relation to extractivism varies, and is a function both of the location of the communities themselves, and also of the size of the family holding within communities. The migration and resettlement process triggered by the collapse of the rubber trade resulted in relatively high rural population densities in the Vaca Díez province. Family holdings within the communities in this area range between 20 and 80 hectares in size, and peasant proprietors dedicate themselves mainly to a mix of subsistence and market-oriented slash and burn agriculture.[28] The city of Riberalta is a main outlet for agricultural produce such as rice, bananas and, more recently, some agro-forestry products promoted by non-governmental organizations. Brazil nut production takes a subsidiary role, given the relatively small size of the family parcels. After harvesting crops on their own parcel, many families also join the workforce harvesting on the *barracas*, in order to obtain a monetary income [*Henkemans*, 2001].

The inhabitants of communities in the less populated Department of Pando have access to significantly larger areas of forest. Here agriculture is mainly subsistence-oriented, due to the distance from urban markets. Brazil nut production is a major source of monetary income for these communities. Nuts may be sold directly to a *beneficiadora* or through an intermediary. Communities have tended to cluster along the Riberalta–Cobija road. It is the competition over access to the road and to Brazil nut stands that underlies the potential for conflict between the emerging *comunidades libres* and the *barracas* in this region, a latent antagonism that manifested itself in the Third Indigenous-Peasant March during July 2000. Understanding the nature and dimensions of this conflict requires some further consideration of the dynamics of the regional economy, as well as the role in this of the new land and forestry legislation introduced in 1996.

As noted, the *beneficiadora* owners have become a key group in the regional economy, overshadowing the once dominant *barraqueros* who have become increasingly dependent on the *beneficiadora* owners to finance their operations during the Brazil nut harvest. By the mid-1990s this economic imbalance resulted in the takeover or purchase of *barracas* belonging to indebted *barraca* owners by the owners' *beneficiadoras*. A process of vertical concentration was taking shape through the elimination of the *barraquero* from the production chain. While some of the *beneficiadoras* had been created through investment by *barraqueros*, others had been created through investment from outside the sector. Through vertical integration the *beneficiadoras* sought to control part of their own supply of wild nuts. Most of them acquired *barracas*, where the Brazil nut crop would be harvested by a seasonal labour force recruited from nearby urban areas.

This tendency towards vertical integration casts some doubts on the expectations about a 'democratization' of the Brazil nut industry, according to which the role of the *comunidades libres* in supplying its raw material might gradually expand. This in turn would benefit the peasant sector, among other things by raising their monetary income, and at the same time contribute to forest conservation [*DHV*, 1993a]. In view of the tendency toward vertical integration, the expectations about a democratization of the industry have been the subject of criticism [*Assies*, 1997a]. It was argued that production by the *comunidades libres* would complement that of the *barracas* for two reasons. In communities near the urban centres, parcel sizes tend to be relatively small, and the commercial output of Brazil nuts is therefore less significant than subsistence agriculture. By contrast, the more remote communities face logistical problems in getting their harvest out of the forest.[29] Aside from assuring a steady supply of raw material, in this context vertical integration and harvesting by means of urban-based gang labour might yield a competitive advantage, and may beome a profitable option.

This argument has raised some controversy. According to Stoian [2000a: 139] it is a 'pessimistic outlook'. He argues that in the context of a booming Brazil nut economy and growing production, the relative shares of nuts produced by *barracas* and communities remained the same, but that the greater volume produced by the communities implied competition over access to resources. Communities pushed the *barracas* into less accessible areas.[30] Furthermore, he points to the ongoing conversion of *barracas* into communities. Finally, the vertically integrated *barracas* produce no more than one-fifth of the harvest, the remainder coming from peasant communities and *barracas patronales*. The peasantry not only benefited economically from the Brazil nut production boom through higher prices, therefore, but also produced more. It is not at all clear, however, just how this process corresponds to 'democratization'. What it does underline is the dependence of the profitability of vertical integration on an additional condition: namely, that world market prices for Brazil nuts are high. As we will see below, in 2001 prices plummeted and local demand for raw nuts contracted. Under such conditions *beneficiadora* owners may desist from or reduce exploitation of their *barracas*, and instead purchase their raw material from peasants whose logic is subsistence- rather than profit-oriented, and for whom Brazil nuts are an important source of cash income. Under such conditions the relative share of the peasantry in the production of raw nuts may increase, but this would be a democratization of poverty.

In contrast to this critical view, Bojanic [2001: 101] asserts that vertical integration increases transaction costs, which might lead eventually to a reversal of the vertical integration process itself, with *barracas* being returned to the *barraqueros*. Evidence for such a reversal is hard to find, however. If the process of vertical integration and concentration of landholding halted, it would be for other reasons, such as the uncertainty about future implementation of the agrarian and forestry legislation and the irregularity of tenure rights. By the year 1999, when the issue of conversion of the *barracas* into concessions under the 1996 Forestry Law had become a major issue, the organizations of *barraca* owners presented a list that distinguished between 'traditional' and 'non-traditional' *barracas*, the latter being those claimed by enterprises involved in the process of vertical integration. According to that list, ten enterprises claimed ownership of 38 *barracas* covering a total of 1,675,781 hectares, whereas 162 smaller *barracas* – the 'traditional' ones – claimed a total of 1,719,010 hectares. It was such claims, which according to a letter of the *Superintendencia Agraria* (16 November 1999) implied that 'there would be hardly any land left for the communities', that provoked the 'Third March'.[31] We now turn to a consideration of the 1996 land and forestry legislation which, together with Supreme Decree No. 25532, allowed for the conversion of the *barracas* into new concessions and thus triggered the 'Third March'.

THE 1996 LAND AND FORESTRY LEGISLATION, THE BARRACA DECREE, AND THE 'THIRD MARCH'

By the 1990s it had become clear that an overhaul of Bolivian land and forestry legislation was in order. The existing legislation was outdated, and its implementation had become thoroughly corrupt. While debate over reform had started in the 1980s, this would eventually be introduced under the Sánchez de Lozada government (1993–97) as part of a far-reaching package of 'second generation' institutional reforms complementing the structural adjustment policies introduced in 1985. The 1996 Bolivian land and forestry legislation reforms, however, stood out among similar changes carried out in Latin America for not simply following the neo-liberal *zeitgeist*. While the World Bank, for example, pressured Latin American governments to adopt only market-oriented reforms which, it was believed, would not only promote efficiency but also benefit the poor [*Deininger and Binswanger*, 2001], the Bolivian reforms incorporated both market-oriented and social justice elements [*Urioste and Pacheco*, 2000].

The 1953 revolutionary land reform had sought to expropriate properties that were either unutilized/underutilized *latifundia* or operated under pre-capitalist tenure and labour relations. It effectively eradicated the hacienda system in the Andean highlands of Bolivia, but failed to resolve the demand for land. The redistribution of land in the Bolivian highlands eventually resulted in minifundization, while the occupation of the eastern tropical lowlands, which accelerated in the 1960s, was characterized by the formation of huge landholdings, surrounded by smallholding colonists. Meanwhile, the institutions involved in land policies became seriously corrupt. The 1953 land reform law had created the *Servicio Nacional de Reforma Agraria* (SNRA) and in 1965, when the redistribution in the highland region was declared complete, an *Instituto Nacional de Colonización* (INC) had been created to promote the occupation and settlement of the eastern lowlands. Both institutions were charged with the distribution of public funds, and were supposed to complement each other's activities. Complementarity, however, was absent in practice, and the two institutions dedicated themselves to the distribution of lands through far from transparent procedures. While in the western highlands of Bolivia peasant and community holdings were subject to a process of land fragmentation, in the eastern lowlands by contrast huge land holdings emerged as a result of policies pursued by the authoritarian military governments of René Barrientos (1964–65 and 1966–69), Hugo Banzer (1971–78) and the narco-dictatorship of Luis García Meza. In the eastern lowlands, particularly around Santa Cruz, most land became monopolized by a small group of large landholders and agribusiness enterprises, dedicated to industrial farming (soya and oilseeds) and/or extensive livestock ranching.

By the 1980s it was clear that land distribution had become extremely skewed, though exact data on tenure patterns were not available due to the irregular and corrupt distribution practices. It is estimated that between 30 and 60 per cent of the land may be subject to overlapping claims, and that 60 per cent of the owners do not have regular titles. The 1984 agrarian census suggests that out of 22.6 million registered hectares, 15 per cent was possessed by 308,000 small and medium-sized holdings, against 85 per cent occupied by 6,000 large owners [*Solón*, 1995]. Other estimates also suggest extreme polarization. [*MACPIO*, 2001: 51–3; *Hernaíz and Pacheco*, 2000: 156–61]. In 1992, after yet another case of corruption had been denounced, it was decided to 'intervene' the land reform and colonization institutions, and their actions were suspended in order to open the way for a *saneamiento* (clarification) of land rights. This required reform of the 1953 legislation. A further issue that required attention was the demands made by the indigenous peoples of the eastern lowlands who had made themselves 'visible' through their 'First March' in 1990, which had resulted in the recognition of eight indigenous territories.[32] During their 'Second March' in 1996, in the context of the debate on new agrarian legislation, they would present 16 new territorial demands. This, too, had to be dealt with in new legislation.

It took four years of negotiations among government officials, indigenous peoples, peasant and landowners representatives before the *Ley del Servicio Nacional de Reforma Agraria* was adopted in 1996 [*Assies*, 2000; *Salvatierra*, 1996; *Solón*, 1995]. The outcome of the negotiation process was a 'hybrid' law that did not fully satisfy anyone but seemed to be acceptable. It introduces some elements of market-oriented reforms but at the same time retains important elements of the social justice orientation embodied in earlier legislation [*Urioste and Pacheco*, 2000]. The law thus recognizes various types of landholding that fulfill a 'social function'. It is assumed that these lands are used primarily for subsistence production by peasants or indigenous peoples. These lands are either prohibited from being bought and sold, or – where such market transfers are permitted – subject to specific conditions/restrictions; furthermore, they are not liable to land tax. The *solar campesino* (peasant yard) and the smallholding cannot be divided or mortgaged, but may be sold only insofar as not expressly prohibited by law. Collectively titled community properties and *tierras comunitarias de origen* (TCO), the much larger holdings, cannot be sold at all. By contrast, medium-sized properties and property held by agricultural enterprises, fall into a category of lands that are supposed to fulfil an 'economic-social' function. These holdings may be sold and mortgaged, and are subject to a land tax. The law thus seeks to guarantee the tenure rights of middle and large properties on the condition that they fulfil an economic-social function, and that they pay taxes. Abandonment would be cause for a reversion of land to the state.[33] This was meant to remedy the concentration of land. Holdings which reverted to the state would fall into the category of public lands (*tierra fiscal*), and as such could then either be granted (*dotación*) at no cost to peasant and indigenous communities or sold off (*adjudicación*) at market value through public auction. Land grants would be given priority over selling off. In its initial clauses, the 1996 law contains stipulations regarding the rapid titling of the eight indigenous territories that had been recognized in the wake of the 1990 indigenous march, and admitted 16 new claims, which were immobilized pending future regularization within ten months. These territories, with a total surface of nearly 15 million hectares, are to be regularized as *tierras comunitarias de origen* (TCO). The implementation of the new legislation would involve the clarification (*saneamiento*) of tenure rights and subsequent titling. This process should be completed within ten years (i.e., by the year 2006).

The 1996 Forestry Law was also the outcome of a negotiation process [*Pavez and Bojanic*, 1998], an attempt both to remedy the flaws of the 1974 forestry legislation and to provide a better fit between land tenure and forest exploitation. As a result of the earlier law, grants made independently of tenure rights and logging concessions overlapped with communal/indigenous lands and other forms of possession or property. Furthermore, the 1974 law had enabled an enormous concentration of concessions by a small number of enterprises, it had failed to promote sustainable forest use, and its administration was plagued with corruption [*Contreras-Hermosilla and Vargas*, 2001]. The 1996 law foresees a regime of concessions of 40 years' duration where state-owned forests (*tierras fiscales*) are concerned. Such concessions can be transferred, are heritable, and they can be renewed. Private owners and indigenous peoples can be authorized to exploit forest resources within their property or TCO. Indigenous peoples are granted the exclusive rights over forest resources within their TCOs. Within the Bolivian municipalities, up to 20 per cent of the state-owned forests can be set aside for use by locally based social associations.[34]

The new forestry regime made exploitation of resources conditional upon the elaboration of management plans, and also introduced a new licence system. Whereas the 1974 law linked payment for a licence to the volume of forest resources extracted, under the new law the licence fee for timber exploitation was set at a minimum of US$1.00 per hectare for concessions of state-owned forests to the timber industries. Private owners can be authorized to exploit forest resources on their land merely by paying the minimum licence fee. Since the concessions would be auctioned, the expectation was that in this case the licence fee would rise above the US$1.00 level. The law allowed for the conversion of existing concessions into new ones under the present regime, but it was expected that the licence fee system would prompt a reduction in the number of concession areas. The remaining areas would revert to the state, which might then allocate them to indigenous communities or auction them off as new concessions. Indigenous peoples would have to pay the same licence fee, but only for the area effectively exploited within their TCO. For non-timber forest products, the licence fee was set at US$0.30 per hectare.

As will be seen below, these two laws provide the framework for the disputes over land and resources in the northern Bolivian Amazon region. Generally speaking, it can be said that the implementation of the *Ley INRA* has been extremely slow. By November 2001 title clarification had only taken place for 13 per cent of the rural lands, while 33 per cent were still being processed. Final titling was proceeding even slower. At the same time, very little land has been reverted to the state, so in the event the concentration of landholding has scarcely changed. In the absence of clear stipulations about the social–economic function of land, decisions were left to the discretion of INRA officials. In the case of the TCOs clarification has made some progress, due to international support, but at the same time the process of clarification has meant that holdings of third parties were consolidated, resulting in a significant reduction of the area to be granted to indigenous peoples. Similarly, 'studies of spatial necessities' often resulted in significant reductions of the area recommended for titling. By the year 2000, only one TCO had been titled, together with part of another. Furthermore, in 1997 the Forestry Superintendency allowed the 'voluntary conversion' of logging concessions, part of which overlapped with TCOs, that were in the process of consolidation.[35] Finally, the INRA law brings no solution whatever for the specific problems of the highland peasantry. It is in this context that demands for the modification – or, in the case of the radical highland peasant movement, even abrogation – of the INRA law have emerged. On the other hand, large landowners have become increasingly militant in the defence of their interests. The disputes that cropped up in northern Bolivia are to be understood in this general context.

Supreme Decree No. 25532

Although the 1996 Forestry Law provided for the possibility of converting existing concessions into new ones under the new forestry regime, *barraqueros* had made little effort to do so. For one thing, they had never really bothered to acquire concessions: their claims were based rather on 'custom'. Moreover, they argued that the new licence fee system was inadequate for Brazil nut production. In the past they had paid a fee per volume extracted (though one may doubt that this system ever really worked). Finally, they argued that the new forestry authorities did not accept their proposals for conversion of their claims. All in all, little had been done to implement the new legislation in the region and *barraqueros* probably would have liked to leave things just like they had been in the past. Emerging pressures for regularizing land tenure and forestry rights under the new laws, however, prompted them, and particularly the larger ones represented in CADEXNOR, to move on this issue, and to lobby for their interests. In October 1999 their efforts were rewarded with Supreme Decree No. 25532 of 5 October 1999, also known as the *Decreto de las Barracas*.[36]

The decree mentions that the 1996 Forestry Law establishes that – where areas with Brazil nut, rubber, palm heart and similar resources are concerned – concessionary preference will be given to traditional users, peasant communities and local social associations. Although the notion of 'traditional' is taken generally to mean either peasant or indigenous users, the decree then argues that the *barracas* are traditional rubber and Brazil nut producing establishments which cover extensive forest areas in the north of the country, where they have enjoyed 'inveterate and traditional' access to these resources which are the principal socio–economic mainstay of the region. On the basis of such considerations the decree then stipulates that the *barracas* should be recognized as concessions for the exploitation of non-timber forest products under the new regime, respecting the legally acquired rights of third parties. The Forestry Superintendency should directly convert these areas, through administrative act and without an auctioning process. The decree further mentions a list of requirements and a formula for the calculation of licence fees to be paid, and in one of its final dispositions establishes that this process of voluntary conversion will not imply the renunciation of titling procedures initiated or pursued with the competent authority. This opened up the possibility for a further conversion into property under the agrarian legislation.[37]

Chronicle of a Conflict Foretold

Soon after the decree was issued, the Agrarian Superintendency wrote a letter to the Minister of Sustainable Development and the Environment in which it recognized that the decree constituted a positive step towards the recognition of the customary rights of the *barraca* owners, but that it might generate some conflict with peasant communities and other 'equally traditional possessors'.[38] The decree seeks to be careful in respecting the rights of peasant and indigenous communities, the letter argues, but in fact at the moment it is impossible for such communities to sustain their property rights, since they are no more than simple possessors as long as the process of *saneamiento* has not been concluded. Out of the 6.3 million hectares in the Department of Pando, only 330,000 (5 per cent) have been distributed under the agrarian reform legislation, which means that the vast majority of the rural population does not have duly regularized property rights. Moreover, the *saneamiento* process has not even started in the region, and the Pando branch of the *Instituto Nacional de Reforma Agraria* (INRA) has not yet been institutionalized. Under such conditions the Decree means that the communities will be deprived of property rights and the use of resources, although they should be considered traditional settlements. The Agrarian Superintendency then calculates that the decree would hand over some 3 million hectares of land (48 per cent) to the *barracas*. If one takes into account that in the Department of Pando an area of 126,000 hectares (2 per cent) has been reserved for cattle raising, that timber concessions occupy some 250,000 hectares (4 per cent), that natural parks cover a further 14 per cent, and if water resources and ecological obligations are also taken into account, the conclusion can only be that hardly any land will be left for the communities.[39] Given the potential for conflict, the Superintendency proposed that the property rights of communities and others should be clarified through the *saneamiento* process before proceeding with any conversion of the *barracas*. Finally, the Superintendency suggests that, given the particularities of the economic activities in the region, the areas to be allocated to the different types of users should be discussed in the context of new regulations for the implementation of the *Ley INRA* instead of leaving the issue to the discretion of the INRA.

With this letter the Superintendency outlined in unambiguous terms the potential for conflict in the region, but its words of warning went unheeded. Instead, the Bolivian government decided in May 2000 to extend the period for applications for conversion of *barracas*, initially set at the end of April 2000, to the last day of July 2000. By then conflict was brewing [*Betancur*, 2000].

A War of Manifestos

Shortly after the Agrarian Superintendency had hoisted its early warning signals, peasant communities and indigenous peoples of the northern Amazon region issued a declaration invoking, among other things, ILO Convention 169, which establishes that indigenous peoples should be consulted over legislation that affects them. Arguing that the decree would result in the expulsion or eviction of peasant and indigenous communities to the benefit of the *barraqueros*, the signatories of the declaration rejected the decree and demanded that titling of community lands should precede any conversion. They also decided to ask for the intervention of the *Defensor del Pueblo* (human rights ombudsman), and announced an intention to undertake action if their demands were ignored or overruled. This declaration was soon followed by an open letter addressed to 'public opinion' issued by the indigenous people's organization CIRABO on 1 December 1999. The next day saw a demonstration in Cobija, capital of the Department of Pando, organized by the rural workers' organization; the latter announced that to indicate its rejection of Decree 25532, roadblocks would be set up on 13 December 2000.

The *barraquero* sector did not fail to react. In its own open letter, similarly addressed to public opinion, ASPROGOAL replied to the letter issued by CIRABO, which it accused of having initiated a disinformation campaign. According to ASPROGOAL Decree 25532 aimed at the recognition of the *barraqueros*' historical and legally acquired rights. ASPROGOAL argued that the *barraca* owners historically had undertaken sustainable development and protection of the forest in the region, and that their economic activities depended on the extraction of non-timber products, which did no harm to the forest. It claimed recognition of the *barraca* owners' rights 'passed down from father to son' through a policy that would grant 'juridical security', and would thus legalize their conservation activities and allow for the elaboration of a socio-economic development strategy for the region. It further questioned some of the assertions and claims made by CIRABO. According to ASPROGOAL, not only were the rights of peasant and indigenous communities fully guaranteed in the decree, but the lands immobilized for future titling as TCOs also stood in no relation to the actual numbers of the indigenous populations involved. It suggested that CIRABO was manipulated by 'foreign' interests outside the region, to the detriment of the local entrepreneurs 'who at present help some 12,000 families, which work in the collection of the *castaña* and other fruits of the forest, improving the internal product of the Bolivian Northwest'.[40] ASPROGOAL announced that it would defend Decree 25532 at 'whatever cost' (*hasta las últimas consecuencias*). About the same time the Civic Committee of the Riberalta Region, the 'Thought and Muscle of the Bolivian Amazon', issued a public manifesto following a similar line of reasoning, this time reproaching the Agrarian Superintendency for its comment on Decree 25532. The Manifesto was signed by several urban organizations that participate in the Civic Committee, such as the Federation of Neighborhood Associations, the President of the Vigilance Committee, the President of the Federation of Rubber and Brazil Nut Workers, and the President of the Federation of Factory Workers. An urban coalition was being forged in support of the claims made by the *barraquero* sector, though in a reply to the ASPROGOAL and Civic Committee statements CIRABO called into question the real degree of support among urban organizations.[41] CIRABO's reply also refers to 'conditions of semi-slavery' in the *barracas*, and once again rejects Decree 25532 which, it pointed out, would benefit only those who 'claim to be entrepreneurs' (*quienes dicen llamarse empresarios*). In support of their campaigns, both the peasantry and the *barraqueros* invoked the 'struggle for poverty reduction', one of the slogans of the Banzer Government. However, whereas the peasant and indigenous organizations pressed for redistribution of land to achieve that goal, the *barraqueros* merely presented themselves as the protagonists in the struggle against poverty.

In the event, the threatened roadblocks announced by peasant organizations for 13 December 1999 did not materialize, since the Department of Pando Prefecture called for a dialogue, which was to take place on 22 December. The meeting was postponed until 15 January 2000, and peasant organizations expected that it would be decisive. The meeting ended in failure. First of all, the Pando Prefecture had 'forgotten' to send official invitations to the peasant federation and the civil society organizations supporting it. Furthermore, the composition of the governmental delegation remained unknown until the last moment. When the meeting finally took place, the representatives of national and local peasant and indigenous organizations, and the civil society organizations with whom they worked, found that the governmental delegation consisted of the INRA director and Senator Peter Hecker, one of the principal landowners and *barraqueros* of the region. Since this delegation had no power of decision, and because the choice of Senator Hecker as a principal delegate was considered insulting in view of the Hecker family's history of confrontation with peasant and indigenous organizations, the latter walked out. They later agreed to talk with the INRA Director and the Pando Prefect, but no point of convergence or consensus was found. As allowed for by the

INRA law, peasants insisted that *saneamiento* should precede any conversion of *barracas*, and any attempt to implement Decree 25532 would be met with legal, political and other kinds of opposition to prevent this.

Marching for 'Land, Territories and Natural Resources'

In April 2000 an 18-point Manifesto was launched by indigenous peasant organizations, and in June a 31-point platform of demands was issued, to be pressed for with a march for 'Land, Territories and Natural Resources'. A few days later the *Defensoría del Pueblo* (national human rights ombudsman) demanded that Decree 25532 be declared anti-constitutional, and on 28 June some 500 peasants and indigenous people started their march from the region to participate in the Great National Assembly of Indigenous Peoples (GANPI) that was to take place in the city of Santa Cruz, where they arrived on 5 July. The next day both CIRABO and the *Coordinadora de Pueblos Etnicos de Santa Cruz* (CPESC) withdrew from the GANPI, accusing the CIDOB leadership of brokering a deal with the government, and announced that they would continue their march, now heading for the national capital itself, La Paz. An agreement between CIDOB and government delegates who had arrived to negotiate at the GANPI was indeed signed on 7 July. According to the dissidents, it postponed solutions and contained empty promises. They resumed their march on 11 July, and reached the town of Montero two days later. Negotiations with a government delegation resulted in another agreement in the early hours of 16 July.

By then, in an effort to stop the march and keep it from growing, the Council of Ministers had on 10 July annulled Decree 25532, well within the 12-day term that had been agreed earlier with CIDOB. Important points of the Montero agreement were the cancelling of an internal INRA resolution that made it possible to declare land available for concessions without first duly clarifying the rights of local people, the setting of clear terms for the titling of four TCOs, the creation of a fund with a starting capital of US$10 million for the reactivation of the peasant, indigenous and colonist economy, and a modification of the regulations of the *Ley INRA*. These modifications accepted, among other things, the following two crucial arguments. First, that the minimum surface area to be granted to families in peasant and indigenous communities in the northern Amazon region should be 500 hectares.[42] And second, that clarification of property rights in the northern Amazon region, as well as in the Gran Chaco region of the Tarija Department, should start immediately and be concluded within a year.[43] Furthermore, the procedures for titling in favour of peasants, colonists and indigenous peoples were simplified, and a series of technical norms were modified, including a clearer definition of the norms regarding the economic-social function of land on farms up to 500 hectares.[44]

The Aftermath of the March and the Crisis of the Brazil Nut Trade

After the march, implementation of the 1996 legislation gradually got underway in the region. In the Department of Pando, the INRA structure finally became more or less institutionalized, though it remained subject to strong political pressures. 'Polygons' were defined, that is areas where the demarcation of properties was to start, and in some cases INRA brigades initiated their evaluation of tenure claims, accompanied by peasants who were trained by local NGOs to keep watch over the process, and denounce irregularities such as the creation of 'phantom communities' by *barraqueros*, the deforestation of areas to prove the presence of economic activity, or the 'lending' of livestock by cattle raisers to one another, so as to provide visiting INRA brigades with the necessary 'proof' of economic activity. In the Vaca Díez Province the process proceeded somewhat more rapidly. The density of settlement implied that boundaries between holdings had often already been established, and political pressures from the departmental government were less frequent than in Pando. Regularization of TCOs in favour of indigenous peoples in the region also made some progress. Out of the four demands for TCOs, titles were issued for part of the area demanded in two cases.

Meanwhile, the question of what to do with the *barracas* remained on the agenda. After the abrogation of Decree 25532, the *barraquero* sector had started to lobby for a law that would permit the conversion of the areas they claimed into new concessions under the Forestry Law, or into properties under agrarian legislation. By October 2001 a draft law was circulating and a provisional agreement was brokered among *barraquero* associations and the leadership of the Pando Peasant Federation, which however soon withdrew its support for the proposal. The draft law foresaw the 'voluntary conversion' of traditional *barracas* into new concessions and established an upper limit of 25,000 hectares, although *barraquero* organizations continued to pressure for conversion of their *barracas* into property under the agrarian legislation. It will, however, be difficult for them to prove that the *barracas* fulfil an economic–social function, since labour relations are informal, debt-peonage relations persist, and production is not mechanized in any way. On the other hand, one large *barraquero*, ADN Senator Peter Hecker, claimed that a huge concession should be granted for the exploitation of *sangre de grado*, a small tree locally used for medicinal purposes. A US firm was interested, and this could be a million-dollar business. The venture would increase regional income and at the same time promote forest conservation, he claimed.

The push and pull over a law on the conversion of *barracas* developed amid a crisis in the Brazil nut trade. After years of low exports, Brazil increased its own production significantly in 2001; Bolivia itself also produced more than in previous years, and was finally left with a stock of 157,000 boxes of shelled nuts. With the world market saturated, prices plummeted, and the *beneficiadora* owners announced that in the 2001/2002 harvest they would not be able to pay more than 4 *bolivianos* per crate of raw nuts. They later offered 8 *bolivianos* (about US$1.25), but this was still much less than the 20 *bolivianos* paid in the forest during the 2000/2001 season. Furthermore, they decided that the harvest would be limited, in order to stabilize prices and to allow them to sell the surplus production from the previous season. The obvious consequence would be unemployment for thousands of people in the region. Some 4,000 *zafreros* from the urban areas would be left without employment during the harvest season, and employment of some 3,000 *quebradoras* and their 4,000 'helpers' would be severely cut back.[45] To solve the problem, it was proposed that the Bolivian state should create a special fund to reactivate the regional economy and pay an additional 10 *bolivianos* per crate harvested to the *zafreros*. In the forest, the *zafreros* would receive coupons worth 100 *bolivianos* for every 10 crates of Brazil nuts delivered, and after the harvest they could cash their coupons in town. By mid-December, when harvesters are usually shipped to the *barracas*, a government representative visited Riberalta to announce that the scheme had been approved, but that some technical details still had to be worked out.[46] By then, the president of the *zafrero* union was already selling official membership cards to his clients at 10 to 20 *bolivianos* apiece. Peasant organizations, however, vehemently rejected the proposal, since it might be used to demonstrate that the *barracas* did indeed perform an economic–social function. The government sought to tie approval of the subsidy scheme to support for a new *barraca* law and, after its failed 'Earth Summit', announced that it would organize regional encounters to find solutions for regional problems.

CONCLUDING COMMENTS

Conflicts over land and resources have become increasingly frequent in Bolivia over recent years. This suggests, among other things, that the land and forestry legislation introduced in 1996 has failed to resolve the problems it was meant to address. It generated expectations that were not fulfilled due to a lack of political will. Moreover, it is often hard to apply in particular local situations. This article has discussed the implementation of the new legislation and the issues it brought to light in the specific regional context of the northern Bolivian Amazon.

To do so, it was necessary to outline the historical development of the regional rural economy, tracing the emergence and consolidation of the rubber estate system and its fragmentation after 1940. It has been argued that there is little reason to revise the prevailing view of the rubber economy in the region and its forms of organization, which are usually characterized as rather harsh and exploitative. Labour recruitment during the early period of rubber extraction was often coercive, and the workforce was not treated particularly well, although excesses like those reported from the Peruvian Putumayo region did not occur. Debt-peonage was the prevailing mode of labour recruitment and control, and there is no convincing evidence in support of the oft-heard argument that this was a relatively benign and, under the conditions, 'rational' system. The interpretation of Barham and Coomes has been shown not to apply in the region, because it hinges on the idea of generalized competition for clients among patrons and merchants. Such conditions did not obtain in the northern Bolivian Amazon region up to 1940. In a similar vein, the evidence presented by Stoian in support of his argument that fixed-wage relations for rubber tappers prevailed during the early rubber era, and that this would shift most of the risk to the patron, was found to be far from convincing. Some of the contracts he cites actually confirm the presence of indigenous slavery, while others point to piece rates for rubber tapping and fixed wages for off-season activities. The workforce could not be considered to have been 'salaried in the strict sense of the term', a point emphasized by Sanabria.

This, however, does not lead to a disagreement with Stoian's characterization of the early rubber era as one of 'primitive capitalism', although a caveat is in order. As noted, even Marx considered North American plantation owners as capitalists, because they exist as 'anomalies in a world-market based in free labour'. For this reason it does not seem useful to frame the discussion in terms of the feudalism/capitalism debate. Instead, it has been suggested that Chevalier's view of simple commodity production may be combined with the pervasive notion of 'captivity', which conveys the element of employer/patron domination and monopoly, and the virtuality of a 'cash economy' in which cash hardly ever materializes. Rubber tappers in the northern Bolivian Amazon region can thus be viewed as simple commodity producers, formally subsumed under capital and subject to the extraction of absolute surplus value through monopolistic domination by a patron who brokers their relation to the market. Their economy, however, was fully 'commodified', in the sense that rubber was exchanged for subsistence goods in the penumbra of a captive market operating through the patron's ledger. Establishing 'free communities' can be understood as the antithesis of this 'captivity', and thus as an emancipatory response on the part of simple commodity producers.

Free communities emerged in the context of a sustained crisis of the rubber economy. It was precisely this crisis that shaped the conditions of emergence of the *comunidades libres*, since it prompted the 'internalization of the conditions of reproduction'. On the one hand, the crisis opened the way to the emergence of an agro-extractive cycle, which combined rubber tapping, agriculture and Brazil nut gathering as complementary activities that could potentially sustain what was in effect a peasant household established by the rubber tapper. The development of rubber tapper subsistence production, one might say, entailed a process of de-commodification, while rubber tapping and Brazil nut gathering were to become sources of cash income. On the other hand, the crisis promoted the formation of households through a new patron strategy to perpetuate 'captivity' by promoting household life, often deciding who was to marry whom, and establishing fictive kinship relations with the parents and offspring, for what it was worth. While the internalization of the conditions of reproduction had occurred in the wake of the 1913 crash in rubber prices, after 1940 the process of socio-economic differentiation between patron-run (instead of 'administrator managed') estates and *comunidades libres* gathered momentum.

The final unravelling of the rubber economy after 1985 brought a new dynamic to the region. It accelerated the decline of the estate system and the formation of independent communities. Rural–rural migration modified the pattern of spatial occupation of the region. The location of the independent communities correlates with the size of parcels within the communities and the relative weight of agricultural and extractive activities. At the same time, a process of rural–urban migration contributed to the formation of an industrial reserve army of urban labour that lacked employment opportunities. During the Brazil nut season, harvesters are recruited from this labour pool to work in the *barracas*, where the permanent population has been drastically reduced and conditions have deteriorated. Although in remote *barracas* debt peonage still persists, in the urban context the *habilito* system as a form of labour recruitment for the Brazil nut harvest has entered into a crisis with uncertain outcomes. The system may either be extinguished or substantially modified, in tandem with a formalization of labour relations.

Decree 25532, which allowed for the conversion of *barracas* into new concessions under the 1996 Forestry Law, and left open the possibility for further conversion into property under the INRA Law, brought to light the latent conflict between *barraqueros* on the one hand and the peasantry and indigenous rural population on the other. Whereas the decree allowed for the consolidation of *barracas* first and the subsequent clarification of peasant and indigenous tenure rights, the 'Third March' successfully pressured for abrogation of the decree and the implementation of the INRA Law in the region while at the same time modifying the norms and procedures for its implementation. According to the new regulations, the peasant communities should be granted at least 500 hectares per family, which would allow them to generate a reasonable income basically derived from the extraction of forest products.

Whether and how the norm will be applied remains to be seen. In Vaca Díez Province, where rural population is densest, parcels in the peasant communities vary between 20 and 80 hectares, whereas in the Department of Pando they have access to larger areas. There too, however, location is important. *Barraqueros* argue that the peasantry seeks to occupy their lands and installations and that, if peasants want land, they should move to the more remote areas. The *barraquero* sector itself has introduced a distinction between traditional and non-traditional *barracas*. According to the leader of an organization of traditional *barraqueros*, the non-traditional ones could be reduced in size so as to make it possible to grant peasant communities sufficient land, albeit in more remote areas. As the clarification of tenure rights gets under way, both communities and *barraqueros* seek to consolidate their claims. Communities are constructing infrastructure with the help of local NGOs that apply for funding from Bolivian poverty relief schemes. For their part, *barraqueros* have cleared forest areas in order to establish their presence, an important consideration in the light of future property claims.

The outcome of the implementation of a new tenure regime in the region will be politically determined. Neither the peasantry nor the *barraqueros*, despite their entrepreneurial rhetoric, are in favour of a market-led reform process, although there is an element of deception here. Peasants and indigenous people seek tenure according to the INRA regulations for land that fulfills a social function and which, at least at the moment, may not be sold or mortgaged.[47] *Barraqueros* seek conversion of their *barracas*, which they claim fulfill an economic–social function, through an administrative procedure. If concessions were ever put up for auction, they argue, they would lose out against transnational capital.[48] And they continue pressuring for the conversion of the *barracas* into regionally defined medium-size properties under the tenure regime of the INRA law, which would bring them 'juridical security'. Their discourse of 'juridical security' is extremely ambiguous, however. They present it as a 'freezing' of their 'inalienable rights', rather than as a condition for the operation of market forces, but various interviewees soon got into difficulties when asked how this type of 'juridical security' was to be reconciled with their claim to perform an economic–social function, which implies that they would fall under the market-oriented regime of the INRA law. They simply want full property rights over their *barracas*, and while some might indeed want to work them, others will surely want to sell them as soon as it becomes opportune and profitable to do so. This outcome would, of course, re-launch the process of vertical integration and concentration of forest-land in the hands of a few agribusiness enterprises.

Market-led reform is not a viable option in the region. Experience shows that land markets are highly segmented.[49] There may be a considerable volume of land transactions within farm-size groups, but land sales across farm-size group boundaries are either absent or contribute to further polarization. Simply put, the land market is not a level playing field.[50] In Bolivia, the mechanisms that were meant to correct such tendencies towards concentration have been rather effectively sabotaged as a result of the lobby for the reduction of the taxes and licence fees that were to stimulate the market process. Under the questionable premise that such reductions will contribute to economic reactivation, the Bolivian government has been quite willing to grant such reductions.

A further issue that emerges is the question of 'poverty reduction'. Peasant organizations and sympathizing NGOs maintain that redistribution of tenure rights in favour of the peasantry and indigenous peoples is a precondition for improving their livelihood. *Barraqueros* and *beneficiadora* owners view themselves as the protagonists of poverty alleviation. The by now familiar Hecker brothers regularly come up with grandiose schemes that would require the granting of huge concessions for the exploitation of natural resources in the region, or for conservation and carbon dioxide capturing. The areas to be set aside for such schemes often coincide with indigenous peoples' territorial claims, and it is not very clear how the profits would eventually 'trickle down'.[51] Neither is there much to be expected from the smaller 'traditional' *barraqueros*. They lack capital, and mostly seem keen to rid themselves of the 'responsibilities' that went with the moral economy of the *barraca patronal*, while at the same time seeking 'juridical security', perpetuating forms of debt-peonage, and claiming the monopoly over the trade in products extracted from their *barraca*. In some cases *barraca* owners have entered local politics, and managed to become mayor of the municipalities created under the 1994 Popular Participation Law, while in other cases *barraqueros* have set up a Territorial Base Organization under the same law, thus creating 'phantom communities' where they hold sway. For their part, peasant and indigenous communities, with the help of NGOs, are engaged in consolidating their claims, constructing infrastructure to justify these claims, and diversifying their production through agro-forestry schemes. They also seek funding from governmental poverty alleviation programmes and the Popular Participation Law.

Meanwhile, preliminary data from the 2001 census suggest that the decline in absolute numbers of the rural population registered between 1976 and 1992 has been reversed. In the period 1992–2001 urbanization continued apace, while the rural population of the region grew by 1.8 per cent annually. Although the data are still preliminary, this reversal of the tendency toward absolute decline may be due both to the efforts of NGOs to improve rural living conditions and also to the increased investment in rural areas under the Popular Participation Law. The data also suggest that rural population growth in Vaca Díez Province is higher than in the Pando Department.[52] This points to continuing concentration of the population in the vicinity of urban centres, where people can combine involvement in agricultural or agro-forestry activities with the benefits of urban services, such as education. The demographic dynamics of the region need further research when more detailed and definitive census data become available, for example to assess the growth of the emerging regional sub-centres. However, one may safely assume that the bulk of this population growth takes place in the *comunidades libres*, through migration from the *barracas*, natural growth, and perhaps some return migration from the urban areas. What the future will bring will very much depend on the outcome of the current struggle over land and access to resources between agribusiness enterprises and simple commodity producers, itself merely the latest stage in a long history of such conflict in the northern Bolivian Amazon.

GLOSSARY AND ACRONYMS

adjudicación: sale by auction of public lands to private enterprises or farmers who perform an economic-social function
barraca: (rubber and/or Brazil nut) estate
barraca patronal: patron-run *barraca*, in contrast to 'adminstrator'-run *barracas* in the context of the more 'entrepreneurial' organization model that characterized the House of Suárez
barraquero: owner of a *barraca*
beneficiadora: processing plant where Brazil nuts are shelled
centro: forest settlement of a few huts in a *barraca* from where rubber trails start
Centro de Desarrollo Forestal: Centre for Forest Development, local executive agency under the 1974 Forestry Law
chaco patronal: field cultivated under supervision of the patron
comunidad libre: free community
Corporación Boliviano de Fomento: Bolivian Development Corporation
Defensor del Pueblo: (human rights) ombudsman
dotación: land grant to peasant or indigenous communities; land that performs a social function
enganche: coercive form of labour recruitment, literally 'hooking' a worker
fregues: subcontractor on a rubber estate
granja: medium-sized farm
habilito: advance payment, known in Brazil as *aviamento*
Ley del Servicio Nacional de Reforma Agraria, Ley INRA: Law on the National Service for Agrarian Reform, also known as INRA-Law (1996)
Ley Forestal: Forestry Law (1996)
motosierrista: chain-saw owner
payol: storage place in the forest for Brazil nuts
pulpería: company store
quebradora: worker (usually a woman) who shells Brazil nuts in a *beneficiadora*

saneamiento: clarification of land rights
solar campesino: peasant yard
tierra fiscal: public land
trabajadores empatronados: workers in a *barraca patronal*
zafrero: Brazil nut harvester

ABAN: *Asociación de Beneficiadoras del Nordeste*, Association of *Beneficidoras* of the Northeast
ADN: *Acción Democratica Nacionalista*, Nationalist Democratic Action (political party)
ASPROGOAL: *Asociación de Productores de Goma y Almendra*, Association of Producers of Rubber and Brazil nuts (*barraqueros*)
CADEXNOR: *Camara de Exportadores del Norte*, Chamber of Commercial Exporters of the North
CAO: *Camara Agropuecuaria del Oriente*, Chamber of Commercial Agriculturalists of the East
CIDOB: *Confederación Indígena del Oriente, Chaco y Amazonía Boliviana*, Confederation of Indigenous Peoples the Bolivian East, the Chaco and the Amazon
CIRABO: *Central Indígena de la Región Amazónica de Bolivia*, Indigenous Central of the Bolivian Amazon Region
CPESC: *Coordinadora de Pueblos Étnicos de Santa Cruz*, Coordinating Organization of Ethnic Peoples of Santa Cruz
CPIB: *Central de Pueblos Indígenas del Beni*, Central Organization of the Indigenous Peoples of Beni
GANPI: *Gran Asamblea Nacional de Pueblos Indígenas*, Grand National Assembly of Indigenous Peoples
ILO: International Labour Organization
INRA: *Instituto Nacional de Reforma Agraria*, National Agrarian Reform Institute
NGO: Non-Governmental Organization
TCO: *Tierras Comunitarias de Origen*, Original Community Lands (legal figure for the regularization of indigenous territories)

NOTES

1. From the 1970s onward the indigenous peoples of the eastern lowlands had begun to organize with the help of anthropologists and NGOs. This led to the formation of an umbrella organization, the *Confederación Indígena del Oriente, Chaco y Amazonía de Bolivia* (CIDOB), in 1982. In 1990, on the initiative of the *Central de Pueblos Indígenas del Beni* (CPIB), which confronted logging interests in that Department, the peoples of the lowlands undertook a much publicized 'March for Dignity and Territory'. In response to this march, which suddenly made the lowland indigenous people visible, the then President Paz Zamora signed a series of decrees recognizing indigenous territories, and Bolivia ratified ILO Convention 169 (Concerning Indigenous and Tribal Peoples in Independent Countries). A 'Second March', under the banner of 'Land and Territory', took place in September 1996 in the context of the debate and negotiations over new agrarian legislation. The *Ley del Servicio Nacional de Reforma Agraria*, which will be discussed below, was adopted in October 1996 [*Assies*, 2000]. A glossary and a list of acronyms can be found at the end of this article.
2. It should be noted that this periodization departs from the conventional one that takes the collapse of rubber prices in 1913 as a major conjunctural break. Although, as we will see, the 1913 crisis had important effects, the power of the Casa Suárez remained intact.
3. It is estimated that between 250,000 and 500,000 people, mostly males, moved into the Brazilian Amazon region, particularly after a drought hit the Northeast in 1877. About one-third of them are estimated to have moved into the Acre region, which soon became the most important rubber producing area in Brazil [*Costa*, 1992: 39; *Martinello*, 1988: 38]. Sanabria [1988: 94] estimates that, between 1860 and 1910, some 80,000 people from the Bolivian side moved northward, particularly from the Santa Cruz region. According to

Stoian [2000a: 63] this figure may well be a gross overestimate.

4. In Brazil this system is known as the *aviamento*.
5. Though its effects in northern Bolivia were rather limited, the 1953 agrarian reform law contributed to the consolidation of such communities [*Ormachea*, 1987; *Ormachea and Fernández*, 1989]. Officially, according to the 1953 law, rubber tappers would have received two trails to exploit and a small property for agricultural use, totalling up to 500 hectares. The larger properties would be affected according to the norms established for agriculture or cattle-raising in the tropical or subtropical regions, and their maximum extension would be 50,000 hectares in the cases involving cattle herds in excess of 10,000 head. The remaining land would revert to the state.
6. It should be stressed that in view of the highly irregular process of land allocation these data refer to claims rather than to properties. Of the smallholders, at best 5 per cent ever managed to get hold of a title to their parcels, while titles acquired for large holdings are often questionable and frequently unclear as to the real size and location of the area. On the other hand, concessions for forest product exploitation had been given out ever since 1920, and some were reconfirmed during the 1940s by the *Corporación Boliviano de Fomento*. When this agency was dissolved in 1985, the Regional Development Corporation took over this task, though the 1974 Forestry Law made the *Centros de Desarrollo Forestal* responsible for granting permits. In fact, exploitation was based on traditional claims and a few renewed permits. In the early 1990s registration of such permits was non-existent [*DHV*, 1993b] and fees due for exploitation of Brazil nuts were hardly ever paid. In 1996 the Riberalta Forestry Development Centre tried to negotiate payment with the owners of Brazil nut processing plants.
7. Based on a survey of 163 rural settlements, Stoian and Henkemans [2000] have elaborated a detailed classification, which distinguishes four types of *barracas* and six types of independent community. Their analysis of demographic trends details the increase in population in the communities and the decline of the population in *barracas*, as well as the influence on this process of location. They point to the emergence of some regional sub-centres, often located at river crossings where, in the absence of bridges, cars have to be brought over by boat. The rise of these sub-centres was also influenced by the 1994 Popular Participation Law, the aim of which was administrative decentralization and a strengthening of the municipal level. In fact it not only strengthened the few actually existing municipalities but created over 250 new municipalities where they had been virtually non-existent before [*Calla*, 2000; *Nijenhuis*, 2000].
8. Part of the crop is often sold at harvest time, when prices are low, and staples then have to be bought later in the year when prices are on the rise. This is due partly to the need for cash and partly to the lack of adequate storage facilities. In 1994–95 the Riberalta municipality promoted a relatively successful food security programme in some nearby communities, where as a result storage capacity was installed and marketing was improved, resulting in better prices. In 1996, peasants in the area expressed their satisfaction and stated their intention to expand rice production. In remoter areas subsistence agriculture predominates and agricultural produce is bartered, rather than sold [*Assies*, 1997a: 63].
9. For a discussion of the 'urban question' in Riberalta, see van Beijnum [1996] and Verheule [1998].
10. This caused a temporary surge in international prices due to competition among buyers on the Bolivian scene, and a misreading of events by Brazilian exporters, who attributed the reduction in supply to a harvest shortfall in Acre rather than to the newfound market outlets for Bolivian producers who now shipped their produce through the Pacific port of Arica [*Holt*, 1992]. Export prices for shelled nuts went from around US$0.90 per pound in the mid-1980s to US$1.70 per pound in 1989, and then dropped again, according to data from the *Instituto Nacional de Promoción de Exportaciones* (INPEX) and La Fleur [1992].
11. Data supplied by the *Asociación de Beneficiadoras del Norte* (ABAN), and also from my own field data for 1994–97. See also Bojanic [2001: 61] and Coesmans and Medina [1997: 150].
12. For a discussion of resources and resource use in the region, see Beekma, Zonta and Keijzer [1996]. See also the DHV [1993b] studies, as well as Bojanic [2001], Henkemans [2001] and Stoian [2000a].

13. Some processing plants have experimented with mechanical shelling, freezing shells and then projecting them against a hard surface, all with variable success.
14. Letter from Federico G. Hecker H. to Monseñor Luis Morgan Casey, Vicario Apostólico de Pando, Riberalta, 3 March 2000. The letter, written on the occasion of a land dispute, elicited an ironical reply from the local indigenous organization, the *Central Indígena de la Región Amazónica de Bolivia* (CIRABO). The latter first thanks Mr Hecker for acknowledging the genocide perpetrated by his forebears, then enumerates the surviving indigenous peoples, and finally tells Mr Hecker to go and claim property in his homeland, Switzerland, instead of telling the Tacana to return to their homelands, from whence they were dragged by his ancestors [CIRABO, 'Rechazamos guerra sucia en contra de los derechos de los pueblos indígenas en el Norte amazónico de Bolivia,' Riberalta, 8 March 2000].
15. The debate concerns the failure of sustained development in the Amazon region. In contrast to the claim about the draining off of surplus, Weinstein [1993] argues that the failure of Amazon development was due to the persistence of pre-capitalist relations, which she attributes to a tapper–trader alliance. Tappers preferred a certain autonomy rather than engaging in wage labour on plantations, which would have allowed for the development of significant internal markets. Barham and Coomes [1994b; 1996; *Coomes and Barham*, 1994], in contrast, argue that the *habilito* system was an efficient institutional arrangement under the circumstances, and that it allowed for significant local surplus retention. They propose a Dutch disease model to explain the failure of Amazon development. As to the possibilities for plantation production, it should be noted that Dean [1989] has argued that efforts to do this failed basically because of an endemic American leaf blight. In other words, whereas Weinstein locates the difficulty at the level of production relations, Dean attributes the same difficulties to the nature of the productive forces.
16. According to the contract Mr Barbery 'authorized' the Casa Suárez to pay the workers 10 Bolivianos per month, 'in merchandise or money', whereas he himself would receive 100 Bolivianos per worker per month. At the time the nominal exchange rate was 12.5 Bolivianos for every pound sterling [*Sanabria*, 1988: 130].
17. Sanabria [1988: 129] notes that there were cases of upward mobility among this group, but also that many, when receiving payment (in English pounds) at the end of the season, rapidly spent it, and had to reopen an account. The message of such stories is as clear as it is moralizing and apologetic: a dedicated and hardworking rubber tapper, who does not fall ill, despite rampant malaria and snake bites, and who does not squander his credit at the end of the season, could become a subcontractor (*fregues*) and even a patron. No examples are given of rubber tappers becoming patrons at this time, and claims regarding the possibility of upward mobility are consequently problematic.
18. The law is reproduced in Roca [2001: 114–16]. See also Sanabria [1988: 97] and Pacheco [1992: 73–4].
19. Fawcett also reported ill-treatment of rubber tappers to the British Foreign Office [*Fifer*, 1970].
20. When in the 1880s La Paz-based explorers entered the northern Bolivian Amazon to stake out their claims, they met with fierce resistance from the Santa Cruz-based pioneers [*Sanabria*, 1988: 59–67; *Roca*, 2001: 209–13]. The situation became monopolistic with the consolidation of the Suárez empire. According to one of the heirs of the Riberalta-based Braillard Company, later Seiler and finally Hecker Hnos. (Hecker Brothers), it was not for nothing that its main *barracas* were called *Conquista* (Conquest) and *Fortaleza* (Fortress). This reflected their confrontation with the Suárez monopoly (personal communication from Peter Hecker in 1996). The imagery of free access and unbridled competition among a variety of entrepreneurs and merchants to win the clients' favour does not hold in this case. Just like a single swallow does not a summer make, so an occasional 'interloper' does not make for generalized competition.
21. Note that I do not follow the translation by Jack Cohen in Eric Hobsbawm's edition of the *Formen* [*Marx*, 1965: 119]. The translation states: 'If we now talk of plantation-owners in America as capitalists, if they *are* capitalists…'. The German text, however, is quite clearly affirmative: 'sondern daß sie es *sind*…' A more accurate translation might have saved a lot of ink and paper.

22. Although it was invariably a legal fiction, rubber tappers were formally viewed as the owners of their product, which they, contractually, were obliged to sell only to the patron who had 'enabled' them to produce it. The patron thus was the 'mediator' and the 'threshold' between the rubber tapper and the market, and in effect controlled the circulation of goods within his realm, a 'virtual market', an arrangement that was the basis of his 'paternalist exploitation' [*Geffray*, 1995: 13–36].
23. Patron domination relies on a combination of violence and 'favours' that create strong, though ambiguous feelings of dependency and mutual obligation [*Geffray*, 1995]. A striking example of such contradictory feelings can be found in a document of the Brazilian *Conselho Nacional de Seringueiros*, the organization of 'autonomous rubber tappers' founded by Chico Mendes, when it complains that '[N]ot one government ever made the necessary social investment that could cover the costs previously met by the patrons, the *seringalistas*, with the object of maintaining their domination. The whole weight fell on the rubber tapper, as government evaded its obligations' [*CNS*, 1991]. On this point, see also Aramburu [1994].
24. In his famous study of hunger as a man-made phenomenon, Josué de Castro [1963: 106–7] noted that the decline of the rubber trade was accompanied by an improved diet, due to the expansion of subsistence agriculture. The phenomenon is also noted by Romanoff [1992: 131].
25. It was reported that a number of 'free communities' came into existence at this time, either as a result of patrons abandoning their *barraca* or by people moving into unoccupied areas [*Ormachea*, 1987].
26. As Costa Sobrinho [1992: 65] notes, women might even be imported by the patrons as one more item among the *aviamento* supplies, the Brazilian equivalent of the *habilito*.
27. It should be noted that since the early 1990s attempts have been made to formalize labour relations obtaining in the Brazil nut harvest and also in the processing plants, but with limited success. Formalizing labour relations during the harvest would require that the real employers, the *beneficiadora* owners and the *barraqueros*, assume direct responsibility as employers, rather than transferring it to the contractors [*Assies*, 1997a: 55–6]. As to profitability, *beneficiadora* owners complain a lot, and the Hecker brothers like to tell anyone who wants to hear it that actually they are 'socialists of sorts' by virtue of providing employment to the population of a backward region while earning hardly anything themselves. During my research in 1995 and 1996, however, I was shown some feasibility studies for *beneficiadoras*, which showed rather handsome profit expectations, and I made an approximate calculation of the distribution of benefits from the nut trade in Bolivia. This showed that out of the world market price for a kilogram of shelled nuts, 16 per cent goes to the *zafrero* (harvester), 11 per cent to the *barraquero*, and 8 per cent to the *quebradora* (the women who shell the nuts in the *beneficiadoras*). The remaining 64 per cent consists of operating costs for the processing plants, transportation costs, intermediary costs, and profits. I concluded that the *beneficiadora* owners had no reason at all to complain [*Assies*, 1997a: 59]. According to Stoian [2000a: 144 n.], who does not address the methodological issue of the calculation involved, my view is an 'impressionistic' one which unjustifiably attributes 'excessive gains to the entrepreneurial class'. Implying that 'erroneous – but perhaps politically motivated – results can be produced', he then argues that 'the facts [...] are different', and that 'the profit after taxes of a typical processing plant is rather modest'. Although he does estimate the share of *beneficiadora* owners, which I did not do, Stoian's [2000a: 146] calculation does not contradict my findings where the other actors are concerned. The harvester's share in the world market price of a pound of nuts could go from 14 per cent to 34 per cent in an exceptionally good year (1997/98), the *barraquero* share is 14 per cent in that same year, and the *quebradora* share is 8.4 per cent. According to this calculation the *beneficiadora* owner's share was 11.3 per cent. Bojanic [2001: 70] provides some insight into how this translates into incomes from the nut trade. The 25 *beneficiadora* owners earn US$5,000 per month, all year round, which means an annual income of US$60,000. The 5,800 harvesters are employed for three months a year, and during this period earn only US$173 per month, or US$520 per year. The 2,500 *quebradoras*, who are formally employed to work nine months per year and themselves earn US$160 per month, or US$1,443 per year, while their 4,000 informally employed 'helpers' also work nine

months annually, but earn only US$40 per month or US$360 per year. Three hundred and fifty *barraqueros* earn US$500 during six months or US$3,000 per year. According to Bojanic [2001: 82] such data not only do 'not reflect a high inequality in the distribution of income', but they show that the lower income groups (harvesters and *quebradoras*) get a daily or monthly wage higher than that paid by other forms of employment available to non-skilled labour. He recommends calculating Gini coefficients and Lorenz curves. Elsewhere Bojanic [2001: 174] shows that 80 per cent of the households in the region live below the US$2 line and 44 per cent live below the US$1 line: in other words, they are extremely poor. The 18 per cent who are 'not poor' account for 36 per cent of the regional income and the 4.5 per cent in the 'higher income' bracket for 15 per cent.

28. The average parcel size in the area is about 50 hectares. This is barely sufficient for sustainable slash and burn agriculture, based on the cultivation of about 2 hectares and a regeneration period of about 25 years. Soils in the region as a whole are extremely poor, and hardly apt for agriculture. One study [*DHV*, 1993b] suggests that the costs of slash and burn agriculture are economically higher than the value it produces. Extraction of forest products would therefore be an alternative, and at the same time would contribute to forest conservation. According to a document prepared by an NGO in Riberalta, in order to earn about US$1,727 per year, a peasant household containing six persons and relying on a combination of agriculture and extractivism would need access to between 300 and 500 hectares of forest land. Similar calculations have been made for the Brazilian extractive reserves, which were created in response to the rubber tappers movement led by Chico Mendes [*Allegreti*, 1990; 1994; *Brown and Rosendo*, 2000; *Mendes*, 1992].
29. Henkemans [2001] discusses the problems of a remote community attempting to become independent from a patron.
30. On the other hand, Stoian points out that vertical integration was accompanied by a tendency toward horizontal integration, that is a diversification of production into palm heart production and logging.
31. In the course of the year 2000, when clarification of land rights had finally started, and after the 'Third March', a technical commission made up of interested parties and various civil society organizations identified 167 communities in the Vaca Díez Province and 307 in the Pando Department. The total number of *barracas* may be around 300 to 350.
32. In Bolivia the highland Indian population rejects the term *indígena* and instead insists on being called *originario*, which in their view better indicates that they were there before either the Spanish conquest or the subsequent formation of the Bolivian state. The indigenous population of the lowlands is estimated at some 220,000 people belonging to 30 different groups. The Quechua, Aymara and Uru of the highlands would number over 4 million.
33. In practice the paying of tax was taken as proof that land fulfilled its economic–social function, a point that was immediately challenged by peasant organizations.
34. This is meant basically to provide an area to be used by chainsaw owners (*motosierristas*), who until then had exploited resources in a highly irregular way. They now should form an association and work according to a management plan.
35. In March 1999 the International Labour Organization (ILO) issued a series of recommendations on this case [*Tamburini*, 2000].
36. Possibly the decree was also a reward for support given to *Acción Democrática Nacionalista* (ADN), the main party of President Banzer's governing coalition, during the 1997 elections.
37. Throughout the debate over the Forestry Law the timber industry has lobbied for full private ownership of forest-lands [*Pavez and Bojanic*, 1998].
38. See *Superintendencia Agraria, 16 November 1999, Despacho 715/99.*
39. Later the INRA produced maps showing the area claimed by *barracas* and the distribution of communities that had obtained legal personality under the Popular Participation Law of 1994, which are by no means all the existing communities. These maps show clearly the extent to which these rival claims overlap.
40. *Castaña* is the local term for Brazil nuts.
41. *Beneficiadora* owners regularly invoke doom-laden scenarios to defend their interests, and threaten to shut down their operations. The support on the part of the President of the

Federation of Rubber and Brazil Nut Workers partly reflects the interests of the urban-based work force that participates in the Brazil nut harvest. It should be noted, however, that both the role and representativeness of this organization are rather doubtful. It holds office in ASPROGOAL – that is, under the auspices of the employers' organization. The Civic Committee Manifesto mentioned various local NGOs with which it claims to cooperate, but it is far from clear that these organizations would support the manifesto.

42. The stipulation that 500 hectares should be the minimum seems to be the result of a lapse by one of the government delegates during the Montero negotiations. Consultants had recommended that the families should be granted between 300 and 500 hectares.
43. The lack of advance in the Gran Chaco region possibly contributed to the conflict between the emerging movement of landless peasants and allegedly paramilitary 'peasants with land', a clash that claimed seven lives in November 2001.
44. Included in the agreement was the fact that at least 50 per cent of the land on such farms should be worked. An earlier modification of the regulations already introduced the norm that such properties should be worked with wage labour, that technical/mechanical productive forces should be used, and that production should be destined for the market. As noted, initially the payment of tax was taken as sufficient evidence for the performance of the social–economic function.
45. Only part of the workforce employed in the shelling plants is officially registered as such. These workers – mostly women – are often 'helped' by family members who are not themselves officially registered as part of the labour force.
46. Obviously, the scheme is rather questionable. At issue is who really benefited. Clearly, the harvesters receive more, provided that the system works, but the *beneficiadoras* would at the same time receive an indirect subsidy, receiving their raw material at an extremely low cost. On the whole, the scheme proposed could not help but end in a huge fraud.
47. There are pressures from the business lobby to reform the constitution on this point.
48. The argument is not terribly convincing. As we saw, the bottom price for exploitation licences was set at US$1, and it was expected that it would rise as a result of competition. That has not been the case, since the fee was lowered to promote 'economic reactivation'.
49. On this point, see Zoomers [2000: 299].
50. On this point, see Carter [2000] and Carter and Salgado [2001].
51. Kaimowititz and Bojanic [1998] provide another example. In the late 1990s, when Freddy Hecker was Mayor of Riberalta, he proposed that the municipal forest reserve, defined in a way to make it overlap with an indigenous territorial claim, should be exploited by a Cuban enterprise, rather than by local 'social associations' of chainsaw operators.
52. This poses a problem. As we saw, parcel sizes in Vaca Díez Province are relatively small. Although until now the communities have sought to accommodate newcomers, the latter receive increasingly smaller parcels, and within the communities some people have no holding at all. Peasant organizations have started to raise the question of a redistribution of land within the communities once they have received their collective title.

REFERENCES

Allegretti, M.H., 1990, 'Extractive Reserves: An Alternative for Reconciling Development and Environmental Conservation in Amazonia', in A.B. Anderson (ed.), *Alternatives to Deforestation, Steps Toward Sustainable Use of the Amazon Rain Forest*, New York: Columbia University Press.

Allegretti, M.H., 1994, 'Policies for the Use of Renewable Natural Resources: The Amazon Region and Extractive Activities', in M. Clüsener-Godt and I. Sachs (eds.), *Extractivism in the Brazilian Amazon: Perspectives on Regional Development*, Paris: UNESCO (MAB Digest 18).

Aramburu, M., 1994, 'Aviamento, Modernidade e Pós-Modernidade no Interior Amazónico?', *Revista Brasileira de Ciências Sociais*, No.25.

Assies, W., 1997a, *Going Nuts for the Rainforest: Non-Timber Forest Products, Forest Conservation and Sustainability in Amazonia*, Amsterdam: Thela.

Assies, W., 1997b, 'The Extraction of Non-Timber Forest Products as a Rainforest Conservation Strategy', *European Review of Latin American Studies*, No.62.

Assies, W., 2000, 'Multiethnic Constitutionalism, Territories and Internal Boundaries: The Bolivian Case', in CEDLA (ed.), *Fronteras: Towards a Borderless Latin America*, Amsterdam: CEDLA.

Barham, B.L. and O.T. Coomes, 1994a, 'Wild Rubber: Industrial Organization and the Microeconomics of Extraction During the Amazon Rubber Boom (1860–1920)', *Journal of Latin American Studies*, Vol.26, Part 1.

Barham, B.L. and O.T. Coomes, 1994b, 'Reinterpreting the Amazon Rubber Boom: Investment, the State, and Dutch Disease', *Latin American Research Review*, Vol.29, No.2.

Barham, B.L. and O.T. Coomes, 1996, *Prosperity's Promise; The Amazon Rubber Boom and Distorted Economic Development*, Boulder CO, Oxford: Westview Press.

Beekma, J., A. Zonta and B. Keijzer, 1996, *Base ambiental para el desarrollo; Departamento de Pando y la provincia de Vaca Diez*, Riberalta: SNV (cuaderno de trabajo 3).

Beijnum, P. van, 1996, *Problemática Urbana Riberalta*, Riberalta: SNV (cuadernos de trabajo 4).

Betancur, A.C., 2000, 'La conversión de la barracas al régimen de concesiones; Nueva expropiación a comunidades campesinas e indígenas en el Norte amazónico', *Artículo Primero*, Año 4, No.8.

Bojanic Helbingen, A.J., 2001, *Balance is Beautiful: Assessing the Sustainable Development in the Rain Forests of the Bolivian Amazon*, Utrecht: Faculteit Ruimtelijke Wetenschappen, PROMAB Scientific Series 4.

Brown, K. and S. Rosendo, 2000, 'Environmentalists, Rubber Tappers and Empowerment: The Politics and Economics of Extractive Reserves', *Development and Change*, Vol.31, No.1.

Calla, R., 2000, 'Indigenous Peoples, the Law of Popular Participation and Changes in Government: Bolivia, 1994–1998', in W. Assies, G. van der Haar and A.J. Hoekema (eds.), *The Challenge of Diversity: Indigenous Peoples and Reform of the State in Latin America*, Amsterdam: Thela.

Carter, M.R., 2000, 'Old Questions and New Realities: Land in Post-Liberal Economies', in A. Zoomers and G. van der Haar (eds.), *Current Land Policy in Latin America; Regulating Land Tenure under Neoliberalism*, Amsterdam, Frankfurt/Main: KIT, Iberoamericana/Vervuert Verlag.

Carter, M.R. and R. Salgado, 2001, 'Land Market Liberalization and the Agrarian Question in Latin America', in A. de Janvry, G. Gordillo, J-P. Plateau and E. Sadoulet (eds.), *Access to Land, Rural Poverty and Public Action*, Oxford: Oxford University Press.

Castro, J. de ,1963, *Geografia da Fome, Vol. I*, São Paulo: Brasiliense.

Chevalier, J.M., 1983, 'There is Nothing Simple About Simple Commodity Production', *The Journal of Peasant Studies*, Vol.10, No.4.

CNS, 1991, *Relatório do Seminário: Alternativas Econômicas para as Reservas Extrativistas*, Rio Branco: Conselho Nacional de Seringeiros.

Coesmans, K. and M. del Carmen Medina I., 1997, *Entre contradicciones y suerte; Una mirada en la realidad cotidiana de las mujeres campesinas y quebradoras de Riberalta y sus alrededores*, Riberalta: Unidad de la Mujer-Radio San Miguel.

Contreras-Hermosilla, Arnoldo and María Teresa Vargas Ríos, 2001, 'Dimensiones sociales, ambientales y económicas de las reformas en la política forestal de Bolivia', Center for International Forestry Research, CIFOR working paper.

Coomes, O.T. and B.L. Barham, 1994, 'The Amazon Rubber Boom: Labor Control, Resistance, and Failed Plantation Development Revisited', *Hispanic American Historical Review*, Vol.74, No.2.

Costa Sobrinho, P.V., 1992, *Capital e Trabalho na Amazônia Ocidental*, São Paulo, Rio Branco: Cortez, UFAC.

Dean, W., 1989, *A luta pela borracha no brasil; Um estudo de históriao ecológica*, São Paulo: Nobel.

Deininger, K. and H. Biswanger, 2001, 'The Evolution of the World Bank's Land Policy', in A. de Janvry, G. Gordillo, J-P. Plateau and E. Sadoulet (eds.), *Access to Land, Rural Poverty and Public Action*, Oxford: Oxford University Press.

DHV, 1993a, *Desarrollo de la Amazonia Boliviana. De la Actividad Extractiva hacia un Desarrollo Integral Sostenible, Resumen Ejecutivo*, Bolivia, Proyecto de Desarrollo

Agropecuario, Banco Mundial/Gobierno de Holanda.

DHV, 1993b, *Tenencia de la Tierra en la Región Castañera de la Amazonia Boliviana*, Bolivia, Proyecto de Desarrollo Agropecuario, Banco Mundial/Gobierno de Holanda.

Fifer, J.V., 1970, 'The Empire Builders; A History of the Bolivian Rubber Boom and the Rise of the House of Suárez', *Journal of Latin American Studies*, Vol.2, No.2.

Geffray, C., 1995, *Chroniques de la servitude en Amazonie brésilienne*, Paris: Karthala.

Genovese, E.D., 1976, *Roll, Jordan, Roll; The World the Slaves Made*, New York: Vintage Books.

Henkemans, A.B., 2000, 'Social Fencing: Forest Dwellers and Control of Natural Resources in the Northern Bolivian Amazon', in A. Zoomers and G. van der Haar (eds.), *Current Land Policy in Latin America; Regulating Land Tenure under Neoliberalism*, Amsterdam, Frankfurt/Main: KIT, Iberoamericana/Vervuert Verlag.

Henkemans, A.B., 2001, Tranquilidad *and Hardship in the Forest: Livelihoods and Perceptions of* Camba *Forest Dwellers in the Northern Bolivian Amazon*, Riberalta: PROMAB.

Hernáiz, I. and D. Pacheco, 2000, *La Ley INRA en el espejo de la historia; Dos siglos de reformas agrarias en Bolivia*, La Paz: Fundación Tierra.

Holt, J., 1992, 'The Brazil Nut Market: an Analysis Prepared by Amazonia Trading Company Ltd for Sr. Victor Flores Veia, Executive Director of INPEX, La Paz, Bolivia'.

Jones, J.C., 1995, 'Environmental Destruction, Ethnic Discrimination, and International Aid in Bolivia', in M. Painter and W.H. Durham (eds), *The Social Causes of Environmental Destruction in Latin America*, Ann Arbor, MI: University of Michigan Press.

Kaimowitz, D. and A. Bojanic H., 1998, 'Riberalta: extractivistas bajo una elite tradicional', in P. Pacheco and D. Kaimowitz (eds.), *Municipios y gestión forestal en el trópico boliviano*, La Paz: CIFOR.

LaFleur, J.R., 1992, *Marketing of Brazil Nuts*, Rome: FAO.

Lema Garret, A.M. (comp.), 1998, *Pueblos indígenas de la Amazonía boliviana*, La Paz: AIP FIDA-CAF.

Lescure, J-P. (ed.), 1993, 'Les Activités Extractivistes en Amazonie Centrale: Une Première Synthèse d'un Projet Multidisciplinaire', Paris: ORSTOM/INPA (working paper).

Lescure, J-P., F. Pinton and L. Emperaire, 1994, 'People and Forest Products in Central Amazonia: the Multidisciplinary Approach of Extractivism', in M. Clüsener Godt and I. Sachs (eds.), *Extractivism in the Brazilian Amazon: Perspectives on Regional Development*: Paris: UNESCO (MAB Digest No. 18).

MACPIO, 2001, *Pueblos indígenas y originarios de Bolivia, diagnóstico nacional*, La Paz: Ministerio de Asuntos Campesinos, Pueblos Indígenas y Originarios.

Martinello, P., 1988, *A 'Batalha da Borracha' na Segunda Guerra Mundial e suas Conseqüências para o Vale Amazônico*, Rio Branco: UFAC.

Marx, K., 1974, 'Formen, die der kapitalistichen Produktion vorhergehen', in K. Marx and F. Engels, *Staatstheorie; Materialen zur Rekonstuktion der Marxistische Staatstheorie*, Herausgegeben und eingeleited von E. Henning, J. Hirsch, H. Reichelt and G. Schäfer, Frankfurt/M, Berlin, Wien: Ullstein.

Marx, K., 1965, *Pre-Capitalist Economic Formations*, with an introduction by E.J. Hobsbawm, New York: International Publishers.

Mendes, C., 1992, 'Chico Mendes – The Defence of Life', *The Journal of Peasant Studies*, Vol.20, No.1.

Nijenhuis, G., 2000, 'Shifting Borders: The Impact of Bolivia's Decentralization Process on the Local Level', in CEDLA, *Fronteras: Towards a Borderless Latin America*, Amsterdam: CEDLA.

Ormachea , S. E., 1987, *Beni y Pando, Latifundio y Minifundio en el Norte Boliviana*, La Paz: CEDLA.

Ormachea S. E. and J. Fernández, 1989, *Amazonía Boliviana y Campesinado*, La Paz: Cooperativa Agrícola Integral 'Campesino'.

Pacheco, B. P., 1990, *La Situación Socio-Economico de los Trabajadores Asalariados de la Goma y la Castaña*, Riberalta, Guayaramerin: CEDLA.

Pacheco, B. P., 1992, *Integración Económica y Fragmentación Social: El Itinerario de las Barracas en la Amazonia Boliviana*, La Paz: CEDLA.

Pacheco, Balanza P. and H. Ávila, 2000, 'Amazonía boliviana', in M. Urioste and D. Pacheco (eds.), *Las tierras bajas de Bolivia a fines del siglo XX*, La Paz: PIEB.

Pavez Lizarraga, I. and A. Bojanic Helbingen, 1998, *El proceso de formulación de la Ley Forestal de Bolivia de 1996*, La Paz: CIFOR, CEDLA, TIERRA, PROMAB.

Paz, R.V., 1999, *Dominio Amazónico*, La Paz: Plural.

Pinto, N. P. Alves, 1984, *Política da Borracha no Brasil: A Falência da Borracha Vegetal*, São Paulo: Hucitec.

Roca, José Luis, 2001, *Economía y Sociedad en el Oriente Boliviano (Siglos XVI–XX)*, Santa Cruz: COTAS.

Romanoff, S., 1992, 'Food and Debt among Rubber Tappers in the Bolivian Amazon', *Human Organization*, Vol.51, No.2.

Salvatierra G.H., 1996, 'Ley INRA; Entre la realidad del latifundio y la necesidad del cambio social en el mundo agrario boliviano', *Artículo Primero*, año 1, no. 2.

Sanabria Fernández, H., 1988, *En busca de El Dorado*, La Paz: Librería Editorial 'Juventud'.

Solón, P., 1995, *La tierra prometida; un aporte al debate sobre las modificaciones a la legislación agraria*, La Paz: CEDOIN.

Souza, M., 1980, *Mad Maria*, Rio de Janeiro: Civilização Brasileira.

Stoian, D., 2000a, *Variations and Dynamics of Extractive Economies: the Rural–Urban Nexus of Non-Timber Forest Use in the Bolivian Amazon*, Inaugural-Dissertation zur Erlangen der Doktorwürde der Forstwissenschaftlichen Fakultät der Albert-Ludwigs-Universität Freiburg im Bresigau.

Stoian, D., 2000b, 'Shifts in Forest Product Extraction: The Post Rubber Era in the Bolivian Amazon', *International Tree Crop Journal*, Vol.10, No.4.

Stoian, D. and A.B. Henkemans, 2000, 'Between Extractivism and Peasant Agriculture: Differentiation of Rural Settlements in the Bolivian Amazon', *International Tree Crop Journal*, Vol.10, No.4.

Tamburini, L., 2000, 'Otorgamiento de concesiones forestales en territorios indígenas en Bolivia', *Artículo Primero*, Año 4, No. 8.

Urioste, Miguel and Diego Pacheco (eds), 2001, *Las tierras bajas de Bolivia a fines del siglo XX*, La Paz: PIEB.

Urioste, M. and D. Pacheco, 2000, 'Land Market in a New Context: the INRA Law in Bolivia?', in A. Zoomers and G. van der Haar (eds.), *Current Land Policy in Latin America; Regulating Land Tenure under Neoliberalism*, Amsterdam, Frankfurt/Main: KIT, Vervuert Verlag.

Verheule, E., 1998, *Work and Housing in the Periphery of Riberalta, Bolivia*, Utrecht: University of Utrecht, Faculty of Spatial Sciences (MA thesis).

Weber, J., 1994, *Población indígena de las tierras bajas de Bolivia*, Santa Cruz: APCOB.

Weinstein, B., 1993, *A borracha na Amazônia: Expansão e decadencia (1850–1920)*, São Paulo: Hucitec.

Woortman, E.F., 1996, 'Família, mulher e meio ambiente no seringal', Trabalho apresentado na ANPOCS, 1996, GT: Familia e Sociedade.

Zoomers, A., 2000, 'Searching for a New Land Policy: Options and Dilemmas', in A. Zoomers and G. van der Haar (eds.), *Current Land Policy in Latin America; Regulating Land Tenure under Neoliberalism*, Amsterdam, Frankfurt/Main: KIT, Iberoamericana/Vervuert Verlag.

The Impact of Neo-liberal Economics on Peruvian Peasant Agriculture in the 1990s

JOHN CRABTREE

INTRODUCTION

During the 1990s, Peru was among the Latin American countries that underwent the most rapid and radical transformation towards a liberal economy. This had the effect of changing the rules affecting economic agents of all sorts, including peasant producers. Although the collectivist aims of the 1969 agrarian reform legislation had long since been abandoned in favour of policies that sought to privilege market relations in the rural sphere, the liberalization of the agricultural economy became much more explicit in the 1990s. The virtues of free market economics were extolled as a panacea – even for sectors like peasants at the very margins of the economic system. State intervention for agriculture of all sorts was reduced, while producers were forced to compete on more open terms with imports. Such a major transformation naturally brought with it winners and losers in agriculture, just as it did in other sectors of economic life.

The 1969 agrarian reform and its effects on Peruvian agriculture gave rise to a substantial literature in the 1970s, but the changes that have taken place since 1990 have received less attention, especially with regard to peasant economy.[1] Although rural poverty has recently become a major topic of debate, much of the writing has focused more on the provision of different types of social support than on resolving the underlying problems of agriculture. The purpose of this article is to examine the ways in which peasant agriculture has responded to the changes in the economic environment in which it operates and the ways it has impacted on those dependent on it for their livelihood. Overall, the conclusion reached here is that, 12 years after it was originally launched, liberalization has probably

---

John Crabtree is Research Associate at the Centre for Latin American Studies in the University of Oxford. The article is based on an unpublished earlier study for Oxfam on economic liberalization and its impact on rural poverty and inequality in Peru. The author is grateful to Tom Brass for editorial comment and suggestions.

brought more losers than winners, and that many peasant producers have been relegated further to the margins of the economic system. This is a conclusion that has worrying implications for those concerned with reducing rural poverty levels.

This is a discussion that has wider implications for the whole debate surrounding the impact of globalization on those sectors that are ill-equipped to compete in the worldwide marketplace for agricultural commodities of one kind or another. What longer-term economic future do peasant producers have in such a framework? Will we see the same disappearance of the peasantry in Peru that Hobsbawm [1994] has noted elsewhere as being one of the hallmark features of the twentieth century? As we shall see, such producers in Peru – despite continued urbanization – are more numerous than they were 30 years ago, casting doubt on this hypothesis [*Mesclier*, 2000]. Indeed, they still constitute a very significant proportion of the total workforce. Assuming that they will not 'disappear' as such, what sort of future therefore awaits them?

The answer to such questions can be only tentative at best, but the experience in Peru over recent years provides some important pointers as to the dynamics affecting peasants and small-scale producers in Latin America more generally and possibly elsewhere. The approach adopted here is essentially of a 'political economy' nature. While changes in economic policy have major implications for different sectors of agriculture and alter the relations of power among actors, such policies themselves exist within a wider political framework that favours them in some circumstances and prejudices them in others. Therefore, as well as analysing the impact of structural adjustment on small-scale producers, it is also necessary to understand the political transformations that have taken place in the past two decades which made such structural adjustment possible in the first place.

The article therefore seeks to highlight both the economic policies employed and their impact, along with the declining significance of 'producer politics' at the national level during the 1980s and 1990s. It begins with a short characterization of the agricultural sector generally, its heterogeneity and volatility, before moving on to considering the key policies followed since 1990 and their effects. It continues with an evaluation of the extent to which producers' ability to articulate their interests and negotiate policy was circumscribed during these years.[2]

However, before going into detail, it is important first to provide some elements of the geographical and historical context and to say a little about what we mean by the 'peasant economy'. As will become clear, this article follows a fairly wide definition of 'peasant producers', defining these as small-scale, independent producers whose workforce consists mainly of family labour.[3] Such producers are not necessarily delimited to the highlands of Peru (where they still predominate) but abound also in other areas of the country. Equally, there are peasant farmers, so defined, working in the jungle and on the coast. Nor are we necessarily talking about those for whom subsistence agriculture is the only or even the main activity, since many such producers have long been highly integrated into the market economy, even in some instances as exporters. It is therefore no longer possible to isolate peasant producers from the rest of the agricultural sector; rather they need to be viewed as a key and integral part of an overall economic system that is no longer limited to a single geographical or ecological zone, even though a large number of those we classify as 'peasants' may still reside in the highlands (*sierra*).

The article will also include some reflections on the implications that this may have for policies to reduce poverty. Since poverty – especially extreme poverty – is concentrated in the rural sector and since the majority of those who live in poverty live off the land, it is not possible to hive off discussions about agricultural policy from those designed to alleviate poverty. The ways in which agricultural policies are designed have an obvious and immediate impact on social conditions in rural areas, irrespective of other policies that may be pursued. Despite the large sums expended by the Fujimori administration (1990–2000) on programmes of social relief in rural areas, the logic of these was largely assistentialist and often unrelated to improving the productive economy of producers in rural areas. Rather, the consequence of economic liberalization seems to have been to increase rather than diminish social inequality, contributing little to the problems afflicting the poorest farmers. That this appears to be the case also reflects the political weakness of peasant producers in making their interests felt in spheres of decision-making. The return to a more democratic government in 2001, committed to improving levels of political participation as well as tackling poverty, may create a more propitious environment for peasant agriculture. Whether this happens remains to be seen.

THE PEASANT ECONOMY IN PERU

The first (and perhaps the most obvious) point that needs to be made about Peruvian agriculture is its extreme heterogeneity. This heterogeneity is defined both by the country's highly differentiated geography and ecology, as well as by widely differing degrees of commercialization, levels of productivity and access to markets. There are few countries in the world where farmers operate in such a broad range of ecological zones, producing such a wide diversity of agricultural output. Equally, the social composition of the agricultural sector is highly differentiated, ranging from subsistence agriculture in the *sierra* to cash-crop agriculture in the irrigated valleys of the coast (*costa*) and the Amazonian jungle (*selva*), geared more to meeting urban and export demand. The social, political and cultural conditions in rural Peru reflect this heterogeneity, greatly complicating the challenges for framing public policy.

The country divides naturally into these three major areas, although there is also a great deal of diversity within each of them.[4] Firstly, there are the irrigated valleys of the coast. This is where Peru's more profitable farms are located, benefiting from high levels of irrigation and relatively easy access to key urban centres and export markets. In the past 20 years, coastal agriculture has benefited from a number of large, high-cost irrigation projects (e.g. Majes and Chavimochic) which have absorbed the lion's share of agricultural investment, albeit to the benefit of relatively few producers. Agriculture in the coastal desert area is almost entirely dependent on irrigation. Secondly, there is the *sierra*, where mostly peasant farmers produce both for their own subsistence and the market (or a combination of the two). Peasant communities still predominate, although in practice most production is now organized on the basis of individual landholding [*Eguren*, 1999]. Some areas of the *sierra* (e.g. the Mantaro valley) are important sources of food for coastal cities, but under increasing competitive pressure from coastal agriculture and imports. Yields in the *sierra* are typically much lower than on the coast, good agricultural land is scarcer and rates of poverty higher. Thirdly, there is tropical agriculture in the *selva.* Typical crops include rice, coffee and citrus, but this is also where Peru's illegal coca is grown and coca competes with other legal crops. For good or for ill, coca has been one of Peru's most dynamic cash crops during the last 20 years. Most farmers in the *selva* are of highland origin, although units of landholding tend to be larger and more productive than in most parts of the sierra. The region suffers from distance from markets and poor communication with the outside world, except possibly in the case of coca, which has its own distinctive marketing mechanisms (see Map 1).

This pattern of heterogeneity is as true for small-scale peasant agriculture as it is for agriculture as a whole, perhaps even more so. The universe of peasant production incorporates not just the *sierra* but also the *costa* and *selva*. Although the majority of subsistence farmers are still concentrated in the *sierra*, small-scale agriculture is dominant in terms of the number of units in the other two main regions as well. According to the 1994 agricultural census – the most recent comprehensive source of data at the time of writing – small-scale units of landholding represented 92 per cent of all productive units in Peru, an even higher proportion than ten years earlier. Of these, the huge majority are independent households [*Ministerio de Agricultura*, 2001]. Even around 60 per cent of agricultural exports came from small-scale units of landholding, principally coffee and cotton (not to

MAP 1

COLOMBIA
0° Equator
ECUADOR
Tumbes
TUMBES
Iquitos
LORETO
PIURA
Piura
AMAZONAS
Chachapoyas
Moyobamba
CAJA MARCA
LAMBAYEQUE
Chiclayo
Cajamarca
SAN MARTIN
BRAZIL
LA LIBERTAD
Trujillo
Pucallpa
ANCASH
Huaraz
HUANUCO
Huanuco
PASCO
UCAYALI
Cerro de Pasco
JUNIN
LIMA
Huancayo
MADRE DE DIOS
Callao
Lima
Huancavelica
Pto Maldonado
Ayacucho
HUANCA VELICA
CUZCO
Pacific Ocean
Cuzco
Abancay
APURIMAC
Ica
AYACUCHO
ICA
BOLIVIA
PUNO
Lake Titicaca
Puno
AREQUIPA
Arequipa
MOQUEGUA
Moquegua
TACNA
Tacna
CHILE
Land over 2000 metres
Departmental boundary
Departmental capital
0
100
200
300 miles

Peru

mention coca). The highest concentration of small units is found, as one would expect, in the *sierra*, especially in the departments of Puno, Cusco, Cajamarca and Ancash.

The definition used in the census of a 'small-scale producer' is one with up to 20 hectares of land. Such an upwards limit is perhaps excessive, especially in view of the fact that there is an enormous difference in the productive potential of 20 hectares of irrigated land on the coast and the same amount of non-irrigated land in the *sierra.* If we take a rather more conservative definition (subject to the same caveats about differentiation between areas) of 5 hectares or less, 'small-scale' production still represented over 70 per cent of all agricultural units in 1994, among which great diversity was also to be found.[5] In terms of geographical distribution, the areas of the country where the average unit of landholding was 2 hectares or less were concentrated in the *sierra*, notably the highland zones of Apurímac, Moquegua, Junín, Lima and Pasco. The average for the *sierra* as a whole was below 3 hectares, whilst the largest average units were to be found in the jungle areas of the country.

This pattern of heterogeneity among small-scale producers has became more pronounced because of the generalized tendency, dating from the early 1980s, towards the subdivision of the large, collective units established both in the *sierra* and in the *costa* under the agrarian reform legislation. The abandonment of the policies associated with agrarian reform led to the *parcelación* of land into small, family-based units of independent producers. Small-scale units are now the predominant forms of landholding in many of the coastal valleys, increasing substantially the proportion of small-scale producers in this part of the country. However, the same tendency is observable in the *sierra* as well, leading to increasing differentiation among highland *parceleros*, a dynamic that emerges clearly from a comparison of the 1972 agricultural census data with that of 1994. In 1972, just after the agrarian reform, the number of independent small-scale producers stood at just under 50 per cent of the total, while by 1994 this had increased to 63 per cent. Indeed, *parcelación*, coupled with demographic pressure on land, has given rise in many cases to a renewed *minifundización* along the coast, with the proportion of very small units (e.g. 1 hectare or less) increasing quite notably in the 1980s and 1990s.

Other key defining characteristics that differentiate sectors of agriculture (especially among small-scale producers) include the application of technology and practices of marketing. An overall characteristic of Peruvian agriculture is its low rate of productivity when compared with other sectors of the economy, but the rates of application of even fairly basic technology vary enormously between the *costa* and *selva* on the one hand and the *sierra* on the other. Again, the 1994 census shows that the highly differentiated use of improved seeds, chemical inputs, mechanization and electrical (or other) sorts of energy, with much higher rates on the coast than in the highlands. At the same time, there is an ever-increasing differentiation among small-scale producers in terms of the markets they serve. While the overall trend is clearly towards increasing participation in the market economy with an increase in the proportion of tradeables, the great majority of land in the hands of small-scale producers in highland Puno in 1994 was still devoted to subsistence farming, whereas in coastal Piura most small-scale farmers were involved in commercial agriculture selling into urban markets.

The performance of agriculture has been fairly volatile in the past three decades, with growth rates considerably less dynamic in the *sierra* than in other parts of the country. Between 1975 and 1990, agricultural production grew at an annual rate of 1.9 per cent, well below the overall rate of demographic growth, let alone that of rural Peru. Agriculture's contribution to global GDP fell from 23 per cent in 1950 to 12 per cent in 1989. It currently stands at around 14 per cent of GDP.[6] This decline is particularly noticeable in the area of foreign trade, with agricultural exports accounting for only 11 per cent of exports compared with over 50 per cent in 1950.

Volatility of output from one year to another is primarily a function of three key factors. The first of these is variation in the level of demand, particularly in the urban economy. Aggregate demand in the economy has been even more volatile in Peru than in most other Latin American countries, with protracted periods of recession interspersed by sudden (unsustainable) spurts of growth.[7] A succession of macroeconomic stabilization packages under the aegis of the IMF has sought to rectify disequilibria on the balance of payments basically by controlling aggregate demand. Given Peru's skewed pattern of income distribution, such demand management tended to hit demand for food particularly hard, thereby impacting on agricultural prices and output. The second major source of short-term volatility is climatic variation. The country's exposure to the periodic El Niño phenomenon has a direct and sometimes dramatic bearing on agricultural output.[8] The Niño results in changed patterns of rainfall, generating drought conditions where harvests depend on timely rainfall and floods that disrupt communications (and therefore channels of marketing) in areas where normally there is scant rainfall. The two most disastrous Niños of recent times were those of 1983 and 1998, although there have been less severe ones in the intervening years and since 1998. The third major factor was the effect of political violence in the 1980s and early 1990s. This had a major impact on output, especially in parts of the *sierra* like Ayacucho, that underwent severe depopulation with the consequent interruption that this caused for the agricultural economy.[9]

Of course, agriculture has also been affected by the direction of sectoral policy under a succession of different governments. The agrarian reform implemented by the military government in the 1970s changed the structure of landholding through the expropriation of landed estates and the reorganization of these into cooperatives of varying types. By providing land to those who had been previously landless, it represented a major step towards greater equity in the countryside. It also established new channels of participation. However, it failed to provide the ancillary services (such as training, credit and technical inputs) required to make the new system economically viable in the longer run [*Caballero*, 1980]. Also, as a reform imposed 'from above' rather than emanating 'from below', it was particularly susceptible to shifts in government policy. As output levels dwindled in the years after the reform, pressure built up to change the model. In the late 1970s and early 1980s, the agrarian reform was abandoned and the process of dividing up the cooperatives began. The implementation of stabilization policies from the late 1970s on – coupled with the negative effects of political violence from 1980 onwards – created a situation that was particularly damaging to peasant interests, especially in the *sierra*. As we shall see, the decline in the organized political strength of the peasantry dates from this period. The García government (1985–90) gave rhetorical support to the need to boost the peasantry as one of the least favoured sectors of society, but in practice did little to redirect policy to this end. While the abandonment of IMF orthodoxy in favour of demand-led heterodoxy created a short-term economic boom in agricultural prices in 1985–87, this policy proved unsustainable. The return to (unsuccessful) stabilization policies in the late 1980s had a devastating effect on agricultural prices (and therefore rural incomes) from which most of the agricultural sector found it hard to recover in the 1990s.

One of the main conclusions of most studies on the long-run performance in Peruvian agriculture is the negative impact of overall policy – one way or another – on the rural sector, particularly those small-scale farmers most dependent on domestic demand for food [*Figueroa*, 1992]. Broadly speaking, this was because one of the strategic constants was the need of successive governments to provide a sufficiently plentiful supply of cheap food to an increasingly urban population. Whereas in 1950 Peru was one-third urban and two-thirds rural, 30 years later these proportions had been inverted. Partly through exchange rate policies, partly through price controls, this 'anti-agrarian bias' encouraged an increased reliance on food imports that competed on advantageous terms with locally produced staples. Over the long term, changes in consumption patterns – strongly promoted by importers – would further marginalize local products, to the disadvantage in particular of small-scale producers in the *sierra*. Peruvian agro-industry has resorted to importing the inputs for the food industry – notably grains, milk products and vegetable oils – used to make basic food products. In 1970, for instance, Peru imported 500,000 tonnes of food, whilst itself producing 2.7 million tonnes. By 1998, it was importing 3.2 million tonnes of food, whilst producing 3.8 million.

THE NEO-LIBERAL AGENDA

The liberalizing agenda took shape soon after the inauguration of Alberto Fujimori in July 1990. Although there had been moves in this direction in the early 1980s, these had been half-hearted and had encountered stiff political opposition. Fujimori's approach to stabilization – the so-called 'Fujishock' of August 1990 – was full-blooded and implemented 'without anaesthetics'. The series of stabilization packages that began in 1988 sought to change the pattern of relative prices within the economy. They had dramatic short-run effects on living standards, the rate of aggregate demand in the economy and – consequently – prices for agricultural goods. Fujimori was able to bring rampant inflation under control and therefore move to the sort of restructuring of the economy that had been impossible previously. His strategy was to push ahead with a radical restructuring of the economy along neo-liberal lines, removing the last vestiges of the state-oriented ISI model introduced in the 1970s. This involved a drastic reduction in public sector activity, the deregulation of markets (including the labour market), the encouragement of privatization and foreign investment, the dismantling of industrial protection and the gradual reorientation of the economy towards export-led growth.

These two strategies – one short-term stabilization and the other longer-term structural adjustment – were regarded as distinct (there were some inconsistencies between them) but complementary. They were enthusiastically backed by the IMF and World Bank, which rewarded Fujimori by facilitating the restructuring of the foreign debt.[10] Policy followed IMF prescriptions to the letter, irrespective of the short-term social costs. It was pursued with particularly single-minded zeal under Carlos Boloña, appointed finance minister in 1991, driven more by macroeconomic exigency than by the needs of individual economic sectors. For most of the Fujimori period, the role of the agriculture ministry was subservient to that of the finance ministry, its capacity to intervene in the sector increasingly limited by the government's rejection of state intervention in the productive sphere. Agriculture, indeed, received less priority than other sectors (such as mining and energy), and within it greater attention was given to boosting the more commercially viable sectors (especially the export sector). Resolving the problems of small-scale producers was not a major priority [*Hopkins*, 1998].

Meanwhile, the compression of domestic demand, first under García after 1988 and subsequently under Fujimori, had an immediate and very negative impact on those sectors of agriculture producing for the domestic, urban market. The Fujishock involved a dramatic adjustment of domestic prices, a major one-off devaluation and a sharp rise in domestic interest rates, all of which had important implications for agricultural producers. However, the structural and institutional reforms that followed were to have more profound and lasting effects. These included trade liberalization, exchange rate appreciation, the ending of state subsidies in marketing, the closure of the agrarian bank (Banco Agrario), institutional downsizing and the promotion of land titling.

In 1990 and 1991, the Fujimori government radically altered the nature of tariff and non-tariff protection for agriculture, as well as other sectors of the economy. The purpose of trade liberalization was to reorient the economy away from ISI towards export-led growth, and at once to improve the efficiency and lower the costs of domestic production. In agriculture, the idea was that cheaper inputs would help boost exports and make Peruvian output more internationally competitive. At the same time, it was hoped that trade liberalization would lower domestic food prices and therefore contribute to reducing inflation. Tariffs (with some exceptions) were thus reduced from an average of 56 per cent to two basic rates of 15 per cent and 25 per cent, and were lowered still further in 1996. In order to compensate specific agricultural sectors, a system of fixed and variable surcharges was introduced in 1992, effectively taxes on five basic commodity imports: hard maize, rice, sugar, milk powder and wheat. These helped shield some agricultural producers from cheap foreign imports, but were vigorously opposed by well-organized lobbies of importers. In 1998, for instance, lobbying from the Alicorp consortium (an amalgam of the powerful Nicolini and Romero groups) encouraged the government to drop the surcharge on imported wheat.

The effects of trade liberalization were compounded by exchange rate policy [*Gonzales de Olarte*, 1996]. Following the 1990 devaluation, the central bank managed the currency in such a way as to lead to progressive appreciation in real terms. This made it cheaper to import agricultural commodities, but reduced the effective protection afforded to domestic producers. The extent of overvaluation at any one point is difficult to determine, but the devaluation of the *sol* lagged well behind domestic inflation for much of the 1990s.

Fujimori inherited a system that involved heavy state intervention in the agricultural sector through price controls and a state monopoly over the trading of food and inputs. Amongst his first moves was to scrap price controls, allowing these to be set by market forces. This, it was argued, would work to the advantage of agriculture generally, since price controls had not benefited producers. Fujimori also abolished two institutions which had played a key role as intermediary between producer and consumer since the time of Velasco government (1968–75): the *Empresa Comercializadora de Arroz* (ECASA) and the *Empresa Nacional Comercializadora de Insumos* (ENCI). The former had had a legal monopoly over the trading of rice, a key staple in the Peruvian diet, ensuring politically influential rice producers an above-market return on their crop. The latter controlled imports of food and fertilizer.

As well as closing ECASA and ENCI, the new government eliminated the Banco Agrario as a source of subsidized credit to producers. At its height, the Banco Agrario had been lending up to 1 billion dollars a year in cheap credit. Although an important source of finance to the agricultural sector, the bank had become a nexus for corruption and influence-peddling, especially during the García administration. In its place, it was hoped that commercial lenders would provide the finance required, or otherwise the *cajas rurales.* In practice, commercial lenders showed little interest in lending to the agricultural sector, particularly to small-scale producers, perceiving it as high-risk and lacking adequate collateral. The experience of the *cajas rurales* also proved disappointing. Between 1993 and 1995, 12 were established, their number subsequently rising to 17. By 2001, only five were still functional, all on the coast and many lending for purposes other than agriculture.

As mentioned above, the agriculture ministry underwent a radical reformulation as the role of the state in agriculture was reduced [*Santa Cruz*, 1999]. This was largely at the behest of the multilateral financial organizations, the size of whose past loans to the agriculture sector gave them considerable leverage. The ministry, accused by its critics of waste and corruption, was reduced in size from 23,000 employees in 1990 to just 5,000 in 1996. As with other reforms to the public administration, this downsizing was conducted in an ad hoc fashion with little prior planning. In many instances, ministry programmes were abruptly suspended or handed over to private sector entities. Lacking state capacities, Peru was poorly placed to enter into the sort of 'second generation' reforms pursued elsewhere in Latin America.

The attempt to create a functioning market economy in rural Peru was one of the more ambitious of the Fujimori reforms. Consonant with the drift of neo-liberal reform, this represented the most decisive break with the spirit of the agrarian reform. It was hoped that the widening of private ownership would extend the benefits of liberalization to a large number of small-scale producers. The aim of building a market in land was clear in Decree Law 658 of 1991, but was made more explicit with the 1995 Land Law (*Ley de tierras*) [*Del Castillo*, 1997]. This provided property guarantees to titleholders, abolished the previous upper limits on personal landholding and allowed the state to sell land currently in public ownership.[11] By promoting individual land ownership through titling, the new law sought to open the way to the capitalization of agriculture by enabling holders to raise mortgages. It reflected the thinking of those, like Hernando de Soto [2000], who saw the unlocking of private assets as key to development.[12] It also reflected the views of the World Bank, which supported similar schemes in neighbouring countries like Bolivia's *Ley INRA*. Separate legislation sought to extend private ownership to water rights – a conflictual issue in an arid country where control of water is arguably as key to production as access to land – as well as the forestry sector in the *selva*. In practice, the government's land titling programme, launched in 1993 with support from the Inter-American Development Bank (IDB), proved over-ambitious. Between 1996 and 2000, only half as many titles were authorized as planned. Most of these were given to coastal producers. Even in the *costa* there is little to suggest that they helped create a viable market in agricultural property, partly owing to negative perceptions about the value of land, partly to the lack of financial backup.

THE IMPACT ON AGRICULTURE

Identifying the ways in which such policies, along with the effects of macroeconomic and climatic change, impacted on different strata of the rural population is by no means an easy matter. As well as problems of pinpointing the differences between sectors within this heterogeneous universe, there are serious problems with regard to the quality of the statistical data available. The 1994 agricultural census provides the most complete set of figures on production and living standards in rural areas, but only gives information for the first years of the Fujimori period when most of these changes were only incipient. The value of output data for agriculture is also questionable, not least because in 2000 the government changed the base year on which such data was collected from 1979 to 1994, altering significantly some of the suppositions about the relative weight of agriculture in the economy as a whole.[13] Furthermore, the household surveys used to measure poverty in rural areas as well as urban ones do not provide much information on such key variables as land ownership, agricultural output and the technologies used. Still, bearing in mind the limitations of the data available, it is possible to give some idea of the effects on the sector as a whole and small-scale producers in particular.

Overall, performance in the agricultural sector since the 1960s has been sluggish. In the 1970s, this was attributable to the dislocations caused by the agrarian reform. In the 1980s, agriculture was hit by the impact of the debt crisis on demand for food, the effects of rural violence over large parts of the country and the 1983 Niño. Between 1970 and 1979, agricultural GDP grew on average by 1.53 per cent each year. Between 1980 and 1989, it grew by 2.13 per cent, slightly above the otherwise far from dynamic average rate of GDP growth for the economy as a whole. During the 1990s, in somewhat improved macroeconomic and political circumstances, growth in agriculture picked up to 3.73 per cent, fractionally above the 3.69 per cent average registered for the economy as a whole. Small-scale producers, like others, benefited from such factors as the ending of hyperinflation, the quelling of Sendero Luminoso and the return to more normal rainfall patterns after the droughts of the late 1980s.

As we have suggested, the long-term agricultural growth figures mask a great deal of shorter-term volatility caused by, amongst other things, sudden variations in the climate and sharp annual changes in the pattern of demand. The relative recovery in production towards the mid-1990s owed much to the revival of domestic demand and the return to more normal weather patterns. However, towards the end of the 1990s, these two key motors went into reverse: the return of El Niño in 1997/98 had a major impact on supply, whilst the economy entered a period of stagnation from which there were few signs of recovery even at the end of 2001. The longer-term data also mask an important change in the structure of agricultural production, with a notable increase in the share of tradeable goods (such as rice, hard maize, wheat, soya, sugar, milk etc.) and a decline in the proportion of non-tradeables (such as potato, quinua and other Andean grains). Policy under Fujimori tended to benefit larger-scale producers oriented primarily towards agro-industry and foreign markets. Some took advantage of new 'niche' markets, such as asparagus which, albeit briefly, became a boom industry in parts of the coast.

The effects of trade liberalization – and indeed other forms of liberalization – are difficult to disentangle from the other factors that determine the rhythm of growth in agriculture. However, the reduction of protective tariffs, in conjunction with the maintenance of an overvalued exchange rate, created a difficult environment for producers of tradeable goods who found themselves increasingly subjected to competition from cheap food imports. Although agricultural exports have increased in value terms since the mid-1980s, they have been overtaken by the increase in imports. Imports of agricultural goods averaged US$488 million in the period between 1986–90, rising to US$687 million in 1991–95, and reaching US$1,035 million in 1996–99. In volume terms (eliminating the effect of price variations) food imports rose from 1.6 million tonnes (1986–90) to 2.1 million tonnes (1991–95) and 2.8 million tonnes (1996–99). Peru's average annual agricultural trade balance, which until 1980 had been consistently in surplus, registered deficits of US$216 million in 1986–90, US$383 million in 1991–95 and US$346 million in 1996–99.[14]

These figures suggest that Peruvian agriculture is satisfying an ever decreasing proportion of domestic demand for food, a clearly worrying trend for a country in which a large proportion of the workforce is employed in agricultural activities.[15] As we can see in Table 1, imports per capita of the population have risen steadily since 1970, whereas production per head of the population has declined. Imports now account for roughly 40 per cent of food needs. As well as having important implications for domestic producers, this makes food provision increasingly dependent on the existence of foreign exchange to pay for imports.

TABLE 1
IMPORTS OF BASIC FOODS (AVERAGES)

Years	Production (000mt)	Imports (000mt)	Population (m)	Production per/cap (kg/person)	Imports per/cap (kg/person)
1970–75	2,781.70	953.43	14.16	193.6	67.3
1976–80	2,648.76	1,172.18	16.44	161.1	71.3
1981–85	2,797.84	1,481.20	18.63	150.2	79.5
1986–90	3,202.10	1,668.30	20.75	154.3	80.4
1991–95	2,955.00	2,126.80	22.74	129.9	93.5
1996–99	3,905.00	2,820.20	24.02	162.6	117.4

Source: Central Bank, Ministry of Agriculture, CEPES

The sectors most vulnerable to the inflow of cheap agricultural produce are the producers of tradeables who, as we have noted, represent an increasingly large proportion of those classified as small-scale peasant producers. At the same time, the increase in imports has also accelerated a change in consumption patterns away from traditional crops, mainly those associated with highland agriculture. The increase in consumption of rice and pasta at the expense of potatoes is particularly notable, even in the *sierra*. Such changes are, of course, not new; they are a consequence of 50 years of progressive urbanization and have defied attempts of various governments to persuade consumers of the value of traditional Andean crops, especially grains. Still, the availability of cheap imported grains has accelerated the decline of such traditional crops as quinua, kiwicha, oca, olluco and beans. Arguably, these may have proved to be more 'tradeable' than was previously thought. Symptomatic of this problem is cultivation of wheat, grown in the *sierra.* Wheat imports nearly doubled in volume terms between 1990 and 2000, without even taking into account donations by organizations such as the European Union (EU) and the US Agency for International Development (USAID). The removal in 1998 of the surcharge that protected producers of wheat, at the insistence of local manufacturers of bread and pasta, further reduced the potential for small-scale domestic wheat producers. A study in Lima and provincial cities on consumption of traditional grains shows just how difficult it is to reverse changing patterns of consumption once these are set in motion [*Smith and Trivelli*, 2001].

Patterns of local demand, coupled with cheap imports, had a direct and dramatic impact on domestic agricultural prices, the most important single economic incentive for producers. These peaked in 1987–88, following the demand-driven boom of García's first two years in office. The years that followed brought a collapse in prices, afflicting all but those engaged exclusively in subsistence farming and those producing for export. Trade liberalization and the overvalued exchange rate reinforced this effect after 1990. Table 2 shows how real farm-gate prices (i.e. those actually received by farmers) varied in the 1990s, but never remotely regained the levels they had reached in the mid-1980s. This decline had a major impact on the prosperity of the agricultural sector in all parts of the country, affecting small-scale and larger-scale producers alike. Typical of those affected were rice producers, mainly small-scale farmers in the southern coastal valleys (Arequipa), those of the north (Piura, Lambayeque and La Libertad) and in the jungle department of San Martín. Prices tumbled between 1988 and 1990 in response to the contraction in urban purchasing power, reaching their nadir in 1994. The problem of low prices was compounded by an increase in rice imports from lower-cost producers like Thailand. Another crop hit by low prices was potatoes, a key crop in the *sierra* but one of growing importance among small-scale producers in the *costa* where yields are higher and marketing much easier. Partly as a result of changing patterns of consumption, demand for potatoes slumped from 100 kg per person per year in 1990 to only 38 kg in 2000.

The institutional reforms introduced by Fujimori in the early 1990s also impacted on agricultural performance. Possibly the most important was the disappearance of the Banco Agrario which, despite its inefficiencies in the past, had been the sole source of credit to an important number of producers, mainly on the coast. As it turned out, private lenders proved extremely reluctant to lend, even to larger-scale, more prosperous landowners with privileged market access either at home or abroad. When they did lend, the interest rates charged reflected a perception of high risk.[16] The appetite for lending was also reduced by bankruptcies in sectors (such as asparagus) that

TABLE 2
FARM-GATE PRICES FOR KEY CROPS (1985–2000)

(Real terms: New soles (1994) per metric ton)

Year	Rice	Potatoes	Wheat	H. Maize	Milk	S. Maize	Coffee	Cotton
1985	1,806.1	1,058.0	2,379.3	1,708.6		2,149.4	11,593.9	5,267.9
1986	2,106.5	1,741.9	2,704.2	1,865.3	2,114.2	2,671.9	18,977.5	4,594.1
1987	2,113.2	1,113.1	2,247.6	1,642.2	2,205.5	2,280.7	7,959.9	6,443.4
1988	1,081.5	857.8	1,734.3	1,031.5	2,005.4	1,749.1	6,824.0	4,011.3
1989	903.0	1,072.2	1,007.5	683.0	968.5	1,191.3	2,184.5	2,333.4
1990	585.9	485.4	941.6	649.2	975.6	1,398.6	1,821.7	1,343.5
1991	543.3	550.5	760.2	449.2	669.9	899.3	1,753.6	1,698.6
1992	491.4	481.4	561.6	454.6	615.1	683.6	1,260.3	1,256.9
1993	506.3	466.4	618.7	402.6	559.6	684.3	1,367.7	1,626.6
1994	370.0	422.5	533.3	406.7	547.5	743.3	3,410.0	1,610.8
1995	457.4	263.2	552.7	416.2	542.1	704.1	3,492.9	1,771.2
1996	555.1	474.4	567.3	427.4	529.1	637.0	2,581.3	1,284.7
1997	471.9	366.0	509.7	344.3	498.7	621.2	3,839.7	1,519.1
1998	547.8	470.5	496.9	357.3	506.3	668.0	2,684.9	1,368.2
1999	406.1	251.0	463.2	344.3	545.8	675.4	2,363.6	1,458.6
2000	384.0	252.2	450.2	330.2	545.4	604.0	2,163.2	1,211.2

Source: Ministry of Agriculture, CEPES

had briefly seemed to offer endless possibilities.[17] The closure of ENCI and ECASA also hit specific sectors. ENCI, for instance, had been the only institution that was allowed to import milk and its disappearance removed a source of support to the local dairy industry; as imports surged in the early 1990s (mainly from New Zealand, but also Australia, the United States and even Poland) many smaller-scale producers went to the wall in areas like Cajamarca and Arequipa. The abolition of ECASA liberalized the market in rice, removing an institution which had maintained prices artificially high for the benefit of producers. Some of its functions were taken over by the *Programa Nacional de Asistencia Alimentaria* (PRONAA), the government's subsidized food programme for the poor, which bought direct from small-scale producers.[18]

Such institutional changes probably had relatively little impact on the poorest farmers, particularly those in the *sierra* who had never benefited from state programmes of any sort. However, they had a direct effect on those producers more integrated into urban markets who found themselves forced to rely on intermediaries or agro-industrial firms for credit.[19] The disappearance of the Banco Agrario thus made it more difficult for such producers to capitalize their operations. The withdrawal of the agriculture ministry from its various activities in such areas as veterinary work and extension also made it harder for small producers to increase their competitiveness, although such services had seldom reached those of the *sierra*.

The land titling programme, designed to assist the capitalization of small-scale agriculture, also provided little by way of immediate help to farmers in buying, selling or mortgaging their land to raise capital. Land titling went furthest on the coast, arguably accentuating the differences between coastal and highland agriculture. However, even on the coast, there is little to suggest that it helped create a viable property market [*Larson et al.*, 2001]. With the commercial banks unwilling to lend and the *cajas rurales* ill-equipped to fill the breach, property owners were thus not much closer to raising the capital that they needed. At the same time, the land titling programme exposed numerous longstanding disputes over land rights that it was unable to resolve. This was particularly the case in areas like Puno in the *sierra* where the agrarian reform and its denouement had led to widespread conflicts over land rights between excluded peasant communities and those who received land under the reform.[20]

PEASANT AGRICULTURE AND RURAL POVERTY

The impact of agricultural liberalization on income inequality and poverty in the rural sector has not been studied in a systematic or comprehensive way. Not only are the patterns of causation often indirect, but the lack of adequate tools for measurement once again renders such a task extremely difficult. Agricultural production data for specific crops do not mesh easily with the poverty data which are broken down only to the level of broad geographical areas. The relationship between agricultural performance and poverty levels in rural areas therefore requires further elucidation, but the linkage is clearly very important since agriculture provides the main source of income for those living in rural areas.

TABLE 3
GEOGRAPHICAL DISTRIBUTION OF POVERTY (1985–2000)

(% of households living in poverty and extreme poverty)

	1985	1991	1994	1997	2000
NATIONAL TOTAL					
Poverty	41.6	57.4	53.4	50.7	54.1
Extreme poverty	18.4	26.8	19.0	14.7	14.8
Metropolitan Lima					
Poverty	27.4	47.6	42.4	35.5	45.2
Extreme poverty	3.4	10.1	5.5	2.4	4.7
Urban areas (other than Lima)					
Coast					
Poverty	42.1	54.9	51.9	58.3	53.1
Extreme poverty	11.1	23.2	12.2	7.6	8.4
Sierra					
Poverty	36.4	53.2	51.6	37.7	44.3
Extreme poverty	15.4	22.4	14.6	7.7	6.6
Jungle					
Poverty	48.2		43.0	44.2	51.5
Extreme poverty	23.3		12.1	7.2	11.6
Rural areas					
Coast					
Poverty	50.0		63.4	52.8	64.4
Extreme poverty	26.6		26.5	23.6	27.3
Sierra					
Poverty	49.2	72.7	64.7	68.1	65.5
Extreme poverty	32.3	54.5	37.7	32.6	30.2
Jungle					
Poverty	68.0		70.1	64.9	69.2
Extreme poverty	43.9		38.6	36.4	31.5

Source: Instituto Cuanto, 2001
Based on Encuesta Nacional de Niveles de Vida (ENNIV) for 1991, 1994, 1997, 2000
INEI Encuesta Nacional sobre Medicion de Nivels de Vida 1985–86

So far as income distribution is concerned, studies for Peru as a whole suggest that inequality in the 1990s probably became more skewed than before, since the benefits of resumed growth were very unequally shared.[21] This had important implications for class differentiation in rural areas. Some small-scale producers were pushed back into subsistence agriculture or into selling labour, whilst others managed to increase the assets at their disposal, becoming economically and politically predominant. The sectors that made most gains were those with higher levels of productivity, especially those linked to foreign capital such as mining, energy and telecommunications. Agriculture was not one of the sectors that attracted foreign investment, although there were specific types of agriculture (such as asparagus) that responded positively to international market stimuli. Although agricultural growth rates in the 1990s may have picked up on earlier decades, the fruits of it were unequally distributed. Among small-scale producers, the most dynamic were those that managed to retain some access to credit and sold into fairly buoyant markets (like agro-industry) without having to depend on a chain of intermediaries. With regard to the poverty data, the evidence suggests that while extreme poverty in rural areas may have fallen, the proportion of the total population living in poverty was higher in 2000 than six years earlier, a finding that is also true of the rural population (see Table 3).[22] The decrease in extreme poverty, especially in rural areas of the *sierra*, was more a consequence of the Fujimori government's social programmes, particularly the supply of subsidized food to the poor, than the result of any improvement in agricultural incomes among more marginalized producers.[23] Such programmes create a dependency on handouts and may well prove unsustainable in the longer run.[24]

The patterns of real farm-gate agricultural prices, noted in Table 2, provides compelling evidence as to why rural livelihoods suffered serious erosion during this period. As we have seen, the impact of downward moving agricultural prices was particularly dramatic at the end of the 1980s when hyperinflation and deep recession severely eroded demand for food crops and other agricultural produce. However, it is also noteworthy how agricultural prices failed to recover in the period between 1993 and 1995 when demand in the economy picked up strongly. Again, one explanation of this is the effect of trade liberalization and the consequent rapid increase in imports after 1992, which meant that these supplied an increasingly large proportion of the market. The differences between the growth period 1985–87 and that of 1992–96 are clear-cut in this respect.

We have already noted that those agricultural producers most at risk from sudden changes in patterns of domestic demand are those more closely integrated into the market economy, whilst those least likely to be affected are those involved in subsistence agriculture and those that export.

Exporters are, of course, susceptible to variations in international prices.[25] The vast majority of small-scale producers produce for the domestic market and are therefore vulnerable to changes in relative prices, especially during periods of recession. By the end of the 1990s, many such producers were being pushed back into subsistence agriculture and/or selling their labour power elsewhere. This was also the case in the *sierra*, where relatively few small-scale producers are entirely independent of the market.[26]

The impact of agricultural prices on living standards will depend in many instances on the extent to which, faced with low prices, small-scale producers are able to switch into other activities that compensate for the loss of agricultural income [*Castillo*, 1994]. In this sense, highland peasants probably enjoy greater protection than other small-scale producers. They often have a more diversified economic base, producing not only crops but livestock. They also can often complement agricultural earnings through non-agricultural activities such as handicrafts. The ability of small-scale producers to weather the effects of a downturn in relative prices will hinge on the quality and quantity of the resources at their disposal. Faced with low prices, those with less land (or land of poorer quality) will probably be forced more quickly into working for others as labourers. The impact of low prices may thus accentuate inequalities within specific rural areas, with wealthier and more resilient producers managing to survive at the expense of others.

The extent to which migration to other areas was a mechanism for survival for the poorest rural producers in the 1990s is also difficult to measure with accuracy, but this has clearly long been a response to deprivation among impoverished Andean farmers and/or their families. The available evidence suggests that patterns of urban migration continued during the 1990s, but probably at a slower rate than in earlier decades. In specific areas like Ayacucho, afflicted by political violence in the 1980s, some earlier migrants even returned to their original communities, often after lengthy periods of displacement. Some highland peasants migrated to the coast (either seasonally or permanently) to work as wage labourers, for example on asparagus farms.[27] Throughout the 1980s and 1990s, the existence of coca agriculture along much of the jungle fringe (*ceja de selva*), also provided an occupational shock absorber for peasant producers forced to migrate from the highlands, whether out of economic necessity or in response to political violence. Through the links that increasingly exist between small-scale producers in one place and those of another, the economic influence of coca is widespread. US-backed policies to eradicate coca therefore have important implications for small-scale producers, not only in the *ceja de selva* but further afield.

WEAKENING THE RURAL 'VOICE'

A key factor in the evolution of the rural economy is the capacity of producers to articulate their problems and to influence policy in such ways as to alleviate or resolve them. In seeking to understand that evolution, we therefore need to focus on the strength of collective identities at the local level. The degree of organization among a group or community of producers is a key factor in their ability to negotiate with the outside world, whether it takes the form of those to whom they sell or those who make policy. As we shall see, the progressive weakening of the rural 'lobby' has been one of the salient features of rural politics over the last 30 years. Arguably, this is both a cause and effect of the process of economic liberalization.

The 1969 agrarian reform and the state policies that accompanied it gave pride of place to the state as the key actor in the rural sphere, just as in other areas of economic life. As we have seen, the state undertook such varied and critical functions as defining landownership, setting agricultural prices, undertaking marketing functions, providing credit and extension services, amongst others. The reform and its aftermath was thus fertile ground for the emergence of an array of organizations, each claiming to represent rural or sectoral interests which sought to influence state decisions of one kind or another. Some were quasi-official, such as the *Confederación Nacional Agraria* (CNA), established by the Velasco government to develop and consolidate regime support among the new cooperatives. Others, like the *Confederación Campesina del Peru* (CCP), were more critical of the agrarian reform and its shortcomings, seeking to radicalize the process and push it further. The CCP had strong links with some of the more radical parties of what became in 1980 the United Left (*Izquierda Unida*) coalition. Some organisations, like the *Organización Nacional Agraria* (ONA) sought to oppose the direction of the agrarian reform, representing the interests of private landowners. Others represented the interests of specific types of rural producers, such as the *Fondos de Ganadería Lechera* (Fongales), and even ethnic entities like *Asociación Interétnica de Desarrollo de la Selva Peruana* (Aidesep). In the context of the late 1970s, and particularly the incipient process of democratization, most of these organizations adopted strong ideological stances – albeit divergent ones – often reinforced by their ties to specific political parties.

The abandonment of official support for agrarian reform by the Belaunde government in the first half of the 1980s undercut the influence enjoyed by some of these organizations, while limited moves were made towards reducing the role of the state in the agriculture and other spheres. Although the García government adopted a rhetoric of support for peasant agriculture, it did little to privilege relations with representative organizations such as the CNA or the CCP. During the economic crisis of the late 1980s, rural lobbies and pressure groups saw their power to influence official policy much diminished. Indeed, hit by hyperinflation and deep recession, popular organizations of all kinds – trade unions and neighbourhood associations as well as those representing rural interests – saw their capacity to mobilize protest greatly reduced. The political parties with which they were associated also went into decline. In such conditions, those that otherwise would have opposed the sort of economic liberalization unleashed by Fujimori in 1990, found themselves unable to do so. Indeed, it is one of the remarkable features of the Fujimori reforms that they sparked so little organized opposition.[28]

Rural pressure groups, especially those of the *sierra*, were also debilitated by the spread of *Sendero Luminoso* (and to a lesser extent the *Movimiento Revolucionario Túpac Amaru* – MRTA) during the course of the 1980s.[29] Sendero's frontal assault on the local institutions of the Peruvian state, as well as on parties and other grassroots institutions that stood in its way, had a highly damaging effect on autonomous peasant organization, especially in the *sierra*. The effect was compounded by the militarization of large parts of the country during the course of the 1980s, with its legacy of killing, intimidation and human rights abuse. Peasant communities were effectively caught in the crossfire between Sendero and the military. Previously important regional peasant federations, like the *Federación Agraria Departamental de Ayacucho* (FADA), suffered greatly as a result. Increasingly autonomous peasant protest became an unfeasible option where dissent was immediately seen by the military authorities as evidence of support for Sendero. In such circumstances, it became impossible, or even irrelevant, to represent the economic interests of peasants or small-scale producers. Indeed, for many communities the primary need was defence, and this was a need met by the formation of *rondas campesinas* at the behest of the military.[30] In departments like Ayacucho, Apurímac and Huancavelica, the interruption of the rural economy and the massive flight of rural producers to the relative safety of urban areas had a major debilitating effect on social organization of all types. In the *selva*, both Sendero and the MRTA also came to control large areas of departments like Huánuco and San Martín. This, coupled to the growth of coca cultivation and drug trafficking, led to a marked change in the nature of community organization.

When Fujimori took over in 1990, the sources of potential rural opposition to his liberalizing agenda had already been greatly weakened. However, his policies weakened them still further. Three factors are relevant here. Firstly, the process of *parcelación* and the atomization of ownership in most rural areas made it increasingly difficult for producers to organize themselves on a collective basis. As we have seen, the progressive dismantling of the associative structures of the agrarian reform led to a large increase in the numbers of smallholders, many of them living on plots close to the margins of economic viability. This also led to a dispersion of crops, again making collective action more difficult to organize.

Second, the withdrawal of the state from such areas as credit provision, extension and marketing support reduced the importance of collective action across a wide field of activities. Some former state functions were taken up by private interests, but many were simply abandoned. Producers were obliged to consider different ways of resolving their problems. Under Fujimori, the government made it clear that it was not prepared to negotiate terms with *gremios* that represented specific farming sectors, still less once-politicized federations of peasants ideologically opposed to liberalization. The reduced role played by the ministry of agriculture in rural areas further limited the possibilities for negotiation.

Third, Fujimori was able to achieve a new relationship with rural producers, especially those of the *sierra*. By channelling large sums into poverty relief programmes, he was able to use the patronage and clientelism that this encouraged at the local level to forestall open opposition to the government. Local officials knew that the flow of resources from the centre was conditional on their support for the regime. This produced a new level of centralized control, a process facilitated by the demise of political parties. The increase in social spending in rural areas – particularly in the years after 1994 – tightened this control and reduced the scope for interest representation. Still, these clientelistic ties were not of equal strength in all places. Nor did they entirely obliterate 'associational autonomy'. And once Fujimori stood down as president in 2000, they ceased to have much relevance.

The main state agencies active in the rural sphere during this time were, on the one hand, the ministries of health and education, and on the other a number of programmes driven by the newly created ministry of the presidency, the most important being the *Fondo de Compensación Social* (Foncodes). Foncodes, along with PRONAA and other schemes, established a new form of state presence in rural areas, distinct from what had gone before. Whilst their ostensible objective was to reduce poverty (especially extreme poverty), they also operated on a political logic to boost Fujimori's standing. Tightly controlled from above, they tended to discourage grassroots participation and worked in such a way as to bypass elected local government. As such they reinforced the control of central government at the expense of representative institutions.

The Peruvian experience stands in rather striking contrast to that being implemented in neighbouring Bolivia, where the Sánchez de Lozada administration's Participación Popular programme aimed to promote administrative decentralization and build channels for grassroots involvement in local affairs (see McNeish, this volume). The programme was designed to give some sort of 'voice' to rural areas previously excluded from budget assignations. Although Participación Popular had its limitations – it provided more a blueprint for decentralization than a recipe for tackling poverty (still less promotion of agriculture) – it represented an important innovation in policy that opened up new spaces for the articulation of popular demands [*Gray-Molina*, 2001]. The story under Fujimori in Peru was very different; his main concern was to thwart any real devolution of power.

Although the various *gremios* representing agricultural interest groups in general lost capacity to influence policy during the 1990s [*Porras Martínez*, 1999], some were clearly more affected than others. Broadly speaking, those which managed to retain greater influence were those that represented sectors that were economically more powerful or politically more resilient. Organizations such as the CCP and CNA found themselves largely eclipsed, no longer able to articulate the interests of peasants and small-scale producers, and officially ignored as valid intermediaries. Those *gremios* that survived were typically those that represented interest groups associated with the more dynamic sectors of agriculture. A good example is that of the milk producers (Fongales) who managed successfully to mitigate the more dramatic effects of trade liberalization.

One of the main weaknesses of agricultural *gremios* during this period was their disunity – they were at loggerheads for instance on the creation of a free market in land – although on some questions they spoke with more of a common voice than others [*Alfaro Moreno*, 1994]. The emergence of Conveagro as an umbrella organization bringing together disparate *gremios* as well as non-governmental organizations (NGOs) showed how on certain issues a united position could be presented and taken seriously by the authorities.[31] One of the more powerful *gremios* to emerge during the late 1990s was the *Comité de Usuarios de Riego*, an entity that staged important mobilizations among coastal agricultural interests in the twilight years of Fujimori. The election of a more democratic government in 2001 provided greater scope for such *gremios* to play a role in support of agricultural producers, but from a much weaker starting point than in the 1980s.

CONCLUSIONS

Economic policy in Peru has long been conducted in such a way as to benefit the largely urban consumer at the expense of rural producers. This does not appear to have changed in any fundamental way in the 12 years since neo-liberal policies were applied. Indeed, it could be argued that the lack of a pro-agricultural policy as such has led to a deepening of this process, a phenomenon encouraged by the weak pressure exerted by groups representing agricultural producers of one kind or another. The fate of small-scale producers is perhaps typical. In themselves a heterogeneous grouping that includes the majority of producers in the *costa* and *selva* as well as in the *sierra*, these have not been among the prime beneficiaries of policy. Rather, as we have seen, they have had to weather the impact of adverse macroeconomic policies that reduced domestic demand for food, trade policies that encouraged competing imports, and sectoral policies designed to remove the state from active involvement in agriculture. Variations in the real farm-gate prices for key products grown by small-scale producers underline the difficulties these producers had to face.

What we have observed over this period is the following three developments. First, increased disparities in performance between agricultural producers in different parts of the country. The area that has probably benefited most – albeit unevenly – were the irrigated valleys of the coast, where larger and more profitable farms are more integrated into the market and better able to access the reduced amounts of credit available. By contrast, agriculture in the *sierra* has not benefited by any great increase in productivity, although the traditional peasant economy has to some extent been shielded from negative variations in prices. Government spending in the *sierra* has been geared primarily to providing social support rather than developing the agricultural base. The jungle has fared worse than the coast, due in part to its distance from markets, although the coca economy has provided an important source of employment and of income to many small-scale producers.

Second, within agricultural sectors it appears to be the case that there has been a concentration of economic power among the larger and more efficient producers to the detriment of small-scale producers. Where farmers enjoy good access to land (and water), credit and markets, they are better placed to prosper than those who lack these advantages. The retreat of the state from active involvement in agricultural development probably magnified such differences. Larger, more organized producers are better placed to influence policy and to defend their interests than smaller ones. Although agricultural *gremios* lost influence during the 1990s, this was particularly prejudicial to small-scale and peasant producers.

And third, trade liberalization compounded the effects of longer-term shifts in patterns of food consumption to the detriment of small-scale highland producers. This is particularly true in the case of wheat, but also of a number of other traditional Andean grains.

In sum, the effects of economic liberalization in agriculture have probably hit hardest those who produce predominantly (or entirely) for the market but who are integrated into it on the least preferential terms. Those whose economy is largely one of subsistence may well have been partly shielded from the fall in prices and the effects of the increased imports, whilst being less exposed to the withdrawal of subsidized credit and marketing supports (which they never received previously). Small-scale producers dependent on urban demand and competing directly with imports were among those most at risk, whether in the *costa, sierra* or *selva.* For these, the alternative to being small-scale producers was either to return to subsistence agriculture, to seek alternatives to agriculture (such as petty commercial activity) or a combination of both. According to Carlos Amat y León, the agriculture minister under the interim Paniagua administration (2000–2001), the shake-out from small-scale, market-oriented agriculture in the late 1990s was 'truly massive'.[32] But until there is a new agricultural census, it will be difficult to know just how many small-scale producers were forced to sell/abandon their land and the extent to which this has led to renewed concentration of ownership.

GLOSSARY AND ACRONYMS

cajas rurales	small-scale rural lending agencies
campesino	peasant or small-scale rural producer
ceja de selva	jungle fringe
comité de usuarios de riego	committee of irrigation users
costa	coast
foquismo	rural guerrilla strategy
gremio	professional or occupational organization
minifundio	small unit of landholding
parcelación	land sub-division
parceleros	those occupying sub-divided land
rondas campesina	peasant militias
selva	jungle
sierra	highlands

Aidesep	Asociación Interétnica de Desarrollo de la Selva Peruana
APRA	Alianza Popular Revolucionaria Americana
CAN	Confederación Nacional Agraria
CCP	Confederación Campesina del Perú
CEDEP	Centro de Estudios para el Dessarrollo y la Participación
CEPES	Centro Peruano de Estudios Sociales
CIES	Consorcio de Investigación Económica y Social
Conveagro	Convención Nacional del Agro
ECASA	Empresa Comercializadora del Arroz
ENCI	Empresa Nacional Comercializadora de Insumos
FAO	Food and Agriculture Organization
Foncodes	Fondo de Compensación Social
Fongal	Fondo de Ganadería Lechera
GDP	Gross Domestic Product
IDB	Inter-American Development Bank
ILD	Instituto Libertad y Democracia
IMF	International Monetary Fund

INEI	Instituto Nacional de Estadística e Informatica
INRA	Instituto Nacional de Reforma Agraria
IRD	Institut de Recherche pour le Développment
ISI	Import Substitutive Industrialization
ITDG	Intermediate Technology Development Group
MRTA	Movimiento Revolucionario Túpac Amaru
NGO	Non-governmental Organization
OGPA	Oficina General de Planificación Agraria
ONA	Organización Nacional Agraria
PRONAA	Progama Nacional de Asistencia Alimentaria
SEPIA	Seminario Permanente de Investigación Agraria
USAID	United States Agency for International Development

NOTES

1. Among the key sources of published research is *Debate Agrario*, the respected bulletin produced by the Centro Peruano de Estudios Sociales (CEPES), and the proceedings of the Seminario Permanente de Investigación Agraria (SEPIA).
2. Over the last 30 years Peru has experienced a fairly wide range of different governments. The leftward leaning, nationalist, military government of General Juan Velasco (1968–75) gave way to a much more conservative military regime under General Francisco Morales Bermudez (1975–80), which shied away from the social reforms initiated by Velasco. The return to constitutional rule brought to power the centre-right government of Fernando Belaunde (1980–85) which initiated some of the liberalizing changes that were taken much further in the 1990s. The 1985 elections brought to office Alan García (1985–90), whose centre-left administration in some ways harked back to the Velasco period, but which ended in economic crisis. The 1990 elections were won by Alberto Fujimori who, having changed the constitution, was re-elected in 1995. Fujimori, backed by the army and shunning all opposition, spearheaded the process of neo-liberal transformation. Having fraudulently secured re-election in 2000 for a third term, he was obliged to flee Peru when details emerged of the extent of the corruption and political manipulation that had taken place during his government. He was replaced on an interim basis by Valentín Paniagua, a centrist politician, pending further elections in 2001 that were won by Alejandro Toledo.
3. The term *campesino* embodies this sort of wide definition. The literature on this subject is extensive. For longstanding theoretical debate about the class position of the Peruvian peasantry, see among others Bradby [1975], Scott [1976], Martínez-Alier [1977], Painter [1986; 1991], Assies [1987], Smith [1979; 1989] and Deere [1990].
4. Much of the writing on Peruvian agriculture focuses on the particularities of these different areas, both in terms of diagnosis of problems and suggested solutions. Following Murra [1975], proponents of the 'verticality' thesis [*Fonseca Martell*, 1973; *Alberti and Mayer*, 1974; *Figueroa*, 1984] have in the past argued that ownership of landholdings situated at different ecological levels in the Peruvian Andes enabled individual peasant proprietors or peasant communities to draw on and exchange different staple products throughout the year, and thus not only secure their subsistence requirements but also resist class differentiation and capitalist penetration. There are still important linkages that bind these economies together, not least in terms of internal trade and migration. It is quite common to find small-scale producers active in more than just one geographical ambit. It is therefore useful to see these as aspects of an overall system in spite of the spatial differences.
5. As we have suggested, a problem arises in equating the units of landholding mentioned in the census with more analytical typologies of different types of peasant and small-scale producer. In practice, there is a wide spectrum of small-scale producers, varying from family-based subsistence farmers at one end through to family farms employing substantial quantities of labour at the other. Many of the smallest producers are forced either to work for others or to involve themselves in non-agricultural activities for at least part of the time. At the other extreme, those units with most land are typically peasant communities dedicated to livestock agriculture at the highest altitudes. According to the census data there were 875,000 peasant producers in 1994, who were preponderantly subsistence farmers, a further 650,000 'intermediate' small-scale producers, producing mainly for the market and

some 38,000 small-scale producers employing other labourers and with access to irrigated land. Differentiation within similar productive areas is also very marked, as Cotlear [1989] observes in his important work on *sierra* agriculture.

6. According to Eguren [1999], agricultural GDP per head was lower in 1997 than it had been 50 years earlier.
7. This underlines the validity of the ECLA prognosis, made half a century ago, that ultimately answers about smallholder productivity had to be linked to questions about the consistency (or the lack of it) of domestic consumer demand.
8. The El Niño phenomenon occurs when the cold waters of the Humboldt Current, which normally flow northward up the west coast of South America from Antarctica, are temporarily displaced by warm waters flowing southwards from the tropics. Sea temperatures can rise by as much as 10 degrees. Dry offshore winds are thus replaced by more humid ones. The phenomenon upsets normal climatic conditions over other parts of the Pacific and elsewhere [*Davis*, 2001]. The exact reasons why Niños occur is something of a mystery. 'Mega-Niños' appear to be becoming rather more frequent occurences.
9. The number of people displaced as a result of political violence in Peru between 1980 and 1997 is reckoned at 430,000. The death toll was nearly 26,000 and a further 6,000 people 'disappeared'. All in all, the population affected is put at 1.6 million [*Coronel*, 1999]. Others have put the number of displaced higher [*Aprodeh*, 2000].
10. Peru had challenged the Bretton Woods institutions and the policies of structural adjustment when Alan García had come to power in 1985. He sought to limit debt servicing to 10 per cent of exports and introduced heterodox policies that challenged liberal orthodoxy [*Crabtree*, 1992].
11. Possession of a title to land occupied was seen by many smallholders as an important advance in claiming their rights.
12. De Soto, who argues that the state is the main obstacle to those in the informal sector being able to realize their suppressed economic potential, worked as an advisor to Fujimori during the early years of his government. His Instituto Libertad y Democracia (ILD) was among the pioneers in seeking to extend the benefits of economic liberalization to the poor.
13. The need to update the base year (1979) on which GDP growth figures were calculated became ever clearer as the 1990s drew on. The hyperinflationary period of the late 1980s had distorted relative prices. However the update was repeatedly postponed, basically for political reasons. The changeover to 1994 was finally made in 1999.
14. The data come from AgroData/CEPES and are based on official agriculture ministry statistics.
15. Most agricultural producers are engaged in producing food for Peru. In the case of non-food output, trade liberalization also often affected production of tradeable goods. A small but telling example is that quoted by Víctor Agreda [1994] of the jute producers in the Amazon areas who were hit by the decision of Paramonga (the sole purchaser of jute) to switch to imported jute to make sacks.
16. The main commercial bank to lend to smaller-scale producers was the Banco Wiese, which did so on an experimental basis using well-established NGOs to help it evaluate risk. The Wiese appears to have been influenced by the model of Bancosol in Bolivia. It ended up losing much of the money it had lent to, for example, coastal potato growers.
17. The banks found themselves confronted with large bad debts by asparagus producers when Peru was undercut in the world market by other lower-price producers, notably China.
18. Although PRONAA generally paid above-market rates to farmers, the benefits seldom accrued to poorest of these. PRONAA was also widely criticized for operating along lines of political favouritism and patronage [*Rebosio and Rodriguez*, 2001].
19. The 1994 census records that the main reason for land lying idle on small-scale units was because credit had become unavailable.
20. In the late 1970s and early 1980s members of peasant communities had occupied lands previously redistributed to others under the reform. Land titling did nothing to resolve these disputes.
21. According to data from Cuanto [1997; 2001], the Gini coefficient for inequality in Peru as a whole in 1999 was 46.2. This compares with 44.9 in 1994. An increase in inequality is also evident (both in the rural and urban spheres) in figures produced by the World Bank [1998].

22. In numerical terms, the numbers of people living in poverty increased substantially. According to Herrera [2001], these rose by 20 per cent between 1997 and 2000, or by more than 2 million. Herrera reworks the official poverty data produced by INEI and concludes that the official statistics were manipulated for political reasons under the Fujimori government.
23. According to INEI [2000], 46 per cent of all households in Peru were in receipt of food assistance of one kind or another in 1998. In the rural sphere, the proportions were higher. In the *costa* it was 51.8 per cent, *selva* 68.5 per cent and *sierra* 69.4 per cent.
24. Trivelli [2000] also makes the important point that the numbers of 'non-poor' in rural parts of the *sierra* whose incomes are only marginally above those of the 'poor' is higher than for the rural 'poor' as a whole. The 'non-poor' are therefore at particular risk of becoming 'poor'.
25. Some small-scale producers were able to take advantage of exports in spite of unpropitious world market conditions. Small-scale coffee producers, for instance, took advantage of the market for better priced organic coffee and tapped into 'fair trade' programmes with help from NGOs. In Piura, for example, in 2001, producers with less than a hectare of coffee were managing profitably to access the export market, despite very low international coffee prices.
26. Iguíñiz [1994] makes the point that what needs to be measured is the extent to which producers are 'net exporters' or 'net importers' in the sense that they sell more in the market than they acquire from it or vice-versa. A fall in prices for those who are 'net importers' of food may be beneficial.
27. It is interesting to note that many of those employed on such farms were women working part-time or on a shift basis. Working conditions were exploitative even by the standards of Peruvian agriculture. As in countries like Chile, some rural employers seem to opt for a casual workforce.
28. Politically an outsider, Fujimori came to power in 1990 on a wave of public revulsion against the political class in Peru. In 1992, he took advantage of this mood – as well as the popularity he won by overcoming hyperinflation – to stage a palace coup in which he closed down the Congress elected in 1990. This paved the way for his rewriting of the constitution the following year. As well as reducing congressional powers, the new constitution lifted the bar on immediate presidential re-election. Fujimori was re-elected in 1995 with an absolute majority, the election confirming the weak standing of the political parties. But as Fujimori resorted to ever more manipulative methods to secure yet another period in office in 2000, the public mood turned against him. Crabtree and Thomas [1998] provide a synopsis of the Fujimori government.
29. *Sendero Luminoso* (Shining Path) was originally a splinter group from Peru's main Maoist Communist Party. With its roots in Ayacucho, it first launched its armed struggle in 1980 at the time of the presidential elections of that year. It took advantage of the weakness of state institutions in the *sierra* to mount a war against the Peruvian state. It came to pose a major threat to regime stability in the late 1980s when the scope of its operations covered much of the country. Fujimori added to his prestige when the capture of Sendero's leader, Abimael Guzmán, precipitated the dismantling of Sendero's hierarchical structure. The MRTA, by contrast, owed its ideological origins to the pro-Cuban *foquista* guerrillas of the 1960s and to dissident factions within APRA. It never reached the scale of the Senderista insurgency. Its most spectacular attack (and its death knell) was the assault on the Japanese ambassador's residence in 1997, and the hostage taking and three-month siege that followed.
30. The *rondas campesinas* were originally modelled on the peasant patrols that became common in northern Peru in the 1980s as a method of dealing with the ever-present problem of cattle rustling.
31. Conveagro began life as an attempt by Absalón Vásquez, the agriculture minister in the early 1990s, as a one-off attempt to discuss problems in the sector. Following Vásquez's removal, it became institutionalized and gained an important margin of autonomy from the government.
32. Interview with the author, April 2000.

REFERENCES

Agreda, Víctor, 1994, 'El impacto del ajuste en la economia y los recursos naturales de los productores ribereños', in O. Dancourt, E. Mayer and C. Monge (eds.), *Sepia V. Peru: El Problema Agrario en Debate*, Lima: SEPIA, IRD, ITDG.

Alberti, Giorgio, and Enrique Mayer (eds.), 1974, *Reciprocidad e intercambio en los Andes Peruanos*, Lima: IEP.

Alfaro Moreno, Julio, 1994, *Los gremios rurales: rol de la organizaciones rurales en la década de los noventa*, Lima: Fundación Friedrich Ebert.

Aprodeh (Asociación Pro Derechos Humanos), 2000, *Los desplazados,* Lima: Aprodeh.

Assies, Willem, 1987, 'The Agrarian Question in Peru: Some Observations on the Roads of Capital', *The Journal of Peasant Studies*, Vol.14, No.4.

Bradby, Barbara, 1975, 'The Destruction of Natural Economy', *Economy and Society*, Vol.4, No.2.

Caballero, José Maria, 1980, *Agricultura, reforma agraria y pobreza campesina*, Lima: IEP.

Castillo, Marco, 1994, 'Impacto de la política de ajuste sobre la agricultura campesina en la sierra del Perú', in O. Dancourt, E Mayer and C. Monge (eds.), *Sepia V. Perú: El Problema Agrario en Debate*, Lima: SEPIA, IRD, ITDG.

Coronel, José, 1999, 'Balance del proceso de desplazamiento por violencia política en el Perú 1980–97', in V. Agreda, A Diez and M. Glave (eds.), *Sepia VII. Perú: El Problema Agraria en Debate*, Lima: SEPIA, IRD, ITDG.

Cotlear, Daniel, 1989, *Desarrollo Campesino en los Andes*, Lima: IEP.

Crabtree, John, 1992, *Peru under Alan Garcia: An Opportunity Lost*, Basingstoke: Macmillan.

Crabtree, John, and Jim Thomas (eds.), 1998, *Fujimori's Peru: The Political Economy*, London: Institute of Latin American Studies.

Cuánto, 1997 and 2001, *Perú en números: anuario estadístico*, Lima: Instituto Cuanto.

Davis, Mike, 2001, *Late Victorian Holocausts: El Niño Famines and the Making of the Third World*, London: Verso.

Deere, Carmen Diana, 1990, *Household and Class Relations: Peasants and Landlords in Northern Peru*, Berkeley, CA: University of California Press.

Del Castillo, Laureano, 1997, 'Propiedad rural, titulación de tierras y propiedad comunal', *Debate Agrario*, 26.

De Soto, Hernando, 2000, *The Mystery of Capital,* London: Bantam Press.

Eguren, Fernando, 1999, 'Agricultura y sociedad rural en el Perú', *Debate Agrario*, 29–30.

Figueroa, Adolfo, 1984, *Capitalist Development and Peasant Economy in Peru*, Cambridge: Cambridge University Press.

Figueroa, Adolfo, 1992, 'La agricultura peruano y el ajuste', *Debate Agrario*, 13.

Fonseca Martell, César, 1973, *Sistemas económicos andinos*, Lima: Biblioteca Andina.

Gonzáles de Olarte, Efraín, 1996, *El ajuste estructural y los campesinos*, Lima: IEP.

Gray-Molina, George, 2001, 'Exclusion, Participation and Democratic State-building', in John Crabtree and Laurence Whitehead (eds.), *Towards Democratic Viability: The Bolivian Experience*, Basingstoke: Palgrave.

Herrera, Javier, 2001, *Re-estimación de la pobreza en el Perú 1997–2000, avances de investigación*, Lima: INEI, IRD, CIES.

Hobsbawm, Eric, 1994, *Age of Extremes: The Short History of the 20th Century*, London: Michael Joseph.

Hopkins, Raúl, 1998, 'The Impact of Structural Adjustment on Agriculture', in John Crabtree and Jim Thomas (eds.), *Fujimori's Peru: The Political Economy*, London: Institute of Latin American Studies.

Iguíñiz, Javier, 1994, 'Desarrollo nacional, agro campesino y ajuste en el Perú', *Debate Agrario*, 20.

Instituto Nacional de Estadística e Informática, 2000, 'Impacto de los programas de apoyo alimentario en las condiciones de vida: resultado de la Encuesta Nacional de Hogares 1997–98', Lima: INEI.

Larson, Janelle *et al.*, 2001, 'Titulación de tierras en el Perú: se está cumpliendo la promesa?' *Debate Agrario*, 32.

Martínez-Alier, Juan, 1977, *Haciendas, Plantations and Collective Farms*, London: Frank Cass & Co.

Mesclier, Evelyne, 2000, 'Trente ans apres la réforme agraire peruvienne: le discours des investisseurs contre la voie paysanne', *Problemes de Amérique Latine*, No.38.

Ministerio de Agricultura, Oficina General de Planificación Agraria (OGPA), 2001, *La economia campesina en la última década*, Lima: OGPA.

Murra, John V., 1975, *Formaciones económicas y políticas del mundo andino*, Lima: IEP.

O'Brian, Jay, and William Roseberry (eds.), 1991, *Golden Ages, Dark Ages: Imagining the Past in Anthropology and History*, Berkeley, CA: University of California Press.

Painter, Michael, 1986, 'The Value of Peasant Labour Power in a Prolonged Transition to Capitalism', *The Journal of Peasant Studies*, Vol.13, No.4.

Painter, Michael, 1991, 'Recreating Peasant Economy in Southern Peru', in Jay O'Brian and William Roseberry (eds.), *Golden Ages, Dark Ages: Imagining the Past in Anthropology and History*, Berkeley CA: University of California Press.

Porras Martínez, Juan, 1999, *Reformas estructurales, institucionalidad y dilemas en la acción colectiva del empresariado agricola en América Latina: un estudio comparado del caso peruano y boliviano*, Santiago: FAO.

Rebosio, Guillermo, and Enrique Rodríguez, 2001, *Ingreso campesino y compras estatales de alimentos en el Perú*, Lima: CEDEP/CIES.

Santa Cruz, Francisco, 1999, *Nueva institucionalidad rural: el caso del Perú*, Lima: FAO/CEPES.

Scott, C.D., 1976, 'Peasants, Proletarianisation and the Articulation of Modes of Production: The Case of Sugar Cane Cutters in Northern Peru, 1940–69', *The Journal of Peasant Studies*, Vol.3, No.3.

Smith, Gavin, 1979, 'Socio-economic Differentiation and Relations of Production among Rural-based Petty Producers in Central Peru, 1880–1970', *The Journal of Peasant Studies*, Vol.6, No.3.

Smith, Gavin, 1989, *Livelihood and Resistance: Peasants and the Politics of Land in Peru*, Berkeley CA: University of California Press.

Smith, Stephen and Carolina Trivelli, 2001, *El consumo urbano de los alimentos tradicionales*, Lima: IEP.

Trivelli, Carolina, 2000, 'Pobreza rural: investigaciones, mediciones y políticas públicas', in I. Hurtado, C. Trivelli and A. Brack (eds.), *Sepia VIII. Perú: el problema agraria en debate*, Lima: SEPIA, IRD, ITDG.

World Bank, 1998, *Poverty and Social Development in Peru 1994–9*, Washington, DC: The World Bank.

Whither *O Campesinato*? Historical Peasantries of Brazilian Amazonia

STEPHEN NUGENT

Brazilian Amazonian peasantries have attracted relatively little scholarly attention, and even with the opening up of Amazonia via the TransAmazon Highway (*c.*1970) and a significant expansion of social science research in the region, recent frontier colonists and environmental crises have been the major *foci*. This article examines some of the factors contributing to the relative invisibility of historical peasantries in the region and tries to show the relevance of such peasantries to debates concerning agrarian structure, economic transformation and state-led modernization efforts. A key feature in the portrayal of Amazonian peasantries (and Amerindians) has been the unique role attributed to the neo-humid tropical landscape in restricting the possibilities for an elaborated social landscape. Drawing on anthropological, archaeological and historical studies, the article advances the notion that these simplifying assumptions are unwarranted and are impediments not only to a more accurate understanding of the legacy of colonial society in Amazonia, but also to efforts to mitigate social conflict and environmental depredation.

The visibility of Amazonian peasantries in scholarly or general literature has been highly variable over time. Currently and in the recent past, the activities of the Landless Workers Movement (MST) and the Rubber Tappers Union (CNS)(see glossary) have provided concrete examples of what an Amazonian peasantry might represent, but these are hardly representative of the diversity of Amazonian peasantries, and in the main, Amazonian peasantries have tended to be subsumed under a rigid structure of naturalism within which social life – whether Indian or *mestiço* – is treated as contingent and burdened by what Blaut [1994: 70] has referred to as the 'Doctrine of Tropical Nastiness'.

The main purpose of this article is to try to account for the relative absence of studies of Brazilian Amazonian peasantries from the anthropological and

---

Stephen Nugent, Department of Anthropology, Goldsmiths College, University of London and Institute of Latin American Studies. Email: snugent@gold.ac.uk. Thanks are extended to Tom Brass for editorial suggestions and comment.

peasant studies literature. The effort is directed at trying to insert the notion of Amazonian peasantry – a relatively minor footnote – into existing models or current debates as well as making exceptionalist claims based on: (a) the historic configuration of anthropological research in the region; (b) the structural position of the region in relation to the post-World War II modernization strategy of the state; and (c) the imprecision of the agrarian metaphor as a defining feature of the Amazonian peasantry.[1]

The first sections of this study are descriptive and somewhat didactic, and for a reason: despite the great historical depth of Amazonian peasantries, despite the vast increase in social science research in recent decades (especially following the planned and spontaneous colonization accompanying the construction of the TransAmazon Highway) and, currently, the attention paid to the Landless Workers Movement, the category 'Amazonian peasant' is inchoate. There are very few monographs: such standard works as *The Brazilian Peasantry* [*Forman*, 1975] have relatively little to say on the subject; and recent 'peasant' literature has focused mainly on migrations from the Northeast and Centre-South instigated by the machinations of the National Security State (1964–85). Additionally, the profusion of debate surrounding ecology and resource issues has tended to overwhelm historical and sociological matters. Thus, it is important to establish in clear form the basis upon which one might set about characterizing historical peasantries of the region and restoring, to some degree, their provenance as a significant feature of the Amazonian landscape.

It is a cruel irony that the rise of – and attention granted to – the Landless Workers Movement (MST), one of the most promising developments in recent Brazilian history, should be so difficult to relate to the peasantries of Amazonia, for the genesis of the MST lies in a Brazil far removed from Amazonia and far removed from the agrarian conditions characteristic of historical Amazonian peasantries. The MST is typically cast by commentators as a New Social Movement, and while that characterization is valid in crucial respects (the MST has been extremely measured in terms of allying itself with other and more official opposition tendencies, including PT – The Workers Party), it may be ease of *au courant* categorization that takes precedence over appreciation of underlying causes that raises interest in the prospects of MST. Existing Amazonian peasantries are poorly positioned to join forces with MST. The former are highly dispersed, highly atomistic, denied organizational opportunities for several generations (due to the imposition of National Security State measures), and more accustomed to patron–client politics than class politics. The latter are veterans of an aggressive agro-industrial export system in which declining labour absorption has resulted not in super-exploitation, but super-exclusion. While they represent a reserve army of labour redundant in terms of further suppressing agricultural wages, much like the super-reserve identified by Quijano [1971] and others many years ago, it is unclear whether unproductive Amazonian estates afford the same agricultural possibilities available on unproductive lands elsewhere in Brazil, and almost certainly not in terms of large-scale monoculture.[2] Agriculture in the Amazon has been, for compelling – although perhaps suppressible – environmental reasons, constrained in ways that confound the expectations of those accustomed to large-scale monoculture or an agrarian structure in which extactivism is subordinate to farming. The dynamic qualities of Amazonian agriculture are tied intimately to its coexistence with diverse forms of extraction (terrestrial and riverine) and pastoralism that many outsiders view as eccentric and opportunistic. A fisherman is also a farmer is also a taxi driver is also gold miner is also a 'wise forest-manager'. Certainly there are Amazonian peasants who are landless labourers or woodcutters or charcoal makers, but Amazonian peasantries are not in the main so specialized. The apparent equivalence in social position between historical peasantries and MST peasants should not be mistaken for the basis of a natural alliance, yet both are indicative of the still active role of peasantries both in Brazil and Amazonia.

PEASANT ANTECEDENTS

With qualification, in much of Latin America there are some significant continuities between pre-contact indigenous social formations and contemporary peasantries, and not infrequently there is a strong association between ethnicity and class position (along *indio* v. *ladino* lines, for example). This is not the case in Brazilian Amazonia (hereafter, simply Amazonia). The contemporary Indian population of Brazil as a whole (with the majority living in Amazonia) is around 300,000 (out of a national population of 160 million), and those few live in relative isolation in remote inter-fluve areas. This is not to say that contemporary Amazonian peasants do not have indigenous antecedents, but it is to say that peasant society is not modernized Indian society. Indeed, Indians in Brazil are officially regarded as 'relatively incapable' (see Ramos [1998] for an extended discussion) and are sharply distinguished from other forest peoples (see Schwarcz [1999] for the history of racial politics). While Indians are treated as 'real' Amazonians (hyper-real in Ramos' astute analysis), non-indigenous Amazonians, such as peasants, are 'inhabitants', 'populations', '*caboclos*', '*ribeirinhos*', 'colonists' or other non-specific or specific (Jewish, French, Lebanese) designations which are not seen as derivative of pre-historical Amazonians.

The consequences of this non-equivalence of native peoples and peasants are numerous and strongly influenced by the early twentieth-century nation-building projects focused around racial democracy and associated with pronouncements of national intellectuals such as Gilberto Freyre and Euclides da Cunha (see Schwarcz [1999]). Amazonian peasants have been, by and large, regarded as relinquished to nature: social beings lacking the integrity of Indians as well as a clear role as national citizens, Amazonian without being exotic, national but atypical (see Verissimo [1970]).

A further complication arises from the fact that the livelihoods of Amazonian peasants were (and are) substantially different from those of other Brazilian peasantries in at least two important respects: the slavery-based plantation systems of the northeast of Brazil (with parallel growth of an independent peasantry – see Schwartz [1985]) in the early colonial period were not replicated in Amazonia (environmental constraints, lack of terrestrial access), hence the trajectory of Amazonian peasants deviated from that of the national economy, and in addition, the importance of riverine production in Amazonia places peasants outside the frame of the ideal-typical rural producer in relation to Brazilian peasantries as a whole.[3]

In emphasizing the significance of the discontinuity between indigenous peoples and non-indigenous Amazonian peasants, and also drawing attention to the special features of Brazilian ethno-racial discourse (there are some 160 racial categories acknowledged by the national statistics bureau, IBGE), it should also be noted that extant Indian groups themselves (with important exceptions, such as the Yanomami) are highly discontinuous with regard to pre-contact indigenous social formations. Recent archaeological research – especially that of Anna Roosevelt [1980; 1991; 1994], anticipated by the work of Donald Lathrap [1968] – has revised received notions of the social landscape of pre-sixteenth century Amazonia in a way that has ramifications for the characterization of contemporary peasantries. Roosevelt's work suggests that the dominant Amazonian societies were sedentary, river-bank, proto-states and that extant Indian societies represent either those driven into the upland, inter-fluve interior or who fled there post-contact (for overview of historical sources see Porro [1996]). To put this another way, not only are contemporary historical peasantries of Amazonia not significantly derived from acculturated indigenous peoples, but extant Indian peoples' distribution in Amazonia does not represent an accurate pre-contact baseline from which to analyse the cultural ecology of contemporary Amazonians (see Beckerman [1991]). What is common to pre-contact social formations, extant Indian societies and historical peasantries is extractive production (see Bunker [1985] for an extended discussion), especially – although not exclusively – riverine, in combination with agricultural production. That the significance of riverine production has not featured prominently in discussions of Amazonian peasantries can be traced to three sources: (1) the relative absence of long-term ethnographic work among historic Amazonian peasantries; (2) the relative neglect of archaeological work; and (3) the developmentalist (since around 1970) emphasis on terra firme, smallholder colonist peasants as well as large-scale commercial extraction.[4]

A fourth and more general source is the overwhelming dominance of environmental determinism in shaping Amazonian research. Roosevelt [1991: 134] argues that this theory 'had its origin in ethnographic evidence and in ethnocentric, historical, Neocolonial attititudes of Euroamerican anthropologists to the tropics rather than primarily in environmental, historical and archaeological evidence from Amazonia', and that the theory has led to an incorrect characterization of human adaptation in prehistoric and historic Amazonia such that 'the effect on anthropological empirical research was to limit strategies, inhibit collection of certain kinds of data, and cause misinterpretation of the data that was collected' [*Roosevelt*, 1991: 134].

Attempts to characterize the Amazonian peasantry are doubly disabled, first by the tenuousness of their relationship with pre-capitalist social formations of the region and second by the dominance of a theoretical orthodoxy – environmental determinism – that has presumed to have answered key questions about the possibilities for socio-cultural florescence in the region. If pre-conquest Indian society was, according to received anthropological wisdom [*Gross*, 1975; *Meggers*, 1977] an impoverished victim of rigid environmental constraints, it is not surprising that its successor should be regarded as an ephemera.

To conclude this section: whatever the outcome of archaeological and ethno-historical research informed by a revisionist scepticism, the emergence of an Amazonian peasantry does not represent the transformation of pre-capitalist social formations. Amazonian peasants are not autochthonous, although their best life chances may well lie in attempts to replicate forms of resource-use that characterized their indigenous predecessors [*Roosevelt*, 1991].

THE INADVERTENT CREATION OF AN AMAZONIAN PEASANTRY

Regardless of differences in the estimates of the pre-contact population of Amazonia (five to ten million plus, according to Hemming [1987] and Hecht and Cockburn [1989] respectively), there is no disagreement about the fact that the region suffered a rapid demographic collapse commencing in earnest in the seventeenth century (see Hemming [1987]). Eighteenth-century attempts to encourage local population recovery through miscegenation (a policy associated with the Pombaline reforms) were relatively fruitless. Given the regional economy's dependence on extractive production (high volume, low price tropical goods) in which output was directly related to the scale of mobilization of labour, there was intense competition for free and indentured labour [*Alden*, 1969]. The importation of African slaves was modest, not only because of the difficulty of mounting plantation agriculture (largely for ecological reasons), but also because of the difficulty of controlling extractivist producers (and there remain today interior, runaway slave communities – *quilombos*).

At the time of Brazilian independence (1822), Amazonia represented a mercantile economy focused around the major interior city of Manaus and the near-coastal city of Belém, but despite its marginality in relation to developments (mainly in the form of export agriculture) elsewhere in the country, Amazonia was far from pre-modern and in mid-century was the site of civil war (*o cabanagem*) the set of antagonists of which gives some idea of the complexity of transformation the region had undergone over two centuries of colonial experimentation. The *cabanagem* was a conflict among three elite fractions of the metropolis of Belém (and outlying cities such as Cametá and, further afield, Santarém and Manaus) representing monarchists, republicans and supporters of regional independence. Followers were drawn from the fragments of Indian communities still functioning, agro-pastoral landowners and their workers, freed slaves, and peasant producers. The outcome – which saw many deaths among the metropolitan Belenense population [*Loureiro*, 1989] – was a republican victory and coincided with the rise of the rubber industry and the ascendancy of the region as a significant economic enclave.

While the *cabanegem* has relatively little attention given the scale of social conflict, the rubber industry – which, after all, lasted for a century and was central to the acceleration of industrialization in Europe and North America – has hardly been better treated. Two standard works in English [*Dean*, 1987; *Weinstein*, 1983] and one in Portuguese [*Santos*, 1980] prevail. Both the *cabanagem* and the rubber industry, however, are key to understanding the development of an Amazonian peasantry, the former because of what it reveals about the class structure of late colonial Amazonia, the latter because of what it reveals about two aspects of economic integration, within the region and between the region and the world economy. The former is important in illustrating the character of Belém as a mercantile city, an entrepôt to 'green hell' (not least for European scientists), as well as its role in nationbuilding activities (the Emilio Goeldi Museum was founded in 1855, the first of its type in Brazil). The *cabanagem* was not a frontier forest shoot-out, but a conflict driven by competition over the control of extractivist, petty commodity and manufacturing interests. The production of rum, for example, manufactured in tidally driven sugar *engenhos* in the estuary complex, played a key role in upriver trade (rum serving as the primary currency for acquiring diverse forms of interior forest produce; see McGrath [1989] and Anderson [1993]).

The rubber industry is no doubt more significant in terms of the creation of a peasantry in as much as it provided uniquely stable conditions for the proliferation of petty commodity production and profitable extractivism for many decades, a linking of multifarious producers (hundreds of thousands) through the circuit of merchant capital.

The production (= extraction) of rubber was undertaken by independent producers typically tied to merchants through stronger or weaker forms of debt-bondage. Although remnants of the vastly reduced Indian populations were engaged as rubber tappers, the industry was capable of absorbing far more labour than was available regionally, and many conscripts from the declining plantation economies of the northeast (coffee production had begun in the south in 1855, signalling the end of a major epoch of northeastern domination of export agriculture) were introduced into Amazonia. Responsible for their own collections of rubber trees (confusingly described as 'estates'), such imported tappers were tied economically through debt, were physically contained (through control of river transport), and were dependent on the exchange of rubber to meet their subsistence needs (the diversion of extractive labour time into agricultural production was heavily proscribed). Through a pyramid trading structure leading from the direct producer through a chain up to the major trading houses of Manaus and Belém, the system was a paragon of merchant capitalism: buying cheap and selling dear.

In retrospect – following the precipitous collapse prompted by the appearance of plantation-grown rubber in Southeast Asia – the agents of the Amazonian rubber industry, both tappers and merchants, have indirectly borne the blame for the failure of the industry precisely for the peasant-like organization of production (quasi-/semi-independent, dispersed producers), the allegation being that it was the failure of the industry to modernize and rationalize production that led to its demise (see Coomes and Barham [1994] and Weinstein [1983]). Against this, as Dean [1987] has argued robustly, there are constraints within the humid neo-tropical ecosystem which subvert large-scale intensive monocultural production, and in addition there is no shortage of failed attempts to replicate the Southeast Asian model (by Henry Ford, for example, at two sites on the Tapajós River).[5] Additionally, there would appear to have been little reason for mercantilists to intervene in a system that: (a) had a virtual monopoly on production of rubber (*hevea brasiliensis*); (b) had producers implacably locked into a debt-peonage system; and (c) could meet rises in costs through the steadily increasing market price of rubber in New York and Liverpool.

While some attention is given to the rubber industry in the abstract, little is given to the extractive-agrarian system it created and which outlived the industry itself.[6] In the first place, the rubber industry introduced to Amazonia a new kind of social actor – a peasant direct producer – closely linked through a mercantile network to regional and global economies, and did so with little in the way of backward linkages. The infrastructure of the rubber industry was largely represented in steam transport and warehousing. The product as delivered by the direct producer was untransformed until it reached a remote industrial metropolis. The labour regime was relatively unsupervised, and relations between trading partners were highly personalistic. One of the durable features of this system was the *aviamento* according to which direct producers made regular deliveries of rubber to local traders in exchange for subsistence goods (with or without augmentation of debt). It would be foolish to romanticize what was clearly – from vantage points near the bottom of the pyramid – a highly exploitative relationship, but the system was – and continues to be – viable from the point of view of social reproduction.

With the collapse of the rubber industry, just prior to World War I, a number of pathological expressions came to be used to characterize Amazonian society – for example, 'decadence', 'economic stagnation' – and the once direct link to the global economy (the passage from Manaus to Liverpool was quicker than that from Manaus to the national capital, Rio) was seen to be severed. As the commercial lustre wore thin, so the notion that the peasantry of Amazonia retained coherence lost plausibility.

The previous section concluded with the suggestion that the Amazonian peasantry was not autochthonous, and was not a derivative of pre-capitalist social formations. In the concluding part of this section this suggestion is augmented with the following one: the Amazonian peasantry is a creation of capitalist intervention, albeit a kind of capitalism that, as the dominant mode of accumulation, is largely consigned to the periphery of contemporary debate: merchant capitalism. The factors prevailing in the development of the rubber industry in Amazonia – the framework for the contemporary peasantry, or one of them at any rate – are uniquely combined: a natural, virtual monopoly on a scarce tropical presicosity (*hevea*); a labour shortage that can be mollified through inter-regional migration facilitated by the collapse of an archaic agrarian economy; a restricted (riverine) transport system; a regular increase in commodity prices on the world market; an extensive distribution of overhead costs through a wide system of trade; and finally, the inadvertent establishment of communities of petty commodity producers linked through a network of small trading houses/companies. While the ocean-going trading vessels disappeared from the scene and warehouses lay empty, Amazonia did not involute or become dormant; rather, direct producers extended the repertoire of activities necessary to maintain a livelihood. New crops were introduced (jute and malva, for example, and black pepper – introduced by Japanese Brazilians in Tomé-Açu – which represented a major addition), and extractivist industries (Brazil nut, pelts, fish, shrimp, cacao) proliferated.[7] None of these in any sense replaced rubber as the prevailing force in the regional economy, but nor did the economy disappear. It just became super-peasant: not peasant as retrograde agrarian actor, but peasant as disarticulated from the national trajectory.

WHERE IS THE ANTHROPOLOGICAL PEASANT IN AMAZONIA?

As should be clear from the discussion above, the relationship between the Amazonian peasantry and the agrarian question is not treated as a privileged area, for it is unclear whether the agrarian question – in its narrow formulation – is apposite in this context. What is of more interest is how generous in some respects is the default category 'peasant' (pick any spot along the line: auto-subsistent, formal subsumption, real subsumption) and how exclusive it is (closed corporate; depending on less than 50 per cent of labour time in proletarian guise [*Kearney*, 1996: 58], etc.). In the case of anthropological treatments of Amazonian peasantries there is yet another issue: how particular academic/disciplinary culture industries render product, and again, I wish to make an exceptionalist case, this time addressing Amazonianist anthropology. The purpose here is not to criticize, but to try to clarify how it is that a field – anthropology – has come to discriminate between coexisting Amazonian social fields, that of the indigene and that of the ersatz peasant.

Anthropological Amazonianist literature is largely ethnographic-monograph based. This is not to disregard key contributions that have appeared in other forms, but by and large, the literature is a collection of detailed case studies of peoples defined by their cultural homogeneity, the *x*-tribe, the *y*-tribe and so on. This has resulted in a highly valorized literature (the term 'fine-grained ethnography' is a supreme commendation), but a literature that has not allowed of much in the way of pan-Amazonian generalization. Three authoritative overviews [*Jackson*, 1975; *Overing*, 1981; *Viveiros de Castro*, 1996] as well as the magisterial *Historia do Indios no Brasil* [*Carneiro da Cunha* (ed.), 1992] concede that as yet, the literature is additive rather than synthetic.

There are good reasons for this state of affairs. For one thing the Brazilian government has not – to put it lightly – been particularly sympathetic to the idea that it should have to deal with a multiplicity of sovereignties. 'The Indian' will do as far as it is concerned, yet anthropological research has continually emphasized the diversity of Indianness and the close attention to the distinctiveness of Indian societies by anthropologists has underwritten notions of authenticity that have aided groups in pursuing particular and collective political programmes (land demarcation, halting development projects), and as the field has matured, a number of anthropologists acknowledge that the conduct of field research cannot be separated from overt advocacy on the part of subject peoples [*Ramos*, 1998; *Albert*, 2001], an additional headache for a government long accustomed to regarding indigenism as a problem.

Thus, we have a highly productive academic Amazonianist anthropology and one that is demonstrably politically vital to the life-chances of the few remaining indigenous peoples.

Given these conditions, Amazonian peasants appear to fall well beyond the remit of anthropology and are – often accurately – depicted as representing malign social forces, not least in the context of a government-mounted assault on 'the resource frontier' characterized by unregulated and volatile forms of predation. For example, the Amazon gold rush – commencing around 1980 – introduced perhaps one million gold miners into the region, generating high levels of social conflict, the invasion of Indian lands and the spreading of fatal diseases.

Assuming the plausibility of an argument for a residual peasantry in Amazonia, there are four marked ways in which peasantries are conceptualized within Amazonian agrarian/extractive structure. First, as antagonistic cohabitees (with Indians) of public land subject to valorization (i.e. made private); these are largely denigrated in the anthropological literature (see Nugent [1993]). Second, as actual, bounded corporate communities linked to mercantile networks via extensive repertoire of petty commodity forms (as well as via real subsumption in primary, secondary and tertiary sectors); these have been the subject of a very small number of anthropological monographs [*Wagley*, 1953; *Moran*, 1981; *Nugent*, 1993; *Harris*, 2001; *Pace*, 1985; see also the collection edited by Parker, 1985]. Third, as environmentalist actors, ranging from the pathological *caboclo com moto serra*, or 'peasant with a chainsaw', to the aspirant utopian 'wise forest manager'. And fourth, as frontier colonists inserted into the region post-TransAmazon Highway (*c.*1970); in the literature, these are mainly treated as economic actors.

In view of the relative paucity of empirical studies, it is not surprising that macro-models (three and four) have achieved greatest visibility, a fact no doubt strongly associated with the aggression with which the federal government has pursued its policies of so-called integration. Of these, the environmentalist (underpinned by panglossian sustainability arguments) commands greatest attention at the moment, but the 'frontier colonist' model(s) laid the strongest basis for an analysis of Amazonian agrarian/extractive structure that integrated historical and recent frontier peasantries.

Articulation and Penetration

Although some authors [*Browder and Godfrey*, 1997: 35–9] distinguish quite sharply between intersectoral articulation and capital penetration perspectives in relation to Amazonia, there are strong grounds for collapsing them. According to Browder and Godfrey [1997: 37], the two approaches differ on three points: (1) while the articulation model presumes a discrete category of peasantry, the penetration model is basically sectoral; (2) while the articulation model emphasizes the logic according to which pre-capitalism is maintained under capitalism, the penetration model 'stresses the logic by which we countenance the dissolution of the peasantry under capitalism'; and (3), while the articulation model emphasizes the appropriation of labour congealed in undervalued peasant products (e.g. cheap foodstuffs), the penetration model emphasizes the appropriation of means of production.

The articulation model addressed by Browder and Godfrey is one in which the expression 'pre-capitalist' underwent significant modification from the time of the work of early structural–Marxist anthropologists (working mainly in Africa) until its insertion into more wide-ranging debates about the agrarian question in Latin America (see Goodman and Redclift [1981]). Not least of the consequences of these modifications was a shift in meaning from a rigorous definition of pre-capitalism to a rather ersatz one (not quite capitalist). It would be fair to say that anthropological attention to substantivist and formalist economic logics was hardly galvanizing outside the field, but equally, the articulation arguments of Meillassoux [1972], Terray [1972], Dupré and Rey [1978], Godelier [1972], Wolpe [1972] and O'Laughlin [1977] are based on a notion of social reproduction in which pre-capitalist characterization (bearing on the substantivist/formalist distinction) is of some theoretical and empirical significance. In the case of Amazonia, it would be difficult to characterize peasant production as pre-capitalist in the sense first mounted in the articulationist arguments: Amazonian peasantries were products of capitalist penetration of the region, not the transformations of extant pre-capitalist social formations, but articulation – of petty commodity producers, say – still bears compelling implications.

Second, the peasantries of Amazonia are not being dissolved (and from what initial state in any case?), but being transformed, unquestionably further subsumed under a national economic structure, and it is an unanswered empirical question whether real subsumption is more potent than formal subsumption.[8]

Third, the appropriation of labour and the appropriation of means of production are parallel processes that have centre–periphery (e.g. region and nation, region and world economy) implications as well as internal ones (Amazonia itself represents a significant internal market, see Browder and Godfrey [1997] for detailed account of modern urbanization). Additionally, the appropriation of means of production (land) in Amazonia probably represents more a hedge against inflation than it does the establishment of *latifundios* (see Hecht and Cockburn [1989]) for other examples of agrarian capitalism.

What is little allowed for in much of the literature on neo-Amazonians, whether or not one maintains a distinction between articulation and penetration models, is the prior existence of a complex peasantry. When the frontier image is invoked (under whatever theoretical banner) the historical peasant appears to become a non-person, and the significance of actual existing peasantries becomes an antiquarian footnote to a projected future Amazonia (whether that be one of signed-up wise forest managers, independent small farmers, disorderly colonists or a region of grand projects – Tucuruí, Carajás, Jarí).

There are a number of possible explanations for this lacuna, some of which have been already been alluded to. One of these is that unlike many other Latin American societies, modern Brazilian peasantries have few significant cultural continuities with indigenous peoples, and in Amazonia itself historical peasantries are mainly represented by refugees from other quarters of the colonial project (e.g. chronic migration of *nordestinos* to the region). Even in the immediate period, the visible profile of 'Amazonian peasantry' is due more to the activities of the MST, arising more in reaction to conflicts in the agro-industrial south of the country than in – as yet – a distinctively Amazonian form.

A further possible explanation lies in the ascendancy of Brazil as a major semi-peripheral power such that the focus of compelling questions of agrarian transformation were closely linked with regionally specific matters of national significance from which Amazonia was excluded. In this regard, Amazonia has been marginal, as it was during the period in which slave-based plantation systems the Northeast were the national cynosure.

A further explanation – and one the aspects of which are taken up more fully later – has to do with the importance of extractivism (terrestrial and riverine) in the livelihoods of Amazonian peasantries, forms of extensive rather than intensive production which have militated against the formation of a rural class structure comparable to those typically encountered elsewhere in Brazil.

In the absence of a clear picture of 'Amazonian peasantry' it might seem perverse to suggest that an idealization may provide a partial solution to the problem of characterizing such a peasantry: an idealization of what extant examples?

For the purposes of this discussion an idealization is proposed: settled cultivators of land (which may or may not be titled, more often the latter) who are also extractivists (terrestrial and aquatic *foci*) and who may also engage in other livelihoods (drivers, artisans) including wage-labour.[9] This idealization is not intended to form the basis for an argument of unwarranted exceptionalism, but to try to frame the peculiarities of 'Amazonian peasantry' in a way that permits recognition of particular socio-historical features as well as some discussion of comparative value.

There are several reasons for this strategy. First, the non-person/agent status of historical peasantries in Amazonia has meant that they have been subject to redefinition/characterization by virtue of cavalier, external fiat. The *caboclo indolente* (= lazy peasant) of the 1920s is reconceived as potential 'wise forest manager' in the 1980s and 1990s on the basis of a theoretical shift requiring virtually no examination of empirical evidence.[10] Their inclusion in the larger programme of environmental awareness and concern is cynical, and has been promoted by the same autocratic agencies and interests that have been responsible for the pillage of the past quarter century: the deforestation of the region (around 14 per cent), threats to biodiversity, pollution, and rapacious mining, not to mention the engendering of intense social conflict.

Second, the plausibility of a critical social science depends significantly on challenging official and self-serving credos according to which the subjects of, say, anthropological investigation are rendered mute objects in a field of geopolitical strategizing.

ACTUALLY EXISTING PEASANT SOCIETIES

While the relative isolation of Amazonia from the main path of Brazilian national development may account for the lack of theoretical attention granted regional agrarian structure, it is also the case that the 'problem' of the Amazonian peasant would appear to have been solved by recourse to a crude environmental determinism: peasant societies are as they are because of environmental features that preclude socio-economic – not to mention cultural – complexity. Even those Amazonian peasantries that have been subject to detailed analysis tend not to be named peoples, but marked by geographical referents ('in the lower Amazon', 'in Tocantins-Araguaia', etc.).[11] In a tradition commencing with Steward's cultural ecology declarations and sustained today by much more sophisticated – but still resource-focused – research [*Moran*, 1993], peasants are portrayed as relatively incapable of surmounting the intrinsic natural defects of the humid neo-tropics.

An interesting commentary, although one largely based on Africanist and Asianist rather than New World material, is provided by J.M. Blaut [1994] in his discussion of 'The Doctrine of Tropical Nastiness', according to which widely acknowledged, common sense depictions of tropical societies and civilizations maintain a plausible stereotypical façade despite empirical refutation.[12] The three tenets of this theory do not withstand much scrutiny, but that has hardly subverted their firm grounding as folk wisdom. They are: (1) the negative effects of a hot, humid climate on the human mind and body; (2) the inferiority of tropical climates for food production; and (3) the prevalance of disease in tropical regions (on which, see Blaut [1994: 70]). The specifically Amazonian version of the Doctrine of Tropical Nastiness is embodied in the imagery of 'green hell'.

Amazonia as 'Green Hell'

The theory of 'climatic energy' invoked in tenet 1 has not been seriously defended since the 1950s. The theory of intrinsic impoverishment of food resources is not supported by historical, pre-historical and ethnographic evidence (see Beckerman [1991] for an Amazonia-specific discussion). Third, public health scourges associated with the humid neo-tropics are largely diseases of poverty introduced during the early colonial period. Whatever the facts of the matter, however, the enduring vision of 'Amazonian society' (whether Indian or peasant) is one of contingency: there are limits to what is socially possible, enforced by Tropical Nastiness. The constraints attributed to 'green hell' have been used in the past to explain – if not justify – the brutality of labour regimes in the region, from the debt-bondage of rubber tapping to the 'culture of terror' referred to by Taussig [1987] in the context of the Putumayo scandal. While few would deny the significance of ecological constraint, it need not invoke a pathological reading (see Baleé [1998], Esterci [1987], and Souza Martins [1997]).

'Green hell' and The Doctrine of Tropical Nastiness have a direct bearing on characterizing Amazonian peasants because they have aided in pre-empting serious study of such peoples on the grounds that peasant society is inchoate and it must either be approached through a resource/carrying capacity model (environmental determinism writ large) or though a broader model of national agrarian reform (in relation to which Amazonian agrarian structure is manifestly exceptional and hard to incorporate within the agro-industrial export programme).[13] The results of empirical case studies attending to actual existing peasant societies, few though they may be, tend to converge around a couple of key points: a broad though shifting range of peasant livelihoods; the durability of social organization; the long-term interpenetration of wage and non-wage forms of labour; and petty commodity production conducted under the regime of merchant capital.

Amazonian Peasants: The Discipline of Research Priorities

A recent monograph on the people of Parú in the lower Amazon [*Harris*, 2000] draws attention to the way the seasonality of riverbank existence matches shifts in both intensive and extensive forms of production, none of which provides an accurate focus for characterizing the economic structures embracing the people of Parú. Intense, seasonal commercial fishing is certainly a key feature for a significant proportion of Paruenses, but typical household production also depends on pastoralism, terra firme extraction, food agriculture, non-food agriculture and gardening. This is a monetized economy, but one that has shifted its cash crop basis (from jute to fish, for example) without necessarily transforming basically auto-subsistent regimes in the course of that shift. As noted above, this seems hardly an issue of articulation versus penetration, for the viability of the local community is premised on the existence of a market sufficient to absorb surplus, but insufficient to compel (or permit) proletarianization. This kind of system is often portrayed as an adaptation (cf. Moran [1974]), but an adaptation to what?

MAP 1

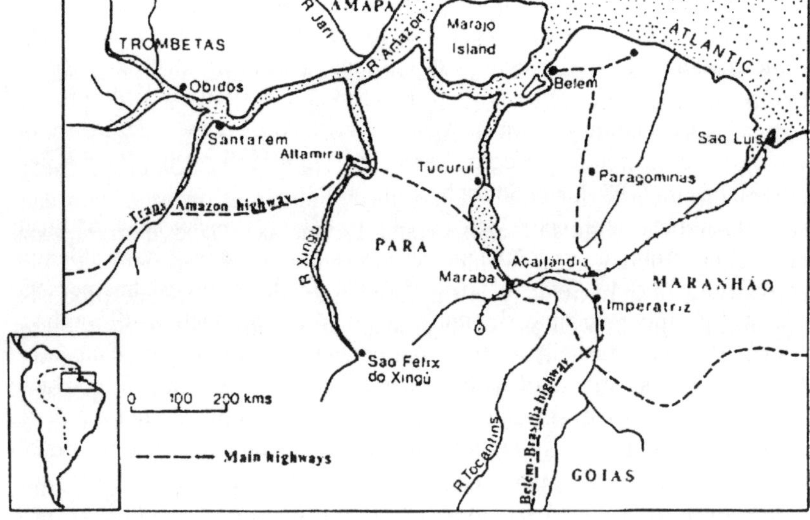

Source: *Journal of Development Studies*, Vol.23, No.4 (July 1987).

Otavio Velho [1972] offered a partial answer to this question in a discussion focused around frontier expansion that took place following the construction of the TransAmazon Highway (see Map 1). Small-scale frontier colonists cultivating untitled public lands were producing cheap foodstuffs (through engagement of non-valorized domestic labour) that subsidized both the growth of an expanding urban labour market and capital intensive export agriculture in the south of the country. A not dissimilar argument was later employed by Foweraker [1981] in arguing that state promotion of frontier agricultural expansion (largely through the provision of roads and a modicum of further infrastructural support) made possible the clearing – and hence commodification – of forest land that could then be usurped by large farmer/ranchers with the resources necessary to claim and title the land.

In both cases, the emphasis is on frontier expansion, but in many respects both arguments have pertinence in relation to the conditions of non-frontier Amazonian peasants as well: peasants persist in a permanent condition of ambiguity *vis-à-vis* peasant autonomy and formal subsumption.

An example from the Eastern Amazon, the town of Igarapé-Açu (see *Sousa Filho et al.* [n.d.]), shows how the frontier status need not be considered a transitional one in the sense that the collapse of the spatial frontier need not imply a collapse of the social frontier (i.e., a commodified agrarian structure does not imply proletarianisation). Established in the late nineteenth century as a community of peasant producers linked to urban markets only by river systems, the people of Igarapé-Açu produced a surplus of locally consumed foodstuffs (rice, maize, beans and *farinha*) as well as extractive produce (fish and game) conveyed to urban markets by local traders. In the period 1895–1940, with the construction of a railway linking the town to the state capital, the immigration of *nordestino* and Spanish settlers with sufficient capital to purchase land outright saw significant differentiation within the peasant category as well as the introduction of agro-industry in the form of various sugar-cane products (sugar and rum) as well as cotton production. As the authors note, these changes represent both an intensification and diversification of production, a point valid when considering a broad range of Amazonian peasant societies during the period between the collapse of the rubber industry and the modernizationist programmes of the late twentieth century.

The enhancement of local value-added activities (processing of cotton and rice) led to further differentiation in terms of household resources, but not to proletarianization. Indeed, the direct producers in Igarapé-Açu were linked to final markets via the system of *compra na folha* according to which personalized credit relations were established between direct producers and traders. With the addition of road transport (and gradual decline of the railway), improved access to peripheral regions led to more land being brought into cultivation and notable environmental degradation. Still, however, the diversification of agricultural activities proceeded with permanent cultivation (e.g. black pepper and *dendê* palm) as well as semi-permanent (e.g. *maracujá* – a fruit). The outcome of one hundred years of incremental peasant production expansion is summarized by the authors as follows: (1) the commodification of land; (2) the ascendancy of cash-only crops (black pepper, *dendê*); and finally, (3) the creation of a labour market [*Sousa Filho et al.*, n.d: 7].

This region is, notoriously, one of the most intensely deforested in Amazonia, and hardly a peasant paradise, but the transformation of the peasantry is hardly captured by the concept of frontier occupation and exploitation. Instead, there is a gradual, rather benign interpenetration of use-value and commodity production maturing over a period of 100 years, rapidly defeated at the end by the valorization of land prompted by road-building.

Both examples attest to a far more dynamic conception of Amazonian peasant than is evident in current or previous discussions of the modern Amazonian social landscape, and raise the question: why the invisibility/anonymity of such a cardinal feature of post-indigenous Amazonia? The relegation of neo-Amazonians by anthropologists has already been alluded to, as has the effect of the National Security State on peasant political organization from 1964 to 1985. An overriding factor, however, concerns the concept of agrarian reform in the Brazilian context.

Brazil, as is well known, has one of the highest concentrations of land ownership in the world. About 2 per cent of all agricultural landowners control 60 per cent of the arable land while half the agricultural labour force is landless, and in the face of pressure for agrarian reform, landowners have argued that reform should apply only to unoccupied public land, e.g. in Amazonia. A gloss on this is that agrarian reform is not about altering agrarian structure, but on stopping excessive growth in the coastal metropolises [*Leroy*, 1997], and in relation to such a goal, actually existing peasantries of Amazonia are an irrelevance. They are already part of the solution (they are structurally marginalized) and to them should be added many more of the dispossessed.

One measure of the structural marginality of Amazonian peasants is the scale of the informal (and hence untaxed) economy of the region. While there are some sectors that are subject to scrutiny (production for export, large-scale monoculture and ranching, major city markets), economic activity that goes unreported/unacknowledged is extensive to an astonishing degree. To take one minor, but indicative, example: a major extractive product in the Belém estuary is the fruit of the *açaí* palm. *Açaí* fruit landed at Ver-o-Peso is subject to *fiscalização* (taxation) and no doubt accounts for a substantial portion of that consumed in the city. What is landed at other wharves is also substantial, and given that there are some 2,000 retailers of *açaí* in Belém, one can with confidence refer to a grey economy in *açaí* of not inconsiderable economic proportions, and *açaí* is but one of the numerous products that make their way virtually directly from producer to consumer. Cleary [1990] has made this point in another context, that of gold production: the bulk of the 100 tonnes per annum of gold extracted from Amazonia during the 1980s and (dwindling) the 1990s found its way to market without the scrutiny of state operatives. The river trade from Belém to the upper reaches of the Brazilian Amazon River – *regatões* carrying manufactured goods to be exchanged for forest and river produce – occurs on a scale far beyond the reach of the statisticians at IBGE. The main point here is that there is an endogenous commercial Amazonia of considerable historical depth that has yet to be factored into generic accounts of 'rural Brazil'.

WHAT IS SO INFORMAL ABOUT THE INFORMAL SECTOR?

Over 25 years ago, Perlman's [1976] work on *favelas* of Rio and Brazilian internal migration drew attention to rural-urban relations that are suggestive in terms of thinking about the dynamics of Amazonian agrarian structure. Among her observations were three of particular salience: (1) the fact that *favelados* were not, as commonly assumed, just rural refugees, but also migrants from other urban areas and home-grown; (2) the fact that immigrants tended to be better skilled and educated than those who remained in the countryside; and (3), the fact that *favela* occupancy conferred certain material advantages – transfer of land from public to private 'ownership' and evasion of *fiscalização*. In the Amazonian context, these three observations draw attention to dynamic features that might help to account for the difficulty of situating the peasantry. With regard to forms of migration, for example, there are three considerations: immigration into Amazonia (from the north-east, classically); migration within Amazonia (in micro-region scale, between Belém and Santarém, for example); and systematic migration within micro-regions, in response to the annual flooding of the *varzeas*, for instance.[14]

Immigration to Amazonia is relatively well documented, certainly for the late modern period, and attention has mainly been drawn to the ways colonists adapt to new agricultural conditions (see Moran [1981]). This is, in effect, a frontier colonist literature attending more to the accommodations that have to be made by peasants unfamiliar with regional environmental conditions as well as the novelty of the prospect of independent smallholder status (see Wood and Carvalho [1988] for a demographic overview). Cleary's [1990] book about the Amazon gold rush documents a dramatic instance of opportunistic mass migration (see also MacMillan [1995]), but in general terms, this kind of migration is treated in national terms, one result of which is that the baseline for comparison is not Amazonian agrarian structure per se.

Migration within Amazonia by historical peasants is poorly documented. There is a set of case studies that allude to the fact that there are region-specific factors that prompt migratory shifts (e.g., the creation of large projects at Jarí and Carajás) that reflect something of the character of existing Amazonian peasants, but the broad features are not well documented. Systematic movement of historical Amazonian peasants among various livelihood possibilities are also weakly documented. A handful of monographs referred to above comprise – at best – a very fragmented set of empirical studies.

The threefold relevance of Perlman's observations is as follows.[15] First, marginal Amazonians have not become so through some simple route ('a land without people for a people without land'); there is a researchable (although largely ignored) Amazonian peasantry that persists, perhaps in interesting ways. Second, Amazonian *favelado* analogues have polymath attributes that are infrequently acknowledged. The straw-hatted, canoe-paddling fisherman could well be a former taxi-driver, lottery ticket salesman – hardly unusual, one would have thought, except that deviation from stereotype is so rarely recognized. Somehow, the notion that the boat going into town filled with forest produce is going to return to the margins with automobile batteries in service of television sets that will broadcast (in houses on stilts, palm frond roofs, a couple of bottles of tepid beer) the World Cup, doesn't scan, despite the fact that it obviously does. And third, as a largely (although now decreasingly) unregulated set of public resources, Amazonia has afforded numerous possibilities for opportunistic exploitation by peasants and large commercial entities as well as a middle range of land speculators and ranchers. The variety of strategic appropriations of natural wealth has been subsumed under the gross notion of 'frontier conquest' without sufficient heed being paid either to internal differentiation – one per cent of landowners control 57 per cent of officially registered lands [*Flavio Pinto*, 2001] – or to the long-term viability of particular kinds of resource appropriation (see Peters, Gentry and Mendelsohn [1989] for discussion of various sustainability trajectories).

As with Perlman's critique of the myth of marginality, re-evaluation of the dynamic features of Amazonian peasantries confounds received wisdom about the character of a self-provisioning plus petty commodity producing rural sector linked to the national economy *a là* Velho [1972] and Foweraker

[1981] through its capacity to supply cheap foodstuffs, and through the subsidy to land valorization (by bearing the significant primary costs of land clearing), and significantly disarticulated from that national economy (there is a vast internal, regional market).

The pressures under which Amazonian farmers/extractivists have found themselves in recent years are increasingly framed by developments in the national sphere, especially the federally directed assault on Amazonia as an untapped resource domain and the growth of large-scale, capital intensive agro-pastoral holdings, yet there is still capacity for accommodation within the existing repertoire of viable peasant livelihoods. What is less clear is whether national tendencies toward concentration of agricultural land will in the long term preclude the social reproduction of historic peasantries of the region.

Thiesenhusen [1996], for example, has drawn attention to the possible consequences of regional and national agricultural market integration by emphasizing the historic tendency for frontier regions such as Amazonia to lose their labour absorption capacity. There is an inverse relation between farm size and production per hectare, as there is an inverse relation between farm size and labour use per hectare. Data from 1980 indicate that farms of 1–10 hectares employed almost ten workers per hectare (with farms under 50 hectares accounting for 71 per cent of the total farm labour [*Thiesenhusen and Melmed-Sanjak*, 1990: 398] such that 12 per cent of the country's farmland accounts for more than half the value of farm income) and farms in the 2,000–10,000 hectare range employ 0.25 of a labourer per hectare (a ratio of 500:1). Returns on small farms, however, appear to be declining as resource depletion occurs (and such farms are weakened by subdivision with successive generations) and large farms – increasingly mechanized, therefore less labour absorptive – tend both to replace agriculture with pasture and maintain large unproductive holdings (35 million hectares according to the 1985 census). The consequence, as observed by Fearnside [1985: 246] – a veteran observer of the Amazonian scene – is that: 'At some point the flow of migrants to the Amazon may slow when the last remaining *minifundios* in Paraná and São Paulo are finally replaced by mechanized soya beans, wheat and sugar cane'. Or to put it another way, the proletarianization of Centre-South small farmers may insulate Amazonian peasants from the same tendencies while simultaneously the extractivist predation promoted by the state subverts the unique agro-pastoral–extractivist material base of a diffuse, marginal peasantry.

What is proposed here, echoing Mintz's [1974] analysis of the Jamaican peasantry, is that the Amazonian peasantry is best viewed as a particular kind of reconstituted peasantry, not one at the heart of Brazilian agrarian structure, but one shaped from a distance. Unlike the Jamaican peasantry, however, for which resistance was a hallmark of reconstitution, the Amazonian peasantry's reconstitution is better characterized – to use Harris's [2000: 25] expression – as resilience, an accommodation not to the disappearance of one agrarian regime (for it would be difficult to characterize colonial Amazonia as agrarian in any strict sense) but accommodation to an unusual set of historical and material conditions.

CHAYANOV AND THE ECOLOGICAL IMPERATIVE

In recent years the question of the Amazonian peasantry has been increasingly implicated in the question of sustainable development.[16] Perhaps the most potent example is provided by the efforts of Chico Mendes and the Rubber Tappers Union who forced on to the agenda the notion of extractive reserves, an *ejido*-like arrangement whereby collectively owned forest could be protected from the incursions of unregulated resource plunderers. Regardless of the mixed results of these efforts, the equation of social justice and ecological justice has been brought to the fore.[17]

While the dominance within Amazonian anthropological discourse of environmental determinism has long provided a shared frame of reference, with the massive increase in biological resource-oriented research commencing in the 1970s, there has been a notable segregation of social science and natural science camps, and a curiosity is the ecological fit of Chayanov [1966] in providing the missing link: with the increasing recognition by geographers, ecologists, economists and others of the particular social character of historic and frontier peasantries, Chayanov's attempts to explain socio-economic differentiation on the basis of demographic variation are particularly appealing. At the simplest level, the notion of 'carrying capacity' represents more than just a condensation of the social-landscape = natural-landscape pairing that has so long prevailed in Amazonianist discourse. If for Chayanov's Russian peasant it was the consumer:worker ratio that was key, it is the parallel social reproduction:natural reproduction that is now (inadvertently) substituted (see Perz [2000] and Porro [1997]).

The current Chayanovian discussion in Amazonianist literature is in many respects a marked advance, for it draws attention to an aspect of Amazonian peasantries that has long been excluded from serious discussion: actual Amazonian societies with dynamics worthy of examination as opposed to the mystical operators programmed into the macro-visions of state planners. That being said, the conception of Amazonian peasant sociality currently bolstered by a Chayanovian approach is still lacking in much historical depth. Chayanov has been invoked to provide a fairly adaptationist, strategy-seeking model for the peasantry rather than one that addresses the long-term formation of a peasantry reconstituted in the way suggested by Mintz [1974] for the Caribbean or, as I have intimated, derivative of the narrow constraints imposed by the domination of merchant capital. What it attends to particularly well, however, is the immediacy of peasant response to the state (and its agents) and highly variable environmental prerogatives, a response that belies the longstanding perceptions of the passivity supposedly afflicting the most marginal of the marginal.[18] A crucial difference between Chayanov's peasants and those of Amazonia, though, is that while for the former subsistence strategies represented (in part) a response to the capitalist/market transformation, for the latter the capitalist/market transformation has been a precondition. There may well be a 'logic of peasant production', but that logic mutates, and does so in ways that defeat attempts to anticipate a formulaic outcome. It may be the case, for example, that Amazonian informal sector/petty commodity participation in the market evades both the constraints of state-sector domination of Amazonian development (enacted, for example, via the Greater Carajás Project, see Hall [1989]), and those of the environment (see Mattos, Uhl and Gonçalves [n.d.]).

CONCLUDING REMARKS

That there are historical Amazonian peasantries is not an issue; that these peasantries remain largely invisible and thereby excluded from socio-historical analysis is, and it is a sad irony that even the heightened attention to the plight of Amazonia in the late twentieth and early twenty-first centuries has not secured a more prominent role for such peoples. There is no focal explanation, but a set of nested explanations that can account for the structural marginality of Amazonian peasantries not only in relation to the Brazilian state, but also in relation to scholarship. A key one of these is the persistence of a Eurocentric construction of the pathologies of 'green hell' that has bolstered a fundamentally ahistorical characterization of the region and its peoples. Another is the marginality of the region – episodically interrupted – and its retention as a resource domain whose primary products have gained appeal only with the decline of more accessible resources (e.g. bauxite in the Caribbean; tropical woods in Africa and Asia). Yet another is the atypicality of peasant livelihood prospects (with a strong riverine and extractivist base) in light of the prominent and normative agro-industrial structure of the Centre-South and other regions of Brazil. Additionally, the anthropological gaze has, for various reasons, been directed elsewhere such that Amazonian peasants have been trapped in a grey area between rural sociology/development studies and pristine ethnographic investigation. Last, the ascendancy of ecologically driven research, both in concert with and in opposition to top-down modernization, has tended toward crisis-focused solutions to the assault on the Amazon in which historical peasantries are conceived as minor players.

GLOSSARY

Açaí: a palm fruit (*Euterpe oleracae*) of considerable commercial value to small-scale extractivists.
Aviamento: debt-credit system according to which tappers exchanged rubber for consumer essentials.
Cabanagem: mid-nineteenth century uprising in Lower Amazon region involving all social classes.
Caboclo: in Amazonia, person with varied ethnic antecedents; peasant.
Compra na folha: to buy on credit.
Dendê: African palm oil (*Elaeis guineensis*).
Ejido: generic term for communally owned, non-partible land (based on Mexican agrarian reform device).
Engenho: sugar-mill – in Amazonia, tidally driven.
Favela: shanty town built on public land. Inhabitants: *favelados*.
Hevea braziliensis: the major species of rubber tapped in Amazonia.
IBGE: Brazilian Institute of Geography and Statistics.
Índio: Amerindian.
Ladino: in some South/Latin American countries, person identified as having European rather than Amerindian attributes.
Landless Workers Movement: The MST (*Movimento dos Trabalhadores Rurais Sem Terra)* has, since 1985, sought to occupy unproductive agricultural land in the name of landless labourers. To date, some 250,000 families have won title to more than 15 million acres.
Latifundio: large estate. In Brazil, a significant proportion of *latifundio* land is unproductive.
Mestiço: person with varied ethnic antecendents.
Nodestino/a: person from the northeast of Brazil (especially Ceará and Pernambuco). Many 'traditional' Amazonians have *nordestino* antecedents.
Quilombo: community of descendants of runaway slaves.
Regatão/ões: long-distance river trading vessels.
Ribeirinho: peasant cultivator/extractivist mainly living on river.
Rubber Tappers Union: The CNS (*Conselho Nacional dos Seringueiros*), based in Western Amazonia and, until his assassination in 1988, led by Chico Mendes, has promoted the idea of extractive reserves as a means of promoting both social and environmental justice.
Várzeas: refers generally to nutrient-rich, annually inundated lands of the Amazon Basin.
Workers Party: The PT (*Partido Trabalhista*) emerged as the major left opposition party in the wake of the 'redemocratization' of Brazil following the demise of the National Security State (1964–85). Notably more successful in cities rather than the countryside, PT has gained a number of significant victories.

NOTES

1. The physical size of Brazilian Amazonia as well as its socio-cultural and natural diversity militate against the notion of a generic 'Amazonian peasantry'. On the other hand, the region's historic marginality in relationship to the emergence of Brazil as a major semi-

peripheral state makes possible a degree of generalization: petty commodity-producing extractivists, agriculturalists and pastoralists occupying land that may or may not be titled and exploiting a range of terrestrial and riverine habitats. Although urbanization is pronounced – and has accelerated since the road construction projects commenced in the 1960s – many Amazonian peasants maintain both rural and urban identities. Most Amazonians are descended from immigrants – or are themselves first-generation immigrants – especially from the northeastern states of Brazil, and although there is a significant sub-set of *nordestinos* who maintain that identity within the Amazonian peasantry, there is a pronounced assimilationist tendency, not least because of national perceptions that Amazonia is a frontier region ineptly occupied not by members of distinctive societies (except in the case of Indians, who are definitely not a category of peasant), but by 'populations', 'inhabitants', 'settlers' or colonists.

2. See Dean [1987] for a detailed case study of ecological constraints on large-scale plantation agriculture.
3. Although there is an old – archaic? – debate in the anthropological literature concerning the appropriateness of characterizing fishing peoples as peasants, such discussion does not seem to have had much salience in relation to the agrarian question in Latin America. That a degree of Eurocentrism should afflict progressive attempts to analyse the course of development/underdevelopment in the New World may not be too surprising, but in the case of attempting to come to grips with 'the Amazonian peasant/agrarian question' two options present themselves: (1) make an exceptionalist claim in which the dominance of the (literally) agrarian question is attenuated by considering the full range of material conditions characteristic of peasant livelihoods, such as fishing/extractivism; or (2) place the Amazonian peasant outside the whole theoretical discussion of the agrarian transition. J.M. Blaut, in *The Colonizer's Model of the World* [1994], vigorously dissects the anti-tropicalist bias that would favour the latter.
4. In recent years, in the context of sustainability claims forged in the alliance of eco-politics and developmentalism, there has been a marked shift by some NGOs toward riverine peasant production. Mark Harris's *Life on the Amazon* [2000] is a rare example of a study of a *ribeirinho* peasantry; Lourdes Furtado's *Curralistas e Redeiros* [1987] is a massively detailed account of Lower Amazonian agriculturalists/fisherfolk (see p.125 for detailed illustration of the integration of riverine and terra firme activities); Violetta Loureiro in *Os Parceiros do Mar* [1985] provides an account of fishing communities forced from the littoral on to smallholding farming plots. The links between environmentalist and developmentalist arguments, however, are multifarious, often converging in Amazonianist discourse (see Anderson [1990]), but elsewhere critically opposed (see Latouche [1993; 1996] and Shiva [1988; 1991]).
5. The late twentieth-century attempt by Daniel Ludwig to create a similar 'factory in the field' project – the Jarí complex – was notably unsuccessful.
6. But see the contribution by Martins to this volume.
7. On the subject of the important economic role of Brazil nuts in Amazonia, see the contribution to this volume by Assies.
8. The extent of the informal economy in Amazonia is unknown, but there are few field researchers of long experience in the region who would not acknowledge the significance – if not dominance – of unmonitored economic activity. Even an activity as visible and specialized as gold mining is largely carried out in the informal sector.
9. This idealization excludes recent frontier colonists and commercial entrepreneurs such as ranchers while acknowledging that there is a high degree of drift (see Mattos, Uhl and Gonçalves [n.d.] for discussion of entrepreneurial peasants).
10. Which is not to say that the latter characterization is inaccurate. Its emergence is ideologically convenient.
11. Chico Mendes and the Rubber Tappers Union represent an important exception, the threat of which no doubt accounts in significant part for the vehemence with which Mendes' assassination was pursued.
12. The 'Doctrine' plays a relatively small, but crucial, part in Blaut's analysis, which is mainly devoted to the ways in which the writing of history from a European standpoint tends to

make special cases for societies on the periphery.

13. Despite its high industrial profile, Brazil is still dependent on the export of primary goods for over half of its foreign earnings. Amazonian exports are largely extractive and include not only minerals (e.g. iron ore and bauxite) produced in large enterprises, but exotic woods, shrimp and fish.
14. *Várzea* refers to low-lying riverbank that is annually – to an unpredictable degree and for an unpredictable duration – flooded during the period December–June. In the estuary of the Amazon (which is tidal for several hundred miles) there are numerous sub-categories. In the Middle and Lower Amazon (Manaus–Santarém, Santarém–Belém, roughly) *várzea* land is heavily exploited agriculturally and pastorally, its fertility guaranteed by alluvium originating in the weathering of the Andes. In pre-history, permanent settlement of the *várzea* was made possible through the construction of large-scale earthworks. In the modern period accommodation of the flood is more difficult and excessive flooding often results in large-scale migration to terra firme and/or cities/towns.
15. And it should be noted that despite her demonstration that the growth of *favelas* is not a pathological add-on to the 'development process', but central to it, there is still a tendency to regard them as epiphenomenal.
16. See Peters, Gentry and Mendelsohn [1989] for a succinct analysis.
17. One by-product has been government enthusiasm for biological reserves, the implementation of which often takes little heed of the fact that such reserve areas are not pristine ahuman environments, but social as well as natural communities.
18. Rod Aya's [1992] sympathetic critique of Wolf's [1969] *Peasant Wars of the 20th Century* is apposite. Aya argues that Wolf makes two historical generalizations, one of which holds, the other of which does not. The latter is that peasants react to capitalism in a uniform manner. The former is that there are a variety of tactical reactions. While Wolf may have been focusing on the revolutionary potential of peasantries, there is no reason not to consider more prosaic circumstances within the analysis. The military metaphors ('assault on the Amazon'; 'conquest of the tropics') are widely deployed, but the reality (which is by no means bereft of gross brutalities) is more often conducted under the terms of neo-colonialist and post-colonialist protocols, those of: neo-liberalism, bureaucracy, consultants, experts, 'officials', researchers, NGOs.

REFERENCES

Albert, B., 2001, 'Reflections on *Darkness in El Dorado*, Pts. I-III', *Documentos Yanomami*, Brasilia: CCPY.

Alden, D., 1969, 'Economic Aspects of the Expulsion of the Jesuits from Brazil: a Preliminary Report', in H.H. Keith and S.F. Edwards (eds.), *Conflict and Continuity in Brazilian Society*, Columbia: University of Southern Carolina Press.

Anderson, A. (ed.), 1990, *Alternatives to Deforestation*, New York: Columbia University Press.

Anderson, S., 1993, 'Sugar Cane on the Floodplains: A Systems Approach to the Study of Change in Traditional Amazonia', unpublished PhD thesis, University of Chicago.

Aya, R., 1992, 'Capitalism and Tactical power in Eric Wolf's Theory of Peasant "Revolt" in Revolutionary Situations', in J. Abbink and H. Vermeulen (eds.), *History and Culture: Essays on the Work of Eric R. Wolf*, Amsterdam: Het Spinhuis Publishers.

Balée, W. (ed.), 1998, *Advances in Historical Ecology*, New York: Columbia University Press.

Beckerman, S., 1991, '*Amazônia Estava Replete de Gente en 1492?*' in W.A. Neves (ed.), *Origens, Adaptacões e Diversidade Biológica do Homem Nativo da Amazônia*, Belém: Museu Goeldi.

Blaut, J.M., 1994, *The Colonizer's Model of the World*, New York and London: Guildford Press.

Browder, J. and B. Godfrey, 1997, *Rainforest Cities*, New York: Columbia University Press.

Bunker, S., 1985, *Underdeveloping the Amazon: Extraction, Unequal Exchange and the Failure of the Modern State*, Urbana and Chicago, IL: University of Illinois Press.

Chayanov, A.V., 1966, *The Theory of Peasant Economy*, D. Thorner, B. Kerblay and R.E.F. Smith (eds.), Homewood: American Economic Association.

Cleary, D., 1990, *Anatomy of the Amazon Goldrush*, Basingstoke: Macmillan and St Anthony's College.

Coomes, O.T. and B.L. Barham, 1994, 'The Amazon Rubber Boom: Labor Control, Resistance, and Failed Plantation Development Revisited', *Hispanic American Historical Review*, Vol.72, No.2.

Da Cunha, M.C. (ed.), 1992, *A História dos Índios no Brasil*, São Paulo: Editora Schwarcz.

Dean, W., 1987, *Brazil and the Struggle for Rubber: A Study in Environmental History*, Cambridge: Cambridge University Press.

Dupré, G. and P.P. Rey, 1978, 'Reflections on the Relevance of a Theory of the History of Exchange', in D. Seddon (ed.), *Relations of Production: Marxist Approaches to Economic Anthropology*, London: Frank Cass.

Esterci, N., 1987, *Conflito no Araguaia: Peões e Posseiros contra a Grande Empressa*, Petropolis: Editora Vozes Ltda.

Fearnside, P., 1985, 'Deforestation and Decision-making in the Development of Brazilian Amazonia', *Interciencia* 10 (September–October).

Flavio Pinto, L., 2001, 'Losing Eden', *Brazil Network*, www.brazilnetwork.org/amazon.htm

Forman, S., 1975, *The Brazilian Peasantry*, New York: Columbia University Press.

Foweraker, J., 1981, *The Struggle for Land: A Political Economy of the Pioneer Frontier in Brazil, 1930 to the Present*, Cambridge: Cambridge University Press.

Furtado, L., 1987, *Curralkistas e Redeiros de Marudá: Pescadores do Litoral do Pará*, Belém: Museu Goeldi.

Godelier, M., 1972, *Rationality and Irrationality in Economics*. London: New Left Books.

Goodman, D. and M. Redclift, 1981, *From Peasant to Proletarian: Capitalist Development and Agrarian Transitions*, Oxford: Blackwell.

Gross, D., 1975, 'Protein Capture and Cultural Development in the Amazon Basin', *American Anthropologist*, Vol.77, No.3.

Hall, Anthony L., 1989, *Developing Amazonia: Deforestation and Social Conflict in Brazil's Carajás Programme*, Manchester: Manchester University Press.

Harris, M., 2000, *Life on the Amazon*, Oxford: Oxford University Press.

Hecht, S.B. and A. Cockburn, 1989, *Fate of the Forest*, New York and London: Verso.

Hemming, J., 1987, *Amazon Frontier: the Defeat of the Brazilian Indians*, London: Macmillan.

Jackson, J., 1975, 'Recent Ethnography of Indigenous Northern Lowland South America', *Annual Review of Anthropology*, Vol.4.

Kearney, M., 1996, *Reconceptualizing the Peasantry*, Boulder, CO, and Oxford: Westview Press.

Lathrap, D., 1968, 'The "Hunting" Economies of the Tropical Forest Zone of South America: An Attempt at Historical Perspective', in R. Lee and I. DeVore (eds.), *Man the Hunter*, Chicago: Aldine.

Latouche, S., 1993, *In the Wake of the Affluent Society: An Exploration of Post-Development*, London: Zed Books.

Latouche, S., 1996, *The Westernization of the World*, Cambridge: Polity Press.

Leroy, J-P., 1997, 'Security, Livelihood and the Politics of Space in Brazil', interview by F.V. Mello, *Political Environments*, No.5 (Fall), www.cwpe.org/issues/environment_html/mello.html

Loureiro, V.R., 1985, *Os Parceiros do Mar: Natureza e Conflito Social na Pesca da Amazonia*, Belém: Museu Goeldi.

Loureiro, V.R., 1989, 'A Historia Social e Economica da Amazonia', in *Estudos e Problemas Amazonicos*, Belém: *Instituto do Desenvolvimento Econômico-Social do Pará.*

MacMillan, G., 1995, *At the End of the Rainbow? Gold, Land and People in the Brazilian Amazon*, London: Earthscan.

Mattos, M.M. de, C. Uhl and B. de A. Gonçalves, n.d., 'Economic and Ecological Perspectives on Ranching in the Eastern Amazon in the 1990s', Belém: Imazon.

McGrath, D., 1989, 'The Paraense Traders: Small-scale, Long-Distance Trade in the Brazilian Amazon', unpublished PhD thesis, University of Wisconsin, Madison.

Meggers, B.J., 1971, *Man and Culture in a Counterfeit Paradise*, Chicago: Aldine.

Meggers, B.J., 1977, 'Vegetational Fluctuation and Prehistoric Cultural Adaptation in Amazonia: Some Tentative Correlations', *World Archaeology*, Vol.8, pp.287–303.

Meillassoux, C., 1972, 'From Reproduction to Production: a Marxist Approach to Economic Anthropology', *Economy and Society*, Vol.1, No.1.

Mintz, Sidney W., 1974, *Caribbean Transformations*, Chicago, IL: Aldine Publishers.

Moran, E., 1974, 'The Adaptive System of the Amazonian Caboclo', in C. Wagley (ed.), *Man in the Amazon*, Gainesville, FL: University of Florida Press.

Moran, E., 1981, *Developing the Amazon*, Bloomington, IN: University of Indiana Press.

Moran, E., 1993, *Through Amazonian Eyes: The Human Ecology of Amazonian Populations*, Iowa City: University of Iowa Press.

Nugent, S., 1993, *Amazonian Caboclo Society: An Essay on Invisibility and Peasant Economy*, Oxford and Providence, RI: Berg.

O'Laughlin, B., 1977, 'Production and Reproduction: Meillassoux's "Femmes, Greniers et Capitaux"', *Critique of Anthropology*, Vol.2, No.8.

Overing, J., 1981, 'Amazonian Anthropology', *Journal of Latin American Studies*, Vol.13, No.1.

Pace, R., 1985, *The Struggle for Amazon Town: Gurupá Revisited*, Boulder, CO, and New York: Lynne Rienner.

Parker, E. (ed.), 1985, *The Amazon Caboclo: Historical and Contemporary Perspectives, Studies in Third World Societies, 32*, Williamsburg, VA: College of William and Mary.

Perlman, Janice E., 1976, *The Myth of Marginality: Urban Poverty and Politics in Rio de Janeiro*, Berkeley, CA: University of California Press.

Perz, S.G., 2000, 'Household Demographic Factors as Life Cycle Determinants of Land Use in the Amazon', paper prepared for the 2000 meeting of the Latin American Studies Association, www.136.142.158.105/2000PDFF/Perz.pdf

Peters, C., A. Gentry, and R. Mendelsohn, 1989, 'Valuation of an Amazonian Forest', *Nature*, Vol.339, pp.655–6.

Porro, A., 1996, *O Povo das Águas: Ensaios de Etno-Historia Amazônica*, Petropolis: Editora Vozes.

Porro, R., 1997, 'Peasant Decision-Making and Political Economy: Economic and Environmental Effects of the Variation in Resource Allocation within a Brazilian Agro-Extractive Peasantry', paper prepared for the 1997 meeting of the Latin American Studies Association, www. 136.142.158.105/LAS97/porro.pdf

Quijano, A., 1971, *Nationalism and Capitalism in Peru*, New York: Monthly Review Press.

Ramos, A., 1998, *Indigenism: Ethnic Politics in Brazil*, Madison, WI: University of Wisconsin Press.

Roosevelt, A.C. (ed.), 1994, *Amazonian Indians: From Prehistory to the Present*, Tucson, AZ: University of Arizona Press.

Roosevelt, A.C., 1980, *Parmana*, New York: Academic Press.

Roosevelt, A.C., 1991, *Moundbuilders of the Amazon*, New York: AcademicPress.

Santos, R. dos, 1980, *História Econômica da Amazonia, 1800–1920*, São Paulo: Queiroz.

Schwarcz, L., 1999, *The Spectacle of the Races*, New York: Hill and Wang.

Schwartz, S., 1985, *Sugar Plantations in the Formation of Brazilian Society, Bahia, 1550–1835*, Cambridge: Cambridge University Press.

Shiva, V., 1988, *Staying Alive: Women, Ecology and Survival in India*, London: Zed Books.

Shiva, V., 1991, *The Violence of the Green Revolution: Third World Agriculture*, London: Zed Books.

Sousa Filho, F.R. de, *et al.*, n.d.,'A Dinâmica Histôrica da Reprodução Agricultura em Area de Fronteira na Amazônia Oriental: o Exemplo do Igarapé-Açu, no Pará', www.dataterra.org.br/Documentos/chicopb.2.htm

Souza Martins, J., 1997, 'The Reappearance of Slavery and the Reproduction of Capital on the Brazilian Frontier', in T. Brass and M. van der Linden (eds.), *Free and Unfree Labour: The Debate Continues*, Berne: Peter Lang AG.

Steward, J., 1949, *Handbook of South American Indians*, Washington, DC: US Government Printing Office.

Taussig, M., 1987, *Shamanism, Colonialism and the Wildman: A Study in the Culture of Terror*, Chicago: University of Chicago Press.

Terray, E., 1972, *Marxism and 'Primitive' Societies*, New York: Monthly Review Press.

Thiesenhusen, W.C., 1996, 'Trends in Land Tenure Issues in Latin America: Experiences and Recommendations for Development Cooperation', Berlin: GTZ.

Thiesenhusen, W.C., and Melmed-Sanjak, 1990, 'Brazil's Agrarian Structure: Changes from 1970 through 1980', *World Development*, Vol.18, pp.393–415.

Velho, O., 1972, *Frentes de Expansâo*, Rio de Janeiro: Zahar.

Verissimo, J., 1970, *Estudos Amazonicos*, Coleção Amazonica, Serie José Verissimo, Belém: Universidade Federal do Pará.

Viveiros de Castro, E., 1996, 'Images of Nature and Society in Amazonian Ethnology', *Annual Review of Anthropology*, Vol.25.

Wagley, C., 1953, *Amazon Town: A Study of Man in the Tropics*, New York: Macmillan.

Weinstein, B., 1983, 'Capital Penetration and the Problems of Labor Control in the Amazon Rubber Trade', *Radical History Review*, Vol.27.

Weinstein, B., 1983, *The Amazon Rubber Boom, 1850–1920*, Stanford, CA: Stanford University Press.

Wolf, E., 1969, *Peasant Wars of the Twentieth Century*, New York: Harper and Row.

Wolpe, H., 1972, 'Capitalism and Cheap Labour Power in South Africa: From Separation to Apartheid', *Economy and Society*, Vol.1, No.4.

Wood, C. and M. de C. Carvalho, 1988, *The Demography of Inequality in Brazil*, Cambridge: Cambridge University Press.

From Dependency to Reform and Back Again: The Chilean Peasantry During the Twentieth Century

WARWICK E. MURRAY

LATIN AMERICAN PEASANTS – AN UNCERTAIN FUTURE?

Although the Latin American peasantry remains comparatively important in terms of livelihood generation and identity formation, the rise of neo-liberal economic theory and policy and its application across the continent arguably spells the demise of peasant economy and society.[1] There can be little doubt, therefore, that the economic liberalization associated with the most recent penetration of global capital represents an important – if not epochal – watershed in the transformation of Latin American peasantries. The latter notwithstanding, debates about this process, its causes and outcome, rage unabated. Views range from the *descampesinistas*, who insist upon the inevitable decline of the smallholding sector, to the *campesinistas*, who emphasize the vitality and adaptability of the peasantry [see *Kay*, 1997b; 2000]; however, the literature is on the whole fairly negative with respect to the implications of the current restructuring phase.[2] This article takes the political economy – arguably structuralist – position that a pre-determined transformation is not possible and that agrarian policy frameworks play a crucial role.[3] It is clear that, in the wake of globalization, the peasantry is being abandoned politically by Latin American governments whose primary concern it once used to be.

At a conceptual level, it appears that there is a simultaneous process of de-peasantization and de-agrarianization occurring throughout Latin America.[4] Despite the recent structural reforms launching economies back towards specialization in agricultural exports, in general the relative economic importance of agriculture is declining both in terms of income

---

Warwick Murray, Institute of Geography and Development, Victoria University, New Zealand. Email: warwick.murray@vuw.ac.nz. I would like to extend thanks to all of the Chilean farmers interviewed for this study. I am grateful to Bob Gwynne and Cristóbal Kay for the generous expert guidance and feedback on the PhD on which some of the article is based. Tom Brass should also be thanked for the extensive and constructive editorial comments and suggestions on the first draft.

and employment [*Murray*, 2002a]. Peasant farmers are being marginalized as a result of the rapid restructuring taking place, in terms of land concentration, earnings and access to inputs and other resources. Although broadly speaking the peasantry is being proletarianized, both the form taken by and the consequences of de-peasantization and de-agrarianization are uneven and contextually specific. In some cases, therefore, what is occurring is disguised proletarianization, where small growers become so dependent on agri-business that they effectively become employees of that concern. Full proletarianization is also increasing as more peasants are affected by the economic pressures of market forces, swelling the ranks of temporary rural labourers, or urban migrants. Perhaps the most important process, however, is semi-proletarianization, whereby peasant farmers are increasingly forced to combine their on-farm income with other off-farm forms of income generation.

The case of Chile is particularly illuminating in this regard, given the relatively widespread agrarian reforms that were undertaken there in the 1960s and 1970s, and the neo-liberal experiment which was conducted by the military dictatorship from the mid-1970s onwards. Chile was the first of the developing economies to experience neo-liberal 'shock' treatment based on the economic doctrines of Milton Friedman of the University of Chicago, and it underwent the purest application of this theory to date. Throughout the 1990s, a period characterized by a return to democracy, the free market economic model has been altered very little. Yet within these overarching macro-economic trends, micro-economic change in response to neo-liberalism unfolds unevenly across nations as they are pulled into the ever-expanding vortex of capitalist accumulation. The specific nature of this insertion, as it affects countries, regions, and rural localities, gives rise in turn to the varying trajectories of agrarian transformation which pattern the broad sweep of epochal change.[5] Perhaps the structuralist idea that national economies are conditioned by externalities, or the nature of their insertion into the broader global capitalist system, has never been as true as it is today; equally true, however, and as the Chilean case studies presented below confirm, is the specific nature of these transformations as experienced by those at the rural grassroots.

This article builds on the observation that, '[t]racing the historically contingent processes of peasant formation and dissolution confirm rather than deny the importance of differences in locality, context and human agency' [*Bryceson*, 2000: 5]. As such, in order to understand the unravelling of the peasantry in specific cases, it is necessary to understand the mechanisms which articulate 'global' processes at the level of the locality, how such processes are conditioned by and re-condition the interaction between the different levels involved, and how resultant patterns are contingent upon different micro-physical and human geographies. This entails a detailed appreciation of the history, political economy and environment of the contexts studied [*Llambí*, 2000], and a careful teasing out of the interaction between the factors responsible for change. Such ideas have long been important, but given the present widespread conceptual ascendancy of the 'global', it is crucial to situate the latter in an understanding of the 'local'.

To this end, the analysis which follows traces transformations in the structure of peasant economy in two localities which were subject to land reform in the 1970s, and were then thrust into the economic orbit of the global fruit complex in the 1980s. By comparing the impact of Chile's neo-liberal agro-export boom on landholders (*parceleros*) in different regional contexts, it is possible to highlight the importance of local contingency on the direction and pace of such macro-economic transformation.[6] Special emphasis is placed on the connection between agri-business enterprises and peasant farmers, since this relationship is the mechanism linking the 'local' to the 'global'. The article begins by considering the recent history of the peasantry in Chile, the creation of the *parcelero* sector, and the adoption of neo-liberal rural policy. Having outlined the characteristics of the fruit export boom, it then presents findings from two localities where fieldwork was conducted in 1995. Following a comparative analysis of the changes taking place in these locations, the conclusion focuses on their implication for rural transformation and agrarian policy in Chile and beyond.

PEASANTS IN CHILEAN HISTORY

The historical trajectory in Chile, from one form of internal dependency up until the 1950s, to the hopes embodied in the various agrarian reform programmes from the mid-1960s to the early 1970s, and the despair represented by the return once again to dependency in the 1980s and 1990s, is not difficult to discern. In order to understand the current fate of the market-oriented *parceleros*, however, it is necessary to put them into a broader context of Chilean history, and in particular to trace how peasants generally have been involved in and affected by the transformations in agricultural production, tenure patterns, and national politics. Broadly speaking, the evolution of peasant smallholding in Chile has followed the same pattern of rural change as that experienced elsewhere in Latin America, and as such its development has been determined by the combined shifts in national and international capitalism structuring the integration of Chile into the global economy.[7] Created in the course of land settlement/alienation that accompanied Spanish colonization in the sixteenth century, the majority of Chilean peasants have since that time operated at the economic margins of existence, and benefited little from the formal process of independence from Spain at the start of the nineteenth century.

During the nineteenth century the *latifundio/minifundio* complex (based on the coexistence of large estate and peasant smallholder) was consolidated, and production relations on the rural estate (or *hacienda*) system in Chile's central valley were structured by a system of internal dependency. The latter condition arose from labour-rent payments made to landlords by livestock-owning tenants (*inquilinos*), peasants who received in exchange grazing/usufruct rights to a portion of estate land.[8] As elsewhere in Latin America, the growth in the external demand for agricultural produce stimulated the expansion of the large *latifundia*. Thus the landlord response to the 1850s wheat boom was to expand labour-intensive cultivation, which entailed settling more tenants on the rural estate, and increasing the amount of labour-rent.[9] From the 1930s onwards, however, raised wheat output by Chilean landlords no longer depended on a settled workforce composed of tenants: the increasing trend towards mechanization led to the proletarianization of labour-tenants (= depeasantization), and the employment of outside migrant workers. This process of workforce restructuring accelerated during the political struggles of the 1950s, as estate tenants resisted proletarianization and welfare legislation increased the cost of tenant labour-power. Although the landlord class still exercised political power at this juncture, through its control over the state apparatus, this was subject to increasing challenge: the latter derived from the extension of the franchise to the peasantry, which ensured that from this point on political parties began to compete for the mass rural vote.

Land Reform and the Peasantry: Internal and External Pressures

A direct effect of increased peasant participation in national politics was that land reform was forced onto the policy agenda, and the three Chilean governments which took office between 1954 and 1973 all addressed this particular issue. The objectives of the reforms changed over time, from an emphasis on productive efficiency to an overriding concern with exploitative social relations of production and rural poverty. Land reform programmes during this period have been categorized in different ways: for example, Kay [1977b] characterizes that undertaken by the Alessandri government (1958–64) as 'technocratic', that of the Frei government (1964–70) as 'reformist', and that of the Allende government (1970–73) as 'radical', and these labels are persuasive. The problems of rural poverty and food supplies, however, were not solved by these agrarian reform programmes, and the import substitution policy of the 1960s was replaced by the free market policies of the mid-1970s, the 1980s and the 1990s.

The domestic agenda of production increases and poverty reduction was in turn combined with external pressure to achieve the same end. Increased food output based on land reform was at the centre of the 1950s development strategy advocated by the United Nations Commission for Latin America (ECLA). Rather than outward-oriented economic growth linked to the export of primary commodities (copper in the case of Chile), ECLA argued for the adoption of inward-oriented development, which would inaugurate and sustain a virtuous economic circle. This consisted of import substitution premised on the expansion of the internal market in Latin America, which necessitated increasing the purchasing power of the rural population by means of agrarian reform programmes. The major obstacle to economic growth, therefore, was the existing inequality in the system of land tenure.[10] By expropriating unproductive landlords, and putting cultivable land hitherto belonging to the latter into the hands of productive smallholders, ECLA argued, all the economic problems associated with inflation and balance-of-payments deficits would be solved.

Interestingly, in the light of events and neo-liberal policies from the mid-1970s onwards, this ECLA argument was made not so much against a laissez-faire economic policy as in the name of the free market: the latter, it was pointed out, could not function properly so long as Chilean landlords were under no *economic* compulsion to surrender their land to more productive economic agents (= smallholders). It was in order to make the market work, therefore, that ECLA recommended that the Chilean state should intervene politically, and expropriate the landlord class.[11] According to this development strategy, a result of land reform would be that land itself became a commodity; peasants with land would then produce food for the nation, saving foreign exchange for investment in domestic industry, and at the same time buy commodities produced by the latter with income generated from the cultivation of food crops. In Chile this ECLA strategy was followed over the period 1964–73 by parties at different points on the political spectrum.

Alessandri's approach, like the party he represented, was conservative and intended to raise productivity only. Land reform legislation was passed, but under pressure from the landed elite it was not implemented.[12] During the mid-1960s, therefore, the agrarian reform programme of the Christian Democrat president Eduardo Frei Montalva attempted a capitalist modernization of the estate system, by expropriating large and/or economically inefficient estates, setting up agrarian cooperatives (*asentamientos*), giving ex-tenants ownership rights, and providing state credit for agricultural production.[13] In 1964, he pledged 'massive, drastic and rapid' land reform to increase both efficiency and equity [*Brown*, 1989]. Frei's initiative was backed by the US anti-communist Alliance for

Progress, which intended to reduce the potential for revolution in the countryside across the continent. It was during this period that the parcellation process was initiated. After initial collectivization, beneficiaries could decide whether to carve up estates into individual plots. Ultimately Frei's reform did not live up to its promise for the peasantry in terms of increased land access.[14]

President Allende's socialist Popular Unity government which was elected in 1970 expropriated all estates, extended the agrarian reform to include hitherto excluded poor peasants and agricultural workers, and introduced food price controls.[15] The response of rich peasants was to withhold foodstuffs which, together with declining imports combined with increased consumption, led to shortages that contributed to the military coup of 1973.[16] Allende's government rapidly accelerated and attempted to fully collectivize the process began under Frei, placing the elimination of rural inequality at the centre of the agenda. Thus all large estates over 80 basic irrigated hectares (BIH) became eligible for expropriation – regardless of efficiency criteria and land use. In 1973, due largely to increased pressure from the peasantry, which had grown dissatisfied with the speed of the programme and had become involved in increasingly violent land seizures (for example, in Melipilla during 1972), a law was passed which allowed the expropriation of inefficient farms between 40 and 80 BIH. Very few land reserves were offered to former owners (*patrones*), and no cash compensation was made available. Undoubtedly this added to the groundswell of dissent among the landed elite and its supporters which helped precipitate the downfall of Allende.

Military Counter-reform and Neo-liberalism

On the advice of the new libertarian economists belonging to the Chicago school, the Pinochet dictatorship restored expropriated land to previous owners, banned political activity, cut wages, and ended food price controls for the urban working class and subsidies to peasant smallholders.[17] With the resulting collapse of domestic purchasing power, and the reversal of the internally oriented development strategy advocated by ECLA, medium-scale capitalist producers began to export traditional staple foods – which locals were no longer able to afford – to international markets. The historical trajectory over the last half of the twentieth century had accordingly come full circle, and peasant producers in 1990s Chile once again found themselves in a precarious economic situation of dependency, but with one major difference: unlike tenants on the estate system in the 1950s, who were dependent on an internal landlord class, peasant producers in 1990s Chile found themselves dependent on an external capitalism.

Soon after the assumption of power the military regime declared its intention to 'normalize' and 'consolidate' the agrarian reform programmes of Frei and Allende. The main objectives of this counter-reform were threefold. First, to dismantle the *asentamiento* system by returning land to former owners; second, to raise the efficiency of agriculture by stimulating competitive forces, principally through parcellation for selected beneficiaries; and third, to fragment and weaken the political power of the collectivized peasantry [*Hojman*, 1985]. Ultimately, this counter-reform would constitute part of a move towards neo-liberalism in the wider economy and society, where individualism and competition became the central pillars of Chilean development policy [*Silva*, 1995].

Of the land worked as cooperative farms in 1973, 30 per cent was returned to the former owners, 30 per cent of the land was auctioned privately, and 7 per cent was kept by the state. Thirty-three per cent of land was converted to *parcelas* [*Collins*, 1979]. Selection for *parcela* ownership would be based on an exacting point-based competition which was ostensibly technical. In practice, political background determined many outcomes. The process of grading was secret, although appeal was possible. Not surprisingly, very few unsuccessful applicants filed complaints. Successful applicants among the peasantry were offered the plots at 50 per cent of market value, often obtaining credit from the reform commission CORA (*Corporación de la Reforma Agraría*).

By 1979 the counter-reform was completed. The increased importance of the small (<5 BIH) and medium–small (5–20 BIH) *parcelero* sector, rising from 22.7 per cent to 42.3 per cent of total land, is shown in Table 1. The new *parcelas* were almost exclusively carved out of formerly collectively owned land – though not all of those who had worked on the collective farms were able to gain from this subdivision and privatization, given constraints in access to credit and the political nature of the selection process outlined above. The growth in the large-scale farm sector, above 80

TABLE 1
PROPORTION OF LAND ACCOUNTED FOR BY DIFFERENT SIZED FARMS, CHILE, 1972–79

Size category	1972	1979
<5BIH	9.7	13.3
5–20BIH	13.0	29.0
20–80BIH	38.9	36.3
>80BIH	2.9	16.9
Collective sector	35.5	0.0
Public agencies	0.0	4.0

Source: *Murray*, 1996
Note: distributions are expressed as percentages

hectares, resulted mainly through the return of land to former *patrones*.

Initially then, the reform increased land access for the peasantry. However, many of the new *parceleros* failed to keep up with payments, thus beginning a process of re-concentration soon after the reform's completion. The prospect of a peasant renaissance was short-lived, as 'savage capitalism' [*Kay*, 1977b] carved a deep swathe of economic differentiation across the countryside and creditors refused to support peasants who had benefited from land sales by the military government [*ICIRA*, 1979]. It is widely accepted, however, that the counter-reform precipitated increased agricultural efficiency [*Cruz*, 1993; *Gwynne and Meneses*, 1994; *Kay*, 1993; *Universidad Católica*, 1991]. With the creation of an active land market, a new class of small-to-medium sized farmers was created. In general, the new *parceleros* were private landowners, commercially oriented, and often employed wage-labour on their plots. De-collectivization, and the concomitant restructuring of the agrarian economy, undoubtedly contributed to the agro-export led growth of the late 1970s and 1980s [*Murray*, 1998].

The Agro-export Boom and Agrarian Policy

In the wider political economy the military pursued a neo-liberal economic model, being the first such example in the Third World periphery. This model placed particular emphasis on the opening of the economy in order to stimulate export growth. New niches in global markets for non-traditional agricultural exports (NTAX) – such as fruit, fish and forestry products – appeared with fortuitous timing. Chile's abundant natural resources, counter-seasonality with respect to major markets, and de-unionized labour force attracted capital investment, precipitating a major boom. The growth of the fruit export sector has become the best-known instance of capitalist restructuring [see *Murray*, 1999], as nominal export values increased from close to zero in 1974 to nearly a billion US dollars in 1991. Fruit became Chile's second largest export sector, and the country became the leader in the southern hemisphere.[18]

Given the fruit specialization in the case studies outlined below, reference must be made to the main species of fruit exported. Grapes and apples became the two leading export items as Chile competed on international markets in price rather than quality terms [*McKenna and Murray*, 2002]. From the mid-1980s, however, the saturation of global markets (a result of increased competition, especially from New Zealand and South Africa), growing protectionism in the USA and EU, and the appreciation of the Chilean peso, all led to sharp decreases in the real price of Chilean fruit exports. Between 1986 and 1994 (that is, up to the point of the fieldwork surveys) the real value of grape exports stagnated. Apple export values declined sharply in the late 1980s, and collapsed in 1993.

The salient question here is: how did this boom and the subsequent stagnation impact on the *parcelero* sector in different markets and localities? What mechanisms allowed these farmers access to such markets initially, and how did these arrangements evolve? Given that policy at the time was anti-interventionist, what implications did global market-orientation have for the economic viability of peasant farmers and the social cohesion of their rural communities? These questions are not merely of historical interest. During the democratic transition, agrarian policy has changed relatively little [*Kay*, 1997a; *Murray* 2002b]. Whilst there is now more explicit concern with rural poverty, and some targeted state intervention, the principal policy for small-scale farmers is to encourage *reconversión* (conversion) into globally oriented, competitive sectors. The ideology underpinning this policy framework is economic Darwinism – failure is seen as an indication of non-competitiveness, and is therefore regarded by the state as an essential and positive element in the economic rationalization and modernization of rural Chile.[19]

The point made by means of the case studies presented below is that such a Darwinist economic perspective ignores the rather obvious structural impediments to successful participation on the part of peasant farmers in global markets. These impediments can only be tackled – if at all – by policy which addresses deep-seated political and economic asymmetries in the capitalist market. In particular, power-relations (and thus policies) tilt heavily in the favour of agri-business enterprises which, in times of market saturation, will inevitably take advantage of these imbalances.

PEASANT DIFFERENTIATION COMPARED

Research was undertaken during the mid-1990s in two localities, El Palqui and East Curicó, in the regions of the Norte Chico (Region IV) and Maule (Region VII; see Map 1) respectively. These areas were subject to extensive land reform in the 1970s, and were affected by major export-oriented booms in the 1980s. Significant *parcelero* specialization has developed: in grapes in El Palqui, and in apples in East Curicó. Semi-structured questionnaires were used to interview the growers (and other informants) owning less than ten hectares, about their agricultural activities and relationships with agribusiness.[20] Sample characteristics are reported in Table 2, broken down into smaller *parcelación* and village units which comprise the wider localities. These case studies are considered in turn, each beginning with a contextual investigation of the impacts of restructuring in the surrounding region.

MAP 1
CHILEAN REGIONS AND FIELDWORK SITES

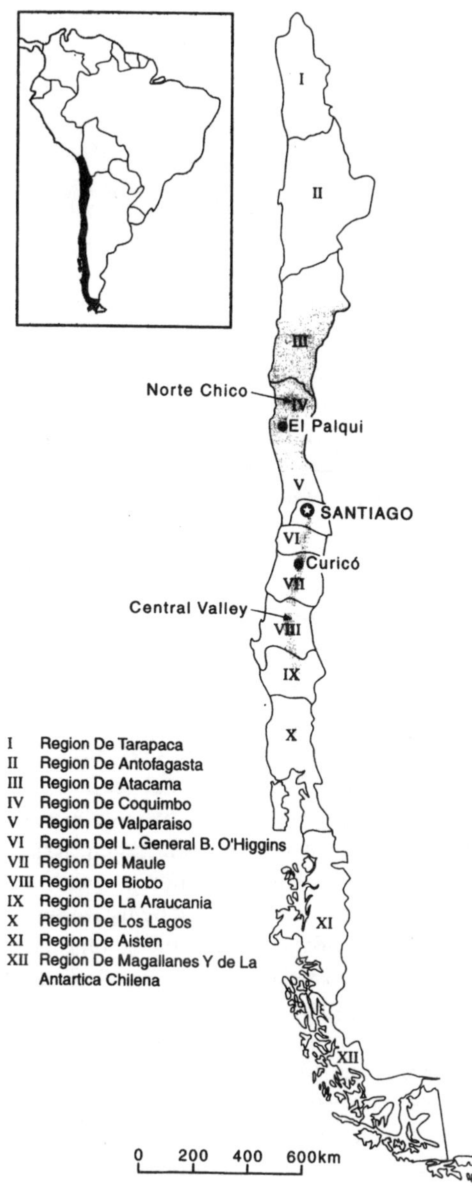

Source: Warwick E. Murray and Kevin Burkhill.

TABLE 2
SAMPLE CHARACTERISTICS, EL PALQUI AND CURICÓ FIELD STUDY 1995/96

Parcelación/ village	Hectares in use*	No. of plots	Mean plot size	No. <10 ha.	Mean sampled plot size	No. of inter-views
El Palqui						
Los Litres	178	34	5.2	34	4.8	11
Santa Rosa	338	50	6.8	45	4.9	9
San Antonio	263	22	12.0	11	7.6	6
Totals	*779*	*106*	*7.3*	*90*	*5.4*	*26*
Curicó						
Los Niches	297.61	12	24.8	6	7.3	3
Chequenlemu	1094.09	48	22.8	19	8.75	4
Cordillerilla	447.69	27	16.58	13	8.9	8
Santa Rosa	29.50	6	2.85	15	8.9	2
Vista Hermosa	373.49	37	10.08	5	7.7	3
Totals	*2242.40*	*130*	*17.25*	*61*	*8.44*	*20*
GRAND TOTALS	3021.40	236	12.8	151	6.72	46

Sources: *Roles* of *Impuestos Internos* for El Palqui and Curicó (1994) and fieldwork.
Note: *Refers to hectares within the *parcelaciones*/ villages in any type of agricultural use. Unfortunately, the *roles* do not provide detail on exact agricultural land use.

Capitalist Restructuring in the Norte Chico

Chile's semi-arid zone, the Norte Chico, has rapidly become Chile's leading grape export region, and one of the major supply zones for this agricultural commodity in the southern hemisphere. Historically, agriculture has been relatively difficult in this zone, given its climatic and topographic characteristics, which partly explain the high incidence of poverty traditionally observed in the region. Much marginal land has been converted to grape production over the last two decades, as the agricultural frontier has expanded rapidly [*Pino*, 1995]. Much of this growth has taken place in the region's five east–west oriented valley systems: Copiapó, Huasco, Elqui, Limarí, and the Choapa valleys. El Palqui is located in the Guatulame valley, which is within the Limarí system (see Map 2). The distribution of temperature and insolation characteristics throughout the year means that the harvesting period, from mid-November to mid-February, has generally coincided with peak prices (around the Christmas festivities) in northern hemisphere markets. Harvest times in the Guatulame can be particularly early, and thus the produce can command excellent prices.[21]

The region's grape economy is almost entirely dependent on an interconnected dam/irrigation infrastructure. Three dams in the Limarí have made export orientation possible – La Paloma, on which El Palqui is located

MAP 2
THE LEMARC VALLEY

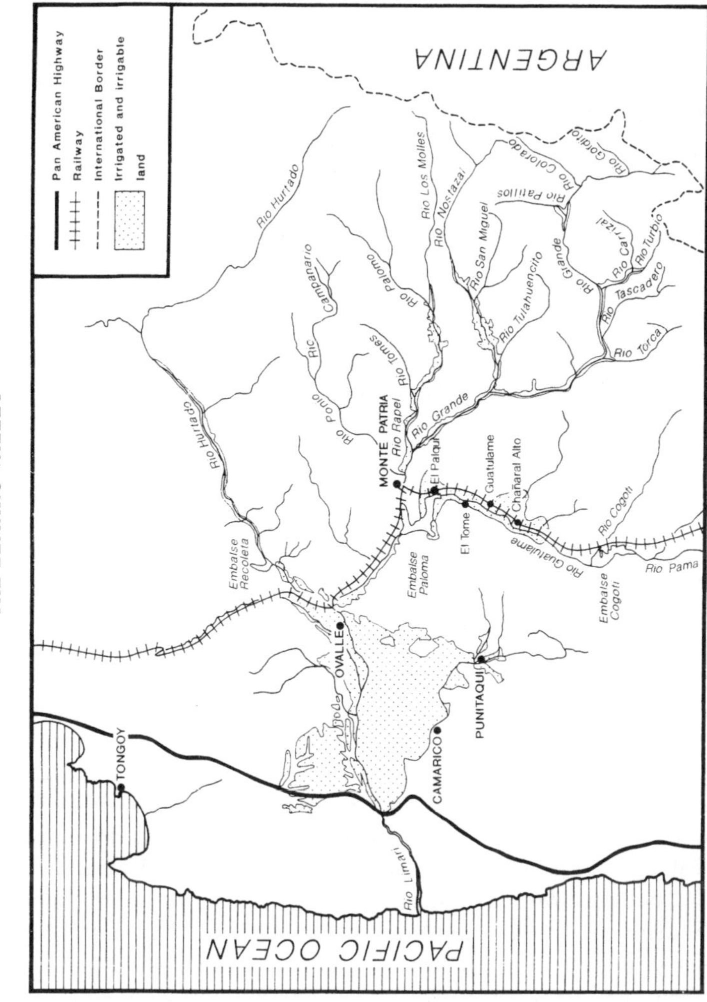

Source: Gwynne and Meneses (1994)

TABLE 3
PRODUCTIVE LAND USE IN THE GUATULAME VALLEY, 1962–88

Land use	Hectares 1962	Hectares 1979	Hectares 1988
Grapes	72.5	128.59	1,514.4
Annual crops	1,222.5	993.43	603.0
Other fruits	10.0	80.69	76.2
Grazing	175.0	172.60	160.0
Totals	1,480.0	1,375.31	2,353.2

Source: *Murray*, 1996

being the largest such facility in South America. The marginality of the regional environment is cause for concern, however, as rainfall declines, dam system losses grow, and water prices rise rapidly [*Gwynne*, 1993].

Natural and constructed advantages in the region, combined with reforms, have shifted the economic base from one oriented towards the production of horticultural products for local and national markets, to one which is directed largely at the northern hemisphere winter fruit market. In the ten years preceding 1992, land devoted to the cultivation of the table grape rose approximately fourfold; from 1,780 to 7,335 hectares [*CIREN-CORFO*, 1982 and 1992].[22] The transformation has been most spectacular in the Guatulame, where between 1962 and 1988 land on which grapes were grown rose from 70 to 1,500 hectares (see Table 3). The region as a whole now exports close to 20 per cent of the Chilean grape export total.

Peasant farmers have played an integral role in this transformation, and in numerical terms dominate the regional export economy.[23] Such growers have been able to participate in the export drive through the provision of capital by agri-business. The first company involved in the region was domestically owned David Del Curto (DDC). Foreign capital entered the regional market in the early 1980s: for example, Unifrutti in 1982, UTC in 1984, and Standard Trading in 1984. Total combined investment in establishing farm production by these enterprises was by 1995 estimated at US$250 million [*Murray*, 1997].

Virtually all of the export companies participating in the regional economy utilize the credit-consignation-contract (CCC) form of procurement in their relations with *parceleros*. In this system, credit is advanced by the companies to growers for the initiation and maintenance of grape plantations; this sum – plus interest and commission – is then subtracted from the final receipts for the product at the port of destination. This system has 'tightened up' in response to market pressures outlined previously. Rates of interest and commission have risen, new debt clauses

MAP 3
EL PALQUI AND LOCATION OF STUDY *PARCELACIONES*

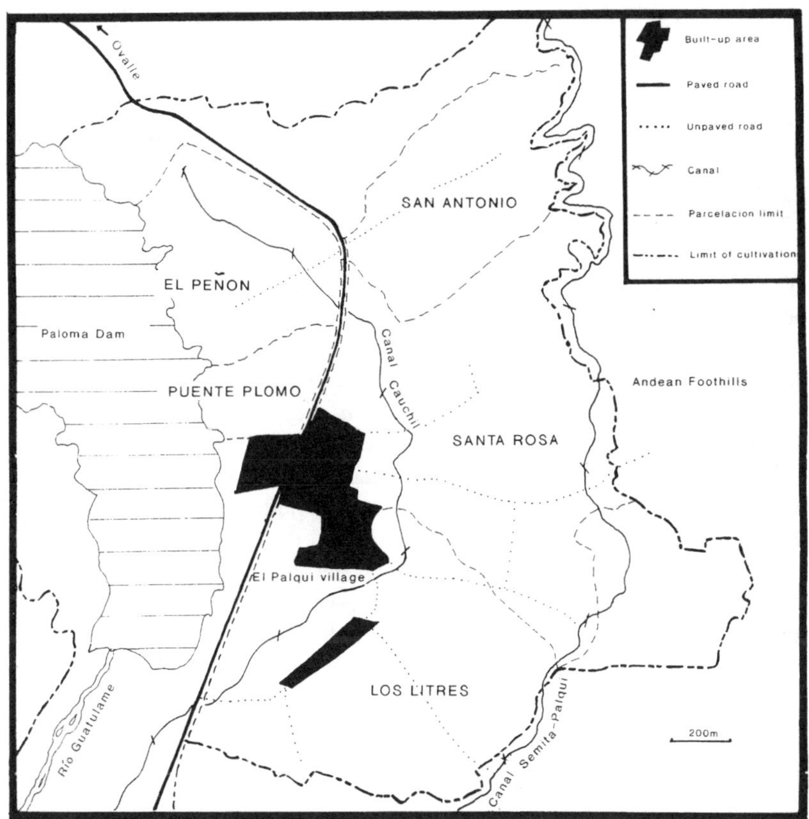

Source: Warwick E. Murray.

oblige growers whose returns do not cover credits and charges to supply exclusively to the firm, and the monopoly provision of inputs, labour and technology is now often required by the firm. In short, firms are able to obtain bilateral monopoly positions with relative ease, acting as banker, advisor and customer to the growers.[24]

Peasant Differentiation in El Palqui

> 'Here things are very bad, and they are going to get worse. Many of my friends are in serious debt with the companies, who will not hesitate to take their land. We were made a lot of false promises in the early days. This system is not for the people, it is for those who are already rich.'
>
> Jose Muñoz, peasant farmer, Los Litres, El Palqui, 1995

A rural settlement of some 5,000 inhabitants located at the edge of the Paloma Dam in the Guatulame valley, El Palqui is one of the most rapidly transformed exporting areas in the whole of Chile.[25] The paved road link to Ovalle completed in 1989 further stimulated the outward economic orientation of the town. The area underwent extensive land reform: expropriated from six large estates during the Frei period, 144 *parcelas* of an average size of 7.3 hectares each were organized into five agrarian reform units (*parcelaciones*) by 1977 [*Silva*, 1993] (see Table 2, and Map 3). Of the five *parcelaciones* within the settlement – Puente Plomo, El Peñon, San Antonio, Santa Rosa and Los Litres – the final three were selected for intensive study. Twenty-six out of 90 growers owning less than ten hectares were interviewed.

The transformation of the local peasantry into grape producers took place in roughly three stages: first, repeasantization, or the creation of *parcelas* and a domestic market-oriented horticultural base (1974–84); second, the incorporation of the *parceleros* into the expanding global

FIGURE 1
PRODUCTIVE LAND-USE IN STUDY *PARCELACIONES*, EL PALQUI 1983–93

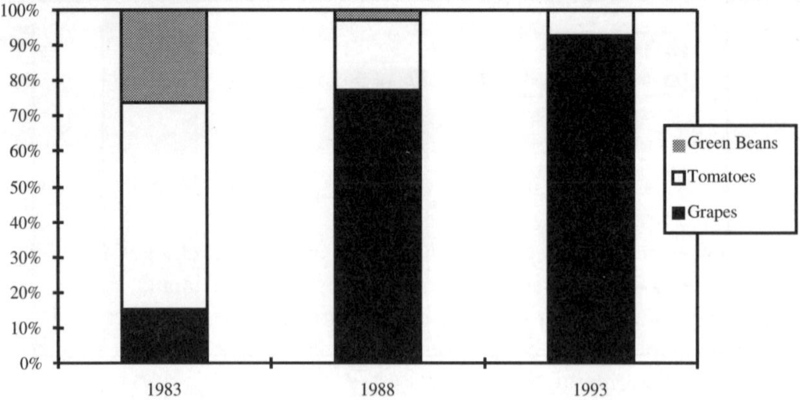

Source: Fieldwork.

market for grapes (1984–90); and third, the proletarianization of the *parceleros* in a stagnating global market for grapes (1990 to the present).

Repeasantization in El Palqui

Historically, local agricultural production in the Guatulame area followed the traditional pattern: that is, cultivation of tomatoes, green beans and other horticultural products. In 1983 all these crops were grown by the producers in the fieldwork sample (see Figure 1). This produce was sold in local markets, and in the 1980s the markets of the national capital, Santiago. The simplicity of the procurement system, which involved a travelling middle man purchasing on the spot, was recalled with nostalgia by a number of the peasant farmers. Many claimed that, when compared to the grape purchasing system now operating, the earlier system was 'transparent', 'understandable', and generally yielded a low but adequate level of profits.[26] High levels of credit were not required for these low-technology activities.

Peasant Incorporation in El Palqui

The second phase in the transformation of the agrarian structure in El Palqui involved the rapid, and almost total, adoption of grape cultivation. Except in the cases of some of the larger growers, this transition was financed largely by agri-business through CCC systems. Set-up and annual maintenance costs are approximately US$25,000 and US$5,500 per hectare

FIGURE 2
PROPORTION OF GRAPE OUTPUT ACCOUNTED FOR BY VARIETY WITHIN THREE SURVEY *PARCELACIONES* 1983–93

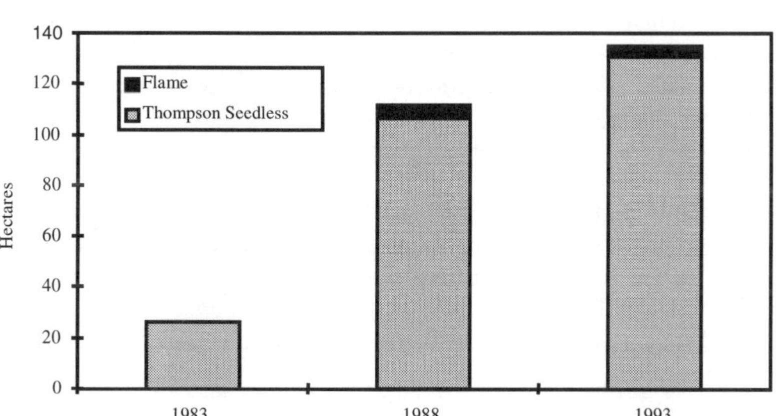

Source: Fieldwork.

respectively – sums representing substantial investments for peasant farmers. One of the growers described this period as 'something like a gold rush' that involved a fight among firms to win suppliers.[27] Large credits were granted, and it was not uncommon for money to be lent to cover non-household and living expenses as well.

The modal year of *reconversión* was 1984, and those peasant farmers who converted early have tended to fare better (given favourable early prices). The adoption of the grape spread through a neighbourhood diffusion process. By 1988, 75 per cent of the sample land was turned over to this crop. Eighteen of the 26 interviewees were practising full monocultural production at this point. Moreover, the green Thompson seedless variety dominated plantations (see Figure 2).[28]

In El Palqui as a whole at this stage there were signs of land concentration.[29] By the late 1980s, 36 of the original 144 *parceleros* – some 25 per cent – had been displaced. According to the *roles* much of this land was purchased by companies or commercial corporations. The greatest number of land transactions took place in 1990, as early 'non-competitive' peasant farmers were expelled from the market.

Proletarianization in El Palqui

Through the economic mechanisms of prices and contracts, external problems were increasingly visited upon the locality from 1990 onwards. By this time, a completely monocultural agriculture was being practised by peasant farmers included in the sample (see Figure 1). This agricultural pattern was encouraged by the agri-business firms, eager to benefit from economies of scale where possible. Many growers were unable to shift out of grape production, as returns consistently failed to cover credits and charges. Their situation worsened considerably in this period, a consequence of the rapid cost-acceleration of the productive forces, in the form of water prices. Water scarcity put the price out of reach of many *parceleros*, and growers reported declining yields due to this.

Agribusiness companies were active in squeezing the *parceleros* during this period, passing on much of the risk associated with increasingly unpredictable trading conditions.[30] All growers remaining in business in 1995 were subject to the monopoly supply of inputs, labour and machinery. Given 'lock-in' clauses, firms were granted enormous power over the pattern followed by local agrarian transformation. Farmers often did not know what their produce was earning in foreign markets, and had few ways of finding out.[31] Many complained that they simply didn't understand balance sheets, and were convinced that items they had not purchased were being included. An additional clause specified that grievances should be heard in Santiago – too far away for many growers to travel to. The CCC

FIGURE 3
PROPORTION OF LAND ACCOUNTED FOR BY DIFFERENT SIZED GROWERS

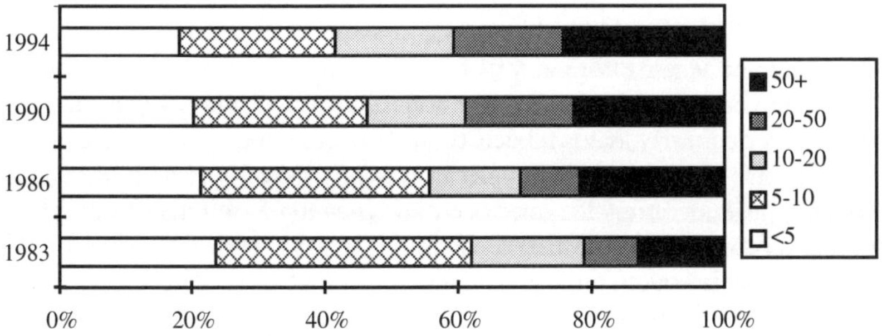

Source: Murray [1993].

system had become increasingly non-transparent and incomprehensible to the farmers, who were now effectively tied labour for the firms concerned.

This squeeze and declining real prices led to crippling levels of debt. Six of the sample had already had to sell their *parcela* to the company in order to pay this by 1995 (receiving lower than market price for the land), and had moved into temporary farm work and petty trading. Of those remaining in business in 1995 the average level of debt was US$50,217. This meant that the average *parcela* value/debt ratio was 3:1. In nine cases properties had been mortgaged to the agri-business firms in order to re-secure this debt. In these specific cases the average *parcela* value/debt ratio was 2:3 – implying very insecure tenure indeed. This level of indebtedness was leading in turn to a significant concentration of landownership. Figure 3 shows a steady decline between 1983 and 1994 in the relative importance of holdings below ten hectares, from over 60 per cent to just over 40 per cent. By 1995, some 39 out of the 144 original *parcelas* in El Palqui – or 27 per cent – were owned by agri-business export companies.[32]

The asymmetry in political and economic strength between peasant farmers and agri-business enterprises allowed the latter to pass any risk on to the former, thereby protecting themselves against market volatility. These asymmetries include (among other things) differential access to finance, organizational capacity, and information levels. Furthermore, the extreme economic vulnerability of the El Palqui *parceleros* was exacerbated by declining environmental conditions and the practice of monoculture. Locked in to highly exploitative contracts, peasant farmers had become almost entirely dependent on agribusiness as the process of disguised proletarianization in the locality increased. It is quite possible, six years after the completion of the original fieldwork, that the remainder of the *parceleros* have now been fully proletarianized.

Capitalist Restructuring in Maule

The region of Maule (Region VII) lies within the upper half of the Central Valley. Favoured by fertile alluvial soils and the Mediterranean climatic regime, agriculture has long been the main economic activity here. Fruit species were traditionally produced in the area. Since restructuring in the 1970s, land under fruit has increased significantly – this has taken place through conversion of existing areas rather than through expansion of the frontier. Specialization in the cultivation of apples has become marked. Intra-annum temperature patterns lead to February–March harvests,

MAP 4
MAULE (REGION VII)

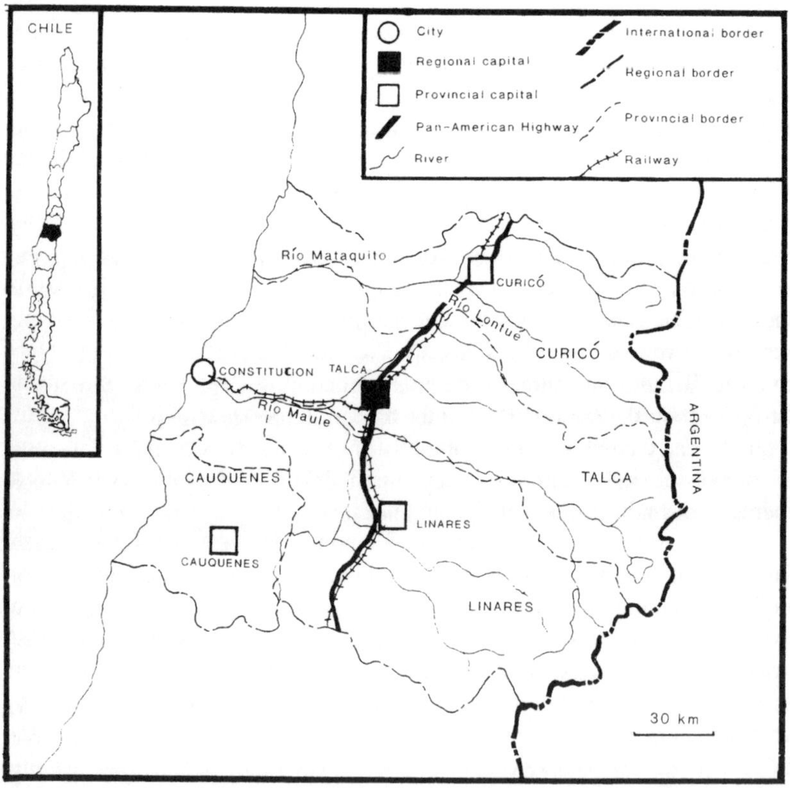

Source: Warwick E. Murray.

coinciding with the period of maximum prices in Chile's major apple market – the EU. Harvests in the province of Curicó are particularly early and highly profitable.[33]

Given the abundance of land, the *parcelas* created during the counter-reform were larger than those in the Norte Chico. This factor help generate a more rapid development of fruit cultivation by peasant farmers in this area than elsewhere [*Riffo-Rosas*, 1993; *Pino*, 1993]. A small export base was built up during the 1960s, following the implementation of President Frei's National Fruit Plan.[34] By the time the free market reforms of the mid-1970s took place, a process of 'learning by doing' had already begun. Unlike the north, however, the boom did not change the nature of the regional economic base overnight, as more step-like transition took place.

Peasant growers in Curicó have been involved in the export economy – although economically they are not as important relatively as they are in the north. Riffo-Rosas [1993] has undertaken surveys which show that the percentage of surplus product destined for global markets increases significantly with farm size in the region. As elsewhere, peasant farmers were incorporated largely through agri-business investment. The history of agri-business enterprise involvement in Curicó, however, is different from that in the Norte Chico. Agri-business production and accumulation in the late 1960s was centred on a collective of large growers called Copefrut. David Del Curto established the prototype CCC system of procurement in 1979, drawing in the first generation of export-oriented peasant farmers. Beginning in the early 1980s, foreign investment has been particularly important in this region. Today there is a marked cluster of large-scale packing and storage plants along the Pan American Highway on the outskirts of Curicó city.[35] By 1994, approximately US$100 million had been invested in the establishment of apple orchards by large firms. Moreover, set-up costs in the region are cheaper than in the Norte Chico.

In the early 1990s the regional marketing structure evolved considerably as 'footloose' export companies began to play a more important role.[36] Such operators did not advance credit, and produce bought was paid for directly at the point of sale. In this way footloose companies absorbed some of the risks generated by market volatility, and extracted correspondingly higher profits. 'Footloose' companies tend to work with small collections of growers, with whom they have built a relationship. A notable separation of procurement mechanisms is occurring in the region's marketing structure. Larger companies are relying increasingly on their own orchards for supply, whilst medium and large growers are increasingly turning footloose. Unable to gain credit to work with 'footloose' companies, and increasingly unattractive to the large firm, peasant farmers face limited choices in marketing their goods.

Peasant Differentiation in East Curicó

> 'Their fixed costs are so high, and their problems so great now, that they need growers in debt so they can treat them like lambs and pay them what they want. That system cannot go on forever. As more people like me enter the market, there will be increasing competition for produce. If the growers can escape debt they will never return directly to the large export companies.'
>
> A 'footloose' company owner talking of large export companies, Curicó, 1995

MAP 5
THE *COMUNA* OF CURICÓ (WEST) AND LOCATION OF STUDY VILLAGES

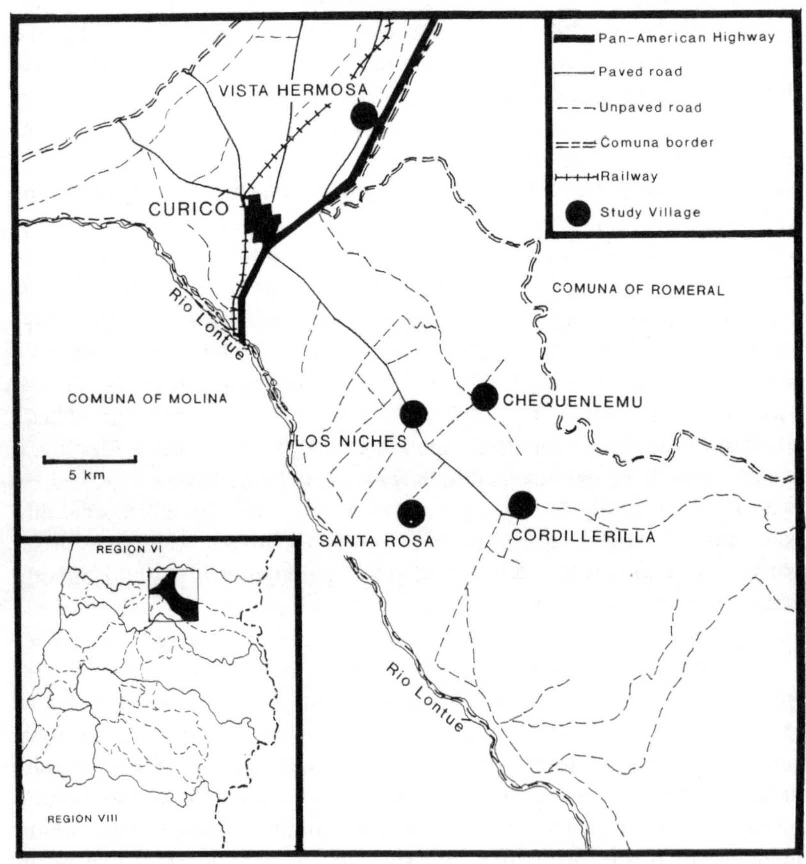

Source: Warwick E. Murray.

As the leading export locality for Chile's second fruit, 16 per cent of the nation's apple area is found in the *comuna* of Curicó. The proximity of the latter to the national capital Santiago has traditionally been an economic advantage that stimulated the commercial production of fruit crops. In Curicó the tenure structure created by the military counter-reform was characterized by the relatively high incidence of large agricultural estates interspersed with small 'pockets' of land. The *parcelas* investigated for the purposes of this study correspond to five such 'pockets' surrounding the villages of Cordillerilla, Santa Rosa, Chequenlemu, Los Niches and Vista Hermosa.[37] Research in the latter contexts involved interviewing 20 out of a total population of 61 peasant farmers (see Table 2 for details of sample).

The transformation undergone by *parceleros* in this locality follows a pattern similar to that experienced by peasant cultivators in El Palqui. First, the creation of *parceleros* producing apples for domestic markets (1974–79); then the incorporation of *parceleros* into an expanding global market for apples (1979–88); and, latterly, the differentiation of *parceleros* producing for the world market (1988 to the present).

Repeasantization in East Curicó

Very few *parceleros* in East Curicó were involved in the production of fruit. Such activity was reserved for larger-scale farmers, not least because of the investment and running costs: at 1994 prices, establishing a hectare of apples required an outlay of US$9,000, and maintenance amounts to US$2,000 per annum per hectare. At this time then, the small-scale farming sector was dedicated mainly to the production of traditional crops, the most important of these being sugar beet, green beans and tomatoes. These products were marketed largely within the region, and occasionally in Santiago.

Two *parceleros* in the sample planted apples for export in 1976. Low availability of credit meant that the growers had to sell a portion of land they had received in the counter-reform in order to finance this. Two further growers planted apples in 1978. The shift to fruit cultivation for export was among the earliest in the country.

Peasant Incorporation in East Curicó

As previously noted, David Del Curto (DDC) entered the local market offering credit in 1979. Of the 20 peasant farmers in the sample, 16 initially entered the market under a CCC arrangement with DDC. By 1984, all 20 of the fieldwork sample had partially reconverted to the production of apples for export. However, unlike El Palqui, land use in the East Curicó sample remained relatively diversified; 46 per cent of land was dedicated to the cultivation of the apple crop, one-third to pears, and the remainder to a

FIGURE 4
APPLE VARIETIES IN EAST CURICÓ SAMPLE 1984–94

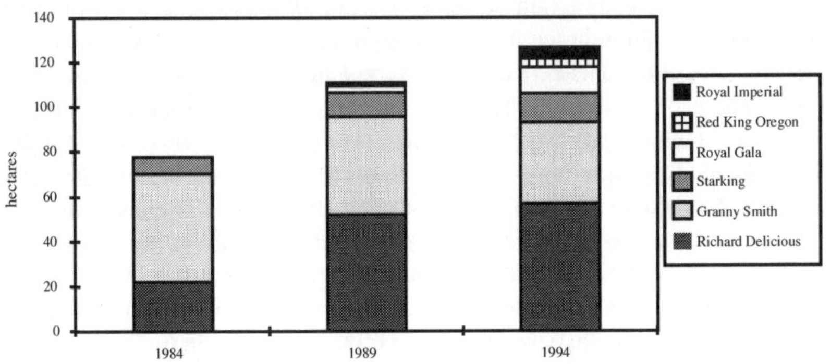

Source: Murray [1996].

mixture of on average three horticultural and fruit products. In 1984 there was an almost even split between red and green apples (in terms of global consumer demand red apples have tended to be the dominant kind), with Richard Delicious and Granny Smith dominating commercial production (see Figure 4).[38]

Overall, the sampled growers were adding to their apple holdings in a step-like fashion, using credit from firms primarily but also ploughing back economic gains to reconvert. In 1986, however, the real price for apples dropped by nearly 25 per cent. As was the case in the north of Chile (see above), large export companies began to tighten up their contract conditions in response to this. By 1988, 13 of the 20 peasant farmers were indebted to export companies.[39]

Semi-proletarianization in East Curicó

By 1994, 75 per cent of the land in the East Curicó fieldwork sample was dedicated to the commercial production of apples, with the remainder set aside for pears, plus an additional range of other fruit and vegetables. Despite this increased specialization, however, crop diversity persisted. Figure 4 shows that six types of apple were being produced in the locality by this time – the new additions such as Royal Imperial and Red King Oregon representing much sought-after innovative reds. All peasant farmers had at least two varieties of apples growing on their land.

In 1993 quota impositions in the EU resulted in a fall of 50 per cent in the real price of apples. Having avoided fully dedicating their lands to just one crop, the *parceleros* were partially shielded from the economic impact of export market restriction. Of the 13 who were indebted to export companies in 1988, nine had re-negotiated or grown out of these problems and shifted to 'footloose' companies (there being four agri-business enterprises of this description operating in the locality at the time). All of those who had made the transformation declared they would not return to work with the large firms. Three of the sample had sold off parts of their *parcela* in order to escape the debt. For those working with 'footloose' companies, an important development has been the increased role of off-farm income. All nine work on other farms and, in many cases, in other industries to supplement their earnings and finance investments. The multi-occupational family is thus very much part of the survival strategy followed by this group.

Two large export companies purchased the output of the rest of the sample (covering approximately 55 per cent of the output). For the 11 peasant farmers under this regime, debts mounted, particularly after 1993, and they became increasing tied into CCC arrangements. Of the 20 growers in 1994, therefore, nine were indebted to companies, the average level of debt being US$3,500. It will be immediately apparent that these levels are far lower than in El Palqui, and the ratio of *parcela* value to debt is not high (26.7 mean). In this respect the tenure status of the growers in East Curicó appears to be relatively secure. It is worth pointing out, however, that many of those worst hit by company debt in the locality had quit farming apples altogether by the time of the fieldwork.

Through the process of capitalist restructuring, *parceleros* in East Curicó have been differentiated into two distinct groups. The first of these is linked to footloose intermediaries, and the other to the larger export companies. The latter group has been squeezed and become economically dependent to a certain degree, but not to the same extent as elsewhere. It is quite possible that some of these *parceleros* may have escaped debt in the period following the fieldwork survey, and have moved into the footloose market. However, they may have been forced to do this, given the increasing reluctance on the part of large agri-business companies to work in conjunction with small peasant farming. Although the footloose group appear to be relatively favourably placed, ironically this group too is somewhat vulnerable: were peasant farmers to suffer economic difficulties, or the locality to experience problems, the footloose intermediaries would be the first to cease their operations. The dominant transformational processes in East Curicó are thus both a disguised variant and a more obvious form of semi-proletarianization.

EXPLAINING PEASANT DIFFERENTIATION

The impact of neo-liberalism on the Chilean peasantry has been broadly

TABLE 4
DIFFERENTIAL CONDITIONS, OUTCOMES AND DEPENDENCY LEVELS IN CURICÓ AND EL PALQUI, 1995

	El Palqui	**Curicó**
Natural antecedents		
Regional/local climate	Marginal. Rainfall low and decreasing.	Ideal rainfall and temperature.
Land quality	Poor. Extensive preparation required.	Very good.
Constructed antecedents		
Timing of peak prices in major market	Sub-optimal for US markets, Shift from Dec. to Nov. in late 1980s.	Optimal for EU markets.
Cooperative behaviour	Little recent history. Fledgling cooperation in Los Litres.	Traditionally strong. Association de Cordillerilla active.
Local 'knowledge' of fruit production	Almost non-existent before boom.	Traditional history of cultivation.
Land reform history	Thorough parcellation. Creation of relatively small plots.	Extensive but not as thorough as El Palqui. Larger plots.
Transport Infrastructure	Good. Road to Ovalle paved 1989.	Excellent. Located around Pan American highway.
Export infrastructure	Numerous pre-packing facilities. Close to port and cool facilities	Port relatively distant. Cool facilities in area.
Irrigation infrastructure	Good. 25% loss in system and rising scarcity.	Excellent. Loss in system but not problematic.
Production costs		
Water costs	US$12,000 per hectare (one payment for rights).	US$10 per annum per hectare.
Set-up costs	Very high. US$25,000 per hectare without land purchase.	US$9,000 without land purchase.
Maintenance costs	Very high (US$5,500 per hectare).	Relatively low (US$2,000 per hectare).
'Global' market conditions and marketing structure		
Market for major export crop	Grape. Reasonable. Some competition from other fruits. Protected.	Apples. Saturated. Demand for novelty. Highly protected.
Prices of major export crop	Peaked in 1986 at 160% of 1980 value. Secondary peak in 1991. In 1994, at 80% of 1980 real value.	Peaked in 1986 at 110% of 1980 value. Collapse in 1993. At 60% of 1980 value in 1994.
Regional marketing structure	Relatively concentrated. CCC system dominant.	Two-tier structure. 'Footloose' and CCC.
'Local' impacts of the boom		
Rapidity of adoption	Rapid neighbourhood diffusion pattern.	'Step-like' adoption.
Land use change	Monoculture of grape and Thompson Seedless variety.	Apples dominant, but diversity in varieties.
Employment effects	Creation of local market for labour. US$5 a day.	Creation of local market for labour. US$7 a day.
Local multiplier effects	Most multipliers concentrated in Ovalle. Some forward and backward linkages.	Multipliers concentrated in Curicó city. Extensive forward and backward linkages
Land transfers and re-concentration	Access vastly reduced, concentration rising.	Access reduced, concentration probably rising.
Income effects	Sharply raised incomes in 1980s. Rapid decline in 1990s.	Steadily rising incomes in 1980s. Decline in the 1990s.
Elements of dependency		
Personal risk levels	Extreme. Passed on by companies.	High. Shielded by diversity and relative autonomy.
Parcela value to debt ratio	3.1 average. Low among mortgaged group (2.6).	26.7 average. Of relatively little concern to those remaining.
'Lock in' contracts	100%. Full bi-lateral monopolies.	45%. Some bilateral monopolies.
Purchase of parcelas by agri-business	High (approx 25%).	Low in study sites. Possibly high in areas around.
Debt	Extreme (US$50,217 mean).	Low (US$3,550 mean).

negative, yet substantially uneven. The El Palqui *parceleros* have clearly fared far worse than those in Curicó. This is despite the fact that the global market for apples has presented deeper problems than the market for grapes. What explains this paradox? A range of factors, including natural and constructed antecedents, production costs, and marketing structure, have led to quite different levels of economic dependence and vulnerability in the two localities. A comprehensive list of these differences, together with the variable outcomes, is presented in Table 4: it is to these differences, and their causes, that we now turn.

In terms of natural antecedents, the Curicó group is favoured by climatic factors which make irrigation relatively unproblematic and cheap, and encourage agricultural diversity. Higher land quality in the Central Valley also reduces the preparation costs of land significantly. Distinctions in the productive forces in agriculture are therefore crucial to the different economic outcomes in the two areas studied. Curicó's history of fruit production, crop diversity, tradition of cooperation, land reform patterns, and infrastructure, have also provided a relatively sound context for peasant farming. Larger *parcela* sizes in particular offer capital a more substantial economic base, facilitate agricultural diversity, provide (albeit limited) economies of scale, and allow step by step adoption patterns of new cropping patterns and varieties. It was the rapid nature of the transition to export monoculture as much as anything that weighed heavily against the El Palqui group, leaving the peasant farmers there exposed to high risk levels.

Of additional critical importance are the divergent levels of production cost between the two localities, those for El Palqui being three times higher than in Curicó. This difference is due both to local environmental constraints (reflected in the differential water costs) and the relatively costly, technology-intensive, requirements of grape production. This, in turn, led to the fact that the growers in northern Chile had to obtain significant levels of credit in order to establish their orchards, and a number of them never managed to escape from this initial debt. Because of the relatively favourable factors at work in Curicó, by contrast, growers there have generally avoided having to go into debt. Ultimately it is because of indebtedness, and because the El Palqui group is forced to work exclusively within the CCC system, that current debt dependency has reached such critical levels. Hence a combination of internal and external economic factors have united to produce either disguised or full proletarianization, a process leading in turn to rapid land concentration.

The fieldwork on which these two case studies are based was completed in 1995/96. Given increasing demand saturation in the world market for fruit, increased southern hemisphere competition, lower prices and raised protectionism, it is unlikely that conditions have improved for the majority

FIGURE 5
PEASANT TRANSFORMATIONS AND CHILE'S FRUIT EXPORT COMPLEX

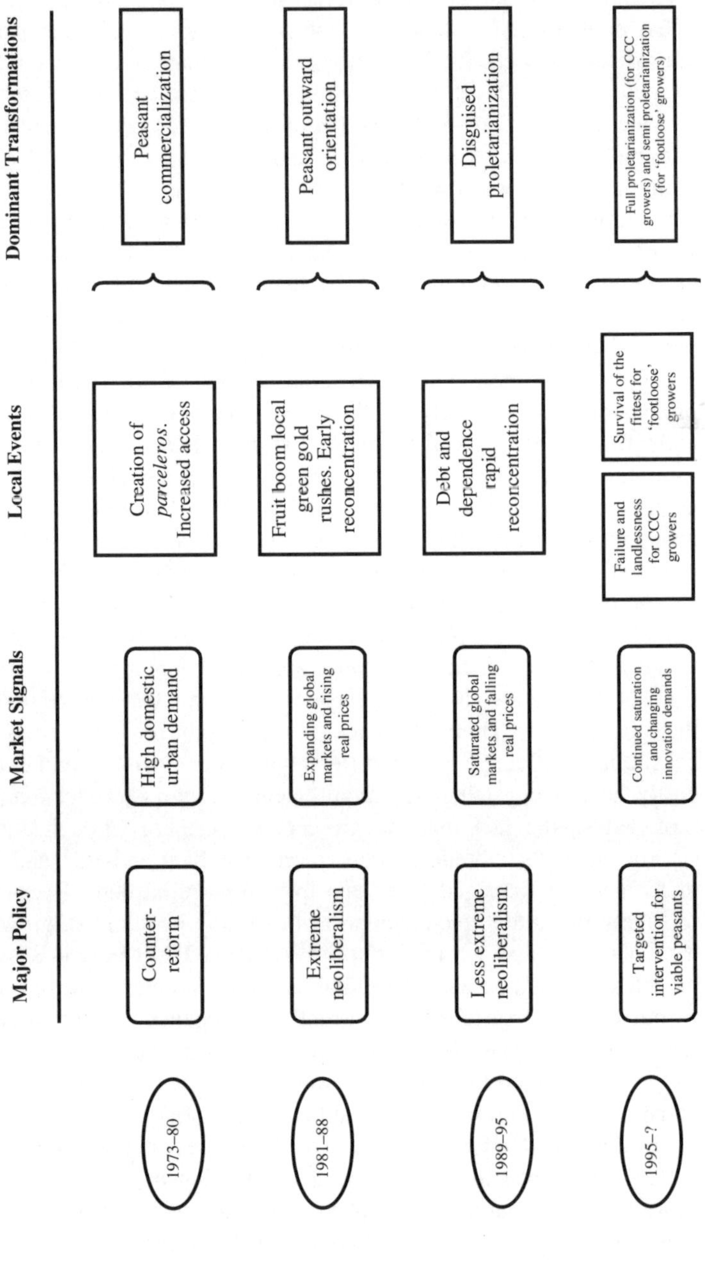

	Major Policy	Market Signals	Local Events	Dominant Transformations
1973–80	Counter-reform	High domestic urban demand	Creation of *parceleros*. Increased access	Peasant commercialization
1981–88	Extreme neoliberalism	Expanding global markets and rising real prices	Fruit boom local green gold rushes. Early reconcentration	Peasant outward orientation
1989–95	Less extreme neoliberalism	Saturated global markets and falling real prices	Debt and dependence rapid reconcentration	Disguised proletarianization
1995–?	Targeted intervention for viable peasants	Continued saturation and changing innovation demands	Failure and landlessness for CCC growers; Survival of the fittest for 'footloose' growers	Full proletarianization (for CCC growers) and semi proletarianization (for 'footloose' growers)

of the Chilean *parceleros*. Although this remains to be confirmed by further research, it is likely that agri-business firms have been moving into the purchase of land, moving away from dealing with small-scale peasant farmers, and generally tightening up the conditions governing access to provision of inputs and credit. Given these factors, land re-concentration, de-peasantization, and debt are likely to have continued.

The fruit boom has deepened inequality in rural Chile, and created an increasingly differentiated peasantry. In the worst cases, this is recreating the bimodal agrarian structure of the past – only this time the *patrones* are the fruit companies.[40] In the best cases, peasant farmers have managed to remain independent of agri-business control, but earn only modest returns. Despite being regarded as the best advertisement for neo-liberal policies in Latin America, therefore, there has been no discernible improvement in living standards even for the more successful *parceleros* in Chile's fruit export sector. Although patterns diverge at the local level, it is nevertheless possible to identify an overarching process of transformation at work. This is represented graphically in Figure 5, which depicts the major changes in policy, market conditions, etc., throughout the period in question. It is suggested here that the transformations affecting peasant smallholders in other export-oriented sectors within Chile, and indeed other Latin American countries, have all followed a roughly similar path.

CONCLUDING COMMENTS

Chile has often been, and remains, a site where significant politico-economic 'experiments' are played out. The outcomes of the resultant systemic shifts offer important signposts for the rest of the global economic periphery. It could be argued that a main shortcoming in the earlier analyses of dependency theorists and ECLA was the assumption that a global division of labour would separate countries in the Third World, where the focus would be on agricultural production, from those in metropolitan capitalist contexts, where nations would concentrate on industrial production. No account was taken of the possibility that, in a laissez-faire global market, peasant producers in less developed countries such as Chile would have to compete with agricultural exports from advanced capitalist countries, not just in international markets but also in their own domestic ones. While peasant cultivators may indeed be economically efficient when compared with unproductive landlords in their own countries – the assumption made by ECLA – this is not the case when they have to compete with efficient high-tech international agri-business enterprises in world markets.

This shortcoming can be linked in turn to one of the more ironical outcomes of ECLA development strategy in Latin America. Many still adhere to the view that, in advocating economic growth, agricultural productivity and agrarian reform, ECLA championed state planning against the free market. On this point, however, the position of ECLA was rather more ambiguous. It was not in fact opposed to the market as such (as many think) but wanted state intervention in order to make the market work. In terms of political objective (= establishing the market), therefore, the neo-liberal policies of the Pinochet dictatorship represent to some degree a realization and not a negation of earlier ECLA development strategy. As this study implies, peasant survival is contingent on more profound and committed state intervention and support than simply 'lubricating' the market. This is unlikely to be forthcoming given the continued dominance of the neo-liberal economic model.

This article has explored the impact of the neo-liberal economic model on the Chilean peasantry as this involves transformations in the agrarian structure of two fieldwork locations, illustrating that changes there are locally contingent and regionally specific. It has also shown the important determining role of market integration on economic differentiation of the peasantry in these fieldwork locations, and thus the manner in which the 'global' is articulated with the 'local'. It is clear that, at the macro level, there are increasing general pressures on the peasantry resulting from the application of neo-liberal economic policies and the corresponding withdrawal of political commitment to the economic reproduction of the peasantry. The reality of the situation is that – barring a major paradigm shift – government support for the peasant farming sector will not manifest itself in the foreseeable future. Increasingly, then, peasant livelihoods and rural community trajectories will be determined by powerful global forces, resulting in dependency for those who survive as peasants and proletarianization for those who do not.

Structuralism has much to say on the implications of asymmetric power relations for global wealth distribution. Relatively little has been said about the impact of asymmetries between individual agents at the micro-level, and how this affects distributive outcomes. Isolating for the impacts of local physical geography and history, a major driving force, and arguably the ultimate determining factor in terms of the scope for survival, is the relationship between agri-business enterprises and *parceleros*. It is this relationship which either constrains or liberates the *parcelero* in the context of the market. Policy which encourages *parceleros* to reconvert by linking into CCC systems tends to end in failure. It is clear that an alternative *reconversión* strategy must involve both the identification of alternative sources of credit and the provision of post-conversion assistance. A major aspect of such assistance would involve the monitoring of fruit contracts and the behaviour of companies, together with the development of mechanisms to deal independently with grower grievances. Without this there simply will be no equality of opportunity, and efforts to increase productive efficiency are likely to be futile.

Neo-structuralist ideas, which have become influential in some Latin American countries (such as Chile under Ricardo Lagos), offer little hope for the peasantry given that the promotion of neo-liberal capitalism remains very much at their core. Agrarian policy in Chile has moved little beyond the law of the jungle associated with the 1970s, and the lessons about the reasons for economic failure have been largely ignored. The decline of Chile's *parceleros* is not inevitable, but it is increasingly likely, given the current overlap between the political and economic interests of international capital and those of the ruling elite within the country itself. About the failure of peasant economy it is possible to say two things. First, the threshold of economic failure is high, affecting as it does those with ten hectares of land. This is a very different, and in some ways more alarming, picture than the one usually presented with regard to rural Latin America, where the expectation is that it is only a minifundist agriculture – that is, smallholders with less than five hectares – that is economically unviable. As the Curicó fieldwork in this article shows, only very few peasant farmers will make it through to become capitalist peasant farmers; once the latter breakthrough has been achieved, moreover, economic reproduction will continue to be precarious. And second, the failure of peasant economy is a political choice rather than the outcome of supposedly inevitable forces of 'globalization'. By continuing to choose this path, the Chilean government also seems prepared to accept the social upheavals and associated costs that will accompany such failure. These include the unsustainable expansion of regional urban centres and Santiago itself, as well as the full proletarianization of those who remain in rural areas; both these outcomes will enhance poverty and economic insecurity in rural areas. The survival of the peasantry in general, and rich peasants in particular, thus becomes a political choice, impossible to effect in the capitalist market without strong state support.

As we move to a food regime characterized by niche markets, novelty tastes and the need for economies of scope, the potential for peasant participation in export markets is likely to be further reduced. Economic viability is about more than size (although it helps). Crucially, successful producers will increasingly have to shoulder personal risk – which is not a favourable option. Given the saturation of global markets, it is inevitable that agri-business companies will continue to restructure and rationalize the agrarian structure of Chile in the future. The asymmetries in the market in terms of knowledge, information, and access to resources and technology are so great, and the incentives to exploit them so strong, that they are likely to be impossible to confront without collective behaviour. There are signs of renewed political activity of this nature in rural Chile, but peasants are not the effective force for social change they once were. In this sense the findings presented here tend to support the *descampesinista* viewpoint: that is to say, given the increased expansion and global penetration of the capitalist system on the one hand, and the absence of state regulation or a state-enforced process of de-regulation on the other, the economic decline of the peasantry is unavoidable. Agrarian reforms are likely to be short-term panaceas at best, and easily reversed if neo-liberal policies continue to prevail.

ACRONYMS AND VERNACULAR TERMS

Asentamiento	Cooperative farms established in the course of President Frei Montalva's agrarian reform programme, and expanded during the Allende period.
BIH	Basic Irrigated Hectares. For reform purposes (and beyond) landholdings were expressed in units of comparable productive capacity. One BIH is equivalent to one hectare of prime irrigated land in the Central Maipo river valley [*Jarvis*, 1989].
Campesinistas	Academics and policy-makers who stress the vitality and adaptability of the peasant economy.
CCC	Credit and Consignation Contracts. Such contracts involve the provision of credit by an agri business enterprise to cover some or all production costs. Payment is made on the basis of what the product commands at the destination port.
Comuna	Government in Chile is administered at the national, regional, provincial and community levels. The administrative unit of the *comuna* represents the smallest of these.
CORA	*Corporación de la Reforma Agraría*, the Chilean agrarian reform agency.
DDC	David Del Curto: A large Chilean-owned fruit export firm based in the Central Valley.
Descampesinistas	Academics and policy-makers who argue that the decline of peasant agriculture is inevitable in the face of capitalist development.
EU	European Union
Latifundio	Large-scale landholding unit, usually a landed estate, created through colonial occupation and conquest.
Minifundia	Small-scale peasant landholding units existing alongside (or, as tenancies, within) *latifundia*. Historically, the *latifundio/minifundio* complex entailed ties of economic dependency linking smallholder to landlord.
NTAX	Non-traditional agricultural exports
Parcelación	A group of individually owned and operated smallholdings (*parcelas*) all created as a result of land fragmentation and subdivision.
Parceleros	Farmers who operate *parcela* landholdings.
Patron	Landowner or landlord owning a *latifundio.*
Roles	Lists which detail land ownership in a given area for the purposes of taxation.
UTC	United Trading Company. A large-scale US-based fruit export company.

NOTES

1. The hegemony of neo-liberal economic policy in the global periphery and semi-periphery (and arguably the core) has been referred to as 'monoeconomics', given the extent to which it has diffused and also the great similarity in the nature of its policy manifestations across

widely differing national contexts.

2. The trajectory followed by agrarian transformation in Latin America, and the role in this of peasants, has provoked great debate. Two opposing viewpoints on the fate of the peasantry are represented by the *campesinista* ('peasantization') and *descampesinista* ('de-peasantization') schools of thought. The former [*Stavenhagen*, 1978] has argued, albeit in slightly different ways, that the peasantry is not being eliminated as a result of capitalist development, and may in fact be strengthening. This view is often associated with the views of Russian populist A.V. Chayanov [1974]. In outlining the views of this group, Kay [1997b: 13] argues, 'they view the peasantry as mainly petty commodity producers who are able to compete successfully with capitalist farmers in the market rather than viewing them as sellers of labour power and being subjected to the processes of socio-economic differentiation'. The second group are far less optimistic about the fate of the peasantry, maintaining that petty commodity producers will be 'de-peasantized' by an expanding capitalism, and will as a result become either rich peasants (= small agrarian capitalists) or wage labourers (= proletarians). This camp is often associated with the ideas of Lenin on the subject of the Russian peasantry. It is possible to conceptualize shades in between the two extreme views as the nature of capitalism is altered and the collective organization of peasants changes across time and space. Ironically, both the political left and the right have appealed to the logic of a *descampesinista* argument. However, the recent growth in peasant movements in Latin America has brought attention to the possibility of multiple peasant futures. See Goodman and Redclift [1982] for an entry point into this debate, and also the contribution by Petras and Veltmeyer to this volume.
3. Structuralism in this context refers to the theory of economic development associated with the ideas of Raul Prebisch and the UN Economic Commission for Latin America (ECLA) during the late 1950s and early 1960s. Essentially the theory conceptualized the globe as divided between an economic core (= advanced capitalist countries in the developed world) and a periphery (= underdeveloped nations of the Third World), a pattern of economic inequality and dependency established historically through imperial conquest. The nature of a country's integration into this world system would largely determine developmental outcomes. This countered earlier ideas of modernization theory, which conceptualized development as an a-historic trajectory. Although it must be said that structuralists were not anti-market, they nevertheless argued that the nature of a Third World nation's insertion into the global economy would – and could only – be altered through state intervention. The two core policies informing ECLA theory about economic development were import substitution industrialization and agrarian reform. This theory, which laid the foundations for later dependency analysis, has seen something of a rejuvenation over the last decade in academic circles, in the form of neo-structuralism (see Sunkel [1993], and Gwynne and Kay [2000]).
4. De-agrarianization refers to the decline in the proportional contribution of agriculture to income generation and employment, a process which has been observed empirically for the continent. Between 1962 and 1999 GDP accounted for by agriculture in Latin America fell from 17 per cent to 7 per cent. Over the same period, agricultural employment as a proportion of total employment fell from 48 per cent to 29 per cent. Due to data collection, calculation and reporting errors, however, these can only be considered approximate figures, although they do reveal a clear trend [*ECLAC*, 2001]. In an absolute sense, real agricultural output has continued to grow, as have certain kinds of agricultural employment. The latter is particularly marked in the case of seasonal harvest jobs and female packing work associated with the recent boom in non-traditional agricultural exports across the continent [see *Murray*, 2002a].
5. In tracing out the implications of different regimes of accumulation for the Latin American peasantry Llambí [1991] offers a useful regulatory framework for conceptualizing epochal change, although it is hazardous to make claims for broad historical transitions of this nature, as does Bryceson [2000].
6. By focusing on *parceleros* – that is, recipients of *parcelas* or subdivided land plots in the agrarian counter-reform – the analysis is shifted away from the minifundistas, temporary workers and other peasant strata who are generally among the relatively deprived. The

advantage of this methodological procedure is simple: by studying *parceleros*, one obtains an idea of where the economic survival threshold is located, precisely because this group should exhibit the greatest scope for economic survival. If, as is argued here, relatively well-placed elements among the *parceleros* are unable to reproduce themselves economically, then this bodes ill for less well-placed elements in the rural population as a whole.

7. On this process, see in particular Kay [2000], who argues that changes in the rural labour force in post-1973 Chile have been very similar to those occurring in other Andean countries. Among other things, these changes include the growth in agriculture of temporary and seasonal employment, as well as the gendering of rural work (= more female labour).
8. Useful accounts, from different political perspectives, of the historical development of the rural estate in central Chile are contained in the texts by Kay [1971; 1977a], Bauer and Johnson [1977: 83-102], Bauer [1975a], and Loveman [1976]. Equally valuable are micro-level accounts of the way in which particular estates developed over time, such as the Hacienda 'El Huique' during the latter half of the nineteenth century [*Bauer*, 1975b: 393–413], and the hacienda – together with its smallholding tenants – in the Putaendo valley [*Baraona, Aranda and Santana*, 1961].
9. For the history and economic dynamics of the 1850s Chilean wheat boom, see Sepulveda [1959].
10. Details of the unequal land tenure system in Chile at this period are contained in texts such as that by Urzúa [1969], and also in the influential countrywide report by CIDA [1966].
11. In a 1956 report prepared for ECLA on the subject of the economic difficulties facing Chile, Kaldor [1964: 233ff.] attributed inflation, a balance-of-payments deficit, and underdevelopment generally to 'social factors which hamper the free development of productive forces'. At the root of the problem was the unequal access to land, a point he made in the following uncompromising manner [*Kaldor*, 1964: 238]: 'In the case of agriculture ... the growth of an efficient enterprise depends not so much on the accumulation of capital but on the acquisition of land. A class of efficient farmers cannot, merely through the forces of competition, deprive the relatively inefficient farmers of their land – particularly if the latter have individual holdings large enough to enable the owners to make a living despite inefficient management and low productivity. Hence, if the land is firmly held by a class of large landowners, the forces making for efficient leadership ... in agriculture are largely inoperative; no amount of market competition can cause the efficient units to grow beyond a certain point, if they cannot force inefficient units with a stagnant outlook to surrender their land.' The conclusion by Kaldor is salutary: 'There can be little doubt that the promotion of a vigorous entrepreneurial class in both industry and agriculture is the main long-term requirement for economic development in Chile – at any rate, so long as she remains, as she is likely to remain, a private enterprise society.'
12. It has been argued that Alessandri's pledge of agrarian reform was made largely in order to capture the vote of the peasant population enfranchised in the early 1950s, and that he had no intention of ever enacting his promised policy [*Bengoa*, 1982].
13. For the agrarian reform programme of the Frei government, see among others, Warriner [1969: Ch. IX], Menjivar [1970], Petras and LaPorte [1971], and Kaufman [1972].
14. Agricultural labourers who worked on the estates, and poor peasant smallholders outside the estate system, received no land. Excluded from the benefits of the Christian Democratic reform, rural labourers and poor peasants voted for Allende's Popular Unity coalition in the 1970 elections. For a case study of peasant land occupations during this period, see Petras and Zemelman Merino [1972].
15. For the agrarian policy of the Popular Unity government, see Allende [1973], Chonchol [1973], and de Vylder [1976: Ch. 7].
16. In this connection it is important to understand that, in the main, shortages in foodstuffs were the result not of economic inefficiency on the part of the reformed agricultural sector (as opponents of Allende claimed), but rather of an increase in the economic capacity to consume among the very poor. As de Vylder [1976: 202] points out, 'the overall availability of foodstuffs in Chile is estimated to have been some 27 per cent higher in 1972 than in 1970 ... there can be little doubt that the Chilean people had both more and better food at their disposal in 1971 and 1972 than before.'

17. The nature of agrarian transformation effected as a result of the Pinochet dictatorship is outlined in the collection edited by Hojman [1993].
18. Outpacing in the process major fruit exporting nations, including South Africa, Australia, Argentina and New Zealand (the former leader).
19. Indeed, by making the policy selective and consigning much of the minifundista and small farm sector to the non-viable category, the state is explicitly admitting what it perceives as the inevitability of the decline of the peasant sector and the desirability of that outcome.
20. The 'populations' from which the grower samples were drawn were derived by checking down the agricultural *roles* and counting off the number of growers with plots of less than 10 hectares.
21. Since the late 1980s, however, the peak price period has moved back to late November, favouring regions further north. Minute changes in demand conditions and price movements can affect spatial outcomes enormously.
22. This measure refers to land already in productive use and land planted with fruit trees in formation [*CIREN-CORFO*, 1992].
23. It is estimated that close to 75 per cent of the region's 16,000 growers have plots of less than 10 hectares [*Gomez and Echeñique*, 1989].
24. A bilateral monopoly is a market characterized by a company which is simultaneously the single seller (monopoly) and single buyer (monopsony).
25. Although contrary to appearances the settlement takes much of its water from another dam in an adjoining valley system.
26. These comments are ascribable to a small grower from San Antonio, interviewed in March 1995.
27. This comment is ascribable to the son of a small-scale grower from Santa Rosa, who was interviewed in September 1994.
28. This variety is the grape for the cautious farmer. It has been a steady performer over the years and is considered relatively predictable. For peasant farmers who are unable to take the risk of venturing into more exotic varieties it represents a sensible choice. In this context, an interesting story was related by a grower who wished to remain nameless. This particular man was advised by an agronomist from Río Blanco to plant grapes of the 'Ribier' variety in 1988. According to this agronomist, this was the 'grape of the future'. The grower followed this advice, and re-planted half of his *parcela* (about 2.5 hectares). Returns for the 'Ribier' were so low that he ran up a debt of nearly US$23,000. He received no compensation for the bad advice from the company. This kind of anecdote preys heavily on the mind of many growers – it was repeated on numerous occasions, and was often used as a good reason not to diversify production.
29. This information was gleaned by an analysis of the *roles* for the district.
30. A new clause which appeared in the early 1990s contracts absolved firms of responsibility for produce until it was in the possession of the purchaser at the final destination. This came about following the 'poison grape' episode where a cyanide-laced grape was allegedly found in a shipment to the USA and the cargo had to be destroyed. By including the 'catastrophe' clause firms would be free of responsibility to compensate farmers in such cases. Needless to say, farmers did not often take out insurance to cover such losses.
31. In this context a local lawyer – who has made his business representing small farmers – estimated that in 60 per cent of cases profit returns were underestimated when reported back to the growers.
32. This probably underestimates the true extent of corporate ownership, however, given the ploy of using private names in order to shield against taxation. This also means that levels of concentration are also underestimated.
33. There is a province of Curicó, a *comuna* of Curicó, and a city of Curicó. Chile is organized into regions, which are subdivided into provinces. These are further subdivided into *comunas*. East Curicó refers to the eastern portion of the *comuna*.
34. This plan involved a range of initiatives intended to stimulate fruit production (especially for export) and laid the seeds of later macroeconomic successes. Investment in infrastructure, training, adaptation and technology was centred on Curicó.
35. This contrasts with the spatial structure existent in the Norte Chico where packing facilities

and cool storage facilities tend to be separated. The former are usually located very close to the inland fruit supply area, whilst the latter are clustered in one area in the port of Coquimbo. The reason for this is that Curicó is located at a greater distance from its port, Valparaiso. Therefore, the fruit must be cooled ready for the relatively long journey (6–8 hours) to port in special 'cool' trucks. In the Norte Chico however, the fruit can be taken the relatively short distance to Coquimbo (1–2 hours) and cooled there.

36. Companies that do not pre-determine from whom they will procure produce through contract arrangements are here referred to as 'footloose' companies. These companies often function with unwritten agreements concerning their suppliers, but never get involved in the granting of credit or any other aspect of the CCC system. Companies determine from whom they will buy according to the nature of the harvest, and the conditions in the global market. They generally pay for produce on the spot. Most of the footloose firms in the Curicó sample were independent (often comprising large-scale growers, or former fruit export company employees) although some were backed by the large-scale firms. The footloose companies tend to hire space from the larger companies in order to pack produce.
37. Strictly speaking, these communities do not represent *parcelaciones* in the same sense as the reform projects in El Palqui.
38. Like the Thompson seedless grape variety, these are the most sensible choices for peasants who cannot take the risk with 'novelty' varieties. Richard Delicious and Granny Smith have performed well globally. However, the markets for these varieties are now almost completely saturated.
39. According to anecdotal evidence many local growers lost their land in the late 1980s. Unfortunately the methodological bias built into the field research (i.e. of 'selecting those that have had already been selected') means that the experiences of these early losers are missed.
40. And ultimately, one might argue, the Northern consumers whose preferences drive the market, demanding ever cheaper fruit from an increasingly over-exploited environment in increasingly vulnerable communities.

REFERENCES

Allende, S., 1973, *Chile's Road to Socialism*, Harmondsworth: Penguin Books.

Baraona, Rafael, Ximena Aranda, and Roberto Santana, 1961, *Valle de Putaendo: Estudio de Estructura Agraria*, Santiago de Chile: Instituto de Geografía de la Universidad de Chile.

Barton, J.R. and W.E. Murray (eds.), 2002, *Chile – A Decade in Transition*, special edition of the *Bulletin of Latin American Research*, Vol.21, No.3.

Bauer, A.J., 1975a, *Chilean Rural Society from the Spanish Conquest to 1930*, Cambridge: Cambridge University Press.

Bauer, A.J., 1975b, 'La Hacienda "El Huique" en la Estructura Agraria del Chile Decimonónico', in Enrique Florescano (ed.), *Haciendas, Latifundios y Plantaciones en América Latina*, Mexico, DF: Siglo Veintiuno Editores.

Bauer, A.J., and Ann Hagerman Johnson, 1977, 'Land and Labour in Rural Chile, 1850–1935', in K. Duncan, I. Rutledge and C. Harding (eds.), 1977, *Land and Labour in Latin America: Essays on the Development of Agrarian Capitalism in the Nineteenth and Twentieth Centuries*, Cambridge: Cambridge University Press.

Bengoa, J., 1982, 'Analisis Histórico de la Agricultura Chilena', *Agricultura y Sociedad*, No.2.

Brown, M.R., 1989, 'Radical Reformism in Chile: 1964–73', in W.C. Thiesenhusen (ed.), *Searching for Agrarian Reform in Latin America*, London: Unwin Hyman.

Bryceson, D., 2000, 'Peasant Theories and Smallholder Policies: Past and Present', in D. Bryceson, C. Kay and J. Mooij (eds.), 2000, *Disappearing Peasantries?*, London: Intermediate Technology.

Bryceson, D., C. Kay, and J. Mooij (eds.), 2000, *Disappearing Peasantries?*, London: Intermediate Technology.

Chayanov, A.V., 1974, *La organizacion de la unidad economica campesina*, Buenos Aires:

Nueva Vision.

Chonchol, Jacques, 1973, 'The Agrarian Policy of the Popular Unity Government', in J.A. Zammit (ed.), *The Chilean Road to Socialism*, Brighton: The Institute of Development Studies at the University of Sussex.

CIDA (Comité Interamericano de Desarrollo Agrícola), 1966, *Chile: Tenencia de la tierra y desarrollo socio-económico agrícola*, Santiago de Chile: Tallares Gráficos Hispano Suiza Ltda.

CIREN-CORFO (Centro de Información de Recursos Naturales), 1982 and 1992, *Catastro Frutícola de Region IV*, Santiago: CIREN-CORFO.

Collins, J., 1979, *Agrarian Reform and Counter-reform in Chile*, San Francisco: Institute for Food and Development Policy.

Cruz, M.E., 1993, 'Neo-liberal Agriculture and Democratisation', in D.E. Hojman (ed.), *Change in the Chilean Countryside: From Pinochet to Aylwin and Beyond*, London: Macmillan.

de Vylder, S., 1976, *Allende's Chile: The Political Economy of the Rise and Fall of the Unidad Popular*, Cambridge: Cambridge University Press.

Duncan, K., I. Rutledge and C. Harding (eds.), 1977, *Land and Labour in Latin America: Essays on the Development of Agrarian Capitalism in the Nineteenth and Twentieth Centuries*, Cambridge: Cambridge University Press.

ECLAC (United Nations Economic Commission for Latin America and the Caribbean), 2001, *Statistical Yearbook 2000*, Santiago: ECLAC.

Gomez, S. and J. Echenique, 1989, *La Agricultura Chilena: Las Dos Caras de la Modernización*, Santiago: FLACSO.

Goodman, D. and Redclift, M., 1982, *From Peasant to Proletarian: Capitalist Development and Agrarian Transitions*, Oxford: Basil Blackwell.

Gwynne, R.N., 1993, 'Outward Orientation and Marginal Environments: The Question of Sustainable Development in the Norte Chico, Chile', *Mountain Research and Development*, Vol.13, No.3.

Gwynne, R.N. and C. Kay, 2000, 'Relevance of Structuralist and Dependency Theories in the Neoliberal Period: A Latin American Perspective', *Journal of Developing Societies*, Vol.16, No.1.

Gwynne, R.N. and C. Meneses, 1994, *Climate Change and Sustainable Development in the Norte Chico, Chile: Land, Water and the Commercialisation of Agriculture*, Occasional Publication No.34, University of Birmingham.

Hojman, D.E. (ed.), 1985, *Chile After 1973: Elements for the Analysis of Military Rule*, University of Liverpool Monograph Series, No.12, University of Liverpool: Centre for Latin American Studies.

Hojman, D.E. (ed.), 1993, *Change in the Chilean Countryside: From Pinochet to Aylwin and Beyond*, London: Macmillan.

ICIRA (Instituto de Capacitación e Investigación en Reforma Agraria), 1979, *Diagnostico de la Reforma Agraria Chilena: Noviembre 1970–Junio 1972*, Santiago: ICIRA.

Impuestos Internos, various years, *Roles de la Tenencia de la Tierra para Curicó y Monte Patria*, Curicó and La Serena: Impuestos Internos.

Jarvis, L.S, 1992, 'Changing Private and Public Sector Roles in Technological Development: Lessons from the Chilean Fruit Sector', unpublished paper, Department of Agricultural Economics, University of California.

Jarvis, L.S., 1989, 'The Unravelling of Chile's Agrarian Reform 1973–86', in W.C. Thiesenhusen (ed.), *Searching for Agrarian Reform in Latin America*, London: Unwin Hyman.

Kaldor, Nicholas, 1964, *Essays on Economic Policy – Volume Two (IV. Policies for International Stability, V. Country Studies)*, London: Gerald Duckworth.

Kaufman, R.F., 1972, *The Politics of Land Reform in Chile, 1950–1970: Public Policy, Political Institutions, and Social Change*, Cambridge, MA: Harvard University Press.

Kay, C., 1971, 'Comparative Development of the European Manorial System and the Latin American Hacienda System: An Approach to a Theory of Agrarian Change for Chile', unpublished DPhil Thesis, University of Sussex.

Kay, C., 1975, 'Agrarian Reform and the Transition to Socialism in Chile, 1970–73', *The Journal of Peasant Studies*, Vol.2, No.4.

Kay, C., 1977a, 'The Development of the Chilean *Hacienda* System, 1850–1973', in K. Duncan, I. Rutledge and C. Harding (eds.), *Land and Labour in Latin America: Essays on the Development of Agrarian Capitalism in the Nineteenth and Twentieth Centuries*, Cambridge: Cambridge University Press.

Kay, C., 1977b, 'Types of Agrarian Reform and their Contradictions: The Case of Chile', *Sociologia Ruralis*, Vol.17, No.3.

Kay, C., 1993, 'The Agrarian Policy of the Aylwin Government: Continuity or Change?' in D.E. Hojman (ed.), *Change in the Chilean Countryside: From Pinochet to Aylwin and Beyond*, London: Macmillan.

Kay, C., 1997a, 'Globalisation, Peasant Agriculture and Reconversion', *Bulletin of Latin American Research*, Vol.16, No.1.

Kay, C., 1997b, 'Latin America's Exclusionary Rural Development in a Neoliberal world', paper presented at the meeting of the Latin American Studies Association, Guadalajara, Mexico, 17–19 April.

Kay, C., 2000, 'Latin America's Agrarian Transformation: Peasantization and Proletarianization', in D. Bryceson, C. Kay, and J. Mooij (eds.), 2000, *Disappearing Peasantries?*, London: Intermediate Technology.

Korovkin, T., 1992, 'Peasants, Grapes and Corporations: The Growth of Contract Farming in a Chilean Community', *The Journal of Peasant Studies*, Vol.19, No.2.

Llambi, L., 1991, 'Latin American Peasantries and Regimes of Accumulation', *European Review of Latin American and Caribbean Studies*, No.51.

Llambí, L., 2000, 'Global–Local Links in Latin America's New Ruralities', in D. Bryceson, C. Kay and J. Mooij (eds.), 2000, *Disappearing Peasantries?*, London: Intermediate Technology.

Loveman, B., 1976, *Struggle in the Countryside: Politics and Rural Labour in Chile, 1919–1973*, Bloomington, IN: Indiana University Press.

McKenna, M.K.L. and W.E. Murray, 2002, 'Jungle Law in the Orchard – Comparative Globalisation in the New Zealand and Chilean Fruit Industries', *Economic Geography* (October edition, in press).

Menjivar, Rafael, 1970, *Reforma Agraria Chilena (Una Visión Global 1965–1969)*, San Salvador: Editorial Universitaria de El Salvador.

Murray, W.E., 1996, 'Neoliberalism, Restructuring and Non-Traditional Fruit Exports in Chile: Implications of Outward Orientation for Small-Scale Farmers', unpublished PhD thesis, University of Birmingham, UK.

Murray, W.E., 1997, 'Competitive Global Fruit Markets: Marketing Intermediaries and Impacts on Small Scale Growers in Chile', *Bulletin of Latin American Research*, Vol.16, No.1.

Murray, W.E., 1998, 'The Globalisation of Fruit, Neoliberalism and the Question of Sustainability: Lessons from Chile', *European Journal of Development Research*, Vol.10, No.1.

Murray, W.E., 1999, 'Local Responses to Global Change in the Chilean Fruit Complex', *European Review of Latin American and Caribbean Research*, Vol.66.

Murray, W.E., 2002a, 'Agriculture in South America – the Need For a New Paradigm?' in P. Heenan (ed.), *South America: Handbooks of Regional Economic Development*, London and Chicago: Fitzroy Dearborn.

Murray, W.E., 2002b, 'The Neoliberal Inheritance: Agrarian Policy and Rural Differentiation in Democratic Chile', in J.R. Barton and W.E. Murray (eds.), 2002, *Chile – A Decade in Transition*, special edition of the *Bulletin of Latin American Research*, Vol.21, No.3.

Petras, James, and Hugo Zemelman Merino, 1972, *Peasants in Revolt: A Chilean Case Study, 1965–1971*, Austin, TX: The University of Texas Press.

Petras, James, and Robert LaPorte, Jr., 1971, *Cultivating Revolution: The United States and Agrarian Reform in Latin America*, New York: Random House.

Pino, F., 1993, 'Caracteristicas Sociogeographicas del Trabajador de Huertos Frutales de las Regiones VI y VII', *Anales de la Sociedad Chilena de Ciencias Geographicas*, Mayo.

Pino, F., 1995, 'La Expansión de la Frontera Agrícola en el Valle Guatulame', unpublished paper, Universidad de Chile, Santiago.

Riffo-Rosas, M., 1993, 'Fruticultura en Chile Central (VI & VII Regiones): Caracterización del

Espacio Productivo Regional y Organización Espacial y Funcional de la Actividad', unpublished paper, Universidad de Chile.

Sepulveda, Sergio, 1959, *El Trigo Chileno en el Mercado Mundial: Ensayo de Geografía Histórica*, Santiago de Chile: Editorial Universitaria, SA.

Silva, M., 1993, 'La Modernización Agrícola y sus Efectos en la Propiedad y Tenencia de la Tierra: Caso de Estudio de los Parronales del Norte Chico', unpublished dissertation, Department of Geography, Universidad de Chile, Santiago.

Silva, P., 1995, 'Modernization, Consumerism and Politics in Chile', in D.E. Hojman (ed.), *Neo-liberalism with a Human Face? The Politics and Economics of the Chilean Model*, Monograph Series No.20, Institute of Latin American Studies, University of Liverpool.

Stavenhagen, R., 1978, 'Capitalism and the Peasantry in Mexico', *Latin American Perspectives*, Vol.5, No.3.

Sunkel, O. (ed.), 1993, *Development from Within: Towards a Neo-structuralist Approach for Latin America*, Boulder, CO and London: Lynne Rienner.

Universidad Católica, 1991, *Impact of Policy Reforms on the Agricultural Sector in Chile*, Informe de Coyuntura No.25, Departamento Economía Agraria, Universidad Católica, Santiago de Chile.

Urzúa, Raúl, 1969, *La Demanda Campesina*, Santiago de Chile: Ediciones Nueva Universidad.

Warriner, D., 1969, *Land Reform in Principle and Practice*, Oxford: Clarendon Press.

Globalization and the Reinvention of Andean Tradition: The Politics of Community and Ethnicity in Highland Bolivia

JOHN McNEISH

INTRODUCTION

Travelling and working beyond the boundaries of their traditional communities, rural populations in the Andean Highlands have never really fitted with earlier categorizations of peasants as easily definable, harmonious and isolated communities wholly reliant on gaining subsistence from working their land. In an age of increasing globalization, in which the distances travelled and the nature of work are changing worldwide, this has never been more true than it is now. Back in 1967, historical events led Eric Wolf [2001: 232] to write that 'peasants are often merely spectators of political struggles, or they may fantasize the sudden advent of millenium, without specifying for themselves and their neighbours the many rungs on the staircase of heaven.' It is argued below that present realities contradict this statement: as a result of recent local government reforms, peasant inhabitants of the community of Santuario de Quillacas in Highland Bolivia have become locked into a negotiation over their identities as individuals and development aspirations as a community with both the national state and the international policy system. The analysis which follows suggests that, although globalization is responsible for an increase in the spread and economic diversification of rural Andean communities, local people continue to ground their different identities in a sense of tradition and past. Described below are the complex ways in which the inhabitants of Santuario de Quillacas mediate present political conditions through an internal discourse,

---

John McNeish is at the Centre for Comparative Research on Poverty (CROP), the University of Bergen, Norway, where he coordinates a research programme on the Caribbean and South America with the Consejo Latinamericano de Ciencias Sociales (CLACSO). The article benefited from helpful editorial observations by Tom Brass.

involving conflicting interpretations of personal and historical memories. Of particular significance, and the central focus of the article, is the way in which an apparently arcane dispute over municipal status and boundaries is used by local people as a means to understand and devise contrasting strategies for dealing with the new economic and political interests created by government reform.

I

In 1994 Bolivia placed itself at the forefront of contemporary institutional reform in Latin America with the announcement to National Congress of the Laws of Popular Participation (*Ley de Participación Popular*) and of Administrative Decentralization (*Ley de Decentralización Administrativa*).[1] By introducing these laws, and making a conscious break with a political past identified with the over-centralization of government and the marginalization of the vast majority of the rural population, the Sánchez de Lozada administration was considered by many commentators to be embarking on the most challenging exercise in social reform seen in the country since the Bolivian Revolution of 1952 [*Blackburn and Holland*, 1998; *Booth, Clisby and Widmark*, 1995, 1997; *Albó* 1996].

GLOBALIZATION, DECENTRALIZATION AND POPULAR PARTICIPATION

Described as a programme for 'municipalization plus popular vigilance', the popular participation legislation had the combined effect of decentralizing a significant percentage of government expenditure to local government budgets, the creation of new opportunities for rural communities to partake in the planning and regulation of local government, and formal recognition of indigenous and popular organizations as political entities with rights. Under the administrative decentralization law, non-payroll responsibilities of central government ministries – including health and education – were devolved to the departmental level, and for the first time prefectural governments at those levels were advised by and made accountable to elected councils representing the municipalities of their area. Although introduced a year later than the popular participation legislation, the administrative decentralization law had in fact been conceived as the functional basis for governmental reform, but had taken longer to pass through Congress as a result of conservative political opposition. Taken in tandem, the two pieces of legislation were claimed by the Sánchez de Lozada administration to provide a comprehensive plan for the creation of a less top-heavy and more integrated and democratic state, in which there would be greater opportunity for formerly disenfranchised groups of non-Hispanic ethnicities to find representation.

Bolivian legislation about popular participation and administrative decentralization has largely been portrayed by government, media and social commentators alike as the radical and original response by the Sanchez de Lozada administration to social pressures within the country.[2] Although the legislation was clearly a response to civil society, this interpretation neglects the way in which it built upon relatively long-established currents in Bolivian politics. It also glosses over the fact that it was both broad public and narrow private sectors of civil society that pushed for change. Importantly for this article, it also ignores the direct and indirect pressure imposed on the country and national government by international economic and political forces.

Peasant and Nation in Bolivia

Over the last 20 years or so, Bolivian politics has undergone great transformation, almost as great as that brought about by the National Revolution in 1952 which ended the conservative rule of large landlords and mine-owners, and resulted in the introduction of universal suffrage as well as widespread agrarian reform [*Kohl*, 1978; *Klein*, 1992]. In 1982, following a break of more than a decade of military rule, Bolivia returned to a representative democratic governmental structure. This return to democracy is largely recognized as the result of pressure by international and national business for the country to restructure and gain control of its corrupt and ailing economy [*Lee Van Cott*, 2000: 131]. However, just as in 1952, there is also some recognition of the centrality of the peasant majority in Bolivia in pushing through political change. Many observers consider the relentless militant mobilization of the country's politicized and well-organized peasant union to be the key to the final destabilization of the military government [*Rivera Cusicanqui,* 1987; *Albó*, 1994].[3] Indeed, it can be argued that despite the radical transformation of politics in Bolivia, the sustainability of political trends and governments remains to a great extent reliant on the goodwill and support of the country's rural population [*Ríos Reinaga*, 1967; *Léons*, 1970].

The necessity of a pact between government and peasantry in Bolivia has resulted in a long-established practice of political bargaining in which 'sweeteners', in the form of favourable legislation and rural development projects, are created by successive governments so as to reproduce a situation in which power is centralized in the hands of the country's urban *criollo* (creoles) and *mestizo* population [*Platt*, 1982, 1984].[4] In this light, the current legislation about popular participation and decentralization can be understood in the same way as the agrarian reform programme of 1953

[*Carter*, 1964, 1971; *Menjivar*, 1969; *Pearse*, 1975; *Hahn*, 1991]. In short, although legislation was formed in response to national and international business interests for greater liberalization of government and economy [*Laserna,* 1994; *Urioste and Baldomar*, 1996], it is evident from the political history and literature written in the country over the last 20 years that its introduction was a pragmatic attempt to respond to growing demands by peasants and the indigenous population for increased political representation, and to secure their acceptance for the wider actions of government [*McNeish*, 2001; *Untoja*, 1992; *Rojas Ortuste*, 1994; *Cárdenas*, 1988; *CIPCA*, 1991; *Medina*, 1992, *Cuadros*, 1991; *Ticona, Rodriguez and Albó,* 1995].

Popular participation and decentralization are now widely celebrated in the development literature as institutional responses to the challenges of economic regionalism, development planning and the distribution and balance of power. In Latin America, schemes for administrative decentralization of the state and participatory development were, with few exceptions, introduced by most governments – including advocates of neo-liberal economic policy – during the 1980s. In Africa, state-run programmes for participatory development and decentralization have been nearly as widespread as in Latin America: for example, Tanzania, Zimbabwe, Uganda, Ghana, the Ivory Coast, Botswana and South Africa to name but a few [*Shou*, 2000; *Crook and Manor*, 1998; *Good*, 1996; *Mohan*, 1996; *Steifel and Wolfe*, 1994; *Erikson, Naustalstid and Shou*, 1999]. In Asia various experiments with state-sponsored programmes for popular participation in development and decentralization have also been undertaken, in India, Bangladesh, the Philippines, Nepal and China [*Crook and Manor*, 1998; *Webster*, 1992, 1999; *Zuo*, 1997; *White*, 1999]. Programmes for democratic local governance have also been introduced as part of the package of reform in a number of European and former Soviet Union countries [*Blair*, 2000].

Governments and supporters of the programmes in NGO circles back administrative decentralization as a way to improve both the efficiency and the responsiveness of governmental institutions. Although claiming the home-grown nature of their respective reforms, national governments appear to learn from each other in including popular participation as the necessary responsive ingredient in their decentralization process [*Martinez*, 1996]. Whilst this learning process appears to originate at home in most countries, the influence both of economics and of international organizations such as the UN, the IMF, and the World Bank on those countries which have continued with programmes of popular participation and decentralization is unmistakable [*Palma Caravajal*, 1995; *Montano*, 1996; *Ospina*, 1997]. In Bolivia the World Bank was a key player in pushing through legislation for local government reform, the financing of the implementation of reform, and the blueprint for participation in planning. In Latin America popular participation and decentralization programmes were not only the result of a regional political mood-swing, but by and large carried out as a part of the structural adjustment process at the behest and with the support of the international community represented by the UNDP (United Nations Development Programme) and the World Bank [*Tendler*, 1999; *Palma Caravajal*, 1995; *Martinez*, 1996; *Stiefel and Pearce*, 1982]. The municipality, a legacy of the centralized Napoleonic state structure shared by many countries in the region, was to be recast and granted a key role in most new programmes for administrative decentralization [*Nickson*, 1997].

THE CONTEXT: SANTUARIO DE QUILLACAS

Santuario de Quillacas is a municipality of principally Aymara-speaking subsistence farmers and pastoralists located on the Southern Bolivian altiplano at an altitude of 3,800 metres (12,500 feet) in the Southern Bolivian Department of Oruro. As is evident from the name itself, the community of Santuario de Quillacas is known to Bolivians not only as a small municipality but also as a major religious sanctuary. Each year on 14 September, people from all over the Bolivian Highlands and from as far away as northern Argentina and Chile descend on the municipal capital of Quillacas, on pilgrimage to celebrate the feast of Señor de la Exaltación. The local image of Christ Crucified, known as *Tata Quillacas*, is held to be a miraculous *suma miriku*, or a doctor with exceptional curative powers.

Despite its current small population of around 2,265 inhabitants, the community of Santuario de Quillacas has had its own municipal government since 1962. Together with environmental change and the reduction of the railway services over the last 30 years, the crash in tin prices and privatization of the mining industry have also been responsible for forcing many Quillacans to leave the area in search of seasonal employment. However, men still seek employment in the nearby mines of Totorani, Collowara and Huanuni.[5] In addition to seasonal work in the mines, short periods of work are also carried out in the cities or richer agricultural areas in the eastern lowlands (Chapare, Santa Cruz). One or two individuals in the town of Quillacas have also managed to make enough money to buy themselves trucks, which they use to tender for haulage work between the major Highland and Lowland cities. On their way they carry local produce from one ecological area to sell or exchange in the next.

Unlike other municipalities in the Highlands of Bolivia, in Quillacas there are no large landowners and no visible remains of a hacienda system.

Modern cantonal divisions within the municipality correspond more or less to the boundaries of pre-existing *ayllu* subdivisions. While there are clearly some common features in this widespread organizational and structural feature of Andean society – the common ownership of land, the Chinese box subdivision of the community, the importance of kinship and ancestors, and connected system of rotating local leadership – the truth is that there exists considerable variance in the form and meaning of the *ayllu*.[6] In Quillacas it is the *ayllu mayor* (main ayllu) which is considered to be the maximal body of people and land that is their community. Within this maximal body the community is segmented into four sections or *ayllus menores* (minor ayllus), which are groups based on kinship and virilocality. It is these *ayllus menores* which correspond with municipal cantonal subdivisions. Within each of the five *ayllu menores* that make up the *ayllu mayor* land is again subdivided. The landscape surrounding each of the villages and settlements is divided, often quite roughly, and people can only work the land, keep animals, or build their *estancias* or *ranchos* (farms or ranches) on parcels belonging to the *ayllu* or sub-*ayllu* into which they are born or marry.

In common with other colonial towns – for example, Yura [*Rasnake*, 1988] or K'ulta [*Abercrombie*, 1998] – this division of territory according to the five *ayllus* is repeated even in the town and villages of Santuario de Quillacas. Neighbourhoods and streets are again divided according to *ayllu*, and people reside side by side with their fellow *ayllu* members. Separately the central square and churchyard are also divided according to *ayllu*. During festivals, religious parades and rituals, *ayllu* members and their musicians take up positions, lead off from and carry out libations, divinations and sacrifices in these areas where – like them – their ancestors are held to reside. In simple terms, then, what the *ayllu* consists of is a classificatory system which locates its subject within a predefined Andean society, and thus a space which, albeit imperfect and frequently broken, emanates out from the church and square of the central *marka*, through the streets, out into the landscape, between different communities to the common borders of their greater community, the *ayllu mayor*.

The Sevaruyo-Soraga Conflict

In April 1998 Don Eleuterio, the Mayor of Santuario de Quillacas, was handed a letter by a town inhabitant returning from market in Oruro.[7] That night the contents were read out at a meeting of the municipal council. The letter announced the holding of an extraordinary meeting of the Civic Committee (*Comité Cívico*), a migrant residents' organization, in Oruro, to which all interested residents were invited. There was a rumour amongst officials of the Departmental Prefecturate that the Bolivian National Senate was in the process of discussing the ending of Santuario de Quillacas's status as a municipality, and the annexation of its political jurisdiction by a neighbouring municipality and province. The meeting in Oruro was aimed at fielding and finding solutions that could address the threat posed to the continued existence of Quillacas' government. The municipality was asked to prepare a report of its accounts, development plan and status in relation to the implementation of the popular participation and decentralization laws; information which the Civic Committee considered important indicators of their chances in government debates about their future.

The reason behind the National Senate's review of Santuario de Quillacas's municipal status lay with the history of conflict between the municipal authorities based in the town of Quillacas and the inhabitants of an outlying canton. In 1996 the municipal government in Quillacas received notification that in carrying out its duty under the popular participation legislation – that is, redrawing territorial and judicial boundaries – the National Boundary Commission (CONLIT) had accepted an application by the canton of Sevaruyo-Soraga, to the southwest of Quillacas, to shift its political and judicial affiliation to the municipality of Huari in the province of Sebastian Pagador (see Map 1). For the municipal government of Santuario de Quillacas, the decision by CONLIT came as shocking news. Although there had been tensions between the government and the canton for some time, cantonal leaders had not received an invitation to the meeting in Pazna where the decision had been taken. Since being returned from Huari to Quillacan administrative jurisdiction in 1994 following the introduction of popular participation, there had been some grumbling amongst cantonal leaders about being forced to join a poorer municipality. However, nothing had been said about a complete change in political affiliation. Although it had been a part of Sebastian Pagador for 12 years, in historical and cultural terms Sevaruyo-Soraga had always been considered an integral member of the greater community of Quillacas. Besides the loss of territory, losing the canton's population of around 700 people [*National Institute of Statistics*, 1992] meant that the per capita resources received by the municipality through provision of popular participation – that is, the *co-participación tributaria* – would now be greatly reduced.

The municipality of Santuario de Quillacas felt cheated by the actions of Sevaruyo-Soraga and Sebastian Pagador. Quillacas had supported the creation of the province of Sebastian Pagador and the municipality of Huari in 1982, even though this had physically separated Quillacas from the rest of the province of Avaroa of which it remained part politically. With this redrawing of the boundaries, Santuario de Quillacas changed from being the third to the second section of the province of Avaroa. Although this improved its administrative status, and the members of the municipal

MAP 1
AVAROA PROVINCE, DEPARTMENT OF ORURO, BOLIVIA

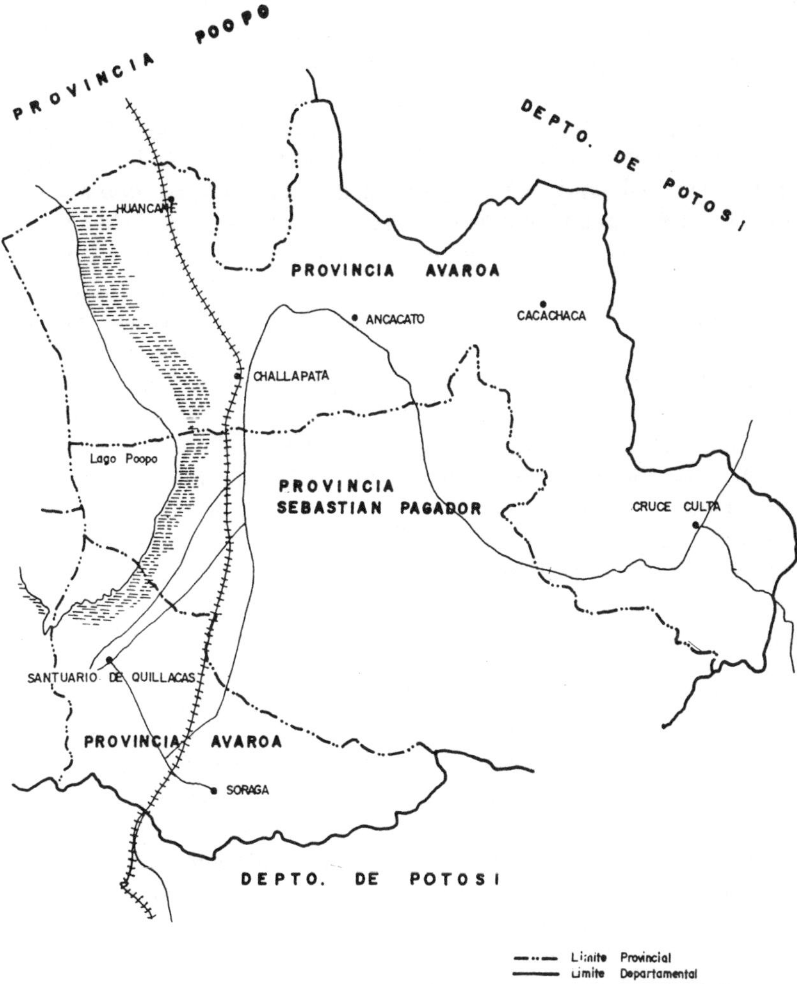

Source: Ministerio de Desarrollo Humano, Secretaria de Participación Popular, Bolivia.

government of Santuario de Quillacas feared that physical separation from Avaroa might harm communication with the provincial government in Challapata, they nonetheless agreed to the creation of Sebastian Pagador. It appeared that the administrative entity Quillacas had helped create had turned against it by agreeing to the annexation of Sevaruyo-Soraga. Envoys from Quillacas travelled to the canton and to the neighbouring municipality to see if they could stop the proceedings. However, in view of the economic value of their decisions, the public representatives of the administrations of Huari and Sevaruyo-Soraga remained unmoved by Quillacan objections.

Since popular participation funding to the municipalities is calculated on a per capita basis, Huari was keen to obtain the financial advantage of raising its overall population. Sevaruyo-Soraga, disappointed at the slow pace of development in the municipality of Santuario de Quillacas, stated that it had been considering such a shift in political affiliation for some time. Indeed, its application to become a canton had been inspired by a desire to secure autonomy from Santuario de Quillacas and redefine its administrative position in relation to the state through permanent administrative union with the wealthier province of Sebastian Pagador. Quillacas knew this. Now with the legal re-demarcation of municipal boundaries carried out under the popular participation law, the opportunity to join the richer municipality of Huari had arisen. The leaders hoped that the shift in political affiliation would see investment in their area rise.

According to municipal authorities in Quillacas they had been powerless to stop this situation from arising. The municipality of Santuario de Quillacas had been severely slowed down in its use of popular participation financing due to a serious error made during the original drafting of the law. In 1994, the Bolivian state issued Supreme Decree No. 23943, which listed the 311 municipalities recognized under Law 1551 as recipients of per capita funding: the list itself was published.[8] It did not include the municipality of Santuario de Quillacas. Without the official recognition conferred by this document, the first year of financing bypassed Santuario de Quillacas, and was transferred entirely to Huari. The following year the municipality's complaints and proof of its right to be recognized under this law stopped the flow of money away from its community. However its municipal accounts were frozen until legislative recognition in May 1996 made its existence official in the eyes of national government.[9] As a result of these problems, the municipality of Santuario de Quillacas experienced severe delay in its efforts to introduce and finance development initiatives throughout its territory. The leaders of the communities within the canton of Sevaruyo-Soraga refused, however, to accept this as a suitable excuse for what they considered to be the poor administration of their area.

Unable to change the decisions of its neighbours, the municipal government of Santuario de Quillacas looked for an alternative way out of the crisis. Together with the Civic Committee in Oruro, it put together a case against the official decision made by CONLIT. The National Senate, the Sub-Secretary of Popular Participation, the National Directorate of Territorial Boundaries and the Military Geographical Institute were each sent a series of documents. These documents not only demonstrated the lawful constitution of the municipality by President Paz Estensorro in 1961, but the historical connection of the canton of Sevaruyo-Soraga to Quillacas. Letters sent with these documents also argued that CONLIT's decision had been unlawful. Contrary to legal procedure, none of the Quillacan officials had been invited to attend the meeting in Pazna. It was pointed out that without the signature of the President of the Republic the document approving the canton's annexation was invalid. Notarized reports that officials of CONLIT had accepted bribes from the municipality of Huari were also included.

Although the case remained unresolved throughout 1996, 1997 and 1998, the submission of a legal case to the correct authorities meant that CONLIT and the province of Sebastian Pagador were temporarily unable to proceed with the annexation of the canton of Sevaruyo-Soraga. Santuario de Quillacas's boundaries remained intact, and with the passing of the 'Law of the Creation of each municipality' the municipality of Santuario de Quillacas began to receive *co-participacion* funds. According to the law of popular participation, they were free for the time being to look for other external sponsors for local development projects. Municipal structures were more or less in place, and Quillacas's annual plan (POA) and municipal development plan (PDM) had received official ratification. To try and demonstrate goodwill to Sevaruyo-Soraga, the canton was earmarked within these plans for a considerable rise in investment and development. However, despite the efforts made by the mayor and the Centre for Training and Socio-Economic Development (CCEDSE) to discuss possible projects with the canton, its leaders and inhabitants refused to negotiate.[10]

As opposition continued and escalated throughout 1997 and into 1998, the conflict began to create such tensions that Don Eleuterio and some of his colleagues were verbally abused and threatened by people in Sevaruyo-Soraga.[11] The road leading from the town of Quillacas to Sevaruyo was blockaded with large boulders, and visiting officials' vehicles were stoned. A few weeks prior to the arrival of the letter, the departmental Prefect and police officers had been called in to try and calm down the situation, and to guarantee both sides that a final decision on their case would be made shortly by the national government.

RURAL GRASSROOTS MOBILIZATION

Given the precious time away from their fields and the long journey they had made to get there, the turnout for the Civic Committee meeting held in the draughty 'Market-Traders' Union Hall' in Oruro was quite impressive. As the numbers rose in the meeting hall the leader of the Civic Committee started proceedings by offering formal greetings to all who had arrived, before going on to describe the subject and direction of the meeting. The meeting first considered the report from the *Alcaldía* before proceeding to the question of how to deal with the current problem. As formal greetings were made, in addition to *vecino* residents the names of outlying village and hamlet representatives were warmly repeated. Given the main topic of the meeting there was a notable exception. Despite the great turnout for the meeting, nobody from the canton of Sevaruyo-Soraga was present.

The Conflict Addressed

In his account of the municipality's current situation, Don Eleuterio began by recounting the problems they had experienced as a result of the conflict with Sevaruyo-Soraga. He explained that although they had received the development funds promised by popular participation legislation, the municipal administrative budget was still struggling to cover the cost of certain functionaries. According to Don Eleuterio, the *Alcaldía* in Quillacas was experiencing problems making the 15 per cent of *co-participación tributaria* funds allocated to the running of the municipal government stretch to cover some of their costs, including the wages of two of its staff (the *Contador*, or accountant, and the *Oficial Mayor*, the general administrator). An inspection made by the Vice-Ministry of Popular Participation of the municipal government the previous month had given their adoption of the new administrative structures the official all-clear. So far they had not been able to produce many visible signs of 'public works' (*obras publicas*), but the municipal accounts had received *co-participación tributaria* financing, as well as further funds, from the Social Investment Fund (FIS) and the Departmental Prefecture for the planned electrification of the towns of Quillacas and Sevaruyo. To this funding a number of international and national NGOs had added considerable sums of money to finance a range of local development projects.[12] However, the conflict with the canton of Sevaruyo-Soraga, and the long drawn out process of change-over in government following the last election, had considerably slowed down the implementation of these projects. Without the cooperation of all the inhabitants of the municipality he feared that any attempts to speed up these works could mean the freezing of their accounts for another year.

Following the *Alcalde*'s account of the current situation, a number of comments made by authorities and individuals in the audience began to reveal hitherto undisclosed opinions and information.[13] First, Don Crecencio Huaylla, President of the Vigilance Committee, stood up and announced that, in adjusting to his new position, he had struggled greatly to understand the complexities and meaning of the reforms for the community and its government. In the municipality of Santuario de Quillacas, grassroots organizations (OTBs) representing the four cantons and a Vigilance Committee had been registered successfully soon after the introduction of reform. Although he had taken over the role of Vigilance Committee president without any previous experience of public office, Don Crecencio complained had been expected to come to terms with the demands of his new job without formal training or a wage. Together with the grassroots organizations, he observed, he had successfully conducted workshops in order to gain an understanding of people's interests and opinions, and what they wanted by way of development planning and investment. In the course of these activities he had encountered other individuals and groups who were similarly confused and struggling to understand the complex legal requirements of the new laws: 'The people of the *rinconada* don't understand why money can't be handed directly to them', he said, 'why does the government need to oversee and control local decisions in this way?'

Building on the Spanish word for corner (*rincón*), the term *rinconada* is used by people in the town of Quillacas to refer to the outlying settlements that belong to their municipal and *Ayllu* area. Although the word is often used in a neutral sense, conversations with inhabitants of Quillacas revealed that the term was often used in a negative context. It conveyed the sense of non-*vecinos* as peripheral, and therefore less aware of or connected to the loci of administrative power and decision-making. Although its critical use is significant in terms of an 'us/them' differentiating mechanism, here Don Crecencio uses it in a way that sets up another 'us/them' distinction. Specifically, he appeals to the mainly *vecino* audience to understand that cantonal views of recent local government reform differed little from those of people living in the town: in his words, 'They had paid the taxes required under governmental decentralization, but under the new system of popular participation was this not meant to be their money, to be directed by them, to address local needs and development? Why did this money have to pass through the state system at all?'

From the sounds of obvious approval and the nodding of heads, these sentiments appeared to find widespread support among those present at the meeting. According to Article 5 of the *Decreto Reglamentario de los aspectos economicos y patrimoniales de la Ley de Participacion Popular*, (*Decreto Supremo, No. 23813, June 1994*), citizens of a municipality are expected to pay tax for their ownership of all urban and rural property and goods, and vehicles. Although older members of the community remembered pre-revolutionary payments of a *tasa*, or poll tax, to the Oruro *Prefectura*, for most Quillacans this was the first time in recent memory they had had to pay any tax other than a small annual fee to the ancestral leaders for community land use.

In response to Don Crecencio, Don Cirilio said that he for one was happy that people in the municipality were complying with new tax requirements. People should recognize that although the system was not as clear as it should be, their taxes were beginning to feed back into the development funds available to the municipality. In reading out the figures from the past three years, Don Eleuterio demonstrated that their account had grown from B$245,000 in 1996 to B$395,000 in 1998.[14] There followed some prolonged discussion before a member from the Civic Committee in Cochabamba rose to his feet. His comment was that the municipal government of Santuario de Quillacas was in need of some constructive criticism; that it appeared to have a problem with communication. For the last two years it had not told the residents what was happening with the money it was receiving. More regular 'economic reports' (*informes económicos*) and more information about the legislation and how it worked were needed before any faith in their possibilities could be created. To this the *Alcalde* openly apologized, adding that 'in an ideal world … we would make more effort to communicate with people.'

However, he went on to say that officially the role of introducing the system of participatory planning, whereby community members could actively participate in municipal development planning sessions, was to have been taken care of by CCEDSE. He now admitted that this was problematic. This was the first time that CCEDSE had dealt with this kind of work. Not only were CCEDSE new to this kind of socio-political facilitation in general, but they also admitted to lacking experience of dealing with the interests of an ethnic rural community such as theirs. This initiated a discussion about political and legal communication. Members of the community in the audience voiced their concern, both about their own vulnerability and about the lack of knowledge (*escaso conocimiento*) regarding the new legislation and its meaning. These concerns were expressed in the following manner:

> The laws express respect for our norms and customs, and promise a positive change in local development, but still they appear to take little account of our lands, customs and culture. When other laws, such as the agrarian reform of 1953, changed our government and rights to land, they too were advertised and initially accepted as positive advances. However, these laws nearly resulted in the destruction of the *ayllus*. What will stop these laws from having the same effect on our communities now? … The reforms of the last government state that they will not disrupt our organizations, but they still do. Popular participation, decentralization and INRA have all divided us more than ever before. Do we not have natural rights to

> land and identity not given by national law? This is what we have to remember!...We can adjust to the new system of government and perhaps receive some benefit from it, but we need to think about our future. At two in the morning another decree can be passed and what will we do? Still hope that the law benefits us?

As well as expressing present difficulties with the Bolivian state, the audience's reactions to what had been said appeared to favour the avoidance of future difficulties of the kind they now faced, through getting hold of more information and improving the community's understanding of national legislation. One member of the audience proposed that perhaps the best source of this knowledge lay with the community's young people. Either the latter, educated as they were in the urban ways of the city, could together with the Bolivian government communicate their knowledge to the Civic Committees, or young people in the secondary school in Quillacas might receive special tuition from CCEDSE explaining the intricacies of political and legislative structures. Don Eleuterio responded that he thought this a good idea. However when he had tried in the past year to interest students in the popular participation legislation, they had shown no interest in coming along to meet the development specialists setting things up in the *Alcaldía*. He had even toyed with the idea of having the specialists run computer classes for a few teenagers on the new computer installed there. However, the simple fact that young Quillacans saw their future linked to the city made these initiatives unworkable. All he could think of doing in the meantime was to ask the Federation of Southern Orureño *Ayllus* (FASOR), a local ethnic political organization based in nearby Challapata, to come and give them another public workshop about the working of the laws.[15] Two months before, on the day of the arrival of a representative of Oxfam America, FASOR had organized a workshop in Quillacas to demonstrate their work in community education about rights, law and identity. A number of other workshops of this kind had been held in the area during the previous year.

Impatient to get on and address the problems at hand, Don Eleuterio now urged the audience to think of what they were going to do in relation to the Sevaruyo-Soraga problem. He repeated his fears that resistance to the government's plans might compound difficulties generated by lack of communication with the state, adding that: 'Central government always seems to have a different perspective from ours. They often seem to have problems integrating our ideas with the Departmental Development Plan.' Nonetheless, he reminded them that what was at stake was not only the possibility of losing their current right to manage their own development projects, but also a complete loss of local self-government. Given this danger, he believed it important to continue trying to win their case with the government and offering the hand of friendship to the canton. Only in this way would they secure the continued existence of the municipality of Santuario de Quillacas. What were their opinions?

The Voice of the Rural Grassroots?

Don Julian, one of the ancestral authorities in the community, stood up for the first time in the meeting. He stated that he for one was opposed to the opinion of some residents that the exercise of physical pressure on the canton was the way to stop their intended separation. He wanted the *alcaldía* to continue down the path they had started. That was, to use existing laws to solve their predicament. Obviously stung by his comment, the *Alcalde* responded that he personally was not satisfied with this response, that he was tired and lacked time to continue dealing with these problems on his own. Now he wanted the ancestral leaders and the entire community to join him in taking on responsibility for the conflict.

One of the municipal council members urged the community to continue down the diplomatic path, but to work through some kind of independent mediator: someone who could not be 'bought', perhaps someone from the Catholic church who was not tempted by money might intervene on their behalf. At this point, criticism was made concerning the loyalties of Don Cirilio Villalobos, the Director of the Civic Committee: 'Why should we listen to the thoughts of Señor Villalobos … he is not going to suffer the consequences, is he? We are the ones who will suffer, aren't we? And if the municipality disappears, we are the ones who will be guilty.' Two men from the audience expressed their opinion that the diplomatic path taken by the *alcaldía* was a waste of time. It was clear to them that to enter a dialogue with the people of Sevaruyo was impossible. Such people should be forced to understand and accept the justice of the municipal government's location in the town of Quillacas: 'They refuse to accept or discuss anything other than their aspiration to join Sebastian Pagador. With this kind of people it is impossible to progress.'

Don René Jallaza, President of the Civic Committee in La Paz, who was clearly bothered by the direction of the preceding discussion, managed to attract the meeting's attention by standing up and waving his hat. A businessman by profession, Don René clearly had learnt some skills in presentation: having received permission to speak, he walked to the front of the audience with a flip-chart and felt-pens. Turning to the audience he commented: 'It's clear that someone has to lose this conflict and, considering all the facts, it looks like it will be Quillacas.' Perhaps by not complying with the letter of the law, he said, CONLIT and Sevaruyo-Soraga had indeed exposed a great weakness in their case. Quillacans, however, should

TABLE 1
COMMUNITIES FOR AND AGAINST ADMINISTRATION BY THE MUNICIPALITY OF SANTUARIO DE QUILLACAS

Community	For administration	Against administration
Quillacas	All for	
Soraga		All against
Villcani	70% for	30% against
Rivera	80% for	20% against
Antatuta		All against
Ichocata		All against
Lucumpaya		All against
Torco	50% for	50% against
Totorani	All for	
Ricotani		All against
Thicomayu	All for	
Antaraqu		All against
Pacollani	All for	

recognize that there were too many factors that would swing the situation in favour of their rivals in Huari. Their municipality's lack of territorial continuity with the rest of the province of Avaroa and insufficient population size – fewer than 5,000 inhabitants – meant that they did not even meet the basic legal requirements for the constitution of a municipality required by the Law of Popular Participation and the will of central government.[16] Sooner or later, these deficiencies would be addressed by the Bolivian State. He reminded his audience that Quillacans should also recognize that, however unfair it might be, Huari had much more money to play with than the Santuario de Quillacas; money which they could not only use to bribe government officials at national and departmental levels, but which also made their claim to exist and expand appear all the more plausible.

Don René continued by saying that it appeared that the leaders and residents refused to accept, or were unaware of the fact that, the majority of communities in the municipality of Santuario de Quillacas were in favour of annexation by another province. To show this, he wrote down the names of all the settlements belonging to the community of Quillacas, and asked the members of the municipal council to report in turn which communities were to their certain knowledge presently for and against its control of local government (see Table 1). The diagram he produced clearly showed that, despite municipal leaders' and townspeople's protestations, the majority of settlements in the municipality were in favour of joining the richer neighbouring province. He said that other settlement leaders were tired of waiting for the municipality to deliver them support. With this, Don René concluded that Quillacans should accept their fate. It would better for their community if they find themselves the best possible deal within the coming annexation. This would reduce the effect on the population and boundaries of their community. After all Santuario de Quillacas was a religious sanctuary and *ayllu* before it was ever a municipality.

A later show of hands would show that the majority of people at the meeting considered this to be defeatist talk. As the meeting drew to a close it became clear that the majority of town residents and municipal representatives were in favour of continuing negotiations with the government and Sevaruyo-Soraga. If a neighbouring province annexed them, they would have to accept a reduction in their political status, from a section to a canton. From this diminution would stem a loss both of their right to self-government and a significant proportion of their population.

Discussion then turned to how they could strengthen their current position as an ethnically distinct people – that is to say, as an Aymara-speaking community – with an independent local government. Surprisingly, although some of the municipal authorities and town residents were aware of this alternative – looking to form a *mancomunidad* with an adjoining municipality (Pampa Aullagas, Ladislao Cabrera) – this option did not enter their discussions.[17] In later interviews with municipal authorities, it was made clear that despite the fact that such an arrangement would have strengthened their numbers and their finances, they were frightened that such a move would mean a reduction in their overall administrative control. It was quite obvious that – where local leaders and the leading families were concerned – there was also a considerable amount of pride involved in choosing to continue to remain independent. Instead, the meeting proposed that in addition to the legal actions already taken by the municipality, some attempt must be made to study the possibility of having the state recognize their status as an indigenous municipality.

It was suggested that perhaps the government might grant their community more secure status if, as in the case of the nearby communities of Coroma and Santa Ana de Chipaya, the special nature of their history as a distinct political and cultural centre was formally recognized. Under the special conditions set by the law of popular participation, ethnic communities can apply for legal recognition as indigenous municipal sections. Within existing municipal structures, this gives them a legal right to have their leaders occupy the local positions of cantonal municipal agents. It also gives them legal right to apply for funding specially allocated by government and other organizations to indigenous peoples and their interests. However, that these communities were recognized legally as dependent indigenous municipal sections, and not as autonomous municipalities in their own right, was a consideration that municipal leaders in Quillacas failed to take into account.

It was with these ideas in mind that the meeting in Oruro finally came to a close. Different opinions, ideas and disagreements had all been voiced, but the municipal government had somehow managed to come out with its existing strategy intact. The idea of becoming an indigenous municipality would be looked into, but the municipal government would continue to rely on the legal case it had submitted.

The Conflict Unresolved

In the weeks and months that followed the meeting in Oruro, the conflict between Quillacas and the canton of Sevaruyo-Soraga remained a major preoccupation of all the inhabitants in the town. The latter discussed the most recent developments in the situation on a daily basis, however small they might be. In conversations about the conflict and legal case it became obvious that opinions in the town were becoming increasingly divided over what was happening, and what should be done to resolve the conflict. As the situation worsened and their efforts appeared to be getting nowhere, a growing number of people were in favour of changing the strategy employed by the municipal government. The Prefectura in Oruro and the National Senate appeared to have forgotten their case. Except for building a block of public toilets and showers in the main square and improvements to the local schools, all other development projects appeared to have been suspended until the end of the conflict. As more town residents aligned themselves with the view that 'perhaps annexation by a neighbouring province wouldn't be so bad', the verbal battle lines for those implacably opposed to compromise became more and more forcefully drawn. For *vecinos* allied with the *alcaldia*, talk of annexation was cowardly. These weren't real Quillacans speaking. Real Quillacans would keep on fighting for their political rights. After all, they had always been the centre of government in the area. They couldn't just give that up now. For other *vecinos* lacking political influence or ties to local government an administrative shift increasingly seemed logical and necessary. Their municipality was too small and too poor to continue on its own. At Don Vicente's home there were regular discussions and occasional arguments between the extended family members and neighbours who met to talk and eat together in the evenings.

As relations between individuals and settlements worsened, Don Vicente was asked as one of the *ayllu*'s ancestral leaders to come and conduct *wilanchas*, or sacrifices, for the local ancestors and spirits of the town, the canton of Sevaruyo-Soraga and other neighbouring hamlets. People hoped that by asking for the ancestors' help, the hostility in the community might be dispelled and peace return to their land. During the procession celebrating the festival of *Santa Vera Cruz*,[18] the priest stopped at each shrine in the churchyard to offer prayers about the conflict with Sevaruyo-Soraga, and asked for peace in the *ayllu* which tended the shrine concerned. In response to calls from local people, the priest held a special mass in the church of Quillacas at the start of July, calling for reconciliation through prayer and blessing. When reports and stories of similar, but much more violent, inter- and intra-community conflicts in nearby rural locations such as Qaqachaka or K'ulta were told or read about in *La Patría*, the main newspaper in Oruro, people in Quillaca made comparisons with their own situation. What could be done, they asked one another, to stop things getting so out of hand?[19] During 1997 and 1998 some 14 people had died as a result of the conflict between Qaqachaka and their Laymi and Jucumani neighbours. A riot in Challapata between opposing K'ulta cantons vying for position as the site of a new municipal capital had put two people in hospital with severe injuries. Aware of such episodes in these neighbouring communities, *vecinos* and *rinconada* alike in the municipality of Santuario de Quillacas were concerned that their own dispute might end in bloodshed. By August 1998, when I departed from the community, these concerns were still apparent. After two years of arguments, blockades, insults, and finally state intervention, the conflict with Sevaruyo-Soraga remained unresolved.[20]

II

As is evident from the above account, the inhabitants of Santuario de Quillacas are not passive onlookers where the recent process of local government reform in Bolivia is concerned. Through their meetings and conflicts with one another and the state, they struggle over the meaning of and form taken by the international development policies they consider to have been imposed on them. This process is not without its problems, and highlights the fact that peasants in this context approach the question of change from different political and economic perspectives. Although it is not possible to address all of these perspectives, the second part of this article will focus on the way in which the antinomic conditions of antagonism and solidarity are formed and reproduced. This is a complex process which, it is argued here, lies at the heart of the different ways in which the government reforms (popular participation, administrative decentralization) have been experienced by and impacted upon the rural population in the locality. Without examining these contradictory processes, neither the significance of local power relations nor the dynamics of linkages with the state and development policies would be evident. A central claim is that in Santuario de Quillacas the past – or rather the way in which the past is understood and (re-) interpreted in the present – is a key ideological and political resource in the course of current decision-making by those at the rural grassroots. In short, peasants with different material and class interests mobilize specific images of the past as part of a specific strategy that is supportive of their own particular interests. To a considerable extent, therefore, these ideological constructions and understandings of the past explain why different segments of the rural population act in the way they do.

LEARNING TO SEE THE PRESENT THROUGH THE PAST

Quillacans draw upon different sources in their efforts to form an understanding of their own past. If they have gone to school to any level they will have received some kind of instruction about the defining moments of the country's history. However, in learning these dates of formation, battles and retreat, no official mention is made of their own community's history and past. The latter has no place in Bolivian children's battered jotters and notebooks. For most Quillacans, therefore, the story about their own particular municipality, *ayllu*, and religious sanctuary, is something they absorb on a quotidian basis, by living in the community and participating in its organization and routines. It is a story that is built cumulatively: a form of knowledge that never arrives all at once, but is rather acquired in fragments throughout their lifetimes. Some families in the village have stores of old documents they try to preserve: papers which their grandparents or ancestors either wrote or received, a record of their past lives. These are occasionally searched for and pulled out, but more commonly they are talked about, as material proof of experience and memory. Rarely are they read. More often it is a process whereby the contents of a particular document are relayed orally, from one individual to another by word of mouth. As in other areas of the Andean region, written histories are not the source of rural grassroots knowledge about the past. Indeed, the process of learning about the past is often more subtle than the spoken word [*Abercrombie*, 1998: 130].

Like most Andean peoples, the past is a lived experience for Quillacans. The longer residents participate in life of the community, the more knowledge they acquire about its formation and constitution. Instead of a narrative punctuated by dates and events like the formal history of Bolivia itself, what they gain on a quotidian basis is an implicit understanding of why things are the way they are.[21] However, what is quite distinct in Andean society is the context in which this process of tacit learning takes place. In the community of Santuario de Quillacas members of the community are said to travel along a 'pathway of life' known as *thakhi* (= 'road/path' in aymara). Although not every inhabitant of the rural community does this, the *thakhi* consists of a series of interconnected positions of service, responsibility and authority through which all residents are encouraged to pass (and most do) during their lifetimes. According to the leaders of Santuario de Quillacas, it is in the course both of the journey through and the carrying out of each of the positions that go to form *thakhi*, that people gain knowledge and understanding of their community's past and reasons for its present organization. It is in essence a system of learning by doing/being, or rather by living.[22]

Given the way that *thakhi* functions as a process of learning, the accounts given by Quillacans of their past are frequently more moral than historical.[23] Constructing the basis of a civil/religious moral order in the community, the understanding of the past embedded in *thakhi* is not as concerned with the accurate depiction of time as Western histories are. Through the activities and responsibilities that *thakhi* entails, the past is bent into the present to construct a singular series of lessons about life and how it should be lived as a member of the community. These lessons are practised through participation in communal work parties (*faena*, *mink'a*), and regularly acted out in the dances and rituals associated with festivals. The costumes worn during these events aim to exaggerate and therefore highlight the moral personality of the mythical and historical characters involved. At the festival of *Señor de la Exaltación*, for example, the practical jokes and general rudeness of dancers wearing a bear costume emphasize the need for propriety amongst people. The long noses, red cheeks, drunkenness, and sword waving of others dressed as Spanish soldiers hint not only at the strangeness and erratic behaviour of their earlier conquerors, but also at the dangerousness and lack of morality of all *gringos* (= white people) or *q'ara* (= non-people).

In common with other Amerindian narratives about the past, the accounts of the past lived out and described in the course of *thakhi* are not chronological [*Rappaport*, 1990]. In the course of re-enacting past events during festivals and rituals, time frames are juxtaposed, causal explanations left out, and narrations of the events themselves are not given in linear form. It is only in conjunction with a whole range of activities – including ritual, pilgrimage, dance and daily work – that an elaborate key to the understanding of these non-sequential narratives can be obtained [*Abercrombie*, 1998]. Indeed, much of this history is encoded in the physical environment in which the people themselves live.[24] Around Quillacas, the mountains, hills, large boulders, wild/domestic animals, changes in weather and season, were all named, and – through their believed connection with one another – seen by local people as active elements with which they interact in daily and ritual life, as had their ancestors before them.

If through *thakhi* Quillacans' knowledge of their past is embodied in a non-chronological expression of time rooted in physical space, ritual and community practice, this is not to say that peasants have no sense of the flow of time in a European sense, that they are unable to distinguish fact from fiction, or that they prefer to confront universal and logical problems as opposed to the specific [*Rappaport*, 1990]. Its prime aim is to initiate individuals into the moral order of a shared community, but this whole system of learning about the rural community and its past does not stand apart from the serious practical questions encountered in everyday life. Indeed, it is deeply engaged with it. Fictitious and fantastic images are employed, but such images are frequently used to reflect on and say something about the real, to comment on present conditions and play out a stock of tried and tested solutions.

Not as remote from daily existence as one would suppose, therefore, the complex and interrelated method both for understanding the past and describing the social and moral order of the local community that is *thakhi* has been subject to change and external influence. The system of ancestral authorities and beliefs, visible in both the daily and ritual life of the present-day community of Quillacas, is – contrary to immediate appearances – the contingent product of long and difficult negotiations with the outside world, or (more pointedly) with the changing and often contradictory demands and projects of the Bolivian state. To stress the changing and contingent historical character of *thakhi* is important, not least because the circumstances that result in change help explain the contrasting forms of ideology and agency in the present.

It is a commonplace that Andean society has been almost completely transformed in the course of history. However, in the form of the ancestral spirits (*achachilas*) to whom rituals and sacrifices are made, a powerful memory of how things were remains in the present. Indeed much of the power of this memory remains embodied in the person, actions and judgements of the *jilaqatas* and *alcalde cobradores*, community authorities who act as intermediaries between ancestors and community, and community and state. Although these positions have not remained untouched by external pressures of political change, their offices have retained a highly influential role in both the spiritual and temporal aspects of community life, even when ancestral authorities have been officially sidelined by state policy and organization. Currently, therefore, the ancestral authorities continue to be active leaders in every area of community decision-making. It is quite clear that, at the same time as the ancestral authority system of *thakhi* has had to adapt to efforts by the national state at local government reform, to a significant degree the local community and leadership of Quillacas have managed successfully to negotiate their own understanding and working of the new systems. The latter have, in short, been adapted so as to defend the importance both of the ancestral authorities and the moral system they represent within community life.

THE REINVENTION OF ANDEAN TRADITION

Up to this point, the picture presented has been one of Quillacan understandings of the past being formed through individuals who embody a commitment to a local system of organization and practice. Broadly speaking, this is an accurate method of depicting what happens in Santuario de Quillacas. It would be wrong, however, to claim that this represents the sum total of knowledge possessed by peasants concerning the past. Personal experience and the experience of a modern education also determine knowledge about what has gone before. Indeed, making a survey of possible sources tells us little more than what kind of 'historical material' is available to people, and from which narratives about the past are constructed. The actual act of remembering is much more complicated and less easily quantifiable as individuals draw on different sources at different times. Rather obviously, the process of remembering is contextually and experientially selective: accordingly, at one conjuncture a specific kind of knowledge is privileged, whereas at another a different set of details are invoked. Most importantly, in the course of conflict at the rural grassroots, memories and/or details about the past become the subject of negotiation and serious disagreement, and are transformed thereby into ideological and political weapons.

To underscore the complexity of remembering is thus of considerable importance, not only because it allows description/explanation of how peasants in Quillaca interpret their past, but also because it permits an insight into the way community members deploy conflicting narratives and discourses about this past in order to justify actions in the present. Much as the structure and functions of local government are the product of negotiation between state and community through history, therefore, they are also the product of ongoing discussions within the community, which are firmly grounded in contrasting visions/versions of the past. Although the discourse of *thakhi* (outlined above) aims to provide a uniform account of the past to which all Quillacans subscribe, it is nevertheless a loosely shared vision, and one which individuals in the community frequently knock down. In recent years the context framing knowledge about the past appears to have changed in Santuario de Quillacas.

Although historical documents kept in a few family homes and a number of cardboard boxes stacked in the corner of the *Cabildo* office are given considerable importance – as symbols of family and community past, and as vital deeds to land and property – until recently few people paid much attention to the actual historical details such records contained. The Quillacans' connection to the past was generally mediated through personal memory or *thakhi*. Over the last decade, however, a number of influential residents in the town of Quillacas have begun to deploy a more detailed kind of historical knowledge in their debates with the rest of the community discourse about leadership and the direction in which the community should go, resulting in a renewed interest in the past of Santuario de Quillacas. The reasons for this are twofold: first, the availability of new external sources of information about the history of the rural community; and second, the appearance of new commentators on the community's history. Since the mid-1980s, Santuario de Quillacas has become a site of interest to a number of academics interested in the previously little studied history and culture of the Bolivian Southern Altiplano area. However, as much as this interest in the past can be explained by the availability of new information and commentators, it is argued here that the heightened interest in it of key figures within the community itself can be explained by the value that these historical interpretations have in supporting or defending ideological positions in current struggles.

Anthropologists Make History

In the late 1980s the Bolivian anthropologist, Ramiro Molina Rivero began conducting research in the Quillacas/Pampa Aullagas area.[25] In so doing it appears that he became an authoritative source and interpreter of local history and culture. Indeed, it was he who helped the ancestral leadership in Santuario de Quillacas to organize and find funding for the setting up of two organizations responsible for giving an impetus to local cultural rejuvenation. The first of these organizations, the Jatun Quillacas Development Cooperation (CODEJQ, *Cooperación de Desarrollo de Jatun Quillacas*) was created to organize and coordinate local development projects, but also to look for ways to strengthen local autonomy and cultural pride. It was CODEJQ which, through its financial support and encouragement, brought about the 'First Regional Assembly of Indigenous Authorities of the *Ayllus Mayores* of Southern Oruro'. Held in Santuario de Quillacas, this assembly brought together ancestral leaders from communities throughout the region to discuss their common cultural heritage and seek solutions to shared problems.

On the back of this assembly another organization was created: namely, the Federation of Southern Orureño Ayllus (FASOR), which defined itself as having both a developmental and cultural aim. Ethnic leaders and authorities committed themselves to search for solutions to the problems and needs of Southern Oruro, which they publicly ascribed to the government having abandoned them. Together with other indigenous organizations in the country, FASOR subscribed to the idea of defending the rights of *ayllus* to local self-government (*auto-determinación*). In 1990 this organization managed to gain sufficient financial support from Oxfam America to build a small centre in Challapata, the provincial capital. Two fulltime members of staff were hired to teach and hold workshops throughout Southern Oruro, covering a series of issues connected to local development and ethnic identity.

In 1991 a history graduate by the name of Ramon Conde, connected to and partially funded by the Andean Oral History Workshop (*Taller Historial Oral Andina* or THOA), a centre for Aymaran cultural activism in La Paz, became attached to FASOR's office in Challapata. As an historian and ex-militant of the Aymara ethnic political *Katarista* movement, Ramon Conde acted as a major contributor of historical knowledge and political direction to FASOR and to the local leaders of Santuario de Quillacas. Under his influence local *ayllu* leaders in the Southern Oruro area were invited to attend workshops on local history, Aymara language and culture in the town of Quillacas and Challapata.[26] During that first meeting a number of speakers were invited to speak on a range of topics, including history, indigenous rights, education, and the Laws of Popular Participation and Administrative Decentralization.

Through FASOR and CODEJQ, the ancestral and municipal authorities in the town of Quillacas became extremely interested in the picture of the past that historical sources furnished them with. As a result of the growing interest in historical sources among townspeople in Quillacas, papers and articles given to the community by the Peruvian historian Espinoza Soriano were dusted off and invested with new value. Historical documents stacked in the corner of the *Corregimiento* office were also looked through and re-evaluated. When I returned to Quillacas with a copy of an article by Espinoza Soriano [1969] publicizing a key sixteenth-century source on the history of the region, this too became an object of intense interest. Now they could read for themselves the contents of documents such as *La Información, La Probanza de Servicio y Meritos* presented by the Quillacan *mallku,* Don Juan Colque Guarachi, to the colonial authorities to describe his family lineage's contribution to government in the area. They could also read about the *senorío* (lordship) of Killaka-Asanaqi, which in the early sixteenth century stretched across the area and secured the allegiance of a great swathe of communities throughout the southern altiplano and southern Asanaqi mountains. Reading about the Killaka-Asanaqi federation's integration into the Inca Empire as a *reino provincial* (= sovereign provincial authority), they learnt additionally of their ancestor's role as a powerful ally of the *zapainca* Tupac Inca Yupanqui.[27] To get an idea of the scale of Killaka-Asanaqi federation at that time, it is sufficient to note one of the titles attributed to Inca Colque: that of *Huno Mallku*.[28] *Huno* signifies 'ten thousand': that is, the number of tributary heads of households subject to his power and over whom he ruled.[29] This suggests that a total population in excess of 50,000 may have been subject to his rule.

Although now based on authoritative and scholarly studies/documents, it becomes clear if what Quillacans say about this history is compared with the works themselves, that the reading FASOR and the ancestral authorities of the town of Quillacas make of the past is somewhat partial. Together with the actions of the ancestors which are less than palatable, therefore, portions of their history are conveniently left out of the picture they portray. That members of the Colque Guarache lineage were more interested in protecting their own positions of power and wealth than in defending their subjects' cultural and political autonomy is never mentioned in the oral versions of history the local leadership and FASOR have put together from documented sources. As in the Inca Empire, during the colonial period the Guarache lineage were able to keep hold of their *cacicazgo* (leadership) privileges through the continued rendering of services to the imperial power. Their access to beasts of burden and herders (which would become extensively used in the moving of minerals and ores from the mines such as Potosi, as well as for the supply of the city), and strategic location of Aullagas (the last *tambo* and substantial settlement of 'peaceful Indians' on the road South) and Puna (a primarily herding settlement conveniently positioned to the Southeast of the Killakas-Asanaqi territory) made them vital allies in the early colonial project.[30] The *mallku* Guarache also demonstrated his new loyalty by directing the Spanish exploitation of the Incan silver mines in Porco [*Espinoza Soriano*, 1969: 15]. However, this history of political pragmatism is not the image of Quillacas presented today.

The image of Quillacas currently projected by the local authorities is of an ethnically integrated and historically fully autonomous community which – in the course of its defence of autonomy – had been divided and cumulatively weakened by the Bolivian state. Neither they, nor the ancestral authorities before them, are responsible for the reductions that have been made to their community's territory or political jurisdiction. Today, as in the past, it is their responsibility, through negotiation with the ancestors and with the state, to ensure the continuation of Quillacan local sovereign autonomy. Based on an interpretation of historical documents, therefore, even comparatively recent events are re-interpreted, repackaged and broadcast as a new foundation story. Now the image of local organization and authority presented to the representatives of the Bolivian state is of a community where *ayllu* and ancestral authority have always been an integral aspect of socio-economic existence. The ancestral authorities informed me that there was an unbroken chain of tradition linking them to their ancestors. However, dig a little deeper and a different story is told. In this story the tradition of ancestral authority is not unbroken. Indeed, following the introduction of peasant union structures after the revolution of 1952, both *ayllu* and ancestral authority disappeared for a time [*Dunkerley*, 1984]. Cultural regeneration took place only in the 1980s, and then because of the confluence of a number of factors either well beyond the control of local people themselves, or dependent on the actions and influence of individual external agents.

A Different History, a History of Difference

In the mid-1980s a changing political and economic climate in Bolivia combined with serious environmental changes to create a situation which undermined both the state policies and syndicalist traditions of the previous 30 years, which had been inspired by the 1952 revolution.[31] In the early 1980s a major fall in the price of tin, and oil prices, led Bolivia into a serious economic crisis, to which the then left-wing coalition government was unable to find a solution. The country was paralysed by hyperinflation and mass demonstrations led by the main workers' union, the *Central Obrera Boliviana* (COB). Hoping that under his direction some stability might return to the country, Bolivian voters in 1985 re-elected for a third time Victor Paz Estensorro as President. Reacting to the situation he found, Paz Estensorro's new administration broke with the tenets of the 1952 revolution in order to try and re-establish favour with foreign governments and international business investors.[32] A neo-liberal structural adjustment programme was introduced at the behest of the World Bank and the international financial community. Although it succeeded in reining in the economy and streamlining government, the social cost of the programme was extremely high [*Crabtree*, 1987; *Nash*, 1993]. Nationalized industries – such as COMIBOL, the National Bolivian Mining Company – were to be sold off. Unable to stop privatization, the Bolivian trade union movement lost much of its membership and, therefore, its political influence and power. Thousands of tin miners were made redundant, as were other public sector employees: left without employment or access to land, some 500,000 people migrated from the highlands to the lowlands in search of alternative sources of income. Often there was no employment to be found other than in illegal coca production. This enforced migration was compounded further by a serious drought that hit the country in 1984, as a result of which numerous rural family farms in the altiplano were unable to reproduce themselves economically. Many peasant households were compelled to abandon their holdings and attempt to find alternative employment, either in urban areas or in lowlands.

This harsh economic climate formed the context in which the ancestral authorities of the Southern altiplano area managed to make a political comeback. In Quillacas, for example, the drought and loss of seasonal employment brought about by the closure of nearby mines forced many families to move out in search of work or land elsewhere. Some moved away permanently, others moved away on a more temporary basis, continuing to return to Quillacas to plant, harvest and take part in the community's ritual and festival life. As the number of peasant households in the community dwindled, those who remained lost faith in the representative power of their peasant unions. It seemed to them as if local leaders and the national union movement were completely ineffectual. In many highlands areas the decline of trade unionism, caused in part by a widespread perception of the failure of left-wing politics, produced a resurgence of interest in an indigenous politics of difference [*Ströbele-Gregor*, 1994; *Ticona, Rodriguez and Albó*, 1995]. Ethnic political paradigms, such as *Katarismo*, began to make a comeback, and not only surfaced in trade union discussions, but also found their way into more mainstream political debates, such as those taking place in Congress or reported in the national media.

By the late 1980s, therefore, political discourse appeared to have changed its view on the subject of the national indigenous population and its various forms of 'traditional leadership'. One way in which this manifested itself was through changes to rural development policy and practice. A programme known as CORDEOR-EU had been set up by the Bolivian government and co-funded by the European Union to encourage rural development in the provinces of the country. In the Department of Oruro, for example, the local representative body of this programme – called 'The Program for Peasant Self-Development' (CONPAC) – had been running a 'consolidatory phase' since 1986. [33] In addition to starting a series of agricultural and infrastructural development projects, therefore, another major task undertaken by CONPAC was to encourage a re-evaluation of local culture and indigenous community organizational structures [*Izko*, 1992; *Ayllu Sartañani*, 1992]. Both these elements (development, culture) informing the strategic approach of CONPAC were designed to solve the serious and continuing problem of out-migration from the area. To this end, CONPAC started an active campaign to re-insert the local ancestral leadership positions within the local government structure. Although now forgotten, it was actually under the auspices of this programme that CODEJQ was established. The anthropologist Ramiro Molina had only brokered the deal between the community and the state's development corporation.

The Modernity of Tradition

For the ancestral authorities in Quillacas, and indeed for many of the people elected to positions within the municipal government who agreed with them, the idea of their town being at the helm of a distinct 'historically recorded' sovereign territory was particularly appealing, if not convenient, as it appeared to support their claim to be the authentic – and hence legitimate – administrative centre of the municipality. For town elites this was an important consideration, as both their social and economic positions relied on this proximity to political power. Currently, therefore, they assert authoritatively that it was their ancestors – not those of Huari, of Sevaruyo-Soraga, or those of the hamlets and villages of the *rinconada* – who had safely steered the community through its history and sustained its cultural integrity. Why change what had always been successful? This was the line of reasoning taken by them in discussions with the rest of the community and, backed up by historical documents, invoked as proof of their municipal jurisdiction at the level of national government.

Although there were some personal tensions between municipal staff and the ancestral authorities as regards the day-to-day running of local government, there was no disagreement between them on the interpretation of reform. Indeed, throughout my stay in the municipality it was quite clear that – in their view – no such opposition between modernity and tradition could be applied in that context. Their role as representatives of a new government regime notwithstanding, most municipal leaders were traditionalists at heart, a situation which can be explained largely by reference to the intertwining of local government and *thakhi* positions.[34] By adopting this 'revised' historical account of their past, much of the leadership in Quillacas, the ancestral authorities and most of the municipal officials, formed a radically conservative position with regard to their shared strategy for the future. They would defend the position of Quillacas as the municipal capital, while simultaneously opposing any moves to reduce the autonomy of the territory under their administrative control. Significantly, this radically conservative approach to the distribution of power in the community did entail opposition to local government reform (represented by popular participation and administrative decentralization). The reforms were interpreted by the conservative section of the community of Santuario de Quillacas as the means not only of defending their local sovereignty, but also of extending it even further (that is, by securing the return of Sevaruyo-Soraga to their political jurisdiction). Popular participation and decentralization appeared to provide the very means whereby Quillaca would become the distributive hub of a system of local development financing.

Whilst it was unsurprising that most municipal government staff were supporters of recent reforms to local government, since their positions depended upon the successful functioning of these structures, rather more surprising was the active support for the reform on the part of the ancestral authorities, the *jilaqata* and *alcalde cobrador*, and the people concerned with the ritual and religious importance of Quillacas. One way of resolving this apparent contradiction is by reference to the 'invention of tradition' framework associated with the work of Hobsbawm and Ranger [1983], who point out how rituals, traditions and/or identities – although often accepted as ancient – are often of a more recent vintage: in short, inventions that have been reintroduced/introduced 'from above' in order to legitimize a specific political objective. This is precisely what seems to have happened in the case of Quillacas, where the concern expressed by the highly influential rural elite for the upkeep of religious practices, and their role as a blueprint for how the community should be run, was in fact a method of defending both the status quo and their own political power within the existing structure. Although the ancestral authorities often voiced their distrust of the local state apparatus, and bemoaned its lack of sensitivity to their cultural interests, they nevertheless conferred legitimacy on government reform by participating in meetings both of the municipal government and the Vigilance Committee. For this small, politically conservative section of the community, popular participation and administrative decentralization were tools to uphold their *vecino*-centred beliefs about the how the community should be organized morally and politically. These are beliefs which, as has been argued above, are tailored to a specific interpretation of past moral and political organization.

Such attempts at the 'reinvention of Andean tradition' did not, however, pass unchallenged. Although the interpretation of Quillacas's 'glorious past' provided *vecino* elites with arguments supportive of claims for their continued rule, other sections of the rural community outside the central canton lacking the same access to, or need for, historical information were less than convinced of its veracity and rationale.[35] For people from the other cantons, the vision of the past shared by the ancestral authorities, municipal government and most *vecinos* of Quillacas served to disguise the reality of recent events. It conveniently covered over the fact that canton Sevaruyo-Soraga had not always been a part of the municipality of Santuario de Quillacas. Between 1982 and 1994 the canton had been under the administrative jurisdiction of the province of Sebastian Pagador, a period which people remembered as being more prosperous than the present. It was this economically advantageous linkage that had overturned as a result of the re-assessment of municipal boundaries following the introduction of popular participation. As a result of this experience, the leaders of the canton had learned to make a distinction between (anti-Quillacas) municipal affiliation and their (pro-Quillacas) *ayllu* allegiances. In short, their interest in changing their political affiliation to ensure local development had in their eyes nothing to do with their continued allegiance to Quillacas as a cultural and spiritual centre. That such a distinction could be made at all was an ideological transformation of which the Quillacan authorities and elites seemed quite unaware.[36]

For the leaders of Sevaruyo-Soraga and people from other rural settlements in the *rinconada* their transfer of provincial and municipal identity was pragmatic. Although involved in municipal decision-making and development planning sessions in Quillacas, they nevertheless felt that over the last few years their economic needs and aspirations had been ignored by the elites in the canton of Quillacas. Although NGOs such as CARITAS and UNICEF had inaugurated useful projects, the municipal government in Quillacas had been unable or unwilling to deliver any concrete programme of change until the canton's petition to move administrative affiliation had been made public. It was, to put it bluntly, a political battle for access to and control over economic resources. Sevaruyo-Soraga had long wanted its own primary school, and had been petitioning the municipal authorities for help with an irrigation project. Recent favourable changes in government and development, however, all appeared to benefit Quillacas. For this reason, Sevaruyo-Soragans' opinions of FASOR were very low. In their view this organization did not understand that, by pressing for the reconstitution and cultural survival of *ayllu* structures such as Santuario de Quillacas, it was sentencing smaller rural communities such as Sevaruyo-Soraga to economic stagnation. They agreed with the organization's politics, but said that its leaders did little for them, and were rarely seen in Challapata except on market days. Another complaint was that, although the leaders from the *rinconada* were invited to FASOR's workshops, they were not offered support for their travel or accommodation. When interviewed, a number of peasants from outlying rural settlements dismissed the validity of FASOR altogether. For them, the self-appointed leaders of FASOR were more interested in lining their pockets and extending their personal political influence than really pushing for political transformation in the area. Even in Quillacas itself there were those who held strongly critical opinions of FASOR, noting that 'they talk about representing us, but really they have no support at the local level'.[37]

Having been passed from one municipal jurisdiction to another, there simply was not the same sense of pride at stake for some of the rural communities in the *rinconada*. It is this receptiveness to change which largely explains the decisions made by the canton of Sevaruyo-Soraga immediately following the introduction of legislation about popular participation and administrative decentralization. Rather than see the reforms as a means to protect the integrity of Santuario de Quillacas as an 'historical community', therefore, Sevaruyo-Soraga chose instead to see them as an opportunity to shake off what, on the basis of their own earlier experience of Quillacas, they saw as inept government.[38] The drawing of municipal boundaries carried out as a preparation for the structural adjustments made by the new legislation provided the rural hamlets of the canton with a window of opportunity: namely, to announce their intention to move their local government allegiance to the neighbouring municipality of Huari. Given the wealth of the neighbouring province, this was a move which for obvious economic reasons offered them better opportunities of development and future viability as a rural community.

CONCLUDING COMMENTS

Although the combination of rural grassroots antagonism and solidarity outlined above with regard to the community of Santuario de Quillacas in the Bolivian Highlands may appear contradictory, such politico-ideological harmony/conflict is common throughout Andean village communities. Similar kinds of situation have been noted, both by Barbara Bradby [1982] in the case of the inter-relationship between the Peruvian communities of Huayllay and Carhuapata in the Department of Huancavelica, and by Thomas Abercrombie [1998] in the case of the nearby Orureño community of K'ulta. Set along side the case of Santuario de Quillacas, the contexts described by Bradby and Abercrombie are revealing, in that they indicate that the harmony/conflict pattern of Santuario de Quillacas is a typical aspect of rural community relationships in Andean history and society. While the details differ (in Quillacas religious loyalties remain intact), the same kind of struggle generated by economic changes taking place in other rural communities gives rise to a similar dynamic informed by a process of politico-ideological action and reaction. Action takes the initial form of changes involving external political and economic forces (emanating mainly – but not only – from the nation state), which push, encourage or require groups or individuals previously on the periphery to question and break with historical or customary linkages and local structures of political power. By contrast, reaction takes the form of what is in effect a conservative political response: the reassertion of historical authority and cultural tradition on the part of those whose local power and 'right to rule' is threatened by this process of participation/decentralization. As has been shown above, this is exactly what has happened in Santuario de Quillacas.

The delimitation of municipal boundaries carried out by CONLIT in compliance with popular participation legislation opened up the opportunity for Sevaruyo-Soraga to establish within the province of Sebastian Pagador conditions (political, financial and developmental) that were to its own advantage. For the municipal government in Quillacas, these efforts to seek separation from their jurisdiction were seen not only as an attempt to subvert their historical right to act as the political centre for the area, but also – by endangering the amount and delivery of their finances – as a threat to their future local government operations. Rather than accept change or entertain the idea of a radical legal solution, such as forming a *mancomunidad* with a neighbouring municipality, the inhabitants of Quillacas pushed instead for a conservative re-emphasis on their historical traditions and pride in their cultural authenticity. This picture suggests that – as has long been argued by many observers of rural Latin America – external pressures are responsible for breaking down the traditional fabric of rural community life, driving a wedge between those who exhibit a continued loyalty to culturally traditional forms of social organization and political allegiance, and those who are willing to forego these traditional forms in order to secure for themselves an economically more advantageous situation within the wider (local or national) socio-economic context. As Bradby [1982: 108] writes about Carhuapata, 'all nostalgia for the past had been rejected and a new ideology of progress and development substituted'.

However, this picture may be incomplete. As Abercombie [1998: 314] notes about the situation in K'ulta, '[w]hile the cantonisation process underlined the seceding groups' lack of commitment to the previous manifestation of the ritual political order, its re-inscription into a more circumscribed social space with the same kind of cultural features characteristic of the old, larger ones proves to be a reaffirmation, rather than a rejection of its commitment to values that motivated participation in their ritual-political synthesis in the first place.' What this suggests is that although a peripheral group or town may separate off from the body of its historic community out of self-interest, this does not mean that it intends to separate itself from the cultural ideas and beliefs it shared with the larger community in the past. The same structure of organization and perceptions of political rights and involvement may be reconstituted within the reduced context. This is an important feature of the situation in Santuario de Quillacas: as much as the community has become divided over different methods of dealing with change, a common perception of cultural identity and organization has been retained.

Just as the political situation in Santuario de Quillacas is comparable with the situations described in Carhuapata and K'ulta, it can also be argued that this conflict/harmony pattern is itself symptomatic of Aymara society generally. It casts doubt on the assumption, still made by some writers [*Apfel-Marglin*, 1998], that there exists an overwhelming grassroots commitment to community within Andean rural society. What is being played out here on the scale of local development politics is reminiscent of what Xavier Albó [1975] has called the 'Aymaran Paradox'. The latter consists, according to Albó [1975: 7], of the fact that although 'the Aymara have a strong sense of group identity … at the same time a typical element of their cultural structure is an internal factionalism, which shows itself at the level of family, politics, religion etc.'. Albó builds the case for the paradox being responsible both for occasional fragmentation of rural communities as well as the articulation of a discourse of solidarity which has enabled Aymara-speaking rural society to adapt to and resist transformations imposed from outside – that is, by the wider Bolivian society. The work of Albó is complemented and amplified by research carried out by Gary Urton [1992] in Pacariqtambo in Peru. Urton demonstrates that the antinomic situation of conflict/harmony, or 'communalism and differentiation', is not specific only to Aymara society, but found to occur throughout Andean rural society in general. Like Albó, he shows that to a great extent the continuing life of Andean communities is dependent on the persistence of forces which pressure peasants both to assert their individual personal identities and to bend their wills to support their life and work of their community. More than this, he suggests that conflict/harmony – or 'communalism and differentiation' – are forces and attributes which actually make Andean social organization dynamic.

To some extent, these observations about the dynamic created by the grassroots rural coexistence of conflict and harmony are representative of an epistemological transformation in the way that agrarian 'communities' are studied by anthropologists. Assumptions about a 'folk mentality' [*Redfield*, 1947] have been replaced by an acceptance that peasants are not locked into a uniformly static 'corporate' [*Wolf*, 1957] acceptance of their world, but often refashion their social structures and institutions to meet their current needs.[39] While it is important to highlight 'difference' as a dynamic in the creation and continuance of rural community, therefore, it is also important to point out that this 'difference' is not necessarily something that has to be resolved. As Urton [1992] suggests, the antinomic process of 'communalism and differentiation' is an ongoing dynamic – there is an unending negotiation between both of these forces, an idea which connects well with Andrew Cannessa's [1998: 244] 'processual and performative' understanding of Andean identity. As well as the symbols for community boundaries [*Cohen*, 1985; 1986], negotiation provides the 'dialectical' tension through which the potentiality for change and transformation of social organization over time is both enabled and made sense of [*Urton*, 1992]. It has often been assumed by social scientists that the outcome of disputes, whatever their content, is a process which leads to reconciliation and the restoration of harmony, itself considered to be the social ideal. Conflict, by contrast, is regarded as the enemy of rural community, a teleology which Urton and other anthropologists [*Caplan*, 1995; *Colson*, 1995; *Gulliver*, 1979] have shown to be false.

The picture presented above with regard to Santuario de Quillacas in the Bolivian Highlands during the 1990s underlines the fact that, in an era of expanding globalization, just as peasants themselves are changing so our notions of peasants have themselves to change [*Kearney*, 1996]. Whilst still linked to land, labour, and a common sense of the past linked to rural community, Bolivian peasants are not restricted by such categories, but are much rather active agents negotiating the very meaning and significance of these conceptual boundaries. Although in recent years Scott [1985; 1990] and members of the Latin American post-colonial school [*Rivera Cusicanqui*, 1998] have highlighted the existence, effects and political importance of peasant agency, there have been few detailed ethnographic examples from Latin America of the way in which local rural communities 'think through' the manifestation of the global in the local (or the 'them' in the 'us'). In this process of thinking through, local notions of history, community and politics are recycled, re-invented and given new meanings. In contrast to Scott [1985], the argument outlined here demonstrates that Quillacan peasants are not restricted to small everyday political deeds within the local arena. Although palpably not on an equal footing with the political elites at the national level, peasants are by necessity frequently engaged in – and have an influence on – the political arena of the nation. Indeed, the argument made here not only describes the way that the local is deeply embedded in both the national and the international, but highlights that this involvement is not necessarily oppositional.[40]

ACRONYMS

CARITAS	The Catholic Agency for Overseas Aid and Development
CCEDSE	*Centro de Capacitación y Dessarrollo Socio Economico*, Centre for Training and Socio-Economic Development
COB	*Central Obrera Boliviana*, Bolivian Workers Central
CODEJQ	*Cooperación de Desarrollo de Jatun Quillacas*, Jatun Quillacas Development Corporation
CONPAC	*Programa de Auto-desarrollo Campesino*, Programme for Peasant Self-Development
CORDEOR	*Coordinación Rural de Desarrollo, Oruro*, Rural Development Agency, Oruro
CSUTCB	*Confederación Sindical Unica de Trabajadores Campesinos de Bolivia*, Rural Workers' Union Confederation of Bolivia
FASOR	*Federación de Ayllus de Sur Oruro*, Federation of Southern Oruro *Ayllus*
FIS	Social Investment Fund
IMF	International Monetary Fund
INRA	National Agrarian Reform Law
MBL	*Movimiento Bolivia Libre*, Free Bolivia Movement
MIR	*Movimiento de la Izquierda Revolucionaria*, Movement of the Revolutionary Left

MNR	*Movimiento Nacional Revolucionario*, National Revolutionary Movement.
MRTKL	*Movimiento Revolucionario Tupak Katari de Liberación*, Tupak Katari Revolutionary Liberation Movement
NGO	Non-Governmental Organization
OTB	*Organización Territorial de Base*, Grassroots Organization
PDM	*Plan de Desarrollo Municipal*, municipal development plan.
POA	*Plan Operativa Annual*, Annual Plan
SNAEGG	*Secretaría Nacional de Asuntos Etnicos, de Genero y Generacional*, National Secretariat for Ethnic, Gender and Generational Affairs
SNPP	*Secretaría Nacional de Participación Popular*, National Secretariat for Popular Participation
THOA	*Taller Historial Oral Andina*, Andean Oral History Workshop
UCS	*Unidad Cívica Solidaridad*, United Civic Solidarity
UNDP	United Nations Development Programme
UNICEF	United Nations International Children's Emergency Fund
USAID	United States Agency for International Development

GLOSSARY (SPANISH/AYMARA)

Achachilas	(Ay.) mountain and ancestral spirits
alcalde	(Sp. From Arabic) Mayor, central position of municipal government
alcalde cobrador	(Sp.) High-level ancestral authority of a major *ayllu*
altiplano	(Sp.) High plateau
ayllu	(Ay) Polity self-formulated through ritual
cabildo	(Sp.) Office of the ancestral authorities in Quillacas
capacitación	(Sp.) Education and training
canton	(Sp.) Smallest administrative division of territory in Bolivia
ch'uspa	(Ay.) Bag for carrying coca
comité civico	(Sp) Representative organization of residents who have migrated to the city or to another area of the country
comuneros	(Sp.) General term used for community members in Santuario de Quillacas
Contador	(Sp.) accountant
co-participación tributaria	(Sp.) The financing of local government from a share of central taxation
faena	(Sp.) *Faena* is an *ayllu*-level agreement in which all heads of families, or their delegated representatives, participate in a communal work project: for example, building works, infrastructural preparations for festivals, development projects, etc.
jilaqata	(Ay.) High-level authority of a major *ayllu*
mallku	(Ay.) Mountain peak, mountain spirit, condor, hereditary authority
marka	(Ay.) Central or capital of a major *ayllu*
mink'a	(Ay.) Involving the exchange of labour between family groups, *mink'a* is a smaller affair than *faena*. It refers to the pooling of labour in order to make production more efficient, but it is also crucial for the preparation of weddings and other festivities.
municipalidad indígena	(Sp.) Indigenous municipality
oficial mayor administrativo	(Sp.) Municipal secretary
pasäru	(Ay.) Community elders who have passed through all the steps of *thakhi*
pollera	(Ay.) The colourful layered skirt commonly worn by women in the Bolivian Highlands
planificación	(Sp.) The system of municipal participative planning introduced by the

participative	Law of Popular Participation
q'ara	(Ay.) Naked, incompletely dressed; figuratively, 'culturally peeled', an insulting reference to nonindians (mestizos, criollos, Europeans)
quinoa	(Ay.) A high-energy value cereal crop grown in the Southern Andes
Rancho	(Sp.) Agricultural holding
Reuniones	(Sp.) Public meetings
Rinconada	(Sp.) Building on the Spanish word for corner (*rincón*), the term *rinconada* is used by people in the town of Quillacas to refer to the outlying rural settlements that belong to their municipal and *Ayllu* area
sumu miruku	(Ay.) Doctor, healer
talleres	(Sp.) Workshops
thakhi	(Ay.) Term with a gamut of meanings linking chronological sequence and landscape. Most prosaically, 'path', 'trail', but modified in a variety of compound terms. Linked here to local organization and moral order.
Vecino	(Sp.) Townsman with fully vested rights (colonial); town resident sometimes non-indian (modern)
Vigilancia	(Sp.) Vigilance
Wilancha	(Ay.) Sacrifice, live offering to the land and ancestors

NOTES

1. Respectively, Ley No. 1551 of the 20th April 1994, and Ley 1654 of 20 July 1995.
2. See Molina and Arias [1996]; also Arrieto and Pinedo [1995].
3. The peasant union is the *Confederación Sindical Unica de Trabajadores Campesinos Boliviano*, CSUTCB.
4. Creoles are the descendants of the Spanish colonizers who, through their appropriation of land, wealth, and power exercised through the legislature, have managed to retain control of the country and government. In simple terms, the Bolivian mestizo population are understood to be people of mixed Spanish and indigenous blood. However, this simple definition often fails to take account of the frequently fluid nature of race and ethnicity in Bolivia. It is not uncommon for a person of one ethnic classification to change to another by transforming cultural habits and costume. In this way people of ethnically indigenous background become mestizo by casting aside their traditional dress (for example, the *pollera*) and adopting urban lifestyles and professions.
5. Usually from June to July, when their plots are lying fallow.
6. On these points, see Ayllu Sartañäni [1992], Skar [1982], Rasnake [1988], Godoy [1984], Bastien [1978], Platt [1982], Murra, Wachtel and Revel [1986], Harris [1985], and Mayer [1985].
7. *Don* (men) and *Doña* (women) are local terms used to show respect for adult members of the community.
8. That is, '*Reglamento y Distribución de Coparticipación Tributaria para los Gobiernos municipales'*.
9. That is, *Ley de Creaciones de cada Municipio, Acta Apocrifa.*
10. *Centro de Capacitación y Desarrollo Socio Economico* – one of the many private companies formed since the introduction of the popular participation law to fulfil the tasks of local *capacitación* in relation to the new procedures of development planning and governmental administration. Based in Oruro, CCEDSE had won a government contract funded by the World Bank to introduce and supervise the new system of *planificanión participativa* in four municipalities of the department.
11. In October 1997 an article in Oruro's newspaper *La Patria* reported the conflict as *Delimitacion de territorio provoca problemas vecinales* (Territorial Redrawing Causes Problems Between Neighbours).
12. For example, CARITAS signed an agreement to fund a drinking water project. USAID had agreed to fund local Health projects. UNICEF had agreed to fund a mother and daughter

health and education programme.

13. It was apparent that local people had been careful to hide their differences from me.
14. That is, from $US47,115 to $US75,982.
15. FASOR stands for *Federación de Ayllus de Sur Oruro*. See below for more on this organization.
16. Article 22 of the Law of Population states that 'those municipalities that don't possess a minimum of 5,000 inhabitants, must form *mancommunidades* [i.e. a federation with another such community]' in order to form a sufficient size of population amongst which *coparticipacion* funds can be shared.
17. That is, an administrative alliance between municipalities.
18. That is, 'the Holy Cross'. A festival held on 3 May which not only marks the death and celebrates the resurrection of Christ but also has a pre-Christian significance: namely, crosses as symbols of fertility. At this particular festival, crosses are paraded and venerated throughout the community.
19. See for example the article 'Conflicto de Límites provoca dos muertes' in *La Razón,* 26/1/1998.
20. At the end of 1999 a decision was finally made by the National Senate, with the result that the municipality has been reduced from four to three cantons.
21. Perhaps this is not so different from the way we ourselves understand our own past.
22. For a full description of this process, see McNeish [2001] and Ticona and Albó [1997].
23. 'Adam and Eve and the Red-Trousered Ant' re-told by Denise Arnold [1993] and Fidencia's story in McNeish [2001] are examples of powerful foundation stories that are both mythical and moral in character, which by stressing the values of solidarity, trust, faith and reward, form a narrative about the present and about continuity.
24. Hence the view that: 'Geography does more than carry important historical referents: it also organises the manner in which these facts are conceptualised, remembered and organised into a temporal framework' [*Rappaport*, 1990: 11; *Rosaldo*, 1980; *Harwood*, 1976].
25. See Molina Rivero and Portugal Loayza [1995] and Molino Rivero [1987].
26. It is to one of these meetings that I was invited to on my first trip to the area at the start of my fieldwork period.
27. On this point, see Espinoza Soriano [1969: 199] and Cieza de Leon [1986/1553: 447].
28. See Espinoza Soriano [1969].
29. On this point, see Espinoza Soriano [1969: 196].
30. An Incaic staging post cum storage facility.
31. Although the National Revolution had tolerated 'traditional' leadership forms, subsequent efforts were made to transform and 'modernize' local political structures. Teams of MNR militants, or revolutionary 'brigades' as they were known, were sent out by the government to instruct peasants about the National Revolution and to create a network of *sindicatos agrarios* (rural unions) to replace pre-existing forms of community organization [*Izko*, 1992; *Arganaras*, 1992].
32. A caveat is in order, since evidence suggests that even in 1952 the populist MNR government of Paz Estensorro was keen to maintain good relations with its powerful northern neighbour, the United States.
33. The *Programa de Auto-desarrollo Campesino.*
34. Although playing the game of party politics required by the government system, authority figures such as Don Eleuterio certainly regarded their positions as part of *thakhi* – that is, as a moral duty.
35. As participants in the everyday life and ritual of *thakhi*, people in the *rinconada* continued to see Quillacas as an important centre. Although at loggerheads with the municipal leadership over their administration, to the surprise of many *vecinos* they continued to play a part in *thaki* and community obligations. As participants in the community festivals, including *Señor de Exaltación*, which are located in Quillacas, they allocate the town a focal position in their relationships with the larger *ayllu mayor*, their ancestors, and the local area. By coming to Quillacas in order to take part in festivals, and showing a continued willingness to meet and take part in communal work parties (*faena*) to look after the church and their *ayllu*'s chapel, therefore, individuals from the *rinconada* demonstrate as much concern with the upkeep of *ayllu* relations as the residents of the town. Through their

participation in these events they not only subscribe to a common ideological discourse (based on shared spiritual and cultural values) with the town but also evince a mutual pride in community history and membership. However, in their decisions both about the present and the future, the vision of the Quillacan leadership ruling over a political and physical territory that encompasses their own land is neither attractive nor useful to those occupying the *rinconada*.

36. However, it is probably what Don René Jallaza was getting at in his comments reported earlier (see above).
37. Although unfair to make sweeping generalizations, it is pertinent to note that the disjuncture between indigenous organizations and the grassroots is a common phenomenon in Latin America. Such a disjuncture has been reported for Bolivia by Ticona, Rodriguez and Albó [1995] and for Guatemalan Mayan movements by Warren [1998].
38. The phrase 'historical community' was one that Don Julian, the Jilaqata in 1998, frequently and proudly used to describe his community, Santuario de Quillacas.
39. As Levine [1993: 2] has noted, 'the objects of any study of culture and power cannot be understood as objects alone: they are created by people, active subjects with lives, interests, and dynamics of their own.' Rural communities are generally understood as being formed out of the complex interlinkage of internal and external discourses over identity and place. Trying to get inside and understand these discourses, it has been suggested, means that we need to 'appreciate the subjective self-understanding of the ethnic group – how the group views its own present situation – as well as its objective circumstances understood in terms of interests, resources and competition' [*Urban and Sherzer*, 1991: 5]. The way outsiders attempt to understand the way rural inhabitants symbolically construct (or perhaps deconstruct) their community is of course – as Cohen [1985] suggested a long time ago – effected by the participant/observation approach to the study of locality and membership.
40. On this latter point, see also Abu-Lughod [1990].

REFERENCES

Abercrombie,T., 1998, *Pathways of Memory and Power: Ethnography and History Among an Andean People*, Madison, WI: University of Wisconsin Press.

Abu-Lughod, L., 1990, 'The Romance of Resistance: Tracing the Transformations of Power through Bedouin Women', *American Ethnologist*, Vol.17, No.1.

Albó, X., 1975, *La Paradoja Aymara: Solidaridad y Faccionalismo*, La Paz: CIPCA.

Albó, X.,1994, 'From Kataristas to MNRistas? The Surprising and Bold Alliance between Aymaras and Neo-liberals in Bolivia', in Donna Lee Van Cott (ed.), *Indigenous Peoples and Democracy in Latin America*, London: Macmillan..

Albó, X., 1996, 'Making the Leap from Local Mobilization to National Politics', *NACLA*, Vol.29, March/April.

Apfel-Marglin, F., 1998, *The Spirit of Regeneration: Andean Culture Confronting Western Notions of Development*, London: Zed Books.

Arganaras, F.G., 1992, 'Bolivia's Transformist Revolution', *Latin American Perspectives*, No.2.

Arias Duran, I., 1996, *El Proceso Social de la Participación Popular: Problemas y potencialidades*, La Paz: SNPP.

Arnold, D., 1993, 'Adam and Eve and the Red-Trousered Ant: History in the Southern Andes', *Travesia: Journal of Latin American Cultural Studies*, Vol.2.

Arrieto, M., and E. Pinedo, 1995, *Hacia una propuesta indígena de descentralización del estado. Etnias y Participación,* La Paz: PROADE/ILDIS.

Ayllu Sartañani, 1992, *Pachamamax tipusiwa: la Pachamama se enoja,* La Paz: Aruwiyiri/Ayllu Sartinani.

Bastien, J., 1978, *Mountain of the Condor*, St Paul: West Publishing Co.

Blackburn, J. and J. Holland, 1998, *Who Changes? Institutionalizing Participation in Development,* London: Intermediate Technology Development Group.

Blair, H., 2000, 'Participation and Accountability at the Periphery: Democratic Local Government in Six Countries', *World Development*, Vol.28, No.1.

Booth, D., S. Clisby, and C. Widmark, 1995, *Empowering the Poor through Institutional Reform: An Initial Appraisal of the Bolivian Experience*, Working Paper 32, Department of Anthropology, University of Stockholm, Sweden.

Booth, D., S. Clisby, and C. Widmark, 1997, *Democratising the State in Rural Bolivia,* Development Studies Unit, University of Stockholm, Sweden.

Bradby, B., 1982, 'Resistance to capitalism in the Peruvian Andes', in A.D. Lehmann (ed.), *Ecology and Exchange in the Andes*, Cambridge: Cambridge University Press.

Canessa, A., 1998, 'Procreation, Personhood and Ethnic Difference in Highland Bolivia', *Ethnos*, Vol.63, No.2.

Caplan, P., 1995, *Understanding Disputes: The Politics of Argument,* Providence, R.I: Berg.

Cardenas,V.H., 1988, 'La lucha de un pueblo', in X. Albó (ed.), *Raices de America: El Mundo Aymara*, La Paz: Alianza/UNESCO.

Carter, W., 1964, *Aymara Communities and the Bolivian Agrarian Reform*, Gainesville, FL: University of Florida Press.

Carter, W., 1971, 'Revolution and the Agrarian Sector', in James M. Malloy and Richard S. Thorn (eds.), *Beyond the Revolution: Bolivia since 1952*, Pittsburgh, PA: University of Pittsburgh Press.

Cieza de León, P., 1986/[1553], *Crónica del Perú – Seguna Parte: (El Señorio de los Incas)*, Lima: Pontifica Universidad Católica del Perú.

CIPCA, 1991, *Por una Bolivia Diferente*, La Paz: CIPCA.

Cohen, A.P., 1985, *The Symbolic Construction of Community,* London: Routledge.

Cohen, A.P., 1986, *Symbolising Boundaries: Identity and Diversity in British Cultures*, Manchester: Manchester University Press.

Colson, E., 1995, 'The Contentiousness of Disputes', in E. Caplan (ed.), *Understanding Disputes: The Politics of Argument*, London: Berg.

Crabtree, J., 1987, *The Great Tin Crash: Bolivia and the World Tin Market,* London: Latin American Bureau.

Crook, R.C., and J. Manor, 1998, *Democracy and Decentralisation in South Asia and West Africa: Participation, Accountability and Performance*, Cambridge: Cambridge University Press.

Cuadros, D. (ed.), 1991, *La Revuelta de las Nacionalidades*, La Paz: UNITAS.

Dunkerley, J., 1984, *Rebellion in the Veins: Political Struggle in Bolivia, 1952–82*, London: Verso.

Erikson, S.S., N. Naustalstid, and A. Shou, 1999, *Decentralisation from Above: A Study of Local Government in Botswana, Ghana, Tanzania and Zimbabwe*, Oslo: NIBR's Pluss Series 4.

Espinoza Soriano,W., 1969, 'El Reino Aymara de Quillaca-Asanaque, Siglos XV y XVI', *Revista Del Museo Nacional*, Lima: Instituto Nacional de Cultura, Peru.

Godoy, R., 1984, 'Ecological Degradation and Agricultural Intensification in the Andean Highlands', *Human Ecology*, Vol.12, No.14.

Good, K., 1996, 'Towards popular participation in Botswana', *Journal of Modern African Studies*, Vol.34, No.1.

Gulliver, P.H., 1979, *Disputes and Negotiations*, New York: Academic Press.

Hahn, D.R., 1991, *The Divided World of the Bolivian Andes: A Structural View of Domination and Resistance*, New York: Taylor & Francis.

Harris, O., 1985, 'Ecological Duality and the Role of the Centre: Northern Potosi', in S. Masuda, I. Shimada, and C. Morris (eds.), *Andean Ecology and Civilisation*, Tokyo: University of Tokyo Press.

Harwood, F., 1976, 'Myth, Memory and the Oral Traditions: Cicero and the Trobriands', *American Anthropologist*, Vol.78, No.4.

Hobsbawm, E.J. and T. Ranger (eds.), 1983, *The Invention of Tradition*, Cambridge: Cambridge University Press.

Izko, J., 1992, *La Doble Frontera*, La Paz: HISBOL/CERES.

Kearney, M., 1996, *Rethinking the Peasantry: Anthropology in Global Perspective*, Boulder, CO: Westview Press.

Klein, H.S., 1992, *Bolivia: The Making of a Multi-ethnic Society*, Oxford: Oxford University Press.

Kohl, J.V., 1978, 'Peasant and Revolution in Bolivia, April 9, 1952–August 2, 1953', *Hispanic American Historical Review*, Vol.38, No.2.

Laserna, R., 1994, *La Descentralizacion: Perspectivas para la Investigacion Social*, La Paz: Ministerio de Relaciones Exteriores de Holanda(DGIS)/Programa de Investigacion Estrategica en Bolivia (PIB).

Lee Van Cott, D., 2000, *The Friendly Liquidation of the Past: The Politics of Diversity in Latin America,* Pittsburgh, PA: University of Pittsburgh Press.

Levine, D.H., 1993, *Constructing Culture and Power in Latin America*, Ann Arbor, MI: University of Michigan Press.

Léons, M.B., 1970, 'Stratification and Pluralism in the Bolivian *Yungas*', in Walter Goldschmidt and Harry Hoijer (eds.), *The Social Anthropology of Latin America: Essays in Honor of Ralph Leon Beals*, Los Angeles, CA: University of California Press.

McNeish, J.A., 2001, 'Pueblo Chico, Infierno Grande: Globalisation and the Politics of Participation in Highland Bolivia', unpublished Ph.D thesis, Dept. of Anthropology, Goldsmiths College, University of London.

Martinez, J.A., 1996, *Municipios y Participación Popular en America Latina: Un Modelo de Desarrollo*, La Paz: IAF/SEMILLA/CEBIAE.

Mayer, E., 1985, 'Production Zones', in S. Masuda, I. Shimada, and C. Morris (eds.), *Andean Ecology and Civilisation*, Tokyo: University of Tokyo Press.

Medina, J., 1992, *Repensar Bolivia: Cicatrices de un viaje hacia si mismo 1972–1992*, La Paz: HISBOL.

Menjivar, R., 1969, *Reforma Agraria – Guatemala, Bolivia, Cuba*, San Salvador: Editorial Universitaria de El Salvador.

Mohan, G., 1996, 'Neoliberalism and Decentralised Development Planning in Ghana', *Third World Planning Review*, Vol.18, No.4.

Molino Rivero, R., 1987, 'La traditionalidad como medio de articulacion al mercado: una comunidad pastoral en Oruro', in Olivia Harris, Brooke Larson, and Enrique Tandeter (eds.), *La Participación Indigena en Los Mercados Surandinos: Estrategias y Reproduccion social: Siglos XVI a XX*, La Paz: CERES.

Molina Rivero, R., and J. Portugal Loayza, 1995, *Consulta de Base a Los Ayllus del Norte de Potosi y Sur de Oruro*, 2nd ed. (Etnias y Participación), La Paz: ILDIS.

Molina, S. and I. Arias, 1996, *De la nación clandestina a la participación popular*, La Paz: CEDOIN.

Montano, J.A., 1996, *Municipios y Participación Popular: Un modelo de desarrollo en America Latina*, La Paz: Produccion Educativa.

Murra, J.V., N. Wachtel and J. Revel, 1986, *Anthropological History of Andean Polities*, Cambridge: Cambridge University Press.

Nash, J., 1993, *We Eat the Mines and the Mines Eat Us*, New York: Colombia University Press.

National Institute of Statistics, Bolivia, 1992, *National Census Population Statistics*, La Paz: INE.

Nickson, R.A., 1997, *Local Government in Latin America*, New York: Lynne Reiner Publications.

Ospina, C.M. (ed.)., 1997, *Procesos y Tendencias de la Descentralizacion en Colombia*, Bogota: Fundacion Universidad Central.

Palma Caravajal, E., 1995, 'Decentralisation and Democracy: The New Latin American Municipality', *CEPAL Review*, Vol.55.

Pearse, A., 1975, *The Latin American Peasant*, London: Frank Cass.

Platt, T., 1982, *Estado Boliviano y Ayllu Andino: Tierra y Tributo en el Norte de Potosi*, Lima: Instituto de Estudios Peruanos.

Platt, T., 1984, 'Liberalism and Ethnocide in the Southern Andes', *History Workshop Journal*, No.17.

Rappaport, J., 1990, *The Politics of Memory: Native Historical Interpretation in the Colombian Andes*, Cambridge: Cambridge University Press.

Rasnake, N., 1988, *Domination and Cultural Resistance: Authority and Power among an Andean People*, Durham, NC: Duke University Press.

Redfield, R., 1947, 'The Folk Society', *The American Journal of Sociology*, Vol.52, No.4.

Ríos Reinaga, D., 1967, *Civiles y Militares en la Revolución Boliviana*, La Paz: Editorial y Librería Difusión.

Rivera Cusicanqui, S., 1987, *Oppressed but not Defeated: Peasant Struggles in Bolivia 1900–1980*, Geneva: UNRISD.

Rivera Cusicanqui, S., 1998, *Debates Post-Coloniales: Una Introducción a los Estudios de la Subalternidad*, La Paz: Sephis/Aruwiyiri.

Rojas Ortuste, G., 1994, *Democracia en Bolivia: Hoy y Mañana*, La Paz: CIPCA.

Rosaldo, M.Z., 1980, *Knowledge and Passion: Ilongot Notions of Self and Social Life*, Cambridge: Cambridge University Press.

Scott, J.C., 1985, *Weapons of the Weak: Everyday Forms of Peasant Resistance*, New Haven, CT: Yale University Press.

Scott, J.C., 1990, *Domination and the Arts of Resistance: Hidden Transcripts*, New Haven, CT: Yale University Press.

Shou, A., 2000, 'Democratic Local Government and Responsiveness: Lessons from Zimbabwe and Tanzania', *International Journal of Comparative Sociology*, Vol.40, No.1.

Skar, H., 1982, *The Warm Valley People*, Oslo : Universitetsforlaget.

SNPP, 1997, *Territorio y Participación Popular*, La Paz: Ministerio de Desarrollo Humano.

Stiefel, M., and M. Wolfe, 1994, *A Voice for the Excluded: Popular Participation in Development, Utopia or Necessity?* London: Zed Books.

Ströbele-Gregor, J., 1994, 'From indio to mestizo...to indio: New Indianist Movements in Bolivia', *Latin American Perspectives*, Issue 81.

Tendler, J., 1999, *Good Government in the Tropics*, Baltimore, OH: The Johns Hopkins University Press.

Ticona, E., and X. Albó, 1997, *La Lucha por el Poder Comunal: Jesus de Machaqa, La Marka Rebelde,* La Paz: CIPCA.

Ticona, E., G. Rodriguez, and X. Albó, 1995, *Votos y Whiphalas: Movimientos Indigenas y Democracia en Bolivia*, La Paz: CIPCA.

UNRISD, 1980, *UNRISD's Popular Participation Programme: A Glance at the Past and Directions for the Future*, Geneva: UNRISD.

Untoja, F.,1992, *Re-torno al Ayllu*, La Paz: CADA.

Urban, G., and J. Sherzer (eds.), 1991, *Nation-States and Indians in Latin America*, Austin, TX: University of Texas Press.

Urioste, M., and L. Baldomar, 1996, 'Ley de Participación Popular: Seguimiento crítico', in *La Participación Popular: Avances y obstaculos* (report of the Secretaria de Participacion Popular, Ministerio de Desarrollo Humano, Bolivia), La Paz: Grupo DRU/SNPP.

Urton, G., 1992, 'Communalism and Differentiation in an Andean Community', in Robert Dover, Katherine Seibold, and John McDowell (eds.), *Andean Cosmologies through Time: Persistence and Emergence*, Bloomington, Indianapolis: Indiana University Press.

Warren, K.B., 1998, *Indigenous Movements and their Critics: Pan-Maya Activism in Guatemala*, Princeton, NJ: Princeton University Press.

Webster, N., 1992, 'Panchayati Raj in Western Bengal: Popular Participation for the People or the Party?' *Development and Change*, Vol.23, No.2.

Webster, N., 2001, 'Local Organisations and Political Space in the Forests of West Bengal', in N. Webster and L. Engberg-Pedersen, *In the Name of the Poor: Contesting Political Space for Poverty Reduction*, New York: Zed Books.

White, S.C., 1999, 'NGOs, Civil Society and the State in Bangladesh: The Politics of Representing the Poor', *Development and Change*, Vol.30, No.2.

Wolf, E., 1957, 'Closed Corporate Communities in Mesoamerica and Java', *Southwestern Journal of Anthropology*, Vol.13, No.1.

Wolf, E., 2001, *Pathways of Power: Building an Anthropology of the Modern World*, Berkeley, CA: University of California Press.

Zuo, X.L., 1997, 'China's Fiscal Decentralisation and the Financing of Local Services in Poor Townships', *IDS Bulletin*, Vol.28, No.1.

Devil Pact Narratives in Rural Central America: Class, Gender and 'Resistance'

KEES JANSEN and ESTHER ROQUAS

INTRODUCTION

Throughout Latin America, and also many other parts of the world, a common theme informing peasant narratives is different kinds of pact in which the recipient obtains the power of the devil in exchange for a soul. The analysis of these narratives is not a mere cultural curiosity; rather, it is a useful way of gaining an insight into how peasants understand and give meaning to the social order in which they live and the social change they experience. Such an approach to devil pact narratives goes beyond conceiving them simply as religious or psychological expressions, and regards such discourse as a method of projecting the language of social relationships and power. It is, however, a hidden discourse not easily accessible to the outside researcher.

Only after we had lived in the village for quite some time did peasants begin to tell us the local narrative of a landlord who signed a pact with the devil. Significantly, the narrative was not told openly, in public, but secretly and in private. The most detailed account of this particular devil pact narrative was obtained after sunset, when we were alone with one of the poorest inhabitants who lived in a mud hut without electric light on the fringes of the village. But does the offstage setting of this discourse imply that peasants tell the story to subvert domination, as some observers argue? This question points to the reason for our interest in understanding precisely what the devil pact narrative, as told in rural Central America, represents. Of particular interest, therefore, is whether the telling of stories about devil pact narratives involving landlords constitutes a form of resistance by

Kees Jansen, Technology and Agrarian Development group. E-mail: kees.jansen@alg.tao.wau.nl; Esther Roquas, Law and Governance group. E-mail: esther.roquas@alg.ar.wau.nl; both at Wageningen University, The Netherlands. We would like to thank The Netherlands Foundation for the Advancement of Tropical Research (WOTRO) for funding the research. We appreciate the helpful comments of Tom Brass, Paul Richards and participants of the Ceres seminar 'Acts of Man and Nature?'

subordinate groups. Our analysis questions a recent tendency in the literature to assume *a priori* that offstage peasant narratives defy forms of domination.

The detailed study by Edelman [1994] of a Costa Rican devil pact narrative will serve as our starting point. The life history of the protagonist in our story, Alfredo Luna (an Honduran landowner), runs surprisingly parallel to the life of Don Cubillo, the man whose history is vividly described by Edelman. Both were wealthy landowners, who had been poor in the past, and each was a notorious womanizer. The structure of the narratives, the language and the details of the various symbols also show clear similarities. However, while Edelman focuses on the connection between the narrative and the womanizing behaviour of Cubillo, our analysis interprets the narrative as an expression of the struggles generated by capital accumulation, as is apparent in the following example:

> The only thing you have to do is to take a bath. Then, you take off your clothes and you lie down under a fig tree (*mata-palo*) at midnight. You lie on your back and start to praise him. A snake will start to pass over you fifteen minutes before midnight, and when its tail passes by you have to watch out. A white flower will drop.[1] When you see it fall, you have to reach out your hand and '*chás*!', you will grab it and you will talk to the devil. He will propose that you sign a paper with blood from your veins, and that you will hand over your most beloved child. Then the devil will give you lots of money (*el gran dineral*) [*Ramos and Valenzuela*, 1996: 45–6].

The quotation links the reasons for entering a pact to securing 'lots of money'. This is but one of the many historical plots of the devil pact narrative.

Doctor Faustus in Central America

The pact with the devil is a discourse of great antiquity, in which progress and development called forth supernatural (either divine or diabolic) retribution, an exchange which entails the acquisition of new knowledge, the power to rule, sexual pleasure, immortality, everlasting beauty and economic advancement. All the latter correspond to what might be termed the up-side of the bargain, and different legends and literary variants emphasize one or more of these aspects. In the legends of the ancient Greeks, Prometheus was punished for having provided humanity with fire stolen from heaven: although humanity benefited, Prometheus himself was made to suffer by being chained to a rock. The acquisition of knowledge as a central feature of the devil's pact is embodied in the legend of Doctor Faustus. From humble peasant stock, he studied theology and medicine, became a medieval magician in late fifteenth- and early sixteenth-century Wittenberg (Germany), and dabbled in the black arts and was said to be in league with the devil.[2] According to the legend, Faustus turned from scholarly pursuits to conjuring up the devil, with whom he then signed a bond (in his blood). The terms of the resulting contract (or pact) with the devil were that, in exchange for providing the latter with his soul, he received not only material wealth and his choice of the most beautiful women, but magical powers to do things no mere mortal could undertake.[3] Sexual liberty and sinfulness as central features are also present in Mariken van Nieumeghen, a late Middle Age Dutch miracle play, and some of the Don Juan interpretations.[4]

Many aspects of the classic European depiction of the complexities and ambiguities raised by the struggle between good and evil are reproduced in the Latin American and Central American versions of the pact with the devil considered below. These all bring forward one particular theme of the legend: new riches.[5] In the acquisition of the latter lies the clue as to the down-side of the Faustian bargain with the devil. Rapid economic advancement, the legend warns, is invariably accompanied by social costs, and this positive/negative combination is accordingly represented symbolically in terms of an exchange, whereby the material benefits obtained by an individual or society (or, indeed, humanity) are offset by long-term disadvantages, either to the individual concerned, or to society as a whole. Current debates about economic development fit neatly into this framework: continuing economic development on a global scale is perceived as having profound negative consequences for the whole of humanity, in the form of environmental pollution and global warming.

The problem of how to understand the Central American narratives is not only a consequence of the different readings of the devil pact narrative that result from the obscurity of an offstage discourse, or the richness of the symbols and the meanings with regard to the acquisition of knowledge, sexual liberty and rapid economic advancement. Two other aspects render interpretation difficult. First, the devil pact narrative we study is a living discourse – and therefore important for understanding current peasant society – but one which nevertheless takes elements from a pre-existing symbolic language to talk about contemporary social processes. The pact is accordingly not simply an imagined idiom but chillingly concrete, and its micro-politics are all-too-real [*Comaroff and Comaroff*, 1993: xxvii]. Explanations of earlier uses of this narrative are thus historically specific; both the symbolic content of the narrative and the context in which the narrative is reproduced explain why it is retold. Local interpretations of the devil are therefore highly modern and constantly changing [*Geschiere*, 1997].

A second problem faced by those reading meanings into this peasant narrative is the shift in theory itself. We therefore intend to analyse and account for an epistemological shift in the way the Faustian pact is interpreted: that is, the shift from Taussig's [1980] positioning of this narrative between different modes of production – reminiscent of the early 1980s theorizing on modes of production (although distinct from modes of production theory) – to Edelman's [1994] focus on gender identity and Foucauldian interpretations of domination – in keeping with the post-structuralist vogue of the late 1980s and 1990s – in order to explore the intertwined modalities of exploitation.

FROM CAPITALIST ALIENATION TO SEXUAL DOMINATION

Any discussion of pacts with the devil in Latin America necessarily begins by addressing the polemical argument in Taussig's *The Devil and Commodity Fetishism in South America* [1980]. Thus Edelman's subsequent contribution to the debate is itself a critique of Taussig's earlier work. Taussig relates how, because they cut more cane and earned more than their fellow workers without added effort, some male Colombian sugarcane workers were said to have entered a pact with the devil. Cane cut by these workers died soon after, while the additional money they earned as a result of this pact was thought to be barren, and used by them to purchase only luxuries. Moreover, the sugarcane workers who made the pact themselves died prematurely and in great pain. According to Taussig, the narrative emerges when former peasants – now rural workers or miners – lose control over their means of production as labour relationships are transformed in the course of a transition towards capitalism. He interprets the change which gives rise to the devil pact narrative as an economic shift, from gift (use-value) to commodity exchange (exchange-value) and from peasant cultivation to wage labour relations. Undergoing these processes of commoditization and proletarianization, and trapped at a point somewhere between full-time cultivation and permanent wage labour, peasants tell a variety of stories about the devil so as to represent the process of alienation they experience with the transition from pre-capitalist to capitalist relations.[6] The devil, with all his ambiguity, serves as a mediator of the clash between petty commodity production and the capitalist mode of production [*Taussig*, 1980: 37]. In this framework, Faustian pact narratives are an indigenous reaction to the supplanting of a pre-existing organic unity between persons and their products by the commodity fetishism of capitalism, with its split between persons and the things they produce and exchange.

Taussig's influential study has been widely discussed and criticized, and the two interrelated objections to it are important for our discussion. A major critique concerns Taussig's eloquently worded, but nevertheless simplifying, representation of a very recent capitalist encroachment on a 'romanticized' or 'idealized' non-market economy.[7] Consequently, and we find this less developed in the critiques, one may question the gist of Taussig's argument, which sees devil pact narratives as a 'counter-capitalist culture' [*Austen*, 1993: 95] or 'oppositional cultural practice' [*Taussig*, 1987]. Taussig lauds the tin miners in Bolivia and sugarcane cutters in Colombia for their attempt to reconstitute the significance of the past in terms of the tensions of the present (imagining the possibility of use-value, of a gift economy, in a capitalist context). In Taussig's view, therefore, everyone is in their debt for having shown us that apparently natural relations are in fact asymmetrical, non-reciprocal, exploitative and destructive relationships between persons. The devil pact narrative is a moral indictment of the new mode of production [*Taussig*, 1995: 390], a rejection of capitalist logic. Although we do not question the possible value that such an analogy may have for 'the finding of meaning for us' [*Taussig*, 1987: 105], we do question – more modestly – whether this really is present in the narrative outlined by us below.

Edelman starts from the many critiques of Taussig's work, and finds the latter's claims too bold, implying as they do a uniformity of peasant beliefs about devil pacts. He points out that Taussig compresses the devil contract into one single perspective: namely, a reaction by peasants to wage labour-based agrarian capitalism. Against such a view, Edelman proposes an alternative framework, the explanatory focus of which is less on wage labour, and more concerned with the intertwined modalities of exploitation. Instead of the alienating effects of wage labour and commoditization, therefore, his interpretation considers the devil pact an expression of the 'variety of socially conditioned anxieties and psychic conflicts' related to gender and ethnic domination [*Edelman*, 1994: 60]. This raises the question as to why, precisely, Taussig remains so important in Edelman's thinking. The answer to this, outlined below, is that both studies share the conceptualization of the devil pact narrative as counter-culture, as a form of resistance to domination: resistance against capitalist alienation in the case of Taussig, and resistance against sexual domination in the case of Edelman.[8] The latter's argument is developed around the history of Don Cubillo, to which we now turn.

Don Cubillo in Costa Rica

Within a few years of arriving in the Costa Rican town of Filadelfia as a poor Nicaraguan immigrant, Don Chico Cubillo turned from a man of humble origins into a wealthy and powerful landowner. In local stories, this abrupt transition was attributed to the fact that Cubillo had signed a pact with the devil. Some rural inhabitants thought that it was this which led to his sudden riches, while others rejected this explanation, and instead pointed out that Cubillo was an intelligent person who knew how to conduct business. Edelman finds it important to note that Cubillo was not considered a greedy and innately evil (= diabolical) person. Many people remembered Don Cubillo as someone who always used to invite people to drink with him. Another typical feature of Don Cubillo that local inhabitants recalled was his seduction of women. He was an inveterate womanizer, and had offspring with many women. Moreover, he recognized many of these children and left them a bequest. It is significant, however, that Edelman does not provide exact information about the way in which Cubillo amassed his wealth. He states that the accumulation of land by Don Cubillo was not perceived as a problem by other people, because at that time – between 1900 and the 1940s – unsettled land was still available in the area. Furthermore, the sale of land to rich landowners was a convenient way for poor peasants to generate much-needed cash.

Three stories about Don Cubillo's life lead Edelman to consider the devil pact entered into by the landlord not as a story that tells something about wage labour and class antagonism but rather as a commentary on sexual domination. Two of the three lead Edelman to the conclusion that rural people themselves identified with Don Cubillo and his wealth, finding little problem in his riches besides common envy. In the story of the lost *alforja* (saddlebag), therefore, a poor man who encounters a drunken Don Cubillo next to an *alforja* bulging with money makes off with the latter. Honest and humble as he is, the man then returns it to a now-sober Don Cubillo. The latter, who has not even missed the bag containing his money, offers the finder a pittance of a reward, just enough to buy a rope with which to hang himself. A second story relates how Don Cubillo visits the famous Hotel Costa Rica in the national capital San José, the best hotel in the country. When the hotel employees refuse to serve him because he is dressed like a poor peasant, he calls over the owner, shows the latter the money in his old *alforja*, and proposes to buy the whole hotel with all the employees in it. Edelman argues that both these stories constitute evidence for the presence of grassroots sympathy towards Don Cubillo, suggesting that rural people identify themselves with his caustic sense of humour. In addition to the fact that he spent his money lavishly within the rural community, for Edelman the fact that the landowner did not even miss the money when it was taken is proof that Don Cubillo was not a greedy person. Furthermore, in the episode set in the Hotel Costa Rica, the latter symbolizes the 'white' townsfolk, whereas Don Cubillo by contrast is the champion of the ethnically different rural population who 'cleverly humiliates representatives of the wealthy, white elite'.[9] The third story deals specifically with Don Cubillo's sexual dominance. It describes what happened in Room 21, a room in one of Cubillo's houses, where he received a great many women who had sex with him in return for money and other material goods. Edelman understands the third story as an attack on the manhood of poor Filadelfinos, in that Don Cubillo's predatory sexuality offended Latin American male supremacist values about the protection of wives, sisters, girlfriends and daughters.

According to Edelman, these stories complicate the interpretation of the devil pact narrative as a simple expression of class antagonism.[10] Rather than the latter, therefore, it is sexual domination and gender antagonism which give rise to the powerful emotions that find expression in the beliefs about diabolical phenomena. By interpreting gender and not class as a key to understanding the meaning of devil pact narratives, Edelman seems to stand Taussig's analysis on its head: it is no longer capitalism but gender that is diabolical. The important issue here, therefore, is the following: by compressing the many stories of Don Cubillo's life into one single cultural interpretation of the devil pact, Edelman may have failed to recognize the multidimensional aspects and the absence of uniformity structuring peasant beliefs. Before discussing his interpretation in more detail, it is necessary to consider a parallel kind of discourse: the life history of Don Alfredo Luna in Honduras.

Our analysis of a similar Faustian pact discourse in Honduras leads us to question the explanatory shift proposed by Edelman, from capitalist alienation to sexual domination. It also leads us to question the main logic informing the analyses of Taussig and Edelman, and one which they both seem to share: the devil pact as a 'from below' cultural discourse that challenges and defies existing relations of power and exploitation.

ALFREDO LUNA AND THE DEVIL IN HONDURAS

We came across a devil pact narrative similar to that involving Don Cubillo while conducting fieldwork research in a village in the Santa Bárbara district of Honduras between 1992 and 1997.[11] Like Don Cubillo, the protagonist in this case was an immigrant who, having once been poor, became a dominant economic figure in the region, was a well-known womanizer, and a man whom it was said had conjured up the devil. When we met Alfredo Luna he was 90 years old and still an active person, living with a wife 40 years his junior. Arriving in the village as a petty trader in the late 1920s, he fell in love with and married a local woman, Doña Aurelia. He established himself as a retailer of consumer goods, but soon became involved in agricultural production and the merchandising of agricultural produce. He started to amass land, and became rich, powerful and the head of a family of wealthy landowners in the village. Significantly, Alfredo did not go in for an ostentatious display of his wealth. When we visited his house, there was nothing to indicate that he had been the richest man in the region. He received visitors in rustic peasant garb: barefooted and stripped to the waist, his old trousers had holes and were held up with a simple piece of string. Other than a pair of the cheapest, locally made chairs, his house contained no furniture. Like Don Cubillo, Alfredo had a reputation as a womanizer. In spite of his marriage to Doña Aurelia, he regularly had affairs with other women. He recognizes paternity of some 40 children, 12 of them already dead, the offspring of two official spouses plus many *pegados* (literally, children 'stuck on' other women). To visitors he recounts at length how much he has spent on the education of his children, both legitimate and illegitimate, and how well they have done: 'I have an engineer, two are in the USA, there are secretaries, nurses, accountants, and my grandchildren are lawyers, engineers and doctors'.[12]

Alfredo Luna, Agrarian Change and Land Appropriation

During the 1920s and 1930s, most of the land controlled by the municipality, the so-called *ejido*, was distributed among villagers, who generally did not lack access to land [*Jansen*, 1998].[13] In the nineteenth and early twentieth century the village economy was connected with external markets through the sale of cattle, pigs, coffee and indigo (the latter in the nineteenth century only), as well as artisan products (mainly sleeping mats produced from natural fibres). Cattle raising as a more specialized commercial production became profitable in the context of the opportunities offered by the national, and Central American, cattle boom of the 1950s and 1960s.[14] This expansion of commercial livestock rearing, and the related concentration of land on which to undertake this kind of economic activity, intensified the conflicts over rural property in many regions of Honduras. The steady growth and intensification of coffee cultivation, led by better-off producers and leading to the emergence of class differentiation of the cultivators into rich, middle and poor peasants, was particularly salient in the 1970s and 1980s.

The basis of Alfredo's fortune lay in his shop, the first one in this municipality of about 1,500 inhabitants. Many people bought drink and drank it on credit.[15] He started to buy small pieces of land close to the village, on which to pasture the mules he used to transport goods and agricultural produce between the village and the district capital. Only later did he begin to invest in livestock rearing and coffee cultivation. He also became an important coffee trader in the village. During the 1930s and 1940s, Alfredo Luna held various political posts on the municipal council, including that of mayor. Along with his trading, producing and banking activities, this political office-holding contributed to his riches.

Throughout 1935, Alfredo frequently travelled as a village representative to the capital in order to secure a piece of land – called Juniapal – as an *ejido* for the village. However, he used these trips to advance his own personal interests, and to make himself the leaseholder of the state, in spite of the fact that the municipality had already received written permission to use the land. Evidence we have seen suggests that Alfredo also bribed the village authorities during the conflict that resulted. The documents proving that the state had assigned the land to the village and not to Alfredo, disappeared mysteriously. After years of submitting new requests to the national authorities, the municipality received approximately half of the Juniapal land, although the boundaries between it and Alfredo's portion of the holding remained the subject of dispute.

Alfredo had also purchased smaller pieces of land adjacent to Juniapal from individual peasants, as well as one large tract of private land onto which peasants had encroached decades earlier, and which they now considered as their own private property. In the disputes that followed, an official survey of the land was carried out, from which (according to information provided by one of his sons) Alfredo benefited enormously. He got all the best land, in a continuous plot, and intensified his cattle raising accordingly. Alfredo changed his agricultural pattern from a maize-pasture-fallow rotation to permanent pasture. Henceforth tenants were no longer able to use this fertile valley land for maize cultivation.

Although in the words of the villagers Alfredo 'grabbed the land' to which the whole village was entitled, there was never a mass protest against and sustained opposition to his behaviour. Nowadays villagers blame this episode on 'the authorities of those days', who in their opinion failed 'to defend the people's interests'. Organized collective action against Alfredo's private appropriation of public land never took place. He nevertheless did not have everything his own way: complete control of the land was not possible, since it was not fully fenced, and some villagers continued to farm plots there.[16] Although he did not evict them because he feared this would lead to violence, Alfredo passed the Juniapal land on to his son Pedro in 1967, not least because he anticipated potentially unfavourable changes in national legislation and politics. His family then commenced legal proceedings to secure legal title, since all leaseholders of the state had the right to convert this into ownership rights. Without the latter, the land would be affected by the agrarian reform.

When, in response to a renewed interest in agrarian reform in the prevailing political climate, some peasants attempted to occupy some of this land during the 1970s, many villagers condemned them, stating that one should not enter another's property (*meterse en lo ajeno*). The ensuing violent confrontation between, on the one hand, several armed Luna brothers and their (military) 'bodyguards', and on the other the peasants who had invaded the land, was seen by the villagers as 'understandable' – that is, the Luna family was justified in protecting what was now perceived as their private property. The attempted occupation failed, and Pedro Luna then sold large parts of the land to his brothers. Despite the fact that nobody knew whether the Luna family had legal title to the land, and that Alfredo had probably manipulated the authorities in order to get and retain access to it two decades earlier, therefore, a certain public legitimacy was conferred on the defensive reaction by his sons to the occupation. In an important sense, this struggle had already been lost much earlier, in that the village seemingly accepted the legitimacy of Alfredo's rights by virtue of not challenging them at the time he appropriated the land (*el pueblo dormido; no se avivaron*), and that his sons had then bought the land concerned. Two local norms – being owner of something you buy (even if it is from another member of the same family) and having rights because you have fenced in the land with the tacit approval of the villagers – were violated by the 1970s land occupation.

The acquiescence in Alfredo's land appropriation of both the municipal authorities and the individual villagers was related in turn to the various ways they were tied to Alfredo. The municipality regularly borrowed money from well-to-do inhabitants like Alfredo in order to carry out public activities, such as buying land for the villagers. Once the division of the Juniapal holding appeared inevitable, it was Alfredo who paid for the land to be surveyed; while he himself did indeed benefit from the latter, it also gave villagers access to an additional and substantial amount of land suitable for maize cultivation. Moreover, Alfredo's network of personal relationships protected him from mass protest: it was said that 'Alfredo dominated the village', or that 'he was the axis of the village'. He was the only merchant in the village from whom peasants either borrowed money or purchased items on credit: it was said that 'everybody was indebted to Alfredo'. The absence of massive opposition to his appropriation of public land was due not just to this economic dependency but also to patronage ties: hence the view that 'you could wake him in the middle of the night to obtain some medicines ... He was a man of prosperity; we saw him as our father, all we asked for he gave us, he did not refuse.' His wife, Doña Aurelia, strengthened his social position; she was called 'the mother to the village' because of her generosity towards the poor. Peasants also admired his strong personality, describing him in positive terms as *vivo* ('alive, shrewd') and *trabajador* ('a hard worker').

Other people in the village stress the far-reaching 'vision' of Alfredo in the following manner: 'After the mayor had divided the land in the 1950s, many people sold their parcels to Alfredo, and he bought everything, but cheaply. I remember that my family sold eight *manzanas* for 100 *lempiras*, which they spent on drinking.[17] For booze they sold him the land; then they went to drink, together with Alfredo, in his shop.' This view includes scarcely veiled admiration for the cunning way in which Alfredo acquired land belonging to other people ('for booze, they sold land'). Furthermore, Alfredo was the only person in the village able to provide agricultural wage labourers with a substantial amount of employment (many orphans considered themselves adopted children of Alfredo, who supplied them with food, housing and work). For all these reasons, villagers perceived Alfredo with mixed feelings. They saw him as friend, father, *compadre*, employer, moneylender, esteemed authority and also land-grabber.[18] These multiple and contradictory relationships with Alfredo influenced how villagers reacted to attempts by him to amass land. It was, however, the dominant presence of dependency relations that enabled him to appropriate land which belonged to the village unopposed. In turn, a combination of merchant and finance capital on the one hand, and primitive accumulation in the form of land grabbing on the other, was the key to Alfredo's later success in cattle raising and coffee production.[19]

The Devil and All His Works

During our conversations with Alfredo, he always looked directly into the visitor's eyes, with a penetrating stare which is much talked about, feared and respected in the village. Reference to the mysterious power of this stare was for many peasants an oblique reference to his contract with the devil. Similar in many respects to other devil pact narratives in Honduras [*Aguilar*, 1989: 150–51; *Chapman*, 1985: 168; *Ramos and Valenzuela*, 1996, 1997], Alfredo had sold his soul to the devil in order to become rich. The most complete story about the devil pact entered into by Alfredo was told us by Fidel Alvarado (b.1941), a poor peasant who lived on the outskirts of the village in a very dilapidated hut. His detailed account of the pact between Alfredo and the devil starts with some observations on his own father.

> My father got to know Alfredo Luna at the time he started to buy and sell *petates* and other stuff in the village.[20] Soon, Alfredo came to live in the village. My father said that he travelled with mules as far as San Pedro to sell *petates*; eight days it took to travel from here to San Pedro. The *petate* was cheap but Alfredo nevertheless became richer very fast. Once when my father went with his *compadre* [Alfredo Luna] to his hacienda they spent the night there. On the way my father said to him that he had seen a man on a black mule counting the cattle of Alfredo. Alfredo answered: 'Just leave him there, these are

sombras (shadows), it is the friend, let him count the cattle'. When they went upstairs to enter the hacienda-house, Alfredo said: 'Wait here for me *compadre*, I have to go out to do something'. My father stayed in the old wooden house a while but then he left to look for his *compadre*. He went down and searched in a small ravine where he saw Don Alfredo sitting at a table with a tall man. In a ravine, you understand. What tables and chairs would be there? The man had a big book open on the table, and a pen; that table was well illuminated. The man was writing, bent forward. I do not know what Don Alfredo Luna was saying because my father returned to the house. When Alfredo Luna came back my father asked him: '*Compadre*, where have you been?' 'I went to do something in the ravine', Alfredo answered, and he continued: 'and you don't have the guts to do such a thing [*usted no tiene valor*]'. Five days later one of his farm labourers died. The labourer went to bathe in the river and simply drowned, even though he was healthy. Labourers of Alfredo died from drowning, or were bitten by insects, for example by ants in the mountains, or from disease. Another died just like that. One guy went to buy eggs, and when he entered the house he dropped on the floor, dead. It turned out that Alfredo handed over many people. The people worked for him because he had work for them to do. In this village we have poverty, we all are poor, so therefore people went to work for the man, because he had ways to pay labourers, many ways. Also, the late Santiago worked for him. The late Santiago was depulping coffee when a tall man, black and with a big sombrero, passed by on a black mule. Then one day Santiago drank milk from a black cow. I was still a boy and told him not to drink the milk. He was caught by cholera, and died lying on a pile of maize leaves. There was a burial; just for drinking a glass of milk! But [I know that] the late Santiago is not there [where the dead are], but stays in the black house. They say it is a black house. Some say it is a white house. One can see the black house only at noon and at midnight. People say that it is the place to enter into an agreement. I have walked a lot in San Pedro, but I have never come across that house, although I want to see it. [To make a contract you have to pass] seven rooms, each one with a big snake, before you meet him [the devil]. He instructs you to deal three blows to Jesus Christ; but Jesus Christ is weeping and shedding tears. Anyone who is timid, who lacks guts, will not make the pact when he sees Christ weeping because of the three blows he will receive. But he who masters his conscience will win; [he] who indeed wants to be rich, will strike Jesus Christ three blows. The deal is for a few days only, and [the devil] will come to collect. People say Alfredo handed over his own

> daughter. They say that those handed over will never die. If, for example, someone is to be shot, Lucifer will make a puppet, and when the shot is fired he throws it, and the bullets will hit the puppet. The puppet will fall dead on the ground, and the person will be taken alive to the black house. They say that my *madrina*, Doña Aurelia, the wife of Don Alfredo, is there too. She died in childbirth, along with her baby.[21] Alfredo sometimes goes to San Pedro, maybe to see her. His sons also travel to San Pedro often. She has told one of her sons that they should take her out there, and should construct a house outside the village. She said: 'The people think that I am dead so how can they then see me alive? You have to bring me a black cat, without any white hair. If you bring it, I will leave.' But no one brought her the cat. All the farm labourers who were handed over by Alfredo are there too. One of his sons told me. He knew all the labourers, and had seen them through a window of the house. He had seen this guy and that; he had seen about eight labourers in the black house. He had also seen my *madrina* with her son, already big now; also some uncles. Nobody was dead, all were alive. Who knows how he managed to bring so many people? In this way Don Alfredo became rich. It is not nothing to make a pact. You have to love the person who is handed over very much. He had an enormous cattle herd. He had fifty pack animals, just to lug coffee. He always had ten, twenty labourers to pay.

Many of the symbols in Fidel's devil pact narrative appear in similar form in other Honduran devil pact narratives. For example, the black mule accompanying the devil, the ravine with a table and a chair at midnight, the sudden and unexpected death of day labourers and family members, the black cat, and the empty coffins, or coffins filled with puppets. Another recurring theme is the pact as a signed document.[22] Significantly, the basement of Don Alfredo's house appears in many versions of the narrative. Alfredo's house was the only one in the village with a basement. One of his granddaughters asked him one day why he had constructed the basement, and he said that he used it to keep 'things' in. But people thought of it as a place of evil.[23] Most stories about Alfredo's devil pact refer to his extraordinary powers. In one of the stories, a certain Anastacio, who lived near the river, left his house on a night of torrential rainfall to check his belongings. It was midnight, and he saw Don Alfredo passing on a black mule. Alfredo went to his hacienda to look for his animals. Anastacio told him not to go because he had to cross the river, which was in torrent and had swept away entire trees. Alfredo nevertheless crossed the flooded river, mounted on his mule, and disappeared entirely under the torrent. Anastacio thought Alfredo had drowned until he heard him shout on the other side of the river. Everybody still wonders how Alfredo succeeded in crossing the flooded river. Another example of his extraordinary powers is his age, about which people say: 'eighty-nine years and he still mounts horses and keeps glaring at people with eyes full of fire. Nobody of that age is so energetic.' These stories have two sides: Alfredo is human, but he is also super-human, as he can do things of which normal people are incapable. These are taken as signs that Alfredo really does have a pact with the devil which gives him everlasting life.

The speed at which Alfredo became rich is important. As one villager expressed it: 'He rapidly became *Don* Alfredo'.[24] Alfredo arrived rather poor and became incredibly rich very fast. He handed over to the devil his own family and his farm workers, he had courage (*valor*) and he possessed super-human powers. The sacrifice of his own family underlines the widespread conviction that he personally handed over his farm workers. Someone who is capable of handing over members of his own family can certainly be expected to hand over his farm workers as well. The fear on the part of day labourers who refuse to work for Alfredo is therefore accepted as plausible and well-founded. 'Having guts' is important because it explains why only he and nobody else made this pact with the devil: only he had sufficient courage to do this. At the same time it conveys respect for those who find it necessary to maintain working relationships with Alfredo. In spite of what he does to his fellow beings, it is possible for some villagers to have dealings with him. Alfredo himself is accordingly not totally evil, he just has the courage to make bargains with evil. The ideological sub-text is inescapable: because he is courageous, Don Alfredo deserves to acquire things of value; his wealth is, in the end, a result of his own work.[25]

CONTRADICTORY ASPECTS OF THE DEVIL PACT

The life history of Don Cubillo, the protagonist of Edelman's devil pact narrative in Costa Rica, is in three important respects very similar to that of Alfredo Luna in Honduras: a sudden economic ascent, a pact with the devil and the reputation of being a womanizer. But is Edelman correct in his assertion that the devil pact of Don Cubillo is primarily a discourse not about his wealth but rather about his sexual liaisons with women? Edelman argues that Don Cubillo's wealth cannot be the source of the devil pact narrative because there were also other rich men in town without a pact with the devil. In support of his claim, Edelman invokes two additional arguments: that peasants tended to identify with Don Cubillo because, first, the regional economy revolved around him, and second, he championed their rural/ethnic 'otherness' against the urban white population. These same peasants, however, do not identify themselves with the sexually predatory behaviour of Don Cubillo: according to Edelman, therefore, the element of devilish evil refers (and is confined) to this particular aspect of Don Cubillo's life. Such a claim is also supported by the fact that the only difference between Don Cubillo and other wealthy men was his womanizing. We will first discuss this problematic epistemological shift in Edelman's explanation, to sexual domination, before discussing the issue of whether or not peasants identified with Don Cubillo.

Sexual Liberty and Male Protection

A central claim made by Taussig, that only men could sign a pact with the devil, has been accepted rather too uncritically: it is certainly not true of the Honduran devil pact narrative.[26] Several of the Honduran narratives chronicled by Ramos and Valenzuela [1996, 1997] relate of women who have entered into pacts with the devil. In the course of our own fieldwork research in Honduras, informants stated that Alfredo's eldest daughter Josefa inherited the pact; they also told us about women in other villages who had made pacts with the devil.[27] In the case of Honduras, therefore, entering a devil pact is not the exclusive preserve of men. One might nevertheless argue that, where Don Cubillo and Don Alfredo Luna are concerned, the pact is not a gender specific one, involving antagonism between males and females, but rather one involving sexual behaviour, a discourse about promiscuity versus marital faithfulness and/or pre-marital chastity (for both men and women).[28]

According to Edelman [1994: 74], Don Cubillo's womanizing and sexual promiscuity 'represented an attack on the manhood of poor Filadelfinos'. This libidinous behaviour generated both admiration and anxiety, an antinomic reaction that provided fertile ground on which the myth of the devil pact could flourish. The story of Room 21 symbolized a twofold attack: not just on the reputation of women, but also on their male relatives who were supposed to protect them. A woman's reputation for virtue can only be lost once, and if this happens men, too, are drawn into the ensuing scandal: it is as much the reputation of males, who are supposed to protect their women, which is dishonoured, and both lose face if this defensive role is not performed. Although the libidinous behaviour of Don Cubillo is the subject of male admiration, therefore, men are nevertheless anxious when this libidinous gaze settles on women under their own protection.

In the event, Don Cubillo chose his women, and 'there was not likely very much that a poor servant girl could do about it' [*Edelman*, 1994: 71]. As depicted by Edelman, however, these women were passive victims of Don Cubillo's libido; they had no capacity to consider the advantages and the disadvantages of such a relationship, and to decide for themselves; they were unable to act in their own right. Because females aspire to conform to the 'traditional Latin American male supremacist values', women's reputations are also important to men [*Edelman*, 1994: 73].[29] Invoking the presence of Latin American male chauvinism (*machismo*), Edelman tends to accept it as standard ideology, the only representation of real practice; in contrast to this interpretation, others (such as Melhuus and Stolen [1996]) have pointed out how the responsibility of men to protect the 'reputation' of women actually varies a lot in practice. Furthermore, many men live with women whose reputation has been 'lost'. The argument that men simply wish to uphold traditional male chauvinist values leaves little scope for any consideration of the ideological variations and contradictions that inform Latin American rural *machismo.*

Alfredo Luna was a womanizer like Don Cubillo, and many villagers liked to gossip about it, but no storyteller linked the devil pact narrative directly with Alfredo's extramarital affairs. Womanizing is not at all uncommon in the village. Many rich and poor men maintain relationships with several women during their lives, and recognize the offspring of several partners as their own. We know of some men who were poor, but who spent alternate nights of the week with different women in different houses. None of these men are said to have made a pact with the devil. Hence, womanizing is not an exclusive preserve of Alfredo alone, nor it is restricted to men who are wealthy. It affects men and women in all social groups.[30]

To substantiate the claim that the devil pact is an expression of gender relations, Edelman refers to other myths and narratives, which combine the theme of reproduction and female sexuality/fertility with evil. In these stories women change to animals, or evil creatures who disguise themselves as beautiful seducers to destroy men. During our fieldwork research we came across numerous similar stories. Sorcery and witchcraft were connected to the night, to certain places (where somebody was murdered, or had died in suspicious circumstances), or to sinful practices such as adultery.[31] However, most of these stories, full of references to sorcery and demonic creatures, never once referred to a pact with the devil. Examining all the different variations in Honduras, our conclusion is that the element of evil generated by the devil pact narrative is connected with the exchange whereby men and women gain a specific advantage, either by becoming rich (the most common attribute that attracts opprobrium), or less commonly by acquiring knowledge (academic titles) which also gives them access to wealth.[32]

One might propose, therefore, an alternative reading of the sexual domination as practised by Don Cubillo in Costa Rica: rather than an attack on Latin American male values, which are not negated but reproduced by inveterate womanizing and the repeated violation of women's 'reputation', sexual domination should be seen as a form of competitiveness between rich and poor men. Males who are poor both admire and fear Don Cubillo's libidinous behaviour, and dread the potential dishonour it brings through the failure to guard against the loss to him of female reputation that it is their responsibility to uphold. That the root of this antinomy is to be found elsewhere is clear from an observation by Edelman [1994: 74] that 'Cubillo could suborn local women and girls by providing significant material inducements that were beyond the ability of "their" men to provide': in other words, he has *the means to buy* women's favours in a way that was denied to those who were poor. Given this, it is unclear why Edelman does not push the argument to its logical conclusion: the narrative about Don Cubillo's devil pact is ultimately one about his wealth, and thus also about class antagonism.[33] Why does Cubillo's money 'upset the balance of control over wealth between the sexes' [*Edelman*, 1994: 74] instead of between classes?[34]

Attraction and Betrayal

A major theme in devil pact narratives is betrayal.[35] Many devil pact narratives contain references to the attraction of new technology and other aspects linked to the process of modernization. Some of the storytellers laid emphasis on Don Alfredo's desire to introduce new technologies into the village as the reason for his pact with the devil. He was the first to own a radio, a water pump next to his house, and a coffee pulping machine; that is, economic innovations which are viewed as attractive but also potentially evil. Other Honduran narratives positing the existence of a contract with the devil often refer to new elements entering peasant village life from the outside world. In the village of Don Alfredo, the engineering company that constructed a hydroelectric power plant during the early 1980s introduced new machinery and, for the first time, industrial employment opportunities into the village. For their part, villagers suspected the company of having made a pact with the devil. The souls of the men who died during the work, it was said, were handed over to the devil and still wander around as *malas espíritus* (evil spirits) on the land near the power plant.[36] This combination of new technology, capital accumulation and new social relationships, is also present in stories about banana, sugar and mining companies operating in Honduras, all of which are said to have signed a contract with the devil.[37]

Most devil pact narratives in rural Latin America refer to one of the following two kinds of betrayal. In the first kind, the subject of the narrative competes strongly with other members of his peer group and threatens group identity. The sugarcane cutter in Taussig's analysis belongs to this category of betrayal.[38] The second kind concerns subjects who transcend a particular class location, or the poor person who becomes extremely rich. The latter is no longer considered 'one of us' since he/she now belongs among the ranks (and is an ally) of the 'other'.[39] The protagonist in this second category, someone who commits an act of betrayal by entering a pact with the devil, is no longer regarded as a co-worker/peasant, but as a patron/capitalist. Often the subject who betrays his fellows does so by securing large tracts of land, a category into which Don Alfredo clearly fits. He arrived poor, with holes in his trousers, and married into the village. However, unlike the other villagers, he then went on to amass much property, became rich within a few years, and was the first villager to employ a substantial amount of farm workers throughout the year. Until that episode, people regarded it as well-nigh impossible for someone to have enough money to pay or provide for so many agricultural labourers. By establishing what was virtually a new kind of labour relation, accumulating lots of land and applying new agricultural technologies, Alfredo became in part the classic non-peasant 'other' of the devil pact narrative and its theme of betrayal, while at the same time remaining an important co-villager. The devil pact represents this shift as a betrayal of existing social relations of production and exchange uniting members of the community (while at the same time it mystifies this relation: see below). This variant of the narrative identifies the source of wealth: the latter not only is generated by earlier riches or by personal endeavour, but also is created as a result of power over others. Alfredo became rich, therefore, because he was able to do two things: first, to hand day labourers over to the devil, that is, to exploit labour-power under his control; and second, to take over land belonging to peasants (including the 'theft' of such property). To accumulate his wealth, therefore, it was necessary for Don Alfredo to cause the death of the farm labourers who worked for him, an exchange which is emblematic not only of the devil pact narrative but also of the theme of betrayal within the narrative itself.

Betrayal does not necessarily result in the destruction of all relationships. The blandishments introduced by the devil cause new relationships to be established, and the power Alfredo gained attracted other villagers to him. Like Don Cubillo in Costa Rica, he developed into a typical Central American *patron*. People sought him out to borrow money, find work, sell their products, find political protection, rent land, get information, ask him to become a *compadre*, drink with him, find a new parental home and so on.[40] In contrast to suggestion made by Edelman, such an identification with the *patron* as co-villager, important as it is for the local economy, does not imply that the *patron* himself is seen as equal with the peasant.[41] To substantiate his analysis of Don Cubillo's social relationships, with sameness/'identification' in the economic field and difference/opposition in the field of gender relations, Edelman identifies the former as the domain of 'good' (= not the devil) and the latter as the realm of 'evil', and therefore the devil.[42] In a similar vein, Taussig tends to characterize the devil in absolute terms, as the embodiment of evil.[43] By doing so, both Edelman and Taussig follow a theologic/Eurocentric epistemology, in which the devil embodies an evil that must be challenged and defeated. In the peasant reading of Alfredo's pact, however, the very strength of Don Alfredo is also a source of his good deeds: that is, the patronage which emanates either directly from him or indirectly from his wife. His economic power made him not only a danger for the village, therefore, but also attractive as an ally to individual peasants and the peasant community/municipality as a whole. The epistemological border between God/virtue and the devil/evil is, in the context of devil pact narratives and their meanings, far too absolute.[44]

Heavenly and Earthly Powers Compared

The argument developed hitherto, about the devil pact narrative in Central America as symbolic reference to new forms of exploitation and the resultant class contradictions (instead of gender/ethnic domination), is essentially one concerning the content of the narrative. A necessary second step is to explain why a narrative about exploitation and class contradictions is located in the realm of the supernatural. Taussig suggests that the narrative offers a much better account of labour relations under capitalism than those who live in a fully developed capitalist society might imagine. Broadly speaking, the latter tend to perceive capitalist relations as natural and thus unchangeable phenomena, and not as actively and socially produced forms of inequality between human beings. By contrast, peasant narratives about the devil pact break with this naturalization of capitalist relationships. The narrative is viewed in essence as a social explanation, either of capitalism (Taussig) or of gender (Edelman).

The devil pact narrative about Don Alfredo does indeed seems to be an alternative to natural explanations. The new and unusual situation, of one individual becoming very rich while living and working in the same socio-economic environment as his co-villagers, is not easily explained away as a natural occurrence. None of the villagers could imagine it possible that one of them could become so wealthy so easily and rapidly. They all worked very hard throughout their life, but nobody had ever managed to amass a comparable fortune. It is true that some were better off than others, but this had always been a result of differences in inherited property and industriousness. This kind of explanation was impossible where Alfredo's wealth was concerned. His rapid and phenomenal economic success could not even be explained by reference to his commercial activities, as these involved low-value produce, such as *petates*, beans and coffee, and high costs in order to transport them to faraway cities. Hence the rapidity of his accumulation did not itself fit into the existing notions of a natural process. But is the devil pact narrative therefore a social explanation? People in the village were, to a certain extent, well aware that Alfredo's riches had something to do with his relationship to them. But why did this lead not to a straightforwardly social explanation, but rather to a devil pact narrative? Why did not a peasant narrative emerge that explains directly how Alfredo exploited labour, made people indebted to him, and practised forms of primitive accumulation in order to expand the amount of landed property he owned? This question – why supernatural and not temporal explanations are invoked – is not answered satisfactorily, either by Taussig or by Edelman.

Rather obviously, the devil is not part of the social environment but belongs to, or comes from, the supernatural realm. Hence the attractiveness of the devil pact narrative as an ideological representation of new forms of social inequality may lie precisely in its supernatural (= 'other worldly') character. By displacing the locus of antagonism, from earth into the realms of the supernatural, it represents the new situation precisely as a non-natural occurrence, and thus precludes a specifically social explanation involving relations of exploitation. The latter kind of explanation, were it to circulate in public discourse, would provoke tensions, anxieties and discomfort among the peasants, not least because its remedy would involve action on their part that undermined the existing social order. If Alfredo's wealth came simply from exploiting his co-villagers, they could and should recover it forcibly, both by taking it back and refusing to participate further in exploitative relationships. But if his wealth emanated from a supernatural source, then this was a situation that lay beyond the capacity of simple human beings to alter. Alfredo's influential position in the village, his wide network of personal and family relations, and his economic and political power, all made organized opposition difficult. Socially and economically, people allied themselves with Alfredo for the reasons outlined above. At the same time, however, these same people, who inhabited an individualized peasant community, were resistant to the idea that they were simply clients – dependent on others and tied into social relations that generated inequality.

Not surprisingly, therefore, villagers occupying the same social and economic domain as Don Alfredo were reluctant to locate the cause of their relative powerlessness in relationships with him in themselves, in their own silence and complicity. Instead, they opted for a classic ideological displacement, and relocated the cause in a realm where they themselves were – quite literally – powerless, thereby justifying their acquiescence and simultaneously presenting their disempowerment in a positive light, both to themselves and to others. Hence what appears as contradictory in natural and social explanations – a rapid increase in riches/accumulation, new exploitative social relationships, all coupled with a 'from below' endorsement on the part of the rural poor – appears as much more logical and acceptable in this supernatural explanation. For villagers who felt betrayed by Don Alfredo's economic success, but at the same time participated in and to a limited degree benefited from this process (= 'trickle down' effect), and for this reason did not offer resistance, a supernatural explanation serves well.

CONCLUSION: PEASANT NARRATIVES AND POLITICAL CONSCIOUSNESS

This article has examined both the structure of and reasons for rural narratives in Honduras about Don Alfredo Luna, who grew from a petty trader to a large landowner, and his pact with the devil. Via Alfredo, villagers became acquainted with a new combination of merchant capital, personal political ties between individual villagers and state-level politicians, permanent wage labour, primitive accumulation (grabbing of land) and new agricultural technologies.[45] As the embodiment of an expanding class of livestock owners, Alfredo took advantage of the new economic possibilities available, installed new technologies and introduced new grassland systems. No one else before Alfredo had been able to expand his farming operations as fast. The devil pact narrative about Alfredo Luna emerged quite clearly in a context where fears generated by this process of rapid accumulation combined with profound changes in the agricultural production system and labour relations. Given this, it is somewhat surprising to encounter explanations of the devil pact narrative in Central America which identify its meaning as being solely about gender and resistance. Against such views, the point made here is that the theme of sexual predation in folkloric accounts of the Faustian bargain entered by Don Cubillo in Costa Rica and Don Alfredo in Honduras does not necessarily mean that gender domination is the main reason why the story is being told. Most Central American devil pact narratives have as their central theme the unnatural acquisition of wealth, a transformation which can be viewed as a form of betrayal. If gender elements are introduced in these narratives, they do not change either the meaning or the central importance of this particular theme.

Equally surprising is the claim that the devil pact narrative corresponds to 'from below' resistance, an empowering form of opposition to exploitation and domination. Hence the problematic nature of the two main approaches to this issue: by Taussig [1980], who views it as grassroots opposition against the capitalist mode of production and the exchange economy, and by Edelman [1994], who sees it mainly as a reflection of grassroots struggle over sexual dominance. The analysis of the latter is based on Crain [1991: 68], who considers the devil pact narrative as an empowering ideology of resistance against dominant interpretations and definitions of the 'real', similar to the everyday forms of peasant resistance theorized by Scott [1985] as the 'weapons of the weak'. Against these kinds of framework, all of which regard the discourse about 'the supernatural' in a positive light (= empowering), it has been argued here that equating devil pact narratives with opposition/resistance from below is problematic.

In contrast to the approach of those such as Taussig, Edelman, Crain and Scott, therefore, the case made here is that the invocation by peasants of the supernatural in the devil pact narrative offered them an alternative to natural and social explanations of Alfredo's wealth. A natural explanation was implausible, since the situation was new, nobody had ever experienced it, and his rapid accumulation of wealth was therefore non-natural. A social explanation, which would connect the exploitation and inequality in the new social relationships to the process of capital accumulation, either onstage or offstage, would in effect be a call for opposition. It would demand that villagers resist the exploitative relationships and land appropriation effected by Alfredo. A resort to supernatural powers in order to account for the origins of Alfredo's wealth, however, offered an alternative to social and natural explanations. Alfredo's practices of exploitation and primitive accumulation were identified as being evil, therefore doing something about this was banished as an option: no one could possibly resist his supernatural power, nor would anyone be expected to attempt this. Not only is the devil the embodiment of evil/betrayal, but he also represents desire. The new *patron* created by the devil was an important economic factor in the livelihood strategies of individual peasants searching for ways to survive in the changed circumstances. This element of ambiguity inherent in the devil, who simultaneously projects 'good' and 'bad', as do those who enter a compact with him, suggests an alternative explanation of the devil pact narrative: not as the empowering cultural expression of 'from below' resistance/opposition to Don Cubillo in Costa Rica and Alfredo Luna in Honduras, but much rather as a conservative representation of difference licensing in turn a disempowering form of accommodation.[46]

Devil pact narratives in rural Central America enable peasants to account for new wealth, new social relations and a new set of circumstances without, however, alluding to the details of what for them are painful revelations about deceit, theft, complicity and consent.[47] It keeps distant, or perhaps even denies, the possibility of social change and political resistance.[48] In doing so, the narrative does not simply reflect underlying social relationships, but also intervenes in social relationships themselves, by representing them in a specific way: in short, it locates them in a realm where, in effect, nothing much can be done to change them. It also helps to create social conventions and the formation of social institutions, that is, new landlord–peasant relationships. A supernatural principle – the pact with the devil – is, it could be argued, an intermediate step in the process of naturalizing new inequalities, in a stage where existing conventions are as yet too fragile to be completely naturalized.[49]

NOTES

1. *Mata-palo* is not the common fig (*Ficus carica*) but a strangler fig (*Ficus glabrata* or *Ficus citrifolia*) [*Williams*, 1981]. Figs, according to peasants, are special trees, as they do not have flowers but do bear fruits (botanically, they have flowers, but these are not visible). Hence, the dropping of the flower is in itself an unnatural act.
2. Among the many literary variants that refer to the theme of forbidden knowledge are Marlowe's play, *The Tragical History of Doctor Faustus* [1589/92], Goethe's *Faust* [1808], and Harry Mulisch's *De ontdekking van de hemel* [1990, translated as *The Discovery of Heaven*]. The expulsion from the Garden of Eden of Adam and Eve, who had eaten the forbidden fruit from the tree of knowledge, inspired this particular theme. In Mulisch's novel, the representations by Marlowe and Goethe of the thirst for knowledge on the part of Faustus are themselves inventions by the devil to obscure another, very real pact that Francis Bacon, in the name of mankind, signed with the devil at the same time as Faustus was alive. In this novel, God tries to recover the two tables of the law, since Bacon had learned from the devil how to institutionalize the scientific method and thus bartered away human morality, as inscribed in the Decalogue, in exchange for knowledge about the origin of the universe.
3. In Marlowe's version, the devil collects an unwilling Faustus at the end of the contract, and takes him down to Hell. Three centuries later, in Goethe's version, angels hoodwink Mephistopheles at the moment his part of the contract is due, and take Faust's body to heaven. Faust's thirst for knowledge is therefore rewarded. Compare this with the much more devotional end in the earlier play about Mariken van Nieumeghen [*anonymous*, *c.*1500] in which the Holy Mother helps Mariken, after a dissolute life, against the accusations of the devil; Mariken does penance for her sins, and dies peacefully in a convent. The peasant narrative we analyse here has no sad, happy or devotional end; the devil pact narrative has been and remains a continuous part of peasant life.
4. The power of seduction, and leading people into sinfulness, is a theme that runs through many devil pact narratives. Thus Mariken van Nieumeghen conjures up the devil and leads a life of sexual debauchery. The devil himself benefits from this when men fight over her and kill each other. Seduction by a diabolic male of females is of course a central theme in Byron's *Don Juan* [1818] and Bram Stoker's late nineteenth-century novel about the Transylvanian Count Dracula.
5. This reproduces the offer by the devil to Jesus, whereby in exchange for worshipping Satan, Jesus would receive as his reward all the kingdoms and power on earth.
6. In Marxist theory, alienation refers to the process whereby the worker undergoes a double separation, both from ownership of the means of production and the means of labour. This in turn is experienced by the subject concerned as a double estrangement: from a capacity to exercise control over the labour process, and from selfhood.
7. Taussig's study has generated much criticism, most of it ably summarized by Edelman [1994: 59–60]. One of the accusations levelled at Taussig is that he idealizes a pre-capitalist

past [*Austen*, 1996; *Turner*, 1986]; consequently, he mistakenly characterizes Latin American peasant societies as non-market economies, whereas most peasants have long been incorporated into the market [*DaMatta*, 1986]. Another is the fundamental opposition between gift exchange and commodity exchange advocated by Taussig and anthropological discourse in general, a point questioned by Appadurai [1986]. Taussig tends to treat the domain of gift exchange as non-exploitative, innocent and even transparent [*Parry and Bloch*, 1989: 9]. Yet another criticism is that Taussig views the key contradiction in the society he studied as one between capitalism and a rural pre-Conquest world, whereas it more likely lies within capitalism itself [*Trouillot*, 1986: 88]. Taussig also fails to account for the specific content of devil pact narratives [*Gross*, 1983]. In a similar vein, Chevalier [1982: 192] finds unanswered the crucial question why only co-workers and not plantation owners are said to have pacts with the devil, when both are equally responsible for the introduction of wage labour. Peasants, too, may have pacts with the devil [*Parry and Bloch*, 1989], so this has to be explained as well. Edelman [1994] himself questions the total rejection by Taussig of any link between devil pact narratives and socially determined fears and conflicts. If these are not to be reduced simply to individual psychology as a way of dealing with problematic situations, it is necessary to locate the reason for the reproduction of such narratives in the wider context (see also Meyer [1994] for devil contracts in Ghana). In his response to some of these critiques, Taussig [1987] insists that his book never described anything resembling a 'natural peasant economy'. Although many critics point to Taussig's idealization of peasant economy, opposed by him to the capitalist economy, little has been said about his schematic view of the ecology of peasant farming as opposed to plantation farming. His claim that peasant economy maintains soil fertility in the rainforest [*Taussig*, 1995] has either been dismissed in its entirety [for example, *Weischet and Caviedes*, 1993] or reinterpreted as an historical and location-specific phenomenon instead of a static, pre-capitalist reality [for example, *Amanor*, 1994]. Between 1980 and 1995 Taussig changed the key feature of the devil pact narrative while retaining the theoretical contrast between the gift economy and the exchange economy. In a later text [*Taussig*, 1995], therefore, devil pact narratives are no longer seen as a commentary on the development of capitalist relations of production but rather as a tale – still reconstituting the past – which shows alternative forms of consumption. It is a discourse about giving without receiving, and as such is a warning about contemporary, capitalist-created luxury and excess consumption.

8. Taussig [1980: 230] sees the devil pact narrative mainly as an effect of imagination and not – or not yet – as an effect of politics, because in his view the latter requires, amongst other practices, political organizing. This view, however, does not prevent him from ascribing many oppositional/resistance characteristics to the discourse about the devil.
9. Edelman suggests that this is an 'ethnic' dimension of the devil pact narrative. He does not, however, explore this further, and this argument remains inferential. The focus here is therefore on the gender element in his analysis.
10. We use here Edelman's terms. Taussig's account is, in fact, not so much about class antagonism – which would exist within one mode of production – but about antagonisms between the different modes of production (or different modes of consumption in his 1995 analysis).
11. The focus of our fieldwork research in Honduras was on peasant perceptions of, on the one hand, agrarian change, natural resource use and agricultural knowledge [*Jansen*, 1998], and on the other the working of law and norms [*Roquas*, 2002]. During our long stays in the village, over different periods, recording local interpretations of Alfredo Luna's position in the village and his contract with the devil became part of our study of peasant narratives. We were unable to persuade Alfredo Luna himself to give us his view about the devil pact narrative. At his age he seemed interested in talking only about his children.
12. This occupational list is very different from the kind of list that most villagers would produce if asked about what jobs their own children held, and as such illustrates the extent to which members of the Honduran landed elite typically invest in educating their children for urban employment and often state jobs.

13. The definition and meaning of the Honduran *ejido* has changed over time (see Roquas [2002] for the different definitions, and disputes about them). For the purpose of the discussion here, it is sufficient to understand *ejido* as state land over which the municipality can claim certain rights, one of them being to concede usufruct rights to individual villagers. Peasants, however, have perceived these usufruct leases as ownership rights to this land, private property which they have subsequently sold, inherited or sublet.
14. These opportunities resulted from improved transport facilities, an emerging export beef market with new packing plants, credit from a developmentalist state, new pasture varieties and cultivation systems, and new cross-breeds and disease control [*Howard*, 1989; *Williams*, 1986].
15. Between 1952 and 1963 at least 906 people received credit from Alfredo (*source*: accounting books of Alfredo Luna).
16. Apart from secretly invading his property, directly stealing his belongings is another individual response Alfredo was required to tolerate, as the following local story illustrates. Juan Perdomo worked as a day labourer in Alfredo's warehouse. One day he ate a combination of raw onions and plantains, and his farts produced a terrible smell. He complained to Alfredo that a bad smell filled the warehouse, adding that 'there must be a dead rat somewhere'. Alfredo ordered him to look for the rat and then to get rid of it. A few hours later, he saw Juan leaving the warehouse with a big box in his arms. He asked what was in the box and where he was going. Juan replied: 'This is the dead rat and I am going to throw it away at the rubbish dump'. Alfredo gave his permission, and Juan left with the big box for the rubbish dump, and dropped it there. At night he went back and collected the box, which did not contain a rat but twenty pairs of shoes stolen from the warehouse. Just like everybody else in the village, Alfredo knew about the missing shoes, but he never claimed them back or pressed charges against Juan.
17. Officially one *manzana* measures 0.7 hectare, but in the village is 0.8361 hectare [*Jansen*, 1998].
18. *Compadre* refers to co-parenthood (*compadrazgo)*, a form of fictive kinship which in many Latin American cultures contains, or has contained, a set of rights and duties between the godfather/mother and the parents of the godchild (which does not imply equality, however). In this particular Honduran region, *compadrazgo* has been relatively unimportant as an agrarian social institution.
19. One informant also stated that he took calves belonging to cattle owned by other villagers, livestock which then was still able to wander freely on common land; Alfredo put his own brand on the calves, and then grazed them on his land. Such thefts made him rich, according to this peasant.
20. *Petates*, or woven sleeping mats, were made by the women of the village.
21. In other versions of the story, she died of fright when a pig that was hanging from the ceiling fell off and dropped into a bin filled with water just beside her.
22. This reinforces the power and importance of signed documents, and the respect with which people treat them. There is another devil pact narrative in a neighbouring village featuring a man who signed it because he wanted to have money to allow his son to study. When his son had completed his studies, the man would hand himself over to the devil. But the son found out about this arrangement, and he went with the chain of the holy saint Francisco to the devil and tied the latter to a chair. The son then demanded that the devil return his father's contract. A contract was indeed returned by the devil, but it was one with another person. The son kept it, and demanded the right contract. Again the devil handed him a contract involving another person, which the son also kept while insisting he be given the right contract. In the end the devil handed over the right document, the contract involving his father. In this way the son rescued not only his own father but also two other individuals from the clutches of the devil.
23. Don Alfredo's granddaughter's own theory was that her grandfather used it to store his cash at a time when there were only coins and no paper money. But she also considered it possible that he used the basement for the illegal production of alcohol. He loved drinking, and frequently organized big parties in his house. The granddaughter remembered how on these occasions alcohol was procured for the party from somewhere inside the house.

24. The word 'Don' is an honorific term of address for a man who is held in respect, on account of his wealth, age, wisdom or professional title.
25. It seems unnecessary to point out that this kind of self-validation is the stock in trade of capitalists everywhere, all of whom claim that their wealth is the result of their own hard work.
26. Although Edelman [1994: 86–7] refers in two notes to other sources which indicate that women made pacts with the devil, he mentions – but does not comment upon – the claim by Taussig that women do not enter pacts with the devil.
27. In the course of conducting fieldwork research in another part of Honduras during the year 2000, we recorded a detailed story of four sisters who had entered a pact with the devil. Although they were poor, they purchased more and more land. Nobody was able to explain from where they got the money to do this.
28. A theme that appears in many versions of devil pact narratives elsewhere (see note 4 above).
29. Edelman [1994: 73] considers men's anxiety lest their women are seduced by Don Cubillo a contrast to the prevalence of 'highly unstable, informal unions, which lessened males' affective attachments to their partners and their concern and capacity for protecting female relatives ...'. Unlike Edelman, however, we did not observe that unstable or informal marital relations (widely present in our research area) automatically implied lessened affective bonds between men and women. Edelman infers that men in (supposedly) monogamous, stable marriages in western capitalist societies love their wives more than men in the Costa Rican hinterlands.
30. Neither does the combination of being rich and a womanizer of itself give rise to devil pact narratives. Several other wealthy men maintained multiple extramarital relationships, but were never said to be in league with the devil.
31. An informant told us the story about her father, a womanizer, who fell in love with one particular woman. 'He regularly followed her to her house and tried to chat with her through the kitchen window. One night, when it was very late and the village was deserted, he saw the woman he admired walking a short way ahead of him. My father immediately tried to attract her attention. She walked out of the village and he followed her. She disappeared and then suddenly reappeared, over and over again. Without warning her appearance changed, and he saw that she was no longer his beloved woman but "*la sucia*" (= 'the dirty one'). My father was seized by panic, but he had brought a cigar with him, and the smoke of a cigar can save you from *la sucia*.' Although this informant's narrative is about evil, linked to her father's adultery, such a story is not of itself evidence that the pact with the devil is necessarily a discourse about female sexuality.
32. About the role of class in the devil pact narrative, Edelman is somewhat ambivalent. His stated intention is to 'challenge the idea that devil pact beliefs are rooted in economic exploitation alone' [*Edelman*, 1994: 78]. Regardless of the degree to which class antagonism plays a role in his interpretation of the devil pact narrative, however, according to him the central theme remains the issue of gender and sexual domination. In our view, Edelman tends to overstate the gender issue and to confuse different social structures. Devil pact narratives may interweave issues of riches and new wealth with symbolic reference to sexuality and knowledge, but his does not necessarily mean that in this case the narrative is a coherent and encompassing explanation of all the behaviour featuring Don Alfredo Luna and/or Don Cubillo. Edelman tries to incorporate every detail of Don Cubillo's life history within the single rubric of his devil pact narrative, which is 'a nearly ubiquitous cultural matrix'. Edelman [1994: 61] argues further that 'the recognition that the rural poor (or others) do not always analytically separate "modes" of exploitation or types of power relations is key to understanding their narratives about domination and subjection. In the case that is the central concern here, intertwined modalities of exploitation are mirrored in stories that mix symbols and levels of meaning but that, in using the metaphor of the devil pact, employ a commonly available idiom or interpretative framework' (for the historical background, see Edelman [1992]). In our fieldwork conversations about Don Alfredo, villagers drew a clear distinction between class (capital accumulation) and gender (that is, sexual predation), using the devil pact narrative exclusively to deal with Alfredo's rapidly acquired riches, changes in the agricultural production system and the use of wage labour.

We think class and gender can be seen as different structures, contingently related, which – as has often been the case historically – may or may not reinforce each other: capitalism without gender oppression is theoretically imaginable, and an objective pursued in most feminist projects [*Sayer*, 1984]. The social structures of class and gender both appear in the life history of Alfredo Luna: the large landowner and the famous womanizer. In contrast to Edelman, who states that rural people cannot distinguish modes of exploitation, the different tales about Alfredo separate out these different structures very clearly. In the case of the devil pact narrative about Alfredo, the story told is of his capital accumulation and not of his libidinous behaviour and his 40 children. Thus the devil pact narrative is not a comprehensive cultural matrix which reflects *all* the behaviour and social relationship of the person involved.

33. Crain [1991] does consider a similar situation in Ecuador as an expression of class antagonism.
34. In fact, gender struggles are absent from Edelman's case study.
35. The structure of betrayal connects centrally with Christian narratives about the transformation of good into evil, and the absolute contrast between them: not only with regard to the expulsion of Adam and Eve from the Garden of Eden, and the Jesus/Judas relationship, therefore, but also to the one involving God/Lucifer/Satan. Satan was a fallen angel: that is, he was initially part of the system against which he subsequently turned, and of which he became the 'other'. In terms of a discourse about betrayal, the devil pact narrative replicates the theme of Satan's fall. Just as the rich man was poor to begin with, and like the poor an honest and virtuous person, so Lucifer – who was originally an archangel in heaven – betrayed God, and consequently became the embodiment of evil and all-that-God-is-not. Like Lucifer/Satan, therefore, those who enter a pact with the devil signal thereby a permanent and enduring process of transformation, or leaving behind 'goodness' (= peasant economy) in order to become something 'other' and 'bad', for example, an accumulator of capital (money = dirt = evil).
36. Such 'undead' – those who are neither in heaven nor in hell – also appear as the people in Alfredo's black house in San Pedro de Sula in the story cited above.
37. Crain [1991] describes a former peasant, now a foreman, who had become so obsessed with a new sawmill which he operated that he regularly remained with the machine at night and fell asleep beside it. His attachment to this symbol of danger and power led ultimately to him being handed over to the devil.
38. Trouillot [1986: 88] argues that piece-work tends to generate resentment in cases where some labourers exceed significantly the average worker's productivity. He advances the persuasive hypothesis that, in the case of the Colombian cane cutters, it was this resentment by fellow workers of the betrayal by some of their number of worker solidarity (= 'rate busting') – and not the clash between two modes of production – that was the source of the devil pact narrative.
39. We leave aside a third category, in which the subject of the devil pact narrative is predominantly an external agent that threatens peasant livelihoods. For example, the agricultural school el Zamorano in Honduras is supposed to have a pact with the devil. It acquired large tracts of the best land in the Zamorano valley on which it erected buildings remarkable for their beautiful architecture. Each year, when its board of trustees meets, it is thought that these 'gringos' have their annual devils' sabbath. The dead souls are handed over to the devil on the last bend of the road that descends from the mountain and enters the valley, a spot where many accidents always result in fatalities. All three categories mentioned are constructed by and circulate within the domain of popular culture. Devil pact narratives may also be constructed by elites who feel threatened by lower classes: for example, the witchcraft trials in European history [*Waardt*, 1989] and the demonization of the Indian population by the Spanish conquerors [*Cervantes*, 1994].
40. Villagers did not perceive Alfredo as completely diabolical or greedy. Many people reported that Alfredo liked to drink and invited them to drink with him. The same is true of Don Cubillo, and Edelman emphasizes that he, too, was not greedy, and thus not entirely evil, which he takes as evidence for the fact it was not his wealth which led to the devil pact narrative. However, the point about Alfredo is that a person in league with the devil always

finds new money in his coffin, and thus is able to keep inviting others to drink with him.

41. According to Edelman, because many storytellers identify themselves in some way with Don Cubillo, the devil pact narrative cannot express hostility or class antagonism. He considers the story of the lost *alforja* as an expression of precisely this identification. However, the lost *alforja* could equally well be interpreted as another form of identification: not with Don Cubillo, who lost it, but with the impoverished finder. The moral of this story could just as easily be that the finder was poor because he was too honest, the inference being that those who are rich become so by being dishonest.
42. Edelman stresses the importance of recording the stories not only from people who believe in the devil pact, but also from those who deny that Cubillo conjured up the devil. He invokes the latter stories as evidence for his assertion that devil pact narratives were not principally about capital accumulation. However, we also recorded stories by those who did not believe in the pact with the devil; although they did not equate the pact with the illicit acquisition of wealth, such people did indeed identify other mechanisms used by Alfredo to become rich. Let us consider the view of one informant, who told us: 'I do not believe in it – no such pact exists. That man loaned half a bag of beans to someone who later had to return him three quarters of a bag. These were loaned out again, and so Alfredo got more and more. Furthermore, he sold everything in his shop … Alfredo also became rich because he took away from the poor animals belonging to them that were wandering free. He branded these animals and put them in his own sheds. This is the way the rich become rich, by taking from the poor'. In this account, Alfredo's wealth is based on accumulation through commanding exchange and credit in kind and through what has been called primitive accumulation: the forcible appropriation of means of production belonging to others. Whilst denying the existence of a pact with the devil, however, this view nevertheless confirms its central theme: the specific ways in which Alfredo became rich – by usury, commerce and dispossessing peasant smallholders. The veracity of devil pact narratives is also denied by those villagers belonging to new evangelical religious movements, who dismiss such beliefs as 'superstition'. One such villager said: 'People say Alfredo has a pact with the devil. I do not believe this. The devil has no money with which to make someone rich. God has not created the rich and the poor for nothing. There have to be rich and poor. The poor can work as farm labourers for the rich and share in some of their wealth. The poor and the rich are there for each other.' This representation of social relationships recurs in the perspective of many poor people. If the rich did not exist, the poor would be unable to find work and receive payment. Although the villager in question rejected the mythological explanation of Alfredo's wealth, he too identified the same link between this wealth and the labourers who work for Alfredo. In his rejection of the devil pact narrative the villager nevertheless confirms that it is centrally about relations between employers and workers. The only difference is that for him it is God and not the Devil who is the source of wealth. In the accounts of both kinds of non-believer, the central theme of the devil pact narrative remains intact.
43. Taussig [1980: 113] acknowledges the importance of the paradoxical and contradictory processes we find in the devil, but his devil is mainly evil, and thus lacks benevolent and attractive qualities. Taussig's *Tío* in the Bolivian tin mines therefore seems more of an European devil than a pre-Columbian deity: the latter possessed malevolent and benevolent qualities, depending on whether or not it received sacrifices, and was only transformed into the 'devil' during the Spanish conquest [*Cervantes*, 1994]. The European version seems to come closer to the characterization of Nash [1979]: 'We eat the mines and the mines eat us'.
44. See Geschiere [1997] for a similar view on the close relationship between evil and good in devil and witchcraft stories in Africa, and Cervantes [1994] for the devil as a god exhibiting both malevolent and benevolent behaviour in post-Columbian Indian religion.
45. This changing context differs from Taussig's case [1980]. When Alfredo Luna arrived, exchange value was already a common element in the village economy.
46. We do not deny the possibility that the devil pact narrative could be used in a process of collective resistance, but we deny the *a priori* connection between peasant culture and empowerment/resistance. If there is any opposition to the landowner in the devil pact narrative, it is a symbolic one only; disagreement and condemnation is permitted, but

outright opposition – in the form of agency to rectify the situation – is not. In keeping with other popular and official Christian/Catholic beliefs, it teaches that rectification or the pursuit of justice is something which is the preserve of God in heaven (not humanity on earth). While on earth, wealth and power are not to be challenged; if punishment is due, this will be meted out only after death. It thus reinforces passivity and fatalism.

47. Those storytellers who thought that Alfredo was in league with the devil generally talked in admiring terms about Alfredo; by contrast, those who did not express admiration for him, and held far more negative views about the kind of person he was, were precisely the ones who explained his acquiring of riches not as a result of a pact with the devil but rather by means of land grabbing, money lending and trading. The argument that such a narrative, as an offstage discourse of gossip and calumniation, undermines the power of the landlord, is not valid in the case of Alfredo. It would anyway be a somewhat one-dimensional explanation, negating the dynamics present in the betrayal/attraction dialectic.
48. It generates consent in this case, not in the sense of an elite discourse imposed upon the peasantry, but as a popular culture giving meaning to its acquiescence.
49. When this grounding in nature through the supernatural is recognized, this fragile convention may collapse or be challenged – for example, when peasants state that it is not the pact with the devil but rental payment which makes Alfredo rich.

REFERENCES

Aguilar Paz, J., 1989, *Tradiciones y leyendas de Honduras*, Tegucigalpa: Museo del Hombre Hondureño.

Amanor, K.S., 1994, *The New Frontier. Farmers' Response to Land Degradation: A West African Study*, London: Zed.

Anonymous, 1982 (*c.*1500), *Mariken van Nieumeghen*, Den Haag: Nijhoff.

Appadurai, A., 1986, 'Introduction: Commodities and the Politics of Value', in A. Appadurai (ed.), *The Social Life of Things: Commodities in Cultural Perspective*, Cambridge: Cambridge University Press.

Austen, R.A., 1993, 'The Moral Economy of Witchcraft: An Essay in Comparative History', in J. Comaroff and J. Comaroff (eds.) [1993].

Cervantes, F., 1994, *The Devil in the New World*, New Haven, CT: Yale University Press.

Chapman, A., 1985, *Los hijos del copal y la candela. Ritos agrarios y tradición oral de los Lencas de Honduras (Tomo I)*, México: UNAM.

Chevalier, J.M., 1982, *Civilization and the Stolen Gift: Capital, Kin, and Cult in Eastern Peru*, Toronto: University of Toronto Press.

Comaroff, J., and J. Comaroff, 1993, 'Introduction', in J. Comaroff and J. Comaroff (eds.) [1993].

Comaroff, J. and J. Comaroff (eds.), 1993, *Modernity and Its Malcontents: Ritual and Power in Postcolonial Africa*, Chicago, IL: University of Chicago Press.

Crain, M.M., 1991, 'Poetics and Politics in the Ecuadorian Andes: Women's Narratives of Death and Devil Possession', *American Ethnologist*, Vol.18, No.1.

DaMatta, R., 1986, 'Review of Chevalier and Taussig', *Social Analysis*, No.19.

Edelman, M., 1992, *The Logic of the Latifundio: The Large Estates of Northwestern Costa Rica since the Late Nineteenth Century*, Stanford, CA: Stanford University Press.

Edelman, M., 1994, 'Landlords and the Devil: Class, Ethnic, and Gender Dimensions of Central American Peasant Narratives', *Cultural Anthropology*, Vol.9, No.1.

Geschiere, P., 1997, *The Modernity of Witchcraft: Politics and the Occult in Postcolonial Africa*, Charlottesville, VA: University Press of Virginia.

Gross, D.R., 1983, 'Fetishism and Functionalism: The Political Economy of Capitalist Development in Latin America', *Comparative Studies in Society and History*, Vol.25, No.2.

Howard Borjas, P., 1989, 'Perspectives on the Central American Crisis: "Reactionary Despotism" or Monopoly Capital?', *Capital & Class*, No.39.

Jansen, K., 1998, *Political Ecology, Mountain Agriculture, and Knowledge in Honduras*, Amsterdam: Thela Publishers (Thela Latin America Series).

Melhuus, M., and K.A. Stolen (eds.), 1996, *Machos, Mistresses, Madonnas: Contesting the Power of Latin American Gender Imagery*. London: Verso.

Meyer, B., 1994, 'Satan, slangen en geld. Betekenissen over duivelse rijkdom in christelijk Ghana', in H. Driessen and H. de Jonge (eds.), *In de ban van betekenis. Proeven van symbolische antropologie*, Nijmegen: SUN.

Nash, J., 1979, *We Eat the Mines and the Mines Eat Us: Dependency and Exploitation in Bolivian Tin Mines*, New York: Columbia University Press.

Parry, J., and M. Bloch, 1989, *Money and the Morality of Exchange*, Cambridge: Cambridge University Press.

Ramos, K., and M. Valenzuela, 1996, *Por cuentas aquí en Choluteca*, Tegucigalpa: Secretaría de Cultura y las Artes.

Ramos, K., and M. Valenzuela, 1997, *Por cuentas aquí en Sabanagrande. Literatura oral de la Zona Sur de Honduras*, Tegucigalpa: Secretaría de Cultura y las Artes.

Roquas, E., 2002, *Stacked Law: Land, Property and Conflict in Honduras*, Amsterdam: Rozenberg Publishers (Thela Latin America Series).

Sayer, A., 1984, *Method in Social Science: A Realist Approach*, London: Hutchinson.

Scott, J.C., 1985, *Weapons of the Weak: Everyday Forms of Peasant Resistance*, New Haven, CT: Yale University Press.

Taussig, M.T., 1980, *The Devil and Commodity Fetishism in South America*, Chapel Hill, NC: University of North Carolina Press.

Taussig, M.T., 1987, 'The Rise and Fall of Marxist Anthropology', *Social Analysis*, No.21.

Taussig, M.T., 1995, 'The Sun Gives without Receiving: An Old Story', *Comparative Studies in Society and History*, Vol.37, No.2.

Trouillot, M.-R., 1986, 'The Price of Indulgence', *Social Analysis*, No.19.

Turner, T., 1986, 'Production, Exploitation and Social Consciousness in the "Peripheral Situation"', *Social Analysis*, No.19.

Waardt, H. de, 1989, 'Met bloed ondertekend', *Sociologische Gids*, Vol.36, Nos.3–4.

Weischet, W., and C.N. Caviedes, 1993, *The Persisting Ecological Constraints of Tropical Agriculture*, Harlow: Longman.

Williams, L.O., 1981, 'The Useful Plants of Central America', *Ceiba*, Vol.24, Nos.1–4.

Williams, R.G., 1986, *Export Agriculture and the Crisis in Central America*, Chapel Hill, NC: University of North Carolina Press.

Representing the Peasantry? Struggles for/about Land in Brazil

JOSÉ DE SOUZA MARTINS

INTRODUCTION

Unlike most other countries in Latin America (particularly Andean and central American ones), a longstanding and thus deeply rooted system of independent smallholding cultivation based on an indigenous peasantry has until relatively recently been absent from Brazilian history. Perhaps because of this, peasants in Brazil have been and are currently more prone than their counterparts elsewhere in the continent to the phenomenon known as the 'invention of tradition', a process which in turn generates claim and counter-claim about identity and entitlement based on this.[1] For this same reason, the domestic and international visibility of the struggle for land in Brazil over the last quarter of a century, and especially during the last decade, challenges the social sciences to update their understanding both of the agrarian question and of the peasant struggles in this country.

At the same time, these struggles over land raise important questions concerning the direction and outcome of such conflict: in short, struggles for land are also struggles about wider socio-economic objectives, or the way in which property rights desired by the protagonists are perceived as desirable by those in Brazilian society as a whole. Recent clashes over the issue of land reform suggest that more attention be paid to the role and agenda of non-peasants, or those who are termed here the *agents of mediation* (= mediating groups). The latter designation covers a variety of groups and institutions – especially the Roman Catholic church – that have played a crucial part in making peasant and Indian protest and resistance viable.

It is necessary, therefore, to dispel some of the more misguided assumptions relating both to the land issue in Brazil and to the ensuing conflicts. First and foremost, one should keep in mind that, in the Brazilian

---

José de Souza Martins, Professor of Sociology, University of São Paulo, Brazil. The article in its present form owes much to the editorial comments of Tom Brass.

case, the agrarian problem does not conform to the standard Latin American format. Historically, Brazil's huge landed estates (*latifundios*) focused on producing tropical goods for export, such as sugar and coffee, and were responsible for the development of an agrarian bourgeoisie that played a key role in Brazilian economic development. In cases such as that of the São Paulo coffee area, this class evolved into a dynamic commercial, industrial and financial bourgeoisie, as early as the nineteenth century. It was this segment of the bourgeoisie, of agrarian origin, that was largely responsible for the industrial development of the country's southeast, currently the core of Brazil's economy. It was a bourgeoisie, furthermore, whose social and political vision had a major social and political impact, such as its involvement with the establishment of the University of São Paulo in 1934, currently Brazil's most important centre of higher education and of the production of technical and scientific knowledge.[2]

The contemporary history of Brazil, especially that which started with the 1964 coup d'état, which installed a military dictatorship that lasted for twenty years (1964-85), suggests that agrarian issues generally and the struggles of the peasantry in particular should be examined through a much broader optic: namely, a perspective that is not confined to episodes and events which occur only in the countryside, but one that includes a wider range of different social categories and classes in Brazilian society. In brief, it is difficult to understand peasant struggle until we cease to regard it merely as a current manifestation of an ancient conflict the protagonists of which have their roots in a distant past, and a past, furthermore, which they are intent on recuperating. For this reason, it would be epistemologically and politically inappropriate to reduce the recent history of Brazil's peasant struggles to a stereotype shared historically with the peasantries of Mexico, Central America, Bolivia or Peru. The genesis of and path followed by agrarian conflict in Brazil is very different, and calls for an interpretation compatible with its own socio-economic specificities.

The presentation which follows contains three sections, each of which corresponds roughly to a particular phase in the agrarian struggle. The first examines what might loosely be termed the 'opening of the agrarian frontier', the ensuing cash-crop production (coffee, sugar, rubber) being dependent for its labour supply on a process of international immigration and settlement.[3] The second looks at the subsequent closing of the agrarian frontier, a situation of double dispossession which gave rise to national migration as land usufruct rights hitherto enjoyed by members of the agricultural work force were cut back at the same time as urban employment opportunities became scarce. The third considers the way in which the land question was then reopened, by whom, and why, while the conclusion investigates the arguments and conflicts surrounding what have in effect become movements by Brazilian Indians and peasant smallholders for the re-possession of and/or the right to work on the land.

I

OPENING THE AGRARIAN FRONTIER

In order to understand what peasant movements consist of in Brazil, as well as to appreciate their aims and difficulties, it is necessary to refer briefly and in passing to the agrarian question. We are all aware of what the agrarian question is in theory: namely, a question about obstacles to accumulation, whereby the existence of land rent blocks the development of capital, and in effect prevents a surplus being generated in agriculture for the purpose of industrialization.[4] Where economic activity depends on the land, and where agricultural land is controlled by a traditional landowning class not directly involved in cultivation, an economically unproductive landlord has the power to demand from the economically productive capitalist what amounts to a charge on accumulation as a condition of setting the agrarian labour process in motion. Such a cost is either passed onto and thus borne by all productive elements in the context concerned, or – more probably – acts as a barrier to capital investment and surplus generation.

In Brazil, however, the modern ownership of land was instituted through the 1850 Land Bill, which had as its purpose the formulation of legal mechanisms that made the cultivation of great landed estates obligatory, especially where coffee plantations were concerned, during the nineteenth century.[5] Its objective was to stimulate a process of primitive accumulation that Brazil did not have, and – in the absence of a large mass of peasants who could be expropriated and then proletarianized – for which the country lacked the necessary pre-conditions. In this respect, it was a different process from the one that took place in European countries, from the reality and history of which the primitive accumulation theory derived. With the abolition of slavery looming, the purpose of the 1850 Land Bill was simple: to create both a shortage of land and a consequent incidence of poverty, so as to ensure the availability to landowners of a work force that was necessary, in large numbers, to tend coffee crops and to maintain the sugar economy. Slave emancipation did indeed take place, in 1888, and deprived plantation agriculture of its captive work force.[6]

By lowering the cost of the agrarian workforce through a system very similar to debt peonage, this measure, to some extent, transferred both the hardships of and the economic burden occasioned by the abolition of slavery onto the new worker. At the same time, it converted surplus portions of this workforce into a reserve army of labour that was essential to the establishment of a cheap source of blue-collar workers necessary for industrialization. In providing medium and small commercial farms, as well as large plantations, with low-cost rural workers, the 1850 Land Bill subsidized the reproduction of the industrial workforce, making it cheaper for industrial capital to employ labour-power. Thus, to some degree Brazil was able to meet its requirements for accumulation from within its own borders, by mobilizing surplus labour for all sectors of the economy (agriculture, industry, trade, banking).

In the Brazilian case, the agrarian question manifests itself on two planes. On one hand, therefore, ownership of the land in a political system that was part of the client-oriented and oligarchic system constituted – at least up to the time of the 1964 *coup d'état* – an economic reward for political loyalty. The republican constitution of 1891 had transferred to the states of the Brazilian federation the ownership of devolved land, and transformed it thereby into the currency of political deals in the market of oligarchic domination. In the more backward areas of the country, land obtained by political means was the source of conflicts with rural workers and consequently of violence against them. On the other hand, land was monopolized specifically in order to enable landowners to exercise control over their work force, and until the 1950s rural labourers were indeed in a relation of dependence on farmers who employed them. With the industrial boom of the 1950s, however, the urban demand for agricultural produce increased the value of land, and rental payments – which hitherto had been a way of obtaining and retaining workers – were now transformed simply into a way of accruing speculative profits.

In this connection, it is important to understand that the current agrarian conflict in Brazil does not stem directly and solely from the undeniable fact of land concentration, notwithstanding the fact that large plantations were and are a focus of struggle. Current agrarian conflict, and political solutions linked to this, stem not from latifundism *per se* as from the transformation in the relations of production that replaced slave labour, and came about as a result of the abolition of slavery in the late nineteenth century. To demonstrate this it is necessary to outline the three different solutions adopted by regional elites in Brazil in order to replace slave labour, and thus to ensure the continuity of large-scale export-oriented commercial agriculture. The key to present agrarian struggles, and to the agrarian question itself, therefore, lies not so much in the system of landholding as in the changes to the labour regime introduced by rural employers.

Land, Slavery and the State

Changes to relations of production within Brazilian agriculture during the nineteenth century were necessitated by the abolition of slavery in the sugar-producing colonies of the Caribbean, itself an effect of inter-imperial rivalries, and the consequent pressure from England to end the slave trade.[7] Shortly after Brazilian Independence from Portugal in 1825, England obtained from Brazil the right for the English navy to board the slave ships headed toward its ports, freeing the captives in their own colonies and confiscating the vessels. But it was only in 1850 that Brazil finally approved a law forbidding the trafficking and entry of slaves from Africa. This sealed the fate of slavery in Brazil.

At that very conjuncture, Brazil also passed a new Land Bill, replacing the *sesmarias* or land-grant system inherited from Portugal and suspended in 1822. According to this older form of tenure, the occupation of land was free and ownership was conferred by virtue of cultivating the land and residing on it permanently. This earlier form of land title extended only to those who were white, free, and Roman Catholic: that is, to those 'pure' in blood and faith. Final disposition over land, however, was vested in the crown (as embodied in the state), which upheld property rights only where land was cultivated. If land granted remained uncultivated, the crown had the right to reallocate such holdings to other interested parties. In essence, the Land Grant Bill (*Lei das Sesmarias*) of the kingdom of Portugal was, in the early fourteenth century, only a usufruct right to land whereby tenure was conditional on the land being cultivated. It is to this law that the establishment of huge landed estates in Brazil is erroneously ascribed; much rather, the consolidation of such latifundia was linked to the availability of slave labour – provided both by the indigenous population and also by Africans. The land grant (*sesmaria*) itself was merely a secondary factor in the establishment of the large landholdings system prevalent in the country.

According to the new Land Bill of 1850, the Brazilian State gave up its rule over granted land (the *dominium*) and made the grantee the full and unquestioned owner of the land, thereby instituting full ownership rights over land property. It simultaneously abolished previous ethnic prohibitions on landownership, while at the same time restricting access to land by establishing economic barriers. In other words, land was henceforth a commodity, and as such could be purchased, either from a private individual or from the State. This law was premissed on two complementary processes. First, the gradual disappearance of slavery, as a result both of the ending of the slave trade, and of an inability to supplement this shortfall by the employment of a captive indigenous population. And second, the recognition that large-scale farming required massive immigration, or the influx of foreign labour to till the land. The interruption of slave trading, however, led to a substantial increase in the price of slaves, which rendered the abolition of slavery inevitable by 1888, for cost reasons.[8] Two years before abolition, the Brazilian government was already fostering immigration schemes, which subsequently resulted in the inflow of hundreds of thousands of families – initially from Italy, Spain, Portugal, Germany, and Switzerland, and later on from Japan – all of which were relocated in the south of Brazil, and especially in the coffee-growing south-eastern region.[9]

Coffee and the Colonato

In the case of coffee, besides the transformation of work relations, one must also take into account that, at that time, cultivation of this crop expanded toward the west of the province of São Paulo, pushing out the economic frontier and occupying virgin land, especially the highly fertile, so-called 'purple' soil. Together with the labour supply crisis occasioned by the abolition of the slave trade, this resulted in an economic decline of the rich but less productive coffee estates in the south-east area, which depended on the port of Rio de Janeiro. These estates suffered economically because of two factors: the comparatively lower productivity of their coffee plantations and the suspension of the slave trade, each of which combined to undermine the position of slave-owning landlords. In the western area of São Paulo, by contrast, commercially dynamic agricultural production based on a new type of labour relation, the so-called *colonato* system employing immigrants from other countries, became the norm [*Beiguelman*, 1968].

Contrary to what is sometimes claimed, chattel slavery in Brazil was not replaced with free wage labour.[10] Commercial farmers made several attempts to create a new work relations that would, above all, ensure the continuation of export-oriented agricultural production on large landed estates managed on capitalist lines. In Rio de Janeiro, for example, one alternative given serious consideration was the introduction of Chinese 'coolies'. The latter, commercial farmers hoped, would become temporary slaves on coffee plantations. This proposal, however, did not work out. Sharecropping was attempted in São Paulo, but this also failed, due to the high cost of obtaining foreign workers, a result of commercial farmers in Brazil themselves having to pay for the passage of such migrants and their families from Europe to the place of work [*Davatz*, 1941].

Instead of these options (coolies, sharecroppers), commercial farmers finally opted for the *colonato* system, which took root and operated for roughly one century. Although there is still debate about this, the *colonato* system in effect combined what were various different types of working arrangement within a single production relation.[11] On any coffee plantation in Brazil at this conjuncture there were three main kinds of agricultural task requiring manual labour. The first was taking care of the coffee plants, by keeping the plantation weed-free, a task which entailed two or three weedings annually. This work was paid for in cash, a fixed amount according to the number of coffee bushes treated. Additionally, a contract labourer (*colono*) was allowed to plant subsistence crops – such as corn, beans and even rice – between the rows of coffee bushes. The second task consisted of harvesting the coffee, work that was paid for either in cash, by volume of coffee picked, or under a sharecropping system. Thirdly, a contract labourer had to provide the landed estate with several days of unpaid work per year: this consisted of jobs such as clearing pasture, cleaning and maintaining paths and roads, fixing fences, and putting out fires. Members of the contract labourer's family also received wages for working in the coffee processing area.

The *colono* contract in fact encompassed the whole agricultural labouring family, all of which was involved in working on the farm, even the children.[12] Accordingly, there was a clear preference on the part of commercial farmers for the recruitment and employment not of single workers but rather of agricultural labouring *families*, and large ones at that. These agricultural labouring families lived in 'colonies' of houses sited within the estate or farm; some of the larger coffee estates had several of these colonies located within their boundaries, forming a veritable rural network of villages. Besides a house, the *colono* workers were entitled to a plot of land on which to plant vegetables and raise farm animals (chickens, goats). Finally, they were also allowed to maintain in the farm's pastures – that is, at the owner's expense – two pack animals (horses, mules, donkeys) for working and transportation purposes. The *colonato* relation included, furthermore, the possibility that at harvest-time a contract labourer might himself hire workers on his own account (i.e., recruited and paid for by him), to help him pick coffee both in the amount and in the time stipulated by his contractual obligations to his employer.

The *colonato* was accordingly a diversified and complex contractual relationship, combining salaried work, the payment of rent in the form of labour and goods, and the rendering of labour services free of charge, in addition to direct production of the means of subsistence. It was, in short, a relational form that united elements of a declining peasantry with aspects of an emerging rural working class, and thus a working arrangement in which cash payment represented less than half of overall pay, in general roughly one third. Researchers who maintain that the *colono* relation indicates the existence of a rural proletariat point to behavioural evidence, citing the participation of contract labourers in strikes. Such episodes were few in number, however, and have little significance when considered in the wider context of the large number of contract workers who did not withdraw their labour-power in this fashion. Most importantly, the dispute about whether or not the *colono* was a proletarian overlooks both the fact and the role of the relation as being that of an agricultural labouring family, and not an individual worker. There is much documentary evidence that the recruitment by rural employers of a family as distinct from a single worker was a deliberate act, designed to achieve two particular ends: not just to obtain access to more labour-power at a lower overall cost, but also to use the family itself as a method of social control. Simply put, the *colono* was dissuaded from participating in class struggles due to the fear of seeing himself and his family – especially his wife and small children – evicted from their smallholding.[13]

The main problem facing commercial farmers using this new labour relation was generated by the fact of worker indebtedness, a result of the trip from Europe. Debt condemned all the agricultural labouring family to many years of serfdom, which contract labourers were unwilling to accept. While the imminent abolition of slavery was being debated in Parliament, a revolt by *colonos* from Switzerland contributed to the decision by the Brazilian government to establish state subsidized immigration. In this it had the support of the government of the province of São Paulo, which also instituted a wide-ranging programme of subsidized immigration in order to obtain workers for its coffee plantations.

It was the Brazilian state which instituted rational, effective ways to manage the landed estates' demand for manpower and the organization of supply. It organized the immigration process, appointing and hiring recruitment agents in Europe, and also created hostels in which to house the immigrants temporarily between their arrival in the country and their transferral to farms and/or estates. Since it was the state which paid for the passage of agricultural labouring families, the labour-power embodied in the latter was in effect gifted to the estate owners. This was, indeed, the form taken by the economic compensation that the Brazilian government offered farmers and/or planters for their acceptance of an end to slavery: namely, socializing the costs of obtaining and establishing a substitute work force, without which the territorial expansion of large coffee plantations would have been impossible. This measure was very important, both in creating the internal market and also in providing a first impulse toward industrialization, shortly after the abolition of slavery.

Sugar after Slavery

In the most important sugarcane growing and sugar-producing area of the country, the north-east, the rural labour supply crisis occasioned by the ending of slavery had other characteristics.[14] At that particular conjuncture, the cultivation of sugarcane differed from the cultivation of coffee in many ways. First, because sugarcane was being grown in what was basically the same area as it had since the sixteenth century; coffee, by contrast, had only become a major crop in the south-east during the nineteenth century, and especially after 1860. This difference in longevity profoundly affected the way in which farmers and workers were habituated to the production regime. Second, for a long time the cultivation of sugarcane was essentially limited to the same part of the north-east, close to the coast. There was a major area of sugarcane plantations also in the inner state area of São Paulo and Rio de Janeiro, but this did not generate the same kind of habituation as was the case in the north-east.

As with coffee, sugar cultivation became a tool for expanding the economic frontier, moving further inland and, over the course of several decades, into new areas of virgin territory covered by native woodlands. Sugarcane production was undertaken by what became over time a well-established planter class, given to conspicuous consumption and the self-image of which was that of an aristocratic agrarian elite, and generally conservative as to property inheritance, social relations, social hierarchy and political outlook. By contrast, coffee produced an agrarian elite that was open to the incorporation of new farmers, precisely because of its rapid and relatively recent territorial expansion. Unlike their well-established counterparts producing sugarcane, therefore, coffee farmers in Brazil were required to start cultivation from scratch: felling the forest, clearing and preparing the soil, seeding the coffee plantation, and waiting for a period of between four and five years before production could commence.[15] All of this groundwork was based on temporary, formally non-capitalist, labour relations; only once all this had been accomplished did the resident *colonos* move in to tend the plantation and harvest the crop.

Because it was older, the cultivation of sugarcane maintained within the great plantations a large mass of creole (*mestizo*) inhabitants descended from Indian freedmen, Indian slavery having been abolished during the mid-eighteenth century. This form of chattel slavery was unknown in the cultivation of coffee. When emancipated, this workforce – equivalent to what the *colono* would become at a later date – did not command sufficient resources enabling them to survive as independent economic agents outside the estate system. For this reason, they continued to live on their former masters' estates, under the paternal regime of the planter class, growing food for their own subsistence on marginal plots of land ill-suited for sugarcane cultivation. In exchange for permission to grow their own crops, these descendants of Indian freedmen paid the landowner labour-rent, an arrangement known as the 'yoke' (*cambão*), whereby they worked for a certain number of days *per annum* in the sugarcane plantation.[16] Although they were allowed to sell surplus product from their plots to anyone they chose, in practice the purchaser was often the landowner himself, who acquired their output at niggardly prices.

Planters were from the outset obliged to acquire black slaves as labour for sugarcane cultivation, not least because of the monopoly over slave trafficking exercised by the Portuguese Crown itself. With the cessation of this trade, slave labour gradually became scarce, both in the sugar-producing north-east and in the coffee-producing south-east, causing the price of such workers to rise. Sugarcane growers began selling their slaves to the large coffee-plantation owners in the south-east, thereby establishing an internal trade in unfree labour. In order to compensate for workers lost in this manner, planters increased the amount of labour-rent their freedmen were required to provide in order to continue having access to smallholdings on the estates. From this emerged a system of tenant farming based on a permanent agricultural worker (*morador*) resident on the sugar plantation, a relational form that lasted until the mid-1950s.

Rubber Tapping in Amazonia

Another area of economic activity possessing its own specific labour regime was the rubber industry located in the Amazon region. Unlike the cultivation of sugar or coffee, rubber was an extractive economic industry based on large tree groves in the heart of the forest. This form of productive activity became more important in the Amazonian region only after 1870, and chattel slavery was therefore relationally insignificant to its economic development. The cultivation and harvesting of rubber depended, much rather, on the labour-power of an internal migrant workforce, composed of impoverished peasants and agricultural workers escaping from the semiarid north-eastern region (not the sugarcane north-east).[17] These migrants were recruited in large numbers and then transported to the Amazon region by labour contractors. Although the latter exercised extra-economic coercion when recruiting workers, usually a process linked to cash advances and debt, the main reason for migration remained hunger and poverty occasioned by severe drought, especially the one that occurred in 1877.[18] Once in Amazonia, these migrants were reduced to serfdom by virtue of debts they owed to the owner's store (*barracão*) that supplied them with staple goods on credit, to be paid for from their accumulated earnings at the end of the agricultural season. Unlike the *colono*, the rubber tapper (*seringueiro*) was a lone worker, living and labouring by himself in the forest, with the owner's store as his sole point of reference.[19] The estate owner forbade the rubber tapper from trading with strangers (either buying from or selling to others), a measure enforced by hired gunmen (*gatos*) who also prevented workers from running away by controlling river access to the rubber-tree groves. Structured by coercion, this type of production relation was in essence a form of slavery: the debt peonage system [*Cunha*, 1946].[20]

Just as the labour regimes of sugar and coffee cultivation differed from that of rubber production, so the economic crisis of the latter was due to an equally distinct cause: the introduction into the world market in 1911 of rubber produced in Malaysia [*Santos*, 1980]. With its comparatively low level of productivity, the extraction of rubber continued in Amazonia, but now stripped of the economic importance it had enjoyed during the 20 years in which its output had dominated world markets. This was the period in which the ostentation and conspicuous consumption by rubber planters ensured that their lifestyle became in effect a tropical extension of Parisian high society. This was particularly true of the town of Belém, the gateway into the Amazon region, the architectural splendours of which reflected the profitability of the rubber economy. In some areas, estates producing rubber were abandoned by their owners, but the rubber tappers continued to work independently as squatters [*Ianni*, 1978]. The extraction of rubber in Brazil was given a new lease of life during World War II, when the West's access to Malay rubber plantations was cut off. As part of the war effort, the Brazilian government developed an incentive program for rubber and encouraged migration from the semi-arid northeast to the Amazon region. These measures, however, did not bring about any changes in production relations. Much rather the contrary, since the economic revitalization of rubber extraction also resulted in a corresponding revitalization of peonage, or the practice of holding persons in servitude to work off a debt.

Peasant Agriculture in the South

There were yet other areas of agricultural production in Brazil the economic problems of which made a contribution to the formation of what now manifests itself as a crisis of the peasantry. This is particularly true of the important family farming sector composed of privately owned smallholdings in the south of Brazil. At a time when it was recruiting workers in Europe for the commercial coffee estates and farms, the Brazilian government intended that at least some of these immigrants should join agricultural colonization projects where they would become peasant family farmers. Not the least important objective of this policy was an ideological one: namely, to demonstrate to prospective immigrants that by working hard on the plantations they, too, could become independent peasant proprietors. The latter was, quite explicitly, held up as a reward for contributing to the economic well-being directly of commercial agriculture and indirectly of the nation itself. In the south of the country, most of the agricultural workers settled in this manner and for this reason were of Italian, German and Polish origin. Theirs was a self-sufficient agriculture, practised by a peasantry transplanted literally from Europe to the south of Brazil, a form of production that remains fairly important to this day.

Each one of these economic processes – sugar, coffee, and rubber production – had its moment of crisis and, consequently, its experience of social transformation. Except for producers engaged in the extraction of rubber, whose crisis came earlier, those who cultivated sugarcane and coffee plus the peasant family farms in the south all faced economic difficulties, but for different reasons, from the 1950s onwards. It was these economic difficulties that are at the root of the social conflict which eventually forced itself onto the national political agenda in the decades which followed. What is important to understand is that, to some degree, it was the shared chronology of change taking place in distinct agricultural sectors located in different parts of the country that conferred ideological legitimacy on the presence of a uniform problem and political solution: that is, on the notion of a uniform set of problems, a uniform political programme, and a uniform agrarian struggle. In short, a rural movement the mobilization of which managed to hide its diverse causes, and – by implication – the different social consequences of this fact for a seeming unified demand for reform.

II

CLOSING THE AGRARIAN FRONTIER

The main outcome of these crises in the different sectors of the agrarian economy was a process of internal migration and westwards expansion within Brazil itself, and the gradual but ineluctable occupation of land on the frontier. From the nineteenth century onwards, therefore, it was this as much as anything which ensured the survival and consolidation of peasant family farming, acting as a safety valve by absorbing migrants from other parts of the country. The capacity of peasant economy to reproduce itself in this manner only really began to diminish in the period of the military dictatorship (1964–85), in the face of what some have defined as 'closing the frontier'.

New land was accordingly occupied not only by coffee planters from the southeast, but also by poor peasants and agricultural labourers from the north-east, midwest and the south. The latter categories became squatters (*posseiros*) who practised shifting cultivation, which involved clearing a small plot of land and cultivating it for a few years, and then moving on to an adjacent plot, where the same procedure was repeated. This permitted the original site to recover its fertility, thereby enabling the squatter to return and cultivate it once again. Thus practised shifting cultivation was sufficient only to provide the squatter and his family with subsistence, and any surplus product generated by this form of peasant economy was sold locally. Because squatters lacked title to the land they occupied and cultivated in this manner, their smallholdings were frequently the subject of ownership disputes, particularly with large landlords or agribusiness enterprises seeking to expand their properties by appropriating all peasant family farms in the vicinity.[21] Thus rural conflicts in the south, such as the Contestado revolt (1912/1916) and the uprising in the state of Paraná (1957), and more recently in the midwest and Amazonia, have all involved disputed land rights and titles.[22]

Closing the Urban Industrial Safety Valve

During the period between the 1930s and the 1960s, a rapid expansion of the Brazilian economy meant that migrants from the rural north-east and south-west were able to find urban industrial employment, particularly in the São Paulo region. Agricultural workers who became unemployed as a result of falling coffee prices in the 1930s, migrated to urban areas and found jobs in labour-intensive capitalist enterprises recruiting new workers. After receiving rural migrants from the coffee estates, industry subsequently absorbed those from the north-east who were fleeing drought and poverty, and also those from Minas Gerais, displaced as a result of the expansion of livestock ranching into areas of peasant economy. However, this capacity on the part of Brazilian industry to employ workers expelled from the land lasted only until the coup d'état of the mid-1960s, when the dynamic of accumulation shifted decisively away from a labour-intensive process to a capital-intensive one.

A crucial result of the technical modernization of Brazilian industry at that conjuncture was a decline in the number of jobs available to rural migrants. Such employment as existed was now open only to skilled workers with higher educational and better technical qualifications than those possessed by agricultural labour. Urban areas continued to receive migrants, but increasingly these entered not the better-paid industrial workforce (= the formal sector) but rather the informal sector economy, where wages were low, working conditions poor, and employment insecure.[23] Over the last three decades, therefore, rural migrants have become slum dwellers (*favelados*) living at the margins of subsistence in the shantytowns, a far cry from kind of life offered them by what they perceived until the 1960s as the welcoming city. In short, migration from the countryside in search of urban employment has ceased to be what it once was in Brazil, a safety valve mechanism.

This decline in urban employment opportunities was itself compounded by transformations in the agrarian economy generally, and in the labour regime on sugar and coffee plantations from the 1950s onwards. In an attempt to stave off the effect of capitalist competition, sugar planters in Brazil increased the amount of labour-rent payable by their plantation workforce. During the 1960s, however, the economic situation improved as a result, ironically, of the Cuban revolution; sugar planters in Brazil benefited from the reallocation by the United States of Cuban sugar quotas to other sugar producing countries. The consequent recovery in the demand for this commodity generated an additional need for plantation labour, and landowners extracted more surplus-labour from their existing permanent workers, converting the latter into rent-paying tenants and the former into a rent-receiving landlord [*Andrade*, 1979].[24] Many smallholding permanent workers, who were unable to meet these demands for additional labour-rent, were evicted from the sugar plantations, only to return subsequently but now as landless casual agricultural labour (*clandestinos*) employed on a temporary or seasonal basis.[25]

A not dissimilar process took place on the coffee estates, where a permanent agricultural workforce was casualized and deprived of its usufruct rights. In well-established and older coffee estates plagued by declining soil fertility, the *colonato* relation was essentially a sharecropping system. To the west of the state of São Paulo, where coffee bushes were by contrast newer, younger, and thus more productive, the *colonato* system combined the characteristics of independent cultivator and wage labourer. Access to land in both coffee growing areas – old and new alike – meant, however, that a *colono* harboured ownership aspirations and perceived his true identity to be that of a peasant farmer. This self-identity sprang from the right of a contract labourer to grow his own staple crops in the rows between the coffee bushes, and either to consume them or sell any surplus produce via the estate owner. From viewpoint of the landlord, this arrangement ensured that the *colono* would regularly and scrupulously clear the coffee groves of competing weeds, if for no other reason than to be able to plant his own crops (corn, beans) in the spaces cleared. Under this system, the *colono* worked simultaneously for himself and for his landowner.

In the course of the century during which the *colono* system prevailed, however, it became clear that growing crops in the spaces between the rows of coffee bushes was counter-productive and thus uneconomic. First, these crops damaged the shallow roots of the coffee bush, affecting the productivity and profitability of this cash crop. And second, the introduction of new and more productive varieties of coffee plant requiring more shade and thus less space between the rows, eliminating the area traditionally cultivated by the *colono*. To compensate for the loss of this usufruct right, *colonos* were provided with alternative plots of land outside coffee estates, which in turn transformed the existing division of labour. As a result of coffee and subsistence crops occupying a separate physical space but coinciding in terms of harvest time, the males in the agricultural labouring family worked on the coffee estate while the women tended the smallholding.

Ironically, the growth of the domestic market for foodstuffs linked to industrial boom of the 1950s gave an added impetus to the peasant farming side of the *colono* relation and simultaneously undermined this. While the increased demand for foodstuffs cultivated on plots leased from coffee growers generated more income for the *colono* family, therefore, it also alerted landlords to the economic potential of such smallholdings. Estate owners began to phase out the *colono* system and its usufruct component, preferring instead to pay such workers a cash wage. Access to land owned by the coffee estate, and with it the possibility of a higher income, was gradually replaced with wage labour for a cash payment. This trend towards the proletarianization of the rural workforce was strengthened by a federal government policy aimed at rationalizing the cultivation of coffee; subsidies were provided enabling farmers and estate owners either to replace old coffee bushes with new ones, to convert portions of their property into pasture, or to diversify into other commercial crops. Consequently, the need to maintain the *colono* system as a means of securing labour-power for estates and large farms declined accordingly.

These changes were pushed through rapidly, not least because of the opposition by organized rural labour to their implementation, the ending of the *colonato*, and the eviction of erstwhile *colonos* and their families from the estates. When the Rural Worker Bill was passed in 1963, giving legal substance to the agricultural worker fightback, landowners and farmers quickly recognized the *colonato* system as being not just an economic burden but also a threat. The rate of evictions increased, and the now landless workers (*bóias-frias*) were frequently re-employed on a temporary basis by the same landowners, who no longer dealt directly with them but with labour contractors.[26] Accordingly, the transition to a casual agricultural workforce in coffee cultivation, from *colonos* to *bóias-frias*, was in essence no different from the transformation from *moradores* to *clandestinos* in the north-east sugar region.

To some degree, these transformations in the patterns of rural employment were accompanied by changes in the productive forces, a result of the adoption by employers of low-cost subsidized technical, mechanized and chemical inputs. Coffee, for example, continued to be harvested by manual labour, but the task of weeding was accomplished through the use of herbicides. In the sugar plantations, tasks such as the annual tilling of the soil and the planting of the cane crop were mechanized, but harvesting of the cane – as in the case of coffee – was still undertaken by labour-power. In other words, capitalist production in Brazilian agriculture became increasingly fragmented into tasks that still required manual labour, and those in which it was no longer employed [*Silva*, 1980]. The effects on agricultural labour of this transformed combination of productive forces and social relations of production were profound: the increasing presence of technical/mechanized inputs meant that agrarian capitalists had to exercise greater managerial control over labour-intensive tasks. Rural workers and their families lost not only their limited and conditional access to land, therefore, but also their equally limited capacity to control the rhythm and pace of agricultural tasks. Moreover, as casual labour they faced long periods of seasonal unemployment coupled with migration to distant areas in search of work.[27]

Land Grabbing and Dispossession in Amazonia

Although in Amazonia the extraction of rubber went into economic decline as early as the first decades of the twentieth century, it recovered during World War II when metropolitan capitalist access to the output of Malaysian rubber plantations was interrupted. It survived until 1965, when for strategic reasons the military dictatorship put into practice a sweeping programme of economic development in the Amazon region. By means of a tax incentives policy, the federal government granted a 50% income tax exemption to those companies already installed in other areas which were willing to expand their activities into the Amazon region.[28] Since most investment was in crop and livestock farming, the demand for Amazonian pasture land increased correspondingly. However, territory that the military dictatorship assumed to be empty was the last refuge of the Indian tribes, both indigenous to the region and those which had fled the Portuguese conquest during the sixteenth century. Amazonia was also the location of on the one hand peasant smallholders, consisting of squatters pushed out from the north-east in previous decades, and on the other rubber-tappers working for masters – especially in the territory of Acre – who actually had no title to the land.[29]

The new Amazon occupation policy revealed the precarious nature of landownership and titles in this region.[30] Those who operated rubber estates, and had government leases to this land, acted as if they had property rights and sold these agreements on to companies interested in the federal government's tax incentives. In a similar vein, forged documents appeared claiming title to the land of Indian tribes and peasant squatters, 'property' thus acquired in the Amazon being sold to enterprises seeking tax incentives. In this situation, paper rather than land exercised power: it was on the basis of such power, however, that Indians and squatters were 'legally' evicted from their holdings by capitalist enterprises.[31] The extent of illegal and dubious transfers of land titles in the Amazon region is underlined by the fact that in the year 2000 the federal government nullified titles to some 63 million hectares of landed property.

Such 'legal' acquisitions of land in Amazonia were also enforced by a process of threats, violence and widespread extra-judicial murder.[32] Peasant squatters were evicted, and not infrequently killed, by gunmen hired by old or new 'owners' of land occupied by the former; squatters reacted weakly and only locally, with actions that had little impact on this incursion. Any attempt to organize resistance was undermined by the isolated nature of small villages and peasant family farms, the inhabitants of which were easily picked off by hired gunmen.[33] Unsurprisingly, therefore, the numbers of peasant families murdered soared, particularly during the seventies and the eighties. Because they were relatively more united and organized, tribal populations fought back with more success, and for 20 years a situation akin to tribal war prevailed in the Amazon region. In order to protect themselves from the attempt to deliver 'Indian-free' land to capitalist enterprises, Amazonian tribes closed or destroyed many of the secondary roads opened by the Brazilian state government in order to form a network linked up to the Transamazon Highway. This resistance notwithstanding, many tribal groups suffered huge losses during this struggle to protect themselves and their lands, and some lost as much as two thirds of their numbers during this period.

These facts confound received theory about the way in which agrarian capitalism is reproduced.[34] Contrary to the assumptions made by current theory on the subject of primitive accumulation, capitalist development still entails the dehumanization of the labouring subject, an objective pursued in the Amazon region not by economically backward enterprises but rather by new investment made by companies that are economically among the most dynamic and advanced representatives of the capitalist system.[35] New companies, not infrequently renowned multinationals, major banks, large industrial concerns, and leading commercial conglomerates, have no problem with the widespread employment on their farms of workers for the slow and exhausting work of felling the forest, clearing the soil and seeding the pastures, who are recruited and retained by means of debt peonage relations – that is, slavery through debt (*peonagem*).[36] It is estimated that, during the 1970s, the number of debt peons enslaved by such modern companies may have been as high as 400,000 people [*Branford and Glock*, 1985]. The current assumption made by evolutionist varieties of Marxism, that accumulation generally and the development of the productive forces in particular necessarily and always entails (and, indeed, is dependent upon) a corresponding transformation in the social relations of production relations, or a transition from unfree to free forms of labour-power, is wholly undermined by the trajectory followed by agrarian capitalism in Amazonia.[37] In the latter context not only did capital give a new lease of life to so-called 'feudal' relations, but the resulting traffic of people was both ubiquitous and open: thus, for example, labour contractors supplied farm managers with receipts for the debt peons bought and sold, as if this were a perfectly normal capitalist transaction – which, in a sense, it is.

The Crisis of Peasant Economy in the South

Family farms in the south of the country also faced crisis from the 1970s onwards, as a consequence of problems in ensuring the social reproduction of peasant economy established by Italian and German immigrants during the nineteenth century. These politically conservative smallholders, who were closely linked to right-wing parties because of their strong religious (mainly Roman Catholic) background, found it difficult to obtain additional land for their offspring. Due to the high prices of rural property, such peasant family farms possessed insufficient resources to compete financially with large capitalist enterprises entering the land market, and were consequently unable to purchase new holdings or expand existing ones. However, as long as the offspring of peasant families were able to migrate to and find well-paid industrial jobs in urban locations, this crisis remained dormant.[38] Peasant economy adopted internal regulatory mechanism in order to cope with a declining land base: among the descendents of Italian immigrants who settled in the state of Rio Grande do Sul, for example, this took the form of ultimogeniture, or the institutionalization of property inheritance by the youngest [*Santos*, 1978]. Sons and daughters of the peasant family married in age order, the last one to marry – the youngest – staying on in the parental home and inheriting the land, in exchange agreeing to take care of elderly parents.

Peasants or Workers?

Agrarian struggles in Brazil generated by these different conflicts became organized around two opposed rural identities and policies that were in conflict with one another. One of these was the reassertion of a smallholder identity, which entailed the restoration of peasant economy by means of land reform; this was the path taken by members of the Peasant Leagues, and also by supporters of the Maoist Communist Party of Brazil (*Partido Communista do Brasil*, or PC do B). In the view of the latter, the struggle in the countryside would be spearheaded by dispossessed peasants for land, and not by landless agricultural workers exploited through the wage relation. The pro-Moscow Brazilian Communist Party (*Partido Communista Brasileiro*, or PCB) took the opposite view, and argued that the struggle would be a peaceful one, involving the implementation of existing rural labour legislation recognizing the claims of both *colonos* and permanent labourers not as peasants with rights to land but rather as agricultural workers with rights to a decent wage, reduced working hours, and improved working conditions. In short, groups with a shared political outlook were fighting for different policy objectives (land reform; improvements in pay and conditions) on the basis of socio-economic identities that were equally distinct (peasants; agricultural wage labourers).

This contradictory and thus debilitating approach to rural identity and policy was inherited by those who subsequently became involved in agrarian issues: the Movement of Landless Rural Workers (*Movimento dos Trabulhadores Sem Terra*, or MST) and Church groups.[39] The latter consisted of the Roman Catholic and Lutheran Churches, both of which took up the question of rural crisis and conflict in the early 1970s, when Brazil was undergoing its severest period of political repression. For these Church groups, what was happening in the countryside generally, and in frontier areas especially, was nothing less than the violation of human rights (of Indian tribes, squatters, agricultural labourers, debt peons, and peasants). Up until the 1964 military coup, the Church generally had not only been reluctant to embrace the policy of land reform but also supported the dictatorship due to a fear on its part that agrarian struggles – and that of the Peasant Leagues in particular – threatened the institution of private property. The reason for this change of mind is complex, but has to do with the way in which the right to private property was seen by Church groups as theologically subordinate to (and thus overridden by) the broader issue of human rights. In short, private property came to be seen by Church groups as being at the root of social injustices inflicted by the powerful against the weak, and thus a motive for the wholesale appropriation by the rich of vast tracts of 'unoccupied' land and the murder of the poor and defenceless who attempted to resist this.

This social awareness on the part of Church groups also stemmed from the findings of their pastoral commissions investigating the situation of native populations and migrant squatters in the Amazon region.[40] In the polarized political climate of the dictatorship, the involvement of laymen in pastoral activities established what amounted to a 'popular front', enabling political cooperation between and coexistence among those who opposed the military régime. These associations were necessarily of varied and contradictory origins, not infrequently involving groups that hitherto had nothing in common except a long history of conflict with one another: Roman Catholics, Protestants, and Communists, the latter split along different political allegiances (pro-Moscow; Maoist) and organizational modalities (legal opposition; armed struggle). When the military dictatorship ended in the mid-1980s, two things happened to this politically heterogeneous opposition: on the one hand, the clergy withdrew from direct political involvement, leaving such activity to laymen, and on the other the MST appeared.[41]

III

RE-OCCUPYING THE AGRARIAN FRONTIER?

Not the least of the many ironies informing Brazilian history is the fact that dispossessed peasants and agricultural workers, the main players in conflicts over land, are not actually the main *political* players in the struggle for agrarian reform. The reason for this, which requires some explanation, lies in the way successive waves of rural population have been inserted within the broader discourse about what it means 'to be Brazilian', and the effect of this ideological exclusion/inclusion on the power of, respectively, members of the urban bourgeoisie and (especially) the intelligentsia on the one hand, and peasants, workers and tribals on the other, both to formulate and thus to delineate the parameters of specifically political solutions to the agrarian question in Brazil.

Like many other countries in the so-called Third World, the non-owning and/or impoverished components of the rural population in Brazil have been either excluded from or marginalized in relation to a broadly defined notion of 'belonging to', being 'part of', and thus in a very basic sense defining the nation. In common with other countries colonized by Europe, Brazil was defined largely by a small element of its urban inhabitants, the wealthier class which, in addition to being urban were also citizens, and citizens, moreover, whose outlook was shaped by all things European (culture, fashion, art, literature, music, ideas, politics). An outlook which, in effect, constituted a backwards glance at (not to say a longing for) its colonial past. The inescapable irony here is that the economic reproduction of this 'civilized' Brazil – urban, wealthy, Eurocentric – was underpinned by the surplus labour of a politically unrecognized and unrepresented plebeian 'other' Brazil: the peasants, workers and tribals employed in commercial agriculture the products of which (sugar, coffee, rubber) were exported to Europe, and whose very profitability made a European lifestyle possible for its Brazilian owners.

This notion of Brazilian national identity defined largely by external criteria – a European culture and society that was a colonial heritage – changed in the 1930s Revolution, when nationalism began to drawn from internal cultural phenomena (indigenous/rural/local artistic/musical influences, etc.) in order to construct a non-European self-awareness, or an authentically modern and forwards-looking Brazilian identity. Although this process of redefinition included what amounted to urban nostalgia for elements of plebeian rural tradition and culture – the hitherto excluded 'other' Brazil – the peasants, workers and tribals whose culture this was were themselves nevertheless excluded from both participation as citizens and an awareness of social/political rights linked to this. It was from the resulting gap – between the recognition of cultural value but the denial of the social and political rights that usually flow from such recognition – that many of the present agrarian disputes and conflicts have received their current impetus.

It is important, therefore, to understand four crucial points about the conflict over land which erupted in Brazil during the 1970s. First, it was a struggle undertaken by members of a rural workforce (especially in the Amazon region) to avoid being expelled from the lands they had occupied under the assumption that these belonged to the government (which would negotiate with them over usufruct rights). Second, theirs was a struggle to obtain or retain access to the means of labour required for survival, and as such had no wider programmatic status, nor did it exhibit a recognizably political form of awareness. Third, the same is true of smallholders in the south and parts of the south-east, who faced impoverishment as a result of being trapped between two rapidly closing frontiers, one in the towns (where secure, well-paid industrial jobs were no longer available to them) and the other in the countryside (where the intergenerational reproduction of peasant economy was blocked by corporate land purchases). And fourth, even casual rural workers, arguably the poorest of the poor, exhibited little interest in joining these struggles for land. All of these categories – squatter, peasant smallholder, potential migrant, and wage worker alike – interpreted politics simply as an act of good will on the part of the state, which in its 'kindness' could (and would) grant the poor land.

Agrarian Struggle for Bourgeois Ends?

The political input to the land issue came from another source altogether, provided by the discourse and agency of those who represented the peasantry, who might be termed the agents mediating peasant struggle: these belonged to party organizations of the left, which saw the struggle for land and agrarian reform as part of a much wider process of class struggle, the end object of which was socialism.[42] Generally speaking, these mediating groups are composed of the bourgeois and intellectual strata, and are frequently religious or party agents, or educators, even though many of them are closely or distantly related to peasant families, especially in the south. This is especially true of the MST leadership and representatives of the Pastoral Land Commission. Furthermore, these groups know that the consciousness of the peasants and rural workers themselves is limited to the immediate objective of survival, and that for this reason it is a consciousness devoid of a wide political dimension.[43] It is precisely because of this that the recent Brazilian history of the politicization of peasant struggles is a history in which the political consciousness of the mediating agents not infrequently shows no consistent link with the objectives of those who are, in theory, the main players on the rural scene.

As a result, the complex social and political realities of what in essence is a *struggle for land* have been reduced to the struggle for *land reform*, or that which is concerned not with the use but with the ownership of land. This has imbued the struggle for land with the characteristics of a 'from above' struggle in order to realize objectives – such as the manoeuvrings by Church group or political party for advantage and dominance – which have tended to be those of the Brazilian bourgeoisie. This kind of intervention by the middle class gives agrarian struggles generally a particular character: the peasantry makes a rapid transition from the role of an outcast and wholly marginalized 'other' to being incorporated with the status of client. From a culture of outright contempt, therefore, the rural subject is absorbed into a culture of patronage, which is nothing more than just another kind of 'otherness' (and, perhaps, even contempt). Underlying this transition is the idea that the rural poor will always need someone to talk/act on their behalf, a perception which downgrades or dismisses their own actions and utterances as politically inadequate, based as they are on an inability to comprehend the struggles of which they are a part.

It was on these kinds of terms – reflecting 'from above' rather than 'from below' objectives – that 'support' networks composed of bourgeois intermediaries were established in rural Brazil. Unquestionably, these were highly motivated and organizationally efficient, far more so than any networks or organization that workers, peasants and tribals could have put in place on their own. The outcome of this process was that the rural poor were now in a dependent position that was no longer economic or electoral, but rather political and party-related.[44] These bourgeois mediations ensured that the different sources of rural conflict, deriving as they did from dissimilar social relations of production and thus from separate and distinct causes, were consolidated politically under the single and all-embracing rubric of land reform. This overlooked the fact that, except for the case of smallholders in the south, all the other conflicts stemmed from production relations which, in different ways, combined the identity of peasant and wage labourer.[45] That is, a hybrid relational form the economic crisis of which could be solved in two opposing ways: either in a politically forward-looking fashion, by recognizing the subject as a wage labourer, whose class interests were those of a rural proletarian, or in a politically backward-looking fashion, by categorizing the subject as a peasant linked to a landlord by rental payments and whose interests were those of a petty-bourgeois. The first of these two distinct identities structured the programme of the Brazilian Communist Party, while the second informed the views of church groups, the Peasant Leagues, and the Maoist Communist Party of Brazil.

The political and programmatic significance of these two identities is that, as a worker, the labouring subject is committed to collective ownership of the means of labour, whereas as a peasant the same labouring subject is locked into an agrarian reform redistributing land on the basis of *individual ownership* – that is, land as private property. This raises, once again, the element of irony, since it is private property in land – as both church groups and Marxists agree (but for different reasons) – which is at the root of the recent and current agrarian crisis in Brazil: for church groups it gives rise to human rights violations, while for Marxists it constitutes an obstacle to socialism.

Of these two identities, it was the first – that of rural proletarian – which was recognized legislatively by the state before the 1964 military takeover, in the form of the Rural Landworker's Bill: it was this which hastened the eviction from large landholdings of resident permanent workers with usufruct rights, and their conversion into temporary wage labourers who were landless. The second identity – that of peasant – structured the claim by the Peasant Leagues to property rights embodied in a land reform programme, which appeared to landowners to be a harbinger of revolutionary socialism.[46] When the military took over the state, it promulgated a Land Bill which, for the first time in Brazilian history, defined what kind of land could be expropriated and redistributed via a land reform. The intention behind this policy, however, was the realization not of social justice but rather of national security as defined by the military dictatorship: namely, to guard against the possibility of a revolutionary transition to socialism.[47]

Over the longer term, the inability of any group or party successfully to address the question of which of these two identities should guide agrarian policy on the one hand, and political agency in the countryside on the other, has been profound. This failure was also an effect of the Cold War, and the prevailing fear among the Brazilian elite of anything resembling an autonomous mobilization of the rural 'voice from below'. Having ideologically constituted the 'enemy' as a uniform peasantry fighting for land reform, the state under the control of the military then reacted to them as if they were, by criminalizing it as 'subversive' and inflicting violent repression on this fictitious domestic 'enemy'. This fight, waged by the state against what in reality was a non-existent *national* entity, continued after the departure of the military.

For their part, those who opposed the dictatorship – church and leftist groups – have, like the military itself, adhered to this same national chimera. Accordingly, leftist groups and parties have persisted in their attempt ideologically to reconstitute a similarly homogenous peasantry out of a widely varying rural population, and to subordinate this politically to the struggle of the urban industrial working class. Thus, for example, both the MST and the Workers' Party (*Partido dos Trabalhadores*, or PT) follow this line, while the MST and the Church continue to act as if the rural stereotype conjured up by the military during the Cold War was real. One irony is that, in an important sense, both the right and left have shared a perception of a uniformly revolutionary peasantry because it is a powerful image that legitimizes and fuels their very different struggles. Another irony which deserves mention here is that the re-emergence in democratic Brazil of a specifically indigenist movement, at the centre of which is an emphasis on the politics of *cultural* identity, has been due in part to the success of the military during the era of dictatorship in suppressing other, politically more threatening forms of rural agency based on *economic* identity.[48]

The Emergence of a 'New' Rural Subject? Brazil is not Mexico...

With the end of the dictatorship and the Cold War, and the dismantling of its longstanding discourse and structure of confrontation, a democratic space was created which licensed freedom of expression, and into this gap emerged what might be termed a new rural subject, a 'voice from below' that no longer coincided with the way in which this had been depicted – either by mediating groups or by the military – in the recent past. Because those actually participating in agrarian struggles ceased to identify themselves as peasants or as wage labourers, such mobilizations were now classified as new social movements composed of 'minorities', native peoples and environmentalists, all of whom were engaged in the defence of nature. Thus, for example, indigenous land rights were included in the 1988 Constitution.[49] Rather than belonging to a proletariat and fighting as a member of the rural working class, therefore, the agricultural labourer is currently depicted as a 'new' subject, defined simply in terms of being poor and excluded, and whose agency is no longer aimed at systemic transition but consists instead of a politically less threatening process of quotidian 'resistance'.

Such a definition, however, raises as many problems as it purports to solve, not the least important of which are the following: to what degree is this 'new' subject any more homogenous – and thus a sociologically concrete category – than that which it replaced, the ubiquitous peasant? Is this 'new' rural subject in fact still the 'old' homogenous peasantry, but in a different guise? And, most importantly, what are the demands made by this 'new' rural subject, and how compatible are its programmatic aspirations with those of Brazilian society generally? Those who argue for the existence of a 'new' rural subject are faced with the same dilemma as earlier advocates of a revolutionary peasantry, in that it raises similar difficulties, not the least of which is that mobilization might take place on the basis of idioms and programmes formulated/constructed once again by 'mediating groups'.

In this connection it is important to recall that both the international media and much academic writing currently draws a parallel between the Zapatista movement in the Mexican state of Chiapas and the MST in Brazil.[50] Although there are a number of similarities between the two in terms of form – such as the active involvement of the Roman Catholic Church in providing each movement with a support network, the possession by both movements of a reasonably efficient level of organization, and the use by each of the same tactics to secure publicity – there is little in common in terms of substance. Unlike its Mexican counterpart, the MST in Brazil is *not* a rural protest movement generated by the continued existence of a large pre-capitalist (= 'feudal' or 'semi-feudal') landholding system that still holds sway in the countryside, much rather the contrary: as has been argued above, the roots of the MST lie in the specifically *capitalist* path of development followed by Brazilian agriculture. For this reason, it is necessary to avoid a facile and unwarranted association with the events in Chiapas.

Another reason for not drawing this parallel is that, by inference, it reduces the diversity and complexity of Brazilian agriculture and agrarian structure, together with the different causes and effects in terms of economic crisis faced by peasants, squatters, agricultural workers, and tribals, to events centred around the MST, merely because it is the latter that generates all the international media publicity and academic interest. Without underestimating the significance of the MST and its achievements, it is necessary to remember that another, equally important, and far older grassroots organization has operated in the Brazilian countryside: that is, the National Confederation of Land Workers (*Confederação Nacional dos Trabalhadores na Agricultura*, or CONTAG). Historically, the latter has been an authentic 'voice from below', at the centre of the social struggle for land, and representing millions of unionised rural workers. There are also other, less visible but no less crucial, rural organizations and unions that operate at the grassroots within specific localities throughout the country. Rather than the more conservative agency (quotidian resistance) attributed by international 'mediating groups' to the 'new' rural subject, these older trade union organizations have fought – and continue to fight – for systemic change in Brazil.

The international media reaction to the Zapatistas in Chiapas and the MST in Brazil is based on the assumption that these are 'new' social movements, and as such constitute a departure from traditional peasant movements.[51] This, however, is to confuse the form taken by the Zapatista and MST – which is certainly new – with the content of the movements, which is not. That the

Zapatistas and the MST have added new tactics to existing forms of struggle is undeniable, especially where the development of international linkages is concerned.[52] The proclamation by Commandante Marcos of the fact of the Zapatista revolt by an email sent to the *New York Times*, at the same time as he actually initiated the revolt itself, is undoubtedly a first in the history of peasant movements.[53] In much the same way, the MST has established contacts with more than two-dozen organizations abroad, especially in Europe, all of which provide it with support.

The existence of both networks stretching to and support in Europe is in part attributable to the political importance there of the burgeoning environmentalist cause. The latter has conferred iconic status on peasants engaged in ('ecologically friendly') subsistence agriculture and tribal populations surviving in forest areas, and consequently these have not only been confirmed in their status as 'new' rural subject but as such have assumed an important role in the anti-capitalist struggle waged in the West.[54] Whilst in a general sense welcome, this ideological development introduces yet another irony: before reopening the frontier, and reoccupying the land, peasants and tribals have first seized the imagination of the elite and the middle class – both at home and abroad – a development that those on the left, beginning with Marx and Lenin, failed to anticipate.[55] That these two agrarian movements in Latin America, the Zapatistas and the MST, have managed to tap into European networks so successfully, not least to secure funding, raises the possibility that the identity of the middle class 'mediating groups' which exercise 'from above' influence on rural mobilization, may have undergone a subtle change, and is now perhaps as much international as it is domestic.

CONCLUDING COMMENTS

It has been argued here that formation of the agrarian structure in Brazil has been shaped historically by the need on the part of commercial landowners to obtain and secure workers, and that the rural struggles arising from this have, in turn, been determined by two phenomena linked to this, one internal to the rural population and one external to it. The internal phenomenon consists of the sheer variety in the many components of the rural population itself, while the external phenomenon has been the influence exercised on the ideological formation/construction of the agrarian question (and thus also its solution) on the part of bourgeois elements in Brazilian society, specifically those with affiliations to political parties and church groups.

In what might be termed the process of opening, closing, and then reoccupying the agrarian frontier, it has been the control of labour-power rather than land that has been crucial to the development of a latifundist commercial agriculture in Brazil. The response of the latter to slave emancipation in the latter half of the nineteenth century was the immigration and settlement of European labour combined with internal migration, a process which gave rise, variously, to the *colono* system in coffee cultivation, to tenant farming based on the *morador* in sugar cultivation, rubber tappers in the Amazon, and independent smallholders in the south. In all these cases, usufruct rights of one sort or another (to land, to crops) enabled members of the rural workforce to unite two distinct identities: that of cultivation for oneself with working for others. This coexistence of peasant economy and agricultural labour, and with it the crucial role of the former as a safety valve mechanism for economic crisis and/or depeasantization elsewhere, was broken as capitalist expansion led to the elimination of traditional usufruct rights, peasant dispossession, the invasion of indigenous territory, and the replacement of permanent workers by casual labour, processes completed under the military dictatorship. However, the dual identity of the workforce was reproduced in the agrarian struggles conducted both against the dictatorship and the subsequent democratic government, not least because of the role played by non-peasant 'mediating groups' (the church, political groups and parties) in the ideological reproduction of each, a process that culminated in the emergence of what is now termed a 'new' rural subject.

The problems generated by this 'new' rural subject stem in turn from the internal phenomenon, or the fact that the rural population in Brazil is not only different from its counterparts in the rest of Latin America, but also more differentiated in terms of background, culture, and class. When compared to the history of other peasant populations in Latin America, therefore, that of what is usually termed 'the Brazilian peasantry' is distinct, as are its formation, culture, and institutions. The difficulties experienced by observers attempting to insert a 'new' rural subject – squatters, peasants, agricultural labourers, rubber tappers, and tribals – into a broader pattern of new social movements in Latin America, merely underlines this fact. At the root of this distinctiveness is the variety of rural subjects, whether 'old' or 'new', that constitute the agrarian history of Brazil: Indians emancipated from slavery in the eighteenth century, but retained by their erstwhile masters within a relation of dependence; nomadic Indians and Creoles with no defined rural status since colonial times; modern descendents of nineteenth century European immigrants who settled as *colonos* or independent peasant cultivators; and freed black slaves who became rural wage labourers. These distinct origins, ethnicities and cultures – not to say social relations of production – make it difficult to speak of 'a Brazilian peasantry', whose characteristics, economic interests and political outlook converge in a single project.

Ironically, this internal phenomenon – the variety and distinctiveness of rural Brazil – is in effect denied by those who compose the external phenomenon: elements of the middle class, of rural petty-bourgeois backgrounds but now mainly urban and cosmopolitan in ideology and political outlook, who – as members of church groups and political parties – have influenced the direction taken by rural struggles in a number of significant ways (the provision of networks, support, finance). It is these 'mediating groups' which have tended to amalgamate all the rural subjects, from distinct cultural backgrounds and in equally distinct economic relations, into a uniform 'Brazilian peasantry' with an uniform political interest. The 'voice from below', embodying the diverse origins and different economic demands of the rural subject, have accordingly been overridden by the 'voice from above' belonging to these mediating groups. When the rural subject has been conservative, the mediating group has tended to be radical, and *vice versa.*

This contradiction is perhaps nowhere more evident than in the different interpretations of what is meant by reform of the Brazilian countryside. First, there are unionized groups, such as CONTAG, with a long history of class struggle against capitalists and landlords, and a political ideology that both addresses and simultaneously requires wider systemic change in Brazilian society. Second, there are church-affiliated and church-inspired groups, such as the MST, which see no need for radical systemic transformation, and adhere much rather to a communitarian vision in which capitalist and worker enjoy a tension-free parity of esteem. And third, there are rural subjects affiliated to both of these groups and none, whose actions are based on the need to have access to land as the means of labour, and yet who are guided by family and religious values, and also by the ideology of 'moral economy'.[56]

It could be argued that these values – family, community, land for subsistence, religion – that are usually associated with backwards-looking forms of agrarian tradition and thus seemingly conservative, are much rather the opposite. That is, they are the product of an undeniably modern capitalism, not least because of the crucial distinction made by the rural labouring subject concerned: namely, between *land as the instrument of labour* (to provide work and basic subsistence for himself and his family) and *land that is owned privately* (to provide the owner with profit, as a result of speculation, or generating rent or surplus-value). In short, when considering the issue of land the labouring subject makes a distinction between use-value for himself and his family and exchange-value, by capital for the purpose of accumulation. In this distinction lies, perhaps, a clue to the modernity of the 'voice from below', and also to the way in which family farming in Brazil might be included in a political future.

NOTES

1. The concept 'invention of tradition' is examined and applied to many different case studies (the British Isles, Victorian India, colonial Africa, and Europe) in the collection edited by Hobsbawm and Ranger [1983]. See also McNeish, this volume.
2. Although their class interests include the appropriation of land rent, and thus also a speculative and economically backward role in the development of capitalism, the class position of big landowners in Brazil is more accurately characterized as that of a bourgeoisie. This does not mean one should ignore that, throughout this period, a powerful faction in this class has acted as land speculators, interested in obtaining the gains from land speculation rather than in making land productive. To define all big landowners simply as belonging to a parasitically pre-capitalist category of rent collectors, however, would be to misunderstand their economic significance in the contemporary history of Brazilian capitalist development.
3. It goes without saying that the notion of an economic frontier is contested. See Wagley [1974] and Hennessy [1978] for the examination of the frontier thesis as applied to Latin America. For a different view, see Cleary [1993].
4. In a very real sense the agrarian question has been – in one form or another – at the centre of most debate about industrialization. Its clearest formulation was by Marxists in their arguments about historical transformation, and especially the presence of (non-capitalist or 'feudal') obstacles to economic development in Russia and Germany at the end of the nineteenth century [*Lenin*, 1964; *Kautsky*, 1988]. It has also surfaced periodically in debates about economic development in Latin America [*de Janvry*, 1981].
5. For important accounts of the labour regime on Brazilian coffee plantations prior to the abolition of slavery, see Dean [1976] and Stein [1985].
6. See Bethell [1970] and Scott *et al.* [1988] for details about slave emancipation in Brazil.
7. On this see the classic interpretation by C.L.R. James [1938] and Eric Williams [1944].
8. In other words, slave labour became too expensive. The same kind of argument has been made with regard to the ending of plantation slavery in the antebellum south; its applicability to the latter context, however, has not gone unchallenged – it has also been the subject of critical analysis by economic historians [*Wright*, 1978].
9. For these migrations, and the subsequent history of the migrants involved, see Denoon [1984], Curtin [1990] and Willems [1948].
10. A recent analysis by Freitas [1994] shows how, after the abolition of the slave trade, the attempt in Minas Gerais to enslave free workers ensured that in effect an illicit traffic in unfree labour continued.
11. See Holloway [1980] for the *colonato* contract in São Paulo.
12. For the role of gender and kinship in *colono*/landowner relations on São Paulo coffee estates from the mid-nineteenth to the late twentieth century, see Stolcke [1988] and Stolcke and Hall [1983].
13. This is a familiar threat, and one that has been utilized by landowners everywhere – not just in Latin America - whenever continued usufruct rights to land were part of the production relation governing the employment of an agricultural workforce. In parts of Europe, for example, this kind of pressure still exists, and takes the form of 'tied' housing, a situation whereby an agricultural worker who loses his job also loses his home.
14. For the economic transformation of Brazilian sugar plantations, and in particular how this entailed changes in the labour regime, see among others Reis [1977], Taylor [1978], Schwartz [1985], and Eisenberg [1989].
15. As one coffee grower confirmed to a Dutch researcher [*Meijer*, 1951: 174] during the early 1950s, the reinvestment of profits in agricultural improvement was always linked to whether or not coffee prices were high, and whether or not landowners thought they would remain high. Hence the view that 'when asked what he was going to do with his profits [one fazendeiro] answered that he was going to buy more coffee soils, or, if he thought a crisis

within a few years likely, that he would probably suggest the purchase of real estate in one of the big cities. The answer "I am investing a big part of my profits in my existing fazenda, by fighting erosion, laying out new plots in the modern way, replacing badly producing trees by young ones, breeding [coffee plants] on my own seed beds from carefully selected material, improving the harvesting methods, cleaning, fermentation and so on" will rarely be given. "Get rich quickly and forget what comes afterward" seems to be still the attitude of the majority of coffee producers.'

16. According to Julião [1972: 11], '*cambão* is the name given to the dry, leafless and earless maize stalk. It also refers to the piece of wood [= yoke] hung around an ox's neck... Finally *cambão* is the day's unpaid labour demanded by landowners once a week from their peasants as rent for their land...'
17. For the agrarian structure of the Brazilian northeast generally at the mid-twentieth century, see Goodman [1977].
18. For the role of drought in driving poor peasants and agricultural workers out of the semi-arid north-eastern region of Brazil, see de Castro [1952], Hall [1978], and Davis [2001: 377ff.].
19. In the case of rubber production in Amazónas at the beginning of the twentieth century, newly recruited labourers were assigned a low-yielding area, the object being precisely to prevent them from being able to cover their subsistence costs and expenses during this period, and thus making debt a necessary outcome [*Ballivián and Pinilla*, 1912: 245–6].
20. As will be seen below, such relations continue to flourish in the Amazonian region.
21. For more details about the struggles conducted by *posseiros* during the military dictatorship, see Souza Martins [1980].
22. The *Contestado* uprising, which took place in the southern states of Paraná and Santa Catarina, involved some 20,000 peasants, many of whom had been dispossessed as a result of railway expansion.
23. The most influential recent contribution to the debate about the role of the informal sector economy in Latin America is that by de Soto [1989].
24. This change, which reduced even further the already precarious economic condition of the plantation workforce, led to the consolidation of the Peasant Leagues (*Ligas Camponêsas*) demanding a radical agrarian reform programme. It was advocacy of the latter policy that led, in part, to the 1964 military coup. For the role of the Peasant Leagues, see Julião [1972] and also Hewitt [1969]; for the mobilization of rural workers in São Paulo prior to the 1964 coup, see Welch [1995].
25. In an important sense, the expulsion from the sugar plantations of permanent workers with usufruct rights to land, and their transformation into temporary landless labour, completed the process of capitalist transition that began when the slave trade ended. In other respects, however, the plantation work regime continued very much as it was, which suggests that accumulation in rural Brazil was able to proceed without undertaking the kind of radical change usually associated with an agrarian capitalist transition [*Sigaud*, 1979].
26. On the socio-economic characteristics and working conditions of *bóia-fria* labour, see Spindel [1985].
27. It is not unusual for the same migrant workers who harvest sugarcane in the north-east to harvest it in the south-east or in the midwest as well.
28. The amount saved through the tax exemption was to be invested in Amazonia, up to a limit of 75 per cent of the capital of the new company.
29. For peasant economy in Amazonia, see Nugent [1993]. See also his contribution to this volume.
30. There were also state-sponsored land colonization schemes at this conjuncture. For an account of just such a project in Rondônia during the 1970s, see Martine [1982].
31. Indian lands were invaded by large corporations, although the Brazilian Constitution expressly forbids the expropriation of land traditionally inhabited by Indian tribes.
32. For an account of this process, see Mendes [1992].

33. It is significant that, despite being faced with the same kind of violent incursion and expropriation, initially no political alliance was formed between squatters and the Indian tribal groupings who inhabited the Amazon region. To some degree, this was an effect of the mutual suspicions with which each regarded the other (perhaps more accurately, the 'other'). For their part, peasant smallholders who were themselves not infrequently of Indian descent, nurtured prejudicial views about tribal populations, a legacy of colonial missionary teachings. This was reciprocated by Indian groups, which for their part tended to categorize all non-indigenous people as potential enemies, a perception bolstered in the late 1980s when independent gold prospectors (*garimpeiros*) invaded lands in the Amazon that were traditionally part of Yanomami territory.
34. It goes without saying that, whereas Marx himself recognized and drew attention to the violence accompanying the accumulation process, many of his more recent followers have tended to underplay or even ignore this aspect of economic development in the Third World. For an account of the link between violence and agrarian capitalist expansion on the Brazilian frontier, see Foweraker [1981; 1982].
35. For the impact of capitalism on the Amazon region, see among others Barbira-Scazzocchio [1980], Bunker [1988], and Hall [1989].
36. On contemporary forms of debt peonage in the Amazon region, see Souza Martins [1990; 1997] and Esterci [1979; 1987; 1994].
37. Evolutionist marxism is associated most closely with the 'semifeudal' thesis, which insists that capitalist development proceeds through stages each one of which is, in terms of labour regime, an improvement on what came before (see the contributions to the collection edited by Brass and van der Linden [1997] for a discussion of the theoretical issues). Upholding a position that is in its essentials not so different from the Whig interpretation of history so beloved of bourgeois academics, exponents of the 'semifeudal' thesis maintain wrongly that where capitalism exists, ('feudal' or 'semifeudal') unfree production relations are absent, and where the latter are present, capitalism is absent. In the case of Brazil, such a notion was challenged by the justly celebrated analysis of Andre Gunder Frank [1971: 249ff. – 'The Myth of Feudalism'].
38. For more on the crisis of peasant smallholders in the south, see Papma [1992].
39. For more on this, see Souza Martins [1989]. The MST appeared in the mid-1980s as a result of Roman Catholic militants connected with the Pastoral Land Commission, and consequently enjoyed the support of the Church.
40. The impact of bodies such as the Pastoral Land Commission (*Comisão Pastoral da Terra*, or CTP), connected to the National Conference of Brazilian Bishops, and the Centre for the Support of the Small Farmer (CAP), funded by the Lutheran Church, should not be underestimated.
41. See Maybury-Lewis [1994] for a useful account of the MST. The latter derived its impetus from struggles conducted by poor and landless agricultural workers from the state of Goiás. These workers started camping out on the strip of government-held land between the barbed wire fences separating farms from the road, an area designed to be used by road maintenance crews and equipment. This strip of land was taken over for a dual purpose: not only for habitation (= the installation of black plastic tents, the squatters' living quarters) but also for cultivation. This tactic rapidly spread and changed, becoming a springboard for the invasion of uncultivated land on neighbouring estates. At first the MST attempted to justify this direct action by invoking existing legislation (the Land Bill), but subsequently used this kind of direct action (land invasions) in order to stimulate state intervention.
42. Dom Tomás Balduíno, retired bishop of Goiás Velho and coordinator of the Pastoral Land Commission, highlights this in a recent interview, observing [*Balduíno*, 2001:18] that 'Indeed, socialism is the horizon...'.
43. The MST is currently engaged in an attempt to formulate a wider political programme, addressing issues such as domestic food security, and the democratization of landownership [*Robles*, 2001]. The emphasis is still very much on what ought to happen in the countryside,

rather than the whole of Brazil.

44. The argument that, in place of traditional domination, a new form of clientage had been established by leftist political groups over Brazil's peasants, was put forward initially by Galjart [1964].
45. Hence the view expressed by Joâo Quartim [1971: 85], a member of the Popular Revolutionary Vanguard, not long after the 1964 coup: 'Whether the likelihood of agrarian reform is a political or economic question is, one can now see, really a side issue. What matters is the content of the reform. Though the regime may have nothing to fear any longer from the latifundists themselves and though it may be fully prepared to dispossess them by slowly transforming the old latifundia into large scale capitalist enterprises, they still have everything to fear from an immiserated peasantry. Such a transformation of landless peasants into agricultural wage-earners could only make the situation in the countryside more explosive.' In short, the assumption is that there is only one 'authentic' rural identity – that of peasants. It is an identity, moreover, that is to be built into an agrarian reform programme.
46. Prior to the 1964 coup, a landless workers' movement *(Movimento de Agriculturos Sem Terra*, or MASTER) had appeared in Rio Grande do Sul, backed by the Brazilian Labour Party of the then already deceased President Vargas. At a time when there were no laws in the country supporting this policy, let alone any public bodies addressing social problems in rural areas, MASTER advocated an agrarian reform as a solution to the problem of small farms. These early pressures for change in the land tenure structure of the south were preceded by a movement composed of permanent workers from the north-eastern sugarcane plantations, which peaked with the organization in 1955 of the Peasant Leagues, led by Francisco Julião, from the Socialist Party.
47. Landowners throughout Latin America still feared both the example and the spread of the 1959 Cuban Revolution and – before that – the 1949 Chinese Revolution. However, it is necessary to question the extent to which those leftist groups (such as the Maoists) really were radical in seeking to subdivide the land into peasant smallholdings, thereby institutionalizing an agrarian system based on an indisputably Chayanovian peasant family farm. Historically, the latter unit is one against which Marxists such as Lenin, Trotsky, Luxemburg, Kautsky and Preobrashensky all fought, pointing out that, once established, peasant economy would effectively prevent the further socialization of land, and its consolidation in large units of production, state-owned, collectively-run, and centrally administered.
48. This argument has been made recently by Ramos [1991].
49. On the connection between the politicization of indigenous land rights and the 1988 Constitution, see Carvalho [2000].
50. See Harvey [1998] for an analysis of the Zapatista movement in Chiapas.
51. An important aspect of this media exposure is the fact that peasants and tribals, together with their struggles, have installed themselves in literary and cinematic discourse of Western capitalism over the past three decades. Thus, for example, films such as *Aguirre, Wrath of God* (1972) and *Fitzcarraldo* (1982), both directed by Werner Herzog, and *The Emerald Forest* (1985), directed by John Boorman, are not only set in the Amazon jungle but have as their sub-text a discourse about 'nature', the 'natural world' and an equally 'natural' group of indigenous inhabitants. Similarly, the film *The Burning Season* (1994), directed by John Frankenheimer, is a fictional portrayal of the struggle by Chico Mendes and the rubber tappers against cattle ranchers and landowners.
52. It is necessary to qualify even this claim to newness, however, given both the fact and the effectiveness of the international campaign mounted in the 1960s to save Hugo Blanco, the leader of the peasant movement in the Peruvian province of La Convención, from the death penalty.
53. Lest the element of irony be missed here, this departure in form is due to the simple fact that all previous agrarian movements in Mexico did not have access to the internet.

54. On this point, see the arguments put forward by the Via Campesina [*Desmarais*, 2002].
55. For more on this point, see Crisenoy [1978]. Such a development also puts in question the perception of Marx [1926] himself that the peasantry was incapable of undertaking political action on any scale other than at a local level.
56. The concept 'moral economy' as used here has the same meaning as when used by Thompson [1993].

REFERENCES

Andrade, Manuel Correia de, 1979, *The Land and People of Northeast Brazil*, translated by Dennis V. Johnson, Albuquerque, NM: University of New Mexico Press.

Balduíno, Dom Tomás, 2001, 'A ação da Igreja Católica e o desenvolvimento rural', *in Estudos Avançados*, No.43 (Setembro/Dezembro), São Paulo: Instituto de Estudos Avançados da Universidade de São Paulo.

Ballivián, M.V., and C.F. Pinilla, 1912, *Monografía de la industria de la goma elástica en Bolivia*, Dirección General de Estadística y Estudios Geográficos, Bolivia.

Barbira-Scazzocchio, Françoise, 1980, 'From Native Forest to Private Property: The Development of Amazonia for Whom?', in Françoise Barbira-Scazzocchio (ed.) [1980].

Barbira-Scazzocchio, Françoise (ed.), 1980, *Land, People and Planning in Contemporary Amazonia*, Cambridge: Centre of Latin American Studies.

Beiguelman, Paula, 1968, *A Formação do Povo no Complexo Cafeiro: Aspectos Políticos*, São Paulo: Livraria Pioneira Editora.

Bethell, Leslie, 1970, *The Abolition of the Brazilian Slave Trade*, Cambridge: Cambridge University Press.

Branford, Sue, and Oriel Glock, 1985, *The Last Frontier: Fighting over Land in the Amazon*, London: Zed Books.

Brass, Tom, and Marcel van der Linden (eds.), 1997, *Free and Unfree Labour: The Debate Continues*, Bern: Peter Lang AG.

Bunker, Stephen G., 1988, *Underdeveloping the Amazon: Extraction, Unequal Exchange and the Failure of the Modern State*, Chicago, IL: The University of Chicago Press.

Carvalho, Georgia O., 2000, 'The Politics of Indigenous Land Rights in Brazil', *Bulletin of Latin American Research*, Vol.19, No.4.

Castro, Josué de, 1952, *The Geography of Hunger*, London: Gollancz.

Cleary, David, 1993, 'After the Frontier: Problems with Political Economy in the Modern Brazilian Amazon', *Journal of Latin American Studies*, Vol.25, Part 2.

Crisenoy, Chantal de, 1978, *Lénine Face aux Mujiks*, Paris: Seuil.

Cunha, Euclydes da, 1946, *À Margem da História*, 6th ed., Porto: Livraria Lello & Irmão, Editores.

Curtin, Philip D., 1990, *The Rise and Fall of the Plantation Complex: Essays in Atlantic History*, Cambridge: Cambridge University Press.

Davatz, Thomas, 1941, *Memórias de um Colono no Brasil (1850) – Translation, preface and notes of Sérgio Buarque de Holanda*, São Paulo: Livraria Martins.

Davis, Mike, 2001, *Late Victorian Holocausts: El Niño Famines and the making of the Third World*, London: Verso.

De Janvry, Alain, 1981, *The Agrarian Question and Reformism in Latin America*, London and Baltimore: The Johns Hopkins University Press.

De Soto, Hernando, 1989, *The Other Path: The Invisible Revolution in the Third World*, London: I.B. Tauris.

Dean, Warren, 1976, *Rio Claro: A Brazilian Plantation System, 1820–1920*, Stanford, CA: Stanford University Press.

Denoon, Donald, 1984, 'The Political Economy of Labour Migration to Settler Societies: Australasia, Southern Africa, and Southern South America, between 1890 and 1914', in Shula Marks and Peter Richardson (eds.) [1984].

Desmarais, Annette-Aurélie, 2002, 'The Vía Campesina: Consolidating and International Peasant and Farm Movement', *The Journal of Peasant Studies*, Vol.29, No.2.

Duncan, Kenneth, Ian Rutledge, and Colin Harding (eds.), 1977, *Land and Labour in Latin America*, Cambridge: Cambridge University Press.

Eisenberg, Peter L., 1977, 'The Consequences of Modernization for Brazil's Sugar Plantations in the Nineteenth Century', in Kenneth Duncan, Ian Rutledge, and Colin Harding (eds.) [1977].

Eisenberg, Peter L., 1989, *Homens esquecidos: escravos e trabalhadores livres no Brasil, séculos XVIII e XIX*, Campinas: Editora da Unicamp.

Esterci, Neide, 1979, 'Peonagem na Amazônia', *Dados*, No.20.

Esterci, Neide, 1987, *Conflito No Araguia: Peões e posseiros contra a grande empresa*, Petrópolis: Editora Vozes Ltda.

Esterci, Neide, 1994, *Escravos da Disugualídade: Um estudo sobre o uso repressivo da força de trabalho hoje*, Rio de Janeiro: Editora Tempo Brasileiro.

Foweraker, Joe, 1981, *The Struggle for Land: A Political Economy of the Pioneer Frontier in Brazil from 1930 to the Present Day*, Cambridge: Cambridge University Press.

Foweraker, Joe, 1982, 'Accumulation and Authoritarianism on the Pioneer Frontier in Brazil', *The Journal of Peasant Studies*, Vol.10, No.1.

Frank, Andre Gunder, 1971, *Capitalism and Underdevelopment in Latin America; Historical Studies of Chile and Brazil*, Harmondsworth: Penguin.

Freitas, Judy Bieber, 1994, 'Slavery and Social Life: Attempts to Reduce Free People to Slavery in the Sertão Mineiro, Brazil, 1850–1871', *Journal of Latin American Studies*, Vol.26, Part 3.

Galjart, Benno, 1964, 'Class and "Following" in Rural Brazil', *América Latina*, No.3 (July–September), Rio de Janeiro.

Goodman, D.E., 1977, 'Rural Structure, Surplus Mobilisation and Modes of Production in a Peripheral Region: The Brazilian North-East', *The Journal of Peasant Studies*, Vol.5, No.1.

Hall, Anthony L., 1978, *Drought and Irrigation in North-east Brazil*, Cambridge: Cambridge University Press.

Hall, Anthony L., 1989, *Developing Amazonia*, Manchester: Manchester University Press.

Harvey, Neil, 1998, *The Chiapas Rebellion: The Struggle for Land and Democracy*, Durham, NC: Duke University Press.

Hennessy, Alistair, 1978, *The Frontier in Latin American History*, London: Edward Arnold.

Hewitt, Cynthia N., 1969, 'Brazil: The Peasant Movement of Pernambuco, 1961–1964', in Henry A. Landsberger (ed.), *Latin American Peasant Movements*, London and Ithaca: Cornell University Press.

Hobsbawm, Eric, and Terence Ranger (eds.), 1983, *The Invention of Tradition*, Cambridge: Cambridge University Press.

Holloway, Thomas H., 1980, *Immigrants on the Land: Coffee and Society in São Paulo,1886–1934*, Chapel Hill, NC: The University of North Carolina Press.

Ianni, Octavio, 1978, *A Luta pela Terra – História social da terra e da luta pela terra numa área da Amazônia*, Petrópolis: Editora Vozes Ltda.

James, C.L.R., 1938, *The Black Jacobins: Toussaint L'overture and the Santo Domingo Revolution*, London: Secker & Warburg.

Julião, Francisco, 1972, *Cambão – The Yoke: the hidden face of Brazil*, translated by John Butt, Harmondsworth: Penguin.

Kautsky, Karl, 1988, *The Agrarian Question*, 2 Vols., London: Zwan Publications.

Lenin, V.I., 1964, 'The Development of Capitalism in Russia', *Collected Works*, Vol.3, Moscow: Foreign Languages Publishing House.

Martine, George, 1982, 'Colonisation in Rôndonia; Continuities and Perspectives', in Peter Peek and Guy Standing (eds.) [1982].
Martins, José de Souza, 1980, 'Fighting for Land: Indians and *Posseiros* in Legal Amazonia', in Françoise Barbira-Scazzocchio (ed.) [1980].
Martins, José de Souza, 1989, *Caminhada no chão da noite: emancipação política e libertação nos movimentos socias no campo*, São Paulo: Editora Hucitec.
Martins, José de Souza, 1990, *O Cativeiro da Terra*, 4ª Edição, São Paulo: Editora Hucitec.
Martins, José de Souza, 1997, 'The Reappearance of Slavery and the Reproduction of Capital on the Brazilian Frontier', in Tom Brass and Marcel van der Linden (eds.) [1997].
Marks, Shula, and Peter Richardson (eds.), 1984, *International Labour Migration: Historical Perspectives*, London: Maurice Temple Smith.
Marx, Karl, 1926, *The Eighteenth Brumaire of Louis Bonaparte*, translated by Eden and Cedar Paul, London: Allen and Unwin.
Maybury-Lewis, Biorn, 1994, *The Politics of the Possible: The Brazilian Rural Workers' Trade Union Movement, 1964–1985*, Philadelphia, PA: Temple University Press.
Meijer, Hendrik, 1951, *Rural Brazil at the Cross-roads*, Wageningen: H. Veenman & Zonen.
Mendes, Chico, 1992, 'Chico Mendes – The Defence of Life', *The Journal of Peasant Studies*, Vol.20, No.1.
Nugent, Stephen, 1993, *Amazon Caboclo Society: An Essay on Invisibility and Peasant Economy*, Oxford: Berg.
Papma, Frans, 1992, *Contesting the Household Estate: Southern Brazilian Peasants and Modern Agriculture*, Amsterdam: CEDLA.
Peek, Peter, and Guy Standing (eds.), 1982, *State Policies and Migration*, London and Canberra: Croom Hill.
Quartim, João, 1971, *Dictatorship and Armed Struggle in Brazil*, London: New Left Books.
Ramos, Alcida Rita, 1991, 'A Hall of Mirrors: The Rhetoric of Indigenism in Brazil', *Critique of Anthropology*, Vol.11, No.2.
Reis, Jaime, 1977, 'From *banguê* to *usina*: Social Aspects of Growth and Modernization in the Sugar Industry of Pernambuco, Brazil, 1850–1920', in Kenneth Duncan, Ian Rutledge and Colin Harding (eds.) [1977].
Robles, Wilder, 2001, 'The Landless Rural Workers Movement (MST) in Brazil', *The Journal of Peasant Studies*, Vol.28, No.2.
Santos, José Vicente Tavares dos, 1978, *Colonos do Vinho*, São Paulo: Editora Hucitec.
Santos, Roberto, 1980, *História Econômica da Amazônia (1800–1920)*, São Paulo: T. A. Queiroz.
Schwartz, Stuart B., 1985, *Sugar Plantations in the Formation of Brazilian Society: Bahia, 1550–1835*, Cambridge: Cambridge University Press.
Scott, Rebecca J., Seymour Drescher, Hebe Maria Mattos de Castro, George Reid Andrews, and Robert M. Levine, 1988, *The Abolition of Slavery and the Aftermath of Emancipation in Brazil*, London and Durham, NC: Duke University Press.
Sigaud, Ligia Maria, 1979, *Os Clandestinos e os Direitos*, São Paulo: Duas Cidades.
Silva, José Graziano da, 1980, 'Progresso Técnico e Relações de Trabalho na Agricultura Paulista', unpublished Ph.D. Thesis, Campinas: Unicamp.
Spindel, Cheywa R., 1985, 'Temporary Work in Brazilian Agriculture: "Boia-fria" – A Category under Investigation', in Guy Standing (ed.) [1985].
Standing, Guy (ed.), 1985, *Labour Circulation and the Labour Process*, London: Croom Helm.
Stein, Stanley J., 1985, *Vassouras – A Brazilian Coffee County, 1850–1900: The Roles of Planter and Slave in a Plantation Society*, Princeton, NJ: Princeton University Press.
Stolcke, Verena, 1988, *Coffee Planters, Workers and Wives: Class Conflict and Gender Relations on São Paulo Coffee Plantations, 1850–1980*, New York: St. Martin's Press.
Stolcke, Verena, and Michael M. Hall, 1983, 'The Introduction of Free Labour on São Paulo Coffee Plantations', *The Journal of Peasant Studies*, Vol.10, Nos.2–3.
Taylor, Kit Sims, 1978, *Sugar and the Underdevelopment of Northeastern Brazil, 1500–1970*, Gainesville, FL: University Presses of Florida.

Thompson, E.P., 1993, 'The Moral Economy of the English Crowd in the Eighteenth Century', in *Customs in Common*, Harmondsworth: Penguin Books.

Wagley, Charles (ed.), 1974, *Man in the Amazon*, Gainesville, FL: The University Presses of Florida.

Welch, Cliff, 1995, 'Rivalry and Unification: Mobilising Rural Workers in São Paulo on the Eve of the Brazilian *Golpe* of 1964', *Journal of Latin American Studies*, Vol.27, Part 1.

Willems, Emilio, 1948, *Aspectos da aculturação dos japoneses no Estado de São Paulo*, São Paulo: Universidade de São Paulo, Faculdade de Filosofia, Ciências e Letras.

Williams, Eric, 1944, *Capitalism and Slavery*, Chapel Hill, NC: University of North Carolina Press.

Wright, Gavin, 1978, *The Political Economy of the Cotton South: Households, Markets, and Wealth in the Nineteenth Century*, New York: W.W. Norton & Company, Inc.

On Which Side of What Barricade? Subaltern Resistance in Latin America and Elsewhere

TOM BRASS

'Subaltern tyrants are ever the most intolerant, and intolerable' – An observation made two centuries ago by J.G. Zimmerman [1800: 4]

'A system of mal-government begins by refusing man his rights, and ends by depriving him of the power of appreciating the value of that which he has lost.' – Maxim CLXXXIV [*Colton*, 1835: 127].

'This is the only way to travel' – Groucho Marx in the film *Duck Soup* (1933), as Rufus T. Firefly, President of Freedonia, sitting on a motorcycle that isn't going anywhere.

INTRODUCTION

Where the study of peasants is concerned, there can be little doubt as to the identity of the most fashionable and influential paradigm exercising intellectual hegemony in academic circles over the past two decades: the Subaltern Studies project, a six-volume series edited by Ranajit Guha that appeared throughout the 1980s.[1] Conceived initially as an alternative historiography of South Asia, it sought to reinterpret both the rural 'voicc from below' and grassroots agrarian mobilization that occurred during the colonial era. Its goal was simple: to expunge the outdated view of South Asian peasants as ideologically passive/disempowered – a tainted legacy of colonialism, it was argued – and replace it with an appropriately (post-) modern (or post-colonial) perception of them as active/empowered rural subjects. For this reason, the epistemological focus of the Subaltern Studies project was from the outset on the idioms of agrarian protest, the object being to rescue and give expression to hitherto subordinated and/or ignored

Tom Brass formerly lectured in the Social and Political Sciences Faculty at the University of Cambridge.

forms of ideological utterance. An important effect of subalternist methodology – uncovering a hidden 'authentic' form of plebeian discourse/agency – was nothing less than the reinstatement of 'the peasant' as the subject of the historical process in South Asia.

The critique which follows focuses on the work of Beverley, Canclini, and Albó, whose symptomatic postmodern/post-colonial theoretical approach inadvertently reveals all the difficulties that arise from the attempt to apply an analytical framework based on the concept 'subaltern' to Latin America.[2] Not only does their work epitomize all that has been wrong with much supposedly 'critical' analysis by those within the domain of cultural studies of agrarian change in the so-called Third World over the past two decades, but the confusions/silences which pervade this approach serve as a useful warning against the perils arising from a superficial acquaintance with Marxism, with its 'other', populism, and with the Subaltern Studies series itself. Like its South Asian counterpart, the Latin American subaltern framework constitutes a reaction to and simultaneously an intervention in longstanding and ongoing debates between Marxists and populists about the agrarian question: that is, the degree to which peasant economy/culture in Latin America is undermined by capitalist development (the *descampesinista* position) or impervious to this process (the *campesinista* position). In contrast to Marxism, which maintains that petty commodity producers are differentiated in the course of class formation/struggle, therefore, the subaltern framework not only reifies peasant economy (= peasant family farming) but also attributes this survival capacity to the efficacy of an empowering cultural resistance against capitalism by smallholders mobilized on the basis of non-class identity.[3]

This presentation is divided into three sections, the first of which examines the search by subalternists for evidence of an 'authentic' and empowering Latin American subaltern identity, as manifested in ancient/indigenous nationhood, the carnivalesque, and literary accounts, plus the questions these quests raise concerning the theorization of subaltern consciousness/agency. In the second section a specifically plebeian pro-peasant ideology not dissimilar to that espoused by exponents of the subaltern framework is considered in relation to the discourse of the political right in Latin America and elsewhere, while the focus of the third is on the unsuccessful attempt to depict contemporary subaltern resistance as a politically progressive form of anti-fascist agency not unlike the 1930s Popular Front. Against the latter view, it is argued that – as Trotsky and other Marxists pointed out at that same conjuncture – an essentialist concept of 'the peasantry' (= subaltern identity) and 'peasant resistance' (= subaltern mobilization) which it generated have tended, historically, to be grassroots identity/agency linked to a reactionary politics.

I

That many current texts about the rural grassroots in the so-called Third World nowadays carry the obligatory word 'subaltern' instead of 'class' in the title, and within such analyses the terms 'struggle', 'revolution' and 'socialism' have been replaced with concepts such as 'resistance', 'identity' and 'democracy', is symptomatic of the present intellectual dominance exercised by the postmodern 'new' populism in general, and in particular the agrarian myth.[4] Given this epistemological *volte face*, it is necessary to ask the following question: what kind of agency is ascribed to those categorized as 'subalterns', and on whose behalf politically is their 'resistance' exercised? In short, on which side of what barricade (for whom and for what) do they fight? This is also a question that it is necessary to ask of those who write about the subaltern.

The provenance and subsequent trajectories of a number of exponents of subalternism resembles nothing so much as an intellectual game of snakes and ladders: having been Marxists, they then discarded Marxism and espoused the postmodern/post-colonial theory redolent of the 'new' populism.[5] Now that the latter is discredited, some have finally begun to abandon postmodernism too, and find themselves in what amounts to an epistemological limbo. That they have nowhere to go has not prevented them, however, from attempting to reinvent themselves, as liberal or even Marxist critics of the 'new' populism. Initially, therefore, some abandoned Marxism in favour of the 'new' populism for reasons to do with the intellectual fashion of postmodernism/post-colonialism, jumping onto a bandwagon because everyone else was on it, and without examining too closely what this transition involved theoretically or politically.[6]

Others changed paradigms because they lacked an understanding of Marxism, and thus failed to recognize – or to appreciate the importance of – the epistemological distinctiveness between it and its 'new' populist (= postmodern/post-colonial) 'other'.[7] For specifically historical reasons, yet others shifted their allegiance because they had forgotten – or perhaps never learned – about the dangers posed by the political right. The latter is perhaps the most worrying aspect of the intellectual realignment that has occurred during the past 20 years. Many of those involved are attempting – unsuccessfully – to disassociate themselves from theoretical positions held earlier, since it is now at last clear to them that such positions are compromised politically in ways which they did not realize at the time.[8] Thus, for example, some erstwhile postmodernists – such as Ulrich Beck, Richard Rorty and Ramachandra Guha – are now trying to reinvent themselves as beleaguered liberals, well-meaning and apolitical centrists trapped between the equally malign and politically discredited 'extremisms' to their political left and right.[9]

Much the same is true of postmodern fellow-travellers like Giddens, who persists in the palpably mistaken belief that 'Third Way' ideology is a weapon against the political right, rather than what it actually is: a weapon *of* the political right.[10] Others, such as Beverley, continue to present themselves as socialists of some sort, whose subaltern framework is – they claim – in essence no different from earlier and more inclusive forms of Marxism (= Gramsci's theory of 'passive revolution', the Popular Frontism of Dimitrov). A prominent exponent of Latin American subalternism, Beverley has produced what is fast becoming a publishing phenomenon: a theoretically confused account by an ex-postmodernist who then proceeds to blame everyone else for the sins of which he himself was guilty earlier.[11] Where exponents of the subaltern framework are concerned, the cause of such multiple and ever-changing epistemological trajectories lies in the problematic nature of the original search for an 'authentic' grassroots identity in Latin America.

THE QUEST FOR AUTHENTICITY

The search by Albó for subaltern 'authenticity' leads him to the holy grail of a pristine 'from below' nationhood underlying and pre-existing what for him is the false 'from above' nationalism associated with European conquest, which – once identified – can then be said to embody this same subaltern 'authenticity'. Accordingly, Albó sets up an opposition between on the one hand the 'from below' nation (= indigenous = 'authentic' = virtuous), which he terms the nation-over-the-state (or 'trans-state nation'), and on the other the 'from above' nationalism imposed by the state (= European/*mestizo* = foreign = 'inauthentic' = evil), or nation-under-the-state (that is, the 'multinational state').[12] The latter corresponds to a situation whereby the 'real' (or 'authentic') nation of the indigenous 'other' throughout Latin America has been – and is – suppressed by and subordinated to the will of an external ('alien'/'other'/foreign) power, a form of rule exercised through an equally illegitimate institutional form (= the state). For this reason, argues Albó, the aim of indigenous people participating in new mobilizations throughout Latin America is nothing less than to reconstitute themselves as a nation, separate from the wider and overarching national designation which is an historical residue of European conquest and colonization. Such a newly-constituted grassroots identity, maintains Albó, would also break with Marxist views which historicize national identity.[13] Underneath the existing nation and its state, therefore, is to be found an earlier and more 'authentic' nationhood – that of the Latin American subaltern; the reassertion of this subaltern identity would require the dissolution of existing national boundaries so as to recuperate territorial spaces occupied by longstanding culturally-constituted nations (or national groups).[14]

In their quest for ever more authentic forms of (subaltern) identity in Latin America, however, postmodern subalternists forget that all forms of 'authenticity' are socially constructed, both by those to whom this designation is applied and also by those who apply this designation: any Latin American identity described as 'authentic' is thus of necessity historically specific. Because the concept 'authenticity' cannot be affixed to a particular socio-economic identity in a particular location at a particular conjuncture, it cannot be essentialized in epistemological terms. This difficulty confronts the attempts by Canclini and Albó to transcend the cultural hybridity that has followed the modernization of pre-Columbian traditions, a process whereby for them a mainly foreign capital appropriates and 'de-authenticates' what was previously an 'authentic' cultural tradition. Thus, for example, Canclini denies that carnival is a site of 'from above' repression/discipline (still less so a context in which false consciousness is reproduced); he insists, much rather, that its rituals 'incorporate the possibility of social transgression'.[15] For Canclini, therefore, an 'authentic' Latin American 'popular culture' (as embodied in the 'transgressive' rituals of carnival) is itself empowering: only in its 'inauthentic' form – that is, in 'from below' manifestations which have resulted from the appropriation by foreign capital of previously 'authentic' traditions/cultures – is 'popular culture' considered by him to be disempowering. In short, the choice presented by Canclini is not of a progressive, forward-looking identity in preference to a backward-looking, traditional one, but much rather between two backward-looking ones: that is, between 'false'/(disempowering) and 'true'/(empowering) forms of indigenous grassroots cultural tradition/'exoticism'.[16]

Celebrated not just by Latin Americanist subalternism but also in postmodern frameworks (resistance theory associated with the work of J.C. Scott) and non-postmodern theory (the 'moral economy' approach of E.P. Thompson) alike as power-exercised-from-below, the 'primordial' rituals of 'crowning/decrowning' associated with Bakhtinian concepts of carnival and carnivalesque discourse/performance are currently presented as the 'natural' voice of the people at the rural grassroots in many so-called Third World contexts, a politically unmediated (= 'authentic') form of 'from below' resistance to any/all types of injustice/oppression/exploitation exercised 'from above'.[17] Broadly speaking, carnival and the carnivalesque entail the inversion – and thus the negation – of existing hierarchy and its structures of control/domination, a situation which licenses in turn a ritual challenge to those who exercise power and its symbolic overturning.[18] In specifically Thompsonian terms, this involves the application of 'moral economy' in a carnivalesque form known as 'rough musicking' (= 'a ritualised expression of hostility').[19] Such a view, however, overlooks the extent to which carnival not merely does not challenge but actually reinforces and justifies the existing social structure, and is therefore – *pace* Canclini – more accurately categorized as a form of social control (or power-exercised-from-above).[20]

For this reason, it is important to remember a number of things about the role of carnival in general, and its particular manifestation as the fiesta in rural Latin America, in the reproduction of the wider socio-economic system.[21] To begin with, the fact that in Latin America (as elsewhere) the main impact of carnivalesque discourse/performance is ideological and not material, and as such involves nothing more than a ritual and symbolic overturning, and one moreover that is only of short duration.[22] Furthermore, insofar as carnival is the site of laughter, this serves not to reinforce but to defuse the anger that prefigures class struggle.[23] In other words, the function of carnival is much rather that of a 'safety valve' mechanism: any grassroots opposition that exists is doubly displaced, from potentially threatening arenas (the labour process) and organizational forms (strikes, trade unions), thus rendering it safe.[24] Opposition is permitted, therefore, but channelled in what is an essentially harmless form (antagonism = symbolic) into an equally harmless site (carnival, the fiesta) in which its manifestation is and remains systemically non-threatening. Equally significant in this regard is the fact that, where disputes over title or access to property have been concerned, often it was poor peasant farmers or labourers who were targets of carnivalesque discourse initiated by authorities or landowners in the vicinity.[25] Far from being a break with the existing socio-economic order, the carnival (and carnivalesque discourse) in some instances ensures its continuation, and allows the dominant class in the context concerned to reproduce the social relations of production and thus to perpetuate its rule.[26]

Evidence from many different contexts/periods in Latin America suggests that ideological conflict in the context of the rural fiesta system – one of the main sites in which carnivalesque performance/discourse has been reproduced historically – has either involved the deployment of traditional (= backwards-looking) identities or been waged by landlords and/or capitalist rich peasants, neither of which is supportive of progressive 'from below' agrarian class struggle. That the rural fiesta throughout Latin America has been, and remains, a localized institution necessarily restricts its potential impact in terms of grassroots mobilization. As important is the fact that the discourse-for/discourse-against circulating in such contexts has been about religion and ethnic identity. Most importantly, however, is the fact that the class view reproduced in carnivalesque discourse is not necessarily that 'from below', nor is it the case that the 'from below' idioms which do circulate in the fiesta context are necessarily progressive in political terms. Thus, for example, carnivalesque discourse/performance associated with one particular fiesta in the central Peruvian Andes during the pre-reform era – a location where agrarian class struggle was endemic – not only served to strengthen ideological ties between landlords and local peasant communities but also reaffirmed the importance of traditional rural identities (religious and ethnic) that transected the class structure.[27]

Even in cases where it is not itself a site in which ethnic or religious discourse/performance takes centre stage, the fiesta does not necessarily correspond to an expression of power-exercised-from-below. Far from regarding the fiesta as empowering, therefore, unionized estate tenants in the eastern lowlands of Peru opposed office-holding sponsorship, and the fiesta itself ceased with the rise of peasant unions.[28] Significantly, the contradiction between landlord ideology about the fiesta, which projected the estate as an undifferentiated and thus harmonious rural community, was challenged not by agricultural workers or poor peasants but by capitalist rich tenants, for whom fiesta office-holding costs formed part of labour-rent imposed by the landlord. Equally significant in this regard is the fact that these same images of an homogeneous rural community were reintroduced by these same rich peasants in the post-reform era along with the fiesta itself, when the latter once more served as a context in which agrarian capitalist producers attempted to disseminate their own class-specific discourse about community identity and resource transfers.[29] It is precisely this 'other' role – enforcing conformity not transgression, licensing continued 'from above' exploitation not 'from below' resistance – that is overlooked or ignored by those postmodern subalternists intent on celebrating carnival and the carnivalesque as sites of grassroots empowerment in Latin America.[30]

'Bringing news'

Just as Canclini and Albó identify nationhood and the carnivalesque as sites where an 'authentic' and empowering form of subaltern identity/resistance manifests itself, so the search by Beverley for a similarly pristine subaltern 'voice'/agency takes him into the domain of literature.[31] Because explanations of capitalism were in his opinion inadequate, Beverley sought a 'new' understanding of culture/identity in literary criticism, and found this in the form of subaltern studies, 'a new form of academic knowledge production' which as a result became 'a conceptual vanguard in Latin American studies'.[32] The futility – not to say the fatuousness – of this vanguardist intellectual aspiration surfaces rapidly when Beverley attempts to contrast non-literary and literary accounts of the Túpac Amaru rebellion against Spanish colonialism during the early 1780s, with the object of revealing the presence in the former of a non-creole national identity constructed by and thus representing an authentic indigenous grassroots voice: 'cultural practices', he proclaims, suggest the existence of 'a vast revolutionary social movement from below, propelled by the poorest and most exploited sectors of the indian artisans and peasantry'.[33] Even some literary sources, such as the play *Ollantay*, written anonymously in Quechua at this time, in his opinion amount to 'the cultural production of a national-popular imaginary by an indigenous peasantry and its organic intellectuals'.[34] This is an astonishing and unwarranted leap: a text which Beverley accepts is anonymous – its author and the socio-economic origin/position of the latter is unknown – suddenly and without any evidence whatsoever becomes the product of 'an indigenous peasantry and its organic intellectuals'.

Beverley attempts to get round this problem by invoking two forms of postmodern aporia (narrative hybridity, subaltern unknowability). Accordingly, much of his analysis is devoted to the conceptual rehabilitation of *testimonio*, or 'narrative … told in the first person by a narrator who is also a real protagonist or witness of the events he or she recounts', as he applied it originally to Rigoberta Menchú, an icon of Latin American subaltern 'otherness'.[35] On discovering that hers was not *testimonio* in the sense he had defined it, however, Beverley reverses its meaning: *testimonio*, he announces, no longer has to consist of a first-hand witness account but can now involve 'a kind of narrative hybridity'.[36] In other words, it is composed of a mixture of truth and non-truth. There is no limit to this kind of inflation: how long before one is told that *testimonio* composed entirely of falsehoods is still acceptable as *testimonio*? Perhaps such a moment will also mark the annexation by literary studies of social science and history, a process whereby all fact finally becomes its 'other', fiction, and the literary critic is accordingly installed as the only true subject of struggle, which he himself constitutes in the realm of literature, the fictional but nevertheless only 'real' world'.[37]

A second form of postmodern aporia involves the claim that, as the subaltern is unknowable, he/she cannot be represented, in effect not only abolishing the intellectual accessibility of peasants and labourers but converting them into the mysterious 'other' of conservative discourse. Those such as Spivak and Kristeva link the 'unrepresentability' of subaltern culture to the 'unknowability' of the subaltern him/herself: a subject thus defined cannot be represented by someone 'other' (= intellectuals) than him/herself, a view that verges on the solipsistic.[38] A consequence of pristine subaltern 'otherness' being both unknowable and intellectually inaccessible, moreover, is that it is unalterable. Just such an epistemology is invoked by conservatives who claim that, as the subaltern likes the way he/she is, and feels empowered by his/her culture (of which the economic is merely a part), consequently no one – and especially not intellectuals on the left – should presume to advise him/her otherwise. This of course leaves power and control in the hands of the bourgeoisie, since according to this kind of argument it is impermissible for an intellectual even to put to a subaltern a non-subaltern idea: because the subaltern is unknowable, the nature of the subaltern and therefore of its 'other' cannot even be posed. Even if it could, intellectuals are disbarred from this, because to do so is to privilege a non-subaltern discourse.

Theorized in this manner, both the subaltern and his/her culture become essentialized and a-temporal forms of existence. Each remains socio-economically hermetic and ahistorical, immune to external change and challenge: neither can be analysed, only reported.[39] This innate and unmediated subaltern consciousness of course forbids its characterization as false, which in turn prevents not only the transcendence but also a political critique by those who are not themselves subalterns of existing cultural identity and agency based on this. Denying the efficacy of 'false consciousness' on the grounds that 'Western Marxism [refuses] class-consciousness to the pre-capitalist Subaltern', therefore, Beverley again follows Spivak and maintains that it is necessary to recognize the existence of a specifically subaltern form of peasant consciousness.[40] Not the least problematic aspect of such an epistemology is that it depoliticizes the link between consciousness and action. Like postmodernism generally, it also licenses the reification of every form of belief, which can then be subsumed within an all-embracing rubric of 'subaltern consciousness'. Trapped within this epistemology, Latin American subalternists are forced to conclude that, since there is no such thing as false consciousness, all from-below consciousness which exists must therefore be an 'authentic' grassroots manifestation. Within this non-judgemental framework, subaltern agency based on any and every conceivable kind of political consciousness – conservative and reactionary as well as socialist and progressive – becomes empowering for its subject, and consequently is regarded not just as legitimate but also as unchallengeable.

Bernays' Sauce, or Postmodern Food for Thought

The political implications of this inability to conceptualize false consciousness and the consequent problems with rural grassroots mobilization based on this are profound. To begin with, the labelling by postmodern theory of all grassroots culture as 'authentic' and 'innate', and mobilization on the basis of this as empowering, is a direct effect of a view that regards subaltern identity/agency as perpetually 'there', and thus 'naturally' desired by its subject.[41] Not only is such a view epistemologically misplaced – ideologically, *nothing* is or can be 'natural' – but it misinterprets as 'from below' or 'authentic' grassroots phenomena forms of identity/behaviour/culture/consciousness that are actually 'from above' creations.[42] In doing this, postmodernism exhibits a gullibility exploited in a systematic fashion from the late 1920s onwards by a nascent public relations industry, which demonstrated clearly how public opinion in the United States could successfully be constructed/channelled.[43] The object was simple: consciously to stimulate anti-rational desire, which could then be harnessed by capitalism for two particular ends. First, to generate additional demand for its commodities; and second, to disguise the 'from above' origin of this initiative, by presenting it as a 'natural' or 'from below' cultural emanation that empowers its subject.

Those who advocated this maintained that the outcome – a situation in which economically unnecessary goods were devoured by those whom big business hoped would become politically passive consumers – would avoid/postpone both economic crisis (due to overproduction) and political crisis (binding workers-as-consumers to capital, in the process pre-empting questions about systemic change). Like postmodernism itself, however, this approach was premissed on a pessimistic view of humanity – one which proclaimed that, as humanity was innately (or instinctively) non-rational, fundamental systemic change was unfeasible.[44] The latter was a philosophy which 1920s capitalists unsurprisingly found congenial, a perception which their contemporaries now extend to the similar postmodern view that economic need (= class identity) – for capital an unpalatable and thus non-negotiable political demand – be replaced with what can be represented as an 'authentic' and thus empowering cultural desire (= ethnic/national 'belonging'), which for capital is an inherently acceptable political demand. For this reason, the justification of 1930s Popular Frontism by exponents of Latin American subalternism such as Beveley (see below) in terms of the realization of a politically empowering 'popular culture' by means of consumer sovereignty is misplaced: not only is such a view nonsense (popular culture ≠ consumer sovereignty) but it also fails to engage with the politics of mass culture (e.g., racism, sexism).

Many examples from Latin America, North America and elsewhere confirm that mass culture is as much a 'from above' as a 'from below' product, a point underlined by the depoliticization/repoliticization of much current popular culture. The case of Disney comics demonstrates both the longevity of and the extent to which 'popular culture' is formed not 'from below' but rather 'from above', and also how the reproduction of the agrarian myth is a central aspect of this process, resulting in the formation of what amounts to false consciousness.[45] Control exercised 'from above' over what precisely constitutes the 'from below' agenda of 'popular culture', together with its reproduction, has always been a political objective pursued globally both by imperial states and by multinational corporations.[46] There is accordingly a remarkable overlap between what are usually represented as being politically divergent processes: on the one hand, the 'natural' identity which both postmodern theory and the subaltern studies project currently insist is culturally empowering for those at the rural grassroots; and on the other, the similarly 'innate'/'authentic'/non-rational – yet palpably disempowering – form of consciousness which capital has attempted historically to create/reproduce 'from above' for its own economic and political ends.

As even commentators sympathetic to post-colonial studies themselves admit, the burgeoning 'alterity' industry in the academy is based on complicity: namely, between local oppositional discourses and capitalism itself, an arrangement whereby the latter commodifies the 'marginality' of the former as 'cultural difference'. In the course of being processed as an ideological commodity, therefore, 'non-Western' identity is rendered 'exotic' (= 'other'), and literary representations of this exoticism are consumed within Western capitalism as one more product.[47] Nor should the role within metropolitan capitalist contexts of travel writing – a widely read genre and hugely influential form of 'popular culture' – in reproducing the agrarian myth about rural populations in the so-called Third World be underestimated.[48] To claim, as Beverley does, that all one has to do in such cases is to 'resubalternize' the issue is to avoid this question, not to answer it. Not the least of the difficulties is that 'resubalternization' will amount in the majority of instances merely to the discursive reinstatement of nationalism, and with it the enduring historical opposition between a stereotypically pristine national identity on the one hand and an all-embracing imperialism on the other. In other words, agency licensing struggle not between classes but between nations, and within the latter between ethnicities.

In contrast to Marxism, for which existing rural grassroots traditions/institutions generate the false consciousness (e.g., national/ethnic/community/religious solidarity) that misinforms/misleads/deflects 'from below' class struggle, both postmodernism and the subaltern approach recast these same non-class ideological forms in a positive light, and regard them as making a positive contribution to (non-class) grassroots agency. The fact that those at the rural grassroots – like people everywhere – tend to act not on reality but on perceptions of reality merely serves to underline the importance of mediation, and thus also of false consciousness, when considering questions of and reasons for such kinds of agency (and, correspondingly, their absence). The falsity of consciousness applies not so much to perceptions of a problem (rural workers are indeed aware of the existence of oppression, injustice, etc.) as to perceptions of what can be done to remedy the situation. That is, the desirability/feasibility/possibility of specific political solutions (fascism, racism and bourgeois democracy instead of socialism or communism) to the problem which exists and of which they are aware.[49] However, the conceptual banishment by subalternists generally of false consciousness, and the corresponding assumption on their part that all from-below agency is necessarily progressive, means that the fact that, historically and currently, grassroots agency has been the result of mobilization by the political right as much as by the left, together with its implications, cannot even be considered.[50]

II

Contrary to the claims made by postmodernism, the subalternist exponents of which eschew cross-cultural comparative analysis because in their view no such undertaking is possible epistemologically, what is significant about the discourse of the political right and the place of the peasantry in this is precisely the remarkable similarity of the 'difference' invoked across space and time. Nowhere is this universality more evident than in the claims made by conservatives and the political right in many different contexts and periods concerning the desirability of redemption linked to the innateness of Nature and thus rural existence and traditional identities based on this. Historically, such arguments have consolidated around what might be termed the aristocratic and the plebeian versions of the agrarian myth, a discourse which is supportive of countryside (= 'good') against the town (= 'bad'). On the one hand, therefore, it valorizes small-scale rural-based uniform/harmonious/'natural' economic activity (artisanry, peasant family farming) and culture (religious, ethnic, regional, village, family identities derived from Nature). On the other, it can be equally supportive of landlordism as part of an ancient – and therefore 'natural' – rural hierarchy to which the peasantry also belong. Both variants of the agrarian myth unite in a symptomatically populist fashion to express their hostility and ideological opposition to urban-based large-scale industrialization (finance capital, the city, manufacturing, collectivization, planning, massification) and its accompanying institutional/relational/systemic effects (class formation/struggle, revolution, socialism, bureaucracy, the state), all of which are perceived as non-indigenous/'inauthentic'/'alien' internationalisms imposed on an unwilling and mainly rural population by 'foreigners', and therefore as responsible for the erosion of hitherto 'authentic' local traditions and values.

All too often rural struggle has been represented by Marxists and non-Marxists alike as one between landlords and peasants, with the twofold result that not only have small agrarian capitalists been banished epistemologically from the ranks of the peasantry but the degree to which the latter category was central to the discourse not of the left but of conservatism and the political right has also been overlooked. The persistence of pro-peasant views among the landlord class and/or the rural bourgeoisie is embodied, for example, in references to the presence and benign character of patron/client relations. A landlord will recognize the worldview of peasants only insofar as it coincides with and reinforces his own (= anti-state, anti-industrialization, pro-nation, pro-tradition), and claim merely that these subjects are culturally and economically different from him. Insofar as they recognize his and their place in the same rural hierarchy, and embody national cultural traditions which he approves of and respects, therefore, he will defend any desire on their part to remain the same and oppose attempts – by them or by others – to change. It is precisely this kind of relativistic conservativism that draws support from postmodern aporia (≠ univocality): both espouse a view in which an inability/unwillingness to make value-judgements merges imperceptibly with a 'refusal of history', positions that mask 'a fear of history' – specifically, of what history tells.[51] The political effect of this aporia is inescapable. If culture lies beyond the realm of value-judgement and satisfies human needs in the way postmodernists claim, then it follows that there is no need to change the material base which sustains cultural activity in the first place. Not the least problematic aspect of such aporia is that it licenses the systemic reproduction of landlordism and peasant farming, each of which can be justified in terms of the cultural empowerment it confers on its constituent subject.

'A FEAR OF HISTORY'

An important and enduring weapon in the ideological armoury of a ruling class in many different contexts and periods has been the capacity to choose to be 'other', or to have an identity 'different' from that which history confers, both on its own followers/supporters and on those to whom it is opposed.[52] This ideological defence, in which a fear of history leads to and combines with an invocation of 'choice', has at times entailed the mobilization by the class in question of a discourse about Nature and 'the natural', and the application of the latter both to itself and also to the category or class threatening its own power.[53] It is often forgotten, therefore, that such claims deployed 'from above' about cultural 'difference'/'otherness' refer not just to those who rule but also to those who are ruled, and that the recipients of this act of labelling have usually been peasants. For this reason, claims about the innate 'difference'/'otherness' of what was regarded as an undifferentiated peasantry have been – and remain – central not just to nationalism, to opposition by conservative philosophy to Enlightenment discourse, but also to the ideology of the far right.[54] Moreover, such claims can be traced through a common discourse about the agrarian myth shared by the political right in Latin American and non-Latin American contexts alike.[55]

Pro-Peasant Ideology and European/North American Conservatism

The aristocratic variant of the agrarian myth projecting seigniorial attitudes/values operates even in advanced metropolitan capitalist contexts, where it forms an important ideological component of historical/contemporary conservative discourse that is supportive of smallholding agriculture. In the case of England, for example, early twentieth-century imperialist discourse warning against the demise of empire, patriotism and the nation itself attributed this to the economic decline of the small farmer (= the military backbone of nation, colonies and imperial possessions) and a correspondingly inexorable process of rural exodus, urbanization and industrialization.[56] Not only is this discourse anti-Semitic, condemning finance capital (= 'a plutocratic caste') for undermining empire/nation/agriculture, but the traditional landlord class is designated the true defender of the small farmer (and, by inference, the nation itself), the conclusion being that agriculture – both at home and in the colonies – should be encouraged/protected.[57] Significantly, at the same conjuncture much the same kind of argument structured the plebeian variant of the agrarian myth in the United States of America, where agrarian populists argued that, by proletarianizing yeoman farmers and transforming them into their 'other' (= the 'mob in the streets') finance capital would destroy not only the peasantry (= warriors) which protected its own class power by defending the latter against the proletariat but also and thereby the nation itself.[58]

Discourse about an undifferentiated/ahistorical peasantry also circulated in both the aristocratic and the plebeian variants of the agrarian myth in Germany. Thus, for example, the eighteenth-century defence of rural tradition and hierarchy against the Enlightenment (*aufklarung*) undertaken by the conservative theoretician Justus Möser did not prevent him from admiring what he regarded as the cultural 'otherness'/'difference' of peasant society, a golden-age version of which in his view constituted the authentic and timeless embodiment of German national identity.[59] Much the same is true of twentieth-century Germany, where Prince Bernard von Bülow, scion of the Junker landlord class, and later Richard Walther Darré, the Nazi Minister of Agriculture, both invoked what each claimed was an unbroken ancient rural lineage – composed of an unchanging/homogeneous peasantry (= a mythical ancestral being closer to Nature, and thus 'more natural') – as evidence for the existence of a pristine nationalism, in terms which were no different from those used by Möser some 200 years earlier.[60] Such pro-peasant views, moreover, are not of themselves incompatible with a view of Nazism as a form of reactionary modernism bent on carrying through a project of capitalist development and industrialization. Accordingly, those linked to the Nazis who espoused pro-peasant ideology perceived no incompatibility between such views on the one hand, and capitalist development and industrialization on the other.[61] And even where such a specifically material incompatibility may have existed, reactionary pro-peasant ideology fulfilled an important mobilizing role in the class struggle.[62]

In the case of 1930s Spain, this fear of history manifested itself in the concern of the ultra-right Falange for the effects on the peasantry of the capitalist crisis, a fear that translated into a reactionary and specifically regressive form of anti-capitalist discourse. The result was a conservative pro-peasant programme of agrarian reform, based on a seemingly contradictory ideological combination: an acceptance by the Falange of the Marxist critique of capitalism, but the rejection of its form of transcendence.[63] Like the political right in Germany, José Antonio Primo de Rivera, founder/leader of the Spanish Falange, endorsed Rousseau's critique of the 'adding-on' inherent in the historical process; that is, the way in which what he regarded as all the 'non-natural' accretions that constitute historical development erode a pre-existing and ahistorical 'primitive goodness' and 'natural community'.[64] The solution to the destructive systemic effects on the peasantry of the 1930s capitalist crisis required liberation from these 'non-natural' accretions – from history itself, in other words – so as to return to an ideologically/institutionally 'spontaneous'/('natural') condition: according to Primo de Rivera, this would be the task of the Spanish Falange.

Instead of a progressive, forward-looking 'going-beyond', therefore, Primo de Rivera sought redemption for rural Spain in the reaffirmation of traditional/feudal values/beliefs embodied 'naturally'/eternally in peasant smallholding agriculture.[65] Because he feared the impact on the latter of the kind of capitalist development that Marx predicted, Primo de Rivera argued that impoverished peasant family farming – the embodiment of nationalism – had to be rescued by the Falange, both from the Marxist policy of proletarianization that would convert peasants into workers (who would then be 'led astray by Marxism'), a transformation that would result in social chaos/collapse, and also from the clutches of finance capitalism, and made economically viable by means of an agrarian reform programme.[66] The object of the latter would be to 'release small farmers, small industrialists and shopkeepers from the gilt claws of the usurious banks', to restore handicraft production in rural areas, and most importantly to reconstitute and protect the future economic and cultural well-being of the peasant family farm itself.[67]

Claims about the desirability of an innate peasant economy/culture continued to be central to both variants of the agrarian myth from 1945 onwards, its ideological complicity with European fascism notwithstanding. The survival during the post-war era of a conservative pro-peasant programme was due at least in part to the fact that it circulated now within the discourse of the victorious bourgeoisies, who were ideologically strongly opposed both to socialism and to collectivization, and – in the context of East European communist revolutions – still feared their own industrial working classes as potentially militant 'mobs in the streets'. Lamenting the fact that 'the doctrine of progress ... still exercises an uncritical and fatalistic influence', therefore, European and North American exponents of this discourse combined the aristocratic and the plebeian variants of the agrarian myth in a symptomatic defence of large landowner and smallholder, both of whom (it was claimed) shared a common rural identity under threat from the urban state and its proletariat.[68] Not only was the post-war trend away from agriculture towards urbanization/industrialization decried as a profanation of Nature and 'natural law', and finance capital blamed for undermining the small farmer, but in some instances this was done in nationalist idioms and barely coded anti-Semitic terms (= 'money-power') not so dissimilar to those circulating in the pre-war discourse of the political right (German fascism, British imperialism).[69] By the mid-1960s, the political right in the USA was arguing strongly in favour of the small farmer: this it managed to do because it had executed a populist reappropriation of existing discourse about political freedom, in the process bolstering the claim of conservatives to be disinterestedly plebeian by linking the concept of 'freedom' simultaneously to a pro-farmer, pro-market and anti-state ideology.[70]

Pro-peasant ideology continues to inform the discourse of the political right in Europe.[71] In what is currently an almost classic restatement of the aristocratic variant of the agrarian myth, therefore, conservative philosophy even now combines a defence of rural hierarchy and tradition based on large landownership with populist concern for the threatened survival of 'natural' forms of rural economy based on small-scale agricultural production.[72] During the period after the Second World War, both components of the English pastoral (landlord estate + small family farm) have been continuously undermined by what for populist conservatives are the interconnected and mutually supportive evils of urbanization, taxation and state regulation, all of which have resulted in the appearance of 'that previously unknown and deeply troubling thing: a landscape without boundaries' (that is, no small privately-owned farms), and a loss of the countryside which is now equated with the loss of national confidence and identity.[73] Like the plebeian variant invoked by the political right in the United States of the 1960s, therefore, the aristocratic variant of the agrarian myth deployed by late 1990s English conservatism is supportive of the free market, decries state 'interference', and is pro-farmer.[74] Significantly, many of these same themes also inform the discourse of the political right in Latin America.

Pro-Peasant Ideology and Latin American Conservatism

It is the acceptability to landlords and rich peasants alike of the pro-peasant discourse informing the agrarian myth, together with the close link between the latter and the politics of nationality and tradition, that poses difficulties for Latin American subalternists. Because the views of those on the ultra-nationalist political right in 1930s Latin America were from the 1920s onwards influenced strongly by the writings and ideas of their European counterparts (José Ortega y Gasset, José Calvo Sotelo and José Antonio Primo de Rivera among them), many commentators equate reactionary discourse in Latin America simply with a harkening back to European culture and tradition (*Hispanidad*).[75] Whilst true in part, this argument overlooks the extent to which a specifically *populist* form of right-wing reactionary discourse about rural society locates its nationalism in idealized forms of popular culture and indigenous tradition *within* Latin America itself.[76] Not the least of the many difficulties faced by those who attempt to apply a subaltern framework to Latin America, therefore, is the crucial role played by the peasantry in the discourse of the political right, where it takes the form of a specifically plebeian national identity deployed by conservatives and reactionaries as a weapon in their struggle with the left.

In describing the subaltern studies project as a new approach Beverley ignores the long history of such ideas in Latin America generally and in the Andean region in particular.[77] Grouped under the rubric *indigenismo*, the lineage in question extends from adherents such as José Carlos Maríategui, Hildebrando Castro Pozo and Hugo Blanco, whose formal position on the Peruvian left masked their populism, to explicitly populist organizations such as the APRA of Victor Raúl Haya de la Torre and the *Partido Indio de Bolivia* of Fausto Reinaga.[78] What the latter have in common are golden age visions of the agrarian myth: on the basis of a shared epistemology, all of them subscribed to the view that the Spanish Conquest imposed an 'inauthentic' and 'foreign' (= European) feudal tenure structure on what each of them interpreted as being a materially self-sufficient and culturally 'authentic' indigenous Andean peasant community that characterized the pre-Columbian era.[79] More important was the fact that for Maríategui, Castro Pozo, Blanco and Haya de la Torre, this discourse also possessed a programmatic status: the socialism of the first three as well as the nationalism of the fourth entailed building on what each perceived as being a still-viable peasant economy, a residue from the golden age of Peru that had survived colonialism. Like their counterparts who focus on Asia, therefore, exponents of the Latin American subaltern studies project have adopted a symptomatically postmodern discourse-for/discourse-against that structures *indigenismo*, populism and the agrarian myth.

Thus, for example, the discourse-against of the agrarian myth deployed by Albó deprivileges class as an analytical category and trade unions as an organizational form, and opts instead for the subaltern category based on the ethnic/cultural identity of what he calls the 'testimonial peoples' of Latin America, composed of 'the modern representatives of old, original civilizations which European expansion demolished'.[80] It is equally clear that Albó also endorses the discourse-for (= 'natural'/harmonious rural community) of the agrarian myth.[81] As the attempts by Albó and Canclini to reconstruct nations based on traditional ethnicity demonstrate, earlier *indigenista* views have merely been recycled, and the same arguments now appear under the rubric of Latin American 'subaltern' identity and resistance.[82] For Albó, therefore, the 'testimonial peoples' constituting the Latin American subaltern are composed of 'small indigenous nations' which exist in a 'primordial relationship of culture with cultivation': as with the Asian subaltern, the 'testimonial peoples' who form the 'authentic'/indigenous nations of Latin American subalterns, and for whom 'the land is also the fundamental base of their cultural identity', correspond to a smallholding peasantry.[83]

The difficulty faced by exponents of subalternism is that the agrarian myth is deployed as – or perhaps more – effectively by Latin American conservatives. Like the Spanish Falange and the German Nazis, the ultra-nationalist political right in Latin America at the same conjuncture also rooted its claims to and view of a pristine national/cultural identity in an indigenous peasantry.[84] The latter category was accordingly regarded as 'natural', eternal and homogeneous, all characteristics with which the Latin American political right imbued its nationalism. This was particularly true of the Andean countries, where since independence nationalist discourse had invariably contrasted the exploitative 'foreign other' to the virtuous indigenous self. In addition to the standard right-wing discourse – invocations of organic unity, authority, hierarchy, family, religion and patriotism, combined with opposition to class, class struggle and the 'foreign other' – the programme for the New Bolivian State (*Nuevo Estado Boliviano*) proposed by the Bolivian Falangists (the fascist FSB, or *Falange*

Socialista Boliviana) during the early 1940s invoked and endorsed peasant economy: not only was an ethnically-specific peasant identity equated with nationalism ('*El indio es la raíz de nuestra nacionalidad*'), therefore, but this culturally delineated rural subject was also to be reinforced and guaranteed economically by an agrarian reform ('*Un plan de reforma agraria le dará su liberación económica*').[85] However, this cultural/economic identity was itself both subordinate and fixed, the structural location and immutability of which its subject was expected to recognize and accept: like every other social category in the 'natural' hierarchy which composed the nation, the Bolivian peasantry had in the view of the FSB its own 'natural' economic role in the new corporate order ('*El individuo participará de la unidad orgánica del estado mediante un regimen corporativo en que cada uno desempeñe su función de acuerdo a la calidad y especialización de su trabajo*').

Even in the southern cone countries of Latin America, where indigenous populations were numerically and economically less significant than in their Andean counterparts, an idealized image of peasant farming still informed the discourse both of nationalism and of the political right. In the case of Argentina, for example, the emergence of the political right at the beginning of the twentieth century was a direct response to the mobilization of the labour movement, and a discourse combining cultural nationalism with anti-modernism, anti-urbanism and anti-cosmopolitanism was central to the class struggle waged 'from above'.[86] From the 1890s onwards, the political right in Argentina was not merely anti-Semitic but its racism mimicked in every respect that propounded by agrarian populists elsewhere at the same conjuncture, and for much the same reasons.[87] Indeed, it was a twofold desire to rescue an 'authentic' indigenous process of family farming in Argentina from the clutches of ('foreign'/'alien'/'Jewish') finance capital and also to prevent depeasantized workers from falling into the clutches of ('foreign'/'alien'/'Jewish') socialism that led to the advocacy by the political right of land reform and rural cooperativization.[88]

During the period following the 1914–18 war, the protection of smallholding peasants and/or the reconstitution of a middle peasantry, was central to Argentinian fascism, as represented by the ultra-reactionary policy and discourse of the Argentine Patriotic League (*Liga Patriótica Argentina*).[89] Along with the gaucho, peasant smallholders were considered by those on the political right not just as indigenous and loyal subjects who upheld private property rights and 'knew'/accepted their 'natural' position in the social hierarchy, but also (and therefore) as the embodiment of an 'authentic' rural tradition that contrasted with an 'alien' urban cosmopolitanism represented by a mainly immigrant proletariat which lived/worked in the cities, as the bearer of 'authentic' national identity and consequently as a bulwark against the spread of socialist and revolutionary ideas to rural areas.[90] Throughout the capitalist crisis of the 1920s, the League maintained a pool of strike-breaking workers that was deployed against organized rural labour in every part of the country; these scab workers (*crumiros*) were made available to farmers and tenants who were in dispute with their hired labour.[91] When workers began to organize or withdrew their labour-power, therefore, it was not just large landowners and owners of agribusiness enterprises but also small farmers, ranchers and tenants – many of who were engaged in struggle with their own labourers (over issues such as wage levels, working conditions and the right to form/join unions) – who called upon the League to come to 'the defence of the cultivator', and it was from these elements of the agrarian petty bourgeoisie that the political right in Argentina received crucial support and recruited much of its membership.

Significantly, pro-peasant ideology continued to be found in the discourse of the bourgeoisie and political right in Latin America throughout the decade and a half after 1945, not least because – like their counterparts in Europe and North America – they were not on the losing side during the war.[92] Thus, for example, an agronomist who was an advisor to the Peruvian landlords' association (*Sociedad Nacional Agraria*, or SNA), and who defended the *hacienda* system on the grounds that it contributed to the national wealth of Peru, also supported the idea of peasant family farming.[93] When equipped with more advanced forces of production, such independent cultivators could, in his view, operate alongside similarly equipped latifundia.[94] In a similar vein, an important vineyard strike by smallholding tenants in Chile during the early 1950s was organized and led by a member of the Chilean Falange.[95] Like its 1930s Spanish counterpart, the mobilizing discourse used by the Falange in Chile during the course of this strike was that of Roman Catholicism, and in particular the social teachings contained in the papal encyclicals *Rerum Novarum* and *Quadragesimo Anno*, both of which upheld the rights of private property and were against socialism and class struggle, advocating instead class compromise between rural workers and their employers.[96] As the case of peasant smallholders among the indigenous Pewenche population confirms, right-wing political candidates and parties in Chile were still able to draw electoral support from among independent cultivators even in the late 1990s.[97] During the same decade, moreover, elements of the Argentinian political right shifted their own discourse, from one which emphasized the necessity of temporal (= military) authority exercised 'from above' to one which invoked the desirability both of religious (= 'natural') and 'from below' plebeian (= populist) legitimacy.[98]

III

That exponents of Latin American subaltern resistance miss the political significance for their project of longstanding conservative pro-peasant ideology not only in Europe but also in Latin America itself is attributable in turn to a corresponding failure on their part to understand political theory, and thus also the connections and contradictions involving a number of crucially similar and radically antinomic discourses. In short, the link between Marxism and populism (subalternism ≠ Marxism), that between populism and subaltern resistance (subalternism = populism = Popular Frontism), and the one between fascism and capitalism (fascism ≠ feudal reaction). Accordingly, the reason behind their misrecognition of the fusion between the subaltern/resistance framework on the one hand and the populist right on the other is not difficult to discern. Since he fails to distinguish populism from its epistemological and political 'other', Marxism, it is in a sense unsurprising that one advocate of Latin American subaltern resistance – Beverley – conflates Marxism not just with the Subaltern Studies project but also with Popular Frontism and Gramscian theory.[99]

THE POLITICS OF SUBALTERN RESISTANCE

In some cases, the merger of subaltern/resistance/populism with the politics and agency of reaction stems from a failure to ask whether those opposed to capitalism were thereby automatically disposed towards socialism. This is particularly true of subaltern 'resistance' generated by issues of ethnicity, nationality, environmentalism, gender and sexuality, where the assumption has been that those who opposed discrimination and/or oppression under capitalism necessarily did so because they were in favour of socialism.[100] For very much the same reasons, it is also true of those who interpreted 'resistance' to capitalism on the part of an undifferentiated peasantry as opposition that prefigured a process of systemic transcendence. The frequent assumption made by exponents of the subaltern framework – as applied to Asia and Latin America – is that all resisters are the same, by virtue of belonging to the same non-class group (ethnic, national, gender), whereas evidence from peasant movements worldwide shows that, in order to understand agrarian resistance/accommodation, such a category must be differentiated along class lines.

The extent of the difficulties informing the arguments made by Beverley may be gauged from the confused attempt to define the relationship between the Subaltern Studies project and Marxism: '[m]y own perspective on subaltern studies', he states, 'is that it is a project of Marxism rather than a Marxist project … I do not think of subaltern studies therefore as a kind of post-Marxism, unless what is meant by post-Marxism is a new kind of Marxism, or a new way in which Marxism acts within the world' [*sic*].[101] Because he conflates Marxism with its 'other', the 'new' populism, Beverley is still able to argue that 'what is most urgent today is a defence and rehabilitation of the project of the left', that the latter is a 'Marxism' purged of social democracy, Leninism and even modernity, and that 'a "postmodernist" form of communism [*sic*] is lodged within the problematic of the subaltern.'[102] This is a claim that verges on the nonsensical, and one that could be made only by someone who misunderstands the antinomic epistemologies and histories of populism, postmodern theory and Marxism.

Not only is the subaltern not a class category, but Marxists in general (and Trotskyists in particular) have been very critical of the whole cultural turn, as embodied in the rise to prominence and subsequent dominance of the subaltern/resistance paradigm. Questions such as who in class terms is the subaltern, and consequently what is resistance designed to achieve, for whom, and why, were asked by a number of Marxists right at the start of the 1990s, when the whole subaltern studies project and its 'everyday-forms-of-resistance' paradigm was in the process of becoming ubiquitous.[103] Rather than a critique which emanates *from* Marxism, therefore, the subaltern/resistance framework was (and is) regarded by Marxists as a nationalist and/or 'new' populist critique *of* Marxism. Moreover, it is a framework which in some instances shares an epistomology and discourse not with the left (to which it is hostile) but – more problematic in political terms – with a globally ascendant 'new' right.

'The old reserve of curses'

That Beverley is unfamiliar with the prefiguring discourse of the subaltern/resistance framework is clear from three things. First, his superficial acquaintance with Marxism; second, an equally slight engagement with the Subaltern Studies series itself, as applied throughout the 1980s to studies of rural Asia; and third, an inability to connect the postmodern epistemology of the latter to the rise of the 'New Philosophers' in France during the previous decade. Most worryingly, therefore, is the fact that Beverley's familiarity with the Subaltern Studies project is confined largely to two anthologies, edited respectively by Guha and Spivak and by Guha, both of which were published in the United States.[104] He does not seem to have read any of the ten volumes (published in India throughout the 1980s and 1990s) which comprise the series, nor is he aware of the large secondary literature which this has generated, both within and outside India. Thus, for example, Beverley claims that the main Marxist critique of the Subaltern Studies project was that by Ahmad, a critique which he then dismisses as irrelevant.[105] Such a view not only overlooks the *Social*

Scientist critique of the early 1980s, but also that Ahmad's principal target was not Subaltern Studies but Said's theorization of orientalism.[106]

More important than this, however, is the fact that the postmodern epistemology of the Subaltern Studies project is rooted in structuralism, which in turn informed the reactionary linguistic/cultural turn of the 'New Philosophers' in France, who emerged in the mid-1970s and in turn prefigured the political right.[107] The rightwards political trajectory of the 'New Philosophers', for the most part ex-Maoists who participated in the May events of 1968, is linked invariably and simply to a disillusion which resulted from the chronicling by Solzhenitsyn of prison life in the Soviet Gulag, a discovery which permitted them to affix the institution of the concentration camp – associated hitherto solely with fascism – firmly within a Marxist lineage, and thus to condemn socialism as irretrievably tainted (Marxism = the State = the Gulag).[108] However, it is equally clear from the views expressed at that conjuncture by Jean-Marie Benoist, one of the 'New Philosophers', that their political roots go much deeper, and are to be found in an espousal of structuralism/(postmodernism), and thus also in the theoretical objections of such theory to Marxism. His structuralist argument is symptomatic, and anticipates all the classic oppositions of postmodern theory: on the one hand, a facile dismissiveness of 'Eurocentrism' coupled with an antagonism towards Marxism, historical materialism, science, development and history, and on the other an endorsement of Heidegger, Neitzsche, an innate concept of difference/'otherness', aporia and the linguistic/cultural turn.[109]

What is particularly significant about both the discourse and the politics of the 'New Philosophers' is the agrarian dimension. Applauding Rousseau's objections to Enlightenment claims about the desirability/possibility of progress and reason, and following anthropologists such as Leach and Lévi-Strauss, Benoist maintained that social relations, myths and beliefs are all informed by a deep and unconscious linguistic structure, which is in turn rooted in Nature (and thus 'natural'/immutable).[110] Just as for Benoist it was a specifically Lévi-Straussian concept of the Third World tribal that was emblematic of this perpetual and unbridgeable element of 'discontinuity' that constituted a natural form of irreducible/eternal 'difference' found in Nature, so for other 'New Philosophers' this same kind of innate rural 'difference' took on an equally specific peasant form.[111] Thus Michel le Bris, who came from a Breton peasant background, and was later active in the Occitanian autonomist movement, was an enthusiastic advocate of what he termed the peasant 'way of life', while (in an echo of José Antonio Primo de Rivera and the Spanish Falange) the 'New Philosophers' Nemo and Clavel sought a transcendence of capitalist alienation in what for them was the more desirable personal bond between master and servant under feudalism.[112] It is this discourse – about the immutability of Nature and the resistance to Marxism/materialism/history on the part of the Third World *rural* 'other' – that is the immediate precursor of the Subaltern Studies approach that Beverley and Albó apply to the Latin American peasantry.[113]

In seeking to displace criticism – why those like him should wish to apply to Latin America, where nations became independent at the beginning of the nineteenth century, a theory about post-colonialism developed in relation to India, which became independent only in the mid-twentieth – Beverley invokes Gramsci's theory about the historical roots of and the reasons for the rise of fascism.[114] The latter process is attributed by Gramsci to Italy, and by others to Germany, to the failure or incompleteness in both contexts of what was seen as the liberal bourgeois project: no bourgeois revolution took place, it is argued, either in Italy during the *Risorgimento* or in Germany during the 1848 revolution. In both contexts, therefore, and in contrast to France in 1789, pre-capitalist landowners not only survived but continued to exercise power, while peasants were excluded from the formation of a 'national-popular will'. The resulting incompleteness of a bourgeois democratic revolution, it is further argued, was the persistence of an authoritarian and pre-bourgeois politics, which culminated in the rise of fascism in Italy during the 1920s and Nazism in Germany during the 1930s.

This theory about 'passive revolution' – the view linking the rise of fascism to the lack of a bourgeois revolution, and consequently a 'weak' national bourgeoisie and bourgeois democracy, and the absence of a peasant 'voice' in national politics – is wrong on a number of counts. First, as has been argued in the preceding section, not only were peasants not excluded from nationalism but they were projected by those on the political right as the very embodiment of the nation itself. Second, it is a theory which decouples capitalism from fascism, and thus exonerates the former from any blame for the latter: if fascism was a feudal reaction against capitalism, then capitalism is recast as an innately progressive systemic form.[115] This idea, as Trotsky, showed throughout the 1930s, is nonsense: fascism was a specifically *capitalist* reaction against the working class, and thus unconnected with feudalism. The latter critique notwithstanding, it was ideas about 'passive revolution' (fascism = feudal reaction) which lay behind the disastrous policy of the Popular Front, or agency which represents the epitome of 'subaltern resistance'.

National Popular or National Geographic?

In keeping with his search for an authentic and from-below 'national-popular', and to counter the objections of those who point out the potentially reactionary components of subaltern identity, Beverley not only draws attention to the similarity between the category of subaltern and the social composition of 1930s Popular Front Marxism (= 'National Popular'), but commends the role of each as an authentically anti-fascist and thus progressive grassroots mobilization.[116] One of the reasons why Beverley endorses 'Popular Front Marxism' is that in his opinion it recognizes popular/mass culture as forms of subaltern agency.[117] Where mass culture 'is popular in the consumer sense', therefore, he maintains that 'it is also "popular" in the political sense; that is, representative of the people, embodying the social will of the people, national popular, "progressive".'[118] Such a view merely confirms the extent of the failure to understand not just the epistemological differences between populism and subaltern resistance on the one hand and Marxism on the other, but also the political consequences of this inability to distinguish between them.

The perils of concessions made by communist parties in order to gain the support of peasants, in terms of the formation of an anti-fascist alliance with the 'progressive bourgeoisie' in defence of democracy and the nation, was pointed out a long time ago. It is important to recall, therefore, the lessons history teaches about the political objective and outcome of Popular Frontism. In order to counter the rise of fascism, Stalin and Comintern instructed autonomous working-class parties and/or organizations throughout the world to ally themselves politically not just with the peasantry and the national bourgeoisie but also with conservatives in their respective national contexts.[119] Popular Frontism in the mid-1930s accordingly entailed the replacement of working-class struggle and revolutionary internationalism with a nationalist and multi-class defence of democratic capitalism. Based on peasant essentialism, this populist strategy has a long history, and Popular Frontism represented the culmination of revisionist views advocated some 40 years earlier by Eduard Bernstein and Eduard David. Of equal length is the history of Marxist opposition to this kind of political strategy.

For example, Leon Trotsky opposed Popular Frontism on a number of grounds.[120] First, he objected to the peasant essentialism it advocated: because an undifferentiated category of 'peasants' included in its ranks small agrarian capitalists whose interests were not merely distinct from but actually opposed to those of workers, Trotsky emphasized the importance of recognizing agricultural workers as part of the proletariat and not as an incipient peasantry. Writing about France during the mid-1930s, he accurately delineated the connection between the populism of the political right and the agrarian myth, and how the latter entailed not only rural mobilization which ignored the existence of class differences within the peasantry but also a discourse-for that idealized the local and a discourse-against that opposed the large-scale (foreign monopoly capital, finance capital, the state).[121] Second, he maintained that the target of working-class mobilization should be capitalism and not feudalism, since fascism was a reaction not by the feudal *ancien régime* but by the bourgeoisie. Third, he warned against the dangers of categorizing the national bourgeoisie in less developed countries as 'progressive', and thus also of the risks to a proletariat of entering supra-class (= Popular Front, 'national-popular') alliances with a colonial or semi-colonial bourgeoisie in order to carry out the tasks of 'democratic' capitalism. And fourth, Trotsky argued that confidence in the existence of a 'progressive national bourgeoisie' itself was misplaced, since it, too, would turn to fascism were its own interests to be threatened by working-class mobilization. In short, the middle classes were not interested in anti-fascist struggle if this in turn opened up the prospect of socialist revolution, as happened in both China during the late 1920s and 1930s Spain.

Instead of Trotsky, however, Beverley symptomatically invokes the views of a prominent Stalinist, Georgi Dimitrov, as emblematic of the supra-class Popular Frontism he wishes to identify with subaltern 'resistance' in Latin America.[122] The folly of this position can be gauged from the fact that the Bulgarian peasantry seen by Dimitrov as the main element of this anti-fascist Popular Front stood not on the left but on the right of the political spectrum. In extolling the virtues of 'people's democracy' in Bulgaria, therefore, Dimitrov invoked the anti-fascist alliance between the Communist Party and the Agrarian Union in the mid-1920s, arguing that fascism triumphed because the working class was isolated from the peasantry, its 'natural' allies.[123] The difficulty with this claim is that, far from being the 'natural' allies of the working class, the mobilizing discourse of the Bulgarian peasantry and its political party, the Agrarian Union, was much rather indistinguishable from that of fascist organizations in Eastern Europe at that conjuncture: all of them adhered to a populist mobilizing discourse that was not only anti-Marxist, anti-urban, anti-industrial and anti-Semitic but also supportive of nationalism and the agrarian myth.[124]

Whereas Marxists who grew up in the first half of the twentieth century did so in the shadow of fascism, at a time when the political right was flexing it muscles, those who grew up during the second half, by contrast, did so in a period when, following the defeat of fascism, the political right was dormant.[125] For this reason, the discourse of the political right, with which most early twentieth century Marxists were familiar and against which a constant guard was mounted, was ignored by many of those who came to Marxism during the latter half of the century.[126] This led in turn to a lack of vigilance and a corresponding false sense of security, with the result that when this same nationalist politics re-emerged in the 1960s and rose to prominence once again during the 1980s and 1990s, many of those who perceived themselves as being on the left were caught unawares, and consequently wrongly identified elements of its discourse as progressive.[127] In short, because socialists have forgotten who their enemy is, too often they have mistaken the latter for a friend.[128] It was perhaps this as much as anything which was responsible for the gasps of surprise from postmodern theorists in the academy when they were presented with evidence of the fascist complicity of a number of prominent intellectuals who were either current exponents of postmodern analysis, or whose theory prefigured postmodernism.[129]

Consequently, during the recent past many of those who regard themselves as on the left have perceived the enemy simply in terms of an external force (foreign capital, the state) clearly visible on the other side of the barricade, rather than – more insidiously – groups on the same side of the barricade. Although it is true that one of the dangers posed by reactionary populist mobilization is that its 'strategy of tension' frequently enables the capitalist state to proscribe all opposition, including that of the left, therefore, as dangerous for those on the left is the risk posed by an unwitting alliance with such mobilizations.[130] This is the problem confronting those such as Beverley, Albó and Canclini, who pin their hopes for a politically progressive grassroots mobilization in Latin America on the deeply problematic category of 'subaltern resistance'.

CONCLUSION

A fairly predictable outcome of the undoubted academic success enjoyed by postmodern/post-colonial exponents of South Asian subalternism during the 1980s was the extension by a similarly self-styled 'alternative' historiography of the search during the 1990s for a culturally 'authentic' rural subject to Latin America. In an age full of ironies, one of the more amusing – and intellectually least sustainable – examples is perhaps the following: just at the moment that the Subaltern Studies project as applied to Asia is sinking under the weight of damaging political criticism, its Latin American counterpart appears to be taking off as a serious academic project. This contradictory juxtaposition might be explained in a number of ways: a project that was inapplicable to South Asia is relevant to Latin America, or the criticisms which have been levelled at the South Asian subaltern do not apply to the postmodern/post-colonial theorization of the subaltern in Latin America. Neither of these explanations, however, is sustainable, not least because, in its essentials, the Subaltern Studies project as applied to rural South Asia is epistemologically indistinguishable from that applied to rural Latin America. The latter is as a result vulnerable to the same kinds of political criticism made of the former.

Arguing that capitalism de-authenticates what is for them a 'natural' and longstanding identity indigenous to Latin America, Beverley, Canclini and Albó all search for and claim to have found evidence of a more 'authentic' grassroots subaltern consciousness and agency. In the case of Canclini and Albó, this quest leads them to the (re-)discovery of a pristine 'other' nationhood suppressed by European conquest, while Beverley locates the presence of a similarly 'authentic' subaltern identity/resistance in literary texts projecting the 'voice-from-below'. These kinds of search for 'authenticity', it has been argued here, cannot but culminate in a return to 1920s and 1930s *indigenismo*, and its attendant romanticization of peasant economy/culture/tradition. Because all grassroots cultural forms are regarded by both postmodern theory and the subaltern studies project as empowering, Beverley, Canclini and Albó conceptually eschew false consciousness. The deleterious political impact of this postmodern epistemology is impossible to avoid.

By agreeing to this essentialization of their discourse, poor peasants and agricultural labourers are permitted by exponents of the postmodern 'new' populism to celebrate their culture, thereby forgoing the right to change the class structure – the very existence of which is denied by these same postmodern 'new' populists – which makes their culture specific to them. In other words, it is a Faustian pact, whereby the celebration of culture is at the same time a celebration of the class system which gives rise to that culture. In exchange for accepting cultural autonomy, poor peasants and workers agree implicitly not to tamper with the underlying class structure. The denial of the falsity of consciousness also has other effects. Thus, the subaltern framework, in both its South Asian and Latin American manifestation, is necessarily silent about the formation and reproduction of 'popular culture' so defined. How, and why, specific forms of cultural identity surface at particular conjunctures is a question that is not asked, a silence which serves to mask the extent to which cultural forms celebrated by subalternism simply as empowering 'from below' manifestations are much rather disempowering 'from above' emanations, reproduced by capital for commercial and political reasons (to combat overproduction and to lock workers into the capitalist system as consumers).

Accordingly, the dominant intellectual trajectory in the social sciences, history, anthropology and development studies over the past two decades suggests that those who remain Marxists are going to have to fight many battles they had long thought settled all over again. The rise of postmodern theory, and its influential progeny the Subaltern Studies project, indicates that – among other things – this battle will involve re-materializing, re-politicizing and re-historicizing the analysis of Asian and Latin American peasantries, who, reclassified as de-materialized/ahistorical/apolitical 'subalterns', have now become trapped in an hermetically sealed discourse about language, literature and culture. Rather than discarding important components of Marxist theory – as even some Marxists now advocate – this battle with the postmodern 'new' populism requires exactly the opposite strategy: reasserting the political validity of these very components. Among the many accusations levelled at Marxism in general, and Leninists in particular, two of the most persistent have been that the insistence of socialists both on the class differentiation of the peasantry and on the international necessity for and similarity of working-class agency are mistaken. Conservative and right-wing critics of Marxism aver that no evidence exists for either of these two processes: not only does class struggle waged by workers possess no international dimension, therefore, but the reason for this is that they – like peasants – are national sociological entities whose specific characteristics (economic conditions, ideology, culture and political interests) are not and cannot be replicated elsewhere.

Of the many ironies raised by these criticisms perhaps the most significant are the two following. First, although it is fashionable nowadays to decry Marxist theory about the class differentiation of the peasantry, the main reason why the latter is still important is invariably overlooked. Marxists opposed the notion of an undifferentiated peasantry on two grounds, of which the less important one was that the reproduction of a middle peasant stratum would prevent class formation, and thus prove an economic obstacle to capitalist development. More important was the political objection (raised by Trotsky) that an undifferentiated peasantry would continue to be invoked as bearers of national identity and culture by those opposed to socialism. It is the second of these two forms which the subaltern project – as applied to Asia – has recuperated, in the process making this discourse academically 'respectable' and thus available to those on the political right in India. This is the danger that confronts those such as Beverley, Canclini and Albó, who wish to extend this same framework – subaltern identity/resistance – to the analysis of rural Latin America.

And second, it is clear that the political right not only possesses an international dimension to its own ideology, but that the latter also allocates similar characteristics and a political role to the peasantry regardless of national context. Against what it categorizes as the 'alien' internationalism of the left (proletariat, class structure, class struggle, socialism), therefore, the right in Germany, Spain, Argentina and Bolivia during the first half of the twentieth century, and in Europe, North America and parts of Latin America during the second half, counterposed its own 'authentic' form of internationalism: namely, the global existence of peasant economy and culture – the embodiment of nationhood and the repository of cherished rural tradition – threatened with destruction by finance capital and depeasantization. This in turn confers legitimacy on historical and contemporary forms of grassroots resistance conducted by peasant cultivators and farmers in defence of their private property against any ('redistributive') state attempting to change existing social relations of production and thus disrupt what conservatives maintain are organic and harmonious rural communities/traditions/hierarchy.

This 'from above' concern for those 'from below' characterizes conservative discourse about peasants as populist, a powerful ideology that combines plebeian and aristocratic versions of the agrarian myth. Its object is to disguise the impact of capitalist development in rural contexts by recasting economic inequality as 'natural', and refocusing 'difference' away from class and onto a town/countryside divide. Such a mutually supportive fusion of above and below forms of 'difference'/'otherness' in general, and arguments concerning the innateness of hierarchically-linked-but-socioeconomically-specific rural identities in particular, are found not just in most European, North American and Asian but also in Latin American variants of conservatism. All the latter lament the loss and simultaneously preach the importance of recuperating an historically innate form of (non-class) national/cultural identity that is virtuous, non-conflictive and rural in origin, and thus unifies the nation, thereby guaranteeing national harmony. For this reason, it is necessary to regard pro-peasant ideology mainly as a *mobilizing* discourse which, by fostering false consciousness among the opponents of capitalism (which include uncompetitive and/or dispossessed peasant proprietors), permits the process of capitalist development to proceed, especially when – as in the case of 1920s and 1930s Europe and Latin America – deployed in a classically populist fashion by groups/parties on the political right.

Although they would not see it as such, therefore, those who now advocate transferring both the subaltern project and its form of 'from below' agency (= 'resistance') from the analyses of rural Asia to approaches to the peasantry in Latin America run the risk of transferring also its nationalist ideology and politically reactionary assumptions. The whole point about the acceptability to the political right of an idealized image of an undifferentiated, ahistorical peasantry is that – once this supposedly homogeneous category is differentiated, and the presence of historically distinct class elements are revealed – it ceases to embody precisely those eternal/ahistorical/traditional virtues that make it acceptable to conservatives. As long as the peasantry remains an epistemologically undifferentiated category, however, it licenses a discourse about the agrarian myth that is central to the populist ideology of the political right. Thus the state/nation duality, and the concept of national identity based on this, which informs the search for a pristine grassroots subaltern 'authenticity' in Latin America has been – and remains – a polarity that underlies the analyses of agrarian populism and fascism. As the cases not only of Germany and Spain but also Bolivia and Argentina in the period between the 1890s and the 1940s all demonstrate, both agrarian populism and fascism seek to realign what they deem to be a pre-existing indigenous – and thus authentic – national identity with a state apparatus that is deemed to be representative of this.

The profoundly conservative subtext to this subalternist discourse has already been noted: no longer permitted by those in the academy to aspire to overturn existing property relations and the division of labour, poor peasants and landless labourers in the so-called Third World are now encouraged to like what they are and to enjoy what they already have. Because 'those below' cannot expect anything better than the status quo, agency in the form of 'assertiveness' is thereby confined epistemologically and politically not to a transcendence of current production relations, but to a defence of the latter on the part of poor peasants and landless labourers. The patronizing sub-text is that 'we cannot expect these people to want more', and consequently their present situation (and class position) represents for them an appropriate aspiration. In short, henceforth they must learn to be empowered by – and thus to be satisfied with – the 'otherness' of their culture, and with it their 'natural' position in the 'natural' socio-economic order. Because it is deemed to be for them a disempowering transformation, therefore, they must eschew economic change (= a Eurocentric metanarrative, the material benefits of which are not for them). In one form or another, this message has always been central to the thinking not of the left but rather of the political right. That such a view can be espoused by those who continue to regard themselves as part of the left is symptomatic of the depoliticization of academic discourse about development, together with a forgetfulness about the hard political lessons learned by an earlier generation of socialists – Gramsci among them – during the 1920s and 1930s, about the tenacity and durability of reaction.

NOTES

1. The Subaltern Studies project is embodied in the series about South Asian history and historiography, edited initially by Ranajit Guha [1982–89] and more recently by Chatterjee and Pandey [1992], Arnold and Hardiman [1994], Amin and Chakrabarty [1996], Bhadra, Prakash and Tharu [1999], and Chatterjee and Jeganathan [2000]. For seriously flawed accounts of the project as applied to South Asia, see Sarkar [1997; 2002: 154–94], Vanaik [1997], Chaturvedi [2000], and Ludden [2001; 2002]. While useful new critiques of the subaltern/post-colonial approach are still being written (see, for example, Veltmeyer [1997], Nanda [2001], Gupta [2001], and Petras [2002]), most of those produced after the mid-

1990s are highly derivative; thus many of the arguments – plus the Brecht quote – in Brass [1995] are also found in Bahl [1997].

2. As well as Beverley [1993; 1999], Albó [1993], and Canclini [1992; 1993; 2001], on whose work this article focuses, others who consider subaltern identity/resistance in relation to Latin America include Aman and Parker [1991], Rappoport [1992], the Latin American Subaltern Studies Group [1993], Mallon [1993: 388ff.; 1994; 1995], Joseph and Nugent [1994], Lowe and Lloyd [1997], Nugent [1998a; 1998b], Chomsky and Lauria-Santiago [1998], Joseph, LeGrand and Salvatore [1998], Bueno and Caesar [1998], Peloso [1999], Fiddian [2000], Mignolo [2000], Masiello [2001] and Aldama [2001]. That the concept subaltern resistance has become so all-embracing as to become meaningless is evident from the way in which it is being applied to specific Central American and Latin American contexts/conjunctures (see, for example, its deployment by Gudmunson and Scarano [1998]). Writing about nineteenth-century Brazil, therefore, Bieber [1999: 11] states: 'Although the term subaltern has typically been applied in the Latin American context to peasants, bandits, women, and the politics of resistance, it may also be fruitfully employed to analyse municipal bureaucrats, who are simultaneously marginal within the political system yet dominant within their local communities.' On this criterion, it would be possible in the case of English history to describe as 'subaltern' those powerful feudal nobles at the apex of the landowning hierarchy who were nevertheless opposed to the exercise of medieval kingship.
3. This epistemological break is one that exponents of the Latin American subaltern framework share with their South Asian counterparts. Both have shifted the analytical locus of grassroots conflict away from class and towards non-class cultural 'difference', the latter becoming as a result a celebration of what in effect is reified by subalternists as a permanent, ahistorical and empowering identity and resistance by peasant smallholders. What Marxism regards as false consciousness – ideas of selfhood based on subsistence cultivation by those whom (subalternists claim) are, have always been, and always will be middle peasants – is accordingly banished at one stroke.
4. Details about the postmodern 'new' populism, together with its connection to the agrarian myth, are contained in Brass [2000a]. The reasons for the intellectual acceptability of the Subaltern Studies project to those in the academy are complex, and have to do with the rejection by many intellectuals/academics of universal categories associated historically with a progressive and forward-looking anti-capitalism, and a corresponding retreat into the national/regional/local/ethnic particularisms/identities that have long been the preserve of a backward-looking, romantic anti-capitalism. It is clear that in some cases (unconnected with the application of a subaltern resistance framework to Latin America) a Faustian bargain has been struck – in exchange for entry into or promotion within the academy, Marxists have 'softened' their views and criticisms, seen the virtues of bourgeois political and/or economic theory, and in effect become 'Marxist' professors.
5. A similar kind of misrecognition informs a recent claim made in what purports to be a history of this journal: namely, that the critique of the postmodern underpinnings of the Subaltern Studies project was prefigured in an early article by Hobsbawm [1973], who 'anticipated so many of the characteristic tropes of "everyday forms of resistance" and "weapons of the weak" [and the subaltern] … none of which he saw as reason for analytical inflation or ideological romance, but rather the opposite, in fact' [*Bernstein and Byers*, 2000]. This, of course, is nonsense, and the reality turns out to be rather different. Leaving aside the obvious difficulty faced by claims that a critique was already in place in the early 1970s of an as-yet unformulated project, or what became the Subaltern Studies series only in the early 1980s, a central question is: if Hobsbawm himself was indeed as prescient as argued, why then was he to be found in the ranks of the 'new' populists a short while after having subjected their views to a class-based critique? Claims made by Hobsbawm [1981] about the decline of the working class as the subject of history were firmly in step with the fashionable anti-Marxist views of the time, and in fact no different from – and thus epistemologically supportive of – those made at that same conjuncture by many of those who were (or became) postmodernists and/or Subalternists.
6. It is clear from what he himself states that Beverley falls into this category. In the preface

to an earlier collection of his essays, covering the period 1989–92, he admits [*Beverley*, 1993: xi] to a 'rather uncritical enthusiasm for postmodernism', and also identifies the reasons for this: namely, that '[i]n jumping on the postmodernist bandwagon [he] was following the dictates of [his] taste', and also that he 'saw postmodernism as a way out of the crisis of the left'.

7. The abandonment of socialism by many of those on the left, and its replacement with one or other variety of the 'new' populisms influenced by postmodernism, has to some degree followed the same intellectual trajectory as that criticized by Deutscher [1955:14–15] some 50 years ago: 'Nearly every ex-communist broke with his party in the name of communism. Nearly everyone set out to defend the ideal of socialism from the abuses of a bureaucracy subservient to Moscow. Nearly everyone began by throwing out the dirty water of the Russian revolution to protect the baby bathing in it. Sooner or later these intentions are forgotten or abandoned. Having broken with the party bureaucracy in the name of communism, the heretic goes on to break with communism itself. He no longer defends socialism from unscrupulous abuse; he now defends mankind from the fallacy of socialism. He no longer throws out the dirty water of the Russian revolution to protect the baby; he discovers that the baby is a monster which must be strangled. The heretic becomes a renegade.'
8. Beverley [1999] falls squarely and self-consciously within the former category, and his book belongs to an increasingly familiar academic genre: the confessional text, which parades and then dismisses the significance of the author's earlier political naïvety, prior to a restatement/reaffirmation of his initial position. For other and earlier examples of this kind, see the texts examined in Brass [2000b]. As a review in this journal (*JPS*, Vol.29, No.1, October 2001, pp.182–91) makes clear, a more recent instance of the same type of *volte face* is Corbridge and Harriss [2000].
9. Ulrich Beck, who, together with Giddens, spent most of the 1990s assuring us that individual 'choice'/risk was innate to all forms of economic activity [*Beck*, 1992], is now attempting unsuccessfully to dissociate his version of individual 'choice' from its conceptualization by neoliberalism [*Beck and Beck-Gernsheim*, 2001]. The same is true of Richard Rorty [1998], an erstwhile postmodernist who, now that he finally accepts that it is unable to address issues such as inequality, advocates a return to liberal values of Dewey and Whitman (his incorrect description of them as 'leftist' notwithstanding). Yet another example of this trend towards self-reinvention is Ramachandra Guha [2001], an agrarian populist sympathizer of the Subaltern Studies project who, much like Beck and Rorty, now attempts to give new relevance to liberalism by arguing that, unlike the political right and left, both of which espoused variants of identity politics (the former advocating a unified Hindu community, the latter a unified lower caste community), liberals like him subscribe to personal choice incompatible with identity politics. In his view, therefore, liberals occupy what amounts to a 'commonsense' position in the centre of the political spectrum, between 'the blinkered polarities' of left and right: 'Fierce political opponents though they may be,' he concludes [*Guha*, 2001: 4669], 'intellectuals of red [= left] and saffron [= right] hues often practice the same methods [and] both tend to equate scholarly worth and scientific truth with ethnic background or cultural affiliation.'
10. For the dubious argument that 'Third Way' discourse is a bastion against the spread of the political right, see Anthony Giddens, 'The Third Way can beat the Far Right', *Guardian* (London), 3 May 2002. What he fails to understand is that fascist mobilization has presented itself historically as an 'above politics' movement that is neither of the left nor of the right, but rather a 'third way' alternative to both.
11. Described on the blurb in a vainglorious manner which goes well beyond the usual hyperbole deployed in such contexts ('one of the most interesting contributions to subaltern studies since Ranajit Guha's definition of the field in the early 1980s'), the book by Beverley [1999] is part of a series identified in somewhat bizarre terms as 'post-contemporary interventions'. At one level, the book, which consists of essays published during 1993–98, can be read as a baroque allegory of the double disenchantment that occurred over the course of this period: first with Marxism, and then with its replacement – the Subaltern Studies framework – as the realization of the latter's theoretically

unsustainable and politically tainted nature gradually dawns on Beverley. By then it is too late, and a final attempt by him to reinstate the concepts which structure Marxist analysis merely confirms the confused nature of the whole approach. Many others who also got it wrong are now trying vainly to persuade everyone either that they did not, or that it does not matter if they did.

12. On the nation-over-the-state versus the nation-under-the-state, see Albó [1993: 24]. The same kind of polarity informs the highly romanticized account of the Peruvian peasantry by Apffel-Marglin [1998: 3–4], who rejects 'Western science/rationality' in the name of what she claims is the 'egalitarian ethos of Andean peasants', so as 'to weaken development efforts and strengthen Andean life'. Significantly, earlier she had applied a subaltern framework to peasants in Eastern India [*Apffel-Marglin and Mishra*, 1995].
13. In contrast to the existing designation of an all-embracing national identity, whereby both nation and state in Latin American countries are historically 'given' categories, even for those who challenge their content, form and political object, Albó [1993: 27] wishes to adopt a wholly 'from below' designation: that is, the nation-as-defined-by-the-(rural)-grassroots. On this he comments: 'The difference between this [former designation], tied to progressive sectors of the hegemonic groups [= the political left], and those originating from indigenous and subaltern groups that have been condemned to a marginal role since 1492 is clear.'
14. In support of his argument that a more 'authentic' indigenous 'nation' overrides the national identity conferred by independence from Spain or Portugal, Albó [1993: 28] cites the example of the Aymaras (= true identity) inhabiting the space on either side of the frontier between Perú and Bolivia (= false identity). Notwithstanding the centrality of grassroots ethnicity to his categorization of 'nation', Albó [1993: 26–7] persists in the view that his project is fundamentally different from ethnic nationalism. Albó [1993: 24] also accepts that the process of decentralization and re-territorialization could extend to include the recognition of other forms of subaltern identity, such as regionalist tendencies (that of Cuzco in Perú, Sucre in Bolivia, and Bahía in Brazil).
15. On the innately transgressive role of carnival ritual, see Canclini [1993: 81]. In making this claim, Canclini is merely repeating an argument that has long circulated within anthropological discourse about rural Latin America.
16. Unsurprisingly, those at the rural grassroots do not themselves share this view, either about the existence or about the desirability of returning to a pristine indigenous culture. In this connection, Canclini [1992: 38] is forced into making the following revealing confession: 'When I first studied these changes I could only deplore the influence that the taste of urban consumers and tourists had on crafts. However, on a field trip eight years ago [i.e., the early 1980s] to a weaving pueblo in Teotilán del Valle, I entered a shop in which a fifty-year-old man and his father were watching television and conversing in Zapotec. When I asked about the wall hangings with images from the work of Picasso, Klee, and Miró, the artisan told me that he began to weave the new designs in 1968 on the suggestion of a group of tourists who worked for the Museum of Modern Art in New York. He then took out an album of clippings of newspaper reviews and analyses, in English, of his exhibitions in California. In the half hour I spoke to him I saw him move comfortably from Zatopec to Spanish and English, from art to craft, from his ethnic culture to mass culture, and from practical knowledge of his craft to cosmopolitan criticism. I had to admit that my worry over the loss of tradition was not shared by this man who easily negotiated three cultural systems.'
17. In keeping with this kind of approach, Dirks [1991] maintains that religious festivals in south India were examples of power-exercised-from-below. For important critiques of the carnivalesque as a 'from below' form of empowerment, see Gupta [2001: 102ff.] and McNeish (this volume).
18. According to Bakhtin [1984: 122-3], the characteristics of the carnivalesque are as follows: 'The laws, prohibitions, and restrictions that determine the structure and order of the ordinary, that is non-carnival, life are suspended during carnival: what is suspended, first of all is hierarchical structure and all the forms of terror, reverence, piety, and etiquette connected with it – that is, everything resulting from socio-hierarchical inequality or any other form of inequality among people (including age). All *distance* between people is suspended, and a special carnival category goes into effect: *free and familiar contact among*

people. This is a very important aspect of a carnival sense of the world. People who in life are separated by impenetrable hierarchical barriers enter into free familiar contact on the carnival square … Carnival is the place for working out, in a concretely sensuous, half-real and half-acted form, *a new mode of interrelationship between individuals*, counterposed to the all-powerful socio-hierarchical relationships of non-carnival life' (original emphasis). In keeping with this view, Scott [1990: 175] identifies the carnival as resistance incarnate, '*the* ritual location of uninhibited speech … the only place where *undominated discourse* prevailed, where there was no servility, false pretenses, obsequiousness, or etiquettes of circumlocution' (original emphasis).

19. According to Thompson [1991: 467ff.], rough musicking is an informal yet powerful type of grassroots sanction, a public method of social disapproval (and thus control) exercised historically by village populations 'against individuals who offend against certain community norms'. The highly stylized act of rough musicking was a customary form of 'from below' retribution in which the whole community participated, and amounted to a display (procession, dancing, construction and burning of effigies) the aim of which was the public humiliation of a specific individual within the community involved: such displays entailed ritual forms of 'unpitying laughter' or 'satiric noise' (= obscenities, rude cacophony, mockery), leading invariably to ostracism or expulsion of the victim. The link with carnival and the carnivalesque is clear: '[r]ough music is a vocabulary which brushes the carnival at one extreme and the gallows at the other' [*Thompson*, 1991: 509].
20. Whereas the majority of ethnographic accounts about the fiesta system in Central America have all tended to depict it as a context in which socially marginal subjects voluntarily assert what for them is an empowering 'from below' ethnic/cultural identity, Smith [1977] by contrast argues that Maya Indians in Guatemala and southern Mexico only go down this path involuntarily, when excluded from participation in the wider economic system. In other words, the kind of 'authentic' identity which postmodern/subaltern theory insists is much sought after is not in fact one that is freely chosen by its subjects (but much rather imposed 'from above'), nor is it regarded by them as a form of power-exercised-from-below.
21. In most rural contexts throughout Latin America the fiesta has been one of the most important sites historically of carnivalesque discourse/performance; such occasions attract large numbers of people to a specific location, and in many cases the whole population from the surrounding area attends and participates in all the fiesta activity – its religious observances, ritual celebrations, and accompanying festivities (street theatre, puppet and firework displays, dancing and drinking, etc.).
22. This replicates a central theme of folkloric discourse, whereby a subject (prince or pauper) discards his true identity for a short period, during which he becomes his 'other' and after which he once again resumes his normal social position in the existing hierarchy. To regard this 'other' identity assumed by the pauper as an empowering transition emblematic of plebeian strength, and thus indicative of the efficacy of 'from below' resistance, is simply to reify power.
23. For the centrality of laughter generally, and Menippean satire in particular, to the supposedly transgressive role of the carnivalesque, see Bakhtin [1984: 133ff.] and Lotman and Uspenskij [1984: 39ff.].
24. This dissonance between carnival and carnivalesque discourse on the one hand, and 'from below' class struggle on the other, is recognized by E.P. Thompson. In the case of nineteenth-century England, therefore, Thompson [1991: 525–6] accepts that 'rough music cannot be claimed as a "working-class" tradition, for the forms were imperfectly integrated into the early organized labour movement … the more sophisticated, organized, and politically-conscious the movement, the less indebtedness it shows to traditional forms of folk violence'. Significantly, he continues: 'This may have been because reformers sensed, in the very forms, a disposition to favour the traditional – or even atavistic – mood of the people. *For it was a form which was used, very consciously, by traditionalists against reformers or out-groups* … Where the rites of rough music survive after 1815, they appear to have an increasingly socially-conservative character' (emphasis added).
25. Thus, for example, Thompson [1991: 502, 504, 507, 516] cites numerous examples of rough musicking initiated by a member of the gentry and/or landowner in an attempt either to evict

'troublesome' tenants from their holdings or to silence their supporters.

26. For the way in which carnivalesque discourse/performance in India has on occasion served to reinforce communalism (= ethnic identity), see Cashman [1975] and Freitag [1989]. The kinds of domestic transgressions (conjugal infidelity, illegitimacy, widow remarriage) and offenders (blacks who challenged racism, women who challenged patriarchal values) punished by 'rough musicking', together with the discourse (monarchism, racism, anti-Semitism) and performance (lynchings) structuring the carnivalesque in many different contexts [*Thompson*, 1991: 486, 487, 523], reveal clearly its potentially/actually reactionary content and form, as well as its compatibility with class struggle waged 'from above', and corresponding incompatibility with a politically progressive notion of 'from below' agency. On this point Thompson [1991: 524] comments: 'Domestic rough music was socially conservative, in the sense that it defended custom and male-dominative tradition ... the elite saw little threat in it and were casual in their attempts to put the practices down'.
27. This particular fiesta, held in honour of the Virgin of Cocharcas in the central Andean province of Huancayo, involved in the period before the early 1940s a large-scale festive re-enactment of the Spanish Conquest by two rival sponsoring groups representing Spaniards and Incas [*Quijada Jara*, 1947]. Central to the carnivalesque performance/discourse of this fiesta were songs/dances reaffirming an autonomous Incaic ethnic/cultural/linguistic/religious identity under threat from the Spanish invaders – for example, offering to pay Pizarro any kind/size of ransom in exchange for the safe return of the imprisoned Inca ('*caballero de luenga barba/ no dés muerte a mi Inca/ si dices plata, si pides oro/ lo que quieras te daré*'), a process which licensed the reproduction of the following ideological oppositions:

Self	Other
Inca	Pizarro
Indigenous/'authentic'	Non-indigenous/'foreign'
Incaic/(Peruvian)	Spanish/(European)
Victim	Conqueror
Non-Christian beliefs	Christianity

For the high incidence of agrarian struggle in the Mantaro region, of which Huancayo is a part, see Samaniego [1978].

28. For this particular case study, which concerns the role of the fiesta in the rural estate system (and subsequently agrarian cooperatives) of the province of La Convención in the Department of Cusco over the period 1940–75, see Brass [1986b].
29. The fiesta officeholders in this instance were capitalist rich peasants, minor bureaucrats from the agrarian reform office, and local merchants, all of whom presented sponsorship of the accompanying festivities in terms of self-sacrifice/service to the benefit of the members of the agrarian cooperative on which it took place. The subtext to this discourse was the necessity in turn of specific forms of material reciprocity on the part of the receiving community (peasants and agricultural labourers) to the officeholders sponsoring the fiesta (selling their produce only to the merchants sponsoring the fiesta, overlooking sponsors' non-fulfilment of conditions necessary for continued membership of the cooperative, etc.).
30. In contrast to postmodern subalternists such as Scott and Canclini, who regard carnival as a site where 'popular culture' and the voice-from-below are reproduced, and consequently for whom the carnivalesque is an unproblematically democratic form of expression, Thompson – who unlike postmodern subalternists also knew his Marx – adopted a more nuanced approach to the form/content/object of rough music. Unsurprisingly, therefore, his analysis of the performance/ritual/discourse/meaning of rough musicking is torn between two contradictory political images of the carnivalesque: on the one hand a benign interpretation that stresses its 'folksy and even reassuring' role as a uniformly 'from below' form of resistance, and on the other a view which recognizes that it can also be a site of politically reactionary discourse/performance. Hence the revealing nature of his concluding observation [*Thompson*, 1991: 530]: 'I make [this] point strongly, arguing in a sense with part of myself, for I find much that attracts me in rough music. It is a property of a society in which justice is not wholly delegated or bureau-criticised, but is enacted by and within

the community. Where it is enacted upon an evident malefactor – some officious public figure or a brutal wife-beater – one is tempted to lament the passing of the rites. But the victims were not all of this order. They might equally be some lonely sexual non-conformist, some Sue Bridehead and Jude Fawley living together out of holy wedlock. And the psychic terrorism which could be brought to bear on them was truly terrifying: the flaring and lifelike effigies, with their ancient associations with heretic-burning and the maiming of images – the magical or daemonic suggestiveness of masking and of animal guising – the flaunting of obscenities – the driving out of evil spirits with noise.'

31. It is important not to confuse a critique of the folkloric images of rural life interpreted by subalternists as 'authentic' with a demeaning attitude to peasants themselves. As Marxists have frequently pointed out, first-hand accounts of peasant/village life emanating from the rural grassroots are usually beset by two kinds of bias: such discourse is not only penetrated by landlord ideology but also localized and parochial in scope. Thus, for example, Trotsky [1925: 72–3], who strongly opposed attempts by Russian populists to romanticize village life, acknowledged that Ivanov, an organic intellectual of the peasantry, 'knows and understands the Siberian peasant, the Cossack, the Khirgiz', but was nevertheless critical of him, observing that 'whether Ivanov wants it or not, he shows that peasant uprisings in "peasant" Russia are not yet revolution. The peasant revolt bursts forth suddenly from a small spark, unevenly, often cruel in its helplessness – and no one sees why it flared up or whither it leads.' It was this absence of the bigger picture – life beyond the village, in other words – that Trotsky found problematic in accounts of village life written by these organic intellectuals. Ironically, the more 'authentic' such literary accounts were, the less they could be said to address the problems of the wider society.
32. For this view, see Beverley [1999: 3, 14–15, 28]. The degree to which those who study/teach literature, and whose knowledge is confined to the latter, remain disconnected from reality (thus disqualifying them from membership of a vanguard of any kind), is perhaps nowhere better illustrated than in the naïve utterance by one such in the course of reviewing the latest collection of postmodern absurdities: 'Who else but Zizek', the reviewer in question gasps, 'could show that the postmodern celebration of difference depends on the radical abolition of class conflict …' (see *Times Higher Education Supplement*, 28 September 2001). Precisely this point ('the radical abolition of class conflict' by postmodernism) has been made time and time again over the past decade by a small number of social scientists who remained Marxists, a fact which appears to escape those who possess knowledge only about literature, or that which according to Beverley is sufficient to endow one with vanguardist potential.
33. See Beverley [1999: 49ff., 53]. Not the least of the many ironies inherent in this privileging of literature as part of a new revolutionary movement, in the vanguard of which are to be found not only post-colonial theorists but also literary representations of the subaltern 'other', is the fact that V.S. Naipaul, one of the principal novelists associated with the notion of post-colonial writing (his family left India for the Caribbean in the 1880s, and his early writings were about Trinidad), is now an unabashed cultural conservative whose literary ideal is the English pastoral, and who appears intent on reinventing himself as an English country gentleman [*Theroux*, 1998: 145, 362]. This kind of rightwards transition on the part of novelists, together with the reasons for it, has long been recognized, not least by writers who are themselves conservatives. Hence the observation about Kingsley Amis, John Braine and others, by fellow novelist and conservative Anthony Burgess [1990: 140] that: 'These former radicals had fulfilled Marx's thesis about economics being at the bottom of everything. A struggling author does well to favour socialism and dream of art as being useful to the state: to prosper with one's books brings capital, and the state had better leave it alone … the literary conservatism that Amis and [Robert] Conquest were adopting seemed to be based on the false premise that literary revolution and political progressivism grow from the same roots. This was never so: the literary innovators have always been bourgeois with a tendency to fascism.'
34. See Beverley [1999: 56].
35. On this point, see Beverley [1999: 65]. For a similar definition and methodological endorsement of *testimonio* by another exponent of Latin American subalternism, see

Canclini [2001: 7–8, 170 n3]. The more perceptive hearers of and commentators on oral history have long warned about the uncritical celebration of the 'voice from below', and the epistemological and political risks attached to its idealization. One such is Jerry White, who two decades ago made the following still relevant observations about the illusory search in the UK for 'representative biographies'; although his criticisms are of the 'new local history' as practised in Britain, they apply with equal force to the celebration of the Third World 'other' by postmodern new populist accounts of the 'voice from below'. '[I]ndividual experience', he notes [*White*, 1981: 36–7], 'can tell us little about the forces which shape our lives make us what we are and where we live what it is. There is a huge reality outside the boundaries of individual consciousness. It is the *critical understanding* of that reality, of the relations of capitalist society and our historical place within them, which must be the object of an actively socialist local history. This critical consciousness of capitalism is missing from the new local history (as it is from much local and political life). It is not that people's reminiscences are necessarily quietist or uncritical: indeed, many of them are fired by a fine anger. But this is criticism without understanding ... Without a socialist understanding, criticism is always in danger of latching onto any apparent "explanation" that happens along: "colour not class" ...or (and just as much) "the council", "the government", "the unions" and whoever and whatever people blame for getting us where we are now. At its worst, and few local oral history publications are free from this, autobiography can reinforce capitalist values so that the whole tone (notwithstanding the angry bits) is politically bland and negative and unprovocative. They give us moving insights which enrich the brotherhood of man and boost the self-confidence of working people, but it all appears to take place in a vacuum ... Work is treated very much as if it were a thing complete in itself, instead of being one part of a social relationship: we do it because we do it. The dignity of labour, stressed by many of the local oral histories which focus on work, disguises what work is for – who owns what we produce, where profits come from, why we are deprived of work, how new jobs are made, the social consequences of the things we do, and so on. We should thus be made to question the function of what, after all, amounts to nearly half the product of our waking lives: unthinking pride in a job well done is just what the capitalist ordered' (original emphasis).

36. For the announcement of this reversal, see Beverley [1999: 69]. On the problematic nature of the *testimonio* by Rigoberta Menchú, see Stoll [1998] and the contributions in Rus [1999].
37. It is perhaps significant that, during the 1960s when the political role of literature was subject to a closer scrutiny than it is now, even those on the political right – like the novelist Simon Raven [1967: 115] – admitted that '[d]eceit, masquerade, metamorphosis, moralization – there is almost no trick class will not try before it is finally made to appear in its own true and proper form and, so to speak, own up'. It goes without saying that such an admission undermines the naïve faith expressed by Latin American subalternists in the unproblematically emancipatory political role of literature *per se*.
38. For the argument that subaltern 'otherness' cannot be represented by anyone other than the subaltern him/herself, see Beverley [1999: 30, 102, 112]. This claim about the innate 'unknowability' of the 'other' is central not just to postmodern/post-colonial theory but also to texts [e.g., *Clifford and Marcus*, 1990] which insist on the impossibility of ethnography (= non-fiction), and maintain that the latter is nothing more than literature (= fiction). Such an approach, which reifies all 'from below' discourse because this cannot be represented by someone who is not him/herself a subaltern, contrasts absolutely with Marxist analyses of literary texts, where the objective/subjective polarity is retained. Thus, for example, both Engels [1976a; 1976b] and Lukács [1950] criticized literary representations projecting rural poverty as ennobling, regardless of whether or not such images circulated at the village level. In a similar vein, Russian writers and poets (Sergei Yessenin, Vsevolod Ivanov, Nikolai Nikitin, Boris Pilnyak) who themselves came from peasant backgrounds, and who also idealized rural life, were characterized by Trotsky [1925: 93–4] as 'the rustic or peasant-singing writers' engaged in legitimizing rural reaction against the urban proletariat ('the *revanche* of the bast shoe over the boot'). His observations on this process are instructive: 'all the rustic writers tend in the direction of a primitive nationalism smelling of

roach … The economic decline [of the peasantry], the strengthening of provincialism, the *revanche* of the bast shoe over the boot, home-brew and drink – all these are pulling (one can even say, have pulled) backward into the depths of centuries. And parallel with this can be seen a conscious return to the "folk" motif in literature. Blok's great development of city couplets ("The Twelve"), the notes of folk song (in Achmatova, and with more mannerisms in Tsvetaeva), the wave of localism (Ivanov) … The advent of workers as a ruling class caused an inevitable reaction against the borrowing of bourgeois patterns … It is quite evident that the return to bast shoes, to home-made rope and to home-brew is not a social revolution, but an economic reaction, which is the main obstacle to revolution. In so far as a conscious return to the past is concerned, everything that has been done is extremely unstable and superficial. It would be unreasonable to expect the development of a new literary form from … a peasant song.'

39. The dismissive comment (cited in Theroux [1998: 127]) applied by novelist V.S. Naipaul to a writer about the working class ('He brings news … from working class people. It's not writing, really. It's news') is, if anything, a more accurate description of the uncritical approach by postmodern/post-colonial theory to the agrarian grassroots in the so-called Third World (= the literary depiction of the rural 'other'). Not the least of the many ironies framing this comment is that the original position occupied by Naipaul himself in the literary salons of metropolitan capitalism was precisely that of a 'bringer of news' (about the non-Western 'other').
40. See Beverley [1999: 100, 101]. What Beverley forgets (or perhaps does not know) is that Marxism does *not* refuse to recognize the existence of a consciousness among peasants: what it *does* refuse are claims that peasant consciousness is a consciousness of class and (thus) politically progressive.
41. As has been pointed out elsewhere [*Brass*, 2000a; 2000b], the political antecedents of this kind of theory ought to generate concern among subalternists (Latin American and others) who subscribe to them.
42. For historical instances of this process, the recent and conscious 'from above' creation of what is widely believed to be a long-standing tradition emanating 'from below', see the seminal text edited by Hobsbawm and Ranger [1983]. See also Philo and Miller [2001] for the impact of cultural studies on the analysis of media, and in particular how postmodern theory recast (and simultaneously depoliticized) such analysis by decoupling economic content (ownership/control of media) from questions of ideological form, the latter as a result being seen (wrongly) as economically non-determined, ideologically free-floating, and thus politically 'autonomous'.
43. This process of *actively* constructing/creating public opinion along lines desired by capital is associated with the highly influential ideas about public relations developed by Edward Bernays (1891–1995), a nephew of Sigmund Freud, who deployed his uncle's theory in the service of corporate North America [*Ewen*, 1996; *Tye*, 1998]. The many successes he achieved in this regard underline both the existence of and the relative ease in reproducing what is palpably a 'from above' form of consciousness, and one which – considered in terms of 'from below' class interests – is undeniably a situation of *false* consciousness.
44. Freudian pessimism about humanity in general, and the possibility of a progressive politics in particular [*Einstein and Freud*, 1933], was transmitted in turn to the influential work of Fanon and Marcuse (on which see Brass [2000a: Ch.5]), where it was responsible in part for the political despair each expressed about the possibility of revolutionary action undertaken by a Western industrial working class co-opted by consumer capitalism, and their consequent espousal of an instinctual (= 'pure'/non-rational) process of mobilization undertaken by peasants and lumpenproletarians in the Third World who had not been co-opted by capital.
45. For the widespread distribution in Latin America and the ideological impact there of Disney comics, plus the centrality to the latter of a 'from above' discourse about on the one hand the desirable innateness of Nature, the countryside, ethnicity, the 'noble savage' and 'primitive otherness', and on the other the corresponding undesirability of technology and the modern city, see Dorfman and Mattelart [1975: 41ff.]; for the reactionary beliefs and political linkages of Walt Disney himself, together with the way these permeated the films

and animated characters (= 'popular culture') that emerged from his Hollywood Studios, see Peary and Peary [1980: 47ff.] and Eliot [1993].

46. After 1945, this ideological control has been ubiquitous, and to a large degree effective: in the ensuing five decades it has encompassed the political content of film, the electronic media (radio, television), and the printed word [*Kahn*, 1948; *Mattelart*, 1979; 1991; *Cumings*, 1992; *Saunders*, 1999].
47. This argument is applied by Huggan [2001] to what might be termed the global literary embrace of post-colonialism, a process extending from the dominance of post-colonial writing where the Booker prize is concerned, and imperial nostalgia for texts about India, to the academic study of post-colonial literature in Canada and Australia. Although he draws attention to the marketing of all the latter by metropolitan capitalism, Huggan himself is nevertheless sympathetic to the post-colonial project; unlike the view taken here – that the quest for any form of 'authenticity' is necessarily self-defeating – he accepts the existence of an essential 'authenticity', and objects only to conceptual misuse of the term by those engaged in searching for it. Like other exponents of postmodernism, Huggan tends somewhat over-optimistically to regard 'exoticism' as a form of political subversion, and – as in the case of Beverley – his critique is itself confined to post-colonial discourse as a purely literary phenomenon; his focus is accordingly on the form of mediation (= literature), rather than between the latter and what is mediated (the material reality existing at the rural grassroots).
48. Thus the idealized Rousseauesque image of the 'noble savage' (= nomadism as 'natural'/primitive humanity) which informed the travel writings of Bruce Chatwin was appropriated by him from anthropological texts [*Shakespeare*, 1999], while a similarly derivative and romanticized account of the Kalahari Bushmen in a correspondingly prelapsarian state structured the equally inaccurate but highly popular narrative in the same genre by Laurens van der Post [*Jones*, 2001]. In the case of the latter writer, this influence not only extended into British ruling class circles but also threatened to have an impact on the shape of the post-apartheid political settlement in South Africa. Dismissing the ANC and Nelson Mandela as 'communists', van der Post (along with the far right in the UK and South Africa itself) championed the separatism of the reactionary Zulu Inkatha movement led by Chief Buthelezi, whose espousal of traditional cultural values represented for the travel writer the embodiment of his own vision of 'natural'/'primitive' man in Africa. From the late 1980s to the early 1990s, van der Post continuously pleaded the Inkatha/Buthelezi cause to the then Conservative prime minister Margaret Thatcher and Prince Charles, with the object of securing their political support for the creation within South Africa of a separate Zulu nation (= KwaZulu-Natal).
49. The corollary of the view that there is no such thing as false consciousness is that all consciousness is true, a position akin to the neoclassical economic argument that individual 'choice'/'preference' is exercised on the basis of 'perfect knowledge', and about as convincing. It should be emphasized that the term 'false consciousness' as theorized by Marxism is not the same as that used by Canclini (see above). The latter differentiates between false/non-authentic and true/authentic forms of indigenous culture/tradition (= rural folkloric beliefs/practices), both of which are consigned by Marxism to the realm of false consciousness.
50. By contrast, the desirability/possibility of mobilizing the grassroots in the pursuit of reactionary ideas/objectives has not escaped those on the political right. Thus, for example, Moeller van den Bruck, who in the early 1920s made an important contribution to Nazi ideology, argued that German reactionaries must wrest the proletariat from the hands of Marxism. His views on this are both prescient and instructive [*van den Bruck*, 1934: 142, 152, 177]: 'To be successful, a leader of today will need to persuade the masses to permit him to act for the whole nation, to preserve or win the values that are essential … If he is to give the masses the opportunity of making the Revolution … ultimately fruitful for the nation, he will require the superiority that springs of an exact knowledge of proletarian problems and persons. He must rejoice at being called to lead the proletarian masses, to direct their will into national channels … Marx had offered to men accustomed for tens of centuries to live for and by ideas, the lure of his materialist thought and his materialist

conception of history. Movements, however, beget counter-movements. When Marxism was swamped in democratic chaos, Nietzsche with his conception of aristocracy came to the fore … the world revolution will not be that which Marx envisaged; it will be rather that which Nietzsche foresaw.' Nor is it the case that such views were confined to Germany. In a similar vein, Patrick Donner, the English conservative MP for West Islington, made the following observation some ten years later: 'It showed our [English] Socialist politicians in their true light, as men out of touch with actualities and times in which they live, that they were not even aware that the days of revolution from the left are over in Europe, and that modern revolutions come, when they do come, from the Right' (see Patrick Donner, 'The Political Outlook in 1933 from the Conservative Angle', *The Bookman Special Christmas Number*, December 1933, p.150). Although wrong on the subject of revolutionary mobilizations from the left, the criticism that the majority of socialists tend to underplay or ignore the counter-revolutionary potential of those on the right was nevertheless correct. More recently, and in a similar vein, a supporter [*Elst*, 2001: 393–4] of the reactionary Hindutva project of the BJP has argued that 'Little wonder that some right-wing "identitarian" groups are taking inspiration from and exploring cooperation with surviving and newly assertive tribal populations … Leftist ecologists and pro-tribal activists plead indignation at the sight of rightists inviting tribal leaders to their meetings [but] if you apply the usual yardsticks of Left and Right to these tribals, it should be obvious that to a man [*sic*], they are in the rightist camp on most issues. They favour…religion over secularism, tradition over progress, tribalism over globalism, identity over the melting-pot.'

51. That conservatives identify as kindred spirits those relativists who claim to be non-conservatives is clear from the following observation by a prominent American conservative [*Buckley*, 1959: 154]: 'There is nothing so ironic as the nihilist or relativist (or the believer in the kind of academic freedom that postulates the equality of ideas) who complains of the anti-intellectualism of American conservatives.'
52. It could be argued that existentialist claims about 'choice' validated not only the choice-making subject of neoclassical economics but also and subsequently the anti-Enlightenment/anti-foundational framework which underlay the relativistic identity politics of postmodernism. This was perhaps one of the reasons why both existentialism and postmodernism ended up unwittingly occupying the same epistemological ground as conservativism. As pointed out at the time by those on the political right, existentialism was for them a central theoretical emplacement of their own ideology. Jacques Maritain, for example, attempted to claw back from Sartre what he regarded as a Thomist concept of existentialism that legitimized and reasserted the anti-rationalistic act of Christian choice as an method of denying/defying what for those on the right were the unpalatable lessons taught by an historical process unfriendly to his/their cause. Hence the observation [*Maritain*, 1957: 11–12] that '[a] Thomist who speaks of St. Thomas's existentialism is merely reclaiming his own, recapturing from present-day fashion an article whose worth that fashion itself is unaware of'.
53. The historical potency of a discourse about Nature, and its role in the ideological armoury of any ruling class engaged in struggle with 'those below' is well-known, and was outlined most succinctly in the late 1920s by Vološinov [1976: 11]: 'Whenever … a social class finds itself in a state of disintegration and is compelled to retreat from the arena of history, its ideology begins insistently to harp on one theme, which it repeats in every possible variation: *Man is above all an animal* … The ideology of periods such as these shifts its center of gravity onto the isolated biological organism; the three basic events in the life of all animals – birth, copulation, and death – begin to compete with historical events in terms of ideological significance and, as it were, become a surrogate history. That which in man is nonsocial and nonhistorical is abstracted and advanced to the position of the ultimate measure and criterion for all that is social and historical. It is almost as if people of such periods desire to leave the atmosphere of history, which has become too cold and comfortless, and take refuge in the organic warmth of the animal side of life. That is what happened during the period of the break-up of the Greek city states, during the decline of the Roman Empire, during the period of disintegration of the feudal-aristocratic order before the French Revolution. The motif of the *supreme power and wisdom of Nature* (above all,

of man's nature – his biological drives) and of the impotence of history with its much ado about nothing – this motif equally resounds, despite differences of nuance and variety of emotional register, in such phenomena as epicureanism, stoicism, the literature of the Roman decadence (e.g. Petronius's *Satyricon*), the skeptical ratiocination of the French aristocrats in the seventeenth and early eighteenth centuries. *A fear of history, a shift in orientation toward the values of the personal, private life, the primacy of the biological and the sexual in man* – such are the features common to all of these ideological phenomena' (original emphasis).

54. This connection is examined by me at length elsewhere [*Brass*, 2000a: Ch.5]. The absurdities arising from this idealization of agrarian custom/practice/tradition can be illustrated from the case of 1930s Germany, where the Nazis presented traditional peasant costume from Bavaria to workers in northern industrial cities as part of their common national identity, the extent of the cultural gap (and corresponding distinctiveness) between their respective urban/rural backgrounds notwithstanding [*Jell-Bahlsen*, 1985: 318]. The same source concludes that this 'abstraction of "cultural unity" in the shape of folklore aided the Nazi regime in imposing a contrived unity from above onto the people below'.
55. Given the idealization by Beverley of literary discourse as a source of knowledge about subaltern identity/resistance, it is perhaps significant that one of the most influential books circulating in the domain not just of 'popular culture' but also of the 'counter-culture' during the latter half of the twentieth century – J.R.R. Tolkien's trilogy *The Lord of the Rings* – is regarded by the Italian 'new' right as an embodiment of its own political beliefs [*Griffin*, 1985]. The reason for this is simple: the fictional portrayal of an alternative mythical cosmology that is both anti-modern and anti-historical shares many of the assumptions that structure conservative ideology.
56. Hence the symptomatic nature of the discourse encountered in White [1901: 95ff., 101ff., 256, 312–13], who not only attributes military setbacks in the Anglo-Boer War to the fact that British soldiers defeated by South African farmers were recruited in towns and cities, but also equates village depopulation and urbanization/industrialization in England with national decline, invokes as ideals both the Russian *mir* and French peasant society ('France is firmly set among the nations by her peasant proprietary'), and concludes on an undeniably fascistic programmatic note ('restore responsibility, enforce it on high and low … [p]atriotism will be taught in our schools, and the gospel of Efficiency will be our national cry').
57. The anti-Semitic nature of this discourse is unmistakeable, 'alien'/'foreign'/'materialistic' Jews being identified as a 'cosmopolitan plutocracy' which threatens empire, nation and small farmer alike [*White*, 1901: 69–70, 74]: 'The great and prosperous Jewish nation … is a caste [that] devotes itself mainly to finance … [this] plutocratic caste is a growing menace to our Imperial position. Many of these gentlemen have no roots in the land. They inhabit town houses, and, if they own a place in the country, it is for display. Their investments being mobile, they themselves are cosmopolitan. The influence they bring to bear upon Governments is noxious, because the British Foreign office learns to recognize the interests of rich men as those which alone require attention. Thus it comes to pass that the interests of the rich and the poor are by no means always identical, and the diplomatic, naval, and military forces of the Crown are utilized in the interests of the plutocratic caste – a proceeding which may, and sometimes does, injure the bulk of the people of England. The material side of life is emphasized, the soul of the nation is shrivelled as the fronds of a filmy fern when exposed to the fumes of an acid.' By contrast, the same discourse [*White*, 1901: 67–8, 74] presents 'authentic' English landlordism in a rather more positive light, as the source of a 'real aristocracy' rooted not in money but in tradition/land/nation, members of which are both the first line of defence against finance capital and also benign protectors of the small farmer: 'The owners of great estates are in a better position to contribute to the welfare of the residents than are the smaller proprietors. They help tenants at a pinch, and assist them to tide over bad times. As a rule, they have more capital than the small owners. They expend it on a system that becomes a family tradition. There is more economy of labour and material. Profit is little, and occasionally, no consideration whatever to the owner of the great estate … The system of land tenure and of primogeniture which have allowed the great estates to descend unimpaired from one generation to another … secures to those

dwelling on the soil material and moral advantages greater than any that are promised under any alternative system, and it enables the heads of great families to take part in public affairs without the imputation of interfering in politics for what they can get out of it. To the real aristocracy of the country I look for a remedy for the disease with which our nation has been infected by bad smart society [= the 'plutocratic caste'].'

58. On this point, see Brass [2000a: 255–6].
59. For the details about Justus Möser (1720–94) see Epstein [1966: Ch.6]. Noting the prefiguring influence of Möser's views on German conservatives such as Adam Muller and Novalis, Epstein [1966: 324, 325] observes that his 'admiration for a society of peasants ... has a Jeffersonian flavour; it did not, however, imply any bias towards egalitarianism. On the contrary, Möser explicitly favoured a hierarchic order of society where everybody knew and kept his place ... Möser admired a society marked by a great diversity of status, where everybody was content to perform his traditional function for the common good. He looked upon inequality as a positive good, not a necessary evil ...'. On the question of a golden age, self-sufficient peasantry as the authentic representatives of German national identity, Möser (cited in Epstein [1966: 329]) observed: 'Where do we find the true German nation? We certainly do not find it at the court of the princes. Our cities today are filled with misshapen and spoiled copies of humanity; ... our countryside with exploited peasants. How different was our nation [in the early Middle Ages], when every Franconian or Saxon peasant cultivated and defended in his own person his *paterna rura*, that is his hereditary allodial lands, free of feudal ties or manorial obligations; and when every freeholder went from his homestead to participate in the work of a popular assembly.'
60. Darré's words (cited in Mosse [1966: 148–50]) are as follows: 'First there was the German peasantry in Germany before what is today served up as German history. Neither princes, nor the Church, nor the cities have created the German man. Rather the German man emerged from the German peasantry. Everywhere one will find primordial peasant customs that reach far back into the past. Everywhere there is evidence that the German peasantry, with an unparalleled tenacity, knew how to preserve its unique character and its customs against every attempt to wipe them out ...' Just as for Darré a direct link joined the German peasant to his *führer*, so for Prince Bernhard von Bülow at an earlier conjuncture there existed a similarly direct link between the peasantry, the Prussian landowning class, and the German kaiser, all united by a common bond of national identity, history, and – by inference – economic and political interest. Hence the view [*von Bülow*, 1915: 136–7] that 'we must not forget what those very classes did in the service of Prussia and Germany. It was the noblemen and peasants east of the Elbe who ... primarily achieved greatness for Brandenburg and Prussia. The throne of the Prussian kings is cemented with the blood of the Prussian nobility ... The praise which the Prussian nobility demand, and which they have a perfect right to expect, is not meant to detract from the achievements and merits of other classes. Without the self-sacrificing loyalty of the middle classes, the peasants and the poor people, the nobility would have accomplished little'. Not only does von Bülow [1915: 233] point with satisfaction to the rising number of peasant smallholdings, which he claims increased by some 180,000 in the period 1895–1907 directly as a result of his 1902 Tariff Law protecting German agriculture, but he also makes clear the political advantage this process confers on Prussian landlordism: namely, to counter the dual political threat posed by a rapidly expanding and class conscious proletariat on the one hand, and the influence of the radical leftwing German Social Democrats on the other. In short, the positive and endorsing views held both by von Bülow and by Darré about the peasantry correspond to class struggle waged not 'from below' but much rather 'from above'.
61. The connection between capitalist development and a conservative pro-peasant discourse is clear from the role of peasant economy in the Nazi project. A fascinating insight into the potentially capitalist economic role of smallholding cultivation as envisaged by Nazism, and thus the importance to the latter of reproducing peasant economy, is provided by the arguments advanced by Professor Konrad Meyer [1939]. He was the representative of *Stabsamt des Reichsbauernsführers*, who led the German contingent of professional economists attending the 1938 International Conference of Agricultural Economists. Among other things, Meyer [1939: 58, 60, 62, 64] claimed that the growth of peasant

economy had effectively refuted Marxist claims about the inexorable nature of land concentration and depeasantization, that the 'internal biological vitality' of the race and nation required material/ideological sustenance by the peasantry, and that the latter formed a solid bulwark in the countryside against the growth in towns of 'class feeling which [originated] in the cities'. The combined economic/political/ideological objectives of fascist pro-peasant discourse, according to Meyer [1939: 58–9], were to kill four particular birds with one stone: first, to retain the political allegiance of the peasantry in a doubly threatening context – from what was perceived to be an external (= 'foreign') menace, and from the unfolding capitalist crisis; second, to prevent the latter from accentuating the process of depeasantization, and consequently the formation of the threatening and much-feared urban 'mob-in-the-streets', which – as an urban proletariat – was the traditional bastion of the political left; third, to include small-scale peasant farming *within* the industrialization process, so as to make it more efficient economically, thereby ensuring that smallholding cultivation made a contribution to Germany's requirement for foodstuffs; and fourth, to settle and populate conquered territories (although, for obvious reasons, this is not made explicit by Meyer). In other words, *as a modernized peasant economy that for Nazis simultaneously embodied all the virtues of a 'traditional', rural and specifically German national identity* (= the economically efficient, socially harmonious, culturally enduring, community sustaining activity of family farming), smallholding cultivation could be said to be part of the fascist project of reactionary modernization.

62. Evidence suggests that between 1928 and 1933 rural voting support for the Nazi Party increased more dramatically than its urban counterpart, the former rising from 2.8 per cent of all votes cast to 52.4 per cent while the latter rose over the same period from 2.4 per cent to only 39.6 per cent [*Knauerhase*, 1972: 42, Table 5]. The role of petty commodity producers in the rise of German fascism is confirmed for the rural areas of Schleswig-Holstein and Hanover where, in contrast to poor peasants and agricultural labourers who supported the Socialists and Communists, the majority of those who voted for the Nazis in the 1932 elections were peasant family farmers [*Loomis and Beegle*, 1946].

63. Far from disagreeing with Marx, therefore, it was because they were familiar with his writings, and thought his prognosis historically accurate, that Falangists were vehement anti-Marxists. In short, they detested and feared Marxism not because it was wrong but much rather because it was right. Throughout his writings Primo de Rivera [*Thomas*, 1972: 160–61, 180] repeats constantly that his anti-Marxism stems from the recognition that Marx was correct in predicting that large-scale capitalism would lead to the ruin of small rural producers and through this the nation itself. Much the same is true of fascism elsewhere at that same conjuncture. Hence the observation made by the leader of the British Union of Fascists [*Mosley*, 1932: 66–7]: 'It is now the declared aim of every great nation to have a favourable balance of trade. *Every nation, in fact, seeks to sell more to others than it buys from them – an achievement which, it is clear, all nations cannot simultaneously attain.* So a dog-fight for foreign markets ensues in which the weaker nations go under, and their collapse in turn reacts upon the victors in the struggle by a further shrinkage of world markets. A continuation of the present world struggle for export markets is clearly the road to world suicide, as well as a deadly threat to the traditional basis of British trade. These phenomena appear at first sight to support Marxian theory … Some of the Marxian laws do actually operate if mankind is not organized to defeat them, and they are operating today in the inchoate society which they envisage … if we rely on Conservatism to defeat Marxism, we shall be defeated by Marxism' (original emphasis).

64. See Thomas [1972: 98]. In attempting to define Spanish nationalism [*Thomas*, 1972: 98ff.], however, Primo de Rivera recognized – but did not resolve – the central contradiction facing those on the political right who wished to formulate national identity on the basis of claims to a geographically innate culture that was pristine, traditional and irreducible. Just as it was possible for him to invoke Spanish nationalism as a 'natural' attribute unique to Spain as embodied in the *existing* nation-state, therefore, so others inhabiting specific areas *within* this same national context could in turn invoke an equally distinct set of regional/local characteristics/identity (ethnicity, language, religion, culture, music, folklore, etc.) in order to justify their claim for the creation of a *new* nation-state (Catalonia being the example he

cited). In the end, he evaded this problem of separatism, settling instead for the nebulous equation (reminiscent of current postmodernism) nationhood = 'otherness', and then asserting the primacy of an overarching Spanish 'otherness' which in his view subsumed all rival local/regional claims.

65. Hence the view expressed by Primo de Rivera [*Thomas*, 1972: 209] that Falangists 'do not see agrarian reform as merely a technical and economic problem … Spain is almost entirely rural. *The open country is synonymous with Spain*; if in the Spanish countryside the living conditions imposed on the Spanish sector of agrarian humanity are intolerable, this is not merely an economic problem. It is a total problem, religious and moral' (emphasis added). His idealization of feudalism and regret concerning its passing is contained in Thomas [1972: 21]. For Primo de Rivera, peasant farming and individual peasant proprietorship were unconnected with capitalism, the capitalist system and the 1930s crisis: much rather, in his view '[o]ne effect of capitalism was just the annihilation, almost entirely, of private property in its traditional forms' [*Thomas*, 1972: 158, 178]. This was due to the fact that he equated capitalism simply with finance capital (= the usurious 'foreign other'), a conflation which in turn licensed a potent relay in statement decoupling property relations both from the crisis and its solution (peasant economy = private property = non-capitalist = 'natural'/Nature, against which were arraigned all its antagonistic 'others': capitalism = finance capital = foreign other = economic crisis).

66. On these points see Primo de Rivera [*Thomas*, 1972: 30, 134, 165, 182, 206–7, 234]. This was a common theme in the discourse of the European political right during the 1930s, and involved blaming not capital or capitalism but finance capital both for the economic crisis and for the dehumanizing impact (= deculturation) of the latter on the peasantry, the embodiment of national identity. In many contexts, this discourse was also ethnicized, and gave rise to a potent ideological opposition between finance capital as the exploitative 'foreign other' (the Jewish 'foreign other' in Nazi Germany) and the exploited peasantry as the national 'self'. For examples of this anti-finance capital stance in the case of the Spanish political right during the 1930s, see Calvo Sotelo [1938] and Primo de Rivera [*Thomas*, 1972: 29, 159]. Socialism was inculpated with the revolutionary destruction of the peasantry and thus by inference of national identity, about which Primo de Rivera [*Thomas*, 1972: 181] observed the following: 'If we really want to prevent the results foreseen in the Marxist prophecy, we have no choice but to dismantle the unwieldy machine whose turning wheels inevitably bring those results; we must dismantle the unwieldy machine of capitalism, which leads to social revolution, to Russian-style dictatorship'. Similarly, the Republican government to which the Falangists were opposed was accused by Primo de Rivera [*Thomas*, 1972: 184] of a trend 'towards the collectivisation of agriculture, the transformation of the peasantry into a gregarious mass, just like the workers in the cities'.

67. On these points, see Thomas [1972: 170, 182]. For the agrarian reform programme of the Spanish Falange, see Primo de Rivera [*Thomas*, 1972: 134] who noted that '[t]he state will recognize private property as a valid means of attaining individual, family and social ends and will protect it against being abused by high finance, speculators and moneylenders.'

68. In the immediate post-war era the concept of an innate 'peasant-ness' was central to the work both of H.J. Massingham, a widely-read writer about the English countryside, and of Wilhelm Röpke, a member of the political right whose ideas influenced European and American conservatism [*Abelson*, 1988; *Hartwell*, 1995]; for examples of their conservative pro-peasant discourse, see the 'Third Way' ideology propounded by Röpke [1948; 1950], and also the contributions collected in Massingham [1945]. Both were vehement anti-communists, and each was influenced by the views of Hayek (see Massingham [1945: 1–2]). Advocating a return to Nature, therefore, Massingham [1945: 7–8] insisted that 'we shall not, in fact begin to understand the meaning of husbandry unless we relate it to the first principles of natural law, which is the earthly manifestation of the eternal law … [t]he pattern of life worked out by pre-industrial rural society was an unconscious obedience to ecological laws.' If Massingham represented the aristocratic variant of the agrarian myth, then the emphasis of Röpke was on the plebeian variant: the significance of his views is that these constitute an epistemological fusion of the agrarian myth, populism, neoliberal economics and the 'traditional' conservatism of the political right. Hence the centrality to

his argument [*Röpke*, 1950: 201ff.; 1948: Ch.IX, 'The Peasant Core of Society – Danger of Agrarian Collectivism'] of an economically viable smallholding agriculture premissed on the recuperation of an idealized peasant proprietorship was itself linked to the wider political project of the right, incorporating ideological support for small-scale rural production/exchange (artisan, petty trading) and opposition to the large-scale (the state, monopolies). For Röpke the importance of peasant family farming was that, since it is immutable and basically individualistic/conservative, it operates as an ever-present economic/political/cultural bulwark against the political dangers represented by economic progress, urbanization, mechanization, class struggle, proletarianization, socialist planning and collectivization. Claiming that smallholding agriculture based on private property 'brings men and nature together' in a way that 'counter-balances the industrial and urban aspects of our civilization with tradition and conservatism, economic independence and self-sufficiency [that derive in turn from a] proximity to nature, ...a natural and full existence near the sources of life ...', Röpke [1950: 202–3] warned that 'the peasant world together with other small sectors of society, represents today [the early 1940s] a last great island that has not yet been reached by the flood of collectivization, the last great sphere of human life and work which possesses inner stability and value in a vital sense. It is a priceless blessing wherever this reserve still exists ...'.

69. Significantly, among the contributors to the collection edited by Massingham were Edmund Blunden, Rolf Gardiner and the Earl of Portsmouth, all of whom had been fellow-travellers of the political right in the 1930s [*Griffiths*, 1983]. In what is an astonishing case of denial, and in defiance of evidence to the contrary, however, Massingham [1945: 3, 4] asserts that German fascism was a 'proletarian vice', an instance of 'state absolutism … all urban in origin', and the result of 'the loss … of the timeless rural values in industrialism'. In keeping with the cold war rhetoric of the political right, he then equates German fascism with Russian communism, in order to dismiss them both as examples of industrialized 'totalitarian' states and also to disassociate himself (and his contributors) from pre-war German sympathies. His coded anti-Semitism is evident from the following [*Massingham*, 1945: 6]: 'A usurious system was built up round this primary sin of abandoning our native land. It not only maintained itself by ruining our own farmers and pushing those of other lands into debt, but handed over all the power and credit in the community from the primary producer to the dealer. Examine the vested interests of this country, and it will be seen that they are nearly all clustered round the breeding of money…'

70. Hence the fact that in North America during the mid-1960s, 'Goldwater showed that with liberals in control in Washington, conservatives could appropriate the tradition of antigovernment populism, thus broadening their electoral base and dispelling their traditional image as elitists.' [*Foner*, 1998: 313]. Where US agricultural policy was concerned, Goldwater [1964; 38ff.] united a critique of high taxation and state regulation with the claim that only the free market would eliminate surpluses and thus deliver higher prices to the farmer ('[f]arm production, like any other production, is best controlled by the operation of the free market').

71. It is necessary to emphasize that, on the question of economic policy generally, the European political right is not a theoretically homogeneous grouping. In the case of Britain, the contemporary political right is usually divided into two distinct ideological tendencies: on the one hand the free market economists assembled under the neoliberal banner, and on the other traditional conservatives less concerned with economic growth than with reasserting ancient privilege. This distinction was accurately delineated in the mid-1980s by David Edgar, who observed that 'an element at least of the impetus behind Thatcherism was to be nothing to do with the release of vital new entrepreneurial energies, but was all about the reassertion of the most ancient of privileges, the most crude and atavistic of class hatreds. That the restitution of seigniorial authority is not the *whole* of New Conservatism shouldn't blind us to the fact that it's a part …' ('Let Them Eat Dirt', *New Statesman*, 26 September 1986, original emphasis).

72. The continuing link between conservatism, the aristocratic variant of the agrarian myth and a pro-peasant ideology is epitomized by the work of Roger Scruton. On the one hand, therefore, the pastoral vision of countryside-as-Englishness he endorses has at its centre an

idealized image of the landlord class: hence his acceptance of the view that country house life amounted to 'the conjunction of liberty and liberality that comes about when affluence coincides with a secure and localized social standing', and that 'the country house came to represent an ideal of English civilization – one in which hierarchy was softened by neighbourliness, and wealth by mutual aid' [*Scruton*, 2000: 237, 239]. This benign perception of rural landlordism as seen from above is then attributed to those below: 'Our countryside is inseparable from the country house and its parklands, and expresses the careful integration of villages, farms and vistas that constituted for the gentry the visible signal of their title. It bears the mark of a mild and deferential despotism, and the nostalgia that people now feel ... for the class-divided and deferential [traditional rural] society' (Roger Scruton, 'In Praise of Mild Despotism: Old families, not the National Trust, can save the countryside', *Business FT Weekend Magazine*, 27 October 2001). Accordingly, this same pastoral vision also requires the inclusion within its ideological framework of a similarly idealized concept of the small family farm: hence the view that in England '[p]rimogeniture, and the abolition of feudal tenures, gave early reality to the small family farm, intact over generations ... [i]t is on such farms that the "yeoman stock" celebrated by Macaulay was raised' [*Scruton*, 2000: 240].

73. On these points, see Scruton [2000: 241]. Symptomatically, this organic unity of English rural society (landlord + small farmer = 'Englishness', or English national identity) is then contrasted [*Scruton*, 2001] with the evils of large-scale urban decay ('Many of our inner-city areas are now unviable. Schools are dreadful, drugs and promiscuity threaten the young, and crime levels are soaring'). Among the reasons that England no longer exists (= 'The Forbidding of England'), therefore, is that '[t]he family farm, which maintained the small-scale and diversified production that was largely responsible for the shape and appearance of England, is now on the verge of extinction' [*Scruton*, 2000: 254]. The principal cause of this multiple and inter-related decline – in 'Englishness', English identity, English culture, and the countryside that embodies them all – is the post-war tax system introduced by the Labour government, which destroyed the country house and now threatens the small family farm [*Scruton*, 2000: 240]. The programmatic imperative of this discourse is not difficult to discern. Lamenting that taxation which penalizes inheritance (= 'broken up landed estates') 'now threaten[s] the family farm', Scruton [2001] calls for 'a wholly new and radical conservative policy' that will reverse this process, both by re-establishing family farming ('[t]he family farm is the backbone of the rural economy, and the most important generator of the distinctive British landscapes') and by rolling back European Union and/or British state control ('it is now clear that regulations are killing off small farms'). Small producers, concludes Scruton [2001: 16], must be protected from 'unfair competition'. That pro-farmer views not only continue to resonate within English conservativism but do so in both plebeian and aristocratic forms, underlines both the centrality of the agarian myth to the populism of the political right, and also the extent to which the discourse of the latter continues to be based on a project of innateness. For this reason, it is necessary to disagree strongly with Cook and Clarke [1990: 140] when they claim that: 'a writer like Scruton is not embarking on a project of innateness but ... one of populism'. Much rather, Scruton's populism is not only based on a project of innateness but actually has no meaning outside this ideological framework.

74. A revealing illustration is the trajectory followed by Richard Mabey, currently an influential writer about nature, conservation and farming in England. During the mid-1960s, when the entrenched power in British society of tradition/privilege/hierarchy was being questioned, he [*Mabey*, 1967] espoused the then commonly-held conservative view that it was the working class, not the bourgeoisie, which objected to attempts to categorize its culture as disempowering. What is of particular interest, however, is the way in which this argument was deployed. Rather than defending tradition/privilege/hierarchy, therefore, the argument took the *opposite* form: *a defence of plebeian cultural 'otherness'*. Hence the view [*Mabey*, 1967: 15] that 'we shall have class groups forming who share not only different standards for living but different standards *of* living. At this point passing some sort of judgement on class inequalities becomes almost impossibly complex' (original emphasis). The insidiousness and effectiveness of this spuriously democratic kind of discourse should not

be underestimated. Conservatives begin by pointing out, uncontentiously, that workers object to attempts by the bourgeoisie to represent their plebeian culture as disempowering; the next step, which is also seemingly uncontroversial, is the conservative claim that, because culture is indeed different, workers are right to make this objection; from this, however, conservatives draw what is palpably a contentious inference. Since cultural formation/reproduction possesses its roots in what one does for a living, conservative political discourse concludes rightly by pointing out that all culture is linked ineradicably to the economics of class. Accordingly, the conservative plea for the innateness of cultural difference becomes in effect a plea also for the retention both of existing class relationships and of the capitalist system itself. Symptomatically, Mabey's [1967: 15–16] opinion is that the problem is not one of class distinctions per se but rather of communication between classes: 'the class problem today is not so much one of privilege … but of communication. [It is] a dangerous and total separation of two sorts of person that it would be to our very great [national] benefit to have, not being the same as each other, but *knowing* each other' (original emphasis). In a conclusion that could easily have been written by a contemporary exponent of postmodern subalternism, he notes [*Mabey*, 1967: 16]: 'We should perhaps be aiming for the class equivalent of a multi-racial society, where ethnic differences are appreciated, not obliterated.' Here the reactionary political role of non-class identity emerges with stark clarity: what conservative discourse is arguing, therefore, is that workers can enjoy *any* identity they want, so long as it is not that of class. The sub-text is equally clear: celebrate your culture, conservatives proclaim, and we – as conservatives – will not only allow but encourage you to do this; you for your part, conservatives swiftly add, must allow us to do the same – namely, celebrate *our* culture and assert *our* cultural difference which, of course, as we all recognize is rooted in *our class position*. As the right-wing novelist Simon Raven [1967: 122, 123] put it at that same conjuncture, 'for [the right] knows that since it will continue to go to its own restaurants, as it were, it will not often be called upon to demonstrate its belief in the new equality', a situation in which '"parity of esteem" is accorded to everyone who fulfils his function conscientiously, no matter how prosaic that function may be.' It comes as no surprise to learn that Mabey [1980; 1983, 1990], who defended tradition/privilege/hierarchy in this seemingly plebeian fashion during the mid-1960s, was during the 1980s – and is in the late 1990s – not only upholding views about the sacredness of nature ('I have a belief that we have an atavistic bond with the natural world … [p]eople are drawn to the countryside to experience the unique rhythms of the natural landscape … [w]hat is exciting about the natural world is precisely that it is autonomous'), advancing a reactionary form of anti-capitalism ('Farmers are utterly in thrall, not to the local rhythms and inward-looking perspectives that have to do with an indefinable quality of rurality, but to a business schedule delivered from factories and companies … you could say that in earlier times we weren't indifferent to nature …'), and advocating small-scale subsistence agriculture ('When we talk about peasant communities we can genuinely talk about rurality, there is a set of conditions of self-sufficiency and of certain kinds of introversion in social living. These are concerned with keeping the integrity of rural communities intact … If you happen to be a lawyer, or a shop-keeper, and you're making a moderate income from that, then you don't have to try so desperately to wring the last ounce of profit from the land … [h]obby farming should be encouraged') but also sharing a platform [*Mabey*, 2000] with Prince Charles and Vandana Shiva. In other words, over the last three decades Mabey has remained politically consistent, both in his defence of rural tradition/privilege/hierarchy and in his advocacy of small farming: that is, in his espousal of the aristocratic variant of the agrarian myth.

75. See, for example, Rama [1981]. Among those on the Latin American political right during the 1930s who were influenced by European fascist ideology, and in particular that of the Spanish Falange (see above), were two important Peruvian political leaders: Luis Flores of the *Unión Revolucionaria*, and the Catholic landowner José de la Riva Agüero (see Klaren [2000: 279–80]).
76. In many ways, these two sources of nationalism – one inside and one outside Latin America – are similar to the two sources of North American right-wing politics: on the one hand the Southern agrarian tradition, linked to visions of European aristocratic culture epitomized by

and reproduced in the context of the antebellum plantation system, and on the other an 'authentic' indigenous plebeian version embodied in the frontier myth and its images of family farming.

77. This misrecognition extends also to Canclini [2001: 11], who observes: 'This is not to say that in Latin America there have not been nationalist and ethnicist fundamentalisms, promoting exclusivist self-affirmations and resisting hybridization by constructing a single absolutist patrimony that illusorily casts itself as pure ... *However, this has not been the dominant tendency in our history. And much less in this era of globalization ...*' (emphasis added).
78. For evidence of which, see Maríategui [1928], Castro Pozo [1924; 1936], Blanco [1972], Haya de la Torre [1936a; 1936b], and Reinaga [1953; 1968; 1969; 1971]. Since these are all examples of a discourse which operates within the domain of 'the political', it is in one sense unsurprising that literary criticism remains unaware of it.
79. In the course of leading an important peasant movement in eastern Peruvian province of La Convención during the early 1960s, therefore, Hugo Blanco believed that 'dual power' corresponded simply to the traditional institutional structure of peasant economy that existed prior to the implantation of the landlord estate.
80. For these points, see Albó [1993: 19] and Ticona, Rojas, and Albó [1995]. The degree to which Albó's subalternism reproduces all the *indigenista* stereotypes is evident from a comparison with the earlier – and in many ways prefiguring – work of Fausto Reinaga, whose views about the presence in Bolivia of an indigenous and undifferentiated Andean peasant community are virtually indistinguishable from those currently held by Albó. Hence the identical claim by Reinaga [1953: 50] that the rural grassroots in Bolivia were not only innately socialist but have also been practising this non-Marxist form of socialism since the pre-Conquest era ('*En la vida económica y social del indio, vive integro en espíritu y cuerpo el sistema comunista incaico, no el de Sorel, Lenin o Marx. El hábito colectivo del trabajo social en la producción, la distribucción y el consumo es toda una evidencia. El indio, como ayllu y comunidad práctica y en alto grado una envidiable vida social socialista.*') The connection between the populism of the Russian narodniks and the conceptualization of Andean peasant community/economy/family is discussed, briefly, by Urquidi [1970: 194ff.].
81. According to Albó [1993: 21], this 'authentic' grassroots identity is an 'image [in which] one can perceive the unity, born in good measure from a common history [that has] led to a shared language of exchange, to similar systems of beliefs and values, and to many shared institutions, such as ... the *compadrazgo* [fictive kinship] systems and rural community'. Much the same point is made about agrarian relations in Peru by another exponent of Latin American subalternism [*Peloso*, 1999: 150], who claims that '[b]ased on mutual trust between the participants, sub-tenantry most frequently occurred between relations and compadres'. As many ethnographic studies conducted in the Andean region confirm [*Sánchez* 1977, 1982; *Brass*, 1986a], these idealized claims are quite simply incorrect: both Andean rural community and its institutional forms – such as fictive kinship – have for a very long time not only been differentiated internally along class lines but also perceived as such by the poor peasants and agricultural labourers involved.
82. For an example of earlier *indigenista* arguments made by those who are now in the Latin American subalternist fold, see Albó [1972; 1987; 1988]. For the deep roots of *indigenismo* in anthropological accounts of the Andean region and Brazil, see Marzal [1990] and Ramos [1998].
83. See Albó [1993: 30–31], where the importance of this nation/culture/land/peasant linkage to subaltern identity in Latin America is underlined in the following manner: 'Perhaps the most fundamental point is that, in contrast to the dominant capitalist models, there persists a collective and self-generating development of the productive forces concerned with maintaining the communal base to a greater or lesser degree in the majority of the indigenous nations we are referring to.'
84. In this connection it is important neither to overlook nor to underestimate the influence of religion on the positions taken by the political right in Latin America (and in Spain). Accordingly, it is significant that, throughout the period from the late nineteenth to the mid-

twentieth century, even the reactionary/conservative discourse of the Roman Catholic Church has consistently advocated the protection/survival of peasant smallholding. This is evident from an analysis by Karin Dovring [1956: Ch.7] of the teachings of Roman Catholicism about land reform, as embodied both in the social encyclicals of and related pronouncements by the Vatican over a 60-year period – from *De Rerum Novarum* (1891) issued by Pope Leo XIII, through *Quadragesimo Anno* (1931), to the Pentecost message of Pope Pius XII in 1941 and the Vatican-influenced ideas of Christian Democratic politicians in Italy during the early 1950s. Throughout this period, therefore, the official discourse-for and discourse-against of a profoundly conservative Catholic Church was uniform in its views. In keeping with the ideology of those on the political right, the discourse-against of the Roman Catholic Church expressed hostility to the theory, practice and institutions/organizations of the left generally (Bolshevism, socialism, communism, class warfare, class hatred, unionization), and argued against collectivization, asserting that socialism threatened family life and was contrary to natural law; it warned continuously against 'state-interference', condemned socialists and left-wing trade unionists as 'crafty agitators', 'seditious' and 'futile', dismissed equality as 'ridiculous', and insisted that common ownership of property was against workers' interests. Over this same period, by contrast, the official teachings of Roman Catholicism not only endorsed private property in all its forms but especially small and medium peasant family farms: the discourse-for of the Vatican and/or Christian Democratic politicians linked to it continuously stressed the value of small- and middle-sized rural landed properties, arguing that Vatican policy was to support 'a society of small owners with farms fit [for] developing family life ...', its ideological focus being on the 'care of the individual male farmer, his workplace and land, his home and the raising of his own family' [*Karin Dovring*, 1956: 302, 305]. On this point the same study concludes: 'The concept of the state, the claim for the right of the individual, private property, negativism against the too rich, the stress on the lawful owner and respect for the law ... are among the concepts the Vatican made its own. A comparative glance at the different documents will disclose more common symbols which definitely conform to the Vatican ideal for a society: small holdings, small lands where the family can be supported' [*Karin Dovring*, 1956: 310]. Two additional points are worthy of note. First, that the two main papal encyclicals reaffirming authority/hierarchy and condemning the left were both issued as ideological guidance during periods of acute economic crisis (1891 and 1931). And, second, that – like the political right generally – the target of Vatican criticism was not the capitalist system *per se* but rather financial capital (= 'greedy capitalist', 'rapacious usury', 'grasping speculators'). This is also true of Argentina, where both the discourse-for (upholding authority, hierarchy, nationalism, family farming) and the discourse-against (anti-socialist, anti-Enlightenment, anti-Semitic) of the Roman Catholic Church were supportive of – and, indeed, indistinguishable from – the discourse of the political right [*Deutsch*, 1986; *Deutsch and Dolkart*, 1993].

85. For the early 1940s political programme of the Bolivian falangists, and the role in this of an indigenous peasantry, see the FSB texts reproduced in Cornejo [1949: 131–8]. For the views of its Secretary General, Oscar Unzaga de la Vega, and the attempt by the FSB to reinvent itself politically during the post-war era, see Lora [1970: 271ff.].
86. Hence the observation [*Deutsch*, 1986: 41–3] that by the start of the twentieth century: 'Some intellectuals blamed foreigners for class conflict [and] urban blight ... The gaucho and the Hispanic past found their greatest defenders in the writers whom historians have called the cultural nationalists ... The cultural nationalists defined the Argentine character in terms equivalent to traditional society – terms that did not threaten the existing order ... the hitherto reviled gaucho now became a model for the masses to follow. Loyal to his employer, content with his station in life, opposed to thrift, rational behaviour, and planning, the idealized gaucho was the antithesis of the successful foreign-born entrepreneur and the labor activist alike.' Such views, the same source notes, 'reflected the extent to which cultural nationalism and intertwined xenophobic and antimodernist sentiments had permeated the upper class'. For the rise of the political right in Argentina, and in particular the role in this from 1919 onwards of the Argentine Patriotic League, see Deutsch [1986; 1999] and Deutsch and Dolkart [1993].

87. In a period of capitalist crisis, therefore, Jews were blamed in the domain of 'popular culture' both for causing the crisis (= finance capitalism) and also for its potential effect (= socialism) [*Deutsch*, 1986: 35, 44–7, 74–5, 78; *Deutsch and Dolkart*, 1993: 38–9]. This discourse informed widely-read anti-Semitic fiction, both in Argentina and in the United States of America: the agrarian populist dystopic book *Caesar's Column* by Ignatius Donnelly [*Brass*, 2000a: Ch.6] in the latter context, and in the former the novel *La bolsa* by Julián Martel [*Deutsch*, 1986: 45–6].
88. On the cooperative credit unions (*cajas rurales*) set up in the countryside by the Argentine Social League, a forerunner of the political right, in order to provide small farmers with loans so that they would not 'have to turn to foreign sources of financing', see Deutsch [1986: 53].
89. The Argentine Patriotic League was a 'from above' response to labour militancy and mobilization during the 1920s, when the bourgeoisie and petty bourgeoisie feared both that the state would be unable to resist this and that – unchallenged – such working-class agency would (as in the case of Russia) lead inevitably to the revolutionary overthrow of the existing socioeconomic order. Its self-professed aims were not just to guard against revolution (= 'to defend the existing socioeconomic order against the left'), but also to maintain national unity ('Fatherland and Order'), to 'help the poor' by 'opposing class hatred', and to protect Argentine nationality and property from 'foreigners', strikes and left-wing ideas/actions. Half its leaders were either themselves landowners or related to members of the landlord class, and many League members had occupations (ranching, commerce) either in agriculture itself or with close links to this [*Deutsch*, 1983: 66ff., 80ff., 102, 104–5, 111].
90. 'Land reform was a matter of special interest for the League and a useful example of its ideas. One reason for the importance of this issue was the postwar agrarian disorders. Another was the fact that League members, like cultural nationalists, believed that the countryside was the storehouse of Argentine traditions and virtues, in contrast to the cosmopolitan cities … In formulating their opinions on this topic, some Liguistas followed [the] dictum that order depended not on abolishing property, but on multiplying it … property ownership gave one a sense of self-worth and a stake in the present order; indeed, the worst enemies of Bolshevism were landholding peasants. Dividing large holdings into smaller ones and facilitating their sale to small farmers would create a large antileftist constituency… In one of the rare instances in which a Liguista mentioned Mussolini, Carlés [the Argentine Patriotic League leader] suggested that Argentina follow the example of the Italian Fascists, whose land reforms were enlarging the independent peasantry' [*Deutsch*, 1986: 168–9].
91. There can be no doubt as to this objective and its long-term political effects. In the view of one commentator [*Deutsch*, 1986: 112, 152] '[the Argentine Patriotic League] spread antileftist publicity, crushed strikes, and replaced unions with [bosses' organizations]. Without serious hinderance from the government, the League helped to weaken the labour movement for decades to come'; unsurprisingly, the number of strikes/strikers declined from 367 and 309,000 in 1919 to an annual average of 90 and 70,000 during the period 1921–28.
92. That is, in the period *before* the development decade of the 1960s, when peasant economy and the issue of agrarian reform became the central focus of discourse about economic growth and planning.
93. The agronomist in question was Gerardo Klinge [1946], who attributed the problems of a minifundist agriculture not to the presence of the *hacienda* system but rather to land fragmentation as a result of inheritance within the context of peasant economy itself.
94. On this point, see Klinge [1946: 369]. Much the same is true of India at that conjuncture, where a report written by representatives of industrial capital [*Thakurdas, Tata, Birla, Dalal, Ram, Lalbhai, Shroff and Matthai*, 1945: 82] similarly advocated 'the establishment of a class of peasant proprietors'. An analogous recommendation was made by yet another capitalist spokesperson [*Zinkin*, 1956: 209–10], who also supported the idea of an individualist agrarian reform in India on explicitly political grounds, because it 'creates new owners by the million', adding that: 'The difference between a man with two acres and a

man with twenty is still great, but it is different in kind as well as in degree from the difference between a man with nothing and a man with two acres.'

95. For a detailed analysis of this strike, see Landsberger [1969].
96. That the vineyard workers' strike was not a success is attributed by Landsberger [1969: 263] to its politically reformist discourse which, by eschewing class struggle, ensured that any 'from below' action undertaken by the strikers stopped short of a challenge to either the property rights of or the power enjoyed by large landowners. An explicitly political objective of undertaking rural grassroots organization in this manner on the part of religious and/or radical right-wing groups was to deny this support to left-wing groups; the latter had been organizing among Chilean vineyard workers since the 1930s.
97. See Fletcher [2001] for evidence of support for the political right by peasant smallholders in the Pewenche indigenous population from the Alto Bío-Bío region of Chile. As this particular case study makes clear, the opposed views held by the Pewenche regarding their displacement by a hydroelectric dam, and consequent resettlement, were themselves an effect of equally distinct employment histories, or the relative importance of experiences as workers or smallholders in the formation of their political consciousness. Whereas males migrated in search of paid work, Pewenche females remained in charge of cultivating the family smallholding. For the women leading the resistance to Pewenche resettlement, therefore, the importance of 'staying put' was because it permitted them to continue as smallholders on ancestral land. In other words, opposition to dispossession stemmed from their economic identity as peasants, and consequently a stated desire to avoid deculturation was an attempt to present this in a politically more acceptable form, by invoking a discourse about legitimacy rooted in ethnic tradition. As is well documented, this kind of defence has a long history in Latin America, where land rights have been defended by recourse to arguments about ethnicity, tradition and culture. Its ideological potency is particularly marked where women are perceived as defenders of a number of mutually reinforcing 'natural' – and thus immutable – traditional identities: of Nature, of the family, of subsistence farming, of indigenous culture, and through all the latter, of the nation itself (female = family = subsistence farming = Nature = nation).
98. As Payne [2000: 74] points out, the political right in Argentina was not only 'unabashed in its appropriation and adaptation of past cultural symbols', but also 'hired a "cultural adviser" rather than a political adviser', the object being – as its arch-enemy, the founder of the Mothers of the Disappeared, put it – to disguise 'a right-wing agenda with left-wing discourse to win working-class votes … the demagoguery of working for the lower echelon of society.'
99. Although he disavows a connection between the subalternist framework and cultural studies on the one hand and populism and nationalism on the other, Beverley [1999: 97, 103, 111, 112] becomes increasingly aware of the unsustainability of this disavowal as his analysis progresses. Hence the profusion of disclaimers such as 'I perhaps run the risk here of idealizing mass culture in the same way that earlier … I seemed to idealize the Popular Front'. Much the same is true of Canclini, another influential exponent of Latin American subalternity, who similarly oscillates between a desire to make the subaltern studies project work and a belated recognition of it populist/nationalist underpinnings.
100. It should be noted that there were two kinds of offender in this regard. The first, and in an important sense the less serious category, was the non- or even anti-socialist (such as Foucault), for whom the presence of non-class issues and discourse merely confirmed what he/she had always maintained was the case: namely, the political irrelevance of Marxism. The second, and far more problematic category consisted of those who continued to regard themselves as socialists (for example, Löwy [1998]), and who endorsed a wide variety of agency as progressive simply because it was 'from below' mobilization against capitalism.
101. Beverley [1999: 21–2]. Symptomatic of this theoretical confusion is the fact that at other points in his book Beverley [1999: 101, 109, 113, 127–8, 171 n22, 172 n32] appears to be not merely non-Marxist but actually anti-Marxist.
102. Beverley [1999: 22, 23, 24]. Although he seeks to distance the Latin American Subaltern Studies project from the Dependency theory of the 1960s and 1970s [*Beverley*, 1999: 10, 47, 91–2], the structure and political discourse of the former inescapably mimics that of the

latter. Just as the economic problems of Latin America were attributed by Dependency theory to external forces (imperialism), rather than on those which existed internally (capitalism, class), in the 1980s and 1990s the ideological problems of Latin America (= crisis of representation) were similarly blamed by postmodernism on exogenous influences ('foundational' Eurocentric metanarratives) rather than on endogenous discourses (nationalism, populism).

103. Marxists who questioned the postmodern theoretical underpinnings and warned about the political direction of subaltern/resistance framework included Petras [1990] and Brass [1991]. These warnings went unheeded, as is clear from the following symptomatic observation about subaltern mobilization by Fox and Starn [1997: 5]: 'Perhaps more than anything else, the rise of a literature on new social movements reflects a new sensitivity on the part of scholars to the multiple vectors of political activity that always exist in any society'. What this complacent statement boils down to is this: resistance and political activity have always taken place, a feature that observers should appreciate. Apart from it being a point that is so self-evident that it hardly requires making, what is avoided by Fox and Starn is the necessity of having to evaluate any/all agency *politically*. To state, as they do, that because it takes place all such 'from below' mobilization is necessarily good is, in effect, to approve of all grassroots agency regardless of its politics and objectives – in other words, to endorse action simply because it corresponds to 'from below' agency. This kind of approach depoliticizes grassroots mobilization, failing as it does to make a political distinction between wage struggles and trade union organization on the one hand, and the lynching of black workers and sharecroppers by racist whites on the other. Both are 'from below' forms of agency, but each is informed by a very different kind of politics.

104. The anthologies in question are Guha and Spivak [1988] and Guha [1997]. The latter are the only Subaltern Studies texts cited by Beverley: see, for example, both the main text [*Beverley*, 1999: 32, 41–2], and the accompanying references [*Beverley*, 1999: 170 n10, 171 n30, 172 n2, n4 and n9, 173 n15 and n18, 174 n1, 175 n3, 178 n28, 181 n1, 182 n5, 184 n21, and 187 n12].

105. On this point, see Beverley [1999: 20].

106. Like every other recent commentator on the intellectual impact of the Subaltern Studies series (about which see Brass [2000b]), Beverley quite simply ignores the critique made by the *Social Scientist* in the early 1980s. This silence is also found in texts by Ahmad [1992; 1995; 2000a], whose initial focus was on the work of Edward Said, and subsequently on Asian politics and the rise of Hindu nationalism. The Subaltern Studies project itself received scant mention in his otherwise useful analyses, a fact which Ahmad [1992: 210] makes clear when he observes 'the actual content of what [Ranajit] Guha or the general Subaltern tendency actually does cannot be an issue here, and all that matters is Said's own construction of it'. By the time he finally turns his attention to the details of the Subaltern Studies project, Ahmad [1997; 2000b] is – not surprisingly – unable to say much that has not already been said in earlier critiques: for example, that the Subaltern Studies approach legitimized postmodern approaches to the 'other' of development theory, that postmodern anti-Enlightenment discourse has its roots in right-wing ideology, that McLuhan and Heidegger are important theoretical precursors of anti-modernism, and that much postmodern theory was prefigured in the emphasis placed by Marcuse on alienation and more generally the events of 1968 [*Ahmad*, 2000b: 451, 454–5, 457, 458, 459, 461–2].

107. On the reactionary politics, the theoretical project, and the media courting of the 'New Philosophers', see in particular Jenkins [1977], Dews [1980], Sheehan [1980], Hirsch [1982; 193ff.], and Lecourt [2001]. In an observation that might have been written about postmodern exponents of subaltern resistance in the 1990s, rather than about the class-collaborationist/reformist policies of French Stalinists in 1935, Trotsky [1970: 11] observed: 'Even now the Communist leaders are already not unsuccessfully picking up drawing room language in their dealings with their allies on the right; the old reserve of curses is preserved only against opponents from the left.'

108. That the Russian Gulags constituted a more specifically located crisis – of Stalinism and not Marxism – was a question ignored by the 'New Philosophers'.

109. It is in fact remarkable just how much the subsequent critique of Marxism by postmodern

theory is prefigured in the earlier project of the 'New Philosophers'. The objections of Jean-Marie Benoist to Marxism (dismissed by him as an 'univocalist causalist scheme' [*Benoist*, 1978: 19]), for example, were framed in terms which are identical to those that postmodernism later made its own: namely, an attack on Marxism that is castigated as Eurocentric, scientistic, historicist, statist and deterministic, all in the name of a pluralist, ahistorical, anti-scientistic, anti-state, aporetic structuralism that is Heideggerian and Neitzschean, and for which 'difference' and a dematerialization of language were epistemologically important [*Benoist*, 1978: 19, 29–30, 37ff, 58ff., 69, 183, 196]. This postmodernism *avant la lettre* is summed up by Benoist [1978: 13] thus: 'Now that the classical ideal of univocality is dead, [a theoretical] work must be allowed to remain free of any attempt to reduce it to a unilateral decipherment: it must remain "pure ambiguity".'

110. On this point, see Benoist [1978: 64–5, 66–7, 71], who observes that 'this deep structure might be called *nature*, because its roots culture back into natural laws … Both Rousseau and Lévi-Strauss see time and history as eroding factors which the frail balance of structures and culture try desperately to arrest: we are far from the ideology of progress in history endorsed by Marxists … and the philosophers of the Enlightenment' (original emphasis). The revival by Claude Lévi-Strauss in mid-1970s French anthropology of Rousseauesque visions of 'the noble savage' is discussed in O'Hagan [1978] and Lemaire [1979].
111. This element of structural 'discontinuity', avers Benoist [1978: 69], permits Lévi-Strauss 'to refute the linear evolutionist pattern according to which so-called primitive societies were conceived as earlier stages of a development of mankind whose Western culture would have represented the latest stage. Such a myth … is a consequence of this subtle Western ethnocentrism … Against this ideology, Lévi-Strauss provides a pattern of discontinuity and differences …'.
112. For the agrarian nostalgia inherent in views of the 'New Philosophers' le Bris, Clavel and Nemo, see Dews [1980: 3, 10].
113. As has been argued elsewhere [*Brass*, 2000a: Ch.5], there are of course earlier precursors (Fanon, Marcuse) of the 'new' postmodern populism.
114. Beverley [1999: 11].
115. Not the least of the many ironies is that such a view is in many respects identical to the semi-feudal thesis, and thus replicates the argument propounded by the Communist Party of India (the need for a 'pure' capitalist stage, which in turn licensed the policy of support for a 'progressive' national bourgeoisie that would realize an equally 'pure' democratic project) to the theory and politics of which the Subaltern Studies project was ostensibly opposed.
116. Beverley [1999: 88ff.].
117. See Beverley [1999: 106].
118. Beverley [1999: 107]. Perhaps uncharitably, it could be argued that a focus on the image/identity/culture of the 'other', the reproduction of folkloric/national stereotypes, and a never-ending search for exotic 'authenticity' are all characteristics that the Subaltern Studies project shares with the popular/populist and widely read magazine *National Geographic*.
119. This class collaborationist policy remained in place long after the demise of the Popular Front itself, and continued to inform Stalinist views about the so-called Third World. In the mid-1970s, for example, one encounters the following [*Ulyanovsky*, 1974: 17, 19]: 'Even today revolutionary anti-imperialist nationalism continues to play a significant progressive role … The foundation for the formation of the patriotic national front is co-operation between Communists, the most consistent champions of the social and national liberation of the working people, with the broad strata of revolutionary democrats. Experience has borne out the idea put forward by the international communist movement to the effect that for the successful development of the national liberation revolutions involving far-reaching socio-economic and political changes, a question of central importance is the co-operation and close friendly relations between the parties of the revolutionary proletariat and the revolutionary democrats. Any lack of mutual understanding and even tense relations between them can only play into the hands of the imperialists and local reactionary forces.'
120. For these objections to Popular Frontism, see for example Trotsky [1936; 1970]. In this connection, there is a revealing contrast between, on the one hand, the Marxist critique of

'popular' culture made by Trotsky (see above), and on the other the palpably non-Marxist analysis of the same domain effected by those associated with the Popular Front. An example of the latter is the review of the film *Duck Soup* (1933) carried in the influential journal *Left Review*, where it was suggested that the appeal of the Marx Brothers derived from their satirical and deflating attacks on '"diplomacy", "dignity", autocracy and [the] pomposity of Governments' – in short, 'giving representatives of upper-class society a warm time' [*Goldman*, 1936–7: 830–31]. The same film review continues: 'The rôle of the Marx Brothers ... is that of rebels against society', that of Groucho being to act 'Prime Minister' or 'Financier' as shyster, 'always acting the part with an unabashed dishonesty that must be very disconcerting to the class of people he is mimicking'. The latter aspect, the review concludes, 'is the secret of the Marx Brothers' popularity with audiences the wide world over. For in each of us, conscious rebel or not, there is a deep instinctive dislike of the myriad shams of this world. It is because the Marx Brothers tear down the flimsy screen covering these shams that we love them so much. It is their healthy contempt of the "mighty" that endears them to us ... We all like to give a jolt to the "comfortable", to act the same against those people whom circumstances (not ability) have placed in authority over us. That is the essence of the Marx Brothers' appeal. They are the free, untrammelled spirit of mankind playing havoc with its would-be oppressors.' The undoubted comic genius of the Marx Brothers notwithstanding, the political discourse of the film *Duck Soup* (anti-state, anti-politics, anti-'shams') which this review endorses so enthusiastically is not so much Marxist as populist. It is difficult to characterize the anti-state discourse which is the essence of the Marx Brothers' attack as politically progressive, therefore, since it makes no distinction between a state oppressing workers on behalf of capital (a conservative or a fascist state) and a state expropriating capital on behalf of workers (a socialist state). The same is true of the theme 'rebels against society', which similarly fails to specify what kind of society: no distinction is made between society that is capitalist and/or fascist (against which socialists mobilize) and one that is socialist (against which conservatives and fascists organize), a view encapsulated in the film *Horse-Feathers* (1932), where Groucho as Professor Quincy Adams Wagstaffe sings 'whatever it is, I'm against it'. Anti-politics is also a specifically populist discourse; the latter attacks *all* politics and *all* government as innately corrupt, regardless of whether this is of the left or of the right. The claim that what is wrong with society is due to 'shams' – namely, the way the system functions, not the system itself – is also populist, in that the latter regards monopoly capital or foreign capital as the problem, not the capitalist system *per se*. This is the reason why populism approves of small-scale capitalist production, which is precisely what many of its (mainly petty bourgeois) supporters – such as peasants – actually do. Finally, the description of the Marx Brothers as 'the free, untrammelled spirit of mankind' is a classically Rousseauesque sentiment, again a hallmark of agrarian populism. All of this would not matter were it not for the fact that the film review is in a left-wing journal; rather than a Marxist politics, the analysis follows a populist line in keeping with the Popular Front. The latter, in turn, is a view that accords directly with the way in which Beverley, Canclini, and Albó perceive 'popular' culture: not just the innate virtue inscribed in the grassroots identity/resistance of the Latin American subaltern, therefore, but also the Menippean/carnivalesque/transgressive form taken by such 'from below' opposition.

121. This argument is embodied, for example, in the following observation [*Trotsky*, 1959: 75]: 'Regionalism is a response to the diversity of agrarian conditions in France. The provincial fascist and prefascist programmes will be varied and contradictory as are the interests of the different categories – the vine growers, truck gardeners, wheat growers – as well as the different social strata of the peasantry. But all these programmes will have in common their hatred of the bank, the treasury, the trust and the legislators.'
122. Significantly, Dimitrov [1935; 1951] was instrumental in the political transformation of Comintern policy during the seventh Congress which took place in 1935. The focus of the latter was on the rise of fascism in Germany, as a result of which Comintern policy switched from one of international working-class solidarity, class struggle against imperialism and the bourgeoisie, with the object of capturing the state and establishing a dictatorship of the proletariat, to one of anti-fascist alliances with what was deemed the 'progressive' national

bourgeoisie in order to defend bourgeois democracy against fascism. The seventh Congress was described by Trotsky [1970: 8–9] as 'Comintern's Liquidationist Congress', signalling a return to the discredited policies of 1914–18 – when nationalist objectives replaced socialist ones in the discourse of the left – that led to the disintegration of the Second International.

123. See Dimitrov [1935: 26] on the role of an undifferentiated peasantry as the 'natural' allies of the working class. For the alliance between the communists and the Agrarian Union in Bulgaria, see Dimitrov [1951: 192–3, 202], who dismissed Trotskyists as advocates of 'narrow' socialism who 'dogmatically defined the peasant commodity producer as a conservative element in society', adding that they 'did not realise that the domination of the trusts leads to the increasing exploitation and pauperisation of the mass of the peasantry, renders them ever more dissatisfied and arouses revolutionary tendencies among them'. That peasants who are 'dissatisfied' exhibit 'revolutionary tendencies' is undeniable: as the example of Eastern European countries during the 1920s suggests, however, these 'revolutionary tendencies' were not of the left but rather of the radical right.

124. East European fascist organizations during the 1920s and 1930s included the Christian Slovak People's Party in Czechoslovakia, the Croatian Peasant Party, the League of the Archangel Michael and the Iron Guard in Romania, and the Hungarian Nationalist Socialist Workers' Party [*Brass*, 2000a: 32ff.].

125. During the 1930s even those more 'moderate' socialists, who rejected a revolutionary overthrow of capitalism in favour of a parliamentary road to socialism, were aware both of the reasons for and the dangers inherent in fascism, and – with the exception of those who advocated a Popular Front strategy – also of the importance to fascism of peasant support and the reactionary character of certain kinds of anti-capitalist discourse. Thus, for example, the analysis by the Austro-Marxist Otto Bauer of what he terms 'populist Fascism' written in the late 1930s (cited in Bottomore and Goode [1978: 168–70]) argued that: 'the economic crises of the postwar period [after 1918] reduced the profits of the capitalist class. With its profits threatened the capitalist class sought to restore them by raising the level of exploitation. It wanted to break the resistance of the working class, and doubted whether it could do this under a democratic regime. It used the Fascist groups and people's militias created by the rebellious mass movements of the petty bourgeoisie and peasantry at first to intimidate the working class and force it on to the defensive, and subsequently to destroy democracy … [Fascism] is typically petty bourgeois, directed against large capital and the proletariat at the same time; for the officer hates the racketeer and the war profiteer, and despises the proletarian. This anti-capitalism is of course only directed against the specific parasitical forms of capital during the period of war and inflation; the officer values war industry but hates the racketeer, so he is hostile to the "profiteering", but not to the "productive" capitalist. [Fascism's] opposition is much more passionate to proletarian socialism … At a time when the power of socialism to attract the masses is at its strongest, fascism represents its own ideal as "national socialism", and in these terms opposes proletarian socialism … [Fascism] represents its fight against democracy to the masses as a fight against the class rule of the bourgeoisie, to the capitalists as a fight against the mob rule of the proletariat, to the nationalist intelligentsia as a fight for the co-ordination of all national forces against the external enemy.'

126. It should be emphasized that this is not generationally but politically determined, in the sense that there is no simple chronological reason why one generation of activists should necessarily forget the lessons learned by the previous one. Those who have not forgotten these lessons, or learned about them, have done so because remembering/learning about fascism and the political right is not only part of politics, but also part of a specifically Marxist politics. Ironically, it is Marxists themselves who have the most reasons for maintaining an interest in the ideas of the political right, and who should therefore insist on the continued visibility of such views. These reasons are as follows: first, in order to ensure that right-wing political theory is subjected to continuous criticism; second, to prevent elements of this political discourse from merging with mainstream ideas; and third, to avoid the endorsement of such views in the mistaken belief that they are somehow progressive. Where postmodernism is concerned, it is precisely this third problem that has materialized,

in the form of the 'new' populist enthusiasm for re-essentialized (or 'other') identities in general, and those of a Third World peasantry in particular.

127. Not only did reactionary populist forms of ideology and mobilization never actually disappear, but evidence of their presence in the Americas was in most instances hard to miss. In the case of Canada, for example, the right-wing populist Social Credit movement emerged initially during the capitalist crisis of the 1930s [*Finlay*, 1972], and 'succeeded in igniting a spark which spread rapidly in the 1940s among the alienated French-Canadian masses who were caught within the vice of rural poverty and were threatened by further decline ... but at the same time wished to preserve their religion, language, culture, and traditional way of life' [*Stein*, 1973: 18]. It re-emerged during the 1960s in Quebec, and secured 26 per cent of the vote in the 1962 Canadian federal election. Espousing the classic discourse-for/discourse-against of a right-wing reactionary populist mobilization (anti-Marxist, anti-socialist, anti-finance capital, anti-monopoly, anti-Semitic, anti-state, anti-taxation, anti-collective and anti-urban; pro-small-scale, pro-individual, pro-'choice', pro-tradition, pro-religion, pro-rural and pro-farmer), the Ralliement Créditiste drew its support from rural areas where 'middle sized farmers' faced economic decline [*Stein*, 1973]. Objecting to what was interpreted as a process of cultural erosion, its 1960s programme was based on the earlier ideas of Major C.H. Douglas (1878–1952), which advocated the restoration of individual choice by means of a return to the 'natural' condition of humanity before its distortion by finance capital (not capitalism). For an analysis of the continuing influence of this populist discourse in Newfoundland, see Overton [2000].
128. Instances of this kind of forgetting abound. Typical, perhaps, is the following observation [*Munck and Waterman*, 1999: ix]: 'Living 150 years later [after the publication of the *Communist Manifesto*], under a high capitalist modernity, both informalized and globalized, we need fundamentally to reconsider the role of [the working] class and its basic organizational form, the trade union. We need to do so in the light of contemporary economic and political developments, of contemporary emancipatory social movements, of the latest critical social theory.' More worryingly, this forgetfulness has in some instances been a sin of commission and not omission, and resulted from what can only be described as 'turning a blind eye', a process from which those on the left have unfortunately not been immune. During the late 1990s, for example, an erstwhile colleague, who regarded himself as a socialist, objected to a critique by me of another self-proclaimed socialist on the grounds that I had pointed out that the latter adhered unwittingly (and thus uncritically) to arguments that had been – and continued to be – deployed by those on the political right.
129. The intellectuals in question were Maurice Blanchot, about whom Mehlman [1989: 329] comments 'what is of interest is simply the omission of the fascist articles of the 1930s from the Blanchot texts discussed by Derrida in his book'; Martin Heidegger, whose complicity with fascism was enduring and unapologetic; and Paul de Man, whose pro-Nazi wartime writings in *Le Soir* – particularly 'The Jews in Contemporary Literature' – were imbued with volkish anti-Semitism. Like many contemporary postmodern theorists, de Man was engaged in a quest for literary authenticity: in his case, a pristine European tradition purged as he saw it of Jewish influence.
130. Hence the view [*Boggs*, 1999: 256]: 'The ruling elites are more likely to use the terrorism of the populist right as an occasion to repress opposition in general in the name of the state than to enter into an explicit alliance with the anti-statist reactionary populist groups. The danger that reactionary populist groups pose for the left is not that they are about to turn into successful fascist parties. It is rather that they could have the effect of inducing a "state of emergency" response from the state which will fail to discriminate (indeed may be only too ready not to try to discriminate) between right-wing terrorism and legitimate left wing political activity.'

REFERENCES

Abelson, Edward (ed.), 1988, *A Mirror of England: An Anthology of the Writings of H.J. Massingham (1888–1952)*, Devon: Green Books.

Ahmad, Aijaz, 1992, *In Theory: Classes, Nations, Literatures*, London: Verso.
Ahmad, Aijaz, 1995, 'Postcolonialism: What's in a Name?', in Román de la Campa *et al.* (eds.), *Late Imperial Culture*, London: Verso.
Ahmad, Aijaz, 1997, 'Post Colonial Theory and the "Post-" Condition', in Leo Panitch (ed.), *Ruthless Criticism of All That Exists – Socialist Register 1997*, London: Merlin Press.
Ahmad, Aijaz, 2000a, *Lineages of the Present: Ideology and Politics in Contemporary South Asia*, London: Verso.
Ahmad, Aijaz, 2000b, 'Postmodernism in History', in K.N. Panikkar *et al.* (eds.), *The Making of History*, New Delhi: Tulika.
Albó, Xavier, 1972, 'Dinámica en la estructura intercomunitaria de Jesús de Machachaca', *América Indígena*, Vol.32, No.3.
Albó, Xavier, 1987, 'From MNRistas, to Kataristas, to Katari', in Stern (ed.) [1987].
Albó, Xavier, 1988, *Raices de América: el mundo Aymara*, Madrid: Alianza Editorial.
Albó, Xavier, 1993, 'Our Identity Starting from Pluralism in the Base', in J. Beverley and J. Oviedo (eds.) [1993].
Aldama, Arturo J., 2001, *Disrupting Savagism: Intersecting Chicana/o, Mexican Immigrant, and Native American Struggles for Self-Representation*, Durham, NC: Duke University Press.
Aman, Kenneth, and Cristián Parker (eds.), 1991, *Popular Culture in Chile: Resistance and Survival*, Boulder, CO: Westview Press.
Amin, Shahid, and Dipesh Chakrabarty (eds.), 1996, *Subaltern Studies IX: Writings on South Asian History*, Delhi: Oxford University Press.
Apffel-Marglin, Frédérique, 1998, *The Spirit of Regeneration: Andean Culture Confronting Western Notions of Development*, London: Zed Books.
Apffel-Marglin, Frédérique, and Purna Chandra Mishra, 1995, 'Gender and the Unitary Self: Looking for the Subaltern in Coastal Orissa', *South Asia Research*, Vol.15, No.1.
Arnold, David, and David Hardiman (eds.), 1994, *Subaltern Studies VIII: Essays in Honour of Ranajit Guha*, Delhi: Oxford University Press.
Bahl, Vinay, 1997, 'Relevance (or Irrelevance) of Subaltern Studies', *Economic and Political Weekly*, Vol.XXXII, No.23.
Bakhtin, Mikhail, 1984, *Problems of Dostoevsky's Poetics*, Manchester: Manchester University Press.
Beck, Ulrich, 1992, *Risk Society: Towards a New Modernity*, London: Sage.
Beck, Ulrich, and Elisabeth Beck-Gernsheim, 2001, *Individualization: Institutionalized Individualism and Its Social and Political Consequences*, London: Sage.
Benoist, Jean-Marie, 1978, *The Structural Revolution*, London: Weidenfeld & Nicolson.
Bernstein, H., and T.J. Byers, 2000, 'From peasant studies to agrarian change' (xerox).
Beverley, J., 1993, *Against Literature*, Minneapolis, MN: University of Minnesota Press.
Beverley, J., 1999, *Subalternity and Representation: Arguments in Cultural Theory*, Durham, NC, and London: Duke University Press.
Beverley, J., and M. Zimmerman, 1990, *Literature and Politics in the Central American Revolutions*, Austin, TX: University of Texas Press.
Beverley, J., and J. Oviedo (eds.), 1993, *The Postmodernism Debate in Latin America*, Durham, NC: Duke University Press.
Bhadra, Gautam, Gyan Prakash, and Susi Tharu (eds.), 1999, *Subaltern Studies X: Essays in Honour of Ranajit Guha*, Delhi: Oxford University Press.
Bieber, Judy, 1999, *Power, Patronage and Political Violence: State Building on a Brazilian Frontier, 1822–1889*, Lincoln, NE: University of Nebraska Press.
Blanco, H., 1972, *Tierra o Muerte: las luchas campesinas en Perú*, México, DF: Siglo Veintiuno Editores.
Boggs, Carl, 1999, 'Warrior Nightmares: American Reactionary Populism at the Millenium', in Leo Panitch and Colin Leys (eds.) [1999].
Bottomore, Tom, and Patrick Goode (eds.), 1978, *Austro-Marxism*, Oxford: Clarendon Press.
Brass, Tom, 1986a, 'The Elementary Strictures of Kinship: Unfree Relations and the Production of Commodities', *Social Analysis*, No.20.
Brass, Tom, 1986b, 'Cargos and Conflict: The Fiesta System and Capitalist Development in Eastern Peru', *The Journal of Peasant Studies*, Vol.13, No.3.

Brass, Tom, 1991, 'Moral Economists, Subalterns, New Social Movements and the (Re-) Emergence of a (Post-) Modernized Middle Peasant', *The Journal of Peasant Studies*, Vol.18, No.2.

Brass, Tom, 1995, 'Old Conservatism in "New" Clothes', *The Journal of Peasant Studies*, Vol.22, No.3.

Brass, Tom, 2000a, *Peasants, Populism and Postmodernism: The Return of the Agrarian Myth*, London and Portland, OR: Frank Cass Publishers.

Brass, Tom, 2000b, 'Unmasking the Subaltern, or Salamis without Themistocles', *The Journal of Peasant Studies*, Vol.28, No.1.

Buckley, W.F., 1959, *Up from Liberalism*, New York: McDowell, Obolensky.

Bueno, Eva, and Terry Caesar (eds.), 1998, *Imagination Beyond Nation: Latin American Popular Culture*, Pittsburgh, PA: University of Pittsburgh Press.

Burgess, Anthony, 1990, *You've Had Your Time: The Second Part of the Confessions*, New York: Grove Weidenfeld.

Calvo Sotelo, José, 1938, *El Capitalismo Contemporáneo y su Evolución*, Valladolid: Cultura Española.

Cashman, Richard I., 1975, *The Myth of the Lokamanya: Tilak and Mass Politics in Maharashtra*, Berkeley, CA: University of California Press.

Castro Pozo, H., 1924, *Nuestra Communidad Indígena*, Lima: Editorial 'El Lucero'.

Castro Pozo, H., 1936, *Del Ayllu al Cooperativismo Socialista*, Lima: Biblioteca de la Revista de Economia y Finanzas.

Chatterjee, Partha, and Gyan Pandey (eds.), 1992, *Subaltern Studies VII: Essays in Honour of Ranajit Guha*, Delhi: Oxford University Press.

Chatterjee, Partha, and Pradeep Jeganathan (eds.), 2000, *Subaltern Studies XI: Community, Gender and Violence*, London: Hirst & Company.

Chaturvedi, Vinayak, 2000, 'Introduction', in Vinayak Chaturvedi (ed.) [2000].

Chaturvedi, Vinayak (ed.), 2000, *Mapping Subaltern Studies and the Postcolonial*, London: Verso.

Chomsky, Aviva, and Aldo Lauria-Santiago (eds.), 1998, *Identity and Struggle at the Margins of the Nation-State: The Labouring Peoples of Central America and the Hispanic Caribbean*, London and Durham, NC: Duke University Press.

Clifford, James, and George L. Marcus (eds.), 1990, *Writing Culture: The Poetics and Politics of Ethnography*, Delhi: Oxford University Press.

Colton, C.C., 1835, *Lacon, or Many Things in a Few Words*, London: Longman, Rees, Orme, Green, & Longman.

Cook, Juliet, and Julian Clarke, 1990, 'Racism and the Right', in Barry Hindess (ed.) [1990].

Cooper, Frederick, Florencia E. Mallon, Steve J. Stern, Allen F. Isaacman, and William Roseberry, 1993, *Confronting Historical Paradigms: Peasants, Labor, and the Capitalist World System in Africa and Latin America*, Madison, WI: University of Wisconsin Press.

Corbridge, S., and J. Harriss, 2000, *Reinventing India: Liberalization, Hindu Nationalism and Popular Democracy*, Cambridge: Polity Press.

Cornejo, Alberto, 1949, *Programas Politicos de Bolivia*, Cochabamba: Imprenta Universitaria.

Cumings, Bruce, 1992, *War and Television*, London: Verso.

Deutsch, Sandra McGee, 1986, *Counterrevolution in Argentina, 1900–1932: The Argentine Patriotic League*, Lincoln, NE: University of Nebraska Press.

Deutsch, Sandra McGee, 1999, *Las Derechas: The Extreme Right in Argentina, Brazil, and Chile, 1890–1939*, Stanford, CA: Stanford University Press.

Deutsch, Sandra McGee, and Ronald H. Dolkart (eds.), 1993, *The Argentine Right: Its History and Intellectual Origins, 1910 to the Present*, Wilmington, DE: Scholarly Resources, Inc.

Deutscher, I., 1955, *Heretics and Renegades*, London: Hamish Hamilton.

Dews, Peter, 1980, 'The "New Philosophers" and the End of Leftism', *Radical Philosophy*, No.24.

Dimitrov, Georgi, 1935, *The Working Class Against Fascism*, London: Martin Lawrence.

Dimitrov, Georgi, 1951, *Selected Speeches and Articles*, London: Lawrence and Wishart.

Dirks, N.B., 1991, 'Ritual and Resistance: Subversion as a Social Fact', in David Haynes and Gyan Prakash (eds.) [1991].

Dorfman, Ariel, and Armand Mattelart, 1975, *How to Read Donald Duck: Imperialist Ideology in the Disney Comic*, New York: International General Editions, Inc.
Dovring, Folke, 1956, *Land and Labor in Europe 1900-1950: A Comparative Survey of Recent Agrarian History*, The Hague: Martinus Nijhoff.
Dovring, Karin, 1956, 'Land Reform as a Propaganda Theme', in Folke Dovring [1956].
Einstein, Albert, and Sigmund Freud, 1933, *Why War?* Paris: League of Nations.
Eliot, Marc, 1993, *Walt Disney: Hollywood's Dark Prince*, New York: Birch Lane Press.
Elst, Koenraad, 2001, *The Saffron Swastika: The Notion of 'Hindu Fascism'*, 2 Vols., New Delhi: The Voice of India.
Engels, Frederick, 1976a, 'The True Socialists', *Marx and Engels Collected Works*, Vol.5 (1845–1847), London: Lawrence & Wishart.
Engels, Frederick, 1976b, 'German Socialism in Verse and Prose', *Marx and Engels Collected Works*, Vol.6 (1845–1848), London: Lawrence & Wishart.
Epstein, Klaus, 1966, *The Genesis of German Conservatism*, Princeton, NJ: Princeton University Press.
Ewen, Stuart, 1996, *PR! A Social History of Spin*, New York: Basic Books.
Fiddian, Robin (ed.), 2000, *Postcolonial Perspectives: On the Cultures of Latin America and Lusophone Africa*, Liverpool: Liverpool University Press.
Finlay, John L., 1972, *Social Credit – The English Origins*, Montreal and London: McGill-Queens University Press.
Fletcher, Robert, 2001, 'What are We Fighting For? Rethinking Resistance in a Pewenche Community in Chile', *The Journal of Peasant Studies*, Vol.28, No.3.
Foner, Eric, 1998, *The Story of American Freedom*, New York: W.W. Norton.
Fox, Richard G., and Orin Starn, 1997, 'Introduction', in Richard G. Fox and Orin Starn (eds.), *Between Resistance and Revolution: Cultural Politics and Social Protest*, New Brunswick, NJ: Rutgers University Press.
Freitag, Sandra, 1989, *Collective Action and Community: Public Arenas and the Emergence of Communalism in India*, Berkeley, CA: University of California Press.
García Canclini, Néstor, 1992, 'Cultural Reconversion', in Yúdice *et al.* (eds.) [1992].
García Canclini, Néstor, 1993, 'The Hybrid: A Conversation with Margarita Zires, Raymundo Mier, and Mabel Piccini', in J. Beverley and J. Oviedo (eds.) [1993].
García Canclini, Néstor, 2001, *Consumers and Citizens: Globalization and Multicultural Conflicts*, Minneapolis, MN: University of Minnesota Press.
Goldman, Willy, 1936–37, 'The Marx Brothers Too!', *Left Review*, No.2.
Goldwater, Barry, 1964, *The Conscience of a Conservative*, London: Fontana Books.
Griffin, Roger, 1985, 'Revolts Against the Modern World: The Blend of Literary and Historical Fantasy in the Italian New Right', *Literature and History*, Vol.11, No.1.
Griffiths, Richard, 1983, *Fellow Travellers of the Right: British Enthusiasts for Nazi Germany, 1933–39*, London: Oxford University Press.
Gudmunson, Lowell, and Francisco A. Scarano, 1998, 'Imagining the Future of the Subaltern Past – Fragments of Race, Class and Gender in Central America and the Hispanic Caribbean, 1850–1950', in A. Chomsky and A. Lauria-Santiago (eds.) [1998].
Guha, Ranajit (ed.), 1982–89, *Subaltern Studies I–VI: Writings on South Asian History*, Delhi: Oxford University Press.
Guha, Ranajit (ed.), 1997, *A Subaltern Studies Reader*, Minneapolis, MN: University of Minnesota Press.
Guha, Ranajit, and G. Spivak (eds.), 1988, *Selected Subaltern Studies*, New York: Oxford University Press.
Guha, Ramachandra, 2001, 'The Absent Liberal: An Essay on Politics and Intellectual Life', *Economic and Political Weekly*, Vol.XXXVI, No.50.
Gupta, Dipankar, 2001, 'Everyday Resistance or Repression? Exaggeration as Strategem in Agrarian Conflict', *The Journal of Peasant Studies*, Vol.29, No.1.
Hamacher, Werner, Neil Hertz, and Thomas Keenan (eds.), *Responses: On Paul de Man's Wartime Journalism*, London and Lincoln, NE: University of Nebraska Press.
Hartwell, R.M., 1995, *A History of the Mont Pelerin Society*, Indianapolis, IN: Liberty Fund.
Haya de la Torre, V.R., 1936a, *¿A dónde va Indoamérica?* Santiago de Chile: Biblioteca America.

Haya de la Torre, V.R., 1936b, *El Antimperialismo y el Apra*, Santiago de Chile: Ediciones Ercilla.

Haynes, David, and Gyan Prakash (eds.), 1991, *Contesting Power: Resistance and Everyday Social Relations in South Asia*, Delhi: Oxford University Press.

Hindess, Barry (ed.), 1990, *Reactions to the Right*, London: Routledge.

Hirsh, Arthur, 1982, *The French Left*, Montréal: Black Rose Books.

Hobsbawm, E.J., 1973, 'Peasants and Politics', *The Journal of Peasant Studies*, Vol.1, No.1.

Hobsbawm, E.J., 1981, 'The Forward March of Labour Halted?', in M. Jacques and F. Mulhern (eds.), *The Forward March of Labour Halted?*, London: Verso.

Hobsbawm, E.J., and Terence Ranger (eds.), 1983, *The Invention of Tradition*, Cambridge: Cambridge University Press.

Huggan, Graham, 2001, *The Postcolonial Exotic: Marketing the Margins*, London: Routledge.

Jell-Bahlsen, Sabine, 1985, 'Ethnology and Fascism in Germany', *Dialectical Anthropology*, Vol.9, Nos.1–4.

Jenkins, Tim, 1977, 'The Death of Marx: A Media Event', *The Journal of the Anthropological Society of Oxford*, Vol.VIII, No.3.

Jones, J.D.F., 2001, *Storyteller: The Many Lives of Laurens van der Post*, London: John Murray.

Joseph, Gilbert, and Daniel Nugent (eds.), 1994, *Everyday Forms of State Formation: Revolution and the Negotiation of Rule in Modern Mexico*, Durham, NC: Duke University Press.

Joseph, Gilbert, Catherine LeGrand, and Ricardo Salvatore (eds.), 1998, *Close Encounters of Empire: Writing the Cultural History of US–Latin American Relations*, Durham, NC: Duke University Press.

Kahn, Gordon, 1948, *Hollywood on Trial*, New York: Boni & Gaer.

Klaren, P.F., 2000, *Peru: Society and Nationhood in the Andes*, New York: Oxford University Press.

Klinge, Gerardo, 1946, *Política Agrícola-Alimenticia*, Lima: Sociedad Nacional Agraria.

Knauerhase, R., 1972, *An Introduction to National Socialism, 1920 to 1939*, Columbus, OH: Charles E. Merrill Publishing Co.

Landsberger, Henry A., 1969, 'Chile: A Vineyard Workers' Strike – A Case Study of the Relationship between Church, Intellectuals, and Peasants', in Henry A. Landsberger (ed.) [1969].

Landsberger, Henry A. (ed.), 1969, *Latin American Peasant Movements*, Ithaca, NY: Cornell University Press.

Latin American Subaltern Studies Group, 1993, 'Founding Statement', in J. Beverley and J. Oviedo (eds.) [1993].

Lecourt, Dominique, 2001, *The Mediocracy: French Philosophy since the mid-1970s*, London: Verso.

Lemaire, Ton, 1979, 'Le Sauvage a la mode', *Dialectical Anthropology*, Vol.4, No.4.

Long, Norman, and Bryan Roberts (eds.), 1978, *Peasant Cooperation and Capitalist Expansion in Central Peru*, Austin, TX: University of Texas.

Loomis, C.P., and J.A. Beegle, 1946, 'The Spread of German Nazism in Rural Areas', *American Sociological Review*, Vol.11, No.6.

Lora, Guillermo, 1970, *Documentos Políticos de Bolivia*, Cochabamba: Los Amigos del Libro.

Lotman, Ju. M., and B.A. Uspenskij, 1984, *The Semiotics of Russian Culture*, Ann Arbor, MI: University of Michigan Press.

Lowe, Lisa, and David Lloyd (eds.), 1997, *The Politics of Culture in the Shadow of Capital*, Durham, NC: Duke University Press.

Löwy, Michael, 1998, *Fatherland or Mother Earth? Essays on the National Question*, London: Pluto Press.

Ludden, David, 2001, 'Subalterns and Others in the Agrarian History of South Asia', in J.C. Scott and N. Bhatt (eds.) [2001].

Ludden, David, 2002, 'Introduction: A Brief History of Subalternity', in David Ludden (ed.) [2002].

Ludden, David (ed.), 2002, *Reading Subaltern Studies: Critical History, Contested Meaning and the Globalization of South Asia*, London: Anthem Press.

Lukács, George, 1950, *Studies in European Realism: A Sociological Survey of the Writings of Balzac, Stendhal, Zola, Tolstoy, Gorki and others*, London: Hillway Publishing Co.
Mabey, Richard, 1967, 'Not On Speaking Terms', in Richard Mabey (ed.) [1967].
Mabey, Richard, 1980, *The Common Ground: A Place for Nature in Britain's Future?*, London: Hutchinson/The Nature Conservancy Council.
Mabey, Richard, 1983, *In a Green Shade: Essays on Landscape, 1970–1983*, London: Hutchinson.
Mabey, Richard, 1990, *Home Country*, London: Century.
Mabey, Richard, 2000, 'A Village Voice', *Resurgence*, Issue 202.
Mabey, Richard (ed.), 1967, *Class: A Symposium*, London: Anthony Blond.
Mallon, Florencia, 1993, 'Dialogues Among the Fragments: Retrospect and Prospect', in Frederick Cooper *et al.* [1993].
Mallon, Florencia, 1994, 'The Promise and Dilemma of Subaltern Studies: Perspectives from Latin American History', *The American Historical Review*, Vol.99, No.5.
Mallon, Florencia, 1995, *Peasant and Nation: The Making of Postcolonial Mexico and Peru*, Berkeley, CA: University of California Press.
Maríategui, J.-C., 1928/[1968], *Siete Ensayos de Interpretación de la Realidad Peruana*, Lima: Biblioteca Amauta.
Maritain, Jacques, 1957, *Existence and the Existent: An Essay on Christian Existentialism*, New York: Doubleday & Company, Inc.
Marzal, Manuel, 1990, 'Antropología e indigenismo en Perú', in Modesto Suárez (ed.) [1990].
Masiello, Francine, 2001, *The Art of Transition: Latin American Culture and Neoliberal Crisis*, Durham, NC: Duke University Press.
Massingham, H.J. (ed.), 1945, *The Natural Order: Essays in The Return to Husbandry*, London: J.M. Dent & Sons Ltd.
Mattelart, Armand, 1979, *Multinational Corporations and the Control of Culture: The Ideological Apparatuses of Imperialism*, Brighton: Harvester Press.
Mattelart, Armand, 1991, *Advertising International: The Privatisation of Public Space*, London: Routledge.
Mehlman, Jeffrey, 1989, 'Perspectives: On De Man and *Le Soir*', in Werner Hamacher, Neil Hertz and Thomas Keenan (eds.) [1989].
Meyer, Konrad, 1939, 'Discussion: The Social Implications of Economic Progress in Present-day Agriculture', *Proceedings of the Fifth International Conference of Agricultural Economists (1938)*, London: Oxford University Press.
Mignolo, Walter, 2000, *Local Histories/Global Designs: Subaltern Knowledges and Border Thinking*, Princeton, NJ: Princeton University Press.
Montague, Ashley (ed.), 1980, *Sociobiology Examined*, Oxford: Oxford University Press.
Mosley, Oswald, 1932, *The Greater Britain*, London: British Union of Fascists.
Mosse, G., 1966, *Nazi Culture: Intellectual, Cultural and Social Life in the Third Reich*, London: W.H. Allen.
Munck, Ronald, and Peter Waterman (eds.), 1999, *Labour Worldwide in the Era of Globalization: Alternative Union Models in the New World Order*, London: Macmillan.
Nanda, Meera, 2001, 'We Are All Hybrids Now: The Dangerous Epistemology of Post-Colonial Populism', *The Journal of Peasant Studies*, Vol.28, No.2.
Nugent, Daniel, 1998a, 'The Morality of Modernity and the Travails of Tradition: Nationhood and the Subaltern in Northern Peru', *Critique of Anthropology*, Vol.18, No.1.
Nugent, Daniel (ed.), 1998b, *Rural Revolt in Mexico: US Intervention and the Domain of Subaltern Politics*, Durham, NC: Duke University Press.
O'Hagan, Tim, 1978, 'Rousseau: Conservative or Revolutionary? A Critique of Lévi-Strauss', *Critique of Anthropology*, Vol.3, No.11.
Overton, James, 2000, 'Academic Populists, the Informal Sector, and Those Benevolent Merchants: Politics and Income Security Reform in Newfoundland', *The Journal of Peasant Studies*, Vol.28, No.1.
Panitch, Leo, and Colin Leys (eds.), 1999, *Necessary and Unnecessary Utopias – Socialist Register 2000*, Suffolk: Merlin Press.

Payne, Leigh A., 2000, *Uncivil Movements: The Armed Right Wing and Democracy in Latin America*, Baltimore, OH: Johns Hopkins University Press.

Peary, Gerald, and Danny Peary (eds.), 1980, *The American Animated Cartoon*, New York: E.P. Dutton.

Peloso, Vincent C., 1999, *Peasants on Plantations: Subaltern Strategies of Labor and Resistance in the Pisco Valley, Peru*, Durham, NC, and London: Duke University Press.

Petras, J., 1990, 'Retreat of the Intellectuals', *Economic and Political Weekly*, Vol.25, No.38.

Petras, J., 2002, 'A Rose by Any Other Name? The Fragrance of Imperialism', *The Journal of Peasant Studies*, Vol.29, No.2.

Philo, Greg, and David Miller, 2001, *Market Killing: What the Free Market Does and What Social Scientists Can Do About It*, London: Longman.

Quijada Jara, Sergio, 1947, *La Tradicional Fiesta de la Virgen de la Natividad o de Cocharcas*, Huancayo: Imprenta Atlántida.

Rama, Carlos M., 1981, *Nacionalismo e Historiografía en America Latina*, Madrid: Editorial Tecnos, S.A.

Ramos, A.R., 1998, *Indigenism – Ethnic Politics in Brazil*, Madison, WI: University of Wisconsin Press.

Rappaport, Joanne, 1992, 'Fictive Foundations: National Romances and Subaltern Ethnicity in Latin America', *History Workshop Journal*, Issue 34.

Raven, Simon, 1967, 'Class and the Contemporary Novel', in Richard Mabey (ed.) [1967].

Reinaga, F., 1953, *Tierra y libertad: La revolución nacional y el indio*, La Paz: Ediciones Rumbo Sindical.

Reinaga, F., 1968, *El indio y los escritores de américa*, La Paz: Ediciones PIB (Partido Indio de Bolivia).

Reinaga, F., 1969, *La revolución india*, La Paz: Ediciones PIB (Partido Indio de Bolivia).

Reinaga, F., 1971, *Tesis india*, La Paz: Ediciones PIB (Partido Indio de Bolivia).

Röpke, W., 1948, *Civitas Humana: A Humane Order of Society*, London: William Hodge & Co., Ltd.

Röpke, W., 1950, *The Social Crisis of Our Time*, Glasgow: William Hodge & Co.

Rorty, Richard, 1998, *Achieving Our Country: Leftist Thought in Twentieth Century America*, Cambridge, MA: Harvard University Press.

Rus, Jan (ed.), 1999, 'If Truth be Told: A Forum on Stoll and Menchú', a special issue of *Latin American Perspectives*, Vol.26, No.6.

Samaniego, Carlos, 1978, 'Peasant Movements at the Turn of the Century and the Rise of the Independent Farmer', in Norman Long and Bryan Roberts (eds.) [1978].

Samuel, Raphael (ed.), 1981, *People's History and Socialist Theory*, London: Routledge & Kegan Paul.

Sánchez, Rodrigo, 1977, 'The Model of Verticality in the Andean Economy: A Critical Reconsideration', *Bulletin of the Society for Latin American Studies*, No.27.

Sánchez, Rodrigo, 1982, 'The Andean Economic System and Capitalism', in A.D. Lehmann (ed.), *Ecology and Exchange in the Andes*, Cambridge: Cambridge University Press.

Sarkar, Sumit, 1997, *Writing Social History*, Calcutta: Oxford University Press.

Sarkar, Sumit, 2002, *Beyond Nationalist Frames: Postmodernism, Hindu Fundamentalism, History*, Bloomington, IN: Indiana University Press.

Saunders, Frances Stonor, 1999, *Who Paid the Piper? The CIA and the Cultural Cold War*, London: Granta Books.

Scott, J.C., 1990, *Domination and the Arts of Resistance: Hidden Transcripts*, New Haven, CT: Yale University Press.

Scott, J.C., and N. Bhatt (eds.), 2001, *Agrarian Studies: Synthetic Work at the Cutting Edge*, New Haven, CT: Yale University Press.

Scruton, Roger, 2000, *England: An Elegy*, London: Chatto and Windus.

Scruton, Roger, 2001, 'A Conservative View of the Countryside', in M. Sissons (ed.) [2001].

Shakespeare, Nicholas, 1999, *Bruce Chatwin*, London: Harvill.

Sheehan, Thomas, 1980, 'Paris: Moses and Polytheism', in Montague (ed.) [1980].

Sissons, Michael (ed.), 2001, *A Countryside for All: The Future of Rural Britain*, London: Vintage Books.

Smith, Waldemar R., 1977, *The Fiesta System and Economic Change*, New York: Columbia University Press.
Stein, Michael B., 1973, *The Dynamics of Right-Wing Protest: A Political Analysis of Social Credit in Quebec*, Toronto: University of Toronto Press.
Stern, S. (ed.), 1987, *Resistance, Rebellion, and Consciousness in the Andean Peasant World*, Madison, WI: University of Wisconsin Press.
Stoll, D., 1998, *Rigoberta Menchú and the Story of All Poor Guatemalans*, Boulder, CO: Westview Press.
Suárez, Modesto (ed.), 1990, *Historia, Antropología y Política: Homenaje a Ángel Palerm*, (Vol.1), México, D.F.: Alianza Editorial Mexicana.
Thakurdas, Sir Purshotamdas, J.D.R. Tata, G.D. Birla, Sir Ardeshir Dalal, Sir Shri Ram, Kasturbhai Lalbhai, A.D. Shroff, and John Matthai, 1945, *Memorandum Outlining a Plan of Economic Development for India (Parts 1 and 2)*, Harmondsworth: Penguin Books.
Theroux, Paul, 1998, *Sir Vidia's Shadow: A Friendship across Five Continents*, London: Hamish Hamilton.
Thomas, Hugh (ed.), 1972, *José Antonio Primo de Rivera: Selected Writings*, London: Jonathan Cape.
Thompson, E.P., 1991, 'Rough Music', in *Customs in Common*, London: The Merlin Press.
Ticona, Estéban, Gonzalo Rojas, and Xavier Albó, 1995, *Votos y wiphelas: campesinos y pueblos originarios en democracia*, La Paz: Centro de Investigación y Promoción Campesinado.
Trotsky, L.D., 1925, *Literature and Revolution*, London: George Allen & Unwin Ltd.
Trotsky, L.D., 1936, *The Third International After Lenin*, New York: Pioneer Publishers.
Trotsky, L.D., 1959, *Trotsky's Diary in Exile 1935*, London: Faber and Faber.
Trotsky, L.D., 1970, *Writings 1935–36*, New York: Merit Publishers.
Tye, Larry, 1998, *The Father of Spin: Edward L. Bernays and the Birth of Public Relations*, New York: Crown Publishers.
Ulyanovsky, R., 1974, *Socialism and the Newly Independent Nations*, Moscow: Progress Publishers.
Urquidi, Arturo, 1970, *Las comunidades indígenas en Bolivia*, Cochabamba: Los Amigos del Libro.
van den Bruck, Moeller, 1934, *Germany's Third Empire*, London: George Allen & Unwin Ltd.
Vanaik, Achin, 1997, *The Furies of Indian Communalism: Religion, Modernity and Secularization*, London: Verso.
Veltmeyer, Henry, 1997, 'New Social Movements in Latin America: The Dynamics of Class and Identity', *The Journal of Peasant Studies*, Vol.25, No.1.
Vološinov, V.N., 1976, *Freudianism: A Marxist Critique*, New York: Academic Press.
von Bülow, Prince Bernhard, 1915, *Imperial Germany*, London: Cassell & Co., Ltd.
White, Arnold, 1901, *Efficiency and Empire*, London: Methuen & Co.
White, Jerry, 1981, 'Beyond autobiography', in Raphael Samuel (ed.) [1981].
Yúdice, George, *et al.* (eds.), 1992, *On Edge: The Crisis of Contemporary Latin American Culture*, Minneapolis, MN: University of Minnesota Press.
Zimmerman, J.G., 1800, *Aphorisms and Reflections on Men, Morals and Things*, London: Thomas Maiden.
Zinkin, Maurice, 1956, *Development for Free Asia*, London: Chatto & Windus.

Abstracts

Latin American Peasants – New Paradigms for Old?
TOM BRASS

Comparing two of the main paradigms utilized in the study of Latin American peasants, this introduction considers the way each interprets grassroots rural identity/agency, as embodied in their respective approaches to the reproduction and survival of peasant economy, the empowering/disempowering nature of specific kinds of agrarian mobilization and labour regime, together with their perception of the role/form of the State. The first of these paradigms is the one used by the 'new' postmodern populists, who – together with neoliberals – theorize rural agency as based on innate peasant/ethnic identity, the aim of which is not to transcend capitalism but to survive within it. This approach to the peasantry in Latin America contrasts with that of the agrarian question, an 'old' paradigm in which rural agency based on class identity is designed to capture and exercise state power, with the political object of transcending capitalism. Their relative merits are examined, and evaluated in terms of the case studies presented in this volume.

The Peasantry and the State in Latin America: A Troubled Past, an Uncertain Future
JAMES PETRAS and HENRY VELTMEYER

This article provides a retrospective overview of peasant/state relations in Latin America. First we assess the adequacy of alternative explanations regarding the dynamics of these relations, and then we review the actual history of peasant/state relations in Latin America, analysing the forces involved in change and struggle. Also examined is the process of regression, displacement and revolution. The analysis concludes by evaluating the kinds of power which structure peasant/state relations, with particular reference to the social forces involved, and to the objectives and outcomes of peasant mobilization.

From Rubber Estate to Simple Commodity Production: Agrarian Struggles in the Northern Bolivian Amazon
WILLEM ASSIES

Rural unrest has been spreading in recent years in different regions in Bolivia, which suggests that the agrarian and forestry legislation introduced in 1996 has failed to solve the problems that it was meant to address. This article examines the background to rural conflict in a specific region, the northern Bolivian Amazon. It reviews the rise and decline of the rubber trade and the subsequent emergence of the Brazil nut economy in the region. In this way it shows how free communities emerged alongside the estate system and compete for access to land and forest resources. This involves a discussion of the evolution of forms of labour recruitment and debt-peonage that takes issue with the neo-institutional economics perspective recently adopted by various authors and students of the region. It is argued that debt-peonage in the Amazon area can be viewed as a specific form of 'captive' simple commodity production, and that this sheds light on the struggle by rubber tappers for autonomy. The article concludes by analysing the 1996 agrarian and forestry legislation, and shows how its landlord-biased implementation made manifest the latent conflict between free communities and estate owners.

The Impact of Neo-liberal Economics on Peruvian Peasant Agriculture in the 1990s
JOHN CRABTREE

The adoption of neo-liberal economic policies by the Fujimori government in the 1990s had major implications for peasant agriculture, as for other sectors. Twelve years after their initial implementation, these policies appear to have brought more losers than winners. Hit in particular by slack urban demand for food and a sharp increase in imports, low agricultural prices undercut peasant incomes. Those most affected were those producing primarily for the market, who were either forced back into subsistence farming or into seeking work in other areas. Rural poverty levels increased over this period, as did inequality in the agrarian sector.

Whither O Campesinato? *Historical Peasantries of Brazilian Amazonia*
STEPHEN NUGENT

Brazilian Amazonian peasantries have attracted relatively little scholarly attention, and even with the opening up of Amazonia via the TransAmazon Highway (*c.*1970) and a significant expansion of social science research in the region, recent frontier colonists and environmental crises have been the major foci. This article examines some of the factors contributing to the relative invisibility of historical peasantries in the region and tries to show the relevance of such peasantries to debates concerning agrarian structure, economic transformation and state-led modernization efforts. A key feature in the portrayal of Amazonian peasantries (and Amerindians) has been the unique role attributed to the neo-humid tropical landscape in restricting the possibilities for an elaborated social landscape. Drawing on anthropological, archaeological and historical studies, the article advances the notion that these simplifying assumptions are unwarranted and are impediments not only to a more accurate understanding of the legacy of colonial society in Amazonia, but also to efforts to mitigate social conflict and environmental depredation.

From Dependency to Reform and Back Again: The Chilean Peasantry During the Twentieth Century
WARWICK E. MURRAY

This article is concerned with the impact of neo-liberal economic theory and resultant policy on peasant farmers in Latin America. In particular, it explores the relationship between agri-business and the peasantry in Chile and traces the evolution of the *parcelero* sector in response to the forces of globalization over the last 30 years. In order to place recent trends in context, the historical evolution of Chile's peasantry, particularly during the last century, is analysed in some depth. To illustrate the impacts of neo-liberalism, two fieldwork-based case studies in areas (El Paqui and East

Curicó) where land reform has taken place and fruit export booms have occurred are presented. Although local transformations are varied, it is contended that the application of a 'free' market policy has increased the dependency of the peasantry, creating disguised, semi- and full proletarianization. The latter process has reversed the various agrarian reforms which took place in the 1960s and 1970s, and returned the Chilean peasantry to the subordinate position it occupied previously. It is argued that the failure of peasant economy is a political effect rather than the outcome of inevitable 'global' economic forces.

Globalization and the Reinvention of Andean Tradition: The Politics of Community and Ethnicity in Highland Bolivia
JOHN MCNEISH

This article examines the complex ways in which a peasant community in the Bolivian Highlands mediates present political conditions through an internal discourse and conflict over personal and historical memories. Highlighted is the way in which existing disputes are used by local people to take advantage of the new economic resources made available by recent government reforms aimed at democratization and decentralization, and how the latter in turn create a space for traditional indigenous authorities to reassert their political power. It is argued that whilst globalization is responsible for an increase in the spread and economic diversification of local communities, peasants in Bolivia are able to negotiate the limits and significance of these changes.

Devil Pact Narratives in Rural Central America: Class, Gender and 'Resistance'
KEES JANSEN and ESTHER ROQUAS

The Faustian bargain, or 'pact with the devil', made by a person who exchanges human souls in order to obtain unattainable riches and power, is a widespread peasant narrative in Central and South America. The narrative expresses various overlapping meanings, of which a sudden increase in wealth and a concomitant shift in social relationships is a central theme. In the case examined, peasants invoke the devil pact narrative and the realm of the supernatural to explain wealth and poverty in order to avoid tensions that socio-economic accounts would provoke. By not referring to the history of deceit, force, robbery, consent and complicity that has led to an unequal distribution of local resources, peasants make new forms of accumulation ideologically manageable. The Faustian narrative offers an ideologically acceptable explanation, and thus provides them with a way of handling the inequality between villagers created as a result of accumulation. It is therefore best seen as an adaptive mechanism in the face of contradictions generated by a modernizing agrarian capitalism, rather than – as in Taussig's interpretation – as a form of resistance by the gift economy against unfolding capitalism, or – as in Edelman's interpretation – as an everyday form of resistance against sexual domination.

Representing the Peasantry? Struggles for/about Land in Brazil
JOSÉ DE SOUZA MARTINS

Arguing that the economic development in Brazil of a commercial latifundist agriculture has depended historically on access to and control over labour-power, the crisis resulting from slave emancipation in the second half of the nineteenth century was met by immigration and settlement of European workers plus internal migration. Usufruct rights in export agriculture (coffee, sugar and rubber) meant the emergence of dual identity, whereby smallholding was combined with working for others. Capitalist expansion in the twentieth century resulted in casualization and/or dispossession of the agrarian workforce in commercial agriculture, undermining the peasant economy. The reproduction of the latter, however, has remained a focus of agrarian struggles, not least because of the ideological role played by non-peasant 'mediating groups' (the church, political parties), a process culminating in the emergence of what is now termed a 'new' rural subject. Such a designation, it is argued, fails to capture both the socio-economic diversity of the rural workforce and also the way in which the 'voice from below' conceptualizes agrarian reform.

On Which Side of What Barricade? Subaltern Resistance in Latin America and Elsewhere
TOM BRASS

Following in the footsteps of their South Asian counterparts, exponents of the Latin American subaltern framework are currently engaged in a quest for evidence of an authentic and thus empowering rural consciousness/agency, as manifested in ancient/indigenous nationhood, the carnivalesque, and literary accounts projecting the 'voice from below'. The consequent essentialization of peasant economy/culture (= subaltern identity) and agency (= subaltern resistance), however, reproduces a specifically plebeian form of conservative discourse, a pro-peasant ideology that has deep roots in Latin American history. This epistemological fusion is attributed here to a failure on the part of the subaltern approach to differentiate the peasantry in terms of class, as well as to decouple Marxism from populism, and fascism from feudalism.

Author Index

Subject Index

Since these terms reoccur throughout the text, this index contains no entries for 'Latin America', 'peasant/s', or 'smallholders'.